W9-CQO-416

PERGAMON INTERNATIONAL LIBRARY
of Science, Technology, Engineering and Social Studies

*The 1000-volume original paperback library in aid of education,
industrial training and the enjoyment of leisure*

Publisher: Robert Maxwell, M.C.

The Global 2000
Report to the President
of the U.S.

THE PERGAMON TEXTBOOK
INSPECTION COPY SERVICE

An inspection copy of any book published in the Pergamon International Library
will gladly be sent to academic staff without obligation for their consideration for
course adoption or recommendation. Copies may be retained for a period of 60 days
from receipt and returned if not suitable. When a particular title is adopted or
recommended for adoption for class use and the recommendation results in a sale
of 12 or more copies, the inspection copy may be retained with our compliments.
The Publishers will be pleased to receive suggestions for revised editions and new
titles to be published in this important International Library.

Pergamon Titles of Related Interest

Related Journals*

*Free specimen copies available upon request.

PERGAMON POLICY STUDIES

ON POLICY, PLANNING AND MODELING

The Global 2000 Report to the President of the U.S.

Entering the 21st Century
Volume I: The Summary Report

Special Edition with the
Environment Projections and
the Government's Global Model

Gerald O. Barney
Study Director

A Report Prepared by the Council on Environmental Quality and the Department of State

Pergamon Press

NEW YORK • OXFORD • TORONTO • SYDNEY • PARIS • FRANKFURT

Pergamon Press Offices:

U.S.A.   Pergamon Press Inc., Maxwell House, Fairview Park,
             Elmsford, New York 10523, U.S.A.

U.K.   Pergamon Press Ltd., Headington Hill Hall,
             Oxford OX3 0BW, England

CANADA   Pergamon of Canada, Ltd., Suite 104, 150 Consumers Road,
             Willowdale, Ontario M2J 1P9, Canada

AUSTRALIA   Pergamon Press (Aust.) Pty. Ltd., P.O. Box 544,
             Potts Point, NSW 2011, Australia

FRANCE   Pergamon Press SARL, 24 rue des Ecoles,
             75240 Paris, Cedex 05, France

FEDERAL REPUBLIC   Pergamon Press GmbH, Hammerweg 6,
OF GERMANY   6242 Kronberg/Taunus, Federal Republic of Germany

Preface Copyright © 1980 Pergamon Press Inc.

Fourth printing, 1982.

Fifth printing, 1983.

Library of Congress Cataloging in Publication Data

United States. Council on Environmental Quality.
  The global 2000 report to the President of the U.S.,
entering the 21st century.

  (Pergamon policy studies on policy planning, and
modeling)
  Includes bibliographical references and index.
  CONTENTS: v. 1. The summary report—special edition
with the environment projections and the Government's
global model.—v. 2. The technical report.
  1. Environmental policy. 2. Natural resources.
I. Barney, Gerald O. II. United States. Dept. of
State, III. Titles. IV. Title: Entering the 21st
century. V. Series.
HC79.E5U49 1980   333.7'0973   80-20264
ISBN 0-08-024617-6 (v. 1)
ISBN 0-08-024616-8 (pbk. : v. 1)

Printed in the United States of America

CONTENTS

PREFACE

When Pergamon Press decided to publish this special edition of materials from the Global 2000 Study, I was delighted to be asked to write the Preface. The Preface provides an opportunity to explain the background, evolution, and structure of this study more fully than has been done to date. It also provides an opportunity, in a few pages, to answer some of the questions that have been asked most often since the Global 2000 Report's release.

The Global 2000 Study was shaped by a very brief directive in President Carter's May 23, 1977 Environmental Message:

> "... I am directing the Council on Environmental Quality and the Department of State, working in cooperation with ... other appropriate agencies, to make a one year study of probable changes in the world's population, natural resources, and environment through the end of the century. This study will serve as the foundation of our longer-term planning."

The idea behind these two sentences was proposed originally by Donald King of the State Department in a conversation with Lee Talbot and George Bennsky, who were working on a draft of the President's Message at the Council on Environmental Quality (CEQ). Talbot and Bennsky liked the idea, and Bennsky inserted the language into the draft Presidential Message, including the one-year schedule for the study.

Many people have asked why the Global 2000 Study took so much longer to complete than the one year specified in the directive. The answer is that the one year specified in the directive was established by Bennsky as an ideal target. Bennsky later told me his reasoning: "I had to write in something. If I wrote in 3 years, the study would take five. If I wrote in 2 years, it would take four. So I wrote in one year."

During the White House clearance of the draft Environmental Message, it was reviewed by Beth Sullivan, newly arrived from the Carter campaign. It seemed to Sullivan that an international study should involve both CEQ and State: she had the language changed making the study a joint responsibility of State and CEQ. The broad perspective provided jointly by these agencies had an important influence on the study.

In 1977 when the Message was signed, Mr. Charles Warren was Chairman of the Council on Environmental Quality, and Ms. Patsy Mink was Assistant Secretary of State for Oceans and International Environmental and Scientific Affairs. They agreed that Mr. Warren, as Chairman of CEQ, was the "senior executive," but that they would co-chair an "executive group" of policy officials representing the participating agencies. They also agreed that the Study's staff would be housed in offices at the Council on Environmental Quality.

In 1977 I was living in New York. Trained as a fusion energy physicist, I had decided after my doctoral dissertation to broaden my background. The first step was a few years of economic studies, operations research, modeling and simulation at the Center for Naval Analyses, followed by a year of postdoctoral study of population, resource and environmental issues at M.I.T. and Harvard in 1970. Then, after working on the Navy's environmental problems for a year, I joined the staff of the Council on Environmental Quality, where I was responsible for the Council's long-range forecasting and technology assessment. Toward the end of President Nixon's first term, long-range forecasting and technology assessment were not particularly high priorities, and after about a year-and-a-half, I moved to New York to work with Russell Peterson, the former Governor of Delaware, who was then directing Governor Nelson Rockefeller's Commission on Critical Choices for Americans. From the Commission, I joined the staff of the Rockefeller Brothers Fund, with administrative responsibility for the Fund's grants relating to population, conservation, and national economics. While at the Rockefeller Brothers Fund, I prepared a book entitled *The Unfinished Agenda,* which draws together the thinking of the leaders of the Nation's largest population and environmental groups on the most important problems the United States must face up to in the years ahead.

At the recommendation of Lester R. Brown, Mr. Warren and Ms. Mink asked me to assume the directorship of the Global 2000 study. Mr. Lawrence S. Rockefeller and Mr. William M. Dietel arranged a leave of absence from the Rockefeller Brothers Fund, and my family and I made a hasty move to Washington.

The first day as Study Director was a shock. There was no budget for the study. During the drafting of the directive, it was felt by both CEQ and State that the Office of Management and Budget would kill the study directive if any money were involved, so the directive had been drafted without any mention of budget. When I arrived on the job, CEQ had enough money to cover my salary, but any additional budget would have to be obtained by going around to other agencies with a tin cup. To round out the day, I discovered that there was no staff, very little office space, and that the "one year" had started the day the President signed the message (May 23), not the day I started work (September 3). Three months of the year were gone before I started. Later that day I checked with the Government Printing Office (GPO) and found that typesetting and printing would require three months at the end of the study. In short, by the end of my first day the time to conduct the analysis and write the report had shrunk to six months, and Mr. Warren had made clear that he wanted the work completed on time.

How is one to study the world and some of its most difficult problems in six months? How could a study done in only six months serve as a foundation for a nation's longer-term planning? These were the questions to be answered the first week of the Global 2000 Study.

Mr. Warren, Ms. Mink, Lee Talbot, Lindsey Grant (then Deputy Assistant Secretary under Ms. Mink) and I all wanted the Global 2000 Study to be made in a way that took into account the many interactions among population, resources and environment. This desire ruled out reusing past government studies in these areas because the past studies neglected virtually all interactions. Some people argued for using one of the privately developed models, for example, The World Integrated Model developed by Mihajlo Mesarovic and Eduard Pestal for the Club of Rome. I argued for another approach.

My concern focused not so much on the projections as on the President's purpose for the Study — to establish "the foundation of our longer-term planning." I argued that the report from any study — especially one done with a non-governmental model, or in only six months — could not provide a foundation for U.S. planning. The needed foundation would have to consist not so much of a report *per se,* but of data, models, and skilled personnel. I argued that the *study process* for the Global 2000 Study could establish a meaningful and useful foundation if, to the fullest extent possible, the Study was performed by U.S. Government personnel using U.S. Government data, and U.S. Government models. An analysis of the assumptions and methods inherent in the Government's current foundation for planning would also be useful, as would a comparison of the Government's models with privately developed models. Mr. Warren and Ms. Mink agreed to this approach. The contributing agencies were then asked to provide the needed data and analysis within an integrating framework, and a small central staff undertook an analysis of the agencies' projection methods.

Two other important decisions were made in the first weeks. One concerned policy, the other technology. Mr. Warren, a veteran of many years in the California legislature, had observed that nothing happens in government when a study is based on the assumption that laws and policies will be changed. As he put it, "The legislators look at the happy ending — and do nothing." Mr. Warren decreed — very wisely, I think — that the Global 2000 Study would assume a continuation of present policies.

As for technology, we decided to ask the agencies to make whatever technological assumptions they normally make in developing long-term projections. We later reviewed these assumptions and found that the agencies are generally assuming a continuation of rapid rates of technological advance. The Department of Agriculture, for example, projects yields per acre to continue increasing throughout the foreseeable future at rates comparable to the peak increases achieved during the "green revolution." The Department of Energy assumes implicitly that rapid advances in nuclear technology will substantially reduce public concern and construction delays, allowing nuclear-powered generating facilities to be tripled over the 1975–1990 period.

With these decisions on the Study's design and approach, Mr. Warren and Ms. Mink brought the members of the executive group together for a meeting in late September 1977. The agencies represented included the National Science Foundation, the Environmental Protection Agency, the

Department of Energy (and its predecdssor, the Federal Energy Administration), the Department of Agriculture, the Department of the Interior, the Department of Commerce, the National Aeronautics and Space Administration, the Agency for International Development, the Office of Science and Technology Policy, the Federal Emergency Management Agency, and the Central Intelligence Agency — in addition to CEQ and State. The overall study plan was described, and each agency was asked to contribute $50,000 to the budget.

It must be noted here that Government agencies generally have a multitude of reasons why they cannot provide money for projects such as the Global 2000 Study, and it is a major credit to Ms. Story Shem that all of the agencies eventually contributed. In addition to her many other contributions, Ms. Shem followed the agencies' paperwork until every contribution was in. The total came to about $600,000, plus about $350,000 that the agencies contributed in analysis and related work. Without Ms. Shem's (usually) gentle pressure, the Study would have faced severe financial problems.

With the overall plan and financing agreed upon, it was necessary to move rapidly into the analysis. The needed experts, data, and models were located with the assistance of a group of agency coordinators. An eight-page memorandum to the agencies' experts indicated what projections were needed — and requested a first draft in six weeks.

Most of the agencies' experts were very excited about participation in the Study. Some had attempted to develop and publish long-term projections previously and had experienced difficulty in having their work cleared and released. But while the agency experts were enthusiastic, some were not given much time or support. One explained that he was told repeatedly that the Global 2000 work was priority ten on a nine-priority system. One contributor was forced to do all of his work for Global 2000 on his own time. The six-week deadline for the first draft was therefore very tight.

After four weeks, little progress was apparent, so a weekend retreat was organized at the Belmont House in Maryland. At this retreat, the agencies' experts were to present their preliminary findings to a group of outside experts who had worked previously on systematic studies of global trends in population, resources, and environment. These outside experts were Anne Carter, Brandeis University; Nicholas G. Carter, World Bank; Anne Ehrlich, Stanford University; Peter J. Henriot, Center of Concern; Mihajlo Mesarovic, Case Western Reserve University; Douglas N. Ross, Conference Board; Kenneth E.F. Watt, University of California at Davis.

In many ways, the weekend at the Belmont House was the highlight of the entire Study. It brought together an exceedingly interesting and stimulating group of people, all of whom had information, ideas, and questions of interest to the others. The retreat was especially helpful to the Government people because the top professional expert on long-term global analysis from each contributing agency was present, and not one of them had ever met someone from another agency with a corresponding responsibility. The first evening was therefore devoted to getting acquainted.

The discussions the next day were stimulating and filled with provocative questions. Did the Department of Energy *really* believe the real price of energy would remain constant at 1973 prices through the end of the century? How did the Department of Agriculture think that world food production could double by 2000? Where would the water, land, energy, and capital come from for both the energy and agriculture projections? What specific technologies did the Department of Interior think would keep the real price of nonfuel minerals constant or declining? These questions and their answers were particularly helpful to Mr. Ned W. Dearborn, who, as a member of the Study's small central staff, analyzed most of the agencies' models used in the Study for consistency of assumptions.

The retreat exposed two major problems: the nonfuel minerals chapter and the environmental chapter were not progressing satisfactorily. By the time of the retreat, the Department of the Interior had written nothing on the nonfuel minerals chapter. Eventually, the Interior simply refused to write the nonfuel minerals chapter, and Mr. Pieter VanderWerf, Mr. Allan Matthews, and I were forced to piece a chapter together.

The problem with the environmental chapter was complex. The memorandum initiating the projections requested each agency to analyze the environmental implications of its projections and to submit the environmental analysis along with projections. The environmental analyses were then to be combined into an environmental chapter. Unfortunately, the agencies' environmental analyses were completely missing or seriously inadequate. About the first of January 1978, it became clear that the agencies' environmental analyses would have to be extensively supplemented. Neither CEQ nor EPA had anyone available who could perform the needed work, and the task fell to Ms. Jennifer Robinson of the Global 2000 central staff.

In the previous three months Ms. Robinson had written Chapters 24-31 of the Global 2000 *Technical Report* reviewing the assumptions and structure of six world models and comparing these models with the Government's models. After this major assignment, Ms. Robinson took on the job of projecting the environmental implications of all of the other projections in the Study. The result — the first version of the environmental chapter of the *Technical Report* — was written largely by Ms. Robinson, again in only three months time.

At this point (March 1978) the study had been in progress for six months, and a decision had to be made. If the report was to be published on time (May, 1978), the manuscript had to go to the printer immediately. The manuscript was reviewed by CEQ and State. The CEQ staff had many concerns and questions about the environmental chapter, and it was decided to take additional time to rework the chapter.

The revision of the environmental chapter was difficult because the primary author, Ms. Robinson, had accepted an appointment at the International Institute for Applied Systems Analysis in Austria and was not available for further work on the chapter. Much clarification and 776 references were required over almost one year to answer all the CEQ questions, but ultimately Ms. Robinson's draft was upheld on virtually every major point.

By the time the environmental chapter was completed and the *Technical*

Report (Volume 2) sent to the printer (Summer 1979), the Study was a year overdue, and pressure was mounting for a quick completion of the summary volume (Volume 1). To complicate matters further, the four Government officials most directly responsible for initiating the Study had all left Government service. Mr. Warren had been succeeded by Mr. Gus Speth; Ms. Mink by Ambassador Thomas Pickering; Mr. Talbot by Ms. Katherine B. Gillman; Mr. Grant by Mr. Wm. Alston Hayne. Since the four new officials were unfamiliar with the design and evolution of the Study, the preparation and review of the summary volume required more time than expected. Along the way there was also one important change of direction.

Mr. Warren had felt that the most important audience for the Global 2000 report would be the general public, and he wanted the summary prepared in the format of a small paperback book suitable for wide public distribution. A book of approximately 150-200 pages would be adequate for a thoughtful synthesis and interpretation of the projections. During the approximately nine months that the summary volume was going through drafts (I think there were finally 14 drafts), the length was reduced substantially and format changed to a larger page size. The synthesis and interpretation was finally reduced to a section of less than 4 pages entitled "Entering the Twenty-First Century."

There have been various suggestions in the press that there were political pressures to "suppress" the report. To my knowledge these suggestions are unfounded. I am not aware of anyone having seriously suggested that the report not be published. There were certainly differences of opinion as to what the *Technical Report* (Volume 2) and the *Summary Report* (Volume 1) should say. With the exception of the environmental chapter, there were no major questions with the *Technical Report,* and all questions on the environmental chapter were resolved satisfactorily.

Most of the questions and differences of opinion centered on the *Summary Report,* but again, there was no suggestion of "suppression," (i.e., not publishing). The questions concerned differences of opinion as to what should be said and emphasized in the *Summary Report.* Ultimately all of what I regard as major points were made without any "suppression." If given the freedom, I would have written the *Summary Report* somewhat differently, including more synthesis and interpretation of the projections and emphasizing further the inadequacies of the Government's current capabilities for longer-term analysis and planning. But in my view, all of the major points are made — at least briefly — in the *Summary Report.*

The Global 2000 Report to the President: Entering the Twenty-First Century is an enormous study. Its three volumes total more than 1,000 pages. Why yet another volume? To serve the needs of professionals and students. The size of the full three volume study will make it difficult for professionals and students to find many relevant portions of the study. This single volume assembles those materials from the entire study most likely to be of interest and use to professionals and students. In addition, this volume explains the importance of other materials in the full report and provides background to the study not found in the Government's edition.

Is it necessary, then, to read more than the *Summary Report* for a full understanding of the Global 2000 Study? Yes. Students and professionals seriously interested in understanding and addressing the problems discussed in this Study will need information beyond that presented in the *Summary Report*. This volume facilitates access to some of the most important pieces of the entire three volume Report.

The *Summary Report* is the first piece reprinted here. It is the place to begin. The "Major Findings and Conclusions" section of the *Summary Report* (Chapter 1 of this volume) covers the highlights of the projections and states the conclusions. The "Study in Brief" section describes each of the projections in a total of only 30 pages and provides references to guide the reader to the sections of the *Technical Report* where many further details can be found. "Entering the Twenty-First Century" provides a short synthesis and interpretaton. The appendix to Chapter 1 presents highlights from the comparison of other global studies with the Global 2000 analysis. The very important matter of inadequacies in the Government's current analytical capabilities is confined to about a page at the beginning of "The Study in Brief."

The second portion of the Study reprinted here, as Chapter 2, is Chapter 13 of the *Technical Report*. This chapter on environment projections is of central importance in understanding the Study and the problems it addresses.

Global environmental analysis is difficult. All of the global studies reviewed in the Global 2000 work were found to be seriously deficient in environmental analysis. So serious are the environmental deficiencies of past global studies that the International Institute for Applied Systems Analysis devoted its last global modeling conference to the problem of incorporating environmental considerations into global models. The reasons for the deficiencies are primarily two: (1) data on global environmental problems are limited, scattered and difficult to obtain, and (2) there are essentially no global environmental models.

The Global 2000 Study made an effort to include environmental analysis, and to a significant degree the study succeeded. From one perspective the Global 2000 Study has the most complete environmental analysis of any global study to date, but from another perspective the Study includes essentially no environmental considerations. On the positive side, about 80 percent of the environmental chapter is devoted to an analysis of the environmental implications of all of the other projections. This analysis is far more extensive and detailed than the environmental analysis in any other global study.

But the environment is not passive in nature. Impacts on the environment in turn have effects back on other sectors — on agriculture, fisheries, forestry, health, etc., — and environmental developments need to be taken into account in developing projections for the other sectors. Again on the positive side, the last 20 percent of the environmental chapter considers such linkages in an important section entitled "Closing the Loops." Unfortunately, however, it was impossible to do more than discuss the many ways in which the projected environmental developments *should* be incorporated into the other projections. The other projections could not be modified to reflect the projected changes in environmental conditions, and in fact the other projections implicitly or explicitly assume that the environment will continue to provide its goods and services in vastly increased amounts, at no increase in cost (usually assumed to be zero) and with no maintenance, assumptions that are brought sharply into question by the environmental analysis. Virtually all of the projections made in the other global studies now available take environmental considerations into account more realistically than the Global 2000 projections do.

While the "Closing the Loops" section of the environmental chapter does not actually close any loops, the discussion in this section of missing linkages does provide additional synthesis and interpretation of the Global 2000 projections as a whole, and is thus a useful supplement to the very brief section "Entering the Twenty-First Century" found in the summary report. It is in "Closing the Loops" that the problem of the "vicious circle" is discussed. Briefly this problem is that in some areas population growth is leading to declining productivity of the land, which in turn leads to social and economic conditions that complicate efforts to reduce population growth, thus leading to still more pressure on the land. The "Closing of the Loops" section also discusses the best available estimate of the earth's ultimate carrying capacity and Census Bureau's estimates of the time to reach this limit at present and projected population growth rates. The estimated time is only a generation or so.

Finally, it should be noted that the environmental chapter begins each of the analyses of the other projections with a summary of the projections being analysed. These summaries were written before the writing of the *Summary Report* began, and they provide a useful supplement to the material in the *Summary Report.*

The third major portion of the Global 2000 Report reprinted here as Chapter 3, is Chapter 14 of the *Technical Report.* This chapter, "The Government's Global Model: The Present Foundation," is one of the most important chapters in the entire Study. It synthesizes and interprets all of what was learned in reviewing and analyzing the Government's present foundation for longer-term planning and analysis. The credit for this chapter and for the analysis that it summarizes belongs primarily to Mr. Ned W. Dearborn.

Many people have been confused by the title of Chapter 3. The Government, they point out, does not have a global model as implied by the title. True, the Government does not have a single, unified global model of population, resources and environment, but the Government does have a set of sectoral models dealing with global trends in population, and resources, and (to a limited degree) the environment. While the Government's sectoral models operate separately, these models have been developed and used under the implicit assumption that separate and distinct sectoral models can provide the executive branch with meaningful population, resource and environmental projections. These sectoral models provide for the executive branch the same projections that a more integrated global model would provide, and it therefore seems both appropriate and necessary to consider these models collectively to be the Government's "global model."

Chapter 3 of this volume points out, however, that the sectoral models that make up the Government's global model are contradictory and inconsistent in many important ways. After looking at all of the pieces and assumptions and making comparisons with other more adequately linked global models, I have the distinct impression that the Government's analysis significantly underestimates the seriousness of the problems the world will face in the decades ahead.

The overall message of Chapter 3 is much more alarming than the brief reference to "inconsistencies" in the *Summary Report* would suggest. The fact of the matter is that one of the most powerful nations in the world is plunging ahead into the future with a vision of the world that is both myopic and astigmatic. This fact is even more alarming when one realizes that the United States probably has better data and better models than the vast majority of other nations in the world. The time has passed when the United States (or any other nation) can afford to base decisions affecting its future economic welfare and national security on an image of the world that is as distorted and out of focus as that produced by the U.S. agencies for the Global 2000 Study.

The fourth and final piece of the Global 2000 Report reprinted in this volume is Appendix A of the *Technical Report*. This Appendix, "Lessons from the Past," is a historic review of the Government's past efforts to take a long-term look at population, or resources, or the environment. While the Global 2000 Study is the first attempt by the Government to look collectively at long-term global trends in population, resources and environment, there is a history that stretches back at least 70 years of Government efforts to examine one or another of these topics separately.

Many of the studies done in the past reached important conclusions which, if they had been acted upon, would have provided long-term benefits, many of which we would be enjoying today. In general, however, the reports were put on the shelf and ignored.

Robert and Patricia Cahn, the authors of Appendix A, point to many lessons to be learned from the failure of past studies to lead to action. They conclude that perhaps one of the most important conditions for a report to be taken seriously is that it not be released during an election year. In this regard the Global 2000 Report has theoretically gotten off to a bad start. The Report's release has received wide coverage in the press, however, including a major segment on ABC Television's "20/20" news program in the middle of the Democratic National Convention, and a citizens' group has been organized under the name "Global 2000: The Challenge to Change" for the purpose of interjecting Global 2000 issues into the Presidential campaign.

The four pieces of the Global 2000 report reprinted in this volume will provide the professional and the serious student with a comprehensive overview of the Global 2000 Study. Further reading will be useful primarily to pick out detailed information on selected topics. The following paragraphs outline where additional information on particular topics may be found.

Details of the agencies projections can be found in Chapters 2-12 of the *Technical Report* (Volume 2). There is much substantive material in these chapters that could not be presented in either the *Summary Report* or in the projection summaries that introduce the sections of the environmental chapter.

The deforestation projections (Chapter 8) provide a particularly interesting contribution. These projections by Mr. Bruce Ross-Sheriff are to my knowledge the first such projections ever made. The comprehensive data presented in the projections, combined with the U.S. embassy reports presented in Appendix C (*Technical Report)* provide a particularly striking picture of the current extent of deforestation and associated problems.

The information presented in Chapter 14 (reprinted in this volume) is only an overview of the penetrating analyses of the projections and the underlying models made by Mr. Dearborn and Mr. Pieter VanderWerf of the Global 2000 central staff. Anyone wishing to understand the analytical basis for the Government's current image of the world will want to read the full analyses presented in Chapters 15-23 of the *Technical Report.*

Chapters 14-23 provide a criticism of the projections and models from the perspective of the Global 2000 mission, but the advisors to the Study had broader criticisms. The advisors' criticisms are presented in Appendix B of the *Technical Report.* They take up a very wide range of methodological and institutional issues. Anyone seriously interested in the question of Government foresight will be interested in the ideas presented in Appendix B of the *Technical Report.*

Since the publication of the *Limits to Growth* in 1972, a number of global models have been developed. Five global models and their assumptions are reviewed in Chapters 24-29. These chapters describe the methodology, model structure and conclusions from these five global studies. The conclusions of the Global 2000 Study have been compared with those of the other global studies. These comparisons are presented very briefly in the Appendix to the summary report (reprinted in this volume). Chapters 30-31 of the *Technical Report* make the comparisons in more detail.

Finally, the third volume of the Global 2000 report, *The Government's Global Model,* presents in a single volume the basic documentation currently available on the Government's long-term global models. Some of this documentation was difficult to obtain, and its collection in a single volume will be of much interest to students, researchers and other professionals concerned with Government foresight.

The central message of the Global 2000 Report is easy to understand. The most knowledgable professional analysts in the executive branch of the U.S. Government have reported to the President that, if public policies around the world continue unchanged through the end of the century, a number of serious world problems will become worse, not better. In addition, the Global 2000 Study reports that the agencies' projections are flawed in many ways and probably understate the seriousness of the problems ahead.

Addressing the problems discussed in the Global 2000 Report is far beyond the resources and responsibility of the United States or of any other individual nation. Effective action will require extensive international cooperation.

President Carter has already begun to bring the Global 2000 Report to the attention of world leaders. Even before the Report was released, the President discussed it with the heads of industrialized nations at the June 1980 economic summit meeting in Venice. Following the release, the President directed the State Department to raise the Global 2000 Report and its issues in every appropriate international forum. The State Department has already briefed foreign diplomatic staffs in Washington and has directed U.S. embassies abroad to bring the Study to the attention of appropriate officials in foreign governments. Secretary of State Muskie referred extensively to the Report in his first speech to the United Nations. The President has further directed the State Department to organize an international conference in Washington at which the Global 2000 Report and related studies by other governments will be discussed.

President Carter has also appointed a high level task force to report to him in six months on specific actions that can be taken by the United States in responding to the Global 2000 Report. The President's task force is chaired by Mr. Gus Speth, the Chairman of the Council on Environmental Quality. The task force members are the Secretary of State, the Director of the Office of Management and Budget, the Assistant to the President for Domestic Affairs and Policy, and the Director of the Office of Science and Technology Policy.

The President's task force has at least two important topics to address. First, the task force must develop responses to the world problems described in the Global 2000 Report. As published, the report analyzes only one policy scenario — continuation of business as usual. The task force will need to identify other policy scenarios and analyze their relative advantages as a basis for specific recommendations. The task force will also need to follow up on the President's purpose for the Global 2000 Study — namely, to establish "the foundation for our longer-term planning." Through the process of the Global 2000 Study, a foundation of skilled professionals, data, and models has been established. The Study also documents in detail the serious weaknesses in this foundation. It is to be hoped that the task force will find ways to strengthen the Government's present foundation for longer-term planning and to institutionalize its use.

The Global 2000 Report is not a prediction of doom. It is, however, a projection of world conditions that could develop by the end of this century if very real problems are ignored. The challenge and the opportunity of Global 2000 were summed up nicely by Secretary of State Muskie on the occasion of the Report's release. The Secretary said: "If we begin our work now, we will say in twenty years that the Global 2000 report was wrong. And we will congratulate ourselves for having had the foresight to build a better future."

Gerald O. Barney
Study Director

xvii

The Global 2000
Report to the President
of the U.S.

1 Major Findings and Conclusions

If present trends continue, the world in 2000 will be more crowded, more polluted, less stable ecologically, and more vulnerable to disruption than the world we live in now. Serious stresses involving population, resources, and environment are clearly visible ahead. Despite greater material output, the world's people will be poorer in many ways than they are today.

For hundreds of millions of the desperately poor, the outlook for food and other necessities of life will be no better. For many it will be worse. Barring revolutionary advances in technology, life for most people on earth will be more precarious in 2000 than it is now—unless the nations of the world act decisively to alter current trends.

This, in essence, is the picture emerging from the U.S. Government's projections of probable changes in world population, resources, and environment by the end of the century, as presented in the Global 2000 Study. They do not predict what will occur. Rather, they depict conditions that are likely to develop if there are no changes in public policies, institutions, or rates of technological advance, and if there are no wars or other major disruptions. A keener awareness of the nature of the current trends, however, may induce changes that will alter these trends and the projected outcome.

Principal Findings

Rapid growth in world population will hardly have altered by 2000. The world's population will grow from 4 billion in 1975 to 6.35 billion in 2000, an increase of more than 50 percent. The rate of growth will slow only marginally, from 1.8 percent a year to 1.7 percent. In terms of sheer numbers, population will be growing faster in 2000 than it is today, with 100 million people added each year compared with 75 million in 1975. Ninety percent of this growth will occur in the poorest countries.

While the economies of the less developed countries (LDCs) are expected to grow at faster rates than those of the industrialized nations, the gross national product per capita in most LDCs remains low. The average gross national product per capita is projected to rise substantially in some LDCs (especially in Latin America), but in the great populous nations of South Asia it remains below $200 a year (in 1975 dollars). The large existing gap between the rich and poor nations widens.

World food production is projected to increase 90 percent over the 30 years from 1970 to 2000. This translates into a global per capita increase of less than 15 percent over the same period. The bulk of that increase goes to countries that already have relatively high per capita food consumption. Meanwhile per capita consumption in South Asia, the Middle East, and the LDCs of Africa will scarcely improve or will actually decline below present inadequate levels. At the same time, real prices for food are expected to double.

Arable land will increase only 4 percent by 2000, so that most of the increased output of food will have to come from higher yields. Most of the elements that now contribute to higher yields—fertilizer, pesticides, power for irrigation, and fuel for machinery—depend heavily on oil and gas.

During the 1990s world oil production will approach geological estimates of maximum production capacity, even with rapidly increasing petroleum prices. The Study projects that the richer industrialized nations will be able to command enough oil and other commercial energy supplies to meet rising demands through 1990. With the expected price increases, many less developed countries will have increasing difficulties meeting energy needs. For the one-quarter of humankind that depends primarily on wood for fuel, the outlook is bleak. Needs for fuelwood will exceed available supplies by about 25 percent before the turn of the century.

While the world's finite fuel resources—coal, oil, gas, oil shale, tar sands, and uranium—are theoretically sufficient for centuries, they are not evenly distributed; they pose difficult economic and environmental problems; and they vary greatly in their amenability to exploitation and use.

Nonfuel mineral resources generally appear sufficient to meet projected demands through 2000, but further discoveries and investments will be needed to maintain reserves. In addition, production costs will increase with energy prices and may make some nonfuel mineral resources uneconomic. The quarter of the world's population that inhabits industrial countries will continue to absorb three-fourths of the world's mineral production.

Regional water shortages will become more severe. In the 1970-2000 period population growth alone will cause requirements for water to double in nearly half the world. Still greater increases would be needed to improve standards of living. In many LDCs, water supplies will become increasingly erratic by 2000 as a result of extensive deforestation. Development of new water supplies will become more costly virtually everywhere.

Significant losses of world forests will continue over the next 20 years as demand for forest products and fuelwood increases. Growing stocks of commercial-size timber are projected to decline 50 percent per capita. The world's forests are now disappearing at the rate of 18-20 million hectares a year (an area half the size of California), with most of the loss occurring in the humid tropical forests of Africa, Asia, and South America. The projections indicate that by 2000 some 40 percent of the remaining forest cover in LDCs will be gone.

Serious deterioration of agricultural soils will occur worldwide, due to erosion, loss of organic matter, desertification, salinization, alkalinization, and waterlogging. Already, an area of cropland and grassland approximately the size of Maine is becoming barren wasteland each year, and the spread of desert-like conditions is likely to accelerate.

Atmospheric concentrations of carbon dioxide and ozone-depleting chemicals are expected to increase at rates that could alter the world's climate and upper atmosphere significantly by 2050. Acid rain from increased combustion of fossil fuels (especially coal) threatens damage to lakes, soils, and crops. Radioactive and other hazardous materials present health and safety problems in increasing numbers of countries.

Extinctions of plant and animal species will increase dramatically. Hundreds of thousands of species—perhaps as many as 20 percent of all species on earth—will be irretrievably lost as their habitats vanish, especially in tropical forests.

The future depicted by the U.S. Government projections, briefly outlined above, may actually understate the impending problems. The methods available for carrying out the Study led to certain gaps and inconsistencies that tend to impart an optimistic bias. For example, most of the individual projections for the various sectors studied—food, minerals, energy, and so on—assume that sufficient capital, energy, water, and land will be available in each of these sectors to meet their needs, regardless of the competing needs of the other sectors. More consistent, better-integrated projections would produce a still more emphatic picture of intensifying stresses, as the world enters the twenty-first century.

Conclusions

At present and projected growth rates, the world's population would reach 10 billion by 2030 and would approach 30 billion by the end of the twenty-first century. These levels correspond closely to estimates by the U.S. National Academy of Sciences of the maximum carrying capacity of the entire earth. Already the populations in sub-Saharan Africa and in the Himalayan hills of Asia have exceeded the carrying capacity of the immediate area, triggering an erosion of the land's capacity to support life. The resulting poverty and ill health have further complicated efforts to reduce fertility. Unless this circle of interlinked problems is broken soon, population growth in such areas will unfortunately be slowed for reasons other than declining birth rates. Hunger and disease will claim more babies and young children, and more of those surviving will be mentally and physically handicapped by childhood malnutrition.

Indeed, the problems of preserving the carrying capacity of the earth and sustaining the possibility of a decent life for the human beings that inhabit it are enormous and close upon us. Yet there is reason for hope. It must be emphasized that the Global 2000 Study's projections are based on the assumption that national policies regarding population stabilization, resource conservation, and environmental protection will remain essentially unchanged through the end of the century. But in fact, policies are beginning to change. In some areas, forests are being replanted after cutting. Some nations are taking steps to reduce soil losses and desertification. Interest in energy conservation is growing, and large sums are being invested in exploring alternatives to petroleum dependence. The need for family planning is slowly becoming better understood. Water supplies are being improved and waste treatment systems built. High-yield seeds are widely available and seed banks are being expanded. Some wildlands with their genetic resources are being protected. Natural predators and selective pesticides are being substituted for persistent and destructive pesticides.

Encouraging as these developments are, they are far from adequate to meet the global challenges projected in this Study. Vigorous, determined new initiatives are needed if worsening poverty and human suffering, environmental degradation, and international tension and conflicts are to be prevented. There are no quick fixes. The only solutions to the problems of population, resources, and environment are complex and long-term. These problems are inextricably linked to some of the most perplexing and persistent problems in the world—poverty, injustice, and social conflict. New and imaginative ideas—and a willingness to act on them—are essential.

The needed changes go far beyond the capability and responsibility of this or any other single nation. An era of unprecedented cooperation and commitment is essential. Yet there are opportunities—and a strong rationale —for the United States to provide leadership among nations. A high priority for this Nation must be a thorough assessment of its foreign and domestic policies relating to population, resources, and environment. The United States, possessing the world's largest economy, can expect its policies to have a significant influence on global trends. An equally important priority for the United States is to cooperate generously and justly with other nations—particularly in the areas of trade, investment, and assistance—in seeking solutions to the many problems that extend beyond our national boundaries. There are many unfulfilled opportunities to cooperate with other nations in efforts to relieve poverty and hunger, stabilize population, and enhance economic and environmental productivity. Further cooperation among nations is also needed to strengthen international mechanisms for protecting and utilizing the "global commons"—the oceans and atmosphere.

To meet the challenges described in this Study, the United States must improve its ability to identify emerging problems and assess alternative responses. In using and evaluting the Government's present capability for long-term global analysis, the Study found serious inconsistencies in the methods and assumptions employed by the various agencies in making their projections. The Study itself made a start toward resolving these inadequacies. It represents the Government's first attempt to produce an interrelated set of population, resource, and environmental projections, and it has brought forth the most consistent set of global projections yet achieved by U.S. agencies. Nevertheless, the projections still contain serious gaps and contradictions that must be corrected if the Government's analytic capability is to be improved. It must be acknowledged that at present the Federal agencies are not always capable of providing projections of the quality needed for long-term policy decisions.

While limited resources may be a contributing factor in some instances, the primary problem is lack of coordination. The U.S. Government needs a mechanism for continuous review of the assumptions and methods the Federal agencies use in their projection models and for assurance that the agencies' models are sound, consistent, and well documented. The improved analyses that could result would provide not only a clearer sense of emerging problems and opportunities, but also a better means for evaluating alternative responses, and a better basis for decisions of worldwide significance that the President, the Congress, and the Federal Government as a whole must make.

With its limitations and rough approximations, the Global 2000 Study may be seen as no more than a reconnaissance of the future; nonetheless its conclusions are reinforced by similar findings of other recent global studies that were examined in the course of the Global 2000 Study (see Appendix). All these studies are in general agreement on the nature of the problems and on the threats they pose to the future welfare of humankind. The available evidence leaves no doubt that the world—including this Nation—faces enormous, urgent, and complex problems in the decades immediately ahead. Prompt and vigorous changes in public policy around the world are needed to avoid or minimize these problems before they become unmanageable. Long lead times are required for effective action. If decisions are delayed until the problems become worse, options for effective action will be severely reduced.

The Study in Brief

The President's directive establishing the Global 2000 Study called for a "study of the probable changes in the world's population, natural resources, and environment through the end of the century" and indicated that the Study as a whole was to "serve as the foundation of our longer-term planning."[3] The findings of the Study identify problems to which world attention must be directed. But because all study reports eventually become dated and less useful, the Study's findings alone cannot provide the foundation called for in the directive. The necessary foundation for longer-term planning lies not in study findings *per se*, but in the Government's continuing institutional capabilities—skilled personnel, data, and analytical models—for developing studies and analyses. Therefore, to meet the objectives stated in the President's directive, the Global 2000 Study was designed not only to assess probable changes in the world's population, natural resources, and environment, but also, through the study process itself, to identify and strengthen the Government's capability for longer-term planning and analysis.[4]

Building the Study

The process chosen for the Global 2000 Study was to develop trend projections using, to the fullest extent possible, the long-term global data and models routinely employed by the Federal agencies. The process also included a detailed analysis of the Government's global modeling capabilities as well as a comparison of the Government's findings with those of other global analyses.

An executive group, established and co-chaired by the Council on Environmental Quality and the State Department, together with a team of designated agency coordinators, assisted in locating the agencies' experts, data, and analytical models. A number of Americans from outside Government and several people from other countries advised on the study structure. The agencies' expert met occasionally with some of these advisers to work out methods for coordinating data, models, and assumptions.

Overall, the Federal agencies have an impressive capability for long-term analyses of world trends in population, resources, and environment. Several agencies have extensive, richly detailed data bases and highly elaborate sectoral models. Collectively, the agencies' sectoral models and data constitute the Nation's present foundation for long-term planning and analysis.[5]

Currently, the principal limitation in the Government's long-term global analytical capability is that the models for various sectors were not designed to be used together in a consistent and interactive manner. The agencies' models were created at different times, using different methods, to meet different objectives. Little thought has been given to how the various sectoral models—and the institutions of which they are a part—can be related to each other to project a comprehensive, consistent image of the world. As a result, there has been little direct interaction among the agencies' sectoral models.[6]

With the Government's current models, the individual sectors addressed in the Global 2000 Study could be interrelated only by developing projections sequentially, that is, by using the results of some of the projections as inputs to others. Since population and gross national product (GNP) projections were required to estimate demand in the resource sector models, the population and GNP projections were developed first, in 1977. The resource projections followed in late 1977 and early 1978. All of the projections were linked to the environment projections, which were made during 1978 and 1979.[7]

The Global 2000 Study developed its projections in a way that furthered interactions, improved internal consistency, and generally strengthened the Government's global models. However, the effort to harmonize and integrate the Study's projections was only partially successful. Many internal contradictions and inconsistencies could not be resolved. Inconsistencies arose immediately from the fact that sequential projections are not as interactive as events in the real world, or as projections that could be achieved in an improved model. While the sequential process allowed some interaction among the model's sectors, it omitted the continuous influence that all the elements—population, resources, economic activity, environment—have upon each other. For example, the Global 2000 Study food projections assume that the catch from traditional fisheries will increase as fast as world population, while the fisheries projections indicate that this harvest will not increase over present levels on a sustainable basis. If it has been possible to link the fisheries and food projections, the expected fisheries contribution to the human food supply could have been realistically reflected in the food projections. This and other inconsistencies are discussed in detail in the Technical Report.[8]

Difficulties also arise from multiple allocation of resources. Most of the quantitative projections simply assume that resource needs in the sector they cover—needs for capital, energy, land, water, minerals—will be met. Since the needs for each sector are not clearly identified, they cannot be summed up and compared with estimates of what might be available. It is very likely that the same resources have been allocated to more than one sector.[9]

Equally significant, some of the Study's resource projections implicitly assume that the goods and services provided in the past by the earth's land, air, and water will continue to be available in larger and larger amounts, with no maintenance problems and no increase in costs. The Global 2000 Study projections for the environment cast serious doubt on these assumptions.[10]

Collectively, the inconsistencies and missing linkages that are unavoidable with the Government's current global models affect the Global 2000 projections in many ways. Analysis of the assumptions underlying the projections and comparisons with other global projections suggest that most of the Study's quantitative results understate the severity of potential problems the world will face as it prepares to enter the twenty-first century.[11]

The question naturally arises as to whether circumstances have changed significantly since the earliest projections were made in 1977. The answer is no. What changes have occurred generally support the projections and highlight the problems identified. The brief summaries of the projections (beginning on the next page) each conclude with comments on how the projections might be altered if redeveloped today.

The Global 2000 Study has three major underlying assumptions. First, the projections assume a general continuation around the world of present public policy relating to population stabilization, natural resource conservation, and environmental protection.* The projections thus point to the expected future if policies continue without significant changes.

The second major assumption relates to the effects of technological developments and of the market mechanism. The Study assumes that rapid rates of technological development and adoption will continue, and that the rate of development will be spurred on by efforts to deal with problems identified by this Study. Participating agencies were asked to use the technological assumptions they normally use in preparing long-term global projections. In general, the agencies assume a continuation of rapid rates of technological development and no serious social resistance to the adoption of new technologies. Agricultural technology, for example, is assumed to continue increasing crop yields as rapidly as during the past few decades, including the period of the Green Revolution (see Figure 1). The projections assume no revolutionary advances—such as immediate wide-scale availability of nuclear fusion for energy production—and no disastrous setbacks—such as serious new health risks from widely used contraceptives or an outbreak of plant disease severely affecting an important strain of grain. The projections all assume that price, operating through the market mechanism, will reduce demand whenever supply constraints are encountered.[12]

Third, the Study assumes that there will be no major disruptions of international trade as a result

---

*There are a few important exceptions to this rule. For example, the population projections anticipate shifts in public policy that will provide significantly increased access to family planning services. (See Chapter 14 of the Technical Report for further details.)

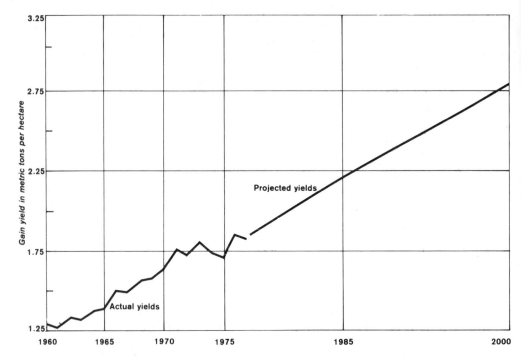

Figure 1. Historic and projected grain yields, 1960–2000. The food projections assume a continued rapid development and adoption of agricultural technology, much of it heavily dependent on fossil fuels.

of war, disturbance of the international monetary system, or political disruption. The findings of the Study do, however, point to increasing potential for international conflict and increasing stress on international financial arrangements. Should wars or a significant disturbance of the international monetary system occur, the projected trends would be altered in unpredictable ways.[13]

Because of the limitations outlined above, the Global 2000 Study is not the definitive study of future population, resource, and environment conditions. Nor is it intended to be a prediction. The Study does provide the most internally consistent and interrelated set of global projections available so far from the U.S. Government. Furthermore, its major findings are supported by a variety of nongovernmental global studies based on more highly interactive models that project similar trends through the year 2000 or beyond.[14]

Population and Income

Population and income projections provided the starting point for the Study. These projections

were used wherever possible in the resource projections to estimate demand.

Population

One of the most important findings of the Global 2000 Study is that enormous growth in the world's population will occur by 2000 under any of the wide range of assumptions considered in the Study. The world's population increases 55 percent from 4.1 billion people in 1975 to 6.35 billion by 2000, under the Study's medium-growth projections.* While there is some uncertainty in these numbers, even the lowest-growth population projection shows a 46 percent increase—to 5.9 billion people by the end of the century.[15]

Another important finding is that the rapid growth of the world's population will not slow appreciably. The rate of growth per year in 1975 was 1.8 percent; the projected rate for 2000 is 1.7 per-

*Most of the projections in the Technical Report—including the population projections—provide a high, medium, and low series. Generally, only the medium series are discussed in this Summary Report.

cent. Even under the lowest growth projected, the number of persons being added annually to the world's population will be significantly greater in 2000 than today.[16]

Most of the population growth (92 percent) will occur in the less developed countries rather than in the industrialized countries. Of the 6.35 billion people in the world in 2000, 5 billion will live in LDCs. The LDCs' share of the world's population increased from 66 percent in 1950 to 72 percent in 1975, and is expected to reach 79 percent by 2000. LDC population growth rates will drop slightly, from 2.2 percent a year in 1975 to 2 percent in 2000, compared with 0.7 percent and 0.5 percent in developed countries. In some LDCs,

growth rates will still be more than 3 percent a year in 2000. Table 1 summarizes the population projections. Figure 2 shows the distribution of the world's population in 1975 and 2000.[17]

Figure 3 shows the age structure of the population in less developed and industrialized nations for 1975 and 2000. While the structures shown for the industrialized nations become more column-shaped (characteristic of a mature and slowly growing population), the structures for the LDCs remain pyramid-shaped (characteristic of rapid growth). The LDC populations, predominantly young with their childbearing years ahead of them, have a built-in momentum for further growth. Because of this momentum, a world

TABLE 1
Population Projections for World, Major Regions, and Selected Countries

	1975	2000	Percent Increase by 2000	Average Annual Percent Increase	Percent of World Population in 2000
	millions				
World	4,090	6,351	55	1.8	100
More developed regions	1,131	1,323	17	0.6	21
Less developed regions	2,959	5,028	70	2.1	79
Major regions					
Africa	399	814	104	2.9	13
Asia and Oceania	2,274	3,630	60	1.9	57
Latin America	325	637	96	2.7	10
U.S.S.R. and Eastern Europe	384	460	20	0.7	7
North America, Western Europe, Japan, Australia, and New Zealand	708	809	14	0.5	13
Selected countries and regions					
People's Republic of China	935	1,329	42	1.4	21
India	618	1,021	65	2.0	16
Indonesia	135	226	68	2.1	4
Bangladesh	79	159	100	2.8	2
Pakistan	71	149	111	3.0	2
Philippines	43	73	71	2.1	1
Thailand	42	75	77	2.3	1
South Korea	37	57	55	1.7	1
Egypt	37	65	77	2.3	1
Nigeria	63	135	114	3.0	2
Brazil	109	226	108	2.9	4
Mexico	60	131	119	3.1	2
United States	214	248	16	0.6	4
U.S.S.R.	254	309	21	0.8	5
Japan	112	133	19	0.7	2
Eastern Europe	130	152	17	0.6	2
Western Europe	344	378	10	0.4	6

Source: Global 2000 Technical Report, Table 2-10.

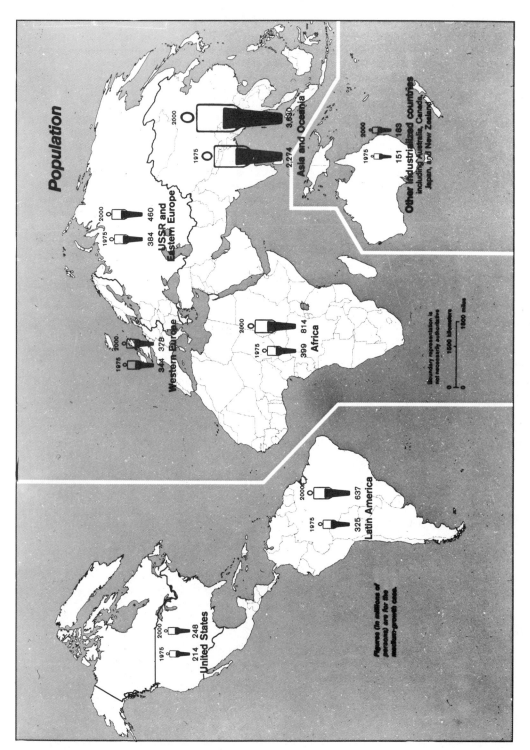

Figure 2. Distribution of the world's population, 1975 and 2000.

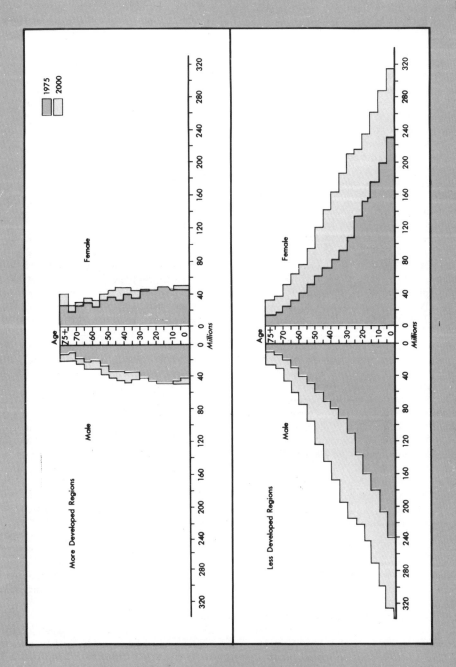

Figure 3. Age-sex composition of the world's population, medium series, 1975 and 2000.

population of around 6 billion is a virtual certainty for 2000 even if fertility rates were somehow to drop quickly to replacement levels (assuming there are no disastrous wars, famine, or pestilence).[18]

The projected fertility rates and life expectancies, together with the age structure of the world's population, are extremely significant for later years since these factors influence how soon world population could cease to grow and what the ultimate stabilized global population could be. The Study's projections assume that world fertility rates will drop more than 20 percent over the 1975-2000 period, from an average of 4.3 children per fertile woman to 3.3. In LDCs, fertility rates are projected to drop 30 percent as a result of moderate progress in social and economic development and increased availability and use of contraceptive methods. The projections also assume that life expectancies at birth for the world will increase 11 percent, to 65.5 years, as a result of improved health. The projected increases in life expectancies and decreases in fertility rates produce roughly counterbalancing demographic effects.[19]

In addition to rapid population growth, the LDCs will experience dramatic movements of rural populations to cities and adjacent settlements. If present trends continue, many LDC cities will become almost inconceivably large and crowded. By 2000, Mexico City is projected to have more than 30 million people—roughly three times the present population of the New York metropolitan area. Calcutta will approach 20 million. Greater Bombay, Greater Cairo, Jakarta, and Seoul are all expected to be in the 15-20 million range, and 400 cities will have passed the million mark.[20] Table 2 shows present and projected populations for 12 LDC cities.

Rapid urban growth will put extreme pressures on sanitation, water supplies, health care, food, shelter, and jobs. LDCs will have to increase urban services approximately two-thirds by 2000 just to stay even with 1975 levels of service per capita. The majority of people in large LDC cities are likely to live in "uncontrolled settlements"— slums and shantytowns where sanitation and other public services are minimal at best. In many large cities—for example, Bombay, Calcutta, Mexico City, Rio de Janeiro, Seoul, Taipei—a quarter or more of the population already lives in uncontrolled settlements, and the trend is sharply upward. It is not certain whether the trends projected

TABLE 2

Estimates and Rough Projections of Selected Urban Agglomerations in Developing Countries

	1960	1970	1975	2000
	Millions of persons			
Calcutta	5.5	6.9	8.1	19.7
Mexico City	4.9	8.6	10.9	31.6
Greater Bombay	4.1	5.8	7.1	19.1
Greater Cairo	3.7	5.7	6.9	16.4
Jakarta	2.7	4.3	5.6	16.9
Seoul	2.4	5.4	7.3	18.7
Delhi	2.3	3.5	4.5	13.2
Manila	2.2	3.5	4.4	12.7
Tehran	1.9	3.4	4.4	13.8
Karachi	1.8	3.3	4.5	15.9
Bogota	1.7	2.6	3.4	9.5
Lagos	0.8	1.4	2.1	9.4

Source: Global 2000 Technical Report, Table 13-9.

for enormous increases in LDC urban populations will in fact continue for 20 years. In the years ahead, lack of food for the urban poor, lack of jobs, and increasing illness and misery may slow the growth of LDC cities and alter the trend.[21]

Difficult as urban conditions are, conditions in rural areas of many LDCs are generally worse. Food, water, health, and income problems are often most severe in outlying agricultural and grazing areas. In some areas rural-urban migration and rapid urban growth are being accelerated by deteriorating rural conditions.[22]

An updated medium-series population projection would show little change from the Global 2000 Study projections. World population in 2000 would be estimated at about 6.18 (as opposed to 6.35) billion, a reduction of less than 3 percent. The expectation would remain that, in absolute numbers, population will be growing more rapidly by the end of the century than today.[23]

The slight reduction in the population estimate is due primarily to new data suggesting that fertility rates in some areas have declined a little more rapidly than earlier estimates indicated. The new data indicate that fertility declines have occurred in some places even in the absence of overall socioeconomic progress.[24] Between 1970 and 1976, for example, in the presence of extreme poverty and malnutrition, fertility declines of 10-15 percent occurred in Indonesia and 15-20 percent in the poorest income classes in Brazil.[25]

Income

Projected declines in fertility rates are based in part on anticipated social and economic progress, which is ultimately reflected in increased income. Income projections were not possible, and gross national product projections were used as surrogates. GNP, a rough and inadequate measure of social and economic welfare, is projected to increase worldwide by 145 percent over 25 years from 1975 to 2000. But because of population growth, per capita GNP increases much more slowly, from $1,500 in 1975 to $2,300 in 2000—an increase of 53 percent. For both the poorer and the richer countries, rates of growth in GNP are projected to decelerate after 1985.[26]

GNP growth is expected to be faster in LDCs (an average annual growth of 4.5 percent, or an approximate tripling over 25 years) than in developed regions (an average annual growth of 3.3 percent, or somewhat more than a doubling). However, the LDC growth in gross national product develops from a very low base, and population growth in the LDCs brings per capita increases in GNP down to very modest proportions. While parts of the LDC world, especially several countries in Latin America, are projected to improve significantly in per capita GNP by 2000, other countries will make little or no gains from their present low levels. India, Bangladesh, and Pakistan, for example, increase their per capita GNP by 31 percent, 8 percent, and 3 percent, respectively, but in all three countries GNP per capita remains below $200 (in 1975 dollars).[27] Figure 4 shows projected per capita gross national product by regions in 2000.

The present income disparities between the wealthiest and poorest nations are projected to widen. Assuming that present trends continue, the group of industrialized countries will have a per capita GNP of nearly $8,500 (in 1975 dollars) in 2000, and North America, Western Europe, Australia, New Zealand, and Japan will average more than $11,000. By contrast, per capita GNP in the LDCs will average less than $600. For every $1 increase in GNP per capita in the LDCs, a $20 increase is projected for the industrialized countries.[28] Table 3 and 4 summarize the GNP projections. The disparity between the developed countries and the less developed group is so marked that dramatically different rates of change would be needed to reduce the gap significantly by the end of the century.* Disparities between the rich and poor of many LDCs are equally striking.

Updated GNP projections would indicate somewhat lower economic growth than shown in the Global 2000 projections. Projections for the member nations of the Organization for Economic Cooperation and Development (OECD) have been revised downward over the past 2–3 years because of the effects of increasing petroleum prices and because of anticipated measures to reduce inflation. In turn, depressed growth in the OECD economies is expected to lead to slowed growth in LDC economies. For example, in 1976 the World Bank projected that the industrialized nations' economies would expand at 4.9 percent annually over the 1980–85 period; by 1979 the Bank had revised these projections downward to 4.2 percent annually over the 1980–90 period. Similarly, between 1976 and 1979 Bank projections for LDC economies dropped from 6.3 percent (1980-85 period) to 5.6 percent (1980-90 period).[29]

Resources

The Global 2000 Study resource projections are based to the fullest extent possible on the population and GNP projections presented previously. The resource projections cover food, fisheries, forests, nonfuel minerals, water, and energy.

Food

The Global 2000 Study projects world food production to increase at an average annual rate of about 2.2 percent over the 1970–2000 period. This rate of increase is roughly equal to the record growth rates experienced during the 1950s, 1960s, and early 1970s, including the period of the so-called Green Revolution. Assuming no deterioration in climate or weather, food production is projected to be 90 percent higher in 2000 than in 1970.[30]

---

*The gap would be significantly smaller—in some cases it would be reduced by about one half—if the comparison were based on purchasing power considerations rather than exchange rates, but a large gap would remain. (See I. B. Kravis et al., *International Comparisons of Real Product and Purchasing Power*, Baltimore: Johns Hopkins University Press. 1978.)

14

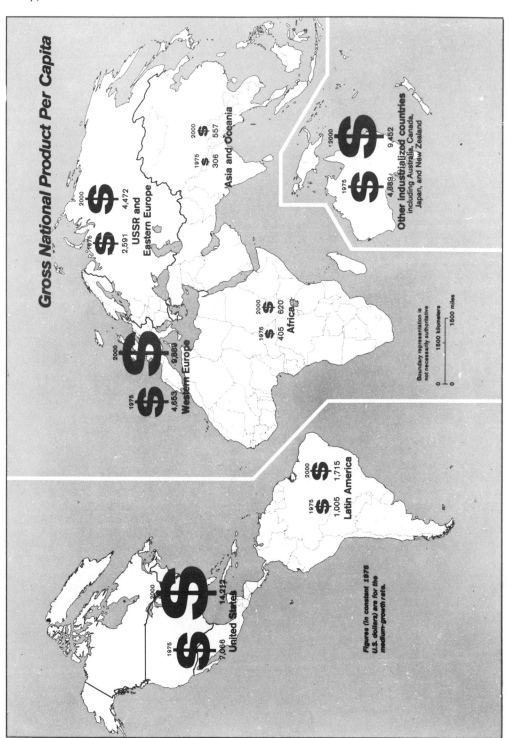

Figure 4. Per capita gross national product, by regions, 1975 and 2000.

TABLE 3
GNP Estimates (1975) and Projections and Growth Rates (1985, 2000) by Major Regions and Selected Countries and Regions

(Billions of constant 1975 dollars)

	1975 GNP	1975–85 Growth Rate	1985 Projections[a]	1985–2000 Growth Rate	2000 Projections[a]
		percent		*percent*	
WORLD	6,025	4.1	8,991	3.3	14,677
More developed regions	4,892	3.9	7,150	3.1	11,224
Less developed regions	1,133	5.0	1,841	4.3	3,452
MAJOR REGIONS					
Africa	162	5.2	268	4.3	505
Asia and Oceania	697	4.6	1,097	4.2	2,023
Latin America[b]	326	5.6	564	4.5	1,092
U.S.S.R. and Eastern Europe	996	3.3	1,371	2.8	2,060
North America, Western Europe, Japan, Australia, and New Zealand	3,844	4.0	5,691	3.1	8,996
SELECTED COUNTRIES AND REGIONS[c]					
People's Republic of China	286	3.8	413	3.8	718
India	92	3.6	131	2.8	198
Indonesia	24	6.4	45	5.4	99
Bangladesh	9	3.6	13	2.8	19
Pakistan	10	3.6	14	2.8	21
Philippines	16	5.6	27	4.4	52
Thailand	15	5.6	25	4.4	48
South Korea	19	5.6	32	4.4	61
Egypt	12	5.6	20	4.4	38
Nigeria	23	6.4	43	5.4	94
Brazil	108	5.6	185	4.4	353
Mexico	71	5.6	122	4.4	233
United States[d]	1,509	4.0	2,233	3.1	3,530
U.S.S.R.	666	3.3	917	2.8	1,377
Japan	495	4.0	733	3.1	1,158
Eastern Europe (excluding U.S.S.R.)	330	3.3	454	2.8	682
Western Europe	1,598	4.0	2,366	3.1	3,740

[a]Projected growth rates of gross national product were developed using complex computer simulation techniques described in Chapter 16 of the Global 2000 Technical Report. These projections represent the result of applying those projected growth rates to the 1975 GNP data presented in the 1976 World Bank Atlas. Projections shown here are for medium-growth rates.
[b]Includes Puerto Rico.

[c]In most cases, gross national income growth rates were projected for groups of countries rather than for individual countries. Thus the rates attributed to individual LDCs in this table are the growth rates applicable to the group with which that country was aggregated for making projections and do not take into account country specific characteristics.
[d]Does not include Puerto Rico.
Source: Global 2000 Technical Report, Table 3-3.

TABLE 4
Per Capita GNP Estimates (1975) and Projections and Growth Rates (1985, 2000) by Major Regions and Selected Countries and Regions

(Constant 1975 U.S. dollars)

	1975	Average Annual Growth Rate, 1975–85	1985 Projections[a]	Average Annual Growth Rate, 1985–2000	2000 Projections[a]
		percent		*percent*	
WORLD	1,473	2.3	1,841	1.5	2,311
More developed countries	4,325	3.2	5,901	2.5	8,485
Less developed countries	382	2.8	501	2.1	587
MAJOR REGIONS					
Africa	405	2.2	505	1.4	620
Asia and Oceania	306	2.7	398	2.3	557
Latin America[b]	1,005	2.6	1,304	1.8	1,715
U.S.S.R. and Eastern Europe	2,591	2.4	3,279	2.1	4,472
North America, Western Europe, Japan, Australia, and New Zealand	5,431	3.4	7,597	2.6	11,117
SELECTED COUNTRIES AND REGIONS[c]					
People's Republic of China	306	2.3	384	2.3	540
India	148	1.5	171	0.8	194
Indonesia	179	4.1	268	3.1	422
Bangladesh	111	0.6	118	0.1	120
Pakistan	138	0.4	144	− 0.1	142
Philippines	368	3.2	503	2.3	704
Thailand	343	3.0	460	2.2	633
South Korea	507	3.5	718	2.7	1,071
Egypt	313	2.9	416	2.2	578
Nigeria	367	3.3	507	2.2	698
Brazil	991	2.2	1,236	1.6	1,563
Mexico	1,188	2.0	1,454	1.3	1,775
United States[d]	7,066	3.3	9.756	2.5	14,212
U.S.S.R.	2,618	2.3	3,286	2.1	4,459
Japan	4,437	3.1	6,023	2.5	8,712
Eastern Europe	2,539	2.6	3,265	2.2	4,500
Western Europe	4,653	3.7	6,666	2.7	9,889

[a]The medium-series projections of gross national product and population presented in Tables 3-3 and 3-4 of the Global 2000 Technical Report were used to calculate the 1975, 1985, and 2000 per capita gross national product figures presented in this table.
[b]Includes Puerto Rico.
[c]In most cases, gross national product growth rates were projected for groups of countries rather than for individual countries. Thus, the rates attributed to individual LDCs in this table are the growth rates applicable to the group with which that country was aggregated for making projections and do not take into account country-specific characteristics.
[d]Does not include Puerto Rico.
Source: Global 2000 Technical Report, Table 3-5.

The projections indicate that most of the increase in food production will come from more intensive use of yield-enhancing, energy-intensive inputs and technologies such as fertilizer, pesticides, herbicides, and irrigation—in many cases with diminishing returns. Land under cultivation is projected to increase only 4 percent by 2000 because most good land is already being cultivated. In the early 1970s one hectare of arable land supported an average of 2.6 persons; by 2000 one hectare will have to support 4 persons. Because of this tightening land constraint, food production is not likely to increase fast enough to meet rising demands unless world agriculture becomes significantly more dependent on petroleum and petroleum-related inputs. Increased petroleum dependence also has implications for the cost of food production. After decades of generally falling prices, the real price of food is projected to increase 95 percent over the 1970–2000 period, in significant part as a result of increased petroleum dependence.[31] If energy prices in fact rise more rapidly than the projections anticipate, then the effect on food prices could be still more marked.

On the average, world food production is projected to increase more rapidly than world population, with average per capita consumption increasing about 15 percent between 1970 and 2000. Per capita consumption in the industrialized nations is projected to rise 21 percent from 1970 levels, with increases of from 40 to more than 50 percent in Japan, Eastern Europe, and the U.S.S.R., and 28 percent in the United States.* In the LDCs, however, rising food output will barely keep ahead of population growth.[32]

An increase of 9 percent in per capita food consumption is projected for the LDCs as a whole, but with enormous variations among regions and nations. The great populous countries of South Asia—expected to contain 1.3 billion people by 2000—improve hardly at all, nor do large areas of low-income North Africa and the Middle East. Per capita consumption in the sub-Saharan African LDCs will actually decline, according to the projections. The LDCs showing the greatest per capita growth (increases of about 25 percent) are concentrated in Latin America and East Asia.[33] Table 5 summarizes the projections for food production and consumption, and Table 6 and Figure 5 show per capita food consumption by regions.

The outlook for improved diets for the poorest people in the poorest LDCs is sobering. In the 1970s, consumption of calories in the LDCs averaged only 94 percent of the minimum requirements set by the U.N. Food and Agriculture Organization (FAO).† Moreover, income and

food distribution within individual LDCs is so skewed that national average caloric consumption generally must be 10–20 percent above minimum levels before the poorest are likely to be able to afford a diet that meets the FAO minimum standard. Latin America is the only major LDC region where average caloric consumption is projected to be 20 percent or more above the FAO minimum standard in the year 2000. In the other LDC regions—South, East, and Southeast Asia, poor areas of North Africa and the Middle East, and especially Central Africa, where a calamitous drop in food per capita is projected—the quantity of food available to the poorest groups of people will simply be insufficient to permit children to reach normal body weight and intelligence and to permit normal activity and good health in adults. Consumption in the LDCs of central Africa is projected to be more than 20 percent below the FAO minimum standard, assuming no recurrence of severe drought. In South Asia (primarily India, Pakistan, and Bangladesh), average caloric intake is projected to remain below the FAO minimum standard, although increasing slightly—from 12 percent below the FAO standard in the mid-1970s to about 3 percent below the standard in 2000. In East Asia, Southeast Asia, and affluent areas of North Africa and the Middle East, average per capita caloric intakes are projected to be 6-17 percent above FAO minimum requirement levels, but because the great majority of people in these regions are extremely poor, they will almost certainly continue to eat less than the minimum. The World Bank has estimated that the number of malnourished people in LDCs could rise from 400–600 million in the mid-1970s to 1.3 billion in 2000.[34]

The projected food situation has many implications for food assistance and trade. In the developing world, the need for imported food is expected to grow. The most prosperous LDCs will turn increasingly to the world commercial markets. In the poorest countries, which lack the wherewithal to buy food, requirements for international food assistance will expand. LDC exporters (especially Argentina and Thailand) are projected to enlarge food production for export because of their cost advantage over countries dependent on energy-intensive inputs. LDC grain-exporting countries, which accounted for only a little more than 10 percent of the world grain

---

*"Consumption" statistics are based on the amount of food that leaves the farms and does not leave the country and therefore include transportation and processing losses. Projected increases in per capita consumption in countries like the United States, where average consumption is already at least nutritionally adequate, reflect increasing losses of food during transportation and processing and might also be accounted for by increased industrial demand for grain, especially for fermentation into fuels.

†The FAO standard indicates the *minimum* consumption that will allow normal activity and good health in adults and will permit children to reach normal body weight and intelligence in the absence of disease.

TABLE 5
Grain Production, Consumption, and Trade, Actual and Projected,
and Percent Increase in Total Food Production and Consumption

	Grain (million metric tons)			Food (Percent increase over the 1970-2000 period)
	1969-71	1973-75	2000	
Industrialized countries				
Production	401.7	434.7	679.1	43.7
Consumption	374.3	374.6	610.8	47.4
Trade	+ 32.1	+ 61.6	+ 68.3	
United States				
Production	208.7	228.7	402.0	78.5
Consumption	169.0	158.5	272.4	51.3
Trade	+ 39.9	+ 72.9	+ 129.6	
Other developed exporters				
Production	58.6	61.2	106.1	55.6
Consumption	33.2	34.3	65.2	66.8
Trade	+ 28.4	+ 27.7	+ 40.9	
Western Europe				
Production	121.7	132.9	153.0	14.6
Consumption	144.2	151.7	213.1	31.6
Trade	− 21.8	− 19.7	− 60.1	
Japan				
Production	12.7	11.9	18.0	31.5
Consumption	27.9	30.1	60.1	92.8
Trade	− 14.4	− 19.3	− 42.1	
Centrally planned countries				
Production	401.0	439.4	722.0	74.0
Consumption	406.6	472.4	758.5	79.9
Trade	− 5.2	− 24.0	− 36.5	
Eastern Europe				
Production	72.1	89.4	140.0	83.2
Consumption	78.7	97.7	151.5	81.7
Trade	− 6.1	− 7.8	− 11.5	
U.S.S.R.				
Production	165.0	179.3	290.0	72.7
Consumption	161.0	200.7	305.0	85.9
Trade	+ 3.9	− 10.6	− 15.0	
People's Republic of China				
Production	163.9	176.9	292.0	69.0
Consumption	166.9	180.8	302.0	71.4
Trade	− 3.0	− 3.9	− 10.0	

market in 1975, are projected to capture more than 20 percent of the market by 2000. The United States is expected to continue its role as the world's principal food exporter. Moreover, as the year 2000 approaches and more marginal, weather-sensitive lands are brought into production around the world, the United States is likely to become even more of a residual world supplier than today; that is, U.S. producers will be responding to widening, weather-related swings in world production and foreign demand.[35]

Revised and updated food projections would reflect reduced estimates of future yields, increased pressure on the agricultural resource base, and several changes in national food policies.

Farmers' costs of raising—and even maintaining—yields have increased rapidly in recent years. The costs of energy-intensive, yield-enhancing inputs—fertilizer, pesticides, and fuels—have risen very rapidly throughout the world, and where these inputs are heavily used, increased applications are bringing diminishing returns. In the United States, the real cost of producing food increased roughly 10 percent in both

TABLE 5 (Cont.)

	Grain (million metric tons)			Food (Percent increase over the 1970-2000 period)
	1969-71	1973-75	2000	
Less developed countries				
Production	306.5	328.7	740.6	147.7
Consumption	326.6	355.0	772.4	142.8
Trade	− 18.5	− 29.5	− 31.8	
Exporters[a]				
Production	30.1	34.5	84.0	125.0
Consumption	18.4	21.5	36.0	58.0
Trade	+ 11.3	+ 13.1	+ 48.0	
Importers[b]				
Production	276.4	294.2	656.6	149.3
Consumption	308.2	333.5	736.4	148.9
Trade	− 29.8	− 42.6	− 79.8	
Latin America				
Production	63.8	72.0	185.9	184.4
Consumption	61.2	71.2	166.0	165.3
Trade	+ 3.2	+ 0.2	+ 19.9	
North Africa/Middle East				
Production	38.9	42.4	89.0	157.8
Consumption	49.5	54.1	123.7	167.3
Trade	− 9.1	− 13.8	− 29.7	
Other African LDCs				
Production	32.0	31.3	63.7	104.9
Consumption	33.0	33.8	63.0	96.4
Trade	− 1.0	− 2.4	+ 0.7	
South Asia				
Production	119.1	127.7	259.0	116.8
Consumption	125.3	135.1	275.7	119.4
Trade	− 6.2	− 9.3	− 16.7	
Southeast Asia				
Production	22.8	21.4	65.0	210.0
Consumption	19.3	17.9	47.0	163.6
Trade	+ 3.4	+ 3.7	+ 18.0	
East Asia				
Production	29.9	34.0	73.0	155.3
Consumption	38.3	42.9	97.0	164.9
Trade	− 8.8	− 9.7	− 24.0	
World				
Production/Consumption	1,108.0	1,202.0	2,141.7	91.0

Note: In grade figures, plus sign indicates export, minus sign indicates import.

[a]Argentina and Thailand.

[b]All others, including several countries that export in some scenarios (e.g., Brazil, Indonesia, and Colombia).

Source: Global 2000 Technical Report, Table 6-5.

1978 and 1979.[36] Other industrialized countries have experienced comparable production cost increases. Cost increases in the LDCs appear to be lower, but are still 2-3 times the annual increases of the 1960s and early 1970s. While there have been significant improvements recently in the yields of selected crops, the diminishing returns and rapidly rising costs of yield-enhancing inputs suggest that yields overall will increase more slowly than projected.

Since the food projections were made, there have been several important shifts in national food and agricultural policy concerns. In most industrialized countries, concern with protecting agricultural resources, especially soils, has increased as the resource implications of sustained

TABLE 6

**Per Capita Grain Production, Consumption, and Trade, Actual and Projected,
and Percent Increase in Per Capita Total Food Production and Consumption**

	Grain (kilograms per capita)			Food (Percent increase over the 1970-2000 period)
	1969-71	1973-75	2000	
Industrialized countries				
Production	573.6	592.6	769.8	18.4
Consumption	534.4	510.7	692.4	21.2
Trade	+ 45.8	+ 84.0	+ 77.4	
United States				
Production	1,018.6	1,079.3	1,640.3	51.1
Consumption	824.9	748.0	1,111.5	28.3
Trade	+ 194.7	+ 344.0	+ 528.8	
Other developed exporters				
Production	1,015.6	917.0	915.6	− 11.3
Consumption	575.4	514.0	562.6	− 5.7
Trade	+ 492.2	+ 415.0	+ 353.0	
Western Europe				
Production	364.9	388.4	394.0	1.0
Consumption	432.4	443.3	548.8	15.5
Trade	− 65.4	− 57.6	− 154.8	
Japan				
Production	121.7	108.5	135.4	6.1
Consumption	267.5	274.4	452.3	54.2
Trade	− 138.1	− 175.9	− 316.7	
Centrally planned countries				
Production	356.1	368.0	451.1	29.6
Consumption	361.0	395.6	473.9	35.8
Trade	− 4.6	− 20.1	− 22.8	
Eastern Europe				
Production	574.0	693.0	921.9	53.3
Consumption	626.6	757.4	997.6	52.1
Trade	− 48.6	− 60.5	− 75.8	
U.S.S.R.				
Production	697.6	711.2	903.2	28.1
Consumption	663.1	796.1	949.9	41.4
Trade	+ 16.1	− 42.0	− 46.7	
People's Republic of China				
Production	216.3	217.6	259.0	17.4
Consumption	220.2	222.4	267.8	19.1
Trade	− 4.0	− 4.8	− 8.8	

production of record quantities of food here become more apparent. Debate on the 1981 U.S. farm bill, for example, will certainly include more consideration of "exporting top soil" than was foreseeable at the time the Global 2000 Study's food projections were made.[37] The heightened concern for protection of agricultural resources is leading to a search for policies that encourage improved resource management practices. Still further pressure on the resource base can be expected, however, due to rising industrial demand for grain, especially for fermentation into alcohol-based fuels. Accelerated erosion, loss of natural soil fertility and other deterioration of the agricultural resource base may have more effect in the coming years than is indicated in the Global 2000 food projections.

In the LDCs, many governments are attempting to accelerate investment in food production capacity. This policy emphasis offers important long-term benefits. Some LDC governments are intervening more frequently in domestic food markets to keep food prices low, but often at the cost of low rural incomes and slowed development

TABLE 6 (Cont.)

	Grain (kilograms per capita)			Food Percent increase over the 1970-2000 period
	1969–71	1973–75	2000	
Less developed countries				
Production	176.7	168.7	197.1	10.8
Consumption	188.3	182.2	205.5	8.6
Trade	−10.7	−15.1	−8.4	
Exporters[a]				
Production	491.0	521.9	671.7	10.4
Consumption	300.1	325.3	287.8	−22.6
Trade	+184.3	+198.2	+383.9	
Importers[b]				
Production	159.4	173.8	180.7	10.8
Consumption	177.7	193.6	202.7	10.8
Trade	−17.2	−24.1	−21.9	
Latin America				
Production	236.1	241.0	311.4	33.7
Consumption	226.5	238.3	278.1	25.1
Trade	+11.8	+2.7	+33.3	
North Africa/Middle East				
Production	217.1	214.6	222.5	−1.8
Consumption	276.2	273.8	292.8	2.2
Trade	−50.8	−69.8	−70.3	
Other African LDCs				
Production	134.9	118.3	113.2	−15.5
Consumption	139.1	127.7	112.0	−19.1
Trade	−4.2	−9.1	+1.2	
South Asia				
Production	161.6	162.4	170.0	4.6
Consumption	170.0	171.8	181.0	5.8
Trade	−8.4	−11.8	−11.0	
Southeast Asia				
Production	244.7	214.5	316.5	35.9
Consumption	207.2	182.6	228.5	14.6
Trade	+37.5	+31.9	+87.5	
East Asia				
Production	137.3	136.0	163.5	22.8
Consumption	176.2	171.5	217.3	27.3
Trade	−40.4	−38.8	−53.8	
World				
Production/Consumption	311.5	313.6	343.2	14.5

Note: In trade figures, plus sign indicates export, minus sign indicates import.

[a]Argentina and Thailand.

[b]All others, including several countries that export in some scenarios (e.g., Brazil, Indonesia, and Colombia).

Source: Global 2000 Technical Report, Table 6-6.

of agricultural production capacity.[38]

Worldwide, the use of yield-enhancing inputs is likely to be less, and soil deterioration greater, than expected. As a result, revised food projections would show a tighter food future—somewhat less production and somewhat higher prices —than indicated in the Global 2000 projections.

Fisheries

Fish is an important component of the world's diet and has sometimes been put forth as a possible partial solution to world food shortages. Unfortunately, the world harvest of fish is expected to rise little, if at all, by the year 2000.* The world catch of naturally produced fish leveled off in the 1970s at about 70 million metric tons a year

---

*The food projections assumed that the world fish catch would increase at essentially the same rate as population and are therefore likely to prove too optimistic on this point. (See Chapters 6, 14, and 18 of the Global 2000 Technical Report for further discussion of this point.)

22

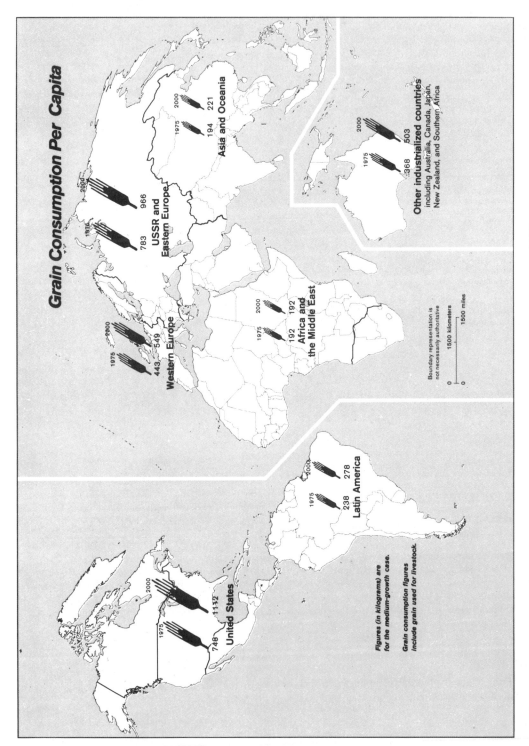

Figure 5. Per capita grain consumption, by regions, 1975 and 2000.

(60 million metric tons for marine fisheries, 10 million metric tons for freshwater species). Harvests of traditional fisheries are not likely to increase on a sustained basis, and indeed to maintain them will take good management and improved protection of the marine environment. Some potential for greater harvests comes from aquaculture and from nontraditional marine species, such as Antarctic krill, that are little used at present for direct human consumption.[39]

Traditional freshwater and marine species might be augmented in some areas by means of aquaculture. The 1976 FAO World Conference on Aquaculture concluded that a five- to tenfold increase in production from aquaculture would be possible by 2000, given adequate financial and technical support. (Aquaculture contributed an estimated 6 million metric tons to the world's total catch in 1975.) However, limited investment and technical support, as well as increasing pollution of freshwater ponds and coastal water, are likely to be a serious impediment to such growth.[40]

While fish is not a solution to the world needs for calories, fish does provide an important source of protein. The 70 million metric tons caught and raised in 1975 is roughly equivalent to 14 million metric tons of protein, enough to supply 27 percent of the minimum protein requirements of 4 billion people. (Actually since more than one-third of the fish harvest is used for animal feed, not food for humans, the contribution of fish to human needs for protein is lower than these figures suggest.[41]) A harvest of about 115 million metric tons would be required to supply 27 percent of the protein needs of 6.35 billion people in 2000. Even assuming that the catch of marine and freshwater fish rises to the unlikely level of 100 million metric tons annually, and that yields from aquaculture double, rising to 12 million tons, the hypothetical total of 112 metric tons would not provide as much protein per capita as the catch of the mid-1970s. Thus, on a per capita basis, fish may well contribute less to the world's nutrition in 2000 than today.

Updated fisheries projections would show little change from the Global 2000 Study projections. FAO fisheries statistics are now available for 1978 and show a world catch of 72.4 million metric tons. (The FAO statistics for the 1970-78 period have been revised downward somewhat to reflect improved data on the catch of the People's Republic of China.) While there has been some slight recovery of the anchovy and menhaden fisheries, traditional species continue to show signs of heavy pressure. As indicated in the Global 2000 projections, the catch of nontraditional species is filling in to some extent. Perhaps the biggest change in updated fisheries projections would stem from a careful analysis of the effects of the large increase in oil prices that occurred in 1979. Scattered observations suggest that fishing fleets throughout the world are being adversely affected except where governments are keeping oil prices to fishing boats artificially low.[42]

Forests

If present trends continue, both forest cover and growing stocks of commercial-size wood in the less developed regions (Latin America, Africa, Asia, and Oceania) will decline 40 percent by 2000. In the industrialized regions (Europe,

TABLE 7
Estimates of World Forest Resources, 1978 and 2000

	Closed Forest[a] (millions of hectares)		Growing Stock (billions cu m overbark)	
	1978	2000	1978	2000
U.S.S.R.	785	775	79	77
Europe	140	150	15	13
North America	470	464	58	55
Japan, Australia, New Zealand	69	68	4	4
Subtotal	1,464	1,457	156	149
Latin America	550	329	94	54
Africa	188	150	39	31
Asia and Pacific LDCs	361	181	38	19
Subtotal (LDCs)	1,099	660	171	104
Total (world)	2,563	2,117	327	253

	Growing Stock per Capita (cu m biomass)	
Industrial countries	142	114
LDCs	57	21
Global	76	40

[a]Closed forests are relatively dense and productive forests. They are defined variously in different parts of the world. For further details, see Global 2000 Technical Report, footnote, p. 117.

Source: Global 2000 Technical Report, Table 13-29.

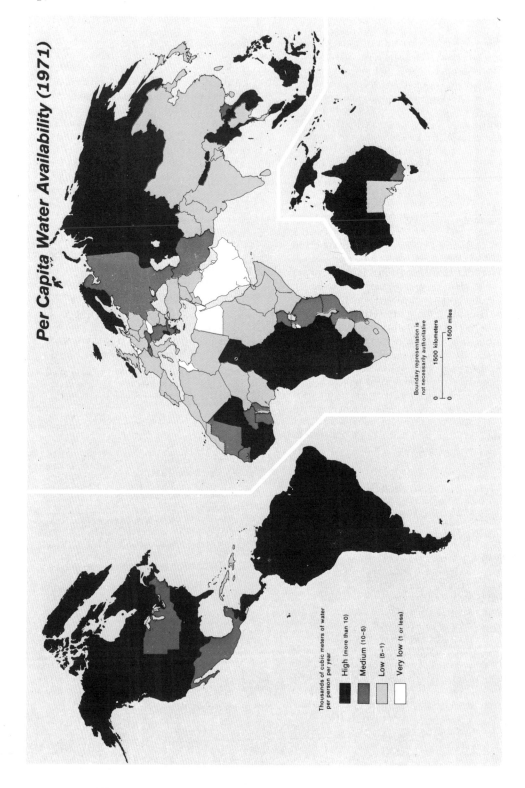

Figure 6. Per capita water availability, 1971.

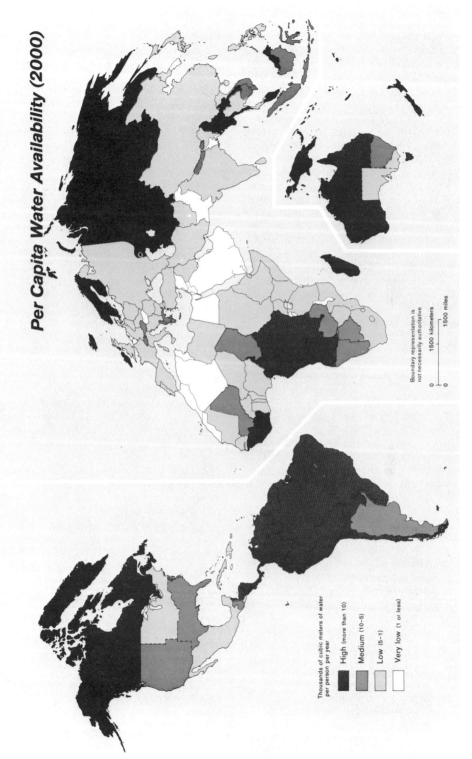

Figure 7. Projected per capita water availability, 2000.

the U.S.S.R., North America, Japan, Australia, New Zealand) forests will decline only 0.5 percent and growing stock about 5 percent. Growing stock per capita is expected to decline 47 percent worldwide and 63 percent in LDCs.[43] Table 7 shows projected forest cover and growing stocks by region for 1978 and 2000.

Deforestation is projected to continue until about 2020, when the total world forest area will stabilize at about 1.8 billion hectares. Most of the loss will occur in the tropical forests of the developing world. About 1.45 billion hectares of forest in the industrialized nations has already stabilized and about 0.37 billion hectares of forest in the LDCs is physically or economically inaccessible. By 2020, virtually all of the physically accessible forest in the LDCs is expected to have been cut.[44]

The real prices of wood products—fuelwood, sawn lumber, wood panels, paper, wood-based chemicals, and so on—are expected to rise considerably as GNP (and thus also demand) rises and world supplies tighten. In the industrialized nations, the effects may be disruptive, but not catastrophic. In the less developed countries, however, 90 percent of wood consumption goes for cooking and heating, and wood is a necessity of life. Loss of woodlands will force people in many LDCs to pay steeply rising prices for fuelwood and charcoal or to spend much more effort collecting wood—or else to do without.[45]

Updated forest projections would present much the same picture as the Global 2000 Study projections. The rapid increase in the price of crude oil will probably limit the penetration of kerosene sales into areas now depending on fuelwood and dung and, as a result, demand for fuelwood may be somewhat higher than expected. Some replanting of cut tropical areas is occurring, but only at low rates similar to those assumed in the Global 2000 Study projections. Perhaps the most encouraging developments are those associated with heightened international awareness of the seriousness of current trends in world forests.[46]

Water

The Global 2000 Study population, GNP, and resource projections all imply rapidly increasing demands for fresh water.[47] Increases of at least 200-300 percent in world water withdrawals are expected over the 1975-2000 period. By far the largest part of the increase is for irrigation. The United Nations has estimated that water needed for irrigation, which accounted for 70 percent of human uses of water in 1967, would double by 2000. Moreover, irrigation is a highly consumptive use, that is, much of the water withdrawn for this purpose is not available for immediate reuse because it evaporates, is transpired by plants, or becomes salinated.[48]

Regional water shortages and deterioration of water quality, already serious in many parts of the world, are likely to become worse by 2000. Estimates of per capita water availability for 1971 and 2000, based on population growth alone, *without allowance for other causes of increased demand,* are shown in Figures 6 and 7. As indicated in these maps, population growth alone will cause demands for water at least to double relative to 1971 in nearly half the countries of the world. Still greater increases would be needed to improve standards of living.[49]

Much of the increased demand for water will be in the LDCs of Africa, South Asia, the Middle East, and Latin America, where in many areas fresh water for human consumption and irrigation is already in short supply. Although the data are sketchy, it is known that several nations in these areas will be approaching their maximum developable water supply by 2000, and that it will be quite expensive to develop the water remaining. Moreover, many LDCs will also suffer destabilization of water supplies following extensive loss of forests. In the industrialized countries competition among different uses of water—for increasing food production, new energy systems (such as production of synthetic fuels from coal and shale), increasing power generation, expanding food production, and increasing needs of other industry—will aggravate water shortages in many areas.[50]

Updated water projections would present essentially the same picture. The only significant change that has occurred since the projections were developed is that the price of energy (especially oil) has increased markedly. Increased energy costs will adversely affect the economics of many water development projects, and may reduce the amount of water available for a variety of uses. Irrigation, which usually requires large amounts of energy for pumping, may be particularly affected.

Nonfuel Minerals

The trends for nonfuel minerals, like those for the other resources considered in the Global 2000 Study, show steady increases in demand and consumption. The global demand for and consumption of most major nonfuel mineral commodities is projected to increase 3-5 percent annually, slightly more than doubling by 2000. Consumption of all major steelmaking mineral commodities is projected to increase at least 3 percent annually. Consumption of all mineral commodities for fertilizer production is projected to grow at more than 3 percent annually, with consumption of phosphate rock growing at 5.2 percent per year—the highest growth rate projected for any of the major nonfuel mineral commodities. The nonferrous metals show widely varying projected growth rates; the growth rate for aluminum, 4.3 percent per year, is the largest.[51]

The projections suggest that the LDC's share of nonfuel mineral use will increase only modestly. Over the 1971-75 period, Latin America, Africa, and Asia used 7 percent of the world's aluminum production, 9 percent of the copper, and 12 percent of the iron ore. The three-quarters of the world's population living in these regions in 2000 are projected to use only 8 percent of aluminum production, 13 percent of copper production, and 17 percent of iron ore production. The one-quarter of the world's population that inhabits industrial countries is projected to continue absorbing more than three-fourths of the world's nonfuel minerals production.[52] Figure 8 shows the geographic distribution of per capita consumption of nonfuel minerals for 1975 and 2000.

The projections point to no mineral exhaustion problems but, as indicated in Table 8, further discoveries and investments will be needed to maintain reserves and production of several mineral commodities at desirable levels. In most cases, however, the resource potential is still large (see Table 9), especially for low grade ores.[53]

Updated nonfuel minerals projections would need to give further attention to two factors affecting investment in mining. One is the shift over the past decade in investment in extraction and processing away from the developing countries toward industrialized countries (although this trend may now be reversing). The other factor is the rapid increase in energy prices. Production of many nonfuel minerals is highly energy-intensive, and the recent and projected increases in oil prices can be expected to slow the expansion of these mineral supplies.[54]

Energy

The Global 2000 Study's energy projections show no early relief from the world's energy problems. The projections point out that petroleum production capacity is not increasing as rapidly as demand. Furthermore, the rate at which petroleum reserves are being added per unit of exploratory effort appears to be falling. Engineering and geological considerations suggest that world petroleum production will peak before the end of the century. Political and economic decisions in the OPEC countries could cause oil production to level off even before technological constraints come into play. A world transition away from petroleum dependence must take place, but there is still much uncertainty as to how this transition will occur. In the face of this uncertainty, it was not possible at the time the Global 2000 energy projections were made—late 1977—for the Department of Energy (DOE) to develop meaningful energy projections beyond 1990.[55] Updated DOE analyses, discussed at the end of this section, extend the global energy projections available from the U.S. Government to 1995.

DOE projections prepared for the Study show large increases in demand for all commercial sources over the 1975-90 period (see Table 10). World energy demand is projected to increase 58 percent, reaching 384 quads (quadrillion British thermal units) by 1990. Nuclear and hydro sources (primarily nuclear) increase most rapidly (226 percent by 1990), followed by oil (58 percent), natural gas (43 percent), and coal (13 percent). Oil is projected to remain the world's leading energy source, providing 46-47 percent of the world's total energy through 1990, assuming that the real price of oil on the international market increases 65 percent over the 1975-90 period. The energy projections indicate that there is considerable potential for reductions in energy consumption.[56]

Per capita energy consumption is projected to increase everywhere. The largest increase—72 percent over the 1975-90 period—is in industrialized countries other than the United States. The

28

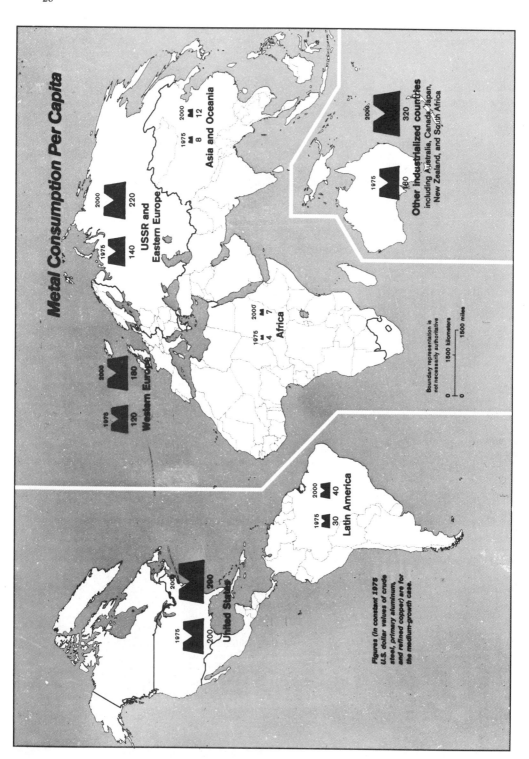

Figure 8. Distribution of per capita consumption of nonfuel minerals, 1975 and 2000.

TABLE 8
Life Expectancies of 1976 World Reserves of Selected Mineral Commodities at Two Different Rates of Demand

	1976 Reserves	1976 Primary Demand	Projected Demand Growth Rate	Life Expectancy in Years[a]	
				Static at 1976 Level	Growing at Projected Rates
			percent		
Fluorine (*million short tons*)	37	2.1	4.58	18	13
Silver (*million troy ounces*)	6,100	305	2.33	20	17
Zinc (*million short tons*)	166	6.4	3.05	26	19
Mercury (*thousand flasks*)	5,210	239	0.50	22	21
Sulfur (*million long tons*)	1,700	50	3.16	34	23
Lead (*million short tons*)	136	3.7	3.14	37	25
Tungsten (*million pounds*)	4,200	81	3.26	52	31
Tin (*thousand metric tons*)	10,000	241	2.05	41	31
Copper (*million short tons*)	503	8.0	2.94	63	36
Nickel (*million short tons*)	60	0.7	2.94	86	43
Platinum (*million troy ounces*)	297	2.7	3.75	110	44
Phosphate rock (*million metric tons*)	25,732	107	5.17	240	51
Manganese (*million short tons*)	1,800	11.0	3.36	164	56
Iron in ore (*billion short tons*)	103	0.6	2.95	172	62
Aluminum in bauxite (*million short tons*)	5,610	18	4.29	312	63
Chromium (*million short tons*)	829	2.2	3.27	377	80
Potash (*million short tons*)	12,230	26	3.27	470	86

Note: Corresponding data for helium and industrial diamonds not available.

[a]Assumes no increase to 1976 reserves.

Source: After Global 2000 Technical Report, Table 12-4, but with updated and corrected entries. Updated reserves and demand data from U.S. Bureau of Mines, *Mineral Trends and Forecasts*, 1979. Projected demand growth rates are from Global 2000 Technical Report, Table 12-2.

smallest increase, 12 percent, is in the centrally planned economies of Eastern Europe. The percentage increases for the United States and for the LDCs are the same—27 percent—but actual per capita energy consumption is very different. By 2000, U.S. per capita energy consumption is projected to be about 422 million Btu (British thermal units) annually. In the LDCs, it will be only 14 million Btu, up from 11 million in 1975[57] (see Table 11 and Figure 9).

While prices for oil and other commercial energy sources are rising, fuelwood—the poor person's oil—is expected to become far less available than it is today. The FAO has estimated that the demand for fuelwood in LDCs will increase at 2.2 percent per year, leading to local fuelwood shortages in 1994 totaling 650 million cubic meters—approximately 25 percent of the projected need. Scarcities are now local but expanding. In the arid Sahel of Africa, fuelwood gathering has become a full-time job requiring in some places 360 person-days of work per household each year. When demand is concentrated in cities, surrounding areas have already become barren for considerable distances—50 to 100 kilometers in some places. Urban families, too far from collectible wood, spend 20 to 30 percent of their income on wood in some West African cities.[58]

The projected shortfall of fuelwood implies that fuel consumption for essential uses will be reduced, deforestation expanded, wood prices increased, and growing amounts of dung and crop residues shifted from the field to the cooking fire. No explicit projections of dung and crop residue combustion could be made for the Study, but it is known that a shift toward burning these organic materials is already well advanced in the Himalayan hills, in the treeless Ganges plain of India, in other parts of Asia, and in the Andean region of South America. The FAO reports that in 1970 India burned 68 million tons of cow dung and 39 million tons of vegetable waste, accounting for roughly a third of the nation's total noncommercial energy consumption that year. Worldwide, an estimated 150-400 million tons of dung are burned annually for fuel.[59]

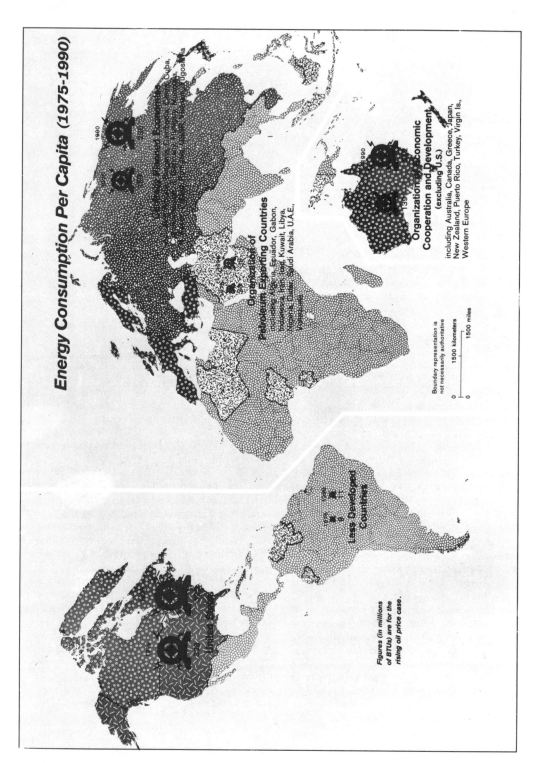

Energy Consumption Per Capita (1975-1990)

Organization of Petroleum Exporting Countries
including Algeria, Ecuador, Gabon, Indonesia, Iran, Iraq, Kuwait, Libya, Nigeria, Qatar, Saudi Arabia, U.A.E., Venezuela

Organization for Economic Cooperation and Development (excluding U.S.)
including Australia, Canada, Greece, Japan, New Zealand, Puerto Rico, Turkey, Virgin Is., Western Europe

Less Developed Countries

Figures (in millions of BTUs) are for the rising oil price case.

Boundary representation is not necessarily authoritative

0   1500 kilometers

0   1500 miles

TABLE 9
World Production and Reserves in 1977 (Estimated), Other Resources in 1973–77 (as Data Available), Resource Potential, and Resource Base of 17 Elements

(Millions of metric tons)

	Production	Reserves	Other Resources	Resource Potential (Recoverable)	Resource Base (Crustal Mass)
Aluminum	17[a]	5,200[a]	2,800[a]	3,519,000	1,990,000,000,000
Iron	495[b]	93,100	143,000[c]	2,035,000	1,392,000,000,000
Potassium	22	9,960	103,000	n.a.	408,000,000,000
Manganese	10[d]	2,200	1,100[e]	42,000	31,200,000,000
Phosphorus	14[f]	3,400[f]	12,000[f]	51,000	28,800,000,000
Fluorine	2[g]	72	270	20,000	10,800,000,000
Sulfur	52	1,700	3,800[h]		9,600,000,000
Chromium	3[i]	780[i]	6,000[i]	3,260	2,600,000,000
Zinc	6	159	4,000	3,400	2,250,000,000
Nickel	0.7	54	103[e]	2,590	2,130,000,000
Copper	8	456	1,770[j]	2,120	1,510,000,000
Lead	4	123	1,250	550	290,000,000
Tin	0.2	10	27	68	40,800,000
Tungsten	0.04	1.8	3.4	51	26,400,000
Mercury	0.008	0.2	0.4	3.4	2,100,000
Silver	0.010	0.2	0.5	2.8	1,800,000
Platinum group[k]	0.0002	0.02	0.05[l]	1.2[m]	1,100,000

[a]In bauxite, dry basis, assumed to average 21 percent recoverable aluminum.
[b]In ore and concentrates assumed to average 58 percent recoverable iron.
[c]In ore and concentrates assumed to average 26 percent recoverable iron.
[d]In ore and concentrates assumed to average 40 percent recoverable iron.
[e]Excludes metal in deep-sea nodules and, in the case of nickel, unidentified resources.
[f]In phosphate rock ore and concentrates assumed to average 13 percent phosphorus.
[g]In fluorspar and phosphate rock ore and concentrates assumed to average 44 percent fluorine.

[h]Excludes unidentified sulfur resources, enormous quantities of sulfur in gypsum and anhydrite, and some 600 billion tons of sulfur in coal, oil shale, and in shale that is rich in organic matter.
[i]In ore and concentrates assumed to average 32 percent chromium.
[j]Includes 690 million tons in deep-sea nodules.
[k]Platinum, palladium, iridium, cesium, rhodium, and ruthenium.
[l]Approximate midpoint of estimated range of 0.03–0.06 million metric tons.
[m]Platinum only.

Source: Global 2000 Technical Report, Table 12-7.

TABLE 10
Global Primary[a] Energy Use, 1975 and 1990, by Energy Type

	1975		1990		Percent Increase (1975-90)	Average Annual Percent Increase
	10^{15} Btu	Percent of Total	10^{15} Btu[b]	Percent of Total		
Oil	113	46	179	47	58	3.1
Coal	68	28	77	20	13	0.8
Natural gas	46	19	66	17	43	2.4
Nuclear and hydro	19	8[c]	62	16[c]	226	7.9
Solar (other than conservation/ and hydro)[d]	—	—	—	—	—	—
Total	246	100	384	100	56	3.0

[a]All of the nuclear and much of the coal primary (i.e., input) energy is used thermally to generate electricity. In the process, approximately two-thirds of the primary energy is lost as waste heat. The figures given here are primary energy.
[b]The conversions from the DOE projections in Table 10-8 were made as follows: *Oil* 84.8 × 10^6 bbl/day × 365 days × 5.8 × 10^6 Btu/bbl = 179 × 10^{15} Btu. *Coal:* 5,424 × 10^6 short tons/yr × 14.1 × 10^6 Btu/short ton [DOE figure for world average grade coal] = 77 × 10^{15} Btu. *Natural gas:* 64.4 × 10^{12}ft³/yr × 1,032 Btu/ft³ = 66 × 10^{15} Btu. *Nuclear and Hydro:* 6,009 × 10^{12} Wh [output]/yr × 3,412 Btu/Wh × 3 input Btu/output Btu = 62 × 10^{12} Btu.
[c]After deductions for lost (waste) heat (see note a), the corresponding figures for output energy are 2.7 percent in 1975 and 6.0 in 1990.
[d]The IIES projection model is able to include solar only as conservation or hydro.
Source: Global 2000 Technical Report, Table 13-32.

TABLE 11
Per Capita Global Primary Energy Use, Annually, 1975 and 1990

	1975		1990			
	10^6 Btu	Percent of World Average	10^6 Btu	Percent of World Average	Percent Increase (1975-90)	Average Annual Percent Increase
United States	332	553	422	586	27	1.6
Other industrialized countries	136	227	234	325	72	3.6
Less developed countries[a]	11	18	14	19	27	1.6
Centrally planned economies	58	97	65	90	12	0.8
World	60	100	72	100	20	1.2

[a]Since population projections were not made separately for the LDC category.
OPEC countries, those countries have been included here in

Source: Global 2000 Technical Report, Table 13-34.

Updated energy projections have been developed by the Department of Energy based on new price scenarios that include the rapid 1979 increase in the price of crude oil. The new price scenarios are not markedly different from the earlier estimates for the 1990s. The new medium-scenario price for 1995 is $40 per barrel (in 1979 dollars), which is about 10 percent higher than the $36 price (1979 dollars) implied by the earlier scenario. However, the prices for the early 1980s are almost 100 percent higher than those in the projections made by DOE in late 1977 for the Study.[60] The sudden large increase in oil prices of 1979 is likely to have a more disruptive effect on other sectors than would the gradual increase assumed in the Global 2000 Study projections.

DOE's new projections differ in several ways from those reported in this Study. Using the higher prices, additional data, and a modified model, DOE is now able to project supply and demand for an additional five years, to 1995. Demand is projected to be lower because of the higher prices and also because of reduced estimates of economic growth. Coal is projected to provide a somewhat larger share of the total energy supply. The nuclear projections for the OECD countries are lower, reflecting revised estimates of the speed at which new nuclear plants will be built. Updated estimates of OPEC maximum production are lower than earlier estimates, reflecting trends toward resource conservation by the OPEC nations. The higher oil prices will encourage the adoption of alternative fuels and technologies, including solar technology and conservation measures.[61]

Environmental Consequences

The population, income, and resource projections all imply significant consequences for the quality of the world environment. Virtually every aspect of the earth's ecosystems and resource base will be affected.[62]

Impacts on Agriculture

Perhaps the most serious environmental development will be an accelerating deterioration and loss of the resources essential for agriculture. This overall development includes soil erosion; loss of nutrients and compaction of soils; increasing salinization of both irrigated land and water used for irrigation; loss of high-quality cropland to urban development; crop damage due to increasing air and water pollution; extinction of local and wild crop strains needed by plant breeders for improving cultivated varieties; and more frequent and more severe regional water shortages—especially where energy and industrial developments compete for water supplies, or where forest losses are heavy and the earth can no longer absorb, store, and regulate the discharge of water.

Deterioration of soils is occurring rapidly in LDCs, with the spread of desert-like conditions in drier regions, and heavy erosion in more humid areas. Present global losses to desertification are estimated at around 6 million hectares a year (an area about the size of Maine), including 3.2 million hectares of rangeland, 2.5 million hectares of rainfed cropland, and 125 thousand hectares of irrigated farmland. Desertification does not necessarily mean the creation of Sahara-like sand deserts, but rather it includes a variety of ecological changes that destroy the cover of vegetation and fertile soil in the earth's drier regions, rendering the land useless for range or crops. Principal direct causes are overgrazing, destructive cropping practices, and use of woody plants for fuel.

At presently estimated rates of desertification, the world's desert areas (now some 800 million hectares) would expand almost 20 percent by 2000. But there is reason to expect that losses to desertification will accelerate, as increasing numbers of people in the world's drier regions put more pressures on the land to meet their needs for livestock range, cropland, and fuelwood. The United Nations has identified about 2 billion hectares of lands (Figure 10) where the risk of desertification is "high" or "very high." These lands at risk total about two and one-half times the area now classified as desert.

Although soil loss and deterioration are especially serious in many LDCs, they are also affecting agricultural prospects in industrialized nations. Present rates of soil loss in many industrialized nations cannot be sustained without serious implications for crop production. In the United States, for example, the Soil Conservation Service, looking at wind and water erosion of U.S. soils, has concluded that to sustain crop production indefinitely at even present levels, soil losses must be cut in half.

The outlook for making such gains in the United States and elsewhere is not good. The food and forestry projections imply increasing pressures on soils throughout the world. Losses due to improper irrigation, reduced fallow periods, cultivation of steep and marginal lands, and reduced vegetative cover can be expected to accelerate, especially in North and Central Africa, the humid and high-altitude portions of Latin America, and much of South Asia. In addition, the increased burning of dung and crop wastes for domestic fuel will deprive the soil of nutrients and degrade the soil's ability to hold moisture by reducing its organic content. For the world's poor, these organic materials are often the only source of the nutrients needed to maintain the productivity of farmlands. It is the poorest people—those least able to afford chemical fertilizers—who are being forced to burn their organic fertilizers. These

nutrients will be urgently needed for food production in the years ahead, since by 2000 the world's croplands will have to feed half again as many people as in 1975.[63] In the industrialized regions, increasing use of chemical fertilizers, high-yield plant varieties, irrigation water, and herbicides and pesticides have so far compensated for basic declines in soil conditions. However, heavy dependence on chemical fertilizers also leads to losses of soil organic matter, reducing the capacity of the soil to retain moisture.

Damage and loss of irrigated lands are especially significant because these lands have yields far above average. Furthermore, as the amount of arable land per capita declines over the next two decades, irrigated lands will be counted upon increasingly to raise per capita food availability. As of 1975, 230 million hectares—15 percent of the world's arable area—were being irrigated; an additional 50 million hectares are expected to be irrigated by 1990. Unfortunately there is great difficulty in maintaining the productivity of irrigated lands. About half of the world's irrigated land has already been damaged to some degree by salinity, alkalinity, and waterlogging, and much of the additional land expected to be irrigated by 1990 is highly vulnerable to irrigation-related damage.

Environmental problems of irrigation exist in industrialized countries (for example, in the San Joaquin Valley in California) as well as in LDCs (as in Pakistan, where three-quarters of the irrigated lands are damaged). It is possible, but slow and costly, to restore damaged lands. Prevention requires careful consideration of soils and attention to drainage, maintenance, and appropriate water-saving designs.

Loss of good cropland to urban encroachment is another problem affecting all countries. Cities and industries are often located on a nation's best agricultural land—rich, well-watered alluvial soils in gently sloping river valleys. In the industrialized countries that are members of the OECD, the amount of land devoted to urban uses has been increasing twice as fast as population. The limited data available for LDCs point to similar trends. In Egypt, for example, despite efforts to open new lands to agriculture, the total area of irrigated farmland has remained almost unchanged in the past two decades. As fast as additional acres are irrigated with water from the

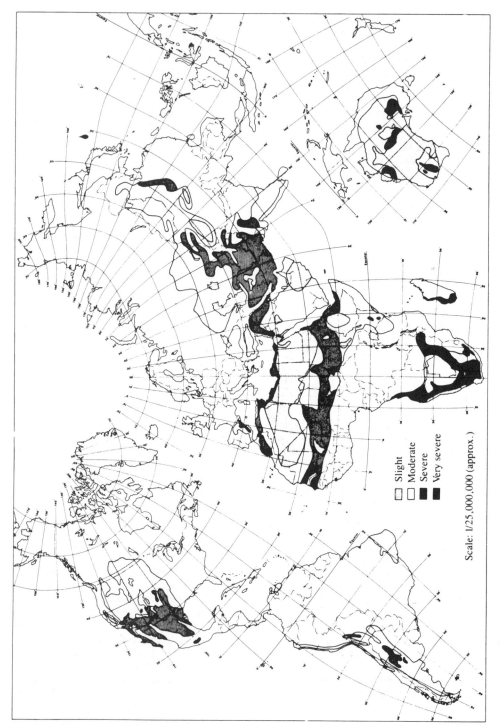

Scale: 1/25,000,000 (approx.)

☐ Slight
☐ Moderate
■ Severe
■ Very severe

Figure 10. Desertification map (*U.N. Desertification Conference, 1977*).

Aswan Dam, old producing lands on the Nile are converted to urban uses.

The rising yields assumed by the Global 2000 food projections depend on wider adoption of existing high-yield agricultural technology and on accelerating use of fertilizers, irrigation, pesticides, and herbicides. These yield-enhancing inputs, projected to more than double in use worldwide and to quadruple in LDCs, are heavily dependent on fossil fuels. Even now, a rapid escalation of fossil fuel prices or a sudden interruption of supply could severely disturb world agricultural production, raise food prices, and deprive larger numbers of people of adequate food. As agriculture becomes still more dependent on energy-intensive inputs, the potential for disruption will be even greater.

Accelerating use of pesticides is expected to raise crop yields quickly and substantially, especially in LDCs. Yet, many of these chemicals produce a wide range of serious environmental consequences, some of which adversely affect agricultural production. Destruction of pest predator populations and the increasing resistance of pests to heavily used pesticides have already proved to be significant agricultural problems. On California farms, for example, 17 of 25 major agricultural pests are now resistant to one or more types of pesticides, and the populations of pest predators have been severely reduced. Many millions of dollars in crop damage are now caused annually in California by resistant pests whose natural predators have been destroyed.

Crop yields are expected to be increased significantly by much wider use of high-yield strains of grains. Unfortunately, large monocultures of genetically identical crops pose increased risks of catastrophic loss from insect attacks or crop epidemics. The corn blight that struck the U.S. corn belt in 1970 provided a clear illustration of the vulnerability of genetically identical monocultures.

Impacts on Water Resources

The quality of the world's water resources is virtually certain to suffer from the changes taking place between now and the year 2000. Water pollution from heavy application of pesticides will cause increasing difficulties. In the industrialized countries, shifts from widespread use of long-lived chemicals such as DDT are now underway, but in the LDCs—where the largest increases in agricultural chemical use is projected—it is likely that the persistent pesticides will continue to be used. Pesticide use in LDCs is expected to at least quadruple over the 1975–2000 period (a sixfold increase is possible if recent rates of increase continue). Pollution from the persistent pesticides in irrigation canals, ponds, and rice paddies is already a worrisome problem. Farmers in some parts of Asia are reluctant to stock paddies and ponds because fish are being killed by pesticides. This means a serious loss of high-quality protein for the diets of rural families.

In addition to the potential impacts on soils discussed above, irrigation adversely affects water quality by adding salt to the water returning to streams and rivers. Downstream from extensive irrigation projects the water may become too saline for further use, unless expensive desalinization measures are undertaken. As the use of water for irrigation increases, water salinity problems are certain to increase as well.

Water pollution in LDCs is likely to worsen as the urban population soars and industry expands. Already the waters below many LDC cities are heavily polluted with sewage and wastes from pulp and paper mills, tanneries, slaughterhouses, oil refineries, and chemical plants.

River basin development that combines flood control, generation of electricity, and irrigation is likely to increase in many less developed regions, where most of the world's untapped hydropower potential lies. While providing many benefits, large-scale dams and irrigation projects can also cause highly adverse changes in both freshwater and coastal ecosystems, creating health problems (including schistosomiasis, river blindness, malaria), inundating valuable lands, and displacing populations. In addition, if erosion in the watersheds of these projects is not controlled, siltation and buildup of sediments may greatly reduce the useful life of the projects.

Virtually all of the Global 2000 Study's projections point to increasing destruction or pollution of coastal ecosystems, a resource on which the commercially important fisheries of the world depend heavily. It is estimated that 60-80 percent of commercially valuable marine fishery species use estuaries, salt marshes, or mangrove swamps for habitat at some point in their life cycle. Reef habitats also provide food and shelter for large numbers of fish and invertebrate species. Rapidly expanding cities and industry are likely to claim coastal wetland areas for development; and increasing coastal pollution from agriculture, industry, logging, water resources development, energy systems, and coastal communities is anticipated in many areas.

Impacts of Forest Losses

The projected rapid, widespread loss of tropical forests will have severe adverse effects on water and other resources. Deforestation—especially in South Asia, the Amazon basin, and central Africa—will destabilize water flows, leading to siltation of streams, reservoirs behind hydroelectric dams, and irrigation works, to depletion of ground water, to intensified flooding, and to aggravated water shortages during dry periods. In South and Southeast Asia approximately one billion people live in heavily farmed alluvial basins and valleys that depend on forested mountain watersheds for their water. If present trends continue, forests in these regions will be reduced by about half in 2000, and erosion, siltation, and erratic streamflows will seriously affect food production.

In many tropical forests, the soils, land forms, temperatures, patterns of rainfall, and distribution of nutrients are in precarious balance. When these forests are disturbed by extensive cutting, neither trees nor productive grasses will grow again. Even in less fragile tropical forests, the great diversity of species is lost after extensive cutting.

Impacts on the World's Atmosphere and Climate

Among the emerging environmental stresses are some that affect the chemical and physical nature of the atmosphere. Several are recognized as problems; others are more conjectural but nevertheless of concern.

Quantitative projections of urban air quality around the world are not possible with the data and models now available, but further pollution in LDCs and some industrial nations is virtually certain to occur under present policies and practices. In LDC cities, industrial growth projected for the next 20 years is likely to worsen air quality. Even now, observations in scattered LDC cities show levels of sulfur dioxide, particulates, nitrogen dioxide, and carbon monoxide far above levels considered safe by the World Health Organization. In some cities, such as Bombay and Caracas, recent rapid increases in the numbers of cars and trucks have aggravated air pollution.

Despite recent progress in reducing various types of air pollution in many industrialized countries, air quality there is likely to worsen as increased amounts of fossil fuels, especially coal, are burned. Emissions of sulfur and nitrogen oxides are particularly troubling because they combine with water vapor in the atmosphere to form acid rain or produce other acid deposition. In large areas of Norway, Sweden, southern Canada, and the eastern United States, the pH value of rainfall has dropped from 5.7 to below 4.5, well into the acidic range. Also, rainfall has almost certainly become more acid in parts of Germany, Eastern Europe, and the U.S.S.R., although available data are incomplete.

The effects of acid rain are not yet fully understood, but damage has already been observed in lakes, forests, soils, crops, nitrogen-fixing plants, and building materials. Damage to lakes has been studied most extensively. For example, of 1,500 lakes in southern Norway with a pH below 4.3, 70 percent had no fish. Similar damage has been observed in the Adirondack Mountains of New York and in parts of Canada. River fish are also severely affected. In the last 20 years, first salmon and then trout disappeared in many Norwegian rivers as acidity increased.

Another environmental problem related to the combustion of fossil fuels (and perhaps also to the global loss of forests and soil humus) is the increasing concentration of carbon dioxide in the earth's atmosphere. Rising CO_2 concentrations are of concern because of their potential for causing a warming of the earth. Scientific opinion differs on the possible consequences, but a widely held view is that highly disruptive effects on world agriculture could occur before the middle of the twenty-first century. The CO_2 content of the world's atmosphere has increased about 15 percent in the last century and by 2000 is expected to be nearly a third higher than preindustrial levels. If the projected rates of increase in fossil fuel combustion (about 2 percent per year) were to continue, a doubling of the CO_2 content of the atmosphere could be expected after the middle of the next century; and if deforestation substantially reduces tropical forests (as projected), a doubling of atmosphereic CO_2 could occur sooner. The result could be significant alterations of precipitation patterns around the world, and a 2°–3°C rise in temperatures in the middle latitudes of the earth. Agriculture and other human endeavors would have great difficulty in adapting to such large, rapid changes in climate. Even a 1°C increase in average global temperatures would make the earth's climate warmer than it has been any time in the last 1,000 years.

A carbon dioxide-induced temperature rise is expected to be 3 or 4 times greater at the poles than in the middle latitudes. An increase of 5°–10°C in polar temperatures could eventually lead to the melting of the Greenland and Antarctic ice caps and a gradual rise in sea level, forcing abandonment of many coastal cities.

Ozone is another major concern. The stratospheric ozone layer protects the earth from damaging ultraviolet light. However, the ozone layer is being threatened by chlorofluorocarbon emissions from aerosol cans and refrigeration equipment, by nitrous oxide (N_2O) emissions from the denitrification of both organic and inorganic nitrogen fertilizers, and possibly by the effects of high-altitude aircraft flights. Only the United States and a few other countries have made serious efforts to date to control the use of aerosol cans. Refrigerants and nitrogen fertilizers present even more difficult challenges. The most widely discussed effect of ozone depletion and the resulting increase in ultraviolet light is an increased incidence of skin cancer, but damage to food crops would also be significant and might actually prove to be the most serious ozone related problem.

Impacts of Nuclear Energy

The problems presented by the projected production of increasing amounts of nuclear power are different from but no less serious than those related to fossil fuel combustion. The risk of radioactive contamination of the environment due to nuclear power reactor accidents will be increased, as will the potential for proliferation of nuclear weapons. No nation has yet conducted a demonstration program for the satisfactory disposal of radioactive wastes, and the amount of wastes is increasing rapidly. Several hundred thousand tons of highly radioactive spent nuclear fuel will be generated over the lifetimes of the nuclear plants likely to be constructed through the year 2000. In addition, nuclear power production will create millions of cubic meters of low-level radioactive wastes, and uranium mining and processing will lead to the production of hundreds of millions of tons of low-level radioactive tailings. It has not yet been demonstrated that all of these high- and low-level wastes from nuclear power production can be safely stored and disposed of without incident. Some of the by-products of reactors, it should be noted, have half-lives approximately five times as long as the period of recorded history.

Species Extinctions

Finally, the world faces an urgent problem of loss of plant and animal genetic resources. An estimate prepared for the Global 2000 Study suggests that between half a million and 2 million species—15 to 20 percent of all species on earth—could be extinguished by 2000, mainly because of loss of wild habitat but also in part because of pollution. Extinction of species on this scale is without precedent in human history.[63]

One-half to two-thirds of the extinctions projected to occur by 2000 will result from the clearing or degradation of tropical forests. Insect, other invertebrate, and plant species—many of them unclassified and unexamined by scientists—will account for most of the losses. The potential value of this genetic reservoir is immense. If preserved and carefully managed, tropical forest species could be a sustainable source of new foods (especially nuts and fruits), pharmaceutical chemicals, natural predators of pests, building materials, speciality woods, fuel, and so on. Even careful husbandry of the remaining biotic resources of the tropics cannot compensate for the swift, massive losses that are to be expected if present trends continue.

Current trends also threaten freshwater and marine species. Physical alterations—damming, channelization, siltation—and pollution by salts, acid rain, pesticides, and other toxic chemicals are profoundly affecting freshwater ecosystems throughout the world. At present 274 freshwater vertebrate taxa are threatened with extinction, and by the year 2000 many may have been lost.

Some of the most important genetic losses will involve the extinction not of species but of subspecies and varieties of cereal grains. Four-fifths of the world's food supplies are derived from less than two dozen plant and animal species. Wild and local domestic strains are needed for breeding resistance to pests and pathogens into the high-yield varieties now widely used.

These varietal stocks are rapidly diminishing as marginal wild lands are brought into cultivation. Local domesticated varieties, often uniquely suited to local conditions, are also being lost as higher-yield varieties displace them. And the increasing practice of monoculture of a few strains—which makes crops more vulnerable to disease epidemics or plagues of pests—is occurring at the same time that the genetic resources to resist such disasters are being lost.

Entering the Twenty-First Century

The preceding sections have presented individually the many projections made by U.S. Government agencies for the Global 2000 Study. How are these projections to be interpreted collectively? What do they imply about the world's entry into the twenty-first century?[64]

The world in 2000 will be different from the world today in important ways. There will be more people. For every two persons on the earth in 1975 there will be three in 2000. The number of poor will have increased. Four-fifths of the world's population will live in less developed countries. Furthermore, in terms of persons per year added to the world, population growth will be 40 percent *higher* in 2000 than in 1975.[65]

The gap between the richest and the poorest will have increased. By every measure of material welfare the study provides—per capita GNP and consumption of food, energy, and minerals—the gap will widen. For example, the gap between the GNP per capita in the LDCs and the industrialized countries is projected to grow from about $4,000 in 1975 to about $7,900 in 2000.[66] Great disparities within countries are also expected to continue.

There will be fewer resources to go around. While on a worldwide average there was about four-tenths of a hectare of arable land per person in 1975, there will be only about one-quarter hectare per person in 2000[67] (see Figure 11 below). By 2000 nearly 1,000 billion barrels of the world's total original petroleum resource of approximately 2,000 billion barrels will have been consumed. Over just the 1975-2000 period, the world's remaining petroleum resources per capita can be expected to decline by at least 50 percent.[68] Over the same period world per capita water supplies will decline by 35 percent because of greater population alone; increasing competing demands will put further pressure on available water supplies.[69] The world's per capita growing stock of wood is projected to be 47 percent lower in 2000 than in 1978[70].

The environment will have lost important life-supporting capabilities. By 2000, 40 percent of the forests still remaining in the LDCs in 1978 will have been razed.[71] The atmospheric concentration of carbon dioxide will be nearly one-third higher than preindustrial levels.[72] Soil erosion will have removed, on the average, several inches of soil from croplands all over the world. Desertification (including salinization) may have claimed a significant fraction of the world's rangeland and cropland. Over little more than two decades, 15-20 percent of the earth's total species of plants and animals will have become extinct—a loss of at least 500,000 species.[73]

Prices will be higher. The price of many of the most vital resources is projected to rise in real terms—that is, over and above inflation. In order to meet projected demand, a 100 percent increase in the real price of food will be required.[74] To keep energy demand in line with anticipated supplies, the real price of energy is assumed to rise more than 150 percent over the 1975-2000 period.[75] Supplies of water, agricultural land, forest products, and many traditional marine fish species are projected to decline relative to growing demand at current prices,[76] which suggests that real price rises will occur in these sectors too. Collectively, the projections suggest that resource-based inflationary pressures will continue and intensify, especially in nations that are poor in resources or are rapidly depleting their resources.

The world will be more vulnerable both to natural disaster and to disruptions from human causes. Most nations are likely to be still more dependent on foreign sources of energy in 2000 than they are today.[77] Food production will be more vulnerable to disruptions of fossil fuel energy supplies and to weather fluctuations as cultivation expands to more marginal areas. The loss of diverse germ plasm in local strains and wild progenitors of food crops, together with the increase of monoculture, could lead to greater risks

39

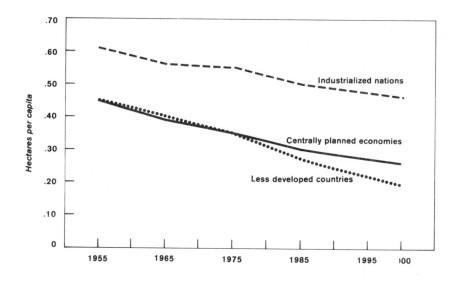

Figure 11. Arable land per capita, 1955, 1975, 2000.

of massive crop failures.[78] Larger numbers of people will be vulnerable to higher food prices or even famine when adverse weather occurs.[79] The world will be more vulnerable to the disruptive effects of war. The tensions that could lead to war will have multiplied. The potential for conflict over fresh water alone is underscored by the fact that out of 200 of the world's major river basins, 148 are shared by two countries and 52 are shared by three to ten countries. Long standing conflicts over shared rivers such as the Plata (Brazil, Argentina), Euphrates (Syria, Iraq), or Ganges (Bangladesh, India) could easily intensify.[80]

Finally, it must be emphasized that if public policy continues generally unchanged the world will be different as a result of lost opportunities. The adverse effects of many of the trends discussed in this Study will not be fully evident until 2000 or later; yet the actions that are necessary to change the trends cannot be postponed without foreclosing important options. The opportunity to stabilize the world's population below 10 billion, for example, is slipping away; Robert McNamara, President of the World Bank, has noted that for every decade of delay in reaching replacement fertility, the world's ultimately stabilized population will be about 11 percent greater.[81] Similar losses of opportunity accompany delayed perceptions or

action in other areas. If energy policies and decisions are based on yesterday's (or even today's) oil prices, the opportunity to wisely invest scarce capital resources will be lost as a consequence of undervaluing conservation and efficiency. If agricultural research continues to focus on increasing yields through practices that are highly energy-intensive, both energy resources and the time needed to develop alternative practices will be lost.

The full effects of rising concentrations of carbon dioxide, depletion of stratospheric ozone, deterioration of soils, increasing introduction of complex persistent toxic chemicals into the environment, and massive extinction of species may not occur until well after 2000. Yet once such global environmental problems are in motion they are very difficult to reverse. In fact, few if any of the problems addressed in the Global 2000 Study are amenable to quick technological or policy fixes; rather, they are inextricably mixed with the world's most perplexing social and economic problems.

Perhaps the most troubling problems are those in which population growth and poverty lead to serious long-term declines in the productivity of renewable natural resource systems. In some areas the capacity of renewable resource systems to support human populations is already being seriously damaged by efforts of present populations to meet desperate immediate needs, and the damage threatens to become worse.[82]

Examples of serious deterioration of the earth's most basic resources can already be found today in scattered places in all nations, including the industrialized countries and the better-endowed LDCs. For instance, erosion of agricultural soil and salinization of highly productive irrigated farmland is increasingly evident in the United States,[83] and extensive deforestation, with more or less permanent soil degradation, has occurred in Brazil, Venezuela, and Colombia.[84] But problems related to the decline of the earth's carrying capacity are most immediate, severe, and tragic in those regions of the earth containing the poorest LDCs.

Sub-Saharan Africa faces the problem of exhaustion of its resource base in an acute form. Many causes and effects have come together there to produce excessive demands on the environment, leading to expansion of the desert. Overgrazing, fuelwood gathering, and destructive cropping practices are the principal immediate causes of a series of transitions from open woodland, to scrub, to fragile semiarid range, to worthless weeds and bare earth. Matters are made worse when people are forced by scarcity of fuelwood to burn animal dung and crop wastes. The soil, deprived of organic matter, loses fertility and the ability to hold water—and the desert expands. In Bangladesh, Pakistan, and large parts of India, efforts by growing numbers of people to meet their basic needs are damaging the very cropland, pasture, forests, and water supplies on which they must depend for a livelihood.[85] To restore the lands and soils would require decades—if not centuries—*after* the existing pressures on the land have diminished. But the pressures are growing, not diminishing.

There are no quick or easy solutions, particularly in those regions where population pressure is already leading to a reduction of the carrying capacity of the land. In such regions a complex of social and economic factors (including very low incomes, inequitable land tenure, limited or no educational opportunities, a lack of nonagricultural jobs, and economic pressures toward higher fertility) underlies the decline in the land's carrying capacity. Furthermore, it is generally believed that social and economic conditions must improve before fertility levels will decline to replacement levels. Thus a vicious circle of causality may be at work. Environmental deterioration caused by large populations creates living conditions that make reductions in fertility difficult to achieve; all the while, continuing population growth increases further the pressures on the environment and land.[86]

The declines in carrying capacity already being observed in scattered areas around the world point to a phenomenon that could easily be much more widespread by 2000. In fact, the best evidence now available—even allowing for the many beneficial effects of technological developments and adoptions—suggests that by 2000 the world's human population may be within only a few generations of reaching the entire planet's carrying capacity.

The Global 2000 Study does not estimate the earth's carrying capacity, but it does provide a basis for evaluating an earlier estimate published in the U.S. National Academy of Sciences' report, *Resources and Man*. In this 1969 report, the Academy concluded that a world population of 10 billion "is close to (if not above) the maximum that an *intensively managed* world might hope to support with some degree of comfort and individual choice." The Academy also concluded that even with the sacrifice of individual freedom and choice, and even with chronic near starvation for the great majority, the human population of the world is unlikely to ever exceed 30 billion.[87]

Nothing in the Global 2000 Study counters the Academy's conclusions. If anything, data gathered over the past decade suggest the Academy may have underestimated the extent of some problems, especially deforestation and the loss and deterioration of soils.[88]

At present and projected growth rates, the world's population would rapidly approach the Academy's figures. If the fertility and mortality rates projected for 2000 were to continue unchanged into the twenty-first century, the world's population would reach 10 billion by 2030. Thus anyone with a present life expectancy of an additional 50 years could expect to see the world population reach 10 billion. This same rate of growth would produce a population of nearly 30 billion before the end of the twenty-first century.[89]

Here it must be emphasized that, unlike most

of the Global 2000 Study projections, the population projections assume extensive policy changes and developments to reduce fertility rates. Without the assumed policy changes, the projected rate of population growth would be still more rapid.

Unfortunately population growth may be slowed for reasons other than declining birth rates. As the world's populations exceed and reduce the land's carrying capacity in widening areas, the trends of the last century or two toward improved health and longer life may come to a halt. Hunger and disease may claim more lives—especially lives of babies and young children. More of those surviving infancy may be mentally and physically handicapped by childhood malnutrition.

The time for action to prevent this outcome is running out. Unless nations collectively and individually take bold and imaginative steps toward improved social and economic conditions, reduced fertility, better management of resources, and protection of the environment, the world must expect a troubled entry into the twenty-first century.

APPENDIX

The Global 2000 Study Compared with
Other Global Studies

In the course of the Global 2000 Study, the Government's several models (here referred to collectively as the "Government's global model") and their projections were compared with those of five other global studies.[90] The purpose was not only to compare the results of different projections, but also to see whether and how different assumptions and model structures may have led to different projections and findings.

The Global 2000 Study's principal findings are generally consistent with those of the five other global studies despite considerable differences in models and assumptions. On the whole, the other studies and their models lack the richness of detail that the Government's global model provides for the various individual sectors—food and agriculture, forests, water, energy, and so on. However, the linkages among the sectors in the other models are much more complete. Many apparent inconsistencies and contradictions in the Global 2000 projections are due to the weakness of the linkages among sectors of the Government's global model.

Another important difference is that the Government's projections stop at the year 2000 or before, while the other global studies project well into the twenty-first century. The most dramatic developments projected in the other studies—serious resource scarcities, population declines due to rising death rates, severe environmental deterioration—generally occur in the first half of the twenty-first century and thus cannot be compared with the Government's projections. Up to the turn of the century, all of the analyses, including the Government's, indicate more or less similar trends: continued economic growth in most areas, continued population growth everywhere, reduced energy growth, an increasingly tight and expensive food situation, increasing water problems, and growing environmental stress.

The most optimistic of the five models is the Latin American World Model. Instead of projecting future conditions on the basis of present policies and trends, this model asks: "How can global resources best be used to meet basic human needs for all people?" The model allocates labor and capital to maximize life expectancy. It assumes that personal consumption is sacrificed to maintain very high investment rates (25 percent of GNP per year), and it posits an egalitarian, nonexploitative, wisely managed world society that avoids pollution, soil depletion, and other forms of environmental degradation. Under these assumptions it finds that in little more than one generation basic human needs could be adequately satisfied in Latin America and in Africa. Thereafter, GNP would grow steadily and population growth would begin to stabilize.

But in Asia, even assuming these near-utopian social conditions and high rates of investment, the system collapses. The model projects an Asian food crisis beginning by 2010, as land runs out; food production cannot rise fast enough to keep up with population growth, and a vicious circle begins that leads to starvation and economic collapse by midcentury. The modelers suggest that an Asian food crisis could be avoided by such means as food imports from other areas with more cropland, better crop yields, and effective family planning policies. Nonetheless, it is striking that this model, which was designed to show that the fundamental constraints on human welfare were social, not physical, does project catastrophic food shortages in Asia due to land scarcity.

The World 2 and World 3 models, which were the basis of the 1972 Club of Rome report *The Limits to Growth,* give much attention to environmental factors—the only models in the group of five to do so. The World models, like the Global 2000 Study, considered trends in population, resources, and environment. However, these

43

models are highly aggregated, looking at the world as a whole and omitting regional differences. In the cases that assume a continuation of present policies, the World 2 and 3 models project large global increases in food and income per capita until 2020, at which time either food scarcity or resource depletion would cause a downturn. The two models do suggest that major changes of policy can significantly alter these trends.

The World Integrated Model, a later effort sponsored by the Club of Rome, is much more detailed than the World 2 and 3 models in its treatment of regional differences, trade, economics, and shifts from one energy source to another, but it is less inclusive in its treatment of the environment. This complex model has been run under many different assumptions of conditions and policies. Almost invariably the runs project a long-term trend of steeply rising food prices. Under a wide range of policies and conditions the runs indicate massive famine in Asia and, to a lesser degree, in non-OPEC Africa, before the turn of the century.

The United Nations World Model found that to meet U.N. target rates for economic growth, developing countries would have to make great sacrifices in personal consumption, saving and investing at unprecedented rates. Personal consumption would not exceed 63 percent of income in any developing region, and none would have a level of private investment of less than 20 percent. To meet food requirements, global agricultural production would have to rise fourfold by 2000, with greater increases required in many places (500 percent, for example, in low-income Asia and Latin America).

The Model of International Relations in Agriculture (MOIRA) confines itself to agriculture; it takes into account the effects of agriculture policies but not those of environmental degradation. Its results are more optimistic than the Global 2000 projections: world food production more than doubles from 1975 to 2000, and per capita consumption rises 36 percent. Even so, because of unequal distribution, the number of people subsisting on two-thirds or less of the biological protein requirement rises from 350 million in 1975 to 740 million in 2000.

The Global 2000 Study conducted an experiment with two of the more integrated nongovernment models to answer the question: "How would projections from the Government's global model be different if the model were more integrated and included more linkages and feedback?" The linkages in the two nongovernment models were severed so that they bore some resemblance to the unconnected and inconsistent structure of the Government's global model. Chosen for the experiment were the World 3 model and the World Integrated Model.

In both models, severing the linkages led to distinctly more favorable outcomes. On the basis of results with World 3, the Global 2000 Study concluded that a more integrated Government model would project that:

- Increasing competition among agriculture, industry, and energy development for capital would lead to even higher resource cost inflation and significant decreases in real GNP growth (this assumes no major technological advances).

- The rising food prices and regional declines in food consumption per capita that are presently projected would be intensified by competition for capital and by degradation of the land.

- Slower GNP and agricultural growth would lead to higher death rates from widespread hunger—or from outright starvation—and to higher birth rates, with greater numbers of people trapped in absolute poverty.

- A decisive global downturn in incomes and food per capita would probably not take place until a decade or two after 2000 (this assumes no political disruptions).

When links in the World Integrated Model (WIM) were cut, outcomes again were more favorable. The results of the unlinked version were comparable to the Global 2000 quantitative projections for global GNP, population, grain production, fertilizer use, and energy use. But in the original integrated version of WIM, gross world product was 21 percent lower than in the unlinked version—$11.7 trillion instead of $14.8 trillion in 2000. In the linked version, world agricultural production rose 85 percent instead of 107 percent; grain available for human consumption rose less than 85 percent because some of the grain was fed to animals for increased meat production. Population rose only to 5.9 billion rather than 6.2 billion, in part because of widespread starvation (158 million deaths cumulatively by 2000) and in part because of lower birth rates in the industrialized countries. The effects of severing the linkages are much less in lightly populated regions with a wealth of natural resources, such as North America, than in regions under stress, where great numbers of people are living at the margin of existence. In North America, the difference in GNP per capita was about 5 percent; in South Asia, about 30 percent.

The inescapable conclusion is that the omission of linkages imparts an optimistic bias to the Global 2000 Study's (and the U.S. Government's) quantitative projections.[91] This appears to be particularly true of the GNP projections. The experiments with the World Integrated Model suggest that the Study's figure for gross world product in 2000 may be 15—20 percent too high.

REFERENCES

1. *The Global 2000 Report to the President: Entering the Twenty-First Century,* vol. 2, *Technical Report,* Gerald O. Barney, Study Director, Washington: Government Printing Office, 1980, App. A.
2. Ibid.
3. Jimmy Carter, *The President's Environmental Program, 1977,* Washington: Government Printing Office, May 1977, p. M-11.
4. A more detailed discussion of the Global 2000 Study process is provided in *The Global 2000 Report to the President,* vol. 2, *Technical Report,* "Preface and Acknowledgments" and Ch. 1, "Introduction to the Projections."
5. *The Global 2000 Report to the President: Entering the Twenty-First Century,* vol. 2, Ch. 14-23; and *The Global 2000 Report to the President: Entering the Twenty-First Century,* vol. 3, *The Government's Global Model,* Gerald O. Barney, Study Director, Washington: Government Printing Office, 1980.

NOTE

Unless otherwise indicated, the following chapter citations refer to the various chapters of *The Global 2000 Report to the President: Entering the Twenty-First Century,* vol. 2, *Technical Report,* Washington: Government Printing Office, 1980.

6. Ch. 13, 14, and 31.
7. Ch. 1.
8. "Closing the Loops," Ch. 13; Ch. 14.
9. Ibid.
10. Ch. 13, especially "Closing the Loops."
11. "Closing the Loops," Ch. 13; Ch. 14 and 31.
12. Ch. 1, 5, 14, and 23.
13. Ch. 1 and 14.
14. Ch. 30 and 31.
15. Ch. 2.
16. Ibid.
17. Ibid.
18. Ibid.
19. Ibid.; "Population Projections and the Environment," Ch. 13.
20. "Population Projections and the Environment." Ch. 13.
21. Ibid.; "Closing the Loops," Ch. 13.
22. Ibid.
23. *The Global 2000 Report to the President,* vol. 3, *The Government's Global Model,* Chapter on population models and the population projections update.
24. Ronald Freedman, "Theories of Fertility Decline: A Reappraisal," in Philip M. Hauser, ed., *World Population and Development,* Syracuse, N.Y.: Syracuse University Press, 1979; John C. Caldwell, "Toward a Restatement of Demographic Transition Theory," *Population and Development Review,* Sept./Dec., 1976.
25. For a discussion of Indonesia, see Freeman, op. cit.; for a discussion of Brazil, see "Demographic Projections Show Lower Birth Rate for the Poor" (in Portuguese), *VEJA,* Oct. 24, 1979, p. 139, citing the research of Elza Berquo of the Brazilian Analysis and Planning Center.
26. Ch. 3.
27. Ibid.
28. Ibid. .
29. World Bank, *Prospects for Developing Countries, 1977-85,* Washington, Sept. 1976, Statistical Appendix, Table 1; World Bank, *World Development Report, 1979,* Washington, 1979, p. 13.
30. Ch. 6.
31. Ibid., "Food and Agriculture Projections and the Environment," Ch. 13.
32. Ch. 6.
33. Ibid.
34. "Food and Agriculture Projections and the Environment," Ch. 13.
35. Ch. 6.
36. U.S. Department of Agriculture, *Farm Income Statistics.* Washington: Economics, Statistics, and Cooperative Services, U.S.D.A., 1978 and 1979.
37. J. B. Penn, "The Food and Agriculture Policy Challenge of the 1980's," Washington: Economics, Statistics and Cooperative Service, U.S.D.A., Jan. 1980.
38. P. Osam, *Accelerating Foodgrain Production in Low-Income Food-Deficit Countries—Progress, Potentials and Paradoxes,* Hawaii: East-West Center, May 1978; J. Gravan, *The Calorie Energy Gap in Bangladesh, and Strategies for Reducing It,* Washington: International Food Policy Research Institute, Aug. 1977.
39. Ch. 7.
40. Ibid.; "The Projections and the Marine Environment" and "Water Projections and the Environment," Ch. 13.
41. Ch. 7.
42. Food and Agriculture Organization, *Fisheries Statistics Yearbook, 1978.* Rome, 1979; Richard Hennemuth, Deputy Director, Northeast Fisheries Center, National Oceanic and Atmospheric Administration, personal communication, 1980.
43. Ch. 8 and App. C.
44. Ibid.
45. Ibid.; "Population Projections and the Environment," "Forestry Projections and the Environment," and "Energy Projections and the Environment," Ch. 13.
46. Norman Myers, *The Sinking Ark,* New York: Pergamon Press, 1979; U.S. Department of State, *Proceedings of the U.S. Strategy Conference on Tropical Deforestation,* Washington, Oct. 1978.
47. See especially Ch. 2, 6, 9, 10, and 12.
48. Ch. 9.
49. Ibid.; "Water Projections and the Environment," Ch. 13.
50. Ch. 9 and 13.
51. Ch. 12.
52. Ibid.
53. Ibid.
54. Ibid.; "Nonfuel Minerals Projections and the Environment," Ch. 13.
55. Ch. 10; "Energy Projections and the Environment," Ch. 13.
56. Ibid.
57. Ibid.
58. Ch. 8; "Population Projections and the Environment," "Forestry Projections and the Environment," and "Energy Projections and the Environment," Ch. 13.
59. Ch. 8; "Forestry Projections and the Environment," "Energy Projections and the Environment," and "Clos-

ing the Loops," Ch. 13.

60. See the IEES Model Projections reported in "International Energy Assessment," in Energy Information Administration, *Annual Report to Congress, 1978,* vol. 3, Washington: Department of Energy, 1979, pp. 11–34; Energy Information Administration, *Annual Report to the Congress, 1979,* forthcoming.

61. See Energy Information Administration, *Annual Report, 1979,* op. cit.; John Pearson and Derriel Cato, personal communication, Mar. 13, 1980.

62. The discussion of "Environmental Consequences" that follows is based on Ch. 13.

63. Thomas E. Lovejoy, "A Projection of Species Extinctions," Ch. 13, pp. 328-31.

64. This section is based largely on material contained in "Closing the Loops," Ch. 13.

65. Ch. 2.

66. Ch. 3.

67. Ch. 6.

68. Ch. 10; "Energy Projections and the Environment," Ch. 13.

69. Ch. 9.

70. Ch. 8.

71. Ibid.; "Forestry Projections and the Environment," Ch. 13.

72. Ch. 4; "Climate Projections and the Environment," Ch. 13.

73. "Food and Agriculture Projections and the Environment," "Forestry Projections and the Environment," and "Closing the Loops," Ch. 13.

74. Ch. 6.

75. Extrapolating from Ch. 10, which assumes a 5 percent per year increase over the 1980-90 period.

76. Ch. 6-9.

77. Ch. 10 and 11.

78. Ch. 6; "Food and Agriculture Projections and the Environment," Ch. 13.

79. Ibid.; Ch. 4; "Climate Projections and the Environment," Ch. 13.

80. Ch. 9.

81. Robert S. McNamara, President, World Bank, "Address to the Board of Governors," Belgrade, Oct. 2, 1979, pp. 9, 10.

82. Ch. 13.

83. "Food and Agriculture Projections and the Environment," Ch. 13.

84. "Forestry Projections and the Environment," Ch. 13, and Peter Freeman, personal communication, 1980, based on field observations in 1973.

85. "Population Projections and the Environment," "Food and Agriculture Projections and the Environment," "Forestry Projections and the Environment," and "Water Projections and the Environment," Ch. 13.

86. "Population Projections and the Environment," and "Closing the Loops," Ch. 13; Erik Eckholm, *The Dispossessed of the Earth: Land Reform and Sustainable Development,* Washington: Worldwatch Institute, June 1979.

87. National Academy of Sciences, Committee on Resources and Man, *Resources and Man,* San Francisco: Freeman, 1969, p. 5; "Closing the Loops," Ch. 13.

88. "Closing the Loops," Ch. 13.

89. Projection by the U.S. Bureau of the Census communicated in a personal letter, Feb. 26, 1980, from Dr. Samuel Baum, Chief, International Demographic Data Center. This letter and projection are presented in vol. 3 of the *Global 2000 Report to the President,* Population section.

90. The discussion in this Appendix is based on the detailed analyses in Ch. 24-31 and on two papers by Jennifer Robinson (author of those chapters) presented at the International Conference on Modeling Related to Environment, sponsored by the Polish Academy of Sciences: "The Global 2000 Study: An Attempt to Increase Consistency in Government Forecasting" and "Treatment of the Environment in Global Models."

91. Further discussion of these and other potential biases in the Government's projections are provided in Ch. 14-23, and App. B.

2 Environment Projections

This chapter is the last of the 12 chapters presenting the Global 2000 Study projections. Chapters 2–4 present the driving-force projections (Population, GNP, Climate), which provide basic inputs to the resource projections presented in Chapters 5–12. Attention turns now to the future of the world's environment.

The term "environment" is not easily defined. To some, the word suggests pristine landscapes and wilderness. While these connotations are certainly inherent in most definitions of the term, "environment" is used in this chapter in a much broader sense.

Literally, the environment is the physical and biological surroundings of the organisms under discussion—in this case *Homo sapiens,* the human species. Humankind depends on this life-supporting environment in many complex ways. So intimate is the linkage between humankind and its environment that the distinction between individual and environment blurs. Some of the air we breathe becomes a part of us. The oxygen metabolizes our foods and becomes a part of our flesh and blood; particulates we breath accumulate in our lungs. Some of the liquids we drink become a part of our bodies, as do the toxic substances the liquids sometimes contain. The soils become our food, which in turn becomes our tissues. In fact, the term "environment"—i.e., human *surroundings*—is an inadequate and inaccurate concept because there is not and cannot be a sharp distinction between humankind and its surroundings. In this chapter, for lack of a better alternative, the term "environment" will be used to describe human surroundings, but throughout it should be remembered that in many important ways we and our environment are one.

In analyzing the future of the human environment, it is also important to note the ways in which humankind shapes its environment. Many anthropogenic changes in the environment are beneficial, but some are not. Houses and communities provide many benefits, including shelter from the elements, predators and pathogens. Other anthropogenic changes—such as the contamination of air, water, and soils—have not been wholly beneficial. Some anthropogenic changes are even

beginning to threaten goods and services that the environment has heretofore provided free or at minimal cost.

Humankind has habitually taken for granted the goods (e.g., soil fertility, clean plentiful water) and the services (e.g., removal of air pollutants) provided by the environment. The habit persists. The projections reported in the previous chapters are based generally on the assumption that the environment will continue to provide goods and services as abundantly and inexpensively in the future as it has in the past. Many of these general assumptions about future environmental goods and services are brought into question by the analyses in this chapter. In the years ahead, humankind will need to consider more carefully both the environmental implications of its activities and the effects that environmental deterioration generally will have on human activities.

In this chapter, two questions will be asked of all of the Study's other projections: *First,* assuming (1) that the developments projected in the previous chapters actually come about and (2) that present environmental policies remain unchanged, what impacts on the world's environment can be anticipated? *Second,* considering all the projected environmental impacts collectively, how might developments and changes in the world's environment influence the prospects for achieving the projections outlined in the previous chapters?

The analyses are conducted in two steps, as illustrated in Figure 13–1. In the first step, the environmental implications of each of the previous driving-force and resource projections are analyzed. In the second step all of the environmental implications are synthesized and their collective impact back upon the driving-force and resource projections are considered. Were it possible to actually reflect these collective impacts in the earlier projections, the two feedback loops in Figure 13–1 would be closed. In practice, it is possible only to note the kinds of effects that could be expected, but without actually modifying the projections. Thus the feedback loops remain open at two points and the projections continue to be

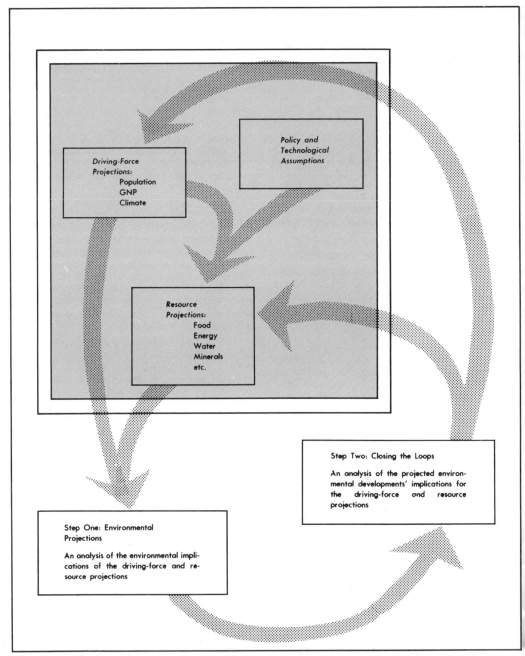

Figure 13-1. The two steps in integrating environment into the analysis. The gray box represents the analysis prior to integration with the environmental analysis.

based on rather optimistic environmental assumptions.

The results of the environmental analyses are presented in the following 11 sections of this Chapter. The first step—the analysis of the environmental implications of the previous projections—is presented in the next 10 sections in this order: Population, GNP, Climate, Technology, Food and Agriculture, the Marine Environment, Forestry, Water, Energy, and Nonfuel Minerals. Each of these sections attempts to analyze the environmental developments that might be expected to follow from the corresponding driving-force and resource projections. To assist the reader in recalling the earlier projections, each of the 10 sections begins with a brief summary of the projections being analyzed (under the heading *The Projections,* as on the following page). The second step—the analysis of the effects of environmental developments collectively on the other projections—is presented in the final section: "Closing the Loops: Environmental Feedback to the Other Projections."

Before proceeding to the first of the environmental projections, a few additional points need to be mentioned.

First, an effort has been made to conduct the entire Global 2000 Study with government personnel, government data, and government analytical tools, but unfortunately this objective could not be met in the case of the "Environment Projections" chapter. There is no agency of the government that has the responsibility and capacity to conduct the kind of environmental analysis and synthesis required by the Global 2000 Study. The Environmental Protection Agency (EPA) has a large staff and substantial resources, but EPA is charged with a regulatory mission, not with developing broad, long-term environmental projections. The National Environmental Policy Act (NEPA) assigns a long-term foresight mission (among other responsibilities) to the Council on Environmental Quality (CEQ), but CEQ has never had the staff and resources necessary to carry out all of its assigned functions.

Faced with the fact that no single agency could be expected to prepare the environment projections, the original Global 2000 Study plan called for each agency to prepare an environmental analysis of its projections, using the capabilities it had developed since NEPA initiated the process of environmental impact analysis. This too proved unworkable. As a result of NEPA, most of the agencies now have a substantial capability for environmental analysis. They have assembled the data and analytical tools needed to analyze the environmental impacts of specific project proposals, but with few exceptions they do not have the data and analytical tools needed to perform environmental analyses of long-term plans and global projections. Nor have such analyses been required of them to date.* As a result, most of the environmental analyses that were appended to the agencies projections were quite limited, and the bulk of the environmental analyses and writing for this chapter had to be done by experts outside the government. But although the Study's objective could not be met entirely in the case of the environmental chapter, many government personnel have been involved in reviewing the analyses that follow.

A second point that must be made before the analyses are presented concerns assumptions. An effort was made to avoid abstract environmental projections by relating the analyses as directly as possible to the driving-force and resource projections, but many of the driving-force and resource projections were not explicit enough to permit detailed analyses of their environmental implications, and it was necessary to base some of the environmental analyses on further assumptions. These additional assumptions are described as they occur throughout this chapter.

Third, the environment projections were frequently difficult to develop because much of the data needed on specific topics was not available. In such cases, the analyst was forced either to omit certain topics or to discuss their implications on the basis of fragmentary information. The latter course was chosen whenever the topic seemed important—in which case the discussion was based on the best information available, even if it was only fragmentary.

Fourth, a variety of technologies for environmental protection are considered in the various sections of the chapter. In general, technologies for solving most environmental problems are now available, but there are exceptions. For example, there is no practical means at present for removing oxides of nitrogen from power plant exhaust stacks. The analyses suggest that in most cases economic and policy considerations—rather than the lack of technology—impede environmental protection efforts.

Fifth, the Environment Projections chapter is far longer than any other chapter in the Global

---

*For example hundreds of environmental impact statements have been prepared on individual highways and power plants, but there are no corresponding environmental analyses for the Department of Transportation's year 2000 plan or the Department of Energy's national energy plan.

2000 Study. Its disproportionate length can be justified on two counts: (1) because future trends in the world's environment is a larger than average topic, and (2) because the development of global environmental models is still in its infancy, the environmental analyses—in contrast to the analysis in preceding chapters—are largely discursive, rather than analytical. It should also be mentioned that organizing this long chapter was complicated by the fact that it was necessary to include several topics in more than one section. Every effort has been made to reduce redundancy, however, through footnotes and occasional cross-references to other sections of the chapter.

Finally, the environment projections proceed from the same policy assumption used in the other parts of the Study—namely, that no changes in public policy are anticipated. When applied to the environment, this assumption has many implications. In situations where there is currently no formal environmental management policy, as for example in management of grazing lands in some countries, it is assumed that present lack of management practices will continue. While the resulting prognostications are occasionally grim, they should not be interpreted as statements of what will actually happen, but rather as indications of what is likely to happen if societies do not develop and implement policies that will sustain the health of the environment. Failing this, the analyses suggest strongly that the collective environmental impacts to be anticipated over the next two decades will be sufficiently severe in many areas to alter significantly—and undesirably—the projected population, GNP, and resource trends.

THE POPULATION PROJECTIONS AND THE ENVIRONMENT

The Projections

Population levels and their rates of change projected by the U.S. Bureau of the Census are summarized in Table 13–1. The average annual world population growth rate will be 1.8 percent per year throughout most of the 1975–2000 period. By the year 2000, a total of 2.3 billion persons will have been added to the world's population, an increase of 55 percent.

The less developed countries will contribute nine-tenths (2 billions) of the world total increase by 2000. The crude birth rates in the LDCs are projected to decline 21 percent, while life expectancies increase 18 percent (from 54.0 to 63.5 years).* The result is a net annual rate of natural population increase averaging 2.1 percent over the 25-year interval. Asia and Oceania experience the largest numerical increases—60 percent of the total projected world growth. The largest rates of increase occur in Africa (leading to more than a doubling) and in Latin America (a 96 percent increase).

The industrialized countries reduce their population growth rates by about a quarter and experience relatively modest numeric increases: 76 million in the Soviet Union and Eastern Europe (a 20 percent increase) and 101 million in the rest of the industrialized world (a 14 percent increase).

Although the projections do not explicitly address migration and urbanization, there are many indications that the LDCs will experience substantial urban growth by 2000.

Introduction

The 5 percent increase in world population projected by the Bureau of the Census and summarized in Table 13–1† has many direct and indirect implications for the environment. For example, the direct effects of excrement from an additional 2.2 billion persons can be expected to have a significant impact on the environment in many areas. Still larger indirect effects can be anticipated as

---

*Calculated from Table 8 in U.S. Bureau of the Census, *Illustrative Projections of World Populations to the 21st Century*, Washington: Government Printing Office, 1979.

†Two sets of population projections are presented in Chapter 2. One set was developed by the U.S. Bureau of the Census; the other by the Community and Family Study Center (CFSC)

at the University of Chicago. Both projections were funded by the Population Office of the U.S. Agency for International Development. The Census projections have been used throughout as the Global 2000 Study base case and are summarized in Table 13–1. The CFSC projections were undertaken with a different methodological approach that assumes a rapid

TABLE 13-1

Increase in World Population, 1975–2000

	1975		2000		Increase	
					Average Annual	Total
	Population	Share	Population	Share		
	billions	percent	billions	percent	percent	
Industrialized regions	1.1	28	1.3	21	0.6	17
Less developed regions	3.0	72	5.0	79	2.1	70
World	4.1	100	6.4	100	1.8	55

Source: Bureau of the Census projections. Chapter 2. this volume.

a result of efforts to meet the growing needs of the projected populations for shelter, food, fiber, educational facilities, transportation networks, and employment sites.

The pervasive environmental consequences (both direct and indirect) of the projected population growth make the subject of "Population and the Environment" unmanageably large. Some boundaries must be drawn and limitations established. There are, of course, a number of ways in which this can be done. The choice here has been to discuss in this section those environmental consequences that are directly related to population. The more indirect environmental consequences of population growth—the environmental consequences of increased demands for food, energy, minerals, forestry, etc., to meet the needs of the projected population—are discussed later in this chapter in the sections devoted to those topics. (There are a few exceptions, however; some indirect consequences of population growth—e.g., increased cattle herds for increased populations of nomadic herders—do not fit well in the other sections of this chapter and are therefore discussed here.) While this choice limits the subject

reduction of fertility rates attributed to large expenditures on family planning programs. Both the Census and the CFSC methodologies are discussed in Chapter 15. Since the writing of Chapters 2 and 15, an extensive criticism of the CFSC methodology and projections has been published and rebutted. The criticism appears in Paul Demeny, "On the End of the Population Explosion." *Population and Development Review*, Mar. 1979, pp. 141–62. The response to the criticism is D. J. Bogue and A. O. Tsui, "A Rejoinder to Paul Demeny's Critique, 'On the End of the Population Explosion,' " which is, at this writing, being considered for publication in *Population and Development Review*. Prepublication copies of the Bogue-Tsui rejoinder are available from CFSC, University of Chicago.

matter of this section somewhat, a few further distinctions relevant to the subjects under discussion should be noted.

One distinction involves the different types of pressures that different cultures exert on the environment. In what follows, the world's cultures are categorized as one of two types: either "traditional" or "industrial." This distinction is admittedly a gross simplification, intended only to indicate the relative closeness of a culture to the environment on which it depends. In traditional cultures, the people depend largely on their local environment and are familiar through personal experience with the environmental implications of their numbers and demands. In industrial cultures, the people depend to a much larger degree on environments that are connected with them only by transportation and trade networks, and as a result, such people are often not familiar personally with the full environmental consequences of their population growth and demands.

Although per capita demands on the environment tend to be higher for industrial cultures than for traditional cultures, the distinction is not strictly between the less developed and the developed countries. LDCs contain within them small industrial cultures that make relatively large per capita demands on environments around the world, and the industrialized countries contain traditional cultures that make demands—relatively small per capita demands—primarily on their local environment. (The Amish communities in the U.S. are an excellent example of a traditional culture within a developed country, as is the community and family life-style practiced by some individual environmental advocates.[1]) While the traditional/industrial cultural dichotomy involves major simplifications, it facilitates discussion of some important relationships between population growth and environmental change.

In the following pages, the relatively localized impacts of traditional cultures on their environments are considered first. The discussion of traditional cultures introduces the problem of managing "common" resources, a problem encountered in various forms throughout this chapter. The discussion then turns to the more dispersed pressures that industrial society places on the environment, after which the environmental consequences of changing population distributions are noted, especially the growing concentration of populations in large settlements with minimal public health and other services. Finally, some of the linkages between environment and health are considered.

Population and the Environment in Traditional Cultures

Traditional cultures, in the sense used here, are cultures that obtain the necessities of life—food, energy, fiber, and shelter—primarily from the local environment with little or no involvement in regional or national trade and commerce. Members of such societies are well aware of their dependence on a healthy environment. Their community values and traditions generally reflect this awareness and encourage a harmonious and sustainable relationship with the environment. [2]

Over the past century industrial cultures have spread and affected, in one way or another, all but a few exceptionally remote traditional cultures. Limited contacts with industrial society have changed some traditional cultures only a little, but in most cases such contacts have set in motion changes significantly affecting the form and function of traditional cultures.

Currently, a majority of the world's rural peoples, who occupy a large fraction of the earth's land, live in modified traditional cultures. There are many such cultures in the less developed countries. Even in the industrialized nations, some native populations still approximate their former traditional cultures—such as the Amish in the U.S., the Eskimos in Canada and Alaska, and the Samis (Lapps) in northern Scandinavia. But trade, medicine, technologies, and other factors have changed practices, values, outlooks, and the relations of such cultures to the environment. The populations of modified traditional cultures often grow at the world's fastest rates and, if unchecked, soon exceed the carrying capacity of the local environments on which they depend. As long as the needs of traditional cultures remain well below the life-support capacity of the local environment, population growth can continue with minimal impacts. As the life-support capacity is approached, however, environmental degradation begins, eroding and reducing the quality of life previously enjoyed. Social tension and conflict over the distribution of increasingly scarce resources often follows. Ultimately, the capability of the environment to support life is undermined and diminished.

Three forms of traditional cultures (and their modified forms) have special significance for the environment: (1) those based on the herding of animals, (2) those based on shifting cultivation, and (3) those who have cut their forests and shifted to settled agriculture. The Global 2000 Study's population projections imply that the populations of all three types will increase significantly over the next two decades, with the result that a number of environmental consequences can be anticipated. The effects of expanding populations of herders and shifting cultivators on the environment are discussed below. The environmental effects of population growth among settled agriculturists are discussed later, in the food and agriculture section of this chapter.

Cultures Based on the Herding of Animals

The world's herding populations, depending upon grasslands or savannas to sustain their livestock, maintain a delicate, often tenuous relationship with their local environments. When herds are managed to sustain the productivity of grassland or savanna ecosystems, grazing can be continued indefinitely without damaging the life-support system. However, when management is neglected, overgrazing often leads to the deterioration or destruction of the rangeland. The extent to which the world's grazing lands are already under pressure is illustrated in the Free Range Grazing Pressure Map in the colored map section of this volume.

Once begun, rangeland deterioration is difficult to control. Most grasslands and savannas are located in semiarid areas, where heavy grazing destroys the ability of plants to resist drought and leads to eventual loss of palatable species in favor of weed species. [3] Range deterioration is almost always accompanied by increased soil erosion. Unfortunately, over much of the world's rangelands today, such overstocking, overgrazing, loss of vegetation, erosion, and associated negative impacts on the hydrologic cycle are accelerating the conversion of productive grazing lands to desertlike wastelands. [4]

The two primary causes of the environmental consequences of overgrazing are (1) expanding human populations accompanied by increasing human demands for larger herds of livestock and (2) efforts to breed and own more livestock as a means of increasing individual and cultural wealth. Together, these two causes lead to accumulating individual pressures on a jointly used, limited resource base.

The protection of such a base in the face of population and economic growth is an exceedingly difficult management problem. [5] Proper management is central to the protection of grazing lands. Unprotected, any jointly used, limited resource suffers a fate often referred to as the tragedy of the commons.*

---

*Protecting a jointly used resource is often an aspect of environmental management. The problems it engenders will be

The tragedy is this: Actions that are in the immediate best interest of each and every individual employing a jointly utilized (common) resource are collectively detrimental to the long-term welfare of the whole society. In his classic essay, "The Tragedy of the Commons," Garrett Hardin describes the tragedy in terms of a grazing commons:

Picture a pasture open to all. It is to be expected that each herdsman will try to keep as many cattle as possible on the commons. Such an arrangement may work reasonably satisfactorily for centuries because tribal wars, poaching, and disease keep the numbers of both man and beast well below the carrying capacity of the land. Finally, however, comes the day of reckoning, that is, the day when the long-desired goal of social stability becomes a reality. At this point, the inherent logic of the commons remorselessly generates tragedy.

As a rational being, each herdsman seeks to maximize his gain. Explicitly or implicitly, more or less consciously, he asks, "What is the utility *to me* of adding one more animal to my herd?" This utility has one negative and positive component.

1. The positive component is a function of the increment of one animal. Since the herdsman receives all the proceeds from the sale of the additional animal, the positive utility is nearly +1.
2. The negative component is a function of the additional overgrazing created by one more animal. Since, however, the effects of overgrazing are shared by all the herdsmen, the negative utility for any particular decision-making herdsman is only a fraction of −1.

Adding together the component partial utilities, the rational herdsman concludes that the only sensible course for him to pursue is to add another animal to his herd. And another. . . . But this is the conclusion reached by each and every rational herdsman sharing a commons. Therein is the tragedy. Each man is locked into a system that compels him to increase his herd without limit—in a world that is limited. Ruin is the destination toward which all men rush, each pursuing his own best interest in a society that believes in the freedom of the commons. Freedom in a commons brings ruin to all. [6]

Hardin points out in his article that human population growth also unavoidably brings with it increasing demands on the environment. These increasing demands are perhaps most easily observed in traditional herding societies where increased populations lead to a need for increased herds, which in turn lend to degradation of the commons.

Degradation of a commons gives rise to a wide range of environmental and societal stresses. In many cases, social conflicts have their source in the deterioration or destruction of a common resource base. One of the earliest recorded illustrations of social stress caused by growing human and livestock populations utilizing a limited-resource commons is the account of the experiences of Lot and Abram (later Abraham) in the 13th chapter of Genesis. In the biblical case, their cattle and herds became so numerous (as a result of the increases in their population and wealth) that "the land could not support them." Eventually, fighting broke out between the herdsmen of the two families. To resolve the conflict, Abram proposed to Lot that the two families separate and gave Lot his choice of where to go. Lot chose to move toward Sodom and the other towns along the river Jordan; Abram chose the hills of Canaan.

The Genesis solution—separation and movement into new, resource-rich commons—is not a true solution to the tragedy of the commons because it is effective only until all of the entire commons is threatened with overuse and destruction. At this point the basic nature of the tragedy can no longer be ignored, and true solutions must be sought. In his essay, Hardin sets forth his recommended solution—mutual coercion, mutually agreed upon—and explains a number of successful applications of this solution.* (Fishing licenses and catch-limits to protect the sport-fish populations of the commons—lakes and streams—are an example of Hardin's "mutual coercion, mutually agreed upon.")

American Indians, Eskimos, Lapps, and many other traditional cultures evolved solutions to the tragedy that limit their demands on resources held in common. [7] Often these solutions are based on myths, traditions, technologies, and cultural practices that are displaced following contacts with industrial society. The results are generally disruptive and sometimes disastrous. [8] In the case of herding societies, the disruptive influences often

---

encountered again later in this chapter in connection with the protection of forests, fisheries, oceans, and the atmosphere. The explanation of "the tragedy of the commons" given above applies wherever the tragedy of the commons is mentioned elsewhere in the text.

*In a more recent essay, Hardin discusses his solution in terms of national efforts to protect biotic resources from the tragedy of the commons and concludes that protection of biotic resources is possible under either socialism or free enterprise but not under the system of unregulated commons (Garrett Hardin, "Political Requirements for Preserving Our Common Heritage," Ch. 20 in Council on Environmental Quality, *Wildlife and America*, Washington: Government Printing Office, 1979). Hardin and John Baden propose other solutions in *Managing the Commons* (San Francisco: Freeman, 1977).

TABLE 13–2

Number of Cattle and Number of Sheep and Goats, 1955–2000

(In millions of head)

	Cattle				Sheep and Goats			
	1955	Annual Growth[a]	1976	2000[a]	1955	Annual Growth[a]	1976	2000[a]
Developing market economies[b]	514.3	1.7	696.3	904.3	587.8	1.3	754.3	944.6
Africa	95.0	1.7	129.9	169.8	150.3	2.1	216.8	292.8
Far East	214.8	0.9	254.0	298.8	130.5	1.7	176.6	229.3
Latin America	175.7	2.4	265.6	368.3	155.9	0.2	161.4	167.7
Near East	28.6	2.9	46.2	66.3	150.8	1.5	199.3	254.7
Asian centrally planned economies	57.5	1.2	71.6	87.7	101.6	2.5	154.8	215.6
Subtotal	571.8	1.6	767.9	992.0	689.4	1.5	909.1	1160.2
Developed market economies[b]	225.0	1.6	302.0	390.0	364.8	−0.1	359.6	353.7
North Africa	106.4	1.6	141.7	182.0	35.3	−2.7	15.0	0
Western Europe	82.0	1.1	100.6	121.9	115.7	−0.5	103.0	88.5
Oceania	21.7	4.7	43.2	67.8	170.1	1.0	205.0	244.9
Eastern Europe and the U.S.S.R.	81.2	3.7	143.9	215.6	146.7	1.1	182.0	222.3
Subtotal	306.2	2.2	445.9	605.6	511.5	0.3	541.6	576.0
World Total	878.0	1.8	1213.8	1597.6	1200.9	1.0	1450.7	1736.20

Source: The State of Food and Agriculture 1977, Rome: Food and Agriculture Organization, Nov. 1977, Ch. 3, pp. 3–16 (draft).

[a] Both the annual growth and the projection to 2000 are based on a linear rather than compound (i.e., exponential) growth model. Reviewers of the manuscript felt that, in view of range conditions, an exponential growth model gave unrealistically large animal populations in 2000.
[b] Including countries in regions not specified.

come through modern medical technology, veterinary medicine, and increased access to water.[9] The consequence is often a growth in human and animal populations that cannot be sustained on the available grazing land.[10]

Lands suitable for grazing are limited, and already available rangelands are overpopulated by livestock in many areas (as in the Free Range Grazing Pressure map in the colored map section of this volume). Data on this problem are limited, but its seriousness is illustrated by recent and projected trends in numbers of cattle, sheep, and goats. Table 13–2 summarizes such livestock data for 1955 and 1976 and projects the 1955–76 trends to the year 2000.

The U.N. Food and Agriculture Organization (FAO) estimates that between 1955 and 1976, world cattle populations grew by more than 330 million head. If these trends continue, approximately 380 million additional cattle will be added to the world's herds by 2000. In North America, the Soviet Union, Japan, and Europe, a significant portion of the growth in herds has been on feedlots, but elsewhere much of the growth is on open rangelands.

Much of the global growth of cattle herds is projected to occur in the developing market econ-omies—from 696.3 million head in 1976 to 904.3 million in 2000, an increase of more than 200 million head. Oceania, Eastern Europe, and the U.S.S.R. have experienced the world's most rapid growth in cattle populations. Oceania's cattle populations, with the world's highest growth rate at 4.7 percent per year, almost doubled in two decades, from 21.7 million in 1955 to 43.2 million in 1976. Eastern Europe and U.S.S.R. cattle populations grew at 3.7 percent per year over the 1955–76 period, from 81.2 million to 143.9 million, and by 2000 are projected to reach 215.6 million, more than three times 1955 levels.

The most rapid recent increases in sheep and goats have been in Africa and the Asian centrally planned economies. Between 1955 and 1976 African sheep and goat populations grew by 66.5 million, and in the Asian centrally planned economies, they rose by 53.2 million. Sheep and goat populations in North America and Western Europe have been declining. If present trends continue, sheep and goats will have largely disappeared from North America by 2000, whereas, worldwide, sheep and goat populations are projected to increase by more than 280 million head between 1976 and 2000.

These recent and projected livestock increases—many of them concentrated in the already heavily utilized, fragile grasslands of Eurasia, the Near East, Africa, the Far East, Oceania, and Latin America—signal accelerating rangeland deterioration, soil erosion, and desertification in these areas. In describing the seriousness of the prospects, the FAO recently reported that global livestock population growth has led to

the serious deterioration of grazing land, particularly in the Sahelian and Sudanian zones of Africa, and in parts of the Near East, the Mediterranean and North Africa. The grazing resources in these areas are to a large extent under arid and semi-arid conditions, and some of them have already been threatened for hundreds and sometimes thousands of years by overuse, leading to complete changes in the vegetation, which have left only shrubs of low palatability. Further increases in grazing pressure and aggravated misuse result in the complete devastation of all vegetation, which finally ends in desertification. The problem has been magnified by the encroachment of cropping onto the grazing area, as a result of faster population growth outside the range area. Similar problems exist in other arid and semi-arid areas, for example, in continental Eurasia, in India and Pakistan, and in Northeast Brazil.[11]

The Global 2000 Study projects further population growth, both within and outside of the world's major grazing lands. Such growth will intensify the pressure on these grazing resources, either for conversion to cropland or for feeding increasing numbers of livestock.[12] In a time when many of the world's free grazing commons have already been overgrazed beyond their ability to recover, the prospect is for even greater devastation of the world's remaining grazing commons by the year 2000.

If the consequences of overgrazing are to be avoided in the areas of the world so threatened, efforts will be needed to relate future herd sizes to the feed resources available. A pioneering global study of livestock feed resources and livestock populations has been completed by the Winrock International Livestock Research and Training Center, Morrilton, Arkansas. The Winrock study starts from an assessment of global livestock feed resources and the potential for their development.[13] This feed potential is then related to herd sizes and composition (to provide projections of possible ruminant populations in 2000) and to the contributions these animals could make toward meeting human needs.

The Winrock projections of feed resources and ruminant populations are summarized in Tables 13–3 and 13–4. Worldwide, the Winrock study foresees the possibility of a 13 percent increase in forage feed sources, a 75 percent increase in grain feed, a 68 percent increase in feed from by-products of the agricultural industry, a 98 percent increase in feed from oilseeds, and a 21 percent increase in feed from crop residues—an overall increase in ruminant feed resources of 18 percent over the 1970–2000 period. Based on these estimates of feed resources and improved livestock management, Winrock projects that the world's herds could increase over the 1972–2000 period as follows: cattle by 27 percent; buffalo by 29 percent; sheep and goats by 40 percent; total ruminants ('cattle, buffalo, sheep, and goats) by 34 percent. The prospects for increases vary markedly from region to region—from a high of 56 percent for sheep and goats in middle America to no increase in a number of other areas.

The Winrock projections differ in important ways from the relatively simple trend projections presented in Table 13–2. The Winrock projections start with the feed resources and attempt an assessment of how these could be developed. Since the projections of Table 13–2 are not as constrained by feed resources, somewhat different results are therefore to be expected. The projected cattle populations, for example, differ in that the Winrock estimates of potential growth are smaller. On the other hand, Winrock believes that the feed resources are potentially available for a larger increase in sheep and goats. However, whatever the animal and whatever the increase, improved range management methods will very much be needed if severe overgrazing of forage resources is to be avoided in the decades ahead. The projected increases in herding populations can only increase the already severe pressure on range and grassland resources in many parts of Asia, the Middle East, north and central Africa, and Central America.

Cultures Based on Shifting Cultivation

Like the herdsmen just discussed, the cultivators of traditional cultures also place intensifying pressure on the environmental commons as their populations grow. According to one estimate, 25 percent of the world's land surface—primarily in tropical or subtropical regions—is occupied by about 300 million people who practice shifting cultivation.[14] (See the Land Use Patterns map in the colored map section of this volume.) In some areas, traditional agriculturists practicing shifting cultivation on lands that cannot sustain continual intensive agricultural use are beginning to damage permanently the productivity of the area and to reduce its carrying capacity.

TABLE 13–3

Winrock Projections of World Feed Resources for Ruminants, by Region

In billions of Mcal (10¹⁵ calories)

Forage Sources and Grain

	Forage Sources						Grain	
	Permanent Pasture and Meadows		Arable Lands		Nonagricultural Lands			
	1970	2000	1970	2000	1970	2000	1970	2000
North America	470	515	615	700	175	125	205	335
Middle America	215	350	60	70	30	15	3	5
South America	1,130	1,170	230	295	230	110	15	15
Western Europe	310	310	220	220	40	30	95	170
Eastern Europe	115	145	85	85	10	10	35	65
U.S.S.R.	300	310	575	670	15	15	50	100
China	250	360	75	85	20	15	2	5
North Africa, Middle East	180	200	150	230	15	10	5	15
Central Africa	850	900	240	300	310	300	1	1
Southern Africa	190	205	25	30	15	15	3	5
India	15	55	415	450	15	10	3	15
South and Southeast Asia	70	445	220	245	130	50	1	5
Japan	5	10	25	25	1	1	5	15
Oceania	580	495	175	360	10	10	15	15
Rest of world	140	140	5	10	3	3	1	1
World total	4,820	5,610	3,115	3,775	1,019	719	439	767

Other Sources

	Agri-Industry By-products		Oilseeds		Crop Residues		World Total		Percent of World	
	1970	2000	1970	2000	1970	2000	1970	2000	1970	2000
North America	15	20	25	55	440	500	1,945	2,250	16	15
Middle America	1	1	1	1	65	80	375	522	3	4
South America	5	10	2	5	195	325	1,807	1,930	14	13
Western Europe	10	15	25	55	275	280	975	1,080	8	7
Eastern Europe	5	10	5	10	175	180	430	505	3	3
U.S.S.R.	25	30	10	15	370	430	1,345	1,570	11	11
China	5	5	1	1	540	595	893	1,066	7	7
North Africa, Middle East	5	20	2	2	110	135	467	612	4	4
Central Africa	10	10	1	1	130	160	1,542	1,672	12	11
Southern Africa	1	1	1	1	25	35	260	292	2	2
India	30	65	5	5	270	350	753	950	6	7
South and Southeast Asia	10	20	1	1	235	300	667	1,066	5	7
Japan	2	2	2	10	45	45	85	108	1	1
Oceania	3	5	1	1	35	105	819	991	6	7
Rest of world	1	1	1	1	35	40	186	196	2	1
World total	128	215	83	164	2,945	3,560	12,549	14,810	100	100

Source: H. A. Fitzhuhg, H. J. Hodgson, O. J. Scoville, T. D. Nguyen, and T. C. Byerly, *The Role of Ruminants in Support of Man*, Morrilton, Ark.; Winrock Livestock Research and Training Center, Apr. 1978.

When conducted in moderation on suitable slopes and at human population levels within the carrying capacity of the environment, shifting cultivation is a sound and appropriate practice. Under moderate demands, shifting agriculture is usually sustainable for long periods of time and with low requirements for energy subsidies or external capital. A recent U.N. report noted that shifting agriculture "achieves high productivity per man-day with small capital investment. . . .

TABLE 13–4

Winrock Projections of World Ruminant Populations, by Region

Stub	Cattle			Buffalo			Sheep and Goats			Camels[a]
	1972	2000	Percent Increase	1972	2000	Percent Increase	1972	2000	Percent Increase	2000
	millions			*millions*			*millions*			*millions*
North America	130	156	20	–	–	–	21	25	19	–
Middle America	39	59	51	–	–	–	16	25	56	–
South America	190	286	51	0.1	–	–	142	214	51	6,154
Western Europe	89	107	20	0.1	0.1	0	94	113	20	–
Eastern Europe	35	42	20	0.3	0.5	67	43	52	21	–
U.S.S.R.	102	123	21	0.4	–	–	145	218	50	307
China	63	82	30	29.7	38.6	30	129	194	50	17
North Africa, Middle East	44	57	30	4.8	6.2	29	216	323	50	6,165
Central Africa	116	150	30	–	–	–	157	235	50	7,656
Southern Africa	16	19	19	–	–	–	45	67	49	–
India	179	179	0	57.9	75.3	30	108	130	20	1,464
South and Southeast Asia	75	112	49	33.2	43.1	30	75	113	51	1,489
Japan	4	4	0	–	–	–	–	–	–	–
Oceania	37	33	19	–	–	–	224	269	20	–
Rest of world	11	13	18	–	–	–	19	27	42	1,059
World total	1,130	1,435	27	126.6	168.8	29	1,435	2,005	40	24,311

Source: H. A. Fitzhugh, H. J. Hodgson, O. J. Scoville, T. D. Nguyen, and T. C. Byerly, *The Role of Ruminants in Support of Man,* Morrilton, Ark.: Winrock International Livestock Research and Training Center, Apr. 1978.
[a] Camel populations were not available for 1972.

If cultivation is not prolonged, rapid regeneration of secondary forest vegetation occurs when the land is abandoned."[15]

The importance of the phrase "if cultivation is not prolonged" must be emphasized. Sustainable shifting agricultural requires periodic fallow periods for the cultivated lands to rebuild soil fertility.[16]

The possibilities for maintaining an adequate fallow cycle are closely related to size of the shifting cultivator population, and to the land area available. The Global 2000 Study's projections suggest that the size of these populations will increase by 50–70 percent by 2000. The amount of land burned* and cultivated each year by shifting cultivators will also increase. Where will this land come from?

Virgin forest lands are not likely to be available to meet all of the increased land needs of shifting

---

*Little has been written about the local and global effects on air quality and climate of burning for agricultural clearing and weed control, but accidental forest fires have somewhat similar effects (see "Air Quality and Smoke from Urban and Forest Fires: An International Symposium," Washington: National Academy of Sciences, 1976). One of the primary atmospheric effects is thought to be a large contribution of particulates. It is now also thought that this burning contributes to the accumulating concentrations of carbon dioxide in the earth's atmosphere (George M. Woodwell et al., "The Carbon Dioxide Problem: Implications for Policy in the Management of Energy and Other Resources," report to the Council on Environmental Quality, July 1979.)

cultivators. In the forestry projections in Chapter 8, approximately one fifth of the world's remaining forests are projected to be removed by 2000. By far the largest portion of the forest losses will occur in developing countries with large populations of shifting cultivators. As a result of reduced forested areas and the spread of settled agriculture, shifting cultivators will be forced to return with increasing frequency to lands previously cleared and cultivated. Fallow periods will unavoidably shorten, leading to nutrient losses, adverse shifts in the species composition in the naturally occurring flora and fauna (a reduction of overall species diversity and an increasing preponderance of weed species), and deleterious alterations of the soil structure.[17] Although crops may be grown temporarily in some areas following a short fallow period, the ultimate result of shortening the fallow cycle is increased nutrient leaching from soils, accelerating competition from weeds, and declining yields.[18]

The projected growth of shifting cultivator populations will also lead to increased use of marginal and submarginal lands. Such lands have generally been avoided in the past because of the known agricultural risks and low yields typical of such areas. However, as good land becomes scarcer, the erosion-prone soils of steep slopes and the lateritic soils of humid tropics are likely to be cultivated. Steep slopes erode rapidly when cleared, increasing flooding, drought, and siltation downstream. Similarly, lateritic tropical soils can quickly become unproductive when misused. If intensive shifting cultivation is continued in such areas, even the forest's ability to regenerate can be threatened. [19]

The populations of traditional cultures—both herdsmen and shifting cultivators—already exert large, population-related environmental effects on approximately a quarter of the world's land area. The Land Use Patterns map and Free Range Grazing Pressure map (in the colored map section) show large expanses of the globe now peopled by herdsmen, pastoralists, and peoples practicing shifting crop culture. Although data on these populations and their effects on the environment are quite limited, most experts agree that large and growing numbers are involved. [20] Already major reductions in the productivity of parts of Eurasia, the Near East, Africa, Oceania, and Latin America have been observed. [21] Some of the productivity losses are very severe. [22] Reductions in land productivity by as much as 90 percent were reported for several areas during the 1977 U.N. Conference on Desertification. [23]

The Global 2000 Study's population projections indicate that by 2000 the populations of traditional cultures will have increased significantly, nearly doubling in some areas. If present trends continue, these populations can be expected to continue growing well into the 21st century,* but in some areas, the trends may change. Evidence is accumulating that agricultural and grazing lands in parts of Africa, Asia, the Near East, and Latin America are already under such heavy stress that they simply cannot be expected to retain their present productivity through another two decades of intensifying human and animal population pressure. [24] In such areas, further population growth makes major losses of biological life-support capacity virtually inevitable.

Population and the Environment in Industrialized Cultures

Like traditional cultures, modern industrial cultures,* place population-related pressures on the environment. They face the same basic problem of the tragedy of the commons, but there are at least three important differences between industrial and traditional cultures. First, an additional person in an industrial society makes larger demands on the world's resources than does an additional person in a traditional society. Second, the environmental pressures produced by an additional person in an industrial society are transmitted by transportation and commerce over a much wider geographic area than are those of an additional person in a traditional society. Third, the economies of industrial cultures are much more complex than those of traditional cultures, complicating the analysis—and even the perception—of population-related environmental impacts of industrial cultures.

It is often asserted that some small percentage (e.g., 6 percent) of the world's population living in industrial cultures consumes some disproportionately large share (e.g., 60 percent) of the world's resources. While this assertion is true in some generalized sense, the percentages often quoted are not as easily developed as the assertions might suggest. One of the major difficulties in comparing the resource consumption (e.g. commercial energy) of an "average" person in an industrial society with that of an "average" person in a traditional society is that the industrial person uses a significant portion of the resources to produce products that are ultimately exported and "consumed" in other countries. Food is probably the resource that is easiest to compare directly because relatively little human energy (the end product of food consumption) is exported as compared to the human energy exported in industrial products,† Tables 13–5 and 13–6 present data on

---

*Erik Eckholm points out that many of the cultivators responsible for deforestation, soil erosion, etc., are not "traditional" shifting cultivators but rather landless castoffs of modern development processes. They are not ecologically skilled like tribal people, but are trying to farm wherever they can. Driven by population growth, unequal land tenure, and unemployment, these people are moving onto hillsides and desert margins. Poverty itself is a cause of some forms of environmental deterioration. (Erik Eckholm, *The Dispossessed of the Earth: Land Reform and Sustainable Development,* Washington: Worldwatch Institute, June 1979.)

*The populations of most industrial cultures and nations are increasing both as a result of natural increase and as a result of immigration. The effects of immigration are discussed briefly in Chapter 2. One of the problems associated with demographics in industrial cultures is that those immigrants who enter a country illegally avoid contact with the government and are often not counted in official census figures. As immigration continues, the demographic importance of uncounted persons will increase. A demographic analysis by Robert Cook (available from the Environment Fund, Washington) suggests that as of mid-1979, the official population figures for the United States are about 3 percent low, in part because of uncounted immigrants residing illegally in the U.S. Concern has already been expressed about the accuracy that will be achievable in the 1980 Census (T. R. R. Reid, "Billion-Dollar Nosecount of '80 Fated to be Wrong," *Washington Post,* June 10, 1979, p. A2).

†Even here, the comparison is not clear-cut because there is a significantly higher human energy content in the goods exported by traditional cultures (such as oriental rugs) than in most industrial goods.

TABLE 13–5
Annual Grain Consumption per Capita in the 20 Most Populous Countries, 1975[a]

	Kilograms
United States	708
U.S.S.R.	645
Spain	508
France	446
Federal Republic of Germany	441
Turkey	415
Italy	413
United Kingdom	394
Mexico	304
Egypt	286
Japan	274
Brazil	239
Thailand	225
People's Republic of China	218
Bangladesh	203
Pakistan	171
Philippines	157
Indonesia	152
India	150
Nigeria	92

Source: Lester R. Brown, The Twenty-Ninth Day, New York: Norton, 1978, p. 200.

[a] Includes grain consumed both directly and indirectly (in the form of meat, milk, and eggs).

TABLE 13–6
Energy Consumption per Capita in the 20 Most Populous Countries, 1974[a]

	Kilograms of Coal Equivalent
United States	11,485
Federal Republic of Germany	5,689
United Kingdom	5,464
U.S.S.R.	5,252
France	4,330
Japan	3,839
Italy	3,227
Spain	2,063
Mexico	1,269
Brazil	646
People's Republic of China	632
Turkey	628
Egypt	322
Philippines	309
Thailand	300
India	201
Pakistan	188
Indonesia	158
Nigeria	94
Bangladesh	31

Source: Lester R. Brown, The Twenty-Ninth Day, New York: Norton, 1978, p. 202.

[a] Excludes firewood and dung.

the food and commercial energy consumption per capita in the 20 most populous countries. The relatively "industrial" nations clearly tend to have substantially higher per capita consumption of both food and energy than the relatively "traditional" nations.

Another approach to comparing the resource and environmental impacts of industrial and traditional societies is to compare the discarded waste from each. In traditional societies very few resources are lost as waste. Even human excrement is returned to the soil where it adds nutrients. In industrial societies, wastes of every kind are extensive and environmentally damaging.

In the United States, for example, industrial solid wastes generated in 1977 totaled about 344 million metric tons, and the amount of these wastes is growing at about 3 percent per year.[25] The Council on Environmental Quality (CEQ) reports that solid wastes from residential and commercial sources were estimated at 130 million metric tons in 1976. Based on present trends and policies, the projection for 1985 is 180 million metric tons. These rising waste generation rates reflect increasing use of raw materials and energy.[26] Currently, the average person in the United States produces about 1,300 lbs. of municipal solid waste annually.[27]

The cost of disposing of this waste is high—$9 billion in 1977—and the rate of resource recovery is low—about 7 percent.[28] CEQ reports* that the recovery rate could be tripled by individuals setting aside recyclable materials such as newspapers, glass, and metal for separate collection or delivery to recycling centers.[29] The composition of municipal refuse generated in the United States in 1977 is illustrated in Table 13–7. In addition to reducing per capita mineral resource demands,[30] recycling has energy-saving and environmental advantages. CEQ reports, for example, that making steel reinforcing bars from scrap instead of from virgin ore takes 74 percent less energy and 51 percent less water, creates 86 percent less air pollution emissions, and generates 97 percent less mining wastes.[31]

Per capita wastes and demands on environmental and other resources in the United States are not typical of all industrial societies, but in general an "industrial person" seems likely to have a larger impact on the world's resources and

*Since this text was written, CEQ has reported further on resource recovery. (See Council on Environmental Quality, "Municipal Solid Wastes," in Environmental Quality: the Tenth Annual Report of the Council on Environmental Quality, Washington: U.S. Government Printing Office, 1979.)

TABLE 13–7

Post-Consumer Residential and Commercial Solid Waste Generated and Amounts Recovered, by Type of Material, 1977

(As-generated wet weight, in millions of tons)

| | Gross Discards | Material Recovery | | Net waste disposed of | | |
		Quantity	Percent	Quantity	Percent of Total Waste	Percent of Nonfood Product Waste
Paper	49.2	10.2	20.7	39.0	28.6	46.9
Glass	14.7	0.5	3.4	14.2	10.4	17.1
Metals	13.7	0.4	2.9	13.3	9.8	16.0
Ferrous	11.9	0.3	2.5	11.6	8.5	13.9
Aluminum	1.4	0.1	7.1	1.3	1.0	1.6
Other nonferrous	0.4	0.0	0.0	0.4	0.3	0.5
Plastics	5.3	0.0	0.0	5.3	3.9	6.4
Rubber	3.3	0.2	6.1	3.1	2.3	3.7
Leather	0.6	0.0	0.0	0.6	0.4	0.7
Textiles	3.0	0.0	0.0	3.0	2.2	3.6
Wood	4.7	0.0	0.0	4.7	3.4	5.6
Total nonfood product waste	94.5	11.3	12.0	83.2	61.0	100.0
Food waste	23.8	0.0	0.0	23.8	17.4	28.6
Yard waste	27.3	0.0	0.0	27.3	20.0	32.8
Miscellaneous inorganic wastes	2.2	0.0	0.0	2.2	1.6	2.6
Subtotal	147.8	11.3	7.6	136.5	100.0	164.0
Energy recovery		+0.7	0.5	−0.7		
Total recovery		12.0	8.1			
Total net disposal				135.8		

Source: Franklin Associates (Prairie Village, Kan.), *Post-Consumer Solid Waste and Resource Recovery Baseline: Working Papers,* draft prepared for the Resource Conservation Committee, U.S. Environmental Protection Agency, May 16, 1979, p. 22.

environment than a "traditional person." Furthermore, the industrial person has less direct experience of the impacts being made on the environment than the traditional person because the industrial person is separated by distance from many of the more severe forms of environmental degradation caused by modern industrial cultures.[32] To many urban members of industrial societies, energy comes from an electrical outlet and food comes from grocery stores. Relatively few have had anything to do with the strip mines, power plants, and nuclear waste facilities involved in producing "clean" electricity or with the air and water pollution associated with steel manufacturing and with the chemicals used in "industrial" agriculture. The complex economic web of trade and commerce extends the environmental impacts of each additional industrial person across oceans and continents (see the map Extent of Commercial Activity in the colored map section of this volume).

The complexities of trade and industrial commerce do not alter the fact that increases in industrial populations and their wealth—like increases in herdsmen and cattle—threaten the resources of the environmental commons. The fundamental population-related problem presented by the tragedy of the commons[33] faces both traditional and industrial societies. As Garrett Hardin has shown, common environmental resources can be protected by "mutual coercion, mutually agreed upon" both under socialist and under market economic systems.[34] The socialist approach is illustrated by the examples of the Soviet Union[35] and China[36]. The market (or mixed) economy approach is illustrated by U.S. efforts, among others.[37] It should be noted, however, that both socialist and market economic systems face two incompletely resolved difficulties in protecting the resources of the environmental commons: They place a monetary value on environmental resources and weigh present and future costs and benefits of resources and protective measures.

Under the theory of market economies, the

price of a good (or service) has a major influence on demand, and to the extent that environmental costs are included in market prices, the market can help control the demand for and use of the environmental commons. A valuation problem arises because many environmental costs (e.g., degraded water and air quality or loss of species and wilderness) are borne by a large portion—or all—of society. Called "externalities" by economists, these costs are generally not included in the price of a particular good or service. Unless environmental costs are included in the market price, the market cannot act to protect the environment.* Similar environmental valuation problems arise under socialist economic systems, because government-set prices often fail to reflect external costs any more adequately than market prices.

The second problem involved in using either socialist or market economic systems to protect the environmental commons is that of intergenerational equity.[38] In most societies, a present-value approach is used in economic decision-making. Under the present value approach, future benefits and costs are valued less (i.e., are discounted) relative to current benefits and costs. The higher the discount rate the more difficult conservation and environmental protection become.[39]

Whatever economic system is involved, increased numbers of people lead to increased environmental pressures. The magnitude and character of these pressures depends significantly on the type of culture. The Global 2000 Study's projections suggest that the populations of traditional cultures will be growing rapidly (at more than 2 percent per year in some cases) in the decades ahead. Increased overgrazing and shortened fallow cycles will aggravate erosion, forest losses, and desertification. In parts of Eurasia, the Near East, Africa, Oceania, and Latin America, the land cannot be expected to retain even its present productivity under another two decades of intensifying stress, as discussed in later sections of this chapter. The Global 2000 Study's projections show the population growth rates of industrial societies falling by about a quarter by 2000. The

population increase in the Soviet Union, Europe, and North America (about 200 million) is small compared to the rest of the world (about 2 billion), but the per capita resource and environmental impacts of industrial societies are relatively large. However analyzed, population increase throughout the world must be regarded as a major source of stress on the common environmental resources of the earth.

Population Distribution and the Environment

The nature of the demands and impacts a population makes on its environment depends in part on how its people are distributed over the land. For both developing and industrialized nations, this distribution has been changing. The trend has been toward a decreasing proportion of the world's population living in rural areas and an increasing proportion living in urban areas.

Over the past two centuries the growth of relatively dense human settlements has been rapid, even more rapid than the growth of the world's population. Between 1800 and 1950, the world's population increased by a factor of 2.6. Over this same period the number of persons living in human settlements of 20,000 or more increased from 22 million to more than 500 million, a factor of 23. The populations of large industrial cities (100,000 or more inhabitants) in America, Europe, Oceania, and the Soviet Union grew still faster, increasing by a factor of 35. Recently, however, urban expansion in developed countries (especially in Europe) has slowed. Large cities in the LDCs grew less rapidly than large cities in the industrialized nations during this period, but since 1900, LDC urban growth has accelerated.[40]

United Nations reports suggest that trends toward urbanization may continue.[41] In 1950, 29 percent of the world's population lived in urban settlements. The urban population share grew to 39 percent in 1975 and is projected to approach 50 percent by 2000.[42] Using the Global 2000 Study's medium world population figure, 50 percent urbanization would mean more than 3 billion urban residents in 2000. Such a population distribution would have significant environmental implications in both less developed and industrialized nations.[43]

Urbanization and the Environment in the LDCs

How much urban growth can be expected in the LDCs by the year 2000? The Global 2000 Study's projections do not include detail regarding

---

*Energy provides an example of the externalities problem. There are many external environmental costs of energy production that are not now included in the market price of energy. Although this problem is not resolved, much thought is being given to alternative methods of including external costs into the market price of goods. William Ramsey's *Unpaid Costs of Electrical Energy: Health and Environmental Impacts from Coal and Nuclear Power* (Baltimore: Johns Hopkins, 1979) provides a useful introduction to this problem.

TABLE 13–8

Urban Population in All Cities of 100,000 or More

	1950	1975	2000
	millions		
World	392	903	2,167
Industrialized countries	262	503	756
Less developed countries	130	480	1,411

Source: Trends and Prospects in the Populations of Urban Agglomerations 1950–2000, as Assessed in 1973–1975, New York: United Nations 1975

TABLE 13–9

Estimates and Rough Projections of Selected Urban Agglomerations in Developing Countries

	1960	1970	1975	2000
	Millions of persons			
Calcutta	5.5	6.9	8.1	19.7
Mexico City	4.9	8.6	10.9	31.6
Greater Bombay	4.1	5.8	7.1	19.1
Greater Cairo	3.7	5.7	6.9	16.4
Jakarta	2.7	4.3	5.6	16.9
Seoul	2.4	5.4	7.3	18.7
Delhi	2.3	3.5	4.5	13.2
Manila	2.2	3.5	4.4	12.7
Tehran	1.9	3.4	4.4	13.8
Karachi	1.8	3.3	4.5	15.9
Bogota	1.7	2.6	3.4	9.5
Lagos	0.8	1.4	2.1	9.4

Source: U.N. estimates and medium variant projections, as published in Department of State Bulletin, Fall 1978, p. 17.

rural or urban populations, but an estimate of the LDCs' urban growth can be obtained from United Nations information.

Projections reported by the U.N. Secretariat indicate that urban areas will absorb 59 percent of the increase in LDC population between 1975 and 2000.[44] The Global 2000 Study projects a net population growth of 2.0 billion persons in the developing nations. Applying the U.N. urban percentage to this figure, the urban populations of the LDCs would increase by about 1.2 billion by 2000. As illustrated in Table 13–8, U.N. projections are similar, but somewhat higher.

Most of the projected increase would occur in existing cities, and as a result many LDC urban populations would become almost inconceivably large. For example, by 2000 Mexico City would house nearly 32 million persons—about 4 times New York City's present population.[45] São Paulo would surpass 26 million.[46] Altogether, more than 400 cities would be expected to pass the million mark, most of them in developing countries.[47] The projected growth of selected LDC cities is illustrated in Table 13–9.

The most rapid urban growth of less developed countries occurs in the "uncontrolled settlements"—urban slums and shantytowns, where sanitation and other public services are nonexistent or, at best, minimal. Already more than half of the populations of many larger cities—for example, Buenaventura in Colombia, Ismir and Ankara in Turkey, and Maracaibo in Venezuela—live in uncontrolled settlements,[48] as do more than a quarter of the populations of Baghdad, Seoul, Calcutta, Taipei, Mexico City, and Rio de Janeiro.[49] Recent estimates indicate that the populations of many uncontrolled settlements are doubling in size every 5–7 years, while the urban populations as a whole double every 10–15 years.[50] The more rapid growth of the uncontrolled settlements means that as time goes on, a larger fraction of the LDC urban population will be living in these settlements. In Bombay, where uncontrolled settlements are among the largest in the world, 45 percent of the 6 million urban population in 1971 was living in squatter villages and slums, and the squatter-slum population was growing at 17.4 per cent per year.[51]

The rapid growth of LDC urban populations will create unprecedented pressure on sanitation and other public services by 2000. Waste disposal, water, health care, shelter, education, food, and employment will be needed for approximately 1.2 billion additional urban residents. Simply to provide in 2000 the same per capita services that now exist, the LDCs will need to increase all of the services, infrastructures, and capital of their cities by roughly two-thirds—and this massive increase would provide no net improvement in services. The degree to which public services are provided will, in large measure, determine future environmental conditions in LDC cities.

Safe drinking water and sewage disposal are two of the most basic indicators of LDC urban environmental conditions. While conditions improved over the 1970–75 period, large numbers of LDC urban residents still do not have access to safe drinking water. A 1975 World Health Organization (WHO) survey[52] indicated that at that time 24 percent of the urban populations in LDCs did not have house water connections, or even access to standpipes, and 25 percent were without even household systems for excreta disposal.*

Progress in providing basic LDC urban services also appears to have varied significantly according to income group. The WHO survey found the

---

*For comparison, 78 percent of the LDC rural population did not have access to an adequate water supply, and 86 percent were without even household systems for excreta disposal.

installation of piped indoor water connections were running well in excess of anticipated rates; thus, it was proposed that the 1980 target for installation of connections from piped public water supplies be moved upward from 60 to 68 percent. On the other hand, service from public standpipes increased slower than anticipated, and the proposed target for this form of service has been moved downward from 40 to 23 percent.[53] These trends suggest that service is being provided more rapidly to the relatively affluent middle-class neighborhoods than to the very poor in the rapidly growing uncontrolled settlements.

Provision of potable drinking water in LDC cities is a service closely related to the problems of sewage treatment and disposal. A 1976 report found that only 3.3 percent of the world's LDC urban population lived in dwellings connected to sewer systems that were in turn connected to some form of conventional treatment facility or oxidation pond. The dwellings of another 23.7 percent were connected to sewer systems without any form of sewage treatment capability. Household systems—pit privys, septic tanks, and buckets— were used by 42.1 percent. The remaining 30.9 percent did not even have a pit privy.[54]

While WHO reports that over the 1970–75 period an increasing percent of LDC residents are served by sewers, the projected growth of slums and uncontrolled settlements projected in the years ahead present an unprecedented challenge. In São Paulo, the number of homes served by sewers increased over the 1940–75 period, but the proportion of urban dwellers served by sewers dropped from 38 percent to 29 percent over the same period.[55] The high capital costs of Western-style sewage systems lead many development specialists to advocate less costly composting toilets as an alternative.[56]

Without basic hygienic facilities, LDC urban populations face the constant threat of epidemics and the daily reality of rampant infectious disease. The health impacts of sewage pollution of water are already serious in LDCs. Growing populations—and the resultant sewage burdens in streams, rivers, and lakes and along coastlines—are spreading several waterborne diseases in many urban communities. Recent figures on the impact of waterborne diseases in developing countries show that such diseases are responsible for 40 percent of the affected countries' mortality and 60 percent of their morbidity. In areas occupied by more than 67 percent of the world's population, dysentery, typhoid, cholera, and hepatitis, the major causes of death, can be linked to inadequate sewage treatment.[57]

Environmental problems in LDC urban areas are by no means attributable to growth only in the poorest classes; growth in the more affluent classes also creates environmental problems. One indicator of the environmental stress produced by growth of the affluent classes is the increasing numbers of automobiles and the associated air pollution. Although statistics on LDC urban air quality are very limited, a few examples will serve to indicate some of the general trends:

- In Caracas, Venezuela, the motor vehicle population grew at an annual rate of around 10 percent prior to 1974. With the increase in incomes brought about by 1973 oil price increases, the figure rose roughly 20 percent during 1974 and 1975. Vehicles now produce 90 percent of the air contaminants in Caracas. At peak traffic hours, the carbon monoxide concentrations reach 40–45 parts per million (ppm); the average urban concentration is 25–30 ppm.[58] An 8-hour exposure to even 20 ppm is described by the U.S. Environmental Protection Agency as "very unhealthful."[59]

- Air pollution problems in most LDC cities are made worse by the fact that many automobiles used are old and in poor state of repair, and their engines release relatively high amounts of carbon monoxide, particulates, and smog-producing hydrocarbons. In addition, other motorized vehicles causing relatively high releases of air pollutants (motorbikes, scooters, motorcycles) are common in LDC cities. LDC urban air pollution problems are further intensified by the lack of vehicular air pollution control laws and associated emission-control devices for internal combustion engines.

- Ecologist Carlos Bustamante of Peru's National University of Engineering noted recently that Lima's serious air pollution problems are not just due to its low diffusion of contaminated air (Lima is surrounded on three sides by Andean foothills). He claimed much of the problem was due to the city's numerous old and poorly maintained vehicles and estimated that such vehicles emit five times more pollution than new cars.[60]

- In the capital city of Ankara, the Turkish Health Ministry recently reported that the air was laden with 2.5 times more sulfur dioxide and four times more smoke than the maximum levels set by WHO. Because of this condition, the Ministry reports that cases of bronchitis, asthma, pneumonia, heart attacks, and other diseases caused by the air pollution have sharply increased.[61]

- Bombay, India, is another city suffering from serious air pollution. A recent government survey found that, largely because of industrial growth, pollutants enter the area's air at the rate of 1,000 tons every four hours.[62] The air pollutants include 38.4 percent carbon monoxide, 33.4 percent sulfur dioxide, and 9.8 percent oxides of nitrogen. In one residential area of Bombay, the residents were found to be inhaling very large amounts of sulfur dioxide every day, and most were suffering from cough, constant sneezing, asthma, bronchitis, chest pain, and fatigue.[63] Bombay's nearly 300,000 automobiles have added to the air pollution caused by local industry, magnifying the respiratory disease impacts.[64]

Migration to cities will continue to be a major component of urban growth in LDC nations as long as rural populations, especially the rural poor, believe that urban areas offer greater economic opportunities than rural areas. As urban populations continue to expand, however, economic and environmental conditions may change. Existing trends indicate that the problems of air and water pollution can be expected to worsen, and the spread of waster-borne diseases—and even the disposal of the dead*—will present increasing threats to human health. Urban economies will be hard pressed to keep pace. Housing and employment are in short supply, and energy will present increasing difficulties, especially for the LDC's urban poor. Many can no longer afford kerosene or gas and depend on firewood and charcoal. In some areas the price of firewood has increased at rates exceeding international oil price increases[65] (see also the forestry section of this chapter). The FAO reports that in some areas of

---

*Disposal of the dead presents fewer physical and health problems in countries where religion and custom encourage cremation. In cultures where burial is preferred and space is scarce, public health issues become more important. The difficulties are most severe in LDC cities following an earthquake or some other temporary cause of high mortality but can occur in industrialized countries as well. A particularly striking example of the cumulative problems that burial can present occurred in France during the late 1700s. The principal cemetery in Paris had accumulated some 2 million bodies in a space of only 131 by 65 yards. The *Smithsonian* magazine reports: "This human compost heap was 30 feet deep and extended seven feet above ground. In 1780, in a catastrophic landslide, the walls of an entire apartment block adjoining the cemetery gave way and 2,000 corpses slid into the cellars, giving off a stench that well-nigh asphyxiated the residents above. It was clear that new arrangements were urgently needed. But the turmoil of the French Revolution and the establishment of the Napoleonic Empire precluded the opening of [the new] Père-Lachaise [cemetery] until 1804." (Robert Wallace, "The Elegies and Enigmas of Romantic Père-Lachaise," *Smithsonian*, Nov. 1973, pp. 108–15.

Asia and Africa, firewood now absorbs 15–25 percent of household income.[66]

Will the trends continue? Some observers are beginning to have doubts. Harold Lubell, project leader for an International Labor Organization study of six major Third World cities, concludes that "there appears to be a saturation point, and when this is reached migration falls off in response to declines in the urban economy."[67] Lester R. Brown, President of the Worldwatch Institute, questions whether sufficient food will be available to LDC cities, either from other countries or from domestic sources in large enough quantities and at low enough prices to allow the urbanization trends to continue for many more years.[68] In effect, negative feedback may slow the growth of already overcrowded cities.

If present trends do continue to 2000, urban populations would approach a majority of the world's population,[69] and the largest urban areas would be in the LDCs. The economic and environmental challenges implied by these trends are enormous. Whether these challenges can be met to the degree necessary if the trends are to continue is an open question.

Urbanization and the Environment in Industrial Nations

Over the past several decades population patterns in most industrial nations have changed significantly. Rural to urban migration has created large national majorities of urban dwellers, declining populations in most small towns and villages, the consolidation and mechanization of farms, and a concurrent decline in the number of small, family-owned farms. Rapid growth of various transport systems (particularly highway and air) has lead to high personal mobility and rapid growth of single-family houses and "townhouse complexes" in suburban areas. Urban and suburban installation of potable-water, sewer, and electric and fossil fuel energy systems for households is nearly complete. Although some of these changes have also been occurring to a degree in some developing nations, such changes are relatively well advanced in industrial nations.

The environmental consequences of these patterns of population distribution and human settlement, many of which have already been touched upon, are numerous. One factor needing emphasis concerns the importance of the low (even the falling) real price of energy and other raw materials during the period of urbanization in the industrialized nations.

During the 1950s and 60s, the low real cost of

energy encouraged a variety of wasteful and inefficient designs. Homes, offices, and factories were built with minimal insulation and energy-conserving features. Labor-saving, but energy-intensive, appliances and machinery spread throughout the culture. Agriculture and industry became increasingly energy-intensive and less labor-intensive. Production of vehicles expanded rapidly, and their weight and horsepower grew substantially. Simultaneous massive investments in highway and road construction led to rapid growth of energy-inefficient single-family homes in suburban communities, often around decaying inner cities. Oil-based chemicals, plastics, and fabrics replaced many natural materials, such as wood, wool, and cotton. All this was made possible by cheap, abundant energy, especially fluid fuels, and all of this has now changed.

Some of the environmental, resource, and economic costs of the past decades of urbanization have been analyzed for the United States in "The Costs of Sprawl," a study prepared by the Real Estate Research Corporation for the Council on Environmental Quality and other federal agencies in 1975.[70] This study documents how, in contrast to urban sprawl, higher-density, better-planned communities require less energy for cooling and heating, stimulate less automobile use, and conserve water. They produce about 45 percent less air pollution than sprawling communities, reduce storm water runoff, and allow more land, wildlife, and vegetation to be protected in parks and open spaces.

Now that the era of inexpensive, widely available energy has come to an end, the implications for both population distribution and environmental quality are likely to be profound. Although the future shape of cities in industrial nations is not yet clear, it is certain that such communities will be confronting radical transformation from energy-wasteful to energy-conserving societies. Smaller, well-insulated homes, and increasing shifts to townhouses and condominiums are trends already underway in housing. Slower driving speeds, smaller and more efficient automobile engines and greater use of public transport are energy-conserving transportation measures already beginning to take effect. Recycling of materials and increased reliance once again on renewable sources of materials (especially wood) may also reduce societal energy requirements[71] but might also increase the competition for land.

The fundamental nature of the long-term change was indicated briefly in the 1977 U.S. National Energy Plan (NEP).[72] The NEP noted that a basic aspect of the energy problem in the U.S. is that abundant cheap energy has led to the development of a stock of capital goods, such as homes, cars, and factory equipment, that uses energy inefficiently.[73] The NEP went on to note that a transition to an era of substantially more expensive and less abundant energy is in progress and that as a part of this transition, changes in capital stocks will be needed.[74] These changes, if started soon, can be accomplished incrementally.

In reviewing the NEP, the Office of Technology Assessment (OTA) noted that energy efficiency in the use of capital stocks depends in significant part on how the stocks are distributed over the nation and that changes in patterns of capital distribution and transportation are long-range and fundamental and will take more than one generation to complete.[75] The OTA report recommends guidelines, leadership and incentives to initiate the process now. Its point might be summed up as follows:

The United States and other industrial nations will face an exceedingly difficult energy problem in 2000 if its patterns of capital distribution are still based on the sprawl that is so characteristic of many industrial cities; yet because of the long depreciation times associated with transportation, communication, sewage, and other systems associated with sprawling types of land-use patterns, the major capital systems of most industrial cities in 2000 will look much like those that existed in 1977 unless the "guidelines, leadership, and incentives" called for by OTA are established immediately. The distribution patterns of major capital systems can be changed only over a period of decades, not within a few years.

At least in the U.S., the dependence on and the passion for the private automobile is not likely to change easily. The U.S. Bureau of the Census recently completed a study of some of the ties between Americans and their automobiles. The study found, among other things, that while the use of car pools and mass transportation probably increased after the 1973–74 Arab oil embargo, the increase was apparently only temporary. By 1975:

- Of 80.1 million Americans going to work each day, 52.3 million (65 percent) were driving alone.

- Another 15.6 million (19.4 percent) were driving, but with other passengers in the car or truck.

- Only 4.8 million (6 percent) used public transportation, and 3.8 million (4.7 percent) walked.

- The remaining 3.6 million (4.5 percent) used bicycles or motorcycles or worked at home.

• The average commuter trip was 9 miles each way and was 20 minutes in duration.[75a]
• The proportion of mass-transit users among those employing vehicles actually *decreased* from 10 percent to just over 6 percent in 1975.

Despite the abiding passion and dependence, the future of the private automobile is in doubt not only in the U.S. but throughout the world. Virtually every other use of dwindling petroleum resources has been found to have a higher priority than that of the private automobile.[75b] However, it will be difficult to eliminate dependence on the private automobile without fundamental changes in population and land-use patterns. As discussed briefly in the energy section of this chapter, the choice of future energy systems and technologies—large-scale centralized systems or small-scale decentralized systems—will have a major influence on the population and land-use patterns than can be expected in the future.

Whether or not in direct response to energy developments, the trend toward urbanization in some industrial nations has begun to change. In the U.S., for example, signs began to appear after 1970 that many of the nation's larger cities—New York, Los Angeles, Detroit, Seattle, Chicago, and St. Louis—were declining in population.[76] At the same time, much of the nation's fastest population growth has shifted to rural areas. From 1970 to 1975, 7 million people emigrated from U.S. central cities to suburbs and other nonmetropolitan areas.[77]

However these trends continue, the industrial nations of the world face a period of perhaps 50 to 100 years of transition. Over the next decades, choices will have to be made, not only in energy development but in many other sectors of industrial society (such as food production and water and minerals supply) that will encounter problems of scarcities and resource degradation. How these choices are made will profoundly affect patterns of future development and human settlement in industrial nations.

Urbanization and the Environment—Summary

Urban growth, due largely to the migration of poor people from rural areas, may have created cities in the developing countries of unprecedented sizes by the year 2000. On the other hand, it is possible that rural development plus a decline in economic and public health conditions in LDC cities will slow the migration somewhat. In any event, it is anticipated that the most rapidly growing parts of these cities will be the uncontrolled settlements where large numbers of the poor exist without access to even basic public services such as potable water and sewage disposal. At anticipated growth rates, it is doubtful that the services of many LDC cities can be increased rapidly enough to provide services at even the present per capita level.[78] Raw sewage, air pollution, lack of housing, poor and crowded transport, inadequate fire protection, and disease will present increasing difficulties within these cities. Immediately outside the cities, firewood gatherers, animal grazers, and charcoal-makers will strip the surrounding areas of accessible trees, shrubs, and grasses. As the area of degradation widens, there are likely to be losses of indigenous plants and animals, aggravated soil erosion, and increased risk of serious flooding.[79]

In the industrial nations, future trends in urbanization are not clear, but designs that conserve resources, especially energy, will become increasingly attractive. The era of rapid growth in industrialized nations fueled by high consumption of resources, particularly relatively clean, inexpensive, and abundant petroleum fuels, has ended. In the future, consumption patterns of both rural and urban settlements of industrialized nations will be altered by inevitable shifts from a high-consumption to a conservation approach.[80] Before the year 2000, industrialized nations will be forced to make major choices relating to their future energy and resource industries and their production technologies—choices that will have profound implications for population distribution and environmental quality throughout the 21st century.

The Population Projections and Human Health

The life expectancy of a population is perhaps the most all-inclusive and widely measured indicator of a nation's environmental health. In the absence of safe drinking water, sewage systems, adequate food and shelter, medical services, and controls over toxic pollutants and disease vectors and hosts, the release of environmental pathogens and pollutants, life expectancies are low. With these basic environmental conditions met, life expectancies are high.[81]

It is generally believed that as economic development proceeds, one of its major benefits is a combination of beneficial environmental conditions that increase the average period of productive life. The increased life expectancy is brought about in three stages according to a theory that has been expressed succinctly by Dr. N.

R. E. Fendall, former director of medical services for Kenya:

1. In the earliest stages of development, the epidemiological picture is determined largely by an endemic infectious disease situation with a high prevalence of parasitosis, gastroenteritis, respiratory diseases, malnutrition, and vector-borne diseases.

2. As living standards rise and environmental conditions improve, the endemic infectious disease problems are brought under control, and measles, whooping cough, poliomyelitis and other bacterial and virus diseases dominate the epidemiological picture.

3. In the final stage of economic development, the degenerative diseases of a cerebrosclerotic nature, hypertension, heart failure, diabetes, psychosomatic diseases, and cancer comprise the major portions of ill health. Undernutrition gives way to overnutrition and the severity of the disease pattern shifts from the child to the aged.[82]

This theory, in effect, underlies the projections of life expectancy made by the Bureau of the Census for the Global 2000 Study. These projections (see Chapter 2) assume that future economic progress and development will lead to environmental conditions that will in turn result in increased life expectancy. For the world as a whole, life expectancy is projected to increase 6.7 years (11 percent) by the year 2000 (from 58.8 years in 1975 to 65.5 years in 2000). For the LDCs, the projected increase is 18 percent (form 54.0 to 63.5 years), and for the industrialized countries, 3 percent (from 71.1 to 73.3 years). In no country is life expectancy projected to decline.

Since the advent of preventive immunization against communicable diseases, life expectancies have improved steadily. The continuing trend of life expectancy is illustrated and compared in Table 13–10 with the Bureau of Census projections developed for the Global 2000 Study. For the world as a whole, a 15 percent increase was achieved over the 1950–70 period. Life expectancies increased everywhere, but the most dramatic increases were in the less developed countries— a 21 percent increase overall. Asia achieved a striking 24 percent increase.

On closer examination, the life expectancy data show another important development: The rate of increase of life expectancy has slowed. For the world as a whole, the average annual increment in life expectancy declined from 0.64 to 0.34 years over the 1950–70 period. Further increases in life expectancy have been particularly difficult to achieve in the industrialized nations, where child mortality is relatively low. Degenerative diseases (e.g., cancer, heart disease, cerebrovascular disease) have proven very difficult to prevent or control. In the LDCs, decreases in infant and child mortality have been difficult to achieve, and progress in increasing life expectancies has slowed there too.

The Bureau of the Census life expectancy projections are based on an examination of past trends, not on an examination of the causes of mortality and the prospects for changes in these causes. The causes are largely associated with environmental problems, and the prospects for change need to be examined. The problems and prospects for improvements are quite different in the industrialized countries than in the less developed countries.

Environment and Health in the LDCs.

Mortality statistics show that in most LDCs high mortality rates among infants and children are the primary statistical contributors to low life expectancies. A 1975 World Bank Policy Paper containing vital statistics for 67 countries lists 19 countries with per capita incomes of less than $200 per year.[83] Of these, only 2 had infant mortality rates below 10 percent, while 10 had rates 15 percent or higher. By contrast, only 4 of the 16 countries with per capita incomes of over $700 had child mortality rates greater than 5 percent; 8 had rates of less than 3 percent.[84]

The World Bank also notes that the rate at which life expectancies have improved in less developed countries has declined since 1955—from 2.7 years in the periods 1950–55 and 1955–60 to 2.6 years in 1960–65 and to only 2.0 years in 1965–70.[85] A particularly significant factor in the slowdown of the decline of LDC mortality appears to be that mortality in childhood has shown a somewhat greater resistance to decline than mortality at some later ages.[86]

The persistence of infectious diseases (above all diarrhea) that cannot be conquered with modern medicine is, in large part, responsible for slowing the decline in infant mortality. Malaria control, antibiotics, and immunization programs have brought some quick, dramatic gains, but further progress depends on improvements in nutrition and sanitation, which are coming along slowly, if at all. According to Dr. John Bryant (formerly with the Rockefeller Foundation, now with the office of International Health, U.S. Department of Health, Education and Welfare):

TABLE 13-10
Levels and Trends of Life Expectancy at Birth, 1950-2000

Life Expectancy at Birth, in Years

	1950/55	1955/60	1960/65	1965/70	1975[a]	2000[a]
World	46.7	49.9	52.2	53.9	58.8	65.5
Industrialized countries	65.0	68.2	69.5	70.3	71.1	73.3
Less developed countries	41.6	45.0	48.0	50.4	54.0	63.5
Africa	36.1	38.5	40.8	43.0	46.2	57.4
Latin America	52.3	55.3	57.7	59.5	63.1	70.3
Asia	42.5	46.3	49.8	52.5	54.3[b]	63.7[b]

Average Annual Increment in Life Expectancy at Birth, in Years

	1950/55-1955/60	1955/60-1960/65	1960/65-1965/70	1975-2000[a]
World	0.64	0.46	0.34	0.27
Industrialized countries	0.64	0.26	0.16	0.09
Less developed countries	0.68	0.60	0.48	0.38
Africa	0.48	0.46	0.44	0.45
Latin America	0.60	0.48	0.36	0.29
Asia	0.76	0.70	0.54	0.38

Source: World Population Prospects as Assessed in 1973, New York: U.N. Department of Economic and Social Affairs, 1977, pp. 138 ff.
[a] Calculated from Bureau of the Census, *Illustrative Projections of World Populations to the 21st Century,* Washington: Government Printing Office, 1979, p. 91 Table 8. Weighting is 105 for males; 100 for females.
[b] Asia *and* Oceania

The great weapons of modern medicine are aimed at the patho-physiology of disease and its susceptibility to pharmaceutical, immunological, or surgical attack. Health services are designed to deliver these weapons mainly through the hands of doctors. The dismal fact is that these great killers of children—diarrhea, pneumonia, malnutrition—are beyond the reach of these weapons.

If children sick with these diseases reach the physician, there are sharp limits to what he can do. Diarrhea and pneumonia are often not affected by antibiotics, and the frequent presence of malnutrition makes even supportive therapy difficult or futile. And even these interventions by the physician, whether or not they are therapeutically effective, are only sporadic ripples in a running tide of disease. We are speaking of societies in which, at any given time, a third of the children may have diarrhea and more than that may be malnourished. Their lives are saturated with the causes—poverty, crowding, ignorance, poor ventilation, filth, flies. [87]

The causes of high infant-mortality rates are well known and closely linked to environmental conditions. As shown in Table 13-11, the diseases most often fatal during early childhood in a developing area (in this case, Latin America) are fecally related and airborne contagious diseases. Although diseases such as cholera, typhoid, and polio all contribute to the mortality statistics, in-testinal parasites and various infectious diarrheal diseases are probably the most devastating of the fecally related types. Surveys of parasite-infected populations frequently show from 70 to 90 percent infestations. [88] In Egypt, Iran, and Venezuela, the *monthly* incidence of diarrhea among preschool children has been estimated to be 40-50 percent. [89]

The effects of diarrhea, pneumonia, and intestinal parasites are greatly aggravated by undernutrition, which is the major underlying cause of death among children. Deaths from infection nearly always result from a combination of undernutrition and infection. When women are undernourished, too frequent pregnancies result in malnutrition for the mother and baby, low average birth weights, and poor resistance to disease.

The prospects for reducing malnutrition are mixed. The Global 2000 Study food projections, in the medium case, show only limited improvement in per capita food availability and, in some instances, declines. Furthermore, when food distribution among income classes is taken into consideration, the number of malnourished, disease-vulnerable children is likely to increase by 2000. Increased death rates in parts of Asia have already been observed during poor crop years. [90]

To further complicate the situation, many of the diseases most threatening health in developing countries are becoming increasingly resistant to drugs now being used in their treatment. [91] Already drug-resistant pathogen strains* have contributed to severe epidemics in several LDCs:

- In Central America between 1968 and 1971, a dysentery pandemic occurred in which the drugs normally used to treat the disease proved ineffective.[92] The strain—*Shigella dysenteriae 1*—had high mortality rates in both Guatemala and El Salvador. In Guatemala alone, an estimated 12,500 people died from the disease in 1968 (200 out of every 100,000 inhabitants).[93]
- In Mexico in 1972, an epidemic of typhoid fever appeared on a scale unprecedented in modern times.[94] The strain—*Salmonella typhi*—has resistance to a wide range of drugs.[95] The outbreak lasted for months and involved four Mexican states. Large numbers of persons of all ages and varying socioeconomic groups were affected.[96]
- In recent years resistance to commonly used therapeutic agents against malaria has increased substantially in South America and Southeast Asia. There is every reason to believe that these resistant strains will spread, thus hampering treatment and eradication.[97]

In short, there is growing evidence that numerous pathogens and vectors† are evolving strains that are resistant to many of the common and least expensive drugs.[98] While new drugs will continue to be developed, the new drugs are often more expensive and effective against a smaller group of pathogens than those that they replace.[99] Excessive use of commom antibiotics both by humans[100] and in animal feed[101] may increase the rate at which resistant strains evolve. The most

---

*Pathogen resistance to drugs is not limited to developing countries; it causes increased mortality in industrialized societies as well ("Rise of Antibiotic-Resistant Bacteria," *Science News*, Aug. 24/31, 1974, p. 119). Certain staphylococcus infections (especially in hospitals) and gonorrhea in particular are growing problems. There are many indications that drug resistance in pathogens will continue to increase throughout the world (Marietta Whittlesey, "The Runaway Use of Antibiotics," *New York Times Magazine*, May 6, 1979, p. 122). Coastal waters off New York have been contaminated with both sewage and mercury. Tests show that bacteria in these waters have developed varying degrees of resistance to ampicillin, tetracycline, kanamycin, and streptomycin, and research with both the genus *Vibro* and the genus *Bacillus* led to the conclusion that ampicillin resistance and mercury resistance are genetically linked (Marine Ecosystems Analysis Program, *New York Bight Project Annual Report for FY 1976–76T*, Boulder, National Oceanic and Atmospheric Administration, 1977, p. 28).

† See the food and agriculture section of this chapter for a discussion of the increasing problems of insecticide resistance and immunities developing in strains of insect vectors.

---

inexpensive, common antibiotics are widely available without prescription even in remote rural LDCs.[102] And the appearance of resistant bacterial strains may not be due only to low probability mutations; it is now thought that epidemic diseases may suddenly acquire resistant traits through higher-probablility contacts with more common, harmless intestinal species that have already evolved their own resistance.[103]

If the reduced LDC mortality figures projected in the population chapter are to be achieved, progress must be made in controlling the fecally related diseases, the airborne diseases, and the increased mortality associated with these diseases as a result of nutritional deficiency. These diseases are largely of environmental origin and can be controlled only through improved environmental and sanitation conditions and through improved nutrition and education, all of which require capital investment, as well as through changes of habits and cultural traditions. As discussed above under urbanization in the LDCs, there is reason to question whether the needed improvements in sanitary and environmental conditions will occur. By the year 2000, sanitary conditions in some areas may even deteriorate. This situation, worsened by increasing scarcities of food and energy in poorer regions, could lead to an increase, rather than a decrease, in mortality rates among some populations.[104]

Environment and Health in the Industrialized Nations

Two important developments in health conditions are occurring in the industrialized nations. First, life expectancies are continuing their trend of many years, increasing slowly. In the U.S., for example, the rate of increase of life expectancy averaged 0.53 years per year over the 1940–50 period but fell to 0.15 years per year for the 1950–60 decade and to 0.12 years per year for the 1960s. Over the first five years of the 1970s, the annual rate has increased to an average 0.32 years, bringing the U.S. life expectancy at birth to 72.5 years.[105]

The second development relates to causes of death. Although there is much dispute over particulars, medical experts generally agree that the causes of the diseases and accidents responsible for most fatalities and prolonged periods of ill health in affluent societies (heart disease, lung disease, cancer, stroke, highway accidents) are now related largely to life-styles and environmental circumstances. Frequently mentioned as con-

TABLE 13-11

Percentages of Deaths of Children Under the Age of Five Due to Fecally Related and Airborne Diseases or Malnutrition, Latin America, Selected Areas

	Fecally Related Disease	Airborne Disease	Nutritional Deficiency	Total
Chaco, Argentina (rural)	40	36	2	79
San Juan, Argentina (central urban)	38	32	3	72
San Juan, Argentina (suburban)	34	38	8	80
San Juan, Argentina (rural)	35	42	8	84
Chaco Resistencia, Bolivia (rural)	52	27	6	84
La Paz, Bolivia (urban)	29	55	3	87
Viacha, Bolivia (rural)	25	65	0	91
Recife, Brazil (urban)	42	41	5	88
Ribeirao Preto, Brazil (urban)	49	36	2	87
Ribeirao Preto, Brazil (rural)	50	29	3	81
Ribeirao, Preto Franca, Brazil (rural)	55	20	7	82
Sao Paulo, Brazil (urban)	40	33	5	78
Santiago, Chile (central urban)	31	37	6	73
Santiago, Chile (suburban)	33	38	3	74
Cali, Colombia (urban)	44	25	15	84
Cartagena, Colombia (urban)	38	23	17	78
Medellin, Colombia (urban)	49	22	11	82
San Salvador, El Salvador (urban)	52	28	6	86
San Salvador, El Salvador (rural)	51	22	13	86
Kingston, Jamaica (urban)	37	21	5	63
St. Andrew, Jamaica (rural)	23	23	23	69
Monterrey, Mexico (urban)	43	35	4	83

Source: Ruth R. Puffer, and Carlos V. Serrano, *Inter-American Investigation of Mortality in Childhood. Provisional Report,* Washington: Pan American Health Organization, Sept. 1971. pp. 133–54.

tributing factors are limited exercise, cigarette smoking, alcohol consumption, exposure to toxic chemicals, chronic psychological stress, and diets high in fats, salt, and refined carbohydrates.[106] Changes in these contributing factors must occur if the increased life expectancy projected in the Global 2000 population projections is to be achieved in the industrialized countries. What are the prospects?

The prospects·for change are mixed, at least in the U.S. The adverse effects of smoking have received much attention since the Surgeon General's report of a decade ago, but smoking habits have changed relatively little. Over the 11-year period from 1965 to 1976 smoking among males declined about 10 percentage points (from 52.4 to 41.9 percent of the male population) and about 2 percentage points for women (from 34.1 to 32.0 percent of the female population).[107] Efforts are being made to control toxic substances, but there will be long lags in identifying and removing toxic substances from the environment.[108] Cancer is the

only major cause of death that has continued to rise from 1970 to 1976, and environmental (i.e., exogenous nongenetic) factors contribute 80–90 percent of the present cancer cases.[109] Little change seems in prospect for the life-styles and institutional demands that are the root cause of much stress. However, many persons are making efforts to improve their physical fitness. Some persons are changing their dietary habits, but the Global 2000 food projections (see Table 13–17) show the industrialized nations increasing· their already high per capita food consumption still further to 130–35 percent of the standards recommended by the Food and Agriculture Organization. Efforts to reduce energy consumption have increased life expectancies in at least one way: Accidental deaths associated with motor vehicle accidents have declined by 25 percent between 1972 and 1975, due primarily to reduced speeds.[110] However, due to lax enforcement of the new speed limits, speed and accidents are both increasing again.

Conclusions

The discussion in this and other sections of this chapter make clear that the projected levels of human population will exert significant pressures on the environment, both directly and indirectly. Environmental impacts will occur in both traditional and industrial cultures.

A number of traditional cultures have existed for centuries in relative equilibrium with their environments. Today, population growth, changing technologies, and altered life-styles have rendered the balancing mechanisms ineffective. Highly evolved social-ecological systems are breaking down with disastrous results for both humans and their life-supporting environment.

The threat to most ecosystems in less developed regions is illustrated in the last four maps in the colored map section at the end of this volume. These maps show the extensive overlap between the areas of high population density, limited agricultural potential, and intense land use. In parts of Asia, Africa, and Latin America, the productivity of the life-supporting ecosystems can be expected to decline as a result of another two decades of intensifying pressure.

The Global 2000 population projections show no significant slowing in growth through the year 2000, and increases can be anticipated well into the 21st century. A large portion of the 6.4 billion persons projected for 2000 will be desperately poor. Biological resources and the environment generally as well as economies will be stressed just to meet basic human needs. Income disparities and limited educational opportunities will compound the difficulties.

Population-related pressures on the environment are also expected to increase in the industrialized countries. Although population growth in these countries is much less than in the LDCs, the resource requirements and waste production of an "industrial person" is large. Trade and commerce spread the environmental impacts of increased industrial populations over very wide areas.

Environmental factors will complicate preventive health measures in both less developed and industrialized countries. Poor sanitary conditions will hamper efforts to eradicate the diseases that have the largest influence on mortality rates in the LDCs. In the industrial nations, environmental factors and life-styles may lead to the continued prevalence of premature deaths.[111] Curative health measures will be complicated in both developing and developed countries as a result of increased pathogen resistance to many common and inexpensive drugs.

THE GNP PROJECTIONS AND THE ENVIRONMENT

The Projections

The medium-growth* Gross National Product (GNP) projections, developed from World Bank, CIA, and nongovernmental data, are summarized in Table 13–12. GNP is projected to grow exponentially at 3.6 percent per year, increasing 145 percent by 2000. The industrialized countries' GNP grows more slowly than the world average, increasing by 129 percent. The less developed countries more than triple their GNP, but the magnitude of the LDC increase ($2.4 trillion) is much less than the magnitude of the increase in the industrialized countries ($6.3 trillion). Nonetheless, the LDC share of the world's total GNP is projected to rise from 18 to 24 percent.

On the average these trends, when combined with the trends inherent in the population projections, imply that real per capita incomes increase by about a third—more in countries with rapid economic and slow population growth, less in countries with slow economic growth and rapid population growth. In some cases (Pakistan, India, Bangladesh), little or no growth in real per capita income is projected. The GNP projections do not address the distribution of GNP (or income) among socioeconomic classes within countries and give no indication of any changes that might occur in the composition of GNP.

---

* The GNP projections in Chapter 3 are based on rates for low, medium, and high growth. Only the medium-growth case is considered here.

Introduction

Although economic activity certainly has many environmental effects, GNP estimates are not an adequate basis from which to deduce detailed environmental impacts. At best, GNP figures provide an indication of the volume of economic activity, but with virtually no hint of the content. The content of GNP is particularly important in connection with the environment; as the U.S. Commission on Population Growth and the American Future observed, "An irony of [present] economic measurement is that the value of goods and services represented by the GNP includes the cost of producing the pollutants as well as expenditures for cleaning up afterward."[112] Without knowledge of the specific goods and bads and the services and disservices to be produced, only a very general discussion of the environmental implications of GNP projections is possible.

Nonetheless, GNP projections do provide some clue to future environmental problems, particularly with respect to pollution and waste generation and resource consumption. By the year 2000, even the slowest growing economy is projected to have nearly doubled its GNP, while more vigorous economies will have more than tripled theirs. Barring major changes in the kinds of goods (and bads) and services (and disservices) produced—and barring major changes in the technologies employed and in the share of GNP devoted to environmental protection—certain rough proportional increases in waste and pollution generation and in resource consumption can be anticipated.*

In the paragraphs that follow, the implications of GNP growth for pollution and waste generation and for resource consumption are considered very briefly. (The specific implications of the projected resource developments are discussed in later sections of this chapter.) Then, toxic substances—a topic that relates more to GNP growth than any of the other projections—are discussed briefly.

Pollution and Waste Generation

Unless there are very significant structural changes in the world's economies, increased eco-

---

* This observation depends to a degree on where sectorally the GNP growth occurs. In industrialized countries, economic growth has become increasingly concentrated in the relatively clean service sector, rather than in the more polluting extractive and manufacturing sectors. GNP growth in the LDCs, which will occur largely in primary and secondary sectors, will probably have relatively larger impacts on the environment over the next two decades. Furthermore, as discussed in Chapter 14, the GNP model assumes that the proportion of GNP allocated to environmental pollution will not increase markedly in the LDCs, and the energy model assumes that the real cost of environmental protection will not significantly increase the cost of building or operating future energy facilities in the industrialized countries.

TABLE 13–12

GNP Trends, 1975–2000, Medium-Growth Rate

(In trillions [10^{12}] of constant 1975 U.S. dollars)

	1975		2000		Increase	
	GNP	Share	GNP	Share	Average	Total
		per-cent		*per-cent*	*percent*	
Industrialized countries	4.9	82	11.2	76	3.4	129
Less developed countries	1.1	18	3.5	24	4.7	218
World	6.0	100	14.7	100	3.6	145

Source: Chapter 2, this volume.

nomic activity can be expected to produce larger quantities of waste materials and more residual wastes. Whether these residual wastes actually enter the environment as pollutants depends on policies for, and expenditures on, environmental protection. The projected economic growth will have one of two effects (or a combination of both): increased release of wastes and pollutants into the environment or increased costs of keeping the waste and pollution out of the environment.

Increased environmental pollution can occur in at least two ways: first, as a result of relaxed or unmet ambient (or source-emission) standards; second, as a consequence of increased numbers of emission sources, all of which meet unchanged source-emission standards. As the number of sources (or the volumes discharged from existing sources) increases, source-emission standards (per unit of effluent discharged) must be tightened just to maintain present environmental conditions.

Tightening standards to compensate for increased economic activity may become quite expensive. For example, if the number of sources meeting a 94 percent emission standard doubles, the standard must be tightened to 97 percent, just to break even. If the discharges triple, increased pollution occurs unless the standards are tightened to 98 percent. As the standard approaches 100 percent, the costs of meeting the standard generally increase very rapidly. Thus, the projected doubling or tripling of economic activity can be expected to lead to either an increasing proportion of GNP being devoted to pollution control, to more pollution, or to both—unless there are innovations in production processes, by which "wastes" are recycled and used (as in the pulp and paper industry, which now uses "waste" as an energy source).

Resource Consumption

The projected increases in GNP imply increased demand for both renewable and nonrenewable resources. Meeting these resource demands will have many environmental implications.

The Global 2000 Study's nonrenewable resource projections (i.e., the energy and minerals projections of Chapters 10–12) are based on various assumed linkages to GNP. For example, as discussed in Chapter 14, the LDC minerals projections assume that LDC economies will become more mineral-intensive as growth continues; the LDC energy projections suggest that LDC economies will not increase in energy intensiveness as industrialization proceeds. In the industrialized economies, the models assume that GNP growth will lead to little change in energy intensiveness and to decreasing minerals intensiveness. Whatever the actual relationship is between GNP and nonrenewable resources, increased environmental impacts can be anticipated in the mining, refining, and energy sectors as a result of increased economic activity. The environmental impacts of the projected increase in demand for nonrenewable resources are considered in other sections of this chapter.

Renewable resources are also of critical importance to the health of the world's economies. As Lester R. Brown, President of Worldwatch Institute, has observed:

Four biological systems—fisheries, forests, grasslands, and croplands—form the foundation of the global economic system. In addition to supplying all our food, these four systems provide virtually all the raw materials for industry except minerals and petroleum-derived synthetics. The condition of the economy and of these biological systems cannot be separated. As the global economy expands . . . pressures on earth's biological systems are mounting. In large areas of the world, human claims on these systems are reaching an unsustainable level, a point where their productivity is being impaired. When this happens, fisheries collapse, forests disappear, grasslands are converted into barren wastelands, and croplands deteriorate.[113]

The environmental impacts of projected increases in demand for renewable resources are considered in other sections of this chapter.

The Use of Chemicals in the Development of Societies*

Reports can be found documenting the use of chemicals dating back to antiquity. The utilization of chemicals to enhance living conditions can be traced to the simple use of metals in the development of glazing materials for ceramic utensils. Other uses of metals are found, for example, in the development of bronze, initially for weaponry, then for the creative arts. Accounts are also found of the use of metals in the development of medical practice, such as the use of mercury for medicinal purposes by the Romans. The reliance by civilizations on chemicals in order to improve their living conditions has had a long history in Western civilization.

By the same token, however, the use of chemicals in an adverse sense also has had a long history, beginning with the use of extracts from the fruit of the hemlock by the Greeks. This was followed by the Romans, who used other forms of poisons, and later still by those who participated in the Italian court intrigues of the Renaissance era. This, of course, continued into the end of the 19th century with the development of trinitrotoluene (TNT) and the use of chemicals in modern warfare in World War I.

It was not until the end of the 19th century that the use of chemicals in society began to become widespread. It was at this point that reliance on natural sources for chemicals became so strong that the sources of supplies began to lag significantly behind the demands society placed upon them. This led to the development of experimental chemistry in Europe for the express purposes of synthesizing new chemicals to replace those originally obtained from natural sources. This development coincided with the discovery that crude oil, which was initially used as a replacement for whale oil, could also be used as a new source of supply for chemicals. A new scientific discipline emerged, to expand the utility of crude oil: organic chemistry.

With the advent of organic chemistry, the synthesis of every imaginable organic compound originating from crude oil feedstock began. In part, this activity was the domain of the scientist in order to further understand the mechanisms of organic chemical reaction rates. Uses for the increasing number of organic compounds synthesized by the organic chemists was left to others,

---

* This section was added at the suggestion of the U.S. Department of State, while Chapter 13 was in press. It is the work of Mr. Jack Blanchard in the Office of the Assistant Secretary for Oceans and International Environmental and Scientific Affairs, Department of State. Since toxic chemicals are a major source of pollutants in the coastal waters of the world's oceans, they are also discussed below, in the section on the marine environment.

however, to develop. An example of such a process was DDT. It was considered a novel compound by organic chemists in the early 1940s. It was not until the latter stages of World War II, however, that it was found to have pesticide activity and was used extensively as a disinfectant. Subsequently, its use as an overall general pesticide expanded enormously after the war. It was used widely and it was inexpensive. Only recently have we realized its adverse effects: pesticide resistance, thinning of eggshells, and its appearance in foodstuffs worldwide. Indeed, the field of organic chemistry spawned an impressive expansion of new pharmaceuticals which led to striking advancements in medical health practices. In time, the advent of novel synthetic organic chemicals quickly found commercial uses, such as plastics and even artificial diamonds. Just before the World War II, U.S. production of synthetic organic materials was less than 1 billion pounds per year. By 1978, U.S. production had risen to approximately 172 billion pounds annually. [114]

The use of chemicals in the 20th century has become so widespread that it can be said that their presence is ubiquitous. Along with this expanded reliance of chemicals, however, has been an increasing awareness in recent years of the unintended adverse impact to the environment and public health due to the widespread use of chemicals. Society has come to rely extensively on chemicals and is now beginning to realize the problems that have been created with the manufacture, use, transportation, and disposal of chemicals. For the advantages that chemicals have given societies, which have been overwhelming, there have also been disadvantages which have proven striking. We are now beginning to realize how extensive these disadvantages are, and in industrialized societies remedial measures are being developed to respond to the more serious problems chemicals pose to the environment and public health.

At the Governing Council meeting of the United Nations Environment Programme in 1978, it was estimated that 4 million identifiable chemicals are in common use, with the worldwide value of chemical sales in excess of $300 million annually and with over 30,000 chemicals in commercial use. There are some 1,000 new chemicals brought on to the market annually. [115] With regard to international trade in chemicals among OECD-member countries, this amounted to approximately $50 billion in 1976. [116]

Along with this expanded use of chemicals, however, has been an increasing awareness in recent years of the unintended adverse impact to the environment and public health following long-term low level exposures to chemicals. Society has come to rely extensively on chemicals in order to improve its living conditions. This heavy reliance on chemicals, however, has begun to elicit concerns about the benefits when evaluated with the unintended risks associated with their use. These risks have been associated with every facet in the utilization of chemicals, from their manufacture and use to their transportation and disposal.

Examples of such risks to chemicals abound, not only in the technical press, but the lay press as well. There can be no dispute that radium, originally used on watch faces for luminescent figures, causes cancer. Similarly that dibromochloropropane (DBCP) developed as a herbicide causes sterility in males following occupational exposures. [117] Also that vinyl chloride monomer, the precursor to polyvinyl chloride, causes angiosarcoma of the liver. [118] Transportation of bulk chemicals has periodically resulted in major accidents requiring the evacuation of whole communities in order to protect them from clouds of poisonous gas, explosives, or other hazards. [119] Similarly, disposal of chemicals until recently has never been regulated. Environmental contamination of the Hudson and James Rivers by PCBs [120] and Kepone, [121] respectively, of the Love canal in New York State, [122] and of Hardeman County, Tennessee, [123] and Seveso, Italy, are examples of large-scale industrial disposals of chemicals, which in time have proven injurious to communities.

Where does the control of chemicals begin in order to provide society with some protection? How will the uses of chemicals be tempered in order to provide a rational basis for their continued use? The projected outcome may not be difficult to develop if current practices are taken into consideration. The major question remains as to whether controls on chemicals will be adequate to allow for their continued use by society while maintaining an acceptable measure of protection from exposures associated with their manufacture, use, transportation, and disposal.

Chemicals will continue to play an integral role in the development of societies of both industrialized nations and less developed countries. The roles played by these societies with regard to the control of toxic substances may not be changed materially by the year 2000.

Industrialized countries have begun to institute regulatory controls on chemicals. As national programs have been developed in the last few years, continued examples of adverse environmental and public health damage coupled with society's increasing concerns, have led to this development. As governments move to implement their respective national programs, two major goals are being addressed: (1) protection of public health and environment and (2) recognition that economic impacts associated with these controls should not impede unduly (or create unnecessary economic barriers to) technological innovation. These issues have international ramifications. Considerable movement has been made in attempting to reach consensus among industrialized countries regarding the control of chemicals. It seems prudent to project that some form of international cooperation will take place in the future, hopefully well before the year 2000.

A different set of problems exist, however, for less developed countries. In these instances, examples already exist with regard to governments who perceive themselves at some disadvantage relative to industrialized countries in protecting themselves from adverse exposures to chemicals. Developing countries, and in some cases less developed countries, have indicated that insufficient data are available to them in order to develop adequate control programs. Few developing countries have the capacity to cope with the sophisticated analyses required to assess the risks of imported or locally manufactured chemicals, and multinational chemical manufacturers are locating plants in the LDCs to avoid the regulations that already exist in many industrialized nations. In view of these problems, the LDCs have asked the United Nations Environment Programme (UNEP) for assistance in developing and strengthening their capabilities for evaluating chemicals, food, drugs, and cosmetics. [124]

The projections for less developed countries for the year 2000 in dealing with chemicals are less amenable to generalizations. It can be said that they will, of course, rely on UNEP as well as other multilateral organizations to provide the basic technical skills for controlling the manufacture, use, transportation, and disposal of chemicals. Some countries may incorporate directly part or all of the control programs implemented by industrialized countries. As such the work of developed countries in harmonizing regulatory controls in chemicals becomes quite important to both the chemical-exporting countries and the chemical-importing countries.

The level of control of chemicals by the year 2000 may be somewhat anticipated on the basis of developments already under way. Within industrialized societies, the environmental movement has established a substantial body of legislative mandates designed to protect public health and the environment from pollutants from industrial sources. This activity has been concerned with toxic chemicals. Many of these programs have been adopted by the World Bank in establishing environmental guidelines for developing countries desirous of undertaking rapid growth in their economies. [125] While environmental controls are being imposed in industrial countries, less developed countries will be able to benefit from these efforts.

With regard to direct controls in chemicals themselves, the picture is a bit less clear. Industrialized countries have identified the characteristics of those chemicals which could be regarded as having unacceptable effects on humans and their environment. These generally are persistence, wide distribution, and bioaccumulation leading to biological effects, and they form the basis of their respective chemical control programs. [126] Since pollution readily crosses political boundaries, there is a definite correlation that can be expected to occur between control programs in industrialized and those in less developed countries, the only mitigating aspects being economics, technical expertise, and societal factors. In time, one would expect that regulatory controls of toxic substances, once initiated by industrialized countries, will also be adopted by nonindustrialized countries.

As less developed countries improve their economies, a transfer of information on the control of chemicals will be expected to occur. In time, the differences will be one of a degree of enforcement from country to country. Society cannot live without chemicals. It is clear, on the other hand, that society cannot live without controls on chemicals. Somewhere in between will be found the position of the broad range of societies, their disparities measured by their willingness to coexist with chemicals in their environment.

Conclusions

The Global 2000 Study projects the GNP of the world to increase from $6 trillion in 1975 to $14.7 trillion in 2000. Because GNP figures include the cost of producing pollution as well as cleaning up afterward, they are an inadequate basis for anticipating environmental impacts. However, the GNP projections imply increasing demand for both renewable and nonrenewable resources. Short of major changes in the structure of the world's economies, meeting the projected resource demands will lead to increases in environmental pollution or increases in the proportion of

GNP devoted to environmental protection, or both. The environmental implications of meeting the projected demands are analyzed in other sections of this chapter.

CLIMATE CHANGES AND THE ENVIRONMENT

The Projections

Because of the difficulty of climatological modeling, it is not possible currently to produce generally agreed-upon quantitative climate projections. Instead, the CIA developed for the Global 2000 Study three climatological scenarios,* each of approximately equal probability, and described the principal characteristics and probable broad-scale effects of each. The three scenarios, discussed in detail in Chapter 4, are, in brief:

CASE I: NO CHANGE. Climate conditions approximate those of the 1941–70 period.

CASE II: WARMING. A general warming, mainly in the polar and higher middle latitudes, is associated with smaller year to year variation in precipitation and with slight increases in global precipitation but, at the same time, with a greater likelihood of continental drought in the U.S.

CASE III: COOLING. Cooling in the higher and middle latitudes is associated with a decrease in precipitation amounts and an increase in month to month and year to year variation in precipitation, a general equatorward shift of storm tracks, more frequent failures of the monsoon over India, and recurrent severe droughts in the Sahel (as during the 1972–74 period).

Aspects of the energy, forestry, food, and GNP projections, which also have the potential to influence (and be influenced by) climate, are listed here in summary form.

The Energy Projecions through 1990 show annual increases in the demand for oil of 3.0 percent; oil will supply 47 percent of the 1990 energy demand. (See Chapters 10 and 20 for an explanation of the 1990 limit to the energy projections.) It is projected that coal will furnish one-fifth of the total energy for 1990. Nuclear and hydroelectricity production will treble and will furnish 16 percent of the 1990 energy demand. Natural gas usage will have increased 43 percent by 1990 to satisfy 17 percent of the demand.

The Forestry Projections anticipate deforestation at rates that will reduce total forested areas on the earth by 16–20 percent by 2000.

The Food and Agriculture Projections foresee a 90–100 percent increase in total world production. This increase is based on a small (5 percent) increase in arable land and a 70–100 percent increase in productivity of land under cultivation. Much of the increased productivity is a result of more than a doubling of fertilizer† use per hectare for the world as a whole, and a quadrupling of fertilizer use per hectare in the LDCs.

The Gross National Product Projections show trends toward increases in real per capita incomes by about one-third, with greater increases in countries with rapid economic growth but slow population growth, and smaller increases in countries with slow economic—but rapid population—growth.

---

* The three climatological scenarios developed by the CIA were based in part on five scenarios developed jointly by the National Oceanic and Atmospheric Administration, the Department of Agriculture, the National Defense University and the Central Intelligence Agency.
† In the USDA projections, the term "fertilizer" is used to denote fertilizers and other yield-enhancing inputs, including pesticides and herbicides.

Introduction

Present comprehension of long-range climatic phenomena is so limited that scientists have no generally accepted bases for predicting with assurance the magnitudes—or even the directions—of possible changes in the earth's climate over the next several decades. Yet it is known that the climate of the 1950s and 1960s was exceptionally favorable and that, on the basis of past experience, the earth can expect both more variable and less favorable climate in the future. Some human activities, especially those resulting in releases of carbon dioxide into the atmosphere, are known to have the potential to affect the world's climate. Whether future climate changes will be predominantly of natural or human origin is not known, and the pace at which they will occur and the severity of their consequences are unknown quantities. Many experts nevertheless feel that changes on a scale likely to affect the environment and the economy of large regions of the world are not only possible but probable in the next 25–50 years.

The Global 2000 Study group, faced with the need to estimate the effects of climate change on the environment over the next quarter century, decided to use the recent survey of expert opinion[127] conducted by the National Defense University as a basis for the three scenarios described briefly above. Environmental implications of each of the Global 2000 Study climate scenarios will be examined here,* together with aspects of some of the other projections that have implications for world climate.

The Climate Scenarios

An analysis of the environmental impacts of the three Global 2000 climate scenarios must begin with a brief glance at the National Defense University (NDU) study on which they are based.[128]

The five climate scenarios of the NDU study were developed by a panel of experts in climatology. All had the same basic information; each had his own ideas and opinions as to the nature, dimensions, and consequences of the climate changes that could be expected over the next 25 years. Both human-caused (anthropogenic) and natural influences were considered. Increased fossil fuel combustion and clearing of forests for food production are examples of possible anthropo-

genic influences. Natural influences are exemplified by changes in solar radiation, volcanic activity, and shifting ocean currents, all of which can have significant effects on climate.

All members of the panel had available detailed evidence of climate variation, both during human history and during the geological history of the planet, indicating that significant natural variations could occur between the present and the year 2000.

The benign climate of the 1950s and the 1960s was by no means typical of the integlacial (or postglacial) period the earth has been experiencing for approximately the last 10,000 years.[129] This 20-year period was most favorable for agriculture and food production over much of the cultivated areas of the industrialized high-technology nations; a climate a few degrees warmer or cooler could have been considerably less favorable.[130]

Consideration of current trends in temperatures and of the history of climate over the past 10,000 years led the NDU panel of experts to five alternative climate scenarios for the next 25 years: (1) Large Warming, (2) Moderate Warming, (3) No Change, (4) Moderate Cooling, and (5) Large Cooling. The three Global 2000 Study scenarios are related to these five as follows: Case I (*No Change*) is essentially identical to the NDU No Change scenario; Case II (*Warming*) falls between the NDU Moderate Warming and Large Warming scenarios; Case III (*Cooling*) falls between the NDU Moderate Cooling and Large Cooling scenarios.

The climatological considerations[131] behind the Global 2000 Study scenarios are, briefly:

Case I: No Change might occur if warming and cooling effects should happen to balance one another between now and 2000.

Case II: Warming might occur if the warming effect of atmospheric carbon dioxide were to predominate over all other effects.

Case III: Cooling might occur if the global cooling trend that began in the 1940s were to continue, possible as the result of an increase in volcanic activity (and related dust) or a (sunspot-cycle-related) decrease in the solar energy reaching the earth.

Environmental Consequences of the Climate Scenarios

Details of the Global 2000 Study's Case I (No Change) scenario are given in Chapter 4 under the heading "Same as the Last 30 Years." The major premise is that the warming effects of increasing CO_2 in the atmosphere will compensate

---

* The probability of occurrence of the Case I scenario (No Change), is 0.30; of Case II (Warming), approximately 0.25; of Case III (Cooling), also 0.25. Estimated from the probability figures for the five National Defense University scenarios given in Tables 4–1A through 4–5A in Chapter 4.

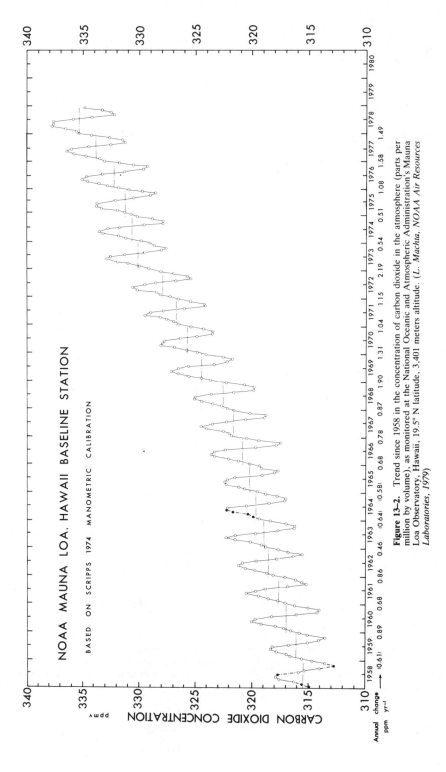

Figure 13-2. Trend since 1958 in the concentration of carbon dioxide in the atmosphere (parts per million by volume), as monitored at the National Oceanic and Atmospheric Administration's Mauna Loa Observatory, Hawaii, 19.5° N latitude, 3,401 meters altitude. (*L. Machta, NOAA Air Resources Laboratories, 1979*)

for the cooling effects of a natural cycle of falling temperatures. The environmental consequences of this scenario on changes in energy usage, agriculture and food production, and forestation are minimal. Furthermore, since none of the government's present long-term global models can utilize climate inputs, *all of the Global 2000 Study environmental impact projections are based on the assumption that the Case I (No Change) scenario will actually occur.* Thus, the environmental impacts of the Case I scenario are incorporated in those projections.

The Case II (Warming) scenario has, of course, somewhat different environmental implications. This scenario leads to an increase of 1° C in global temperatures, with most of the warming in the polar regions and the higher middle latitudes. Precipitation increases are predicted for the higher middle latitudes with little change elsewhere. Fewer extremely cold winters might be expected, but the chance that the interior of the U.S. would experience hot summers and widespread drought conditions resembling those of the mid-1930s is likely to increase. The warming would be substantially beneficial to Canadian and Soviet wheat production; it would be moderately detrimental to wheat in Argentina, Australia, and India and marginally unfavorable to corn (maize) in Argentina and the U.S.[132] The effects on energy usage, while not calculated, are probably negligible. Deforestation would probably increase in the higher middle latitudes as more of the land became arable. Pressures on forests elsewhere would depend on population growth and concomitant needs for food, fuelwood, building materials, and other forest products.

The Case III (Cooling) scenario leads to a global temperature decrease of 0.5° C, with 1° C cooling in the higher and middle latitudes and smaller changes near the equator. Precipitation amounts decrease, and month to month and year to year variability increases. Storm tracks shift equatorward, bringing precipitation to the higher latitudes of deserts, but causing equatorward expansion of these deserts. Monsoon failures would become more frequent and severe in India, and the Sahel would experience more frequent severe droughts. Wheat yields in Canada and the Soviet Union would be reduced, but other key crops would not be severely affected.[133] The demand for energy would increase, particularly in the middle and higher latitudes, where increasing amounts of energy would be needed for heating. Also, greater variability of climate might call for higher levels of heating-fuel reserves. Additional demands for energy might also result from attempts to relieve drought effects in densely populated areas by producing water in massive desalinization programs. Forested areas at higher latitudes of the Northern hemisphere would become less accessible, and grow more slowly.

Impact of the Other Projections On Climate

Climatologists have identified two general types of factors that influence climate: human activity (anthropogenic influences) and natural factors (geological, oceanic, and ice feedback effects and astronomical effects). The following paragraphs focus primarily on the anthropogenic influences implied by the other Global 2000 Study projections, especially the GNP, food and agriculture, forestry, and energy projections. These projections are considered in terms of their potential effects on the factors thought most likely to alter the world's climate.

Most experts agree that the most potentially harmful changes in climate on a global scale would result from increases of atmospheric carbon dioxide and other "greenhouse gases" (such as fluorocarbons and nitrous oxide), from changes in the quantity and character of particulate matter in the atmosphere, or from a partial destruction of the ozone layer. Changes in the earth's surface albedo (a measure of reflectivity), and increases in residual heat released as a consequence of energy use are also known to be factors in local, regional, or—in extreme cases—global changes in climate.

Carbon Dioxide

Carbon dioxide (CO_2) is a colorless, tasteless, nontoxic gas. It is exhaled by all animals as a product of metabolism and is absorbed by plants as part of the process of photosynthesis. CO_2 is a basic product of the combustion of all hydrocarbons, including fossil fuels and wood. It is not subject to economically practical control by any pollution-control technology. The amounts produced annually are so large that the only possible means of disposal is discharge to the atmosphere.

The carbon dioxide content of the atmosphere has been increasing since routine observations began. Preindustrial (ca. 1860–90) atmospheric CO_2 content is estimated by most experts at approximately 290 ppm (parts per million by volume)[134]; measurements show the 1976 content to be 332 ppm.[135] The upward trend is easily seen in Figure 13–2, which shows rather large seasonal variations superimposed on the long-term trend. The average concentration increased by about 5 percent in the 20-year period 1958–78.

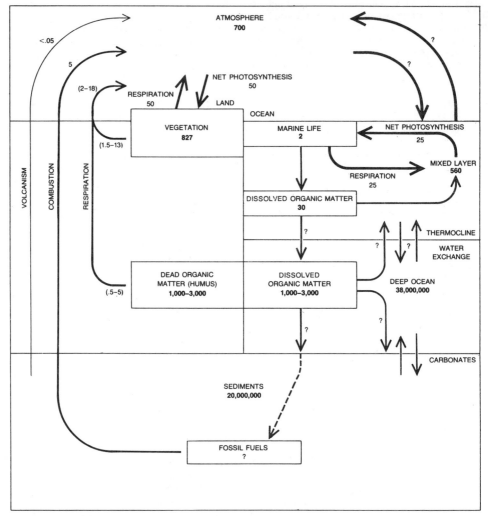

Figure 13–3. Global pools and flows of carbon. Pools are expressed in billions of metric tons of carbon, flows in billions of metric tons of carbon per year. (*From "The Carbon Dioxide Question," by George M. Woodwell, copyright 1978 by Scientific American, Inc., all rights reserved*)

The increasing atmospheric concentration of CO_2 is of concern because of the so-called greenhouse effect. In a greenhouse (or solar collector), shortwave solar radiation (light) from the sun passes through the glass and is re-radiated as infrared longwave, heat radiation from the soil and other surfaces inside the greenhouse. The heat energy radiated upward is trapped inside of the greenhouse by the glass, which cannot transmit longwave radiation to the colder outside environ-

ment. The CO_2 in the atmosphere acts in much the same way as glass, permitting solar radiation to pass through to the earth's surface but intercepting some of the heat radiated upward from the surface toward space and reradiating it back toward the surface. With steadily increasing atmospheric CO_2, the balance between incoming and outgoing radiation can be maintained only if surface and lower-atmospheric temperatures increase.

There is still some uncertainty on exactly where all of the additional CO_2 is coming from, where it goes, and whether the rate of increase will remain constant or change. The general picture, however, is reasonably well established, at least out to the year 2000.[136] Since the total amount of carbon in the earth-atmosphere system is constant, the carbon being added to the atmosphere pool must come from a nonatmospheric carbon pool somewhere within the system. Figure 13–3 shows the various pools of carbon in the earth-atmosphere system and the flows of carbon between pools. Most experts consider that carbon from the combustion of fossil fuels is the main cause of increasing CO_2 in the atmosphere, but recently others have suggested that deforestation (and the associated oxidation of the fixed carbon in plants and humus) may contribute approximately as much to the increase of atmospheric CO_2 as the combustion of fossil fuels.[137]

Global 2000 Study projections are not sufficiently precise to permit accurate calculations of how much CO_2 will accumulate in the atmosphere in the coming decades. However, significant increases in atmospheric CO_2 levels can be anticipated on the basis of the forestry and energy projections: Deforestation and fossil fuel combustion are both projected to increase significantly. On the basis of the Study's projections of fossil fuel combustion alone, the Brookhaven National Laboratory estimates that annual emissions of CO_2 will increase by 35–90 percent by the year 1990.*

Not all the CO_2 released into the atmosphere by these and other processes accumulates in the atmosphere. Past records and computations show that atmospheric carbon dioxide has been increasing by only about 46 percent of the CO_2 released into the atmosphere annually.[138] An amount equivalent to the remaining 54 percent is removed by plants through the process of photosynthesis and by the surface waters of the ocean, which take up the CO_2 in solution.[139] The amount removed from the atmosphere by these processes is dependent on the atmospheric concentration of CO_2. From biology and chemistry it is known that, in general, the greater the concentration of CO_2 in the atmosphere, the more is removed by vegetation and the oceans. However, the increasing concentration of CO_2 in the oceans (which may reduce the ability of ocean surfaces to dissolve CO_2) and the projected deforestation could conceivably reduce the rate of absorption and cause

an acceleration in the current annual rate of increase in atmospheric CO_2. No one knows for sure how these and other[140] circumstances will combine in the years ahead, but after a careful study of the matter, the National Academy of Sciences anticipates that, if present trends continue, a four- to eightfold increase of atmospheric CO_2 concentration is entirely possible by the latter part of the 22nd Century.[141] A four- to eightfold increase in atmospheric CO_2 concentration would have exceedingly serious consequences. Even a doubling would have very serious consequences, and several scientists feel that, if present trends continue, a doubling is likely to occur during the first half of the 21st Century.

The major contribution to an increased concentration of atmospheric CO_2 is the combustion of fossil fuels. Over the past 30 years fossil fuel combustion has increased at about 4.3 percent per year. About half of the CO_2 released by fossil fuel combustion remains in the atmosphere while the other half is taken up by plants and ocean waters, or is otherwise removed from the atmosphere. If these trends continue, the atmospheric content of the atmosphere could reach twice that of preindustrial times by 2025–2050.[142] The rates of increase are dependent on energy strategies yet to be chosen, but an illustrative range of cases is shown in Figure 13–4. The rapid increases shown in the figure are due in part to an assumed continuation in the growth of fossil fuel combustion and in part to a shift toward coal and synthetic fuels produced from coal, both of which produce somewhat more CO_2 per unit of heat produced than do oil and gas.

The increased CO_2 concentrations implied by a continuation of present trends have momentous implications. The Geophysics Study Committee of the National Academy of Sciences has studied the prospects with one of the most complete climate models yet developed for examining such problems. The Committee has observed:

For even a doubling of carbon dioxide in the atmosphere, the model predicts about a 2°–3° C rise in the average temperature of the lower atmosphere at middle latitudes and a 7 percent increase in [global] average precipitation. The temperature rise is greater by a factor of 3 or 4 in polar regions. For each further doubling of carbon dioxide, an additional 2°–3° C increase in air temperature is inferred. *The increase in carbon dioxide anticipated for A.D. 2150 to A.D. 2200 might lead to an increase in global mean air temperature of more than 6° C*—comparable with the difference in temperature between the present and the warm Mesozoic climate of 70 million to 100 million years ago. [Emphasis in the original.][143]

---

* See the Energy System Network Simulator (ESNS) estimates in Chapter 10.

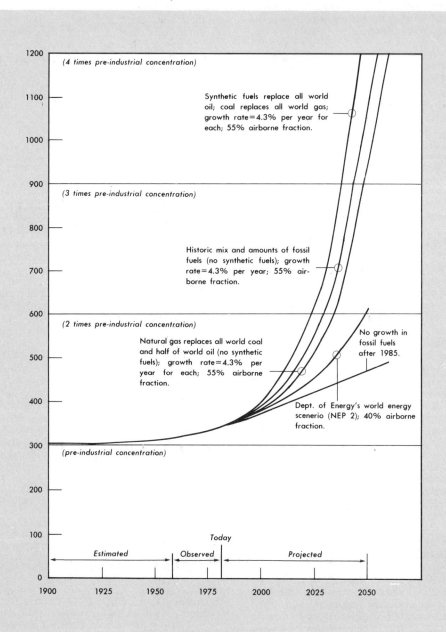

Figure 13-4. Carbon dioxide concentrations implied by various energy scenerios. Synthetic fuels derived from coal are assumed to release 3.4 x 10^{15} grams of carbon in CO_2 per 100 quads of energy. Airborne fraction is the percent of emitted CO_2 that remains in the atmosphere. *(U.S. Department of Energy)*

TABLE 13–13

Global Summary of Sources and Annual Emissions of Atmospheric Particulate Matter

	Natural Sources	Anthropo-genic Sources
	Millions of metric tons per year	
Primary particle production		
Fly ash from coal	–	36
Iron and steel industry emissions	–	9
Nonfossil fuels (wood, mill wastes)	–	8
Petroleum combustion	–	10–90
Incineration	–	4
Agricultural emission	–	10
Cement manufacture	–	7
Miscellaneous	–	16
Sea salt	1,000	–
Soil dust	428–1,100	?
Volcanic particles	4	–
Forest fires	3–150	?
Subtotal	1,500–2,300ᵃ	100–180
Gas-to-particle conversion		
Sulfate from H_2S	130–200	–
Sulfate from SO_2		130–200
Nitrate from NO_x	60–430	30–35
Ammonium from NH_3	80–270	–
Organic aerosol from terpenes, hydrocarbons, etc.	75–200	15–90
Subtotal	350–1,100ᵃ	175–325
Total	2,000–3,400ᵃ	275–500ᵃ

Source: Adapted from George D. Robinson. "Effluents of Energy Production: Particulates," in Geophysics Study Committee. *Energy and Climate,* Washington: National Academy of Sciences, 1977, p. 62.

ᵃ Subtotals and totals do not sum exactly due to rounding.

Particulates

At any given time the earth's atmosphere, at various levels above the ground, carries billions of tons of many different kinds of particles in various concentrations. These particulate accumulations are of both natural and anthropogenic origin.[144]

Table 13–13 lists the kinds, amounts, and sources of particulate matter in the atmosphere. The figures in this table are estimates only; for the most part they were extrapolated from data that are limited both in accuracy and length of record, and assumptions used in the extrapolations were sometimes arbitrary in nature.

The effects of atmospheric particulates on climate are varied. Their size, shape, color, electromagnetic properties, and distribution in the atmosphere determine how they affect the balance of solar and terrestrial radiation, the formation of clouds and rainfall, the surface temperature of the earth, and the quality of air for both plant and animal life.[145]

Naturally produced particulates tend to have more widespread and more chronic effects than those produced by human activity. For example, volcanic activity injects particulates high into the atmosphere, where they tend to reflect much more of the incoming solar radiation than do particles generated by human activity, which tend to remain at lower altitudes.[146] Volcanic particles are known to have been carried completely around the world and to have remained in the atmosphere from one to three years.* Clouds of dust particles from desert areas are sometimes carried thousands of miles by the prevailing winds.[147] These heavy clouds of dust may suppress cloud formation and the occurrence of precipitation, and could be implicated as a cause of drought.[148]

A general atmospheric effect of particulates involves the scattering and reflection of solar radiation back into space, thus reducing the amount of solar energy reaching the earth's surface.† With this effect in mind, it has occasionally been speculated that the cooling effect of anthropogenic particulates might just balance the warming effect of CO_2 accumulations. All the Global 2000 Study's projections of fossil fuel combustion, deforestation, agricultural production, and GNP generally imply increases in particulate emissions. The ESNS (Energy System Network Simulator) findings reported in Chapter 10 indicate that over the next two decades there will be significantly more emissions from energy conversion. If desertification, conversion of forests to agriculture, and general removal of vegetative cover continue, the amount of particulates contributed by windblown dust will increase—perhaps significantly.

Can the effects of increased particulates and CO_2 emissions be expected to be mutually balancing? The definitive study of this question has yet to be done, but on the basis of present information, the answer seems virtually certain to be no. Anthropogenic particulates do not have enough effect. The National Academy of Sciences reports:

---

* The National Defense University global climate scenario for Large Cooling is based in part on the cooling effect of particulates released by several major volcanic eruptions assumed to occur between 1980 and 2000 (see Chapter 4).
† The scattering and reflective properties of particulates vary considerably with the size and other properties of the particles. While the most common effect is as described above, some particles absorb enough solar radiation to produce a warming effect.

We can greatly increase emission of the kind of particle now produced by combustion in industrial communities without greatly changing the integrated radiative properties of our planet's disk as seen from space, unless, as may be the case, the increased particle loading changes the albedo of cloud. . . . [However,] there is little doubt that an increase in particles and sulfurous emissions to a magnitude that might have global climatic consequences would be intolerable from the point of view of community health.[149]

The Academy's passing reference to cloud albedo is significant. Particulates and aerosols are known to provide condensation nuclei important in the formation of clouds, but it is not known how the types of particles and aerosols that are likely to be added to the atmosphere in the years ahead would affect cloud formation. The effect is likely to be quite nonlinear, at least in some respects—i.e., relatively modest changes in particulate loadings may lead to significant changes in cloud cover. The linkage between condensation nuclei and cloud formation has been termed one of the most frequently overlooked, yet potentially most serious consequences of industrial pollution.[150] More research in this area will definitely be needed.

Ozone

The atmosphere consists of two major layers; the troposphere extending upward to 8 to 16 kilometers and, above that, the stratosphere extending up to about 50 kilometers. Temperature decreases with increasing altitude throughout the troposphere, but a permanent temperature inversion exists at the tropopause, with temperatures *increasing* with altitude in the stratosphere. Temperatures rise by roughly 65° C over a height interval of 35 kilometers. The temperature rise is caused by the stratospheric layer of ozone (O_3).[151]

The ozone layer has two important and interrelated effects. First, it absorbs ultraviolet (UV) light in the UV–B band (optical wavelengths ranging from 290–320 nanometers) and so protects all life on the earth from the harmful effects of this radiation. Second, by absorbing the UV radiation, the ozone layer heats the stratosphere, causing the temperature inversion.[152] The effects of temperature inversions in limiting vertical mixing in the atmosphere are well known as a result of the pollution problems of inversion-prone areas such as Los Angeles. This same effect is at work in the stratosphere.* Various waste products produced

in, or migrating slowly into, the stratosphere may remain there for years until they are converted to other substances in the stratosphere or are transported downward into the troposphere, where they can be removed by various processes, including rain. The difficulty is that the effluents of several human activities are being trapped by the temperature inversion in the stratosphere, where they react in ways that deplete the ozone.[153] The human activities now thought to have varying degrees of adverse impact on the ozone layer include the release of chlorofluorocarbons from pressurized cans and other sources,[154] jet aircraft flight† in the stratosphere,[155] and the use of nitrogen fertilizers in agriculture.[156] The Global 2000 Study's projections all suggest that, unless regulatory policies change, these activities and emissions will continue to increase.

The effect of effluents (hydrocarbons and oxides of nitrogen) from jet flights in the stratosphere has been studied in reports by the U.S. Department of Transportation and the National Academy of Sciences.[157] The effect depends greatly on the number of flights and the performance of the jet engines. Concern has centered primarily on supersonic transport (SST), since these aircraft fly higher in the stratosphere than subsonic jets. The Department of Transportation report estimates the size and properties of future SST fleets that would be required to pay off development costs and return a fair profit. On the basis of these estimated fleet sizes, updated for improvements in technology, the National Academy of Sciences estimates that the impact of such a fleet might ultimately be a reduction of ozone by about 6.5 percent, with an uncertainty range of 1–10 percent, whereas current stratospheric flights reduce ozone by less than 0.1 percent.[158]

The effect of chlorofluorocarbon release has been studied by the National Academy of Sciences and others.[159] Using recently updated informa-

---

* While the wastes mix only very slowly vertically, they spread horizontally relatively rapidly, reaching all longitudes of the world in about a week and all latitudes within months. There

is therefore little that any one nation or region can do to protect the ozone layer above it. Like carbon dioxide, the ozone problem is global in scope.
† Based on a 1975 report by the National Academy of Sciences. A very recent opinion by the Academy's Committee on Impacts of Stratospheric Change—as yet unpublished—suggests that jet aircraft may not be as much of a problem as suggested in previously published reports and may actually increase ozone (personal communication, Apr. 3, 1979, from J. Murray Mitchell, Jr., senior research climatologist, National Oceanic and Atmospheric Administration). Opinions, however, are still in a state of flux (see, for example, Anthony J. Broderick, "Stratospheric Effects from Aviation," *Proceedings*, 13th Propulsion Congress, Orlando, Fla., July 1977, and his "Stratospheric Effects from Aviation," *Journal of Aircraft*, Oct. 1978, pp. 643–55). The discussion presented here is based on National Academy of Sciences published reports.

tion,[160] the Academy reports that continued use of chlorofluorocarbons at the 1974 rate would reduce the global ozone by 14 percent over the next 50 years, with a 4–40 percent range of uncertainty. If the rate of production were to increase in proportion to the Global 2000 Study's GNP projections, the impact would be much larger.

The Academy has also studied the impact of anthropogenic nitrogen fixation on stratospheric ozone.[161] The linkage between fertilizer and ozone comes through the release of nitrous oxide (N_2O) during the denitrification of fixed nitrogen. The processes involved are much more complex than for either SST emissions or chlorofluorocarbon emissions, and yet they have been studied far less.[162] Assuming a 2–3 times increase in manufactured and legume-produced nitrogen fertilizer,* the Academy estimates that the global ozone would be reduced by 3.5 percent, with a range of uncertainty of 0.4–13 percent.[163]

It now appears, therefore, that definite and adverse effects on the ozone layer do exist in varying magnitudes as a result of (1) aircraft exhaust in the stratosphere, (2) chlorofluorocarbon and other halocarbon emissions, and (3) nitrogen fertilizer use. The Global 2000 Study's projections suggest that all three activities can be expected to increase by the year 2000. At present, there is tremendous uncertainty associated with the relative magnitude of the impacts of these three human activities, but all three now appear to be within an order of magnitude of each other,[164] with chlorofluorocarbons apparently having the greatest impact. While scientific assessment is still in flux and might shift significantly, the most recent work on the subject continues to support these general conclusions.[165]

How serious are depletions of global ozone? The consequences are related both to climate modification and to the amount of ultraviolet radiation reaching living organisms on the earth. The temperature inversion in the stratosphere is caused by the solar energy absorbed by ozone. A change in the ozone would lead to a significant change in the temperature distribution of the stratosphere, and probably to a small (but as yet uncertain) change in the pattern of temperature and rainfall over the earth's surface as well. These climatic changes are currently thought likely to be small compared to the potential changes that could occur as a result of carbon dioxide accu-

mulations in the atmosphere.[166] The effects of increased amounts of ultraviolet (UV) radiation may be more serious.

Ozone-induced changes in UV radiation would change one of the conditions that has almost certainly influenced the evolution of life on earth so far, and a significant UV increase can be expected to precipitate a disturbance in the existing balance of life virtually everywhere on the planet.[167] The National Academy of Sciences reports:

All unshielded cells are highly vulnerable to sunlight and may be killed by relatively short exposure to full sunlight. While such cells and organisms are generally protected to varying degrees in nature so that they experience sublethal doses of radiation, any increase in UV radiation could be considered to increase the pressure against survival. Because of the relationships between species in ecosystems, damage to one species might jeopardize an entire ecosystem. Hence, the potential effects of any elevation of the present UV–B levels of sunlight reaching the earth's surface should be taken most seriously.[168]

Cancer is the best-established direct threat to the human species. There is compelling evidence that UV radiation is a cause of skin cancer.[169] A 10 percent decrease in stratospheric ozone appears likely to lead to a 20–30 percent increase in this type of cancer,[170] but the increase may vary significantly from area to area (e.g., in the Andean or Tibetan highlands it could be higher than the world average).

The indirect threat of UV radiation to human welfare may be even larger than its direct effect.[171] It is known that, for small changes, UV radiation reaching the ground increases about 2 percent for each 1 percent decrease in stratospheric ozone.[172] It is also known that increased exposure to UV radiation adversely affects plants. Plants that have been exposed to supplemental UV in growth chambers or greenhouses have shown a 20–50 percent inhibition of growth, a 10–30 percent decline in chlorophyll content (and a similar decline in capacity for photosynthesis), and up to a 20-fold increase in the frequency of harmful mutations.[173] Seedlings are even more sensitive to UV radiation than mature plants, and single-celled algae are extremely sensitive. Algae can withstand only a few hours' exposure to even natural sunlight, and enhanced UV is expected to cut the survivable exposure time by as much as a factor of 2.[174] Enhanced UV radiation also appears to be extremely lethal to fish and crustacean larvae, and has been shown to produce burns and induce tumors on those organisms surviving exposure.[175] At the present time, the accumulating research

---

* The Global 2000 Study's agricultural projections are based on a doubling of fertilizer application worldwide and a quadrupling in the LDCs. Over and above these increases, large amounts of fertilizer may be applied in the intensive silvicultural methods projected to occur in forestry.

data seem to indicate that ecosystems may be significantly disrupted by increased levels of ultraviolet radiation.

There are a number of steps that can be taken to limit the reduction of the earth's ozone layer. The emissions of chlorofluorocarbons can be limited by legislation. The U.S. has enacted such legislation[176] and hopes to persuade all industrialized nations to establish similar limitations. Supersonic flying can also be regulated if further research indicates the need.* But the world cannot easily dispense with nitrogen fertilizers even if future research should indicate that they contribute more to ozone depletion than recent findings suggest. The National Academy of Sciences has published an economic analysis† of the costs and benefits of chemical fertilizers and reports that the present discounted value of damages is small because of the distant nature of the projected impacts.[177] On the basis of this analysis, the Academy states that "in our opinion, the current value to society of those activities that contribute to global nitrogen fixation far exceed the potential cost of any moderate (e.g., up to a decade) postponement of action to reduce the threat of future ozone depletion by N_2O [from nitrogen fertilizer use]."[178]

Albedo and Heat

The Global 2000 Study's forestry, energy, minerals, agriculture, and GNP projections all point to significant changes in land use§ and significant releases of waste heat. These changes will certainly influence local climates, and may even affect regional or global climate.

Perhaps the most significant land-use change anticipated is the 16–20 percent reduction in the world's forests over the next two decades, as pro-

jected in Chapter 8. This reduction of 420 million hectares involves roughly 3 percent of the earth's continental land surface and about 1 percent of the earth's total area.

The most direct linkage between change of land use and climate is through change of surface albedo.* Evergreen forests have an albedo of 7–15 percent. Dry, plowed fields have an albedo of 10–15 percent; deserts, 25–30 percent; fresh snow, 85–90 percent; and asphalt, 8 percent.[179]

The global changes in land use over the next two decades are by themselves probably not so extensive as to cause a significant change in global climate, but they are certainly sufficient to cause local changes in many areas. In some cases beneficial changes will occur as, for example, when restored park and forest lands improve local climate, but adverse change—including desert conditions—can also be anticipated.[180]

Urbanization is another land-use trend known to affect local weather and climate. Typical changes resulting from urbanization are shown in Table 13–14.

The energy projections in Chapter 10 anticipate an almost 50 percent increase in energy demand by 1990. All human energy use ultimately ends up as residual heat and much of it—especially in thermal generation of electricity—is converted to heat immediately on use.† Already, residual heat releases are comparable or larger than the solar input in some reasonably large local areas.[181] The anthropogenic energy releases over the 60 square kilometers of Manhattan are almost 4 times the solar energy falling on the area; even over sprawling Los Angeles (3,500 square kilometers) the anthropogenic heat released now totals 13 percent of the solar flux.[182]

Although it has long been known that releases of residual heat influence local climates, it has generally been thought that thermal pollution would probably not affect global climate because anthropogenic heat is now, and is expected to remain, a small percentage of the solar influence on global weather.[183] As shown in Table 13–15, fossil fuel combustion increased by a factor of 8

---

* During the 1976 U.N. Environment Programme's Governing Council Meeting, the U.S. sponsored a resolution calling for an international meeting on the regulation of supersonic flying. The meeting, held in Washington in March 1977, prepared a world plan of action on the ozone layer, which is reported in *Ozone-Layer Bulletin* (U.N. Environment Programme, Nairobi), no. 1, Jan. 1978.
† The Academy's report notes that this economic analysis has limitations and is not a broad-scale assessment of the full costs and benefits of current or projected patterns of global food production and energy use. The analysis addresses a 3.5 percent decrease in stratospheric ozone, using discount rates ranging from 3 to 8 percent. Changes in temperature and in ultraviolet radiation are considered. Increased UV radiation is assumed to have negligible effects on plants.
§ Surface changes are thought to affect climate through (1) changes in albedo, (2) changes in surface "roughness" (by affecting drag on winds), (3) changes in water storage capacity (affecting wetness), and (4) changes in heat storage capacity. Only albedo effects are discussed here.

---

* Albedo (as defined in the National Science Board/National Science Foundation *Patterns and Perspectives in Environmental Science,* 1972, p. 66) is the percentage of the amount of the incident solar radiation reflected by a land or water surface. For example, if the sun radiates 100 units of energy per minute to the outer limits of the atmosphere, and the earth's surface receives 80 units per minute (the atmosphere absorbs 20 units) and then reflects 40 units upward, the albedo is 50 percent.
† Roughly two-thirds of the primary energy needed in the thermal generation of electricity (primarily by coal and nuclear plants) is lost immediately as waste heat.

TABLE 13–14

Typical Climate Changes Caused by Urbanization

Type of Change	Comparison with Rural Environs
Temperature	
Annual mean	0.5–1.0° C higher
Winter minima	1.0–3.0° C higher
Relative Humidity	
Annual mean	6% lower
Winter	2% lower
Summer	8% lower
Dust Particles	10 times more
Cloudiness	
Cloud cover	5–10% more
Fog, winter	100% more frequent
Fog, summer	30% more frequent
Radiation	
Total on horizontal surface	15–20% less
Ultraviolet, winter	30% less
Ultraviolet, summer	5% less
Wind Speed	
Annual mean	20–30% lower
Extreme gusts	10–20% lower
Calms	5–20% more
Precipitation[a]	
Amounts	5–10% more
Days with 0.2 inch	10% more

Source: After H. E. Landsberg, in W. H. Matthews et al., eds., *Man's Impact on the Climate*, Cambridge, Mass.: MIT Press, 1971, p. 168.

[a] Precipitation effects are relatively uncertain.

TABLE 13–15

Selected Annual Energy Supply Rates for the Earth[a]

(Billions of watts)

¼ Solar constant (extra-atmospheric irradiance)	178,000,000
Insolation absorbed at ground level	90,000,000
Dissipated by friction in atmospheric circulations	1,500,000
Photosynthesis (production by living vegetation)	40,000
Geothermal heat (by conduction in crust)	32,000
1970 Rate of fossil fuel burning	8,000
Infrared radiation from full moon	5,000
Dissipated by friction in ocean currents and tides	3,000
Solar radiation received via reflection from full moon	2,000
Dissipated by friction in solar tides of the atmosphere	1,000
1910 Rate of fossil fuel burning	1,000
Human body heat	600
Released by volcanoes and hot springs (geoconvection)	300
1960 Rate of hydroelectric power production	240
Dissipated as heat in lightening discharges	100
Radiation from bright aurora	25
Received from space by cosmic radiation	15
Dissipated mechanical energy of meteorites	10
Total radiation from all stars	8
Dissipated by friction in lunar tides of the atmosphere	5
Solar radiation received as zodiacal light	2

Source: After Office of Research and Development, U.S. Environmental Protection Agency, *Changes in Global Energy Balance*, Washington, Oct. 1974.

[a] These whole globe averages represent annual gigawatts (10^9W) of power totaled over the earth's surface.

between 1910 and 1970, but solar energy is still far and away the most important energy source in human affairs. However, it has been noted that although anthropogenic heat inputs will be localized, they may be strong enough to alter local or regional components of the world climate system.[184] In turn, changes triggered in individual components of the system may have effects throughout the world. Examples of local effects are given in Table 13–16.

The energy research group at the International Institute of Applied Systems Analysis (IIASA)* near Vienna has studied this problem with the general circulation model of the United Kingdom Meteorological Office.[185] The IIASA group found that large heat releases (such as one might expect from "power parks") could trigger changes in re-

gional elements of the global system, and that these in turn produced global effects in the model runs. The kinds of global changes produced depended on where the heat source was located. The IIASA group concluded that the results of these model experiments indicate a possible global atmospheric response to large heat discharges, which must be borne in mind for planning purposes and also investigated further.[186]

Conclusions

Both the National Defense University survey of expert opinion and the analysis of the possible climatic implications of the Global 2000 Study's other projections lead to the same general conclusions: (1) Climate will continue to vary in the future, just as it always has in the past, in a largely unpredictable manner. (2) Apart from this characteristic variability, no substantial net trend of

---

* An international effort to accomplish East-West cooperation through joint work with the use of systems analysis tools. The Institute is well supported by both the U.S and the U.S.S.R.; Canada, Czechoslovakia, France, and German Democratic Republic, Japan, the Federal Republic of Germany, Bulgaria, Italy, Poland, the United Kingdom, Austria, Hungary, Sweden, Finland, and the Netherlands also participate.

TABLE 13–16

Effects of Large Heat Additions to the Atmosphere

Phenomenon	Energy Rate (Mw)	Area (km²)	Energy-Flux-Density (W/m²)
‘Large brush fire[a]	100,000	50	200

Consequences: (Relatively small energy-flux rate, very large area.) Cumulus cloud reaching to a height of 6 km formed over 0.1 area of fire. Convergence of winds into the fire area.

Forest fire whirlwind[b]

Consequences: Typical whirlwind: Central tube visible by whirling smoke and debris. Diameters few feet to several hundred feet. Heights few feet to 4,000 ft Debris picked up—logs up to 30 in. in diameter and 30 ft long.

| World War II fire storm[c] | | 12 | |

Consequences: Turbulent column of heated air 2.5 mi in diameter. Fed at base by inrush of surface air; 1.5 mi from fire, wind speeds increased from 11 to 33 mph. Trees 3 ft in diameter were uprooted.

Fire at Hiroshima[d]

Consequences: (10–12 hr after atomic bomb.) "The wind grew stronger, and suddenly—probably because of the tremendous convection set up by the blazing city—a whirlwind ripped through the park. Huge trees crashed down; small ones were uprooted and flew into the air. Higher, a wild array of flat things revolved in the twisting funnel." The vortex moved out onto the river, where it sucked up a waterspout and eventually spent itself.

| Surtsey volcano[e] | 100,000 | < 1 | 100,000 |

Consequences: Permanent cloud extending to heights of 5–9 km. Continuous sharp thunder and lightning, visible 115 km away. (Phenomenon probably peculiar to volcano cloud with many small ash particles.) Waterspouts resulting from indraft at cloud base, caused by rising buoyant cloud.

| Surtsey volcano[f] | 200,000 | 1 | 200,000 |

Consequences: Whirlwinds (waterspouts and tornadoes) are the rule rather than the exception. More often than not there is at least one vortex downwind. Short inverted cones or long, sinuous horizontal vortices that curve back up into the cloud, and intense vortices that extend to the ocean surface.

| French Meteotron[g] | 700 | 0.0032 | 219,000 |

Consequences: ". . . artificial thunderstorms, even tornadoes, many cumulus clouds . . . substantial downpour." Dust devils.

| Meteotron[h] | 350 | 0.016 | 22,400 |

Consequences: 15 min after starting the burners, observers saw a whirl 40 m in diameter . . . whirlwind so strong burner flames were inclined to 45°.

| Single large cooling tower | 2,250 | 0.0046 | 484,000 |

Consequences: Plume of varying lengths and configurations.

| Array of large cooling towers [48,000 Mw(e) NEC; area 48,000 acres] | 96,000 | 194 | 495 |

Consequences: Unknown.

Source: Ralph M. Rotty, "Energy and the Climate," Institute for Energy Analysis, Oak Ridge Associated Universities, Sept. 1976, pp. 15–16.
[a] From R. J. Taylor et al., "Convective Activity Above a Large-Scale Brush Fire," *Journal of Applied Meteorology,* vol. 12, 1973, p. 1144.
[b] From H. E. Graham, "Fire Whirlwinds," *Bulletin of American Meteorological Society,* vol. 36, no. 3, 1955, p. 99.
[c] From H. Landsberg, "Fire Storms Resulting from Bombing Conflagrations," *Bulletin of American Meteorological Society,* vol. 28, no. 2, 1947, p. 72.
[d] From J. R. Hersey, *Hiroshima,* New York: Bantam, 1946, pp. 50–51.
[e] From A. G. Borne, "Birth of an Island," *Discovery,* vol. 25, no. 4, 1964, p. 16.
[f] From S. Thorarinsson and B. Vonnegut, "Whirlwinds Produced by the Eruption of Surtsey Volcano," *Bulletin of American Meteorological Society,* vol. 45, no. 8, 1964, p. 440.
[g] From J. Dessens, "Man-made Thunderstorms," *Discovery,* vol. 25, no. 3, 1964, p. 40.
[h] From J. Dessens, "Man-made Tornadoes," *Nature,* vol. 193, no. 4810, 1962, p. 13.

climate in the direction of either warming or cooling is anticipated between now and 2000.

These conclusions, however, are not the end of the climate story. Human societies around the world have become (and are becoming increas-ingly) dependent on favorable climate. Less favorable climates are known to have occurred in the past, and the less favorable climate of the 1971–73 period demonstrated just how vulnerable world societies have become to weather and climate change. The Global 2000 Study's projections (all based on the assumption of no significant climatic change) point to a world in 2000 that is even more vulnerable to weather and climate change than the world of today. Furthermore, scientists now know that several human activities have reached a scale that, over periods of several to many decades, has the potential to alter the world's climate significantly. These anthropogenic influences on global climate include carbon dioxide emissions and release of chemicals affecting the ozone layer as well as potential land-use changes, aerosol and particulate generation, and heat releases.

The import of anthropogenic influences on climate lies not in any imminent threat of massive climatic change, but rather in the inadequacy of present knowledge and the inability of institutions to make society respond effectively if evidence of serious consequences develops. Probably the most serious anthropogenic threats to the stability of climate are CO_2 emissions and releases of chemicals that deplete stratospheric ozone. In both cases it is impossible for an individual nation to protect itself against the consequences of other nations' actions. These problems are truly global in scope, and there is no human institution now established that can adequately address them.

In commenting on its carbon dioxide findings, the National Academy of Sciences concluded: "If the preliminary estimates of climate change in the latter part of the twenty-second century are validated, a reassessment of global energy policy must be started promptly because, long before that destined date, there will have been major climatic impacts all over the world."[187] Other studies now underscore the Academy's concern, and point to significant changes in CO_2 concentrations by 2000 or shortly thereafter:[188]

The key word in the Academy's admonition is "promptly." Unfortunately, given the limitations cited above, it is difficult to imagine how a reassessment of *global* energy policy could be undertaken promptly. Considering the uncertainties in the magnitude of CO_2 sources and sinks and the limited research that has been done in these areas, it could easily be more than a decade before a definitive conclusion is reached just on how to project CO_2 concentrations accurately. Even given definitive projections, several decades of intensive research will be required to reach agreement on the climatological implications of increasing CO_2 concentrations. Lacking a world institution with an energy mission, how long would a global reassessment of a world energy policy require? And given a change in policy, how long would be

needed to implement any basic change in the world's energy capital, infrastructure, and economy? By the time the world is prepared to address seriously the climatological implications of world energy policy, commitments (e.g., to intensified use of coal and to deforestation) may have become so well established that a basic change in the global energy economy might be as economically catastrophic as the climatic change itself. Thus, to delay a careful and prompt international assessment of the carbon dioxide problem could lead to capital commitments and forest policies that make irreversible accumulations of CO_2 in the atmosphere essentially unavoidable. Similar difficulties could develop in connection with the stratospheric ozone layer as the world's growing population becomes increasingly dependent on biologically and synthetically produced nitrogen fertilizers.

In the decades ahead, the finite capacity of the atmosphere to absorb various anthropogenic chemical emissions without catastrophic climate change must be recognized as an extremely important resource, a resource vital to and held in common by all nations. Protecting this resource will raise perplexing and troublesome questions: Which nations should be allowed to burn how much coal or to replace how much forest with food crops? How are global CO_2 discharges to be monitored and controlled?

The capacity of the atmosphere to absorb CO_2 may be a resource that is even more limited than either forests or fossil fuels, and questions concerning the allocation of "CO_2 disposal rights" could conceivably overshadow all other energy issues.[189] Similarly, if protecting the ozone layer requires limitations on the emissions from spray cans, air conditioners, supersonic aircraft, and nitrogen fertilizers, the right to deplete the atmosphere's limited ozone resource can be expected to go first to agriculture.

Even within individual nations, the making of major decisions in these regards can be expected to place a strain on existing institutions and to require long periods of time for debate. On a global scale, there is no adequate institution and no precedent for such decisions or the cooperation they would require.

While no major worldwide climatic changes are expected by 2000, anthropogenic forces affecting the world's climates will be accelerating, and unless these forces and their effects are soon studied, monitored, and analyzed much more carefully, human institutions will be ill prepared to make some of the difficult choices that may be required in the 1980s or at the latest in the 1990s.

THE TECHNOLOGY PROJECTIONS AND THE ENVIRONMENT

The Projections

Each of the agencies making projections for the Global 2000 Study made its own projections (and/or assumptions) of technological developments in its particular area of concern. In general, the technological projections and assumptions are implicitly, rather than explicitly, incorporated in each agency's overall contribution to the Study. As a result it is not always possible to state precisely what technological developments are projected or assumed. Nonetheless, a general pattern is discernible. On the whole, the technological projections and assumptions imply that production- and yield-enhancing technologies will continue to be developed and disseminated as fast as they have been over the past few decades—or faster. Further, the agencies generally assume that new technologies will be deployed as fast as (or faster than) they have in the past, and that the technologies will not produce adverse side effects (of an economic, environmental, social, or resource nature) that would limit their application.

The more specific technological assumptions associated with the projections are as follows:

Population Projections. Birth control (family planning) and health care, technologies will be disseminated and used to a greater extent than in the past two decades. The technological developments of industrialization, as they impinge on natality and mortality, will continue at or above historically observed rates.

Gross National Product Projections. In the industrialized world, technology is assumed to contribute to future economic growth as it has in the recent past. The productivity of new investment capital will increase, in part a result of technological change, at about the historically observed rate of 0.5–1.5 percent per year.

Fisheries Projections. The projections assume that technologies for harvesting and processing nontraditional living marine resources will be adopted increasingly through the year 2000.

Food and Agriculture Projections. The projections assume that yields per hectare will continue to increase at rates comparable to those of the past two decades.

Forestry Projections. Continued progress is assumed in increasing forest yields per hectare, and in decreasing losses incurred during processing or from previously underutilized species and from disease.

Energy Projections. Due to technological developments, the real costs of production, refining, and marketing of energy products will remain essentially constant. Large increases in the adoption of existing technologies are assumed to be possible. It is assumed that, collectively, nuclear and hydroelectrical generation (which are lumped together in the Department of Energy projections) will approximately triple between 1975 and 1990. The technologies for fossil fuel production and use are assumed to respond to variations in relative costs, resulting in shifts from oil and natural gas to coal.

Nonfuel Minerals Projections. Technological advances in production technology necessary for continued growth in production will be made. As high-grade ores are depleted, technological developments will hold the real cost of minerals and materials constant. Mineral use per dollar of GNP will tend to decrease as economies enlarge and mature.

None of the projections assumes specific major technological breakthroughs, (such as harnessing of the fusion process for energy production), and none assumes failures of existing technologies (such as the evolution of antibiotic-resistant diseases, or the termination of nuclear power development due to inadequate reactor safety or waste disposal methods).

For three reasons, no attempt will be made to analyze the environmental implications of the technological projections and assumptions made by the contributing agencies. First, the technological projections and assumptions are, for the most part, too inexplicit to permit an adequate assessment of their environmental implications. Second, technology is knowledge—especially scientific knowledge—applied to practical or productive ends, and since the principal environmental implications of a particular technology occur in the economic sector in which it is applied, its environmental implications are analyzed individually in the other sections of this chapter. Third, the interesting and important environmental questions about technologies emerge not from an analysis of a particular technology but from an analysis of alternative technological options. The last point deserves elaboration.

Both developed and less developed nations have had considerable experience with the unforeseen social and environmental impacts of technology and development. Neither Henry Ford nor the purchasers of his Model Ts foresaw that automobile exhaust would become an environmental health problem. Similarly, university agricultural facilities involved in the development of modern agricultural equipment failed to anticipate adverse social impacts—such as unemployment among farmworkers and urban migration—and were taken by surprise recently when 19 farmworkers and a California Rural Legal Assistance group sued the University of California over the development of sophisticated harvesting machines, which the farmworkers alleged were a threat to their livelihood. The suit contends that harvesting machines in the California tomato industry alone have displaced 32,000 workers and that thousands more have been displaced by university-developed machinery in vegetable fields and fruit orchards.[190] One certainly cannot infer from this development that all harvesting machinery is bad, but the farmworkers' suit does illustrate the extent to which questions are being raised about the impact of technology—questions that in even the relatively recent past might have been thought external to decisions concerning technological priorities.

New institutions are developing in response to the growing awareness of the social and environmental impacts that follow in the wake of new technologies. In the United States, the Office of Technology Assessment was instituted to assist Congress in assessing the social, economic, and environmental consequences of new and emerging technologies. Internationally, the United Nations Conference on Science and Technology for Development (UNCSTD) was designed to consider both technological choice and the transfer of technologies among nations.

The international transfer of technologies has important environmental implications. In fact, some of the most serious environmental problems have come from the direct transfer of technologies from temperate-zone industrial societies to tropical environments in less developed societies.[191] Many of these environmental problems are due to lack of understanding of how tropical- and arid-zone ecosystems differ from temperate-zone systems. For example, many tropical river basin development projects have stabilized irrigation systems to provide increased agricultural production, only to discover such stabilized-irrigation agriculture provided ideal environments for the spread (via snail vectors) of such serious water-borne diseases as schistosomiasis.[192]

Economist E. F. Schumacher and his colleagues of the Intermediate Technology Group in London have pioneered efforts over the past two decades to develop "appropriate" technologies, i.e., technologies that are ecologically gentle and adaptable to the economic, resource, and social structures of a particular society. Schumacher presented his thoughts on technology in *Small is Beautiful: Economics as if People Mattered*. In this well-known book, Schumacher goes beyond environmental compatability to identify four basic propositions for choosing technologies for developing societies:

- First, that workplaces have to be created in the areas where the people are living now, and not primarily in metropolitan areas into which they tend to migrate.
- Second, that these workplaces must be, on average, cheap enough so that they can be created in large numbers without this calling for an unattainable level of capital formation and imports.
- Third, that the production methods employed must be relatively simple, so that the demands

for high skills are minimized, not only in the production process itself but also in matters of organization, raw material supply, financing, marketing, and so forth.

- Fourth, that production should be mainly from local materials and mainly for local use.[193]

The industrialized nations face corresponding choices in defining and developing appropriate "postindustrial" technology. The environmental problems that are passed on to the next generation will be greatly influenced by whether industrialized countries—as well as less developed countries—encourage technologies that conserve energy and other natural resources, increase employment, and minimize pollution and other impacts on the environment, or whether these countries continue to develop technological innovation primarily for increasing per capita consumption of goods and services.[194]

Conclusions

Many of the environmental impacts discussed in other sections of this chapter are the consequences of past technological choices. The health of the environment during the 21st century will be shaped significantly in both developing and industrialized countries by the choices of technologies made over the next two decades. Fortunately, a wide range of technologies are available that appear to be environmentally, socially, and economically sound, but it is by no means clear that these technologies will be chosen.[195] How political and social controls affect the choice and diffusion of technologies in the early stages of their development will have monumental implications for the environmental conditions passed on to the next generation. Indeed, the choice of technologies may be the area in which society will have the greatest latitude and leverage in shaping the future of the global environment.

THE FOOD AND AGRICULTURE PROJECTIONS AND THE ENVIRONMENT

The Projections

The food and agriculture projections developed by the U.S. Department of Agriculture* foresee a 90–100 percent increase in total world production over the 1970–2000 period. This increase, however, is the equivalent of only a 10–15 percent increase in per capita production. The real price of food is projected to increase from 30 to 115 percent over 1969–71 prices.

The projections increases are based in part on a projected 4 percent increase in arable area. Although this expansion of arable area involves a substantial increase in the world's harvested area over the record high levels reported for the first half of the 1970s, the rate of increase in arable area is significantly slower than in the postwar period. The slowed expansion is due in large part to the growing capital costs of adding increasingly remote and marginal lands to the production base. The slowed rate of increase leads to an increased number of people supported per hectare. Globally during the first half of the 1970s, 2.6 persons were supported per arable hectare; by 2000 the figure is projected to rise to 4.0. In the LDCs the ratio is projected to rise from 2.9 in the early 1970s to 5.3 in 2000, excluding China.

---

* Half of the Study's food projections reported in Chapter 6 assume that energy prices remain constant in real terms (at 1974–76 prices) to the year 2000. The figures presented under Alternative II (see Chapter 6) assume that energy prices remain constant. The double set of figures presented under Alternative I reflect possibilities ranging from constant to increasing energy prices. (The first of the two Alternative I entries is for constant energy prices; the second entry is for rising energy prices.) Alternative III explicitly presents results based on real energy prices rising as projected in the Study's energy projections in Chapter 10. Alternative III also assumes high population growth rates, lower income growth rates, and weather less favorable than that of the past 25 years. The food projections under this alternative show the real price of food increasing by 115 percent over the 1970–2000 period. For

LDCs overall, average per capita daily calorie consumption remains constant at the 2,165 calorie per capita levels of 1969–71. Per capita calorie consumption declines for the North Africa/Middle East region, other African LDCs, and South Asian areas and increases for Latin America and the Southeast Asia and East Asia areas. The percentages of decline in per capita consumption (relative to 1969–71 levels) are as follows: 1 percent for the North Africa/Middle East area, 16 percent for the other African LDCs, 3 percent for the South Asian area. Fertilizer consumption and increase in arable area are not projected for the specific case of rising energy prices. World grain trade increases 200 percent, from 79.6 million metric tons in 1969–71 to 238 million in 2000. Grain imports increase as follows: 190 percent for developed importers, 650 for centrally planned country importers and 220 for LDC importers.

The remainder of the increase in production comes from a projected 70–100 percent increase in productivity, (i.e., substantially higher crop yields per hectare). Implicit in the projected productivity growth is a more than doubling of fertilizer* use per hectare for the world as a whole and a quadrupling of fertilizer use per hectare for LDCs. The food projections also note a continued diminishing of marginal return to increases in fertilizer use. In simplified terms, a 1-kilogram increase in fertilizer use at the world level appears to have generated about an 8-kilogram increase in grain production in the early 1970s; a 1-kilogram increase in fertilizer use in 2000 is projected to generate less than a 6-kilogram increase in production. Water, which is already a limiting factor in agricultural production in large parts of the world, will become even more of a limiting factor by 2000. As noted in the food and agriculture projections (Chapter 6), the projected increases in food production imply large public-sector investments in irrigation, agricultural extension, and land reclamation.

The projected increases in demand will be generated by the projected increases in population and, to a lesser extent, by increases in per capita income. Increases in both production and demand are likely to be unevenly distributed and are therefore expected to generate both a marked increase in international trade and a widening of the differences between per capita consumption in the different regions of the world. Net declines in caloric consumption per capita are projected for most areas of developing Africa south of the Sahara; negligible gains in caloric consumption are expected for South Asia and parts of the rest of the developing world.

As noted in Chapter 4 ("Climate"), the Study's food projections implicitly assume that no significant change in the climate will occur relative to that experienced over the last several decades. However, the projections do explicitly consider variations in weather by providing for fluctuations in yields similar to weather-related variations experienced during the 1950–77 period. The projections take into account ecological stresses, such as deterioration in soil fertility, and hydrologic irregularity induced by deforestation, but only to the extent that these problems have occurred in the past and—given past experiences—are likely to occur in the future. Ecological stresses are linked to the projections by assuming that steps will be taken to alleviate the impact of these stresses on production. The costs of taking the preventive steps are expensive and contribute significantly to the increased real cost of producing and consuming food. The required capital is assumed to be available.

Introduction

The food projections present a complex picture of interacting factors that will affect the environment. The growing populations and incomes projected increase the demand for food at a time when increasing the stock of arable land will have become more difficult and expensive. A reduced rate of expansion of arable land will place further importance on increasing yields, but yield-enhancing techniques are themselves showing signs

* In the Department of Agriculture's projections for this Study, the term "fertilizer" is used as a proxy for a group of productivity-expanding inputs, including pesticides, herbicides, and high-yield grain varieties, as well as chemical fertilizers in the usual meaning of the term. The projections are not detailed enough to specify any change in the relative proportions of these various inputs.

of limitations. Further, the *nonrenewable* resources on which agriculture is based—fossil fuels, genetic strains, and soils—are being diminished rapidly in some areas. All of these developments will have environmental implications, some of which will directly influence the prospects for future food production.

This point has already been forcefully made by the Council on Environmental Quality. The Council's 1977 report "The Food-People Problem" discusses the situation in the following terms:

In the race to provide food for the expanding world population, improper farming practices—including overly intensive cultivation, too heavy a reliance on marginally productive semi-arid lands, and inadequate conservation measures—

are increasing the erosion and depleting the nutrients of topsoils. The result . . . is reduced fertility of the land, lowering its capacity for food production.

In many parts of the world, hillsides are being deforested to make way for more farms and to provide fuel for cooking food. The rains no longer soak into the ground but run off in the form of uncontrollable torrents which tear away the soil under cultivation, flood the low lying cropland, and clog reservoirs and irrigation canals with silt. Left behind are barren slopes that later become abandoned.

Environmental degradation has been barely noticeable amid increased farm production resulting from the technological improvements of the "Green Revolution," made particularly effective by fertilizers and pesticides. However, rapidly growing population and growing affluence continue to increase the demand for food, while at the same time losses in soil fertility which reduce land's capacity to produce are occurring across the world.

According to a U.S. survey of 69 countries with 1.8 billion people:

• Overgrazing and overcropping, which result in heavy loss of soil by erosion, are serious problems in 43 countries with 1.4 billion people.
• Serious irrigation problems were recorded in eight arid countries attempting to increase food production.
• Heavy loss of forests has occurred in at least 24 developing countries. Principal reason for converting forest to cropland and grazing fields is to meet the demand for food.
• Water problems resulting from deforestation have appeared in 16 countries in the form of critical water shortages, and in 10 countries in the form of increased flooding. Some countries shared both drought and flooding. [196]

The implications of the Global 2000 Study's food projections for the environment are discussed in the following five sections. First, the food projections are analyzed in terms of their implications for human nutrition—an important aspect of environmental quality—and in terms of the kinds of pressures that agricultural activities will exert on other parts of the environment. Other subjects of environmental concern include soil deterioration, the ecological effects of fertilizers and pesticides, crop vulnerability (the genetic instability induced by simplification of ecosystems and reduction of genetic resources), and the implications of the food projections for nonrenewable fossil fuels.*

---

*In addition to the discussions that follow, several direct estimates and broad directional indicators of environmental change are presented in the food and agriculture projections themselves (Chapter 6).

Food and the Human Environment

Food is an essential element in environmental quality for the human population. Without an adequate diet, vulnerability to disease is increased, capacity to perform physical work is limited, and (in children) mental and physical development is impaired. Nutritional requirements vary with age, sex, occupation, height, and weight. As a rough guide to human nutritional needs, the U.N. Food and Agriculture Organization (FAO) [197] has estimated minimum caloric requirements for various regions.* The degree to which the FAO standards are met provides an important indication of the nutritional dimension of human environment and, indirectly, an indication of the pressures on local agriculture.

Table 13–17 compares recent and projected per capita calorie consumption with the FAO minimum standards for various regions of the world. As noted in Chapter 6, real-price increases will be needed to pay for more costly land development and yield-enhancing technologies implicit in the projected figures. Some regions will be better able than others to pay the increasing real prices, and consequently the prospects reflected in the table vary widely from region to region. The prospects are good in the industrialized countries and the centrally planned economies. In the affluent developed countries, diets can be expected to become more diversified while calorie consumption rises to perhaps 135 percent of FAO standards. The increased consumption in these regions brings to mind the problem of malnutrition due to overconsumption (i.e., overeating) cited in several recent studies. [198]

The consumption statistics for the industrialized countries and centrally planned economies do not fully indicate the magnitude of the pressures for increased agricultural production in these regions. Many are critically dependent on imports. In one case, the food projections in Chapter 6 show a food-importing centrally planned economy increasing its grain purchases by 650 percent by the year 2000. Pressure will also be high in those exporting countries experiencing balance of payment problems. Agricultural sales provide a significant amount of foreign exchange for some countries. In 1975–77 in the U.S., for example,

---

* Of course, adequate nutrition also requires protein and other nutrients, many of which will also be increasing in price. The discussion here is limited to caloric requirements. See Joint FAO/WHO ad hoc Expert Committee, "Energy and Protein Requirements," Rome: Food and Agriculture Organization, 1973; and World Food Study and Nutrition, vol. 1, Washington: National Academy of Sciences, 1975.

TABLE 13–17

Daily per Capita Calorie Consumption, Historic and Projected, by Region, with Percent of FAO Minimum Standards

	Historic		Projected for 2000	
	1969–71	1973–74	Alternative II[a]	Alternative III[b]
	Figures in parentheses are percents of FAO minimum standards[c]			
Industrialized countries	3,180 (122)	3,340 (128)	3,500 (135)	3,400 (130)
Centrally planned economies	2,600 (107)	2,665 (110)	2,940 (121)	2,860 (118)
Less developed countries .	2,165 (94)	2,135 (93)	2,390 (104)	2,165 (94)
Latin America	2,525 (106)	2,540 (107)	3,080 (130)	2,710 (114)
North Africa/Middle East	2,421 (104)	2,482 (107)	2,655 (114)	2,390 (103)
Other African LDCs	2,139 (92)	2,071 (90)	1,920 (83)	1,800 (77)
South Asia	2,036 (92)	1,954 (88)	2,230 (101)	1,985 (105)
Southeast Asia	2,174 (98)	2,270 (103)	2,425 (110)	2,310 (105)
East Asia	2,140 (97)	2,205 (100)	2,520 (114)	2,320 (105)

Source: Data for industrialized countries and centrally planned economies are from Table 6–8, Chapter 6, this study; data for LDCs are from Table 6–9. Conversion from the food indexes was performed by the Department of Agriculture.

Note: Caloric requirements and per capita caloric consumption figures are calculated from measures of total food supply (adjusted for nonfood use, and processing losses and waste) divided by midyear population. Intake below 80–90 percent or above 120–130 percent of the FAO minimum requirement is unlikely, given basic body metabolism. Therefore projected per capita caloric levels outside a range of 80–130 percent of caloric minimums reflect an unusually small or large

waste or processing margin rather than a sustained daily per capita intake in the 1,700–1,800 calorie range or in the 3,300–3,400 calorie range.
[a] Real price of energy remains constant, with low population growth, high income growth, and less favorable weather.
[b] Real price of energy increases as projected in Chapter 10, with high population growth, low income growth, and less favorable weather.
[c] FAO's minimum, country-specific caloric requirements imply regional requirements of 2,375 calories per capita per day for Latin America, 2,325 for developing Africa, 2,210 for developing Asia (2,300 for the LDCs as an aggregate), 2,600 for the industrialized countries, and 2,420 for the centrally planned economies.

grain sales provided over 10 percent of all U.S. foreign sales.[199]

Prospects in the LDCs are mixed. Diet improvements for the poorest two-thirds of the world's population are likely to be small or not forthcoming at all. As shown in Table 13–17, diets are projected to improve in Latin America and in Southeast and East Asia. Diets also improve in South Asia under the optimistic assumptions (including constant energy prices) of Alternative II. But under the assumptions of increasing energy prices, high population growth, low income growth, and less favorable weather (Alternative III), average per capita calorie consumption declines in South Asia and in the LDCs south of the Sahara.*

The full implications of these calorie consumption levels depend on an additional measure—the statistical distribution of diets above and below calorie consumption averages. Studies by the U.S. Department of Agriculture and the World Bank[200] suggest that calorie distribution in the LDCs is sufficiently skewed that national average calorie consumption levels would have to be at least 110–120 percent of the FAO minimum before consumption in lower-income groups could be ex-

pected to approach the recommended minimum.* Keeping this added distribution factor in mind, the projected increase in per capita calorie consumption would probably be adequate to improve Latin American diets (under all three alternatives) and Southeast Asian and East Asian diets (under selected alternatives) to the extent that low-income groups would have access to minimum food supplies. Consumption in the rest of the developing regions—and in the LDCs as a whole—would fail to increase fast enough to meet the minimum needs of the lowest-income groups, which possibly make up one-third to one-half of the total world population. The World Bank, taking these inequities into account, estimates that malnourished persons in the LDCs could increase from the current figure (400–600 million) to as many as 1,300 million by the year 2000.[201]

There has been hunger and malnutrition somewhere in the world for virtually all of recorded history, but as National Academy of Sciences President Philip Handler has observed,

The character of malnutrition has changed markedly in the last 40–50 years. The classical defi-

---

* Alternative I (see Chapter 6) presents a range for the medium case. The first number presented in the Alternative I entries reflects conditions with constant energy prices; the second entry is for rising energy prices. The Nutritional implications of Alternative I are presented in Chapter 6.

---

* Policies leading to a more equitable income distribution could reduce this skewness and result in a far larger improvement in diets than reflected in the regional consumption averages. However, the analysis throughout this Study is limited to one policy option, namely the continuation of present policies.

ciency diseases—beriberi, scurvy, pellagra, rickets, sprue—have almost disappeared. Only xerophthalmia due to Vitamin A deficiency continues as a serious problem, causing blindness in large numbers of children. Instead, there is marasmus, and kwashiorkor—both forms of general protein-calorie insufficiency and iron deficiency anemia. Thus, nutritional status is now rarely the consequence of ignorance; malnutrition now reflects lack of food, not lack of scientific understanding. [202]

In short, nations throughout the world will be pressured to substantially increase agricultural output to respond to growth in demand. Demand will be driven by both population and income growth, but in different proportions in different areas. In the LDCs, approximately a third to a half of the world's population will experience a calorie shortfall. Most food-importing nations will produce as much as possible to alleviate negative trade balances. Exporters, especially the U.S., will encourage grain production to help offset the balance of payment pressure created by continued heavy oil imports. While the demand for food will be high everywhere, the strains on the agricultural sector are likely to be highest in South Asia and in LDCs south of the Sahara. These pressures will affect the environment adversely through soil deterioration, through use of pesticides and abuse of fertilizers, and through the consequences of monocultures of inbred crop varieties.

Deterioration of Soils

The amount of land available for cultivation changes when new lands are brought into production, when existing croplands deteriorate and are abandoned, and when croplands are converted to other uses. The projections suggest that, even with substantially higher food prices, only relatively modest amounts of additional land can be expected to be brought into production by 2000. This prospect accentuates the importance of increasing yields and, in turn, of maintaining and improving soil fertility. Yields can be enhanced with fertilizers but only at an increasing cost and only as long as an adequate soil structure remains. The condition of soils is of central importance now, and its importance is likely to increase in the years ahead. The trend, unfortunately, is one of deteriorating soil conditions.

To what extent does soil deterioration on existing croplands affect the world's agricultural potential? The limited data available can only suggest the outlines of an answer to this question, [203] showing scattered but alarming examples

of soil deterioration.* The primary problems include: (1) loss of topsoil to erosion, (2) loss of organic matter, (3) loss of porous soil structure, (4) build-up of toxic salts and chemicals.

Given the limited data, there are several approaches that might be used in assessing the influence of soil deterioration on agricultural production to the year 2000. First, as has been done in the Global 2000 Study's food projections, one can assume that farmers throughout the world will be aware of the potential problems, will successfully charge more for their produce, and will use the additional income to counteract potential ecological problems. The technologies and management techniques now available are assumed to be brought to bear on ecological problems as they emerge, so as to limit their adverse impact on expanding production. This approach does not assume that adverse effects do not occur but rather that the capital, knowledge, and incentives necessary to employ presently known solutions will be available. Under this assumption, the impacts of ecological problems on agricultural production do not increase markedly beyond the current level. This approach is subject to criticism because it is based on assumed developments—specifically, the adoption of environmentally sensitive technologies and management policies—that may or may not occur.

Another approach is to extrapolate on the basis of the present limited knowledge of world soil deterioration. For example, the 1977 U.N. Conference on Desertification projected that if present trends continue, the world will have lost one-third† of its arable lands due to desertification and

---

* Changes in soil quality cannot be directly and accurately measured over large geographic areas, and too few sample measurements have been made to obtain a detailed statistical picture at the global (or even, with few exceptions, at the national) level. Presently, rates of soil deterioration for large geographic areas can be estimated only on the basis of fragmentary evidence: data from experimental plots, studies of stream-water siltation, archeological and historical studies of once verdant lands now turning to desert, and remote sensing satellite images used to assess vegetative and other characteristics. The limited number of cases where site-specific data are available include examples of disastrous soil deterioration, and evidence of deterioration can be found in scattered observations from around the world. [204] The study of world soil conditions is further complicated in many regions by the use of synthetic fertilizers and high-yielding varieties, which may maintain or even increase production for a time, temporarily masking losses of soil and deteriorating soil structure.

† Erik Eckholm has noted in a private communication an inability to find anyone who will take responsibility for this U.N. projection. Eckholm himself sees the problem as serious, but not quite this serious. He has described his own perceptions of the problem in Erik Eckholm and Lester R. Brown, *Spread-*

other causes by 2000. [205] This approach is open to criticism because of the limited knowledge on which it is based. The approach used in the following paragraphs is simply to catalog and describe the principal elements of what is now known of world land degradations.

The five major agents of soil loss are: (1) desertification (the process of land deterioration associated with desert encroachment, usually caused by overly intense grazing, shortened fallow periods, and consumption of woody plants as fuel); (2) waterlogging, salinization, and alkalinization, which commonly occur when irrigation systems, particularly in arid lands, apply water in ways that are incompatible with soil drainage and other soil and water characteristics; (3) soil degradation that follows deforestation on steep slopes and in many humid tropical areas; (4) general erosion and humus loss occurring in major agricultural regions as a consequence of routine agricultural practices; and (5) loss of lands to urbanization, road building, village expansion, and other land-consuming developments associated with economic and population growth.

Desertification.

Desertification* will probably be a major modifier of landscapes between now and 2000. If all the lands identified by the U.N. as having a high or very high probability of desertification were to become desert by 2000, deserts would occupy more than three times the 7,992,000 square kilometers they occupied in 1977. [206] Most of the land lost would be pastureland, but losses in cropland could also be significant. As shown in the accompanying map, most of the losses would probably take place in Africa and Asia. Desertification is

ing Deserts—The Hand of Man, Washington: Worldwatch Institute, Aug. 1977. Present losses to desertification are apparently on the order of 6 million hectares per year (60,000 square kilometers): 3.2 million hectares of rangeland, 2.5 million hectares of rainfed cropland, and 125,000 hectares of irrigated farmland (Margaret R. Biswas, "United Nations Conference on Desertification in Retrospect," Laxenburg, Austria: International Institute for Applied Systems Analysis, Sept. 1978, p. 31). According to "Desertification: An Overview," U.N. Desertification Conference Aug. 1977, areas undergoing severe desertification now cover about 30 million square kilometers, or 23 percent of the earth's ice free land area.

*Desertification is a broad, loosely defined term encompassing a variety of ecological changes that render land useless for agriculture or for human habitation. Deserts rarely spread along well-articulated frontiers; rather, they pop up in patches where abuse, however unintended, destroys the thin cover of vegetation and fertile soil and leaves only sand or inert earth. (Erik Eckholm and Lester R. Brown, Spreading Deserts—The Hand of Man, Washington: Worldwatch Institute, Aug. 1977, pp. 7–8).

an active ongoing phenomenon, and its implications are not a matter of speculation. The economic bases of several West African countries, including Mauretania, Senegal, Upper Volta, Mali, Niger, and Chad have recently been undermined through the extensive desert expansion that occurred during the 1968–73 drought. These countries will find recovery difficult, as the damage done to soils was long-term. Sudan, Somalia, Ethiopia, Kenya, and Tanzania have also suffered degradation of soils associated with the recent drought. [207]

As already stated, one of the leading causes of desertification is overgrazing. As shown in the Free Range Grazing Pressure map in the colored map section, a large amount of land surface is used for free range grazing. Livestock populations have grown rapidly over the last few decades, and in the LDCs much of the increase has been in free-ranging animals. Globally the population of cattle rose by 38 percent over the 1955–76 period—including a 62 percent increase in the Near East and a 51 percent increase in Latin America. Over the same period, global sheep and goat populations increased by 21 percent, with a 52 percent increase in the Asian centrally planned economies and a 44 percent increase in Africa. [208] A portion of this increase has been in countries with rapidly expanding feedlot operations, but in many areas the increases in free-ranging livestock populations have pushed above the levels that can be indefinitely sustained by the land—given current pasture management policies and the limited application of available (but expensive) technologies for the protection of rangelands. In some regions, such as Rajasthan in India, increases in the land under cultivation have reduced available pastureland and intensified pressure on remaining pastures. The result has been severe declines in soil productivity and in some areas the actual creation of deserts of blowing sands. [209]

It is easy to underestimate the statistical probability of a drought. The 1968–73 drought in the African Sahel was so long and so severe that many experts suspected that a climatic shift had occurred. However, several statistical analyses of climatological data prepared for the 1977 U.N. Conference on Desertification suggest that the 5-year Sahelian drought was within the range of statistical expectation and therefore should not be thought of as a climatic shift or a fluke. Moreover, the analyses suggested a statistically significant tendency for dry years to occur in succession. Thus the Sahel can expect a recurrence of such a drought. [210] In most arid areas the oldest people can, on average, remember having experienced

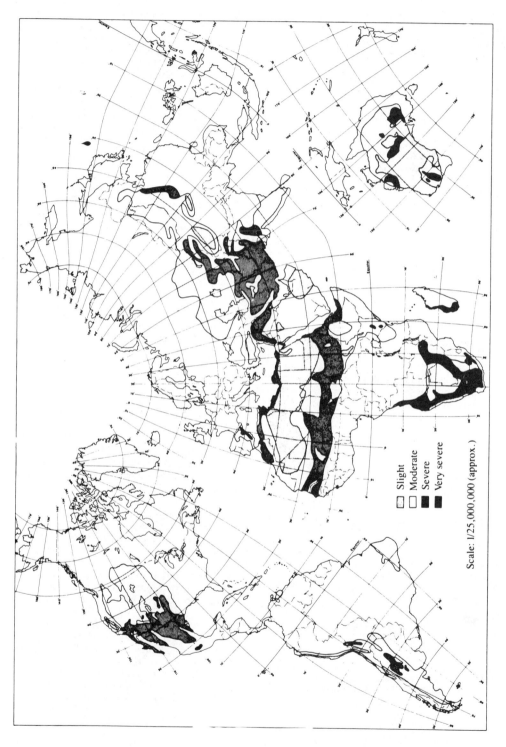

Desertifiaction Map (U.N. Desertification Conference, 1977)

Scale: 1/25,000,000 (approx.)

Slight
Moderate
Severe
Very severe

about four major droughts, some of which extended over several years. While most areas do not experience droughts as frequent or as severe as those in the Sahel, the probability of adverse weather is often underestimated, especially during periods of good weather.

The example of the Sahel also raises questions relating to populations, carrying capacity, and assistance. Drought always means hardship, but in cases like the recent Sahelian drought, where conditions exceed mere hardship and include severe famine and ecological decline, the role of human and animal population levels must be examined as potentially major contributors to suffering.[211] Where drought occurs periodically, the livelihood systems of the peoples there become adapted to coping with the consequences of drought. In these situations, the U.N. notes, great care must be exercised in external efforts to assist so that the adapted livelihood systems are not disrupted.[212]

Waterlogging, Salinization, Alkalinization

Many irrigation projects also take their toll. The causes vary, as discussed below, but worldwide an estimated 125,000 hectares of irrigated land are lost from production each year due to waterlogging, salinization, and alkalinization.[213] This loss rate amounts to only about .06 percent per year of the world's total irrigated land.[214] If it remains constant through the year 2000, about 2.75 million hectares (approximately 1.4 percent of the world's total irrigated land) will be out of production. These losses have more impact than averaged figures suggest because irrigated land is almost always the most productive land in a given region. But even assuming average productivity, 2.75 million hectares represents the food supply (with average yields) for more than 9 million people.*

Problems of waterlogging, salinization, and alkalinization occur in arid regions where irrigation systems supply water to the soil faster than drainage can remove it. The excess water raises the water table to a level near the ground surface. Evaporation brings dissolved soil salts to the surface where they inhibit plant growth and form a mineral crust. The water that returns to local streams and rivers is often so laden with salts that irrigation downstream is impaired (see the water section of this chapter for further information on this point).

Seepage from unlined canals is often even more of a problem than the water intended for irrigation. Canal seepage may cause the water table to rise, waterlogging the soil and transporting salts from lower soil horizons to the surface.

Such problems reach extreme proportions in Pakistan even as early as the 1960s. At that time in the Sind, one of Pakistan's two major provinces, 49 percent of all agricultural land was moderately or severely waterlogged, 50 percent was highly saline, and 27 percent was moderately saline, according to U.N. data. In the Punjab, the other major agricultural province, over 30 percent of all agricultural land was reported suffering from salinization. Massive soil reclamation projects in Pakistan have had some success, particularly in reducing waterlogging, but reclamation of saline soils has been slow.[215]

The situation in Pakistan is far from unique. In Afghanistan, waterlogging, salinization, and alkalinization are evident in most agricultural areas.[216] In Argentina, 2 million hectares of irrigated land are adversely affected by waterlogging, salinization, or alkalinization.[217] And in Peru, 300,000 out of 800,000 hectares of coastal irrigated land are affected by salinization or waterlogging.[218] In fact, virtually every nation with a sizable irrigated area is now adversely affected by these problems.

In the U.S., for example, some of the nation's richest farmlands are threatened. The San Joaquin Valley provides a recent, well-studied example. About 400,000 acres (160,000 hectares) of irrigated farmland in the San Joaquin Valley currently are affected by high, brackish water tables that pose an increasingly serious threat to productivity. Approximately 1.1 million acres (450,000 hectares)—about 13 percent of the total valley—ultimately will become unproductive unless subsurface drainage systems are installed. The salting problems of the valley have been compared to those that resulted in the collapse of civilization in Mesopotania and Egypt's upper Nile when early signs of agricultural overproduction were not heeded. Loss of the productive capacity of the San Joaquin Valley lands would be a serious loss to the people who work them, to the economic community of the valley, to the State of California, and to the country as a whole. The agricultural output of the valley is now estimated at $4 billion annually. To prevent this loss, a comprehensive system for management and disposal of the saline effluent of on-farm subsurface drainage systems has been proposed.[219] Similar problems

---

*A Department of Agriculture representative has pointed out that with higher yields (2,000 kilograms) 2.75 million hectares could feed more than 15 million people. Furthermore, even when lands are not abandoned, waterlogging, salinization, and alkalinization are reducing the yields on ever larger amounts of land—annually and cumulatively.

are also being observed in California's Imperial Valley.

Reclamation of degraded irrigated lands is a slow and costly process, often requiring construction of major public works, drainage, and corrective soil chemistry and structure. Lands that are waterlogged but have no problems with accumulated salts can generally be restored by reducing the water seepage rate and improving drainage, which can be costly but at least shows immediate results. Salinized and alkalinized soils, on the other hand, generally can't be restored without washing the accumulated salts out of the soil. In arid lands where such problems occur, passing enough water through the soil to carry away excess soil salts is difficult, costly, and time-consuming. In most instances, drainage problems make it impossible to simply pour huge quantities of water over the soil, and major hydraulic engineering is required. Furthermore, once washed out, the salts may reach ground-water supplies or become deposited in downstream regions, thus moving the problem rather than solving it. In many cases it is only possible to move the salts down in the soil profile.

In conclusion, history shows that when the desert is made to bloom, it sometimes does so only as a day flower, soon to wither under the stressful interaction of soil and sun. Poorly managed irrigation is often a major cause. The U.N. Conference on Desertification has focused attention on these problems, and the ecological and technological aspects of reclamation and prevention are beginning to be understood.[220] However, many drylands scattered across the world are showing early signs of salinization. By 2000 these areas may have experienced major declines in fertility unless major educaional efforts are made and capital is provided. The technology is available, but high costs and poor management (often including no water charge, thus encouraging overwatering and inadequately designed drainage) may significantly limit its appliction.

Deforestation

In their natural state, most regions of the globe receiving moderate-to-high rainfall would be forested. When forests are cut, particularly in tropical and semitropical lands (where rainfalls are violent and biochemical reactions are relatively rapid) and on steep slopes (where soils are usually thin and easily eroded), accelerated soil erosion occurs, accompanied by increased seasonal flooding, low flows, and siltation.

Haiti is an example of what advanced defores-

tation can do to an agricultural system. With a tight 5.3 persons per arable hectare, Haiti has effectively lost the forests on its watersheds. Farmers looking for a small patch of land, hungry cows and goats, and firewood gatherers have reduced the country's forests to 9 percent of their original extent. Droughts and floods are unmoderated by forest buffers; erosion is rampant; irrigation and hydroelectric systems are silting in; and the quality of the soils is declining.[221]

Information on watershed deforestation from U.S. Embassy officials (see Appendix C) and from the U.S. Agency for International Development,[222] suggests that Thailand, Brazil, Costa Rica, the Philippines, Burundi, the Ivory Coast, Burma, India, Indonesia, and many other nations may be facing similar problems, at least locally, if not on a nationwide scale. For example, the U.S. Embassy in Thailand reports that under the combined influences of firewood gathering, slash-and-burn agriculture, and large-scale illegal poaching of protected forests, the country's entire forest area cover could be effectively cleared by 1987, and even the most optimistic estimates of the rate of destruction offer no hope of significant forest stands in Thailand beyond 1993. As a result of its deforestation, Thailand suffers increasingly from both flood and drought, and while Thailand's arable area is still expanding, the general impression left by the U.S. Embassy reports is that erosion is already serious and likely to become more so.

As will be discussed more fully in the forestry section of this chapter, deforestation, particularly of mountain slopes forming the watersheds to heavily populated agricultural regions, appears likely to create serious obstacles to achieving the food projections summarized above, and hence also to the fulfillment of basic food needs for tens of millions of the world's people.

General Erosion

Given the scenarios developed in the agricultural forecasts in this volume, it can be anticipated that hydrologic destabilization will increase rates of erosion and loss of soil organic matter through the year 2000. By that time many croplands that are now producing well will be facing serious soil problems if current cultivation practices continue.

Because corn (maize) is relatively poor at holding soil, the corn-growing lands—about 7.5 percent of all lands in cultivation, producing roughly one-fifth of the world's grain—will fare the worst. The United States, as the world's largest corn producer, is in particular danger.

The U.S. Soil Conservation Service considers soil losses of 1 ton per acre for shallow soils and 5 tons per acre for deep soils to be the maximum that can be sustained annually without harming productivity. Although difficult to estimate, the extent to which soil losses exceed this figure appears to be great. For example, a survey of 283 U.S. farms in the Midwest, Great Plains, and Pacific Northwest recently conducted by the General Accounting Office (GAO) found that 84 percent had annual soil losses in excess of 5 tons* per acre.[223] In Iowa and Illinois, the two corn-dominated states covered by the GAO study, half the farms surveyed lost betwen 10 and 20 short tons per acre per year. These findings are consistent with those of other studies.[224]

Gently sloping lands planted to corn, millet, or cotton often lose as much as 20 tons of soil per acre per year, at which rate they will have lost approximately 3 inches of soil by the year 2000.[225] Steeper slopes might double or even quadruple these figures and conceivably experience soil losses of 6 inches to a foot or more by the year 2000 wherever the main crop does not provide good soil cover. The significance of these losses depends on local soil depths, but to date the seriousness of such losses have been masked largely by energy subsidies in terms of fertilizers—subsidies that will be increasingly expensive and difficult to maintain in the decades ahead.

Wheat is relatively good at holding soil. Five to 10 tons of soil loss per acre per year are commonly reported losses for wheat, at which rate approximately 1.5 inches of soil could be lost by the year 2000.[226] Terraced rice cultivation appears to be the most soil-conserving of all. It has been calculated that Chinese, Japanese, and Korean practices may add more to the soil, through addition of canal dredging to the fields, than is washed away.[227] Very low rates of erosion can also be attained by crop rotations, such as alternative plantings of corn, wheat, and clover, which restore organic matter and keep the earth well covered at most times.

Loss of organic matter follows trends similar to those observed for erosion. It is particularly severe with crops such as corn and soybeans, which do not provide a dense soil cover or sodlike root structure. Organic matter is also lost if crop residues are burned to protect crops against disease, as they often are in the U.S., or if crop residues and manure are used as fuel, as they are increasingly in developing regions faced with firewood shortages. Rotation schemes, fallow periods, and green manuring can reduce losses or permit buildup. However, until 1973 relatively inexpensive chemical fertilizers and high crop prices discouraged fallowing and encouraged continuous cropping. Since 1973 fertilizer prices have risen, but although the Global 2000 Study's energy projections suggest that the price of energy-intensive fertilizers will increase significantly in the years ahead, the high effectiveness of chemical fertilizers may continue to make the use of organic fertilizers less attractive.

Loss of organic matter is critical for two reasons: (1) organic matter serves to retain soil structure and moisture, and (2) breakdown of soil organic matter adds carbon dioxide to the atmosphere, potentially leading to climatic change. As shown in Figure 13–3, the pool of carbon in soil systems is thought to be larger than that in forests and living organisms. The effects of converting fixed carbon in both forests and soil systems to carbon dioxide are discussed above in the climate section of this chapter.

Losses to Development

When land is subjected to the intense uses characteristic of urban and industrial development, it is in effect permanently lost for food production. Furthermore, urban and industrial developments are often located on some of a nation's, or the world's, *best* agricultural land—rich, irrigated, alluvial soils in gently sloping river valleys. Such lands lost to urban and industrial growth often involve taking lands out of production and therefore represent an *actual* loss of production as opposed to a *potential* loss.

The loss of both producing and potentially producing land has serious implications for food-importing nations. For example, the total irrigated land in Egypt has remained virtually unchanged over the past two decades. Old producing lands are lost to development almost as fast as additional hectares are irrigated with water from the Aswan Dam.[228]

The worldwide losses of agricultural land to development are difficult to estimate on the basis of the limited data now available. A recent report by Lester Brown, President of Worldwatch Institute, brings together most of what is now known.[229] Brown projects that, if present trends in urban development and growth continue, development between 1975 and 2000 will claim 25 million hectares of cropland. While this is only about 2 percent of the world crop base, it is enough land (assuming even average productivity) to feed some 84 million people.

Increases both in urbanization (growth of the urban population) and suburbanization (the geographical spread of urban settlements) have ac-

TABLE 13–18

Loss of Agricultural Lands, 1960–2000, Selected Industrialized Countries

	Average Annual Rate of Loss 1960–70	Projected Cumulative Loss 1978–2000
	Percent	
Austria	0.18	5
Belgium	1.23ᵃ	24
Denmark	0.30	6
Finland	0.28ᵇ	6
France	0.18	4
West Germany	0.25	5
Japan	0.73ᶜ	15
Netherlands	0.48ᵈ	10
New Zealand	0.05	1
Norway	0.15	3
Sweden	0.33	7
Turkey	0.04	1
United Kingdom	0.18	4
United States (excluding Alaska)	0.08	2
Weighted total		2.5

Source: 1960–70 data from Organization for Economic Cooperation and Development, *Interfutures,* Ch. 13,"Physical Environment." Paris. May 16, 1977 (draft). p. 22.
ᵃ 1959–70.   ᵇ 1959–69.   ᶜ 1965–75.   ᵈ 1966–72.

celerated the rate at which agricultural land is lost to development. A recent study by the Organization for Economic Cooperation and Development (OECD) indicates that in the OECD (industrialized) countries urban land area has been growing about twice as fast as the population.[230] This trend is due in part to sprawling residential patterns. In 1972 each additional U.S. suburbanite required 0.15 hectares of land (0.09 hectares of which was taken out of cultivation) for development purposes. This loss is nearly half the *average* agricultural land per capita (0.19 hectares) projected for the LDCs by the year 2000.[231] On a percentage basis, even higher loss rates are being experienced in some industrialized nations (see Table 13–18). Surveys in developing countries show lower per capita land losses to development, but the high rates of population growth and the limited amounts of prime farmlands are likely to make such losses equally important in the LDCs.

In the face of rising energy costs, it is unclear whether the trend toward urban, suburban, and industrial sprawl will continue or reverse. Energy concerns will gradually encourage both greater compactness (for the efficiency needed by large centralized energy facilities) and more decentralization (for the more diffused, land-intensive, and self-sufficient settlement patterns that efficiently use solar and other small-scale renewable sources of energy, such as windmills, biogas plants and biomass). However these forces eventually balance out, it seems likely that significant amounts of land will be removed from cultivation or potential cultivation between now and 2000. The OECD countries again provide an example. Should 1960–70 rates of land loss continue, the OECD countries will have lost an average of 2.5 percent of their agricultural lands by 2000, as shown in the table. A substantial portion of the higher cost of food production projected for 2000 in Chapter 6 is a direct result of the costs of expanding arable area to compensate for development losses.

Over and above losses to urbanization and suburbanization, agricultural lands are being lost to expanding rural populations and villages around the world. The data available on these losses are limited. Lester Brown, who finds evidence that villages frequently expand onto cropland, reports that India, a nation of 600,000 villages, projects nonagricultural land use to expand by 9.8 million hectares (or 60 percent) between 1970 and 2000.[232] Overall, world losses of agricultural land to village expansion have not been estimated.

The food projections in Chapter 6 include explicit consideration of land lost to development.* The above discussion is presented as support for the estimates used and cited in the Study's food projections, although it provides only an indication of the gross changes known to be occurring.

By the Year 2000

This discussion of global deterioration of soils has considered (1) desertification, (2) waterlogging, salinization and alkalinization, (3) the effects of deforestation, (4) general erosion and humus loss, and (5) loss of land to urbanization and village expansion. These problems are widely recognized by national and world leaders and efforts are being made to reduce rates of deterioration and to restore soils. The 1977 U.N. Conference on Desertification is an example of these efforts.

---

*In the GOL (grain, oilseed, and livestock) model used by the Department of Agriculture for the food projections, development-related land losses are specified as a negative function of population growth. Specifically, the assumed losses range from 0.03 hectares per capita in LDCs to 0.1 hectares per capita in the developed countries. The Department notes that to date losses of arable area to development have been offset substantially by larger gains through settlement of new lands or by reclamation of old lands. With the supply of potentially arable area finite and the cost of reclamation increasing, losses due to development are likely to become increasingly important.

Most instances of soil deterioration are reversible, at least in theory. Given sufficiently large commitments of time, capital, energy, technical knowledge, and political will, most land deterioration can be slowed, stopped, or even restored. The problem is that in practice the time and knowledge required and the economic, resource, and political costs involved make many cases of soil deterioration virtually irreversible.

The difficulty in controlling the five types of land deterioration can be seen in examples in the United States. Luther Carter has described the economic problem in part, noting that despite the billions spent on it, the problem of soil erosion persists.[233] The General Accounting Office has recently pointed to the need to give soil conservation top priority in order to meet future food needs.[234] Salinization continues to be a threat to important U.S. croplands.[235] Prime agricultural lands continue to be lost to urban sprawl, resource development, roads, and shopping centers.[236] The Department of Agriculture's Soil Conservation Service (SCS) reported that in 1975 soil losses on U.S. cropland amounted to almost 3 billion tons, an average of about 9 tons per acre. Although this was excessive, it was less than the estimated 4 billion tons of topsoil that would have been lost in 1975 if farmers had followed no conservation practices at all.[237] The SCS report concluded that to sustain U.S. crop production indefinitely at even present levels, soil losses must be cut in half. The SCS has developed a plan for reducing soil losses, but the plan has not been implemented, probably in part because it would lead to a 5–8 percent increase in production costs. It might also reduce food output somewhat in the short run.[238]

Not just in the U.S. but throughout the world, the fate of soil systems depends on societies' willingness to pay the short-run resource and economic costs to preserve soils for long-run benefits. Whether the soils of the world will deteriorate further or be reclaimed will depend in large part on the ability and willingness of governments to make politically difficult policy changes. Soil protection requires a stable society and well-developed institutions. A society stressed by warfare, hunger, internal turmoil, and corruption, or obsessed with modernization to the point that it ignores the fate of its agricultural lands, will be fortunate if the productivity of its land does not diminish significantly in the decades ahead.

The political difficulties cannot be overemphasized. Often solutions to soil problems will require resettlement, reduction of herd sizes, restrictions on plantings, reforms in land tenure, and public works projects that will fail without widespread cooperation from the agrarian population. The costs will be immediately apparent; the benefits will seldom be seen in less than half a decade and in some cases may not be apparent for a generation or more. Unless a government is trusted by its people or can afford to offer long-term financial incentives, it will have difficulty implementing soil conservation programs.

The soil conditions that can be expected by the year 2000 are critically dependent on policy changes during the intervening years. Assuming no policy change—the standard assumption underlying all of the Global 2000 Study projections—*significant deteriorations in soils can be anticipated virtually everywhere, including in the U.S.* Assuming that energy, water, and capital are available, it will be possible for a time to compensate for some of the deterioration by increasing the use of yield-enhancing inputs (fertilizer, irrigation, pesticides, herbicides, etc.), but the projected increases in energy (and chemical fertilizer) costs will make this approach to offsetting soil losses ever more expensive. Without major policy changes, soil deterioration could significantly interfere with achieving the production levels projected in this Study.

Ecological Effects of Fertilizers and Pesticides

Historically, fertilizer use is correlated with the use of a number of yield-enhancing agricultural inputs including pesticides and herbicides. The projections in Chapter 6 are based on the assumption that growth in fertilizer use is representative of the growth in all yield-enhancing inputs. Therefore the "fertilizer" projections are intended to apply to a full package of yield-enhancing inputs.

However, from an ecological perspective, fertilizers and pesticides have very different effects. It is therefore important in the environmental analysis to examine factors that might alter the historic correlation. Thus, the discussions that follow begin with a brief consideration of some of the factors that will influence the relative growth of fertilizers and pesticides and herbicides. Fertilizers are considered first.

Fertilizers

Chapter 6 projects that by 2000 global use per hectare of "fertilizer" (as defined in that chapter) will be 2.6 times that of the record levels reported in the early 1970s. Usage in LDCs is projected to quadruple, and usage in the centrally planned and market economies is projected to increase by factors of 2.3 and 2.1 respectively. Since the area under cultivation is projected to increase only slightly, the *per hectare* usage of fertilizers in all regions can be expected to increase at essentially the same rates as the total applications. In the discussion that follows, it is assumed that actual fertilizer use will follow closely these indicative "fertilizer" projections.

In assessing the environmental implications of the projected fertilizer usage, it is important to obtain some sense of the magnitude of projected fertilizer use relative to natural flows of basic nutrients. The Scientific Committee on Problems of the Environment (SCOPE) of the International Council of Scientific Unions estimated in 1976 that if current rates of increase in nitrogen fertilizer production were to continue, synthetic nitrogen fixation—which then amounted to about 26 percent of natural, terrestrial fixation— would be equal to natural fixation by 1983.[239] The ecological ramifications of an alteration of this magnitude in a basic nutrient cycle are unclear, as are the ramifications of the parallel and equally significant changes in the phosphate nutrient cycle.

While U.S. Department of Agriculture officials regard the global levels of fertilizer use projected for 2000 to be safe when applied carefully by trained personnel, they are aware that improper use leads to increased dangers. Improper use can aggravate rather than alleviate problems of soil deterioration and declining fertility. Furthermore, even with careful application adverse effects of fertilizer usage have been observed, or are suspected, in aquatic and marine systems, in the atmosphere, and in terrestrial ecosystems.

Scientific understanding of atmospheric influences is not yet well developed, but it is reported by the National Academy of Sciences that nitrous oxide from fertilizer usage, when it makes its way into the stratosphere, reacts in a fashion that depletes the ozone layer. If this phenomenon turns out to be serious, the world could find itself in the tragic situation of having to support the human population at the cost of subjecting the world's biota to damaging dosages of cosmic and ultraviolet radiation, at least one effect of which would be increased incidence of skin cancer in human beings.*

From the perspective of ecology, the known terrestrial effects of increased fertilizer usage are surprisingly benign. The addition of large amounts of three critical nutrients (phosphorus, potassium,

and fixed nitrogen) might be expected to produce many changes in soils. The most apparent effect is simply the intended increase in plant growth. One potentially adverse effect concerns the accelerated decomposition of organic matter in soils. As nitrogen is often the limiting nutrient for decomposition of soil organic matter, increased nitrogen usage contributes to reduction of soil organic matter, thus degrading soils and contributing carbon dioxide to the atmosphere.[239a]

As soon as virgin soil is plowed, the decomposition of its organic matter accelerates, and soil quality (especially tilth, porosity, and water-absorbing capacity) begins to deteriorate. It was once thought that the application of nitrogen fertilizer would rebuild the organic matter in croplands by stimulating more plant growth, the residue of which would be added to the soil.[239b] However, it was demonstrated early[239c]—and confirmed again more recently[239d]—that under modern farming methods the organic matter in soils cannot be maintained at anything approaching its virgin state. Generally, soil organic matter declines to an equilibrium value of 40–60 percent of the orginal content. Soil quality deteriorates as well. While in most cases crop yields can be maintained through the continual application of chemical fertilizers, through plowing with large heavy tractors, and through irrigation, the modern methods of farming tend to lock agriculture into a particular mode of cultivation and resource allocation if high yields in degraded soils are to be maintained.[239e]

Consequences of increased fertilizer use for aquatic systems are more serious than terrestrial effects and include eutrophication[240] and nitrate contamination of drinking water supplies.[241] The phosphorus component of fertilizers is thought to contribute most to eutrophication in affected lakes, but nitrogen is also important. Nitrogen contributes most to eutrophication in coastal waters. More than 70 percent of the nitrogen entering surface waters is from nonpoint agricultural sources. Even the input of nitrogen from rainwater is a sufficient nutrient loading in some lakes to support a moderate increase in biotic activity. An important part of the fixed nitrogen in precipitation enters the atmosphere as a result of ammonia volatilization, chiefly from animal wastes.[242]

The levels of nitrogen that pose hazards to human health—about 10 milligrams of nitrate per liter of water—are roughly an order of magnitude higher than the levels that produce eutrophication and are relatively rare at the rates at which fertilizers are now used. The primary population at risk is that of infants under the age of three. In-

---

*See the climate section of this chapter for further information on nitrous oxide and other chemicals that deplete the ozone layer.

fants consuming synthetic milk formula mixed with nitrate-contaminated water may experience the toxic effect known as methemoglobinemia. This disease is readily diagnosed, and is rapidly reversible with clinical treatment. After the age of 3 months, vulnerability to methemoglobinemia decreases rapidly. In the U.S., concentration of nitrates above 10 milligrams per liter are rare. The primary risk is from wellwater on or near farms, especially in areas where soil and hydrologic conditions favor the accumulation of nitrate in groundwater.

While mortality from methemoglobinemia is now extremely rare, the presence of high levels of nitrate in drinking water supplies poses a health hazard that is already a valid concern in at least some regions of the United States, and the projected doubling to quadrupling of fertilizer applications by 2000 could make this disease more serious and more widespread.[243]

Pesticides and Herbicides

The first step in examining the future environmental implications of pesticides is to assess whether their usage globally is likely to continue to be correlated with the "fertilizer" package projected in Chapter 6. This assessment is difficult because data on pesticide use are not published for most countries, and thus it is not possible to quantify past trends in any detail or to project future developments. It is known that a large fraction—probably more than half—of all pesticides are applied to a few high-value, commercial crops (especially cotton, vegetables, and tobacco) and that demands for these crops are expected to continue growing steadily. The applications of pesticides to food grains are relatively small.

The Food and Agriculture Organization succeeded in gathering some data for the LDCs in 1975 and found that pesticide use in the LDCs had increased by about 50 percent over the two year period 1971–73 and that consumption for 1974–77 was expected to increase more slowly, at about 9 percent per year.[244] These figures are significantly influenced by the heavy use of pesticides in India, Mexico, and Argentina. If this slowed rate of increase (9 percent per year) continues, LDC pesticide use by 2000 would still be more than 10 times the 1971–73 rate. The FAO growth estimates are therefore considerably higher than the "fertilizer" projection of Chapter 6.

The FAO survey revealed further that half the pesticides used in the LDCs were generally persistent organochlorines (DDT, aldrin, and other chlorinated hydrocarbons). This is to be expected.

Though more environmentally damaging, organochlorines are markedly less expensive in most applications than the less persistent, more specific alternatives, and are also far safer for farmers to apply because of less short-term toxicity to humans. If the conclusion to the food projections in Chapter 6 is correct—namely, that in most LDCs food demands "are likely to outweigh problems of the environment well beyond 2000"—the use of DDT and other persistent pesticides can be expected to continue in proportions much like those found at present.[245]

The future use of pesticides in the industrialized nations is equally difficult to project both because of data limitations and because of growing interest in changing practices. The "fertilizer" indicator in Chapter 6 implies moderate increases (by a factor of 2.1) over 1971–75 average consumption by 2000. The banning of DDT and other persistent insecticides by much of the industrialized world during the last decade suggests that increases in insecticide usage there will be discriminating, emphasizing compounds with less persistent ecological effects than the compounds likely to be used in the LDCs. Furthermore, there is growing interest in several industrialized nations in the techniques of integrated pest management* (IPM).[246] Although there is not at this time a prevailing policy to encourage IPM, increasing pest resistance and simple economics may encourage a shift. If widely applied, IPM would reduce the use of pesticides.

The rapid increase in the use of herbicides in the developed regions in the last two decades can be expected to continue. If no-till planting, which involves heavy use of herbicides, is widely adopted in the next few decades—and there is reason to expect that it will be—very rapid increases in herbicide usage can be expected.

No-till planting is the practice of eliminating field preparation entirely and planting on top of the residue of the previous crops. Minimum tillage refers to the practice of minimizing field preparation—principally plowing, but also tillage with disc harrows, drags, and cultivators—for planting. There are both advantages and disadvantages in no-till and minimum-till practices. Crop residues

---

*The Council on Environmental Quality defines integrated pest management as follows: IPM employs a combination of techniques to control crop-threatening pests. Maximum reliance is placed on natural pest population controls and a combination of suppression techniques—cultural methods, pest-specific diseases, resistant crop varieties, sterile insects, attractants, augmentation of parasites or predators, or chemical pesticides as needed.

are often breeding places for pests, which increases the need for pesticides or other pest control measures. Fertilizer placement options are reduced and, as a result, fertilizers may be inefficiently utilized and fertilizer runoff increased. Also, extensive use of herbicides is involved. Nonetheless, no-till and minimum-till techniques appear to have potential for reducing energy inputs and for conserving soil resources. The use of these techniques has grown roughly 300 percent in the U.S. since the start of the decade. They account today for roughly a quarter of farmland preparation, and some experts expect them to be used very extensively in the future.

What, then, are the prospects for future utilization of pesticides and herbicides? In the following discussion, it is assumed that world pesticide (and herbicide) use will increase at approximately the same rates as the "fertilizer" indicator in the Department of Agriculture projections in Chapter 6, that is, they will more than double over the 1975–2000 period. In the LDCs the increase is likely to be fourfold, and possibly as much as sixfold if the FAO estimated increase of 9 percent per year is sustained.

The environmental problems anticipated from increases in pesticide use are suggested by problems that have already occurred and can be expected to continue.[247] They include: (1) biological amplification and concentration of persistent pesticides in the tissues of higher-order predators, including humans; (2) development of increased resistance to pesticides by numerous insect pests, and hence possible declines in yields through increased vulnerability to pests; (3) destruction of natural pest controls such as insect-eating birds and predatory insects, and hence further increases in the cost of—and decreases in the effectiveness of—preventing crop losses caused by pests; (4) emergence of new pests previously not troublesome; and (5) increased poisonings of farm workers and families from nonpersistent pesticides.

The first of these problems, biological amplification (or concentration), is familiar because of the extensive attention it received (due initially to the pioneering work of Rachel Carson) in the years preceding the bans in several developed countries on the use of DDT.* Here it is appropriate to note only that biological concentration is a continuing problem. Although monitored concentrations of DDT in the environment have been shown to be declining in those industrialized countries that have banned DDT,[248] concentrations are

virtually certain to continue to increase in those LDCs where DDT is still being used extensively. Unfortunately, very little information is available on DDT concentrations in LDC environments because almost no monitoring is being done.

The second problem, biological resistance, has received less popular attention than the first, but is equally important. Biological resistance to pesticides develops in pest species because repeated pesticide usage places species under an evolutionary pressure such that those individuals in a pest population that possess some immunity to pesticides are the most likely to survive and reproduce. Malaria-transmitting mosquitoes, plant-eating mites,[249] and other insects that have been regularly exposed to pesticides are showing great genetic flexibility in developing tolerance or resistance to insecticides. The three examples that follow were selected from the many available and illustrate the seriousness of this problem.

1. In California, a state that makes heavy use of pesticides, a large number of pest species attacks crops. Of this large number, 25 species have been found to cause major damage (i.e., losses of $1 million or more per species in 1970). The genetic flexibility of these species is indicated by the fact that, at some location in the world, 21 of those 25 species have been found to be resistant to one or more pesticides: 16 to DDT, 16 to organophosphates, and 10 to cyclodines. In California alone, 17 of the 25 species were found to be resistant to one or more types of insecticide.[250]

2. Disease vectors that have been heavily controlled by use of insecticides have shown great ability to tolerate their intended poisons. The National Academy of Sciences (using World Health Organization data) documents the growing number of vector-insect species (e.g., body lice) showing tolerance to important pesticides over an extended period, as shown in the following table.[251]

	DDT	Dieldrin	Organo- phosphate Compounds	Total
1956	27	25	1	33
1962	47	65	8	81
1969	55	84	17	102
1974	61	92	27	109

Of the anopheline (malarial) mosquitoes, 41 have been found resistant to dieldrin and 24 to DDT. One species, *Anopheles albimanus Wiederman,* has become resistant not only to dieldrin and DDT but to malathion and certain other or-

---

*For some uses, that is. The bans do not prevent the use of DDT for controlling health-threatening insect vectors.

ganophosphate and carbonate insecticides, *thus showing itself resistant to all the major chemical groups that are used to combat malaria vectors.*[252] If pesticide resistance becomes widespread in other species of malarial mosquitoes, control of malaria would be badly hampered, and its incidence could be expected to rise sharply.

3. Cotton, which receives about 50 percent of all the pesticides applied in the U.S.,[253] now attracts several pests that have developed immunity to all currently available and registered pesticides. In cotton-growing districts across Central America, the U.S. Southwest, Southern California, and Australia, the situation has become so severe that growers in many places have been forced either to give up cotton growing or to shift to integrated pest management techniques. Some districts have endured the cost of as many as 30–50 pesticide applications a year to a single crop.[254]

As long as pesticides are used, pest resistances can be expected to continue to develop. By the year 2000 there will almost certainly be more pesticide-resistant pests and more crops for which there are no effective pesticides. There will also be more registered pesticides. How the continuing struggle with insect pests will stand in 2000 will depend on pest control policies, chemical technologies, and biological technologies. Newer pesticides are generally more selective, but also more expensive than those they replace. The techniques of integrated pest management offer new hope,[255] but the transmittal of these techniques requires a significant amount of field and laboratory research on insect ecology, and therefore commitments of both time and money. Also IPM methods depend heavily on the very species most seriously threatened by pesticides—the beneficial insect species that prey upon agricultural pests.

The third problem of increased pesticide use is simply that pesticides destroy natural pest controls. The discussion here focuses on predatory insects, but insect-eating birds are also affected.

Insecticides are usually more damaging to predator insect species than they are to pests, because (1) predators may be poisoned through ingesting poisoned pest species as well as directly through the effects of the pesticide*; (2) since predator populations are always less numerous and generally less fecund than their prey, predator populations have less genetic material from which to develop immunities to pesticides, take longer to regain their numbers after insecticide application,

and face a higher probability of being reduced to such a low level that they cannot recover; (3) the predator species are eliminated both directly through the effects of insecticides and indirectly through the loss of their normal food when the insects on which they feed are eliminated.

Often predatory insects are made locally extinct through pesticide applications. When predatory insects are eliminated, herbivorous pest species multiply rapidly leading to severe pest outbreaks. Farmers often respond to such outbreaks with still heavier application of pesticides, reducing further the chances that predator species might be reestablished.

Also, in such predator-free environments, species that have previously been benign become major pests. Mites, which are now major pests in fruit culture, became pests only after the start of heavy use of pesticides in fruit cultivation. Similar histories can be found for many insect species, including Hessian flies, and several major pest species of the cotton plant. Insecticides are probably largely responsible for new insect pests in agriculture.[256]

Successive developments of biological resistance and releases of new pest species will decrease the effectiveness of the projected increases in pesticide use. Diminishing returns on pesticide investments can go on only so long before crop losses will force a major change in strategies of pest control. The techniques of integrated pest management[257] and biological controls appear now to offer good alternatives. Although there are as yet few policy commitments to IPM or biological controls, interest is growing.

By the Year 2000

The pressure to increase agricultural yields is projected to more than double the application rates of nitrogen and phosphorous fertilizers and pesticides. This growth in fertilizer use implies that before 2000 the annual industrial rate of fixing of nitrogen for agricultural purposes will exceed the total global rate of nitrogen fixation by natural systems. The full implications of a modification of this magnitude in a basic nutrient cycle are not clear and have not yet been studied carefully, but potentially adverse effects are known or suspected. Nitrate contamination of fresh water supplies and eutrophication of fresh and estuarine waters are among the adverse effects known to be possible, and potentially serious reductions in the atmospheric ozone layer are suspected by some knowledgeable scientists. The increased use of pesticides can be expected to continue to reduce

---

*In general, predators are more susceptible to pesticides than the pest species they hunt.

pest populations, but with diminishing returns since insect resistances to pesticides will continue to develop and predator populations will continue to be depleted. By 2000 the techniques of integrated pest management and biological controls may be in much wider use than today.

The overall environmental impacts are difficult to estimate because so many uncertain variables are involved. Rising food prices (where people can afford to pay them) may allow producers to endure the higher costs of increased pesticide use at diminished returns; increased resistance to pesticides may increase losses, thereby increasing food prices still more; or increased pesticide prices may make IPM more competitive. The rate at which pest resistance will diminish returns on investments in chemical controls will depend both on the way the chemicals are used and on the progress of chemical technology in finding new insecticides. New chemical pesticides will be developed but will require time and money for registration, adoption, and application.

There are similar uncertainties for the variables relating to fertilizers. Will the LDCs—where the marginal returns on fertilizer investments are greatest—be able to afford fertilizers? How serious a threat do fertilizers pose for the upper atmosphere? How far and how rapidly will the biologically based technologies for nitrogen fixation develop and be applied?

With all this uncertainty, it is not possible to project precisely how these variables will develop over the next two decades. It is only possible to note that the foreseeable trend is one of heavy and increasing dependence—often with diminishing returns—on both synthetic fertilizers and chemical pesticides. The potentially adverse atmospheric effects associated with continued heavy dependence on synthetic fertilizers is one of the most understudied and potentially serious global environmental questions. Pest control strategies also need much further study. Many experts feel that strategies based on biological controls and integrated pest management offer much greater possibilities for improvement than do chemical technologies alone, and a gradual shift toward integrated and biological control techniques seems probable in both the industrialized countries and the LDCs.

Crop Vulnerability: Genetic Considerations

With only modest increases in arable land expected, the food projections imply strong pressures to continue increasing yields through genetic technologies. Following two decades of developments in agricultural genetics, two trends can be expected in response to the continuing strong pressures. The first is for further genetic improvements in key plant and animal species to raise yields.* Developments in this area will entail greater dependence on inbred strains manifesting a high degree of genetic uniformity. The second trend is the shift toward monoculture cultivation of a few relatively high-yielding, low-cost, staple food crops. Together, these two trends will lead to further genetic hybriding and further replacement of lower-yielding, diversified cropping patterns with extensive, often contiguous, patterns. The short-term effect will be increased yields, but in the long run, questions of crop vulnerability must be considered.

These two factors—dependence on inbred strains and the shift toward monoculture cultivation—have become more closely interrelated over the past two decades as pressure to expand food production has grown. It has been estimated that by the early 1970s over four-fifths of the world's food supplies were derived from less than two dozen plant and animal species.[258] One expert estimates that as much as four-fifths of the world's population depends for sustenance on wheat or rice.[259] The exact figures are not important. The point is that the already narrow genetic base of the world's major food crops may become even more narrow. Plant diseases are constantly evolving ways to overcome plant resistances, requiring plant breeders to develop new resistant strains. The tens of thousands of genotypes of the major crop species are the raw materials from which plant breeders work, and these stocks of genetic raw materials are being reduced as natural habitats are lost. Increased reliance on a narrowing gene pool and more extensive monoculture of food staples could lead to sudden unanticipated widespread losses in world food production. How likely and how serious is such a disaster? There is no easy or precise answer to the question. Past history suggests that the probability of a major genetic failure is low but increasing.

The following paragraphs discuss three aspects of increasing genetic vulnerability. The first is historic in nature. Past examples demonstrate both the difficulty of controlling pest or disease infections in areas of extensive monoculture, and

---

*Questions are being raised as to how much further yields can be increased by genetics and technology. See for example N. F. Jensen, "Limits to Growth in World Food Production," *Science*, July 28, 1978, pp. 317–20.

the severe implications of failures. The second and third aspects relate to concerns voiced by plant geneticists themselves: that present trends toward uniform strains and loss of genetic reserves could raise the frequency and severity of pest-related and disease-related crop failures significantly by 2000, and that the costs of even relatively minor genetic failures (genetic in the sense that a crop population is genetically unable to protect itself from pathogens and pests) may ultimately outweigh gains from genetically increased yields, even if major catastrophes do not occur. Such a development would be a catastrophe by itself, eventually.

Historical Examples

One of the best known examples of a genetic/monoculture crop failure is the massive failure of potato crops of the 1840s in Ireland and Europe. An estimated 2 million people starved to death in the wake of the blight, and a similar number were forced to emigrate. [260] The potato famine was not a unique phenomena; there are many other examples. Wheat rust epidemics have caused localized famines since the Middle Ages. The European wine industry was nearly destroyed three times in the last century by three different plant diseases. Between 1870 and 1890 coffee rust transformed Ceylon from the world's largest coffee-growing nation into a country unfit for coffee-growing. Shortly after the turn of the century, two separate, highly destructive epidemics struck the widely cultivated Gros Michael banana. [261] A fungus devastated the Bengali rice crop in 1942, leading to the deaths of tens of thousands. [262] In 1946 a large fraction of the U.S. oat crop, which was comprised almost entirely of a strain called Victoria, was lost to a fungus epidemic. [263] While these genetically related crop failures have all had very serious impacts on the human populations involved, some genetic failures have been even more damaging ecologically. For example, the American chestnut is virtually extinct due to the chestnut blight, and elms are becoming ever scarcer due to Dutch elm disease.

Serious outbreaks of genetically related crop diseases continue. For example, after existing as a minor disease for 14 years, race 15B of the wheat stem rust erupted in the early 1950s into a full-blown epidemic. It destroyed 75 percent of the Durham variety in the 1953 U.S. spring wheat crop as well as 35 percent of the bread wheat crop in that season. [264]

Another example occurred in 1970. A corn fungus disease, *Helminthosporium maydis*, reached epidemic proportions in large areas of the corn belt. An estimated 80 percent of U.S. corn acreage was highly susceptible because of both the genetic composition of the corn and the contiguous monoculture used across large areas of the states involved. The disease did not spread to all susceptible areas, but it did manage to reduce U.S. corn production by 15 percent (710 million bushels). It is no exaggeration to call the response of the seed corn industry heroic. There is a fascinating story of efforts to locate stocks of normal cytoplasm, which were then in short supply. [265] If the U.S. seed industry had not been sufficiently adaptable in developing a technical fix—it replaced approximately 80 percent of its sales with an alternative (and much harder to produce) product*—losses in 1971 and 1972 might have been much greater than in 1970. [266] Nonetheless, the effect on the price of seed was significant. The price of seed corn in 1970–71 was $18–$25 per bushel; the mean price was $20. The price has risen steadily ever since to a mean of $48 per bushel during the 1976–77 season. [267] This 140 percent increase is due in large part to the increased difficulty of producing blight-resistant seed.

The Danger of Present Trends Toward Monoculture and Genetic Uniformity

It is almost always the case that a hard fight on one front means fewer defenses elsewhere. So it is generally with breeding plants for high yields. Modern plant breeding is based largely on the use of inbred, uniform strains, [268] and the most inbred strains appear to have weakened in their natural resistance to pathogens and pests. The inbred products manifest a high degree of genetic uniformity. The increasing cultivation of strains of high-yield varieties will result in great increases in the degree of genetic uniformity of major crops throughout the world. As a result the fraction of the crop at risk in the event of a trait-specific epidemic will also increase, as will the ease with which disease or insect pests can spread across large areas of contiguous monoculture. As a result, the probable geographic extent of the epidemic may expand in the years ahead. Furthermore, since water enhances the transmission of many plant diseases, the projected in-

---

*The vulnerable strain in this case was a male-sterile cytoplasm, which allowed the breeder to cross strains in the field, using natural pollination rather than employing an expensive manual process to avoid self-fertilization of the two strains. The fungus forced the seed industry to go back to hand detasseling. (C. E. Yarwood, "Man-Made Plant Diseases," *Science*, Apr. 10, 1970, pp. 218–20.)

creases in the amount of irrigated cropland may further increase the vulnerability of crops to disease throughout the world.[269] Furrow or flood irrigation, for example, creates conditions that favor the growth of pathogens requiring high soil moisture (e.g., *Pythium*), and sprinkling irrigation favors diseases spread by splashing water and rain (e.g., bacterial blight and anthracnose of bean).[270]

Simultaneously, the genetic resources available for combatting diseases are dwindling. In the event of a major new crop epidemic, plant breeders sort through thousands of varieties of the afflicted plant species, hoping to identify a resistant strain that can be interbred with other varieties to impart disease resistance without reducing productivity or imparting undesirable characteristics. Finding a resistant strain depends on the quality of the available seed bank. In general, the more tough wild varieties available, the better the chance of finding an appropriate resistant strain.[271]

However, the varietal stock is diminishing. The wild strains (from which modern high-yielding varieties were originally bred) are not usually cultivated and are being obliterated by widespread and increasing destruction of habitat. High-yield varieties are being adopted everywhere, replacing the myriad native strains that local farmers have developed over centuries. These strains, often uniquely suited to local conditions, are rarely preserved when farmers shift to high-yield varieties. The increases in the use of high-yield varieties implicit in the food projections of Chapter 6 will worsen this situation.[272]

A recently discovered plant related to corn (maize) dramatically illustrates the potentially catastrophic losses that can occur when plant species are lost. Corn, an annual plant, must be planted every year at the expense of labor, erosion, and fossil fuel subsidies. A plant known as teosinte, an ancestor of corn, was thought to have had several varieties, some annual and some perennial. If a perennial variety of teosinte could be found, modern plant breeding techniques might permit the development of a perennial corn. For many years, only annual varieties of teosinte were discovered. Unfortunately, teosinte grew in only limited areas of Mexico where they were regarded locally as weeds, and it was feared that the perennial varieties—if they ever existed—had been eradicated.

In 1910 a perennial variety of teosinte was discovered.[273] The variety discovered (*Zea perennis*) has the long-sought perennial properties, but unfortunately it has 40 chromosomes and can not be crossed with modern corn, which has 20 chromosomes. The discovery of *Zea perennis* established the fact that a perennial variety of teosinte had in fact existed, but it seemed increasingly likely that the 20-chromosome variety had been lost.

In late 1977 Raphael Guzman, a botany student at the University of Guadalajara, found a new variety of teosinte growing in a remote, mountainous region of Mexico in the state of Jalisco. Guzman's variety (*Zea diploperennis*) has now been examined by Dr. Hugh H. Iltis, Director of the Herbarium at the University of Wisconsin, who reports that *Zea diploperennis* is a perennial variety with the 20 chromosomes necessary for cross-breeding with corn.

The discovery of *Zea diploperennis* opens the possibilities of not only perennial corn, but of corn that can be grown over wide ranges of climate and soil. Furthermore, since *Zea diploperennis* grows successfully in cool, damp places where fungus diseases (such as the 1971 corn blight) abound, cross-breeding may produce varieties that are more resistant to the diseases that now plague corn farming.

Cross-breeding has begun, and fertile offspring have been produced. Dr. Iltis now feels certain that the perennialness of *Zea diploperennis* can be crossed into corn, but cautions that perhaps 10–20 years will be required.

The sobering fact, however, is that the benefits from *zea diploperennis* could easily have been lost, just as the potential benefits from many other plant species are being lost now, especially in the tropics. Dr. Iltis writes of *Zea diploperennis:*

This species could easily have become extinct [before its discovery], and may yet become [extinct] in the wild in the near future. . . . Just this winter I spent 10 weeks exploring for primitive corn in southern Jalisco, Mexico. There is wholesale mass destruction of vegetation [in progress there] on a gigantic scale (e.g., virgin tropical deciduous forest near Puerto Vallarta, 30,000 hectares at a time) by pushing of vegetation into piles with bulldozers, then burning the piles and planting sorghum. . . . The destruction is enormous, terrible and devastating. . . . None of this vegetation has . . . been studied or . . . represented in preserves. Much of such destruction was originally U.S. instigated to "help . . . raise more food." . . . One could not think of a more effective policy . . . to help destroy a livable world![274]

Dr. Iltis has recommended that the mountain range where *Zea diploperennis* was discovered be established as a national park. Instead, he reports, the area is being deforested to provide jobs and to supply wood for making broom handles.[275]

Plant breeders around the world are aware of the rapid rate at which species are being lost, and efforts are being made to protect genetic resources. An International Board for Plant Genetic Resources has been established in Rome with U.N. and national government funding. The Board is encouraging a variety of seed collection, storage, and documentation schemes.[276] The U.S. Department of Agriculture maintains an extensive collection of crop plant specimens which includes more then 60,000 small-grain specimens, but concern is increasing over corporate control of genetic resources. Seed companies owned by multinational conglomerates have large private seed reserves and are lobbying the U.S. Congress to extend patent protection to plant varieties.[276a] The institutes responsible for breeding Green Revolution varieties are developing and expanding their collections, and the Soviet collections are as extensive as our own, if not more so. But as plant geneticist Jack Harlan has pointed out, many of these collections leave much to be desired:

I know these collections too well. Some are better than others; some are better maintained than others. All are incomplete and shockingly deficient in some kinds of materials. They tend to be enormously redundant in certain races showing seemingly endless repetition of combinations and permutations of common items and are cluttered with accessions that float from experiment station to experiment station. On the other hand, some races are hardly represented at all and the wild and weedy gene pools are conspicuously missing. In no collection is there an adequate sampling of the spontaneous races that are the most likely sources of disease and pest resistance. On the whole, the collections we have are grossly inadequate for the burden they will have to bear.[277]

This narrowing of the gene pool may hinder plant breeding in coming years: Traits possessed by local plants (such as tolerance to adverse and eroding soil conditions or insect and bird predation), which may be required by the high-yielding varieties to adapt them to local environmental conditions, may be lost.

Animal genetic resources are facing problems like those affecting the pool of plant genes. Local breeds of livestock are disappearing almost as rapidly as are local crop strains. Due to artificial insemination, changes in livestock populations that might formerly have taken centuries now take place in a few decades. About 80 percent of the cattle strains indigenous to Europe and the Mediterranean are threatened with extinction. Elsewhere, many of the tropical cattle strains are low

in numbers, and programs for their genetic improvement are often weak. Native poultry and pig strains are also threatened in some developing regions. Very little is known about genetic resources for goats, water buffalo, camels, alpacas, llamas, cultivated fish species, and other domesticated animal varieties.[278] Therefore it is not possible to evaluate the loss of genetic diversity among these types of livestock as readily as among crop plants and their progenitors.

Minor Genetic Failure

Regardless of whether major disasters occur, it is clear that further development (or even maintenance) of genetically specialized, high-yield crop strains that are also defensible against pests and diseases will be increasingly difficult. There will be occasional pest and pathogen outbreaks from genetic failures, i.e., when the natural or inbred resistance of a plant (or animal) strain is overcome by pests or pathogens. Many plant breeders now expect a new variety of wheat to last only about a decade before pests and pathogens evolve a way around the variety's defenses.[279] The high-yield Mexican wheats that touched off much of the Green Revolution were carefully bred for resistance to stem rust, leaf rust, and stripe rust. Recently, however, this resistance appears to have begun to break down, and 10 years appears to be the longest that a wheat variety can withstand the constantly evolving attack of the three rusts.[280] As a result, peasant and commercial farmers using high-yield seeds will have to learn to shift varieties when the ones they are using become vulnerable. Furthermore, the production and distribution of seed will have to be developed to the point that one major variety can be substituted for another over large areas on very short notice.*

The trends point to problems for plant breeders. When favored strains cease to be effective, good monitoring and management may be capable of limiting losses, but difficulties will mount. As the probability of plant epidemics increases (due to inbreeding, decreased species disease re-

---

*A far better approach might be to simply avoid monocultures altogether. Plant pathologist J. Artie Browning has described the advantages of diverse cultures modeled on natural ecosystems. He notes: "When used as part of a *diverse* [plant] population, a frequency of only about 30% [resistant plant strain] can be considered adequate protection against the most virulent and prevalent group of strains of the pathogen!" ("Relevance of Knowledge About Natural Ecosystems to Development of Pest Management Programs for Agro-Ecosystems," *Proceedings of the American Phytopathological Society,* 1974, pp. 191–99.)

sistance, and monoculture) and as the number of genetic resources available declines (due to loss of wild habitat and the replacement of local strains with high-yield varieties), major food losses will be increasingly difficult and costly to avoid.

The less developed countries in the tropics may be particularly susceptible to genetic crop failures in the years ahead. The traditional staple foods and export crops of the tropics are often more vulnerable than the global staples, either because they are propagated asexually (with the consequence that all plants in a large area are genetically identical) or because the present collections of their genetic material are very limited—or both.[281] Notable among such vulnerable crops are: plantation crops, such as rubber, oil palm, coffee, and cocoa (whose seeds resist normal methods of storage with the result that the collections of germ plasm are extremely limited); and tropical roots and tubers, such as yams, taro, sweet potato, and cassavas (which are both extremely difficult to store and are commonly propagated by dividing roots, a form of propagation that leads to genetically identical plantings).[282] For crops such as these, the stage is set for disasters on the scale of the coffee blight that ruined Ceylon's coffee industry and the potato blight that struck Ireland.

Genetic engineering may, at some point, reduce dependence on naturally evolved sources of disease-resistant genetic material, but to date there has been little success in the use of induced mutations for generating agriculturally useful plant varieties.[283] Plant cell culturing might eventually improve photosynthetic efficiency and the amino acid balance in plants (from the human point of view) and lead to asexual propagation of crop plants.[284] Should this happen, the world may face even greater genetic uniformity in crops.

Areas in which science and technology could definitely help in combatting genetic vulnerability include increased systematization of existing collections, computerized reference systems, better international exchange of plant disease information, improved warning systems, genetic heterogeneity in agro-ecosystems, and live collections in protected, representative ecosystems.

By the Year 2000

If present trends continue, increasing numbers of people will be dependent on the genetic strains of perhaps only two dozen plant and animal species. These strains will be highly inbred, and the plant strains may have reduced pest and disease resistance and may be planted in large, contiguous monocultures. Plant and animal epidemics will occur as they have in the past, except that in the

future the number of human lives at risk may not be in the millions (as was the case in the Irish potato famine) but in the tens or even hundreds of millions. While the magnitude of the risks involved cannot be measured precisely, the world's history of crop failures due to pests and diseases (including the recent U.S. corn blight) demonstrates that the probabilities of a major failure are not negligible. Furthermore, the costs of even a minor failure would be so high they might offset the gains in yields expected from extensive monocultures of high-yield varieties.

Food and Nonrenewable Fossil Fuels

Modern high-yield agriculture is heavily dependent on fossil fuel inputs.* As Philip Handler, President of the National Academy of Sciences, has observed,

The great gains in cereal production have occurred where modern energy-intensive agriculture—as developed in the United States, largely with federal research support—has combined applied genetics, irrigation, pesticides and herbicides, fertilizer and mechanization to the increase of yields. In effect, modern agriculture utilizes sunlight to transmute fossil fuels into edible crops.[285]

The gains and developments noted by Dr. Handler are illustrated in the U.S. corn (maize) data presented in Table 13–19 (inputs and outputs expressed in common measures) and Table 13–20 (inputs and output expressed in energy equivalents). Perhaps most notable are the declining labor input and the increasing energy inputs through machinery, gasoline, fertilizers, pesticides, herbicides, drying, irrigation, electricity, and transportation. Yields also increase—by 138 percent from 1945 to 1970—but on a list of the 20 major world food crops and nations that regularly achieve the highest yields per hectare of each, the United States, as of 1974, does not appear even once.[286] Furthermore, the energy input table shows that the number of calories returned in food energy per calorie of input energy declines by almost 25 percent over the 1945–70 period. Overall, the U.S. now uses the equivalent of approximately 80 gallons of gasoline to grow an acre of corn.

Increases in energy inputs have been observed throughout the entire U.S. food system. Processing, packaging, and distribution in all ultramodern food systems require about three times as much energy as the production itself.[287] The overall en-

---

*The implications of higher energy prices for the Global 2000 Study's food projections are discussed in Chapter 6.

TABLE 13–19

Average Energy Inputs per Acre in U.S. Corn Production, 1940–70

Input	1945	1950	1954	1959	1964	1970
Labor (*hours per acre*)	23	18	17	14	11	9
Machinery (*thousands of kilocalories*)	180	250	300	350	420	420
Gasoline (*gallons*)	15	17	19	20	21	22
Nitrogen (*pounds*)	7	15	27	41	58	112
Phosphorus (*pounds*)	7	10	12	16	18	31
Potassium (*pounds*)	5	10	18	30	29	60
Seeds for planting (*bushels*)	0.17	0.20	0.25	0.30	0.33	0.33
Irrigation (*thousands of kilocalories*)	19	23	27	31	34	34
Insecticides (*pounds*)	0	0.10	0.30	0.70	1.00	1.00
Herbicides (*pounds*)	0	0.05	0.10	0.25	0.38	1.00
Drying (*thousands of kilocalories*)	10	30	60	100	120	120
Electricity (*thousands of kilocalories*)	32	54	100	140	203	310
Transportation (*thousands of kilocalories*)	20	30	45	60	70	70
Corn yields (*bushel*)	34	38	41	54	68	81

Source: D. Pimentel et al., "Food Production and the Energy Crisis," *Science*, Nov. 2, 1973, pp. 443–48.

TABLE 13–20

Energy Inputs in U.S. Corn Production (in kilocalories)

Input	1945	1950	1954	1959	1964	1970
Labor[a]	12,500	9,800	9,300	7,600	6,000	4,900
Machinery[b]	180,000	250,000	300,000	350,000	420,000	420,000
Gasoline[c]	543,400	615,800	688,300	724,500	760,700	797,000
Nitrogen[d]	58,800	126,000	226,800	344,400	487,200	940,800
Phosphorus[e]	10,600	15,200	18,200	24,300	27,400	47,100
Potassium[f]	5,200	10,500	50,400	60,400	68,000	68,000
Seeds for planting[g]	34,000	40,400	18,900	36,500	30,400	63,000
Irrigation[h]	19,000	23,000	27,000	31,000	34,000	34,000
Insecticides[i]	0	1,100	3,300	7,700	11,000	11,000
Herbicides[j]	0	600	1,100	2,800	4,200	11,000
Drying[k]	10,000	30,000	60,000	100,000	120,000	120,000
Electricity[l]	32,000	54,000	100,000	140,000	203,000	310,000
Transportation[m]	20,000	30,000	45,000	60,000	70,000	70,000
Total inputs	925,500	1,206,400	1,548,300	1,889,200	2,241,900	2,896,800
Corn yield (output)[n]	3,427,200	3,830,400	4,132,800	5,443,200	6,854,400	8,164,800
Kcal return/input kcal	3.70	3.18	2.67	2.88	3.06	2.82

Source: David Pimental et al., "Food Production and the Energy Crisis," *Science*, Nov. 2, 1973, p. 445.

[a] It is assumed that a farm laborer consumes 21,777 kcal per week and works a 40-hour week. For 1970, from Table 13–17: (9 hours/40 hours per week) × 21,770 kcal per week = 4,900 kcal.

[b] The machinery needed to farm 62 acres of corn was estimated to have required 244,555,000 kcal. This machinery was assumed to function for 10 years. Repairs were assumed to be 6 percent of total machinery production. Hence, a conservative estimate for the production and repair of farm machinery per acre of corn for 1970 was 420,000 kcal. A high for the number of tractors and other types of machinery on farms was reached in 1964 and continues. The number of tractors and other types of machinery in 1945 were about half what they are now.

[c] Gasoline: 1 gallon = 36,225 kcal.

[d] Nitrogen: 1 pound = 8,400 kcal, including production and processing.

[e] Phosphorus: 1 pound = 1,520 kcal, including mining and processing.

[f] Potassium: 1 pound = 1,050 kcal, including mining and processing.

[g] Corn seed: 1 pound = 1,800 kcal. This energy input was doubled because of the effort employed in producing hybrid seed corn.

[h] Only about 3.8 percent of the corn grain acres in the United States were irrigated in 1964, and this is not expected to change much in the near future. An estimated 905,600 kcal is required to irrigate an acre of corn with an acre-foot of water for one season. Since only 3.8 percent of the corn acres are irrigated (1964–70), it was estimated that only 34,000 kcal were used per acre for corn irrigation. The percentage of acres irrigated in 1945 was based on trends in irrigated acres in agriculture.

[i] Insecticides: 1 pound = 11,000 kcal, including production and processing.

[j] Herbicides: 1 pound = 11,000 kcal, including production and processing.

[k] When corn is dried for storage to reduce the moisture from about 26.5 percent to 13 percent, 408,204 kcal are needeed to dry 91 bushels (*Corn Grower's Guide*, Aurora, Ill.: Grace and Co., 1968, p. 113). About 30 percent of the corn produced in 1970 was estimated to have been dried, as compared to an estimated 10 percent in 1945.

[l] In 1970, agriculture consumed about 310,000 kcal per acre for fuel used to produce electricity.

[m] The number of calories burned to transport machinery and supplies to corn acres and to transport corn to the site of use was estimated to be about 70,000 kcal per acre in 1964 and 1970 and about 20,000 kcal per acre in 1945.

[n] A bushel of corn was considered to weight 56 pounds, and each pound was assumed to contain 1,800 kcal.

ergy requirements of the U.S. food system are illustrated in Figure 13–5. On a per capita basis, David Pimental estimates that U.S. crop production alone requires about 112 gallons of gasoline per person per year.[288]

The commercial energy requirements for modern and traditional production of rice and corn (maize) are compared in Table 13–21. The only commercial energy input in traditional agriculture is the energy used in making simple tools and implements. But when the commercial energy inputs are low, the yields are also low. In transitional agriculture, more commercial energy is used especially for machinery, fuel, fertilizer, pesticides, improved seeds, and transportation. In transitional agriculture commercial energy inputs may increase by a factor of 10 or more over the commercial energy used in traditional agriculture. Yields may more than double. Modern agriculture involves commercial energy inputs that are more than 100 times those of traditional agriculture. Yields achieved are double to triple those achieved with traditional agriculture.[289]

The energy intensiveness of high-yield agriculture has been studied extensively[290] and is discussed briefly in the food projections in Chapter 6. While the concerns that have emerged cannot be discussed in any detail here, a few need to be mentioned.

The basic concern is that in becoming highly dependent on fossil fuels, modern high-yield agriculture is also becoming vulnerable—both in the short and the long run. In the short run (the next two decades), energy-intensive agriculture will become increasingly vulnerable to the vicissitudes of the energy sector. Even now a sudden price increase or a sudden interruption of petroleum or natural gas supplies could severely affect world agricultural production, raise food prices, and increase the numbers of people who cannot afford adequate food.* If the energy intensiveness of agriculture continues to increase over the next two decades as implied by the projections, the potential disruptiveness (measured in terms of the numbers of persons unable to obtain adequate

nourishment) of an energy supply interruption might well become twice what it is today.

In the long run, agriculture becomes vulnerable through reliance on a depleting resource. David Pimentel estimates that if the world's petroleum reserves were used *exclusively* to provide the world's population with the average U.S. diet as now produced with modern, energy-intensive agricultural methods, the entire 415 billion barrel reserve would last a mere 29 years—or 107 years if all potential reserves (about 2,000 billion barrels) became available. If the world population were to subsist on corn grain only, the same potential petroleum reserves would provide enough energy to supply food for a population of 10 billion for 448 years![291]

The prospect of increasing energy dependence and vulnerability in agriculture has led to some preliminary examinations of alternative approaches.[292] Most of the options so far examined involve relatively small farm units, less substitution of fossil energy for human energy and skill, and the use of "intermediate" or "appropriate" technologies.[293]

The prospect of relatively small farm units raises questions of economic efficiency, and it is encouraging to note that the U.S. Department of Agriculture, in its publication "The One-Man Farm," considers that food production on a small scale can be as efficient as production on a larger scale:

The fully mechanized one-man farm, producing the maximum acreage of crops of which the man and his machines are capable, is generally a technically efficient farm. From the standpoint of costs per unit of production, this size farm captures most of the economies associated with size. The chief incentive for farm enlargement beyond the optimum one-man size is not to reduce unit costs of production, but to achieve a larger business, more output, and more total income.[294]

Encouraging as some of the preliminary investigations are, two points must be kept in mind. First, present trends are overwhelmingly in the direction of further energy intensiveness of agriculture; *major* technological and policy changes would be required to reverse this trend. Second,

---

*In this connection it should be noted that energy-intensive food is "inexpensive" in the United States only because per capita income is high by world standards. U.S. costs of production in the U.S. are high compared to those of many other countries. For example, the cost of producing 1,000 kcal of plant product is estimated to be about $38 in the U.S. and about $10 in India (Pimental et al., "Food Production and the Energy Crisis," *Science*, Nov. 2, 1973, p. 448). Because many LDCs can produce food less expensively than the U.S., some observers expected LDCs to export significant amounts of food

(and cotton and rubber) to earn foreign exchange, even though their own populations are malnourished. Land tenure is a contributing factor. Much good farmland in the LDCs (and increasingly in the industrialized nations) is held by landlords or corporations and is farmed for export, not local consumption. Such exports, if they develop significantly, would also affect the U.S. balance of payments (CIA National Foreign Assessment Center, "The Role of the LDCs in the U.S. Balance of Payments," Washington, Sept. 1978).

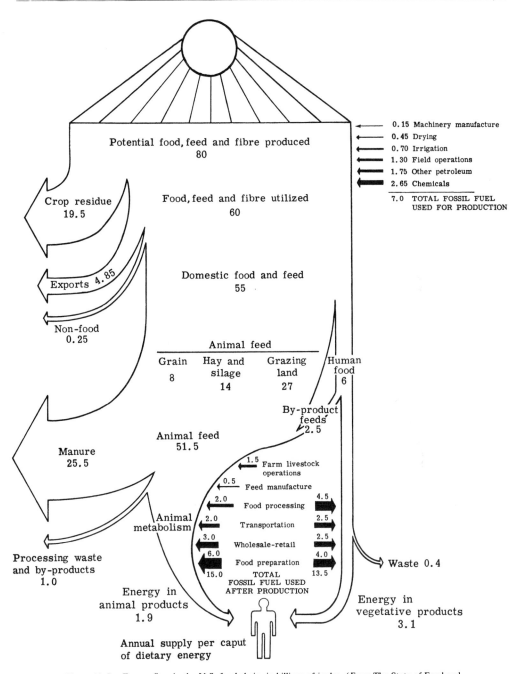

Figure 13–5. Energy flow in the U.S. food chain, in billions of joules. (*From* The State of Food and Agriculture 1976, *FAO, 1977; adapted from F. C. Stickler et al.,* Energy from Sun to Plant, to Man, *Deere & Co., 1975*)

TABLE 13–21

Commercial Energy Required for Rice and Corn (Maize) Production, by Modern, Transitional, and Traditional Methods

Input	Rice — Modern (United States) Quantity per hectare	Energy per hectare	Rice — Transitional (Philippines) Quantity per hectare	Energy per hectare	Rice — Traditional (Philippines) Quantity per hectare	Energy per hectare	Maize — Modern (United States) Quantity per hectare	Energy per hectare	Maize — Traditional (Mexico) Quantity per hectare	Energy per hectare
		10^6 joules		10^6 joules		10^6 joules		10^6 joules		10^6 joules
Machinery and implements[a]	4.2×10^9 joules	4,200	335×10^6 joules	335	173×10^9 joules	173	4.2×10^9 joules	4,200	173×10^6 joules	173
Fuel[b]	224.7 liters	8,988	40 liters	1,600	—	—	206 liters	8,240	—	—
Nitrogen fertilizer[c]	134.4 kg	10,752	31.5 kg	2,520	—	—	125 kg	10,000	—	—
Phosphate fertilizer[d]	—	—	—	—	—	—	34.7 kg	586	—	—
Potassium fertilizer[e]	67.2 kg	605	—	—	—	—	67.2 kg	605	—	—
Seeds[f]	112.0 kg	3,360	110 kg	1,650	107.5 kg	—	20.7 kg	621	10.4 kg	—
Irrigation[b]	683.4 liters	27,336	—	—	—	—	351×10^6 joules	351	—	—
Insecticides[g]	5.6 kg	560	1.5 kg	150	—	—	1.1 kg	110	—	—
Herbicides[g]	5.6 kg	560	1.0 kg	100	—	—	1.1 kg	110	—	—
Drying	4.6×10^9 joules	4,600[h]	—	—	—	—	$1,239 \times 10^6$ joules	1,239	—	—
Electricity	3.2×10^9 joules	3,200[h]	—	—	—	—	$3,248 \times 10^6$ joules	3,248	—	—
Transport	724×10^6 joules	724[h]	31×10^6 joules	31	—	—	724×10^6 joules	724	—	—
Total		64,885		6,386		173		30,034		173
Yield (kg/ha)		5,800		2,700		1,250		5,083		950
Energy input yield per unit (10^6 joules/kg)		11.19		2.37		0.14		5.91		0.18

Source: Food and Agriculture Organization. The State of Food and Agriculture 1976. Rome. 1977. p. 93

a Energy input to produce 1 kg of equipment assumed to be 68.7 × 10^6 joules.
b One liter of fuel assumed to contain 40 × 10^6 joules.
c Production of 1 kg of nitrogen fertilizer assumed to require 80 × 10^6 joules.
d Production of 1 kg of phosphate fertilizer assumed to require 14 × 10^6 joules.
e Production of 1 kg of potassium fertilizer assumed to require 9 × 10^6 joules.
f Production of 1 kg of high-quality seed assumed to require 30 × 10^6 joules in the United States and 15 × 10^6 joules in the Philippines and Mexico.
g Production of 1 kg of pesticide assumed to require 100 × 10^6.
h Assumed to be similar to figures given for maize by David Pimentel et al., "Food Production and the Energy Crisis," Science, Nov. 2, 1973, p. 444

population growth may make energy-intensive agriculture inevitable. The People's Republic of China has probably been more successful than any other country in developing its agriculture with minimum energy requirements. The Chinese experience and other experiments[295] demonstrate clearly that there are alternatives to the most energy-intensive agricultural methods. Yet even China has been forced by the food needs of an expanding population to import energy-rich chemical fertilizers and has contracted for the construction of 13 large nitrogen fertilizer plants.[296]

Conclusions

It has often been observed that agricultural resources are renewable: A hectare of farmland can grow as many as three crops annually; soil fertility can be maintained and often improved; biomass can be consumed and yet grow again another year. While these points are all true, they do not provide an adequate perspective for consideration of agricultural prospects in the decades ahead, particularly beyond the year 2000.

There are three critically important facts to be kept in mind when considering agricultural prospects for the future. First, agriculture is now and will continue to be based largely on depletable resources. Second, at present these depletable resources—crucial to the maintenance and renewal of land, water, and other renewable agricultural resources—are being consumed, extinguished, and eroded at rates that cannot be sustained indefinitely. Third, for the foreseeable future, there is no end in sight to increasing population levels and to escalating needs for agricultural production.

The depletable nature of a number of basic agricultural resources has been given inadequate attention in the past. There has even been occasional confusion as to what the basic resources of agriculture are. Biomass is not a basic agricultural resource, but genetic stocks of crop plants and of domestic animals and beneficial insects are. These agricultural resources are being depleted or rendered extinct at an accelerating rate that alarms many scientists. Soil is a basic agricultural resource, but it is a depleting, salifying, and eroding resource. Lost soil fertility often can be restored, but only after long periods of time and at great cost. Furthermore, in some instances soil fertility simply cannot be renewed: Soils lost by erosion, by urban and industrial expansion, and by hydroelectric development are permanent losses for agriculture. Solar energy is a basic agricultural resource, but fossil fuels are too. Fossil fuels are

a depletable, nonrenewable resource, required for production of chemical fertilizers, pesticides, and fertilizers, and for mechanization and irrigation. Water, too, is a basic agricultural resource, but an exhaustible resource of finite extent, threatened by competing uses, dissolved salts, and acid rain.

The knowledge, technologies, and management techniques needed to protect the basic, depletable resources of agriculture are generally established, but often not known or available where they are most needed. Careful cultivation practices and well-known techniques of terracing, for example, can reduce soil losses. The preservation of habitat for the maintenance of genetic stocks requires no elaborate technologies. But the technological knowledge and capital necessary to successfully use marginal soils is not available to many of the farmers who will be forced to use these soils in the years ahead. Similarly the skills needed for safe and effective use of fertilizers or for alternative methods of pest control are not widely available in many less developed countries.

Although further research is certainly called for (e.g., the atmospheric effects of nitrous oxide from fertilizer applications is not known with certainty), the skills and technologies needed to limit virtually all of the environmental pressures implicit in the Global 2000 Study's food projections are already available. The big question is: Will these skills and technologies be used?

There is no clear answer to this question. Conflicts are involved. The need to increase agricultural production will certainly continue since a large fraction of the world's population is inadequately nourished even now and since throughout the foreseeable future the world's population is projected to continue growing. Historically, increases in agricultural production have come both from increasing the lands under cultivation and from increasing yields per hectare. Options for increasing the lands under cultivation are now limited and expensive, and becoming more so. Therefore efforts to increase yields on lands already under cultivation can be expected to intensify. Unless marginal lands are introduced with skill and moderation, and unless efforts to increase yields are carefully managed, environmental stresses will follow—erosion, laterization, alkalinization, salinization, waterlogging, urban encroachment, and loss of plant, animal, and predator-insect species. If unabated, these stresses could lead initially to a significant reduction in the expansion of food production and in time to a serious reduction in the world's capacity to maintain food production. As noted in the beginning of this section, the Global 2000 food projections are based on the assumption that steps will be taken to keep the impact of these stresses in line with past experience. If these stresses are not controlled, they could bring into serious question even the modest increases in per capita food availability projected in Chapter 6.

To what extent will farmers, governments, and international organizations act to protect the world's depletable agricultural resources? Several nations have already faced the kinds of agriculturally related environmental pressures that are expected to occur worldwide. Some of these nations have successfully maintained or expanded their agricultural capacities. The People's Republic of China and Israel are examples. Several other nations, of which Haiti and Ethiopia are examples, have so far been unable to respond successfully. Most nations have yet to experience the pressures and face the policy decisions.

Success in efforts to protect depletable agricultural resources will require a concerted public effort to set priorities for both food production and environmental protection and to finance ecologically positive technologies and management techniques. Issues relating to land tenure will also be important.[297] Unfortunately, efforts to maintain and expand the productivity of agricultural resources often increase unit costs and reduce production, at least in the short run. In the face of increasing costs of food, it is uncertain that the public support required to accomplish these objectives will be made even in the affluent industrialized nations—and far less certain in the LDCs, which face the greatest pressures to increase food production in years ahead.

The agricultural and population policies that nations develop over the next two decades will have lasting significance. The possibility of a serious erosion and depletion of the world's depletable agricultural resources cannot be ignored. Unless the pressures on these resources are addressed and resolved, at least in part before the year 2000, it appears virtually certain that the world's per capita food production will slow, stagnate, or even decline during the first half of the 21st century.

THE PROJECTIONS AND THE MARINE ENVIRONMENT

The Projections

Many of the Global 2000 projections and their implicit consequences have implications for the future of the marine environment. The projections that are most relevant are as follows:

Population. A 45–65 percent increase in human population will lead to substantial increases in the amount of coastal development.

Gross National Product. Coupled with projected population growth, doubling and tripling of GNPs will lead to global increases in water and airborne pollutants and to increases in economic activities—such as dredging and the construction of port facilities—that alter the coastal marine environment.

Agriculture. An increase by a factor of 2.5 in global use of fertilizer, pesticides, and other yield-enhancing inputs will lead to a marked growth in the quantities of nutrients and toxic chemicals entering the marine environment.

Fisheries. The intense demand projected for fishery resources (83.5 million metric tons by 2000) will result in severe pressure on preferred stocks and increased exploitation of nontraditional, smaller, and shorter-lived species. Pollution and physical destruction of marine habitats will impede the growth of aquaculture in estuarine and coastal areas, effectively reducing the overall potential yields of living marine resources.

Forestry. A 15–20 percent decrease in the area under forest cover, with most of the reduction taking place in LDCs, will lead to a sizable increase in the silt loads of tropical river systems and thus to increased silt deposition in estuaries, deltas, and on adjacent coastal shelves.

Water. Hydraulic engineering of freshwater systems will alter salinity concentrations and cyclic flows in estuaries, and will interfere with the life cycles of organisms that spend part of their lives in the ocean and part in freshwater. Because nutrients will be trapped behind new dams, the quantity and quality of estuarine and coastal productivity will be adversely affected.

Energy. More offshore drilling, more marine transport of oil, and more portside storage and processing facilities will be needed to sustain the projected 3.3–4.4 percent annual increase in demand for oil. More petroleum pollutants will enter the oceans. Proliferation of onshore and offshore power plants will result in extensive use of oxidants and other biocides (especially chlorine) to prevent biological fouling in cooling towers, entrainment, and thermal pollution, altering the habitat of marine organisms. The increased use of nuclear energy may lead to accidental release or to deliberate disposal of radioactive materials into the oceans.*

Nonfuel Minerals. More mining wastes will be produced and more mineral products will be in circulation, due in part to increased production of various minerals from lower grade ores. As a result, more of these wastes will enter the earth's air and freshwater systems and, eventually, the oceans. Of particular concern are toxic wastes resulting from increased production of several heavy metals. Chromium production is projected to increase annually by 3.3 percent, copper by 2.9 percent, lead by 3.1 percent, mercury by 0.5 percent, and zinc by 3.1 percent. Increased industrial dredging for gravel and coral sands will also have significant local impacts. If initiated, deep-sea mining operations will produce locally disruptive effects on open-ocean ecosystems.

In summary, while the projections are usually not sufficiently detailed to provide specific quantitative estimates, they do imply a variety of impacts on the marine environment. Worldwide population growth will contribute to increased economic development of the earth's coastlines and their estuaries. Industrial, agricultural, and domestic pollution, coupled with hydraulic engineering of freshwater systems, will adversely affect biological productivity in coastal waters and interfere with aquaculture. Growing demand for commercially preferred fish will increase pressures on these stocks. Overfishing may increase, and a growing proportion of the global catch will be composed of nontraditional species. Continued deforestation will lead to destructive silt deposition in river estuaries, deltas, and on adjacent coastal shelves. More energy-related pollutants—petroleum hydrocarbons, radioactive materials, and waste heat—will enter the oceans, and the increased production of various minerals will add to the amount of toxic wastes entering coastal waters. Dredging and deep-sea mining will disrupt coastal and oceanic ecosystems.

Introduction

The earth is truly a water planet. The waters of the oceans cover 71 percent of the earth's surface and amount to 97 percent of the earth's total water supply. So vast is this volume that more than 200,000 years would be needed by a river the size of the Amazon to drain the world's oceans.

For an understanding of the future of the

---

*There are two emerging energy technologies that deserve note here — Ocean Thermal Energy Conversion (OTEC) and deep water hydrocarbon exploration. Neither of these technologies are projected to be making a major contribution to the world's energy supplies by 1990 (where the DOE projections stop), but both may be in early growth stages by 2000. Both may have very significant impacts on the marine environment.

The OTEC technology utilizes the temperature difference between the warm surface water and the cold deep water to generate electricity. OTEC plants are likely to be anchored in deep waters close to subtropical and tropical islands. Each plant may take in and discharge as much water as the flow of a large river. Environmental effects could include death of vast numbers of plankton, and larvae of coastal and oceanic fishes and benthic organisms by entrainment through heat exchang-

ers, chemical anti-fouling treatments using chorine or other biocides, and thermal shock.

Hydrocarbon exploration and production will occur in progressively deeper waters, introducing into vulnerable oceanic ecosystems unprecedented quantities of drilling muds and cuttings, well treatment fluids, oily brines, natural gas flared underwater, and oil spills. Oil spills are a special concern because production in oceanic waters will probably be by seabed systems rather than above-water platforms, making blowout repairs and spill cleanup operations particularly difficult. (*Ocean Thermal Energy Conversion 1977: Environmental Development Plan (EDP)*, Washington: U.S. Department of Energy, 1978; James J. Geraghty et al., *World Atlas of the United States*, Port Washington, N.Y.: Water Information Center, 1973.)

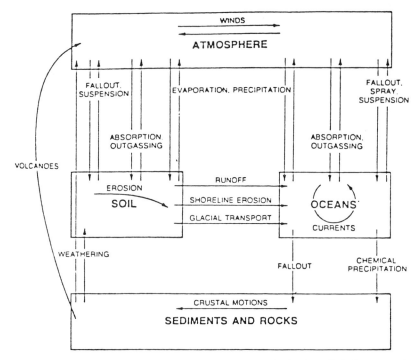

Figure 13–6. Transport mechanisms linking the oceans with the other principal parts of the physical world. (From Ecoscience: Population, Resources, Environment by Paul R. Ehrlich, Anne H. Ehrlich, and John P. Holdren. *W. H. Freeman and Company, Copyright © 1977, p. 69*)

world's environment, the immensity of the oceans is important for two reasons. First, because of their size and other properties, the oceans have a major role in determining the energy flows and the macroenvironment of the entire planet. Thus the condition of the oceans is of planetary significance. Second, the oceans' enormous size provides a large amount of dilution and stability. As a result, change comes slowly to the oceans, and changes are often difficult to detect and even more difficult to control.

The major flows involved in the oceans' influence on the world's macroenvironment are illustrated in Figure 13–6. Through evaporation, precipitation, and runoff, the oceans are linked with the atmosphere and soil in determining the primary flows of solar energy and thus the planet's temperature distribution and climate. The massive heat storage capacity of the oceans is one of the strongest stabilizing influences on the planet's climate.

The absorption and outgassing flows noted in Figure 13–6 are simplified representations of the highly complex carbon and oxygen cycles, which, through photosynthesis in plants and respiration in most organisms, further link oceans, soil, and atmosphere. In the oceans, minute phytoplankton annually fix 40 billion tons of carbon from carbon dioxide and release billions of tons of oxygen.[298] Both oxygen and carbon dioxide gases are exchanged with the atmosphere. Settling and decomposition provide nutrients and energy to life in the lower ocean-water strata.

Although there are still uncertainties, the major stabilizing functions of the oceans—the water, oxygen and carbon cycles—are not likely to be seriously disrupted over the next two decades. The major impacts on the oceans are more likely to occur as a result of yet another function of the oceans, namely, as the ultimate receptacle for much of the world's unwanted waste materials—toxic substances, sediments, agricultural chemicals, oil, sewage, and solid litter.

The flows toward the oceanic "sink" are also illustrated in Figure 13–6. Most of the waste flows start on land and move through runoff, dumping, evaporation, precipitation, fallout, and absorption into the ocean waters. Marine transportation, seabed oil development, and seabed mining also contribute to the flow of damaging wastes.

A major impact on living marine resources is implied by the Global 2000 Study's projections. These resources now make an important contribution to the economics, health, and welfare of many nations. Fisheries contribute about 2 percent of the food calories consumed globally by humans, and directly supply approximately 14 percent of the world's animal protein consumed by humans. In a number of LDCs and industrialized nations, such as Iceland, Japan, the Philippines, and Vietnam, animal protein from ocean organisms is a major component of the national diet, in some cases making up over one-half of animal protein consumption.[299] Any reduction in calories and protein from the oceans will have serious implications for the populations of such areas.

Major changes in the composition of living marine resources are anticipated, especially in the coastal waters. These changes will come about as a result of habitat destruction and waste deposition and concentration, and particularly from pollutants such as synthetic organic chemicals and heavy metals. In some areas habitat destruction is proceeding rapidly and is a major threat. Contamination of the marine environment occurs at different rates in different areas. Its seriousness depends on a number of considerations.

Because of their enormous volume, ocean waters are potentially capable of much dilution of polluting wastes. However, the ocean waters themselves are not the ultimate resting place for many wastes entering the oceans. Some materials are biologically degraded; others are transported by particulate fallout and chemical precipitation to the sediments of the ocean floor, as indicated in Figure 13–6. The rate at which wastes reach various parts of the ocean is therefore important in determining their concentration and ultimate fate. There is extreme variation in the times required.

There are two basic kinds of marine ecosystems: coastal and oceanic. Table 13–22 briefly describes these two ecosystems and indicates (1) the type of pollution affecting each kind, (2) the effects of the pollution, and (3) the duration of the effects. One fact that stands out strikingly in the table is that the highly productive coastal waters—including the world's estuaries, coastal wetlands, reefs, and the many marginal seas over the continental shelves and slopes[300]—account for only 10 percent of the total area of the global marine environment, whereas the relatively less productive (biologically speaking) open oceans constitute 90 percent.

An important distinction between coastal and oceanic waters is the large difference in the duration of effects from various pollutants, many of which have only relatively short-term effects in coastal waters. Although these effects are ex-

TABLE 13–22

Categories of Ocean Areas and Types of Pollution, with Effects on Uses and Their Duration

Types of Pollution	Effects on Uses and Pollution Trends	Duration of Effects
COASTAL WATERS *(10 percent of total area; 99 percent of total fish production[a])*		
Sewage; industrial wastes; litter; petroleum hydrocarbons	Living resources destroyed or rendered unusable; industrial uses of seawater adversely influenced; amenities reduced; recreational values diminished	Short-term; mainly during period of discharge
Synthetic organic chemicals; metals; radioactivity	Living resources decreased or rendered unusable	Long-term; metals and synthetic organic chemicals deposited in sediments may be released for a long time through normal leaching and/or dredging disturbance
OPEN OCEAN *(90 percent of total area; 1 percent of total fish production[b])*		
Synthetic organic chemicals; metals; petroleum hydrocarbons; radioactivity	Increasing concentrations in water and organisms may indicate dangerous trends	Long-term; duration depends on the residence time of pollutant

Source: Michael Waldichuk, *Global Marine Pollution: An Overview,* Paris: UNESCO, 1977, p. 12.

[a] Including fish production from upwelling area.   [b] Excluding fish production from upwelling area.

tremely serious in some instances, their intensity may be reduced rapidly after the discharge is terminated. Other pollutants can have longer-term effects due to bioaccumulation and accumulated sedimentary deposits. In the open ocean, pollutants have the potential to produce delayed effects. In addition to bioaccumulation and interactions with coastal zone sediments, pollutant effects on the open ocean are prolonged, since most ocean waters below a depth of 100 meters exchange with surface and coastal waters relatively slowly—usually over time periods on the order of hundreds or thousands of years.[301]

Because deep open-ocean waters are so different from coastal waters in the rate at which they receive and experience the effects of pollutants, these two major ocean areas will be considered separately. The implications of the Global 2000 Study projections for coastal waters are considered first under the following topics: coastal development; coastal pollution; and overexploitation of living marine resources.

The implications of the projections for the deep open-ocean waters must be examined separately. Not enough time will have elapsed by the year 2000 for projected developments to greatly affect these waters. The discussion of the open ocean, therefore, will be primarily in terms of the trends established over the next two decades that will ultimately have implications for oceanic ecosystems.

Effects of Coastal Development

The earth's coastal waters and ecosystems are important for human society because they are highly productive biologically and because they support a wide range of economic activities. These ecosystems are strongly influenced by changes in the physical and biological conditions of the coastal seabed and adjacent land.[302] Many of the Global 2000 Study's projections suggest a variety of coastal developments that can be expected to cause extensive and adverse changes in the biological productivity of the world's coastal zones.

In the next two decades, a significant consequence of many of the Global 2000 projections will be a dramatic growth in coastal development. Population pressures will lead to rapid rates of coastal settlement and urbanization, especially in LDCs. Rivers emptying into estuaries will be dammed to ensure adequate supplies of water for burgeoning metropolitan areas and agriculture. Rising GNPs and energy demand will encourage the expansion of coastal industrial facilities, and the consequent development will have serious impacts upon the marine environment.

Coastal dredging is likely to be extensive. The Global 2000 Study's minerals, technology, energy, population, and GNP projections indicate that offshore dredging for landfill, improved port and waterway facilities, and construction material can be expected to continue. Coastal dredging of anchorages and channels destroys the immediate benthic area and, through sedimentation, can affect more distant zones. Commercial dredging of gravel, coral, and coral sands is already conducted in many areas in waters as much as 100 meters in depth.

Marine transportation is still the cheapest, most energy-efficient mode of transporting materials in bulk, and the Study's food, minerals, and energy projections suggest that it will accelerate at least as much over the next few decades as in the last few. Gross registered tonnages of ocean vessels have grown by 9 percent annually during recent years, while the volumes transported have increased by 6–9 percent.[303] If present growth rates continue, marine transport will have increased three to sevenfold by the year 2000. To accommodate the increased marine traffic, existing port facilities will have to be expanded significantly, and corresponding increases in secondary economic activities and human settlement in coastal areas can be anticipated. Dredging, filling, paving, and construction of terminals, factories, settlements, and service roads will increase noise, air and water pollution, and will greatly reduce productivity, diversity, and stability of coastal and adjacent ecosystems. Increasing marine traffic may bring proportional increases in catastrophic spills and chronic pollution from discharges of ballast and tank washings. However, international agreements requiring the use of navigation aids, segregated ballast tanks, and other features to reduce oil pollution should diminish adverse effects of increased marine traffic.[303a]

A less widely recognized problem is "biological pollution," the introduction of nonnative species into coastal ecosystems. Newly introduced species freed of their natural predators, parasites, and competitors can severely disrupt food webs, diversity, and stability and may effectively eliminate valuable native living marine resources. Besides marine transportation-related sources of biological introduction such as ballast waters, bio-fouling on vessels and mobile drilling rigs, and sea level canals, nonnative species may be introduced deliberately or accidentally, as in clumps of transplanted oysters.[303b]

Once established, settlements, factories, refineries, power plants, and port facilities along the coastal zones are not easily—nor are they likely to be—relocated. Furthermore there is a limit to the modification feasible should their presence or their delayed, indirect environmental impact prove severely damaging to coastal ecosystems. The expected result of the next two decades of development along coastlines is damaging physical alteration or total destruction of habitat—particularly in estuaries and wetlands and on coral reefs—that will adversely affect marine organisms and natural nutrient and waste cycling processes.

Impacts on Estuaries and Coastal Wetlands

Estuaries,* and the salt marshes and mangrove communities that make up coastal wetlands, are globally widespread. One third of the population of the United States lives and works in regions surrounding estuaries, and of the 10 largest metropolitan areas in the world, seven border existing or former estuarine regions (New York, Tokyo, London, Shanghai, Buenos Aires, Osaka, and Los Angeles). Estuaries and coastal wetlands accumulate natural riverborne sediments as well as wastes from nearby urban areas. Nutrients are cycled in estuaries and wetlands. Large phytoplankton and zooplankton populations responsible for the high productivity of global coastal fisheries, as well as benthic plant production, algae, salt marsh grasses, seagrasses and mangrove communities result from this rich nutrient supply. It is estimated that 60–80 percent of the commercial marine fisheries species are dependent upon estuarine ecosystems during part or all of their life cycles.[304]

Salt marshes and mangrove communities are distributed all over the world and are either associated with estuaries or coastal barrier islands.[305] Intertidal salt marshes are an exceptionally fertile part of coastal zone estuarine ecosystems. Salt marsh grasses recycle mineral and organic nutrients entering the marsh environment, creating an area of biological productivity that can yield 10 tons of organic material per acre per year.[306] Cyclic tidal flooding circulates detritus and dissolved nutrients to other marsh areas and to offshore organisms. Much of the decomposing plant matter goes to the floor of the marsh, producing rich deposits of organic peat. Ultimately, low tidal marshes can actually build themselves up and out of the tidal range,[307] contributing to

coastline stabilization. Lush salt marshes also provide a habitat for a wide variety of fish, shellfish, wildfowl and mammals. Many ducks, geese and other waterfowl use coastal wetlands as resting stations and feeding grounds during migratory movements. Fish such as flounder and bluefish may make transient use of marshes for feeding, overwintering or as nurseries.[308]

Like salt marshes and estuaries, tropical mangrove communities are highly productive. The net primary production from mangrove ecosystems is utilized by a variety of organisms in a complex, detritus-based food web. As a transitional ecological belt, mangroves serve to protect the shoreline, are a source of raw materials for human populations, act as a shelter for bird and mammal species, and are nursery and breeding grounds for freshwater and marine organisms. A large number of commercially important fish and shellfish of the tropical coastal waters depend directly or indirectly on mangrove communities for food and shelter during their lives.[309]

The water, food, climate, and population projections imply that future water-supply and conservation efforts may include construction of freshwater dams and irrigation works. However useful these projects may be, they may reduce the diversity, productivity, and stability of the marine environment. Already, the damming of rivers flowing into estuaries reduces the size of wetlands and diminishes the flow and alters periodicity of freshwater entering the coastal zone. As yet, little definitive information is available with which to anticipate the ultimate effect of such human manipulation of the hydrology of salt marshes and mangrove communities,[310] but it can be reasonably expected that global damming or diversion of estuarine river systems will disturb or destroy many estuarine habitats for fish and wildlife, and will disrupt the normal processes of nutrient supply and cycling. As a consequence, estuarine ecosystems and their distribution and abundance of plants and animals can be expected to be significantly altered.[311]

Salt marshes have historically been filled or dredged to accommodate the needs of human settlements, agriculture, and industry the world over.[312] The alteration of salt marsh wetlands continues today for the establishment of new residences, for recreation, and industry. In the United States, commercial "finger-fill" lagoons have been dredged out of salt marsh to provide docking space for marinas and land for housing sites.[313] Salt marshes have been dredged for boat and ship harbors in the course of commercial development of coastal barrier islands as well.[314] These practices

---

*"Estuary" has been used to describe the lower reaches of a river in which seawater mixes with freshwater. The definition can be expanded to include bays, inlets, gulfs, and sounds into which several rivers empty and in which the mixing of fresh- and saltwater occurs. (Charles B. Officer, "Physical Oceanography of Estuaries," *Oceanus*, Fall 1976, p. 4).

are environmentally detrimental. Instead of the healthy flushing of salt marsh organic matter into adjacent waters, the organic matter collects on the stagnant canal bottoms, depleting the oxygen from the canal waters, thus killing or driving away valuable fish and shellfish.[314a] Leftover dredge spoils from channel and boat basin construction— and from their subsequent maintenance dredging—often have been dumped on nearby undisturbed wetlands, where they smothered established plant life and bottom-dwelling animals, polluted soil and water, and drastically altered the overall topography of the marsh.[315] Dredge spoils are often dumped in offshore coastal waters, and the resulting spoil deposits smother and intoxicate benthic organisms. Sediments mobilized and resuspended by bottom currents and upwellings can also move the spoil material inshore, or pollute more removed areas.[315a]

Salt marsh lands have been regarded globally as prime areas for industrial siting. Marshes also bear the brunt of the often environmentally destructive aftermath of economic development. For example, new refineries, power stations, and dikes are being planned for construction on marshy European coastlines.[316] Rivers carrying industrial pollutants contaminate their own estuarine marshes as well as those adjoining or connected by coastal currents; chemicals, metals, and petroleum pollutants carried to the sea in the Rhine River have tended to move northward to pollute the Wadden Zee tidal flats in the Netherlands.[317]

Mangrove ecosystems are also facing destruction through development. In many countries with large and rapidly expanding populations, mangrove areas are seen as areas for human settlement and zones of more intensive exploitation— as in southern Florida, U.S.A., where extensive areas of mangrove have been bulldozed and then filled with dredged sediments to create land for housing developments.[318]

Mangrove communities have been destroyed to make way for other forms of land use such as fish ponds, urban development, and industrial sites. Coastal mining, logging without replanting, and military defoliation have destroyed mangroves as well.[319] Destructive influences on mangrove communities also include the diversion or regulation of freshwater streams and rivers. The resulting reduction of freshwater flows cause estuarine soils to become excessively salinized, a condition in which mangroves cannot survive. As a result of these varied development practices during the 1960s and 1970s, there has been widespread and rapid degradation or destruction of extensive mangrove areas along the coasts of the Americas, Africa, east and west Malaysia, the Philippines, Indonesia, Vietnam, Singapore, east and west India, east and south Australia, and south Thailand.[320]

Impacts on Coral Reefs

The loss to the marine environment of coral reef ecosystems is great. Coral reefs are among the most extensive and productive shallow marine communities.[321] Reef habitats, comparable in complexity and diversity to tropical rain forests,[322] provide food and shelter for approximately one-third of all fish species and for seemingly countless invertebrates, some of which contain or produce a wide range of pharmacologically active compounds. In addition, reefs function as buffers against ocean forces. As self-repairing, energy-dissipating breakwaters, they protect thousands of miles of continental and island coastlines from erosion in Southeast Asia, the Middle East, the Central and South Pacific and the Caribbean.[323]

Coral reefs in the U.S. Virgin Islands, Micronesia, the Seychelles, Puerto Rico, the Bahamas, Hawaii, and Florida have been damaged or destroyed entirely as a result of poorly planned and managed dredging.[324] Continued destruction of coral reef habitats through dredging activities will ultimately affect the marine environment and its coastal productivity and protection capabilities.

In short, anticipated coastal development will lead to large-scale destruction of estuaries, coastal wetlands (salt marshes and mangroves), and coral reefs. Notwithstanding the vital role of these areas in maintaining coastal productivity and protection, coastal development during the present century has already reduced the total world acreage significantly.[325]

If present trends continue throughout the next two decades, the increases in human population density and industrial and commercial activity will have yet more substantial effects on the biological productivity of the oceans' coastal waters. The habitats provided by estuaries, salt marshes, mangrove communities, and reefs will suffer the stresses of coastline development, and their loss will contribute significantly to changes in size and species composition of the global fisheries catch.

Coastal Pollution

Coastal waters the world over constantly receive direct injections of polluting materials through river discharge, coastal outfalls, dumping, and atmospheric transport.[326] The agriculture, population, minerals, forestry, and energy projections suggest that the amount of pollutants entering the coastal zones will increase between now and the year 2000. Toxic chemical contamination, as yet largely uncontrolled, is likely to have the most damaging impact. While only a small number of all toxic chemicals are of agricultural origin, even the projected increases in pesticide and herbicide use have serious implications for the coastal environment. Pollution from expanding use of fossil fuel energy sources will continue to afflict coastal waters and their living resources. The impact of sewage, silt, and fertilizer nutrients will grow and have critical local and regional consequences. As GNPs rise globally, the volume of solid wastes discarded or deposited in the oceans will increase as well.

Collectively, the anticipated amount of coastal pollution is seen to be a major problem for the marine environment in the future. Pollutant stress on ocean life forms can cause chemical-physical damage to cell membranes or tissues, modification of biochemical reactions, buildup of microbial pathogens, low environmental oxygen levels, viral infections, skeletal anomalies, and genetic abnormalities. Several indicators point to rising levels of pollution in coastal waters. In fish, a degenerative disease syndrome aptly named "fin erosion" is associated with degraded estuarine or coastal environments and has been observed in U.S. coastal waters, in Tokyo Bay, and in the Irish Sea. A similar condition affects crabs, lobsters, and smaller crustaceans.[327] In the New York Bight, heavy municipal and industrial pollution and long-term dumping of dredge, sewage, and industrial wastes has caused fouling of shellfish gills by parasites and detritus.[328] The collection of contaminated shellfish is prohibited in certain areas because of hazards to human health.*

Toxic Waste Pollution

Toxic waste pollution (also discussed above in the section entitled, "The GNP Projections and the Environment.") will be discussed here because many toxic substances eventually find their way into the sea via the atmosphere or continental runoff. By either route, toxic waste pollution is one of the most serious threats to the health of the coastal oceans.

---

*Trends in shellfish contamination and the closure of shellfish beds in the U.S., as well as a description of the innovative Mussel Watch—a monitoring program that uses mollusk tissue pollutant levels as an indicator of estuarine environmental quality—are discussed in "Ecology and Living Resources," Council on Environmental Quality, *Environmental Quality 1979*, Washington: Government Printing Office, forthcoming.

Toxic substances include those that are carcinogenic (causing cancer), mutagenic (producing mutations), and teratogenic (causing birth defects). Many toxic substances possess two—or even all three—of these specific properties.

Over 4 million chemical compounds have been reported to the American Chemical Society for listing in the Society's registry. Of the chemicals listed, about 70,000 are now in production in the United States, 50 in quantities greater than 1.3 billion pounds per year.[329] Unfortunately, not all 70,000 will be adequately tested for toxicity or environmental hazards. Studies to determine environmental persistence, transport, and long-term biological effects are expensive both in time and money, and the substances to be measured are often not only low in concentration but accompanied by other substances that produce synergistic effects and complicate analysis of the data. Relatively few contaminants have been monitored to the point where trends can be detected, and links between human health and the contaminants at the levels at which they occur are only tenuously understood.[330]

One of the gravest perils to human and marine life is that relatively persistent toxic chemicals and metals might build to dangerous levels before being detected, as occurred in the mercury-poisoning incident at Minamata Bay, Japan (see Table 13–28, below). The Minamata Bay tragedy is by no means the only instance in which long-lived toxic chemicals have been released in a way that will ultimately lead to their entry into the oceans. The Kepone contamination of the James River in Virginia provides another example.

Until it was ordered to stop in 1975, a Hopewell, Virginia chemical company under contract to Allied Chemicals had been dumping quantities of chemical waste into the James River in the course of manufacturing the insecticide Kepone. About 1.5 million gallons of highly toxic material were created and dumped. In 1976, the strange symptoms that had been exhibited by workers at the plant manufacturing this white-powder chemical compound were attributed to Kepone poisoning. The acute physical symptoms of this poisoning are evident, but its long-term effects on humans and animals are still unknown. Since Kepone is bioaccumulative and environmentally persistent, aquatic life downriver from Hopewell and in the James River estuary will be affected for many years, even though the source of pollution has been eliminated.[331]

Polychlorinated biphenyls (PCBs) have been in use for half a century. More recently they have been discovered to cause cancer in laboratory animals, and skin diseases, jaundice, and liver damage in humans. In the Baltic Sea, only a few thousand gray seals remain of a population estimated to be 20,000 in 1940, due to the seal's diet of PCB-contaminated fish.[332] In the United States, the Toxic Substances Control Act of 1976 prohibits the sale of PCBs after July 1, 1979, but this persistent chemical will remain in commercial products, municipal dumps, soils, and the sediments of streams, lakes, and ocean coastal zones for years to come.

The Hudson River, already contaminated with a complex mixture of toxic substances, was further contaminated in the early 1970s by approximately 440,000 pounds of PCBs, discharged there by two General Electric capacitor plants. Now, much of the PCB contamination, lodged in the river sediments over a 40-mile stretch between Troy Dam and Hudson Falls, poses a health threat to the 150,000 upstate New Yorkers who drink the river water, as well as a threat to commercial fisheries in the Hudson's estuary. Approximately 6,000 pounds of the accumulated contaminant spills over Troy Dam each year.

In 1976, General Electric agreed to pay the State of New York $4 million for the removal of the polluted sediment. Two years later, the New York State Department of Environmental Conservation was requesting $25 million in federal funds to remove 75 percent of the contaminant from 30–40 of the most contaminated spots in the riverbed. Estimates for dredging the entire 40 miles of polluted sediments are in the hundreds of millions, and would take about 10 years and cause destruction of local sediment life for at least a year or two in each section of the river dredged.[333] In the absence of decontamination, most of the PCBs will ultimately be deposited in the Atlantic Ocean.

Pollution of the James and Hudson Rivers are dramatic illustrations of toxic substance contamination that ultimately is transported to the oceans. While these instances are massive and serious in and of themselves, hundreds of thousands of smaller daily losses of chemicals around the world have even greater implications for the oceans. In the next few pages, marine environmental problems arising from toxic wastes will be discussed by type of pollutant: synthetic organic chemicals, heavy metals, and radioactive materials.

Synthetic Organic Chemicals

Large numbers of different synthetic chemicals enter the oceans through rivers, the atmosphere and offshore coastal dumping of chemical wastes and are now ubiquitous in the oceans.[334] The effects of most of these chemicals has not been carefully studied, and even if the knowledge were available, the numbers of chemicals and their even more numerous effects could not be fully addressed here. The discussion is therefore limited to a few examples from a group of chemicals—halogenated hydrocarbons—about which there is both concern and understanding (albeit limited) of their effects on marine ecosystems. Three heavy halogenated hydrocarbons are considered first, followed by examples of lighter halogenated hydrocarbons.

DDT, polychlorinated biphenyls (PCBs), and hexochlorobenzene are heavy halogenated hydrocarbons over which there continues to be concern. DDT is still widely used in both agricultural and vector control programs in many nations. As discussed in the food and agriculture section of this chapter, the Global 2000 food projections anticipate a large increase—on the order of 2 to 4 times the present amount—in the use of pesticides over the next 20 years. Persistant pesticides such as DDT will almost certainly continue to be used in large and increasing quantities in many areas, especially in the LDCs.

Atmospheric transport is the principal pathway by which DDT and its metabolites reach the oceans.[335] Regional DDT contamination has been shown to have caused reproductive failure in birds and fish. In some cases DDT has proved to be toxic to fish,[336] and has interfered with their chemoreception and natural behavior patterns.[337]

PCBs—stable, relatively insoluble and nonflammable compounds—are now widespread pollutants of the marine environment as a result of inadvertent spills and leakage, breakage of containers, and evaporation. Besides being dangerous to human health, they are toxic to some marine organisms.[338] PCBs (and other heavy halogenated hydrocarbons including DDT and its metabolites, and dieldrin) are known to adversely affect vital estuarine phytoplankton communities. Field and laboratory experiments have shown that a variety of normal functions—including growth, photosynthesis, and cellular development—are inhibited in phytoplankton when they are exposed to chlorinated pesticide concentrations ranging from 1 to 10 parts per billion. Sustained high concentrations were observed to cause cell rupture and ultimate death. As a result, these chemicals in the marine environment may adversely affect natural food chains by altering the quantities and sizes of phytoplankton available for zooplankton grazing. Such changes could in turn disrupt trophic interactions within an estuarine community and could bring about changes in the species composition of many marine ecosystems.[339]

Hexachlorobenzene (HCB) is a stable, unreactive compound used as a grain fungicide and a component in some pesticides. It is produced as a by-product in the manufacture of many chlorinated hydrocarbons. HCB is widely used as a fungicide in the Near East, Australia, the United States, and Eastern and Western Europe.[340] The National Academy of Sciences has identified HCB as a danger to human health and to the environment. Once transferred to the oceans via atmospheric fallout, waste-dumping, or coastal outfalls containing pesticide residues, HCB is resistant to chemical, biological, or physical degradation.[341] It is now present in terrestrial and aquatic food webs, and has been observed to be concentrated in some marine organisms at levels similar to those of DDT and the PCBs.[342]

Halogenated hydrocarbons of low molecular weight are also of concern, but their effects in the environment are different from those of heavier molecules. Compared to the heavy halogenated hydrocarbons, such as DDT, the PCBs, and dieldrin, compounds of lower molecular weight are more water-soluble. They are found in aerosol propellants, fumigants, fire extinguishers, solvents, dielectric insulators, and are used as intermediates of organic synthesis. It is estimated that 6,000 tons of one of these compounds (trichlorofluoromethane) enter the world's oceans annually.[343] These compounds readily evaporate and remain in the atmosphere long enough to make transfer to the oceans highly likely. While low molecular weight compounds are now ubiquitous in the atmosphere and in surface waters,[344] concentrations observed so far in the oceans are six orders of magnitude below the concentrations that cause toxic effects in mammals and aquatic organisms.[345] The long-term impact of these chemicals at low concentrations is unknown, and a continuing buildup of these chemicals could significantly increase both their concentrations and their potential biological consequences.

One aspect of the long-term buildup of synthetic organic chemicals applies to both heavy and light molecules. Unless monitoring increases significantly, pollutant concentrations may grow to unmanageable proportions before they are recognized. By that time, they may have become ecologically dangerous and, even if inputs were to cease, the effects of the materials continuing to circulate in the ecosphere would be manifested for years afterward. DDT use offers an example of this phenomenon.[346] It has been observed that the effects of DDT pollution on a localized or regional scale begin to subside in individual species 3–5 years after input to the ecosystem has halted.[347] On a global scale, however, simulation models suggest that if world application were phased out, a downturn in bioaccumulation and physiological effects might not occur for decades because of the DDT residue remaining in atmospheric, soil, and oceanic reservoirs (Fig. 13–7).

Heavy Metals

All naturally occurring heavy metal elements are found in the oceans at some concentration. Those metals introduced by human society enter via rivers, industrial outfalls and domestic sewers, and through atmospheric transport and offshore dumping of waste materials. As a result, pollution of the marine environment by metals is most evident in the coastal zones, especially where mixing processes between coastal and oceanic waters are slow, facilitating accumulation.[348] Due to their oceanic omnipresence, most heavy metals are now bioaccumulated to some degree in one or more

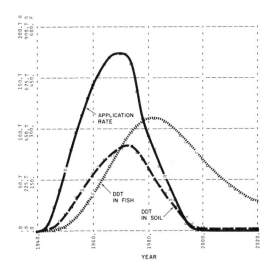

Figure 13–7. The effect of a gradual reduction, starting in 1971, in the use of DDT from a simulation model. The usage rate is assumed to reach zero by the year 2000. The usage rates are historically correct through 1971, when it is assumed that a world decision to phase out the use of DDT is reached. Shortly thereafter, the concentration of DDT in soil begins to decline, but the concentration of DDT in fish continues to increase for 11 years and does not return to the 1971 level until 1995. The response of DDT concentrations in animals further up the food chain—birds and humans, for example—are subject to even longer delays. (*Jørgen Randers, in D. L. and D. H. Meadows, eds., Toward Global Equilibrium, Cambridge, Mass.: Wright-Allen Press, 1973; reprinted by permission of the distributors, MIT Press*)

components of the marine food web.[349] Trace metal concentrations have been measured in fish and shellfish in coastal waters of the United States and New Zealand, the North Atlantic, the North Sea, and other European coastal areas.[350] According to the Global 2000 Study projections, the annual production and circulation of most metals is expected to increase between now and the year 2000. In many cases the rate of accumulation in the oceans of metals injected by human activity is expected to exceed the natural rate (Table 13–23).

The effect of heavy metal concentrations on the development of marine organisms is only beginning to be understood. However, the characteristics of heavy metals are significant. They are among the most environmentally persistent substances. They cannot be transmuted or destroyed and, in concert with certain bacteria, have the insidious attribute of combining with organic substances to form highly toxic metallo-organic compounds. Sometimes these compounds are discharged directly into ocean waters. For example, the "mercury poisoning" at Minamata, Japan, involved spent chemical catalysts containing metallo-organic methyl mercury.[351]

The highest mercury concentrations in ocean organisms are found in the top predators of the food chain. In the past decade there has been concern that the concentration of mercury may increase as more of the metal is released into the environment. However, recent studies suggest that the present mercury levels in these pelagic life forms should not be expected to increase with society's continued use of the metal. The estimated total mercury content of the world ocean mixed layer is currently two orders of magnitude greater than the annual production by human society; therefore, measurable man-made alteration of mercury levels in the open ocean is not probable in the short term. It does appear likely that regional pockets of high-level coastal mercury pollution will continue to exist, due primarily to industrial processes.[352]

Besides input from rivers, urban outfalls, and dumping, concentrations of iron and copper metals in the ocean are atmospherically transported from specific industrial sources, particularly the smelting industry processes for copper and the processes of the iron, steel, and titanium dioxide industries for iron. The National Academy of Sciences has estimated that coal combustion is also one of the most significant human sources of iron and copper introduction to the sea.[353] These metals are partially released during combustion and carried to the oceans in fly-ash particulate matter.

TABLE 13–23

Estimates from Annual River Discharges of Amounts of Metals Injected into the Oceans Annually by Geological Processes and by Man

	By Geological Processes (in rivers)	By Man (in mining)
	(in thousands of metric tons)	
Iron	25,000	319,000
Manganese	440	1,600
Copper	375	4,460
Zinc	370	3,930
Nickel	300	358
Lead	180	2,330
Molybdenum	13	57
Silver	5	7
Mercury	3	7
Tin	1.5	166
Antimony	1.3	40

Source: Michael Waldichuk, Global Marine Pollution: An Overview, Paris: UNESCO, 1977, p. 20.

Current levels of oceanic introduction of iron and copper will not result in major overall concentration changes but will probably increase. Global industrial development will provide a growing source of metallic emissions that will easily enter the world oceans.[354]

Cadmium poisoning in Japan has stimulated an interest in the possible effects of this metal on the marine ecosystem. As with most other metals, cadmium enters the oceans through continental outfalls and the atmosphere. Its bioaccumulation in organisms consumed by humans could potentially be a threat to health. Any significant cadmium pollution would be expected to occur in the coastal zones, and localized high concentrations of cadmium could contaminate marine organisms in coastal waters. However, open-ocean surface water pollution by cadmium metal does not seem probable, at least in the near future.[355]

It appears that, up to this point, lead is the only stable metal element that has exhibited widespread increased concentrations in the ocean. It has been nearly 20 years since concentrations in the oceans were demonstrated to be attaining significant levels through anthropogenic sources.[356] These concentrations have been altered in coastal waters, mainly as a result of the use of lead alkyls as antiknock additives in fuels of internal combustion engines. Lead aerosols have been responsible for the increase of this metal in the coastal surface waters of the Pacific, Atlantic, and Mediterranean Oceans. Once introduced into the sea via coastal runoff and the atmosphere, lead quickly interacts with the marine biota. Concern exists over how human health may be affected by the consumption of lead-contaminated marine resources.[357]

Following a course similar to that of lead in the marine environment, other trace metals still incompletely investigated may have increased their concentration in the surface layers of the global ocean. This is especially possible in northern hemispheric waters surrounding regions of high fossil fuel combustion, cement production, and other industrial activities.[358]

Ultimately, most reactive heavy metals are deposited relatively rapidly in the sediments of the coastal zones, seemingly out of the water layers where they may play a determinate role in biological processes.[359] However, metal accumulation in sediments poses potential problems. Measurement of the extent of metal concentrations have only begun, as have studies of the mechanisms for redistribution of metals back into bottom water and their uptake by benthic organisms.[360] One study has examined the amounts and distribution of six trace metals—cadmium, chromium, copper, nickel, lead, and zinc—in the water and sediments of Raritan Bay, a polluted estuary of the New York Bight. Large amounts of metal-laden municipal and industrial wastes have accumulated in the bay, forcing the termination of shellfish harvesting, decreasing benthic diversity and reducing the yield of commercial fishery species. Metal concentrations in Raritan Bay bottom sediments have been found to be similar to other estuarine areas in the United States and in the United Kingdom.[361] Anoxic coastal sediments containing precipitated mercury sulfide also may release their deposited mercury upon contact with aerated waters.[362]

Artificial Radioactive Materials

The Global 2000 energy projections foresee significant growth in the worldwide development and use of nuclear energy, and this increased nuclear activity may result in increased flows of radioactive materials into the marine environment.

The history of radioactive contamination of the oceans provides a useful context for considering possible future contamination. The largest source of radioactive materials entering the oceans has been nuclear explosions detonated by the United States, the U.S.S.R., the United Kingdom, France, the People's Republic of China and India. Up to 1968 the world's oceans had received much of the radioactive debris from 470 nuclear explosions. Two biologically active fission products—cesium-137 and strontium-90—have been produced at levels of 21 and 34 megacuries, respectively, and much of this material has now entered the oceans.[363]

Although the nuclear test ban has substantially reduced the rate at which radioactive materials enter the oceans, nuclear energy production and the use of radioactive materials has continued the flow of radioactive isotopes into the terrestrial environment and ultimately into the oceans.

The three broad types of radioactive species have been introduced to the marine environment: (1) transuranic elements used as nuclear fuels, such as uranium, neptunium, curium and plutonium; (2) the radionuclides produced as fission products or as induced radioactive species, such as strontium-90 and cesium-137; and (3) the activation products resulting from the interaction of nuclear particles with the components of nuclear reactors and weapons, such as zinc-65 and iron-55. As early as 1972, scientists had detected 52 artificially produced radionuclides in the marine environment.[364]

In the decades ahead, the largest source* of radioactive materials entering the oceans will probably be the nuclear fuel cycle, i.e., the production, use, reprocessing and disposal of nuclear fuels. The Department of Energy projects more than a 200 percent increase in nuclear energy by 2000. How extensive this source will be depends critically on how carefully the fuel cycle is managed.

Table 13–24 presents a projection of the inventory of radionuclides in the world's oceans that has been reported by UNESCO. The total artificial radioactivity in the oceans in 2000 is projected to be of the same order of magnitude as it was in 1970, i.e., about 10^9 curies. Tritium from nuclear reactors increases by three orders of magnitude over the 30-year period, reaching something on the order of 10^8 curies. The largest artificial contribution continues to be tritium from nuclear explosions. The total artificial radioactivity introduced remains two orders of magnitude less than the total natural background of potassium-40 at 5×10^{11} curies, but some of the artificially introduced radionuclides have effects quite different from those of natural potassium-40.[365]

It is not known to what further levels the various radioactive elements could safely be accommodated in the marine environment, especially in crucial coastal zones. So far, only modest efforts have been made to study the environmental impact these substances have upon individual marine organisms or their communities. Transuranics,

---

*Assuming that atmospheric testing of nuclear devices is not resumed.

TABLE 13–24

Total Inventory of Artificial Radionuclides Introduced into the World Oceans, 1970 and 2000

	1970	2000
	Curies	
Nuclear explosions (worldwide distribution)		
Fission products (exclusive of tritium)	$2-6 \times 10^8$	$? \times 10^8$ [a]
Tritium	10^9	$? \times 10^9$ [a]
Reactors and reprocessing of fuel (restricted local distribution)		
Fission and activation products (exclusive of tritium)	3×10^5	3×10^7
Tritium	3×10^5	$? \times 10^8$
Total artificial radioactivity	10^9	10^9
Total natural potassium-40	5×10^{11}	5×10^{11}

Source: A. Preston et al., as reported in Edward E. Goldberg, *The Health of the Oceans,* Paris: UNESCO, 1976, p. 81.
[a] Assuming that atmospheric nuclear testing will continue at about the 1968–70 rate.

fission products, and induced radioactive species are now found in seawater and in the ocean biota almost universally. The biological or environmental significance of this contamination is virtually unknown. [366]

Fossil Fuels

The Study's energy projections anticipate a global growth in commercial energy demand, and a resulting rise in the production and use of fossil fuel energy resources. Driven by expanding GNPs, population needs, and technological advances, this increased energy usage will certainly aggravate the already serious problems of coastal zone degradation by fossil fuel pollutants. The proportions of fuel oil and gas supplies extracted from the seabed are significant and increasing. While large oil spills caused by blowouts and tanker collisions can have disastrous local effects on coastal zone ecosystems, the discharges from the routine transportation, production, and use of oil and gas are greater in volume and may present a long-term threat to the marine environment. Estimates of the quantities of petroleum hydrocarbons entering the oceans annually are presented in Table 13–25.

As oil exploration continues worldwide, increasing numbers of extraction facilities will be established in coastal zone areas. Sublethal and long-term damage to marine organisms and eco-

systems may result from chronic discharges and accidental low-volume spills during normal offshore and dockside operations, from disposal of drilling muds and cuttings, and from disturbance of the seabed and coastal wetlands by platform and pipeline construction. Losses incurred during transportation and processing also contribute to low-level petroleum contamination, as do inputs from the atmosphere, coastal municipal and industrial waste outfalls, and urban and river runoff. [367] Increased coal combustion and conversion can also be expected to contribute to oceanic pollution. Mining wastes, secondary pollutants associated with trade and transport, and the byproducts of processing and primary combustion of coal will enter coastal waters via the land and the atmosphere.

The manner and severity with which fossil fuel pollutants affect the marine environment varies. Different factors—such as oil dosage and type, weather and water conditions, and the seasonal behavior patterns of marine organisms—influence the biological impact of petroleum hydrocarbons on ocean life and habitats. [368] Nearshore petroleum discharges cause more extensive and permanent damage to organisms and life cycles in estuaries and coastal wetlands than those further offshore. Biological recovery of oil-inundated

TABLE 13–25

Best Estimates of Petroleum Hydrocarbons Introduced into the Oceans Annually

Source	Best Estimate	Probable Range
	(millions of metric tons)	
Natural seeps	0.6	0.2–1.0
Offshore production	0.08	0.08–0.15
Transportation		
LOT tankers	0.31	0.15–0.4
Non-LOT tankers	0.77	0.65–1.0
Dry docking	0.25	0.2–0.3
Terminal operations	0.003	0.0015–0.005
Bilges bunkering	0.5	0.4–0.7
Tanker accidents	0.2	0.12–0.25
Nontanker accidents	0.1	0.02–0.15
Coastal refineries	0.2	0.2–0.3
Atmosphere	0.6	0.4–0.8
Coastal municipal wastes	0.3	–
Coastal nonrefining industrial wastes	0.3	–
Urban runoff	0.3	0.1–0.5
River runoff	1.6	–
Total	6.113	

Source: National Academy of Sciences, *Petroleum in the Marine Environment,* Washington, 1975, p. 6.

wetlands is a complex process, and the time required for recovery varies widely.[369]

The coastal effects of oil pollution may be of longer duration than previously thought. Components of oil are now known to remain in estuarine wetland sediments for as long as eight years after an initial spill,[370] continuing to affect benthic organisms and altering biological productivity. A marsh grass community has been observed to have been unable to reestablish itself even three years after an oil spill. Over the three years of observation, erosion rates in the salt marsh were found to be 24 times greater than those in nearby unaffected areas.[371]

If subjected to large enough amounts of oil and petroleum hydrocarbon products, either through accidental spills or extended low level inputs, a sea-surface hydrocarbon microlayer can form to cover the adjacent coastal ocean areas. This hydrocarbon film can act as a differential accumulation layer for trace materials such as toxic heavy metal ions, vitamins, amino acids, and lipophilic chlorinated hydrocarbon pollutants, including DDT residues and PCBs. The combination of these materials near or at the ocean surface could significantly affect coastal ocean ecosystems. Such "microslicks" have been observed to interfere with the normal development of fish eggs during spawning seasons, and some scientists suspect microslicks of inducing changes within phytoplankton communities.[372]

Although the long-term implications of low-level oil contamination are just beginning to be understood, it is now well established that petroleum hydrocarbons adversely affect a wide variety of marine organisms physiologically and behaviorally.[373] Significant petroleum contamination of wetland sediments resulting from repeated small spills and/or effluent discharges have already occurred along West German, British, French, and Italian coastlines, as well as those of the U.S.[374] Such polluting input can be expected to increase globally as fossil fuel production, transportation, and use grow during the next two decades.

As the search for oil and gas intensifies, exploration and extraction will take place in areas previously untouched. The marine environment in parts of the Arctic is now vulnerable to conditions accompanying the exploitation of fossil fuel resources. The construction of artificial drilling islands, dredged up from bay bottoms, will have locally adverse effects on Arctic sea life, as will low level losses of oil incurred during routine production and transportation. Accidental large volume spills or well blowouts would pose serious problems, for the very nature of the far northern

environment would make cleanup efforts and ultimate ecosystem recovery especially difficult.[375] Exploitation of fossil fuel resources in the Antarctic region could create similar difficulties. There would certainly be localized environmental effects of oil processing and transport activities; repeated accidental spills could have serious cumulative effects on Southern Ocean ecosystems.

Sewage, Fertilizer Nutrients, and Sedimentation

The Global 2000 Study projections for water, population, forestry, and food and agriculture imply that there will be a growth in coastal pollution from sewage, fertilizers, and land runoff sedimentation. These problems are seen to be particularly acute in the coastal zones of less developed countries. Unprecedented urban growth will give rise to an increase in the volume of untreated sewage entering estuarine rivers and coastal waters. Intensified agricultural activity and the concomitant twofold to threefold increase in global fertilizer use will add to already large amounts of chemical nutrients carried into estuaries, wetlands, and coral reefs. Projected deforestation will destroy watersheds, exacerbate erosion, and create large nutrient-laden silt loads in rivers running to the sea. Upon entering estuaries and coastal areas, river waters will release their suspended sediment and organic matter, creating conditions of coastal water overproductivity and contributing to problems of sedimentation that are especially destructive of coral reefs. While the dangers of both nutrient and sediment pollution are known, there has been little study of what the ultimate consequences of this pollutant combination may be. In the short term, however, it appears that nutrients and sediments, together with physical alteration of estuaries and reefs, will produce localized cases of estuarine and coastal eutrophication.

Coastal wetlands are naturally able to absorb contaminants from polluted tidal water. Since most salt marshes are either located in estuaries or have freshwater flowing into them, their ability to retain contaminants running off the land help to prevent further transport of pollutants to the sea. Marshes of *Spartina* grasses can biologically fix inorganic nitrogen, creating high levels of plant productivity equal to that of intensively managed agricultural areas.[376] Mangrove soils are effective nutrient reservoirs too and are exceptional environments for the removal of nitrogen in sewage. In salt marshes, extreme enrichment of inorganic nitrogen is counteracted by its bacterial conversion to nitrogen gas. However, as capable as wetlands are in utilizing large volumes of nutrients, the presence of excessive amounts of nitrogen, like those contained in sewage and fertilizer runoff, could eventually result in an overproductivity of coastal waters that takes the form of coastal algal blooms[377] and could cause eutrophication of localized estuarine and wetland areas.

In tropical waters, sewage pollution can also result in the growth of coral-smothering algae, causing reef degradation and sometimes leading to the sedimentary production of toxic levels of hydrogen sulfide. Pollution-intolerant reef species then decrease. The more tolerant species take over the community, and the reef ecosystem is altered, sometimes permanently.

The exposure of reefs to land runoff sedimentation has, so far, been the greatest single cause of reef destruction.[378] Ongoing activities such as deforestation, intensive agricultural practices, livestock grazing, and dredging and filling operations are currently leading to extensive sedimentation of reef waters in tropical coastal waters. Natural growth of reef-forming polyps requires favorable conditions of salinity and relatively warm, turbulent or upwelling water to bring nutrients and cleanse away waste materials.[379] When functioning naturally, a coral reef ecosystem sustains the life cycles of all of its individual components, but when the reef-growth system is disturbed, imbalances develop as certain reef organisms either leave or die. Most corals cannot live if heavily coated or buried by sediment particles, and reduced light intensity caused by turbid waters significantly affect growth rates and species diversity.[380]

Other causes of reef destruction include heavy freshwater runoff due to deforestation, excessive salinity (produced by desalinization plants), and thermal pollution.[381] The resuspension of sediment in dredging operations effectively blocks any regeneration of already damaged coral colonies.[382] Once destroyed, a coral reef has little hope for regeneration. If healing reef growth does occur in the absence of pollutants, the time for restoration to any semblance of its natural state can easily be a matter of decades.[383]

Solid Wastes.

Solid waste disposal in the coastal zones is—for the short term—one of the least serious of marine pollution problems. While foreign material can adversely affect coastal ecosystems, its current impact is generally as a localized nuisance and human health hazard. However, considering the population, GNP, and forestry projections, greater quantities of solid wastes should be expected to enter the oceans between now and the year 2000.

The sea floor, surface waters, and beaches of the earth's marine environment are littered with man-made materials originating from deliberate, incidental, or accidental waste disposal.* Solid waste, often referred to as "litter," is of two types: (1) refuse originating on land, consisting of packaging materials (plastic, metal, cloth, glass, or wood), and (2) refuse from ships released during fishing, recreation, or cargo-carrying operations.[384] The amount of solid wastes entering the world's oceans each year—a large part of which is released in harbors, ports, or other coastal water areas—is estimated to be in the millions of tons (Table 13–26).

Floating litter is mainly a coastal zone problem and affects both commercial and biological activity. Nylon ropes and plastic sheets floating just beneath the sea surface easily foul ship propellors. Wood debris and submerged logs can present sudden and serious navigational problems. The effect of litter on ocean organisms is apparent also. Plastic sheets can also smother benthic organisms. Sheer plastics, mistaken for jellyfish, have been eaten by sea turtles, small plastic objects been injested by fish, and plastic bags caught on the heads of sea mammals are known to have caused suffocation. In coastal waters adjacent to logging and pulp mill activities, solid and liquid wood wastes have been found to be destructive of ocean organisms and habitats.[385]

On the whole, given current practices and the projections of the Global 2000 Study, a growth in marine pollution can be expected in the next 20 years. Outfalls and the atmosphere will inject industrial, municipal, and agricultural chemical and metal wastes into coastal waters. Pollutants from fossil fuel extraction, transportation, and energy production will contribute significantly to spoilation of the marine environment. Population growth, deforestation, and intensive agriculture will all contribute to the volume of sewage, nutrient chemicals, and sediments entering coastal

---

*Disposal of solid wastes in the oceans can be carried to extremes, as it has in the New York Bight, resulting in unpleasant localized impacts on the marine environment. The Marine Ecosystems Analysis Program of the National Oceanic and Atmospheric Administration (NOAA) has described one incident as the infamous "summer 1976 floatables event," during which "beaches along the south shore of Long Island were inundated by a variety of floating litter. Included among the materials washed ashore were tar and grease balls, charred wood, garbage and trash (e.g., watermelon rinds, chicken heads, styrofoam beads, paper, and plastic wrappers), and sewage-related items (e.g., condom rings, diaper liners, and tampon applicators)." (*New York Bight Project: Annual Report for FY 1976*, NOAA Environmental Research Laboratories, Boulder, Dec. 1977, p. 29.)

TABLE 13-26

Annual Ocean Litter Estimates

Source	Litter (millions of metric tons)
Passenger vessels	0.028
Merchant shipping	
Crew	0.110
Cargo	5.600
Recreational boating	0.103
Commercial fishing	
Crew	0.340
Gear	0.001
Military	0.074
Oil drilling and platforms	0.004
Catastrophe	0.100
Total	6.360

Source: National Academy of Sciences. *Assessing Potential Ocean Pollutants.* Washington. 1975. p. 422.

waters. Unsightly and unhealthy solid waste pollution will develop into problems of greater magnitude and areal extent. The most serious impact of pollutants will be on the organisms and ecosystems of the coastal zones. Living marine resources will be affected by disease and by the reduction and spoilation of viable habitat resulting from pollutant increases. The greatest uncertainty over coastal pollution concerns the specific level of the pollution and the future of international efforts to control it.

Overexploitation of Living Marine Resources

The Global 2000 food and population projections point to a growth in global demand for living marine resources. However, the fisheries projections themselves suggest that the trend in ever increasing annual yields may have peaked and that future catch tonnages may not be able to readily meet this demand. Increasing pressure by commercial fisheries will place great stresses on living resource populations and lead to an overexploitation of traditional species. Catch compositions will shift to greater amounts of nontraditional species. A significant proportion of these smaller, shorter-lived species will continue to be utilized in ways other than direct human consumption. The policies and practices applied to marine mammals are in flux. In the face of extinction, the survival of many species depends on rational scientific and societal management decisions.

Fisheries

The Global 2000 Study population and food projections suggest that the demand for seafood will increase, encouraging still more fishing activity. The degradation of coastal zone habitats—either through physical destruction for development or through constant injection of various pollutants—will contribute to changes in species composition and the quantity of the global catch. Future gross catch statistics therefore may show a constant or increasing yield, but the catch will become composed of progressively less traditional products. Advances in fishing and processing technologies, by helping the gross catch figures to remain high, will effectively conceal the degree to which overfishing is undermining the utility and value of the world catch.

The coastal oceans are the crucially important sites of the world's fisheries: At least half of the marine life forms directly utilized by humans come from coastal waters; nearly all of the remainder come from coastal and oceanic upwellings*. Although these upwellings occur in approximately 0.1 percent of all oceanic areas, they are among the world's most productive fisheries.[386]

Over the last three to four decades, intensive fishing activity has produced a shift in the species composition of the global catch away from the traditionally preferred species toward species at lower trophic levels and of less economic value. A growing proportion is being converted to fertilizer and fishmeal for animal feed. Before 1940, a negligible portion of the catch was used in meal production; by the mid-1970s, 35 percent was being used for making meal and oil.[387] Thus the fish catch directly used for human consumption in 1975 was closer to 45 million metric tons than the 70 million often cited. Use of the ocean fisheries for animal feed is somewhat analogous to fattening livestock on high quality grain. The fish catch—like the grain—would be more efficiently utilized if it were consumed directly by humans and if animals were raised primarily on plant species and other foods of no value as human food. Whether the shift to fertilizer and fishmeal can be attributed partially to the need to find a market for the less preferred species or to the fact that fishmeal has been made into a more marketable product, the shift itself is clear.

*Upwelling areas occur where winds and prevailing boundary currents allow cold, nutrient-laden water to rise from below. Upwellings create areas of high primary productivity, which consequently allow the production of large stocks of fish.

Intensive fishing activity appears to have helped reduce the absolute yield of the global fisheries catch. Improved fishery technologies have greatly aided the overexploitation of most traditional stocks. Until 1971, global total fisheries production had increased annually at a rapid rate. However, in 1972 a combination of natural ocean current inversions and the prolonged strain of overfishing on fish populations drastically reduced the population size and thus the yield from the Peruvian anchovy fishery.[388] This reduction in yield appears to have contributed significantly to the 1972 world decline in catch tonnage and to the subsequent fluctuations in total annual yields.[389]

Marine Mammals and the Marine Environment

Constant global demand, shortsighted management of living resources, and overexploitation have caused the severe depletion, and in some cases the extinction, of a number of marine mammal species. Marine mammals—which include whales, porpoises, dolphins, seals, sea lions, sirenians, sea otters, and polar bears—have historically been hunted to the brink of extinction. Some animals, such as whales, have been attacked one species at a time and with increasing technological expertise (see Table 13–27). As marine biologist Kenneth Norris has written, "The contest has now become so grossly unequal that no evasion on the part of the animals has any effect. Their only defense is scarcity."[390]

Abusive overutilization of a living marine resource results in the loss of a full range of benefits—tangible, intangible, realized, or potential—to both present and future generations. Such benefits include economic and nutritive values, aesthetic contributions, and important roles in maintenance of the health and stability of the marine ecosystem.[391]

Ecosystem effects may be a crucially important factor; no species exists alone, and exploitation of one species has some impact on other components of the habitat. Yet present harvesting procedures consider only the effects on individual species, or groups of species in isolation, and do not recognize the need for predicting the impact on the cycle of reciprocal relationships within the ecosystem. The impact of overexploitation may include changes (1) in the population of competing or symbiotic species within the functional group of the exploited species, (2) in the vegetation structure and carnivore populations where the exploited species is a herbivore, and (3) in numbers of prey where the exploited species is a carnivore. These are only first-order responses,

TABLE 13–27

Effect of Whaling on Stocks of Ten Species of Whales

Species	Virgin Stock	1974 Stock	1974 Stock as a Percentage of the Virgin Stock
	(thousands)		
Sperm			
both sexes	922	641	69
male	461	212	45
female	461	429	93
Fin	448	101	22
Minke	361	325	90
Blue	215	13	6
Sei	200	76	38
Bryde	100	(40)?	?
Right*	(50)?	(2)?	?
Bowhead*	(10)?	(2)?	?
Humpback	50	7	14
Gray*	11	11	100
Total	2,367	1,218	51.4

Source: Victor B. Scheffer, "The Status of Whales," *Pacific Discovery*, vol. 29, no. 1, 1976, p. 3.
* Not currently being hunted.

and consequent changes in more remote parts of the system are probable.[392]

International efforts to regulate whaling have been protracted.[393] The somewhat more responsible management techniques now established by the International Whaling Commission are seriously hindered by the lack of accurate whale-population data needed to determine harvest quotas. In the United States, the Marine Mammal Protection Act of 1972 is the first national legislation that makes the healthy maintenance of the ecosystem the primary objective of marine mammal management.[394]

Major uncertainties arise when evaluating the consequences of the Global 2000 Study's projections on the environmental quality of marine fisheries. A good knowledge of the ecological effects of marine resource overexploitation has yet to be gained, and agreement has yet to be reached over whether current reduced catch yields are a trend or only a temporary fluctuation in fisheries population cycles. The productivity of future fisheries depends on the development of cooperative marine management practices. Inherent in this course will be the problem of how to regulate internationally commonly utilized living resources. Unilaterally declared 200-mile economic zones may both aggravate and alleviate the evolution of fisheries overexploitation. Only time, and a clear perception of current and potential environmental conditions, will tell how successful these management efforts will have been.

In conclusion, the Study's projections indicate that loss of habitat, pollution, and overexploitative living-resource management policies will significantly affect the integrity and ultimate productivity of the world's coastal waters. Economic development along the coastal zone will destroy or alter ecosystems crucial to the life cycles of many fisheries species. Chemicals, fossil fuels, solid and sewage wastes, agricultural nutrients, and eroded sediments will pollute ecosystems and degrade marine communities. Growing demand for food to feed rapidly multiplying populations will lead to great stresses on global fisheries and cause a further shift in total yields and species composition. Population pressures, concerted economic development, and an increased need for food will have cyclic effects and eventually impact upon those very areas, the coastal zones, from which basic sustenance and livelihood is derived.

Open Oceans

The open oceans differ from coastal waters, both in the time scales of the processes taking place within them and in their capacity to absorb, dilute, and disperse waste materials. The environmental conditions of the deep sea are quite unique. It is an immense area that is relatively stable over long time periods, has little topographic complexity, and receives low inputs of energy. Most benthic animals are small mud-dwelling and mud-feeding creatures of great variety and long evolutionary history. Natural deep-sea disturbances consist of events such as mud slumps, fish and invertebrate activity, and large objects settling from the surface.[395]

As a result of their vast size and the nature of their ecosystems, environmental change in the open oceans necessarily occurs very slowly. It can be expected that the Global 2000 Study projections will cause no major impact on the earth's open oceans by the year 2000. However, the projections do indicate that over the next 20 years world society will establish certain trends that, sustained over the long term, will eventually cause measurable change in the oceanic environment. Most importantly, long-lived toxic substances will continue to accumulate in open ocean waters and inevitably affect oceanic ecosystems for many years into the future. Deep-sea mining, if initiated without adequate knowledge and precautions will also have the potential to disrupt the ecosystems of extensive benthic and pelagic areas.

Pollution of the Open Oceans

The Global 2000 energy, GNP, nonfuel minerals, and agriculture projections imply that increasing amounts of toxic pollutants will continue to be produced in the decades ahead. Toxic chemicals enter oceanic waters three ways. Major quantities are deposited in coastal waters and subsequently carried into oceanic waters by currents and living organisms. Significant amounts are also deposited directly from the atmosphere. Large and probably increasing amounts will be deposited directly into surface and deeper oceanic waters by accidental spills, operational discharges and intentional dumping.

Oceanic ecosystems differ from coastal ecosystems by assimilating pollutants from land-based, coastal, and oceanic sources over a longer time period. Most pollutants enter marine waters as fine particles, as liquids, or in dissolved form. The pollutants are then adsorbed onto fine sediment and detrital particles that are consumed by zooplankton in the water column. The zooplankton incorporate the pollutants into their bodies and eject them as packaged fecal pellets. Dead organisms and feces settle quickly, leading to a rapid accumulation of chemicals in oceanic depths.[395a]

In the cold oceanic bottom waters, metabolism and natural sedimentation are very slow,[395b] and as a result, pollutants are biologically degraded or immobilized in sediments at a much slower rate than in coastal waters. A related consequence of the slow degradation and immobilization of pollutants is that deep sea communities are exposed to pollutants for long periods of time. Lengthy exposure to even low concentrations of pollutants is likely to be especially damaging to the organisms of the deep oceanic waters because they have evolved in one of the most stable, least varying ecosystems in the biosphere, and have had little need to develop adaptations to deal with environmental change.[395c]

Given their enormous volume, oceanic waters can accept a certain amount of waste material. Yet the oceans' capacity to dilute is ultimately finite. Marine scientist Edward Goldberg has expressed concern that over an extended period of time the introduction of pollutants into the oceans could lead to a long-term buildup of toxic material, causing "widespread mortalities and morbidities" in ocean organisms.[396] Once this condition is reached, Goldberg writes, there would be "no turning back. The great volume of the open ocean makes the removal of a toxic substance, identified by a catastrophic event, an endeavor beyond mankind's capabilities with the technologies of today or of the foreseeable future."[397]

Deep-Sea Mining

The potential environmental implications of mining the deep seabed are not yet fully understood but are being studied by the U.S. National Oceanic and Atmospheric Administration, the International Union for the Conservation of Nature and Natural Resources, and the American Society for International Law.

In a preliminary effort to assess what the ecological impact of deep-sea mining might be, the National Oceanic and Atmospheric Administration (NOAA) has monitored test-mining activities in the Pacific Ocean.[398] The short-term, near-field effects of seabed mining have been evaluated to some extent; they include the action of the ore collector itself, pelagic and benthic plumes generated by deep seabed collection, and damage to benthic and pelagic organisms.

NOAA stated in its preliminary estimates[399] that deep-ocean mining will have very marked impacts on the sea floor and in the 20 to 50 meters of water above the point of discharge of the bottom effluent. The NOAA-monitored mining test has found this to be true in varying degrees. The ore collector contact zone—the portion of the seafloor actually mined and an area of several meters on either side of the collector track—is the site of severe, long-term environmental destruction.[400] Under present techniques, ore collection on the seabed also creates a benthic plume of suspended sediment as thick as a few tens of meters. The resedimentation from a benthic plume is easily measurable near the collector track, yet diminishes rapidly as the distance from the track increases. NOAA concluded that initial test monitoring has shown the resedimentation to not measurably affect benthic organisms at sites removed from the collector track.[401] However, the available study methods constrained the ability of the monitoring team to track the benthic plume and observe its effects on the deep sea benthic organisms.

The surface plume is a cloud of turbid waste water that extends with decreasing intensity and detectability downcurrent from the mining ship after its discharge. After monitoring the mining activity and conducting initial laboratory tests, NOAA concluded that the surface plume has no observable deleterious effects on the rate of primary productivity. The effects of the plume sediments on penetration of light into the euphotic zone are as yet undetermined. Preliminary investigations show no detectable "in-plume" mortality of zooplankton; experiments are being conducted to assess the possible uptake of plume-related particulates by zooplankton.[402]

The International Union for the Conservation of Nature and Natural Resources[403], Morges, Switzerland, feels that the eventual environmental consequences of deep seabed mining may be more serious than anticipated or observed, for the following reasons:

1. Deep sea organisms may have very long generation times—a benthic clam was recently described as taking 200 years to reach sexual maturity—and may be extremely vulnerable to alteration of their environment.*

2. In the process of bringing dredged materials to the surface, sediments and bottom water will be released. Settling times for sediment may be very slow—on the order of 20 meters per year—and intensive dredging operations may create extensive surface plumes. One estimate states that several hundred thousand square miles of the Pacific may be layered with sediment in the 100 meters below the surface by 1990. Clouding of waters may have adverse effects on many organisms, and species composition of the phytoplankton community may be altered due to transport of dormant spores from the bottom to surface waters.

3. An estimated 70–96 percent of the nodules, by volume, will end up as processing waste, and processing them will require large quantities of chemical reagents and energy. The wastes, which will include heavy metals, may be quite toxic to marine life, and regardless of whether the operations take place on the coast or offshore, it is likely that they will produce both chemical and thermal pollution.

On the other hand, a report prepared for the American Society of International Law states that if strict controls and regulations are established soon by the United States and other countries involved, adverse impact could be minimized and deep-sea mining could be made environmentally acceptable.[404]

Conclusions

Overall, what implications do the Global 2000 projections have for the marine environment? In large part, the answer is uncertain. The limited

---

*The deep ocean floor exhibits very low rates of recovery from damage. Even after a period of two years, densities of life in an altered area can be an order of magnitude lower than those of surrounding sediments. Benthic species composition remain different from the undamaged encircling environment for a similiar period of time (J. Frederick Grassle, "Diversity and Population Dynamics of Benthic Organisms," *Oceanus*, Winter 1978, pp. 42, 43, 45.)

detail in the projections, combined with inadequacies in present knowledge of the oceans, leave many questions unanswered. However, a few general conclusions can be drawn.

First, there is no evidence to suggest that the major regulatory functions of the world's oceans will be substantially disrupted during the next two decades. The oceans' heat and energy storage capacity and its influence on global climate are not expected to undergo major modifications. The oceanic role in the global oxygen, carbon, and water cycles will not be drastically affected by the year 2000.

Second, the most significant impacts of the events foretold in the projections will probably occur in the coastal zones. These impacts will stem from the projected pressures of overfishing, the projected increase in the installation of new transportation and industrial facilities, and the projected discharge of toxic wastes and petroleum hydrocarbon products. As a result of these projected developments, the future pollution, alteration and destruction of estuaries, coastal wetlands and coral reefs may be anticipated.

Spoilation of coastal waters and disruption of estuarine and wetland ecosystems may have grave implications for the continued productivity of global fisheries—including aquaculture—and for the general viability of many ocean organisms. It is known that a large fraction of marine fishes depend, during some period in their lives, on estuarine ecosystems, coastal wetlands (including salt marshes and mangroves), and coral reefs. The extent to which the world's potential fish catch has already been affected by losses of coastal wetlands, estuaries and coral reefs is unknown, but certainly large, continuing losses may be expected to produce adverse effects. Furthermore, overfishing will continue to stress coastal fish communities; fisheries catches will be composed of species at lower trophic levels; and the proportion of these species used for animal feed and fertilizer rather than for human consumption will increase.

Coastal zones everywhere will be affected in one way or another. The use of DDT and other persistent pesticides in African, Latin American, and Asian countries for vector control and agricultural pest control is expected to increase in the next few decades, and the quantities of these persistent chemicals entering the coastal waters and the open ocean will increase accordingly.[405] The global input of herbicides and other agricultural chemicals will also increase, as will urban and industrial pollution and the destruction of estuarine and coastal wetland habitats.

In many respects the degradation of the marine environment in the next few decades parallels the terrestrial "tragedy of the commons," with the same complex problem of how to protect a jointly used, limited resource in the face of population and economic growth. No assured source of funds, no unified strategy, and no authority adequately protects the global marine environment from overuse or misuse. Unilaterally declared two hundred mile limits encourage coastal states to protect their ocean resources, but the oceans themselves do not recognize such arbitrary boundaries; they will transport pollutants throughout their environment regardless of political delimitations.[406] International agreements on the control of marine pollution have addressed contamination by petroleum and radioactive materials. Dumping of wastes at sea has also been considered in international conventions, but the largest sources of marine pollution—land-based outfalls, runoff, and atmospheric emissions of synthetic organic chemicals and heavy metals—are largely exempt from regulation by international agreement. The exploration and exploitation of the deep seabed are also still unregulated.[407] The United Nations Environment Programme (UNEP) is helping nations to protect and manage shared oceanic zones through its Regional Seas Programme. Of eight regional seas programs now designated by UNEP, that for the Mediterranean is the most developed. Assessment of coastal and open-ocean pollution is being conducted by most of the states surrounding the Mediterranean; they are also involved in marine environmental planning and management, the development of legislation, and institutional and financial arrangements. Although difficulties remain concerning both individual and collective responsibilities and capabilities, UNEP's Regional Seas Programme is advancing the cause for international cooperation in the prevention of ocean pollution.[408]

To further complicate the management of the marine commons, there are societal delays in responding to even catastrophic environmental problems. The Minamata Bay incident in Japan, involving mercury poisoning through consumption of contaminated fish, is a case in point. As shown in Table 13–28, 17 years elapsed between the time the mercury-laden catalysts were first discharged into the bay and the observation of neurological disorders in the fishermen and their families. Three more years elapsed before the agent causing the disease was identified, and another 14 years passed before the chemical factory was held legally responsible for its actions and ordered to compensate the victims or their fam-

TABLE 13–28

Timetable of Societal Responses to Mercury Pollution of the Ocean, Minamata Bay, Japan, 1939–73

Year		Years Elapsed Since Pollution Began
1939	Chemical production begins on the shores of Minamata Bay; the factory discharges spent catalysts containing mercury into the bay.	0
1953	Birds and cats in the bay area act oddly; the behavior disorder becomes known as "disease of the dancing cats."	14
1956	Neurological disorders observed among Minamata Bay fishermen and their families.	17
1959	High concentrations of mercury ascertained in bay fish and in dead patients; an independent study shows disease was methyl mercury poisoning and factory effluent the likely source.	20
1960	Chemical company denies relationship of mercury to the disease but finds new discharge sites for waste; several new cases break out at new site.	21
1961–64	Very small compensations paid by the chemical company to disease victims and to fishermen for loss of livelihood.	22–25
1965	A second outbreak occurs at Niigata, Japan, where an acetyldehyde factory discharges spent mercury catalysts into the river.	26
1967	Niigata patients initiate a civil action, presumed to be the first large civil suit brought against a polluter in Japan.	28
1971	Niigata District Court pronounces judgment against the Niigata factory; compensation awarded the 77 Niigata victims or their families.	32
1973	Kumamoto District Court finds Minamata Bay factory culpable and orders company to pay reasonable compensation to victims or their families.	34

Source: Edward D. Goldberg, *The Health of the Oceans*, Paris: UNESCO, 1976, pp. 21–23; Paul R. Ehrlich, et al., *Ecoscience: Population, Resources, Environment*, San Francisco: Freeman, 1977, p. 574.

ilies.* And many more years will pass, if ever, before all of the consequences will have run their course. If societal delays on the order of decades are involved in the responses of a single nation, how long a time might be required for all of the nations of the world to respond if the oceans were observed to be evolving into a "toxic broth?"[409]

Global society is currently in a reactionary mode in its dealings with the marine environment:

Problems develop, and society reacts—after a time. Considering the magnitude of the short- and long-term problems to be faced, a determined shift to a more anticipatory mode is now appropriate. Although dead or dying global oceans will not be in evidence by the year 2000, what happens over the next two decades will be a major determinant of the health and productivity of the marine environment in the 21st century.

THE FORESTRY PROJECTIONS AND THE ENVIRONMENT

The Projections

The CIA forestry projections anticipate that the present net global deforestation rate of 18–20 million hectares per year will continue through the end of the century.† About one-fifth of the world's land surface is now covered by closed forests. By the year 2000, the projected deforestation will shrink

---

*Two years later, in 1975, a survey disclosed that there had been 3,500 victims of the disease and that an additional 10,000 persons might develop symptoms of the disease in the future (Paul R. Ehrlich et al., *Ecoscience*, San Francisco: Freeman, 1977, p. 574).

†Estimates of the annual rate of global deforestation vary widely. Data from the governments of tropical countries indicate a net annual deforestation of 6.4 million hectares during the 1975–80 period, and an optimistic projection of those countries' plans indicates the rate will decline to 4 million hectares per year by the 1995–2000 period (J. P. Lanly and J. Clement, *Present and Future Forest and Plantation Areas in the Tropics*,

Rome: Food and Agriculture Organization, Jan. 1979). A more widely used estimate of tropic deforestation is 10–12 million hectares per year (used, for example, by Edouard Saouma in "Statement by the Director-General of the Food and Agriculture Organization," 8th World Forestry Congress, Jakarta, Oct. 16–28, 1978). The substantially higher estimate used in this study takes into account the common disparity between the official designation of areas as forests and the actual use of the land by farmers, as well as the disparity between official intentions and actual accomplishments in the tropical nations.

forest cover to one-sixth of the land surface. As illustrated in Table 13–29, most of the deforestation will occur in the LDCs, whose humid tropical forests and open woodlands are steadily being felled and converted to farmland and pasture. This trend is impelled by several forces: the expansion of agricultural frontiers into forested areas in order to supply food as populations increase; the demand for fuelwood and charcoal; the demand for tropical forest products by industrialized nations; and the demand within the LDCs for paper and other forest-derived products as incomes rise. In North America and the U.S.S.R., on the other hand, only small reductions in forested areas are expected, while in Europe some increase in forests is anticipated.

The combination of increasing population growth and decreasing forest area will result in a decline in stocks of commercial-sized timber per person. In the industrialized countries, such stock will fall from the present 142 cubic meters per capita to 114 cubic meters per capita in the year 2000, with consequent rises in the real price of wood and some increases in the use of substitutes for wood products. In the LDCs over the same period, stocks will plummet from the present 57 cubic meters per capita to 21 cubic meters per capita, resulting in serious shortages of firewood, building materials, and other forest-derived benefits.

Forest management practices will also change. In the industrial nations, forest management will become increasingly intensive as efforts are made to boost commercial wood yields. In the less developed countries, the planting of plantation forests may increase toward the end of the century, but over the next two decades denuded areas and degraded forests resulting from planned agricultural settlement and from unplanned cutting will become far more extensive.

Introduction

Of all the environmental impacts implied by the Global 2000 Study's projections, the forest changes, summarized in Table 13–29, pose one of the most serious problems, particularly for the less developed regions of the world.[410] When forests are removed, water and nutrient cycles are destabilized, and soil is left unprotected from rainfall and from the sun's heat, often leading to a sharp decline in soil fertility and to harsh extremes of temperature and moisture that reduce agricultural potentials.[411] Where catchments are deforested, the result is destabilization of steep slopes and increased flooding, both of which jeopardize downstream land and water use. Where humid tropical lowlands are deforested and recovery does not occur, sterile soils—capable of supporting little more than tenacious inedible grasses—may be exposed. When followed by burning, overcultivation, and overgrazing, deforestation is merely the first step in the process of converting forest lands into barren wastelands. This transformation occurred centuries ago in much of the Mediterranean basin and the Middle East and has already occurred during this century in wide areas

TABLE 13–29

Estimates of World Forest Resources, 1978 and 2000

	Closed Forest (millions of hectares)		Growing Stock (billions cu m overbark)	
	1978	2000	1978	2000
U.S.S.R.	785	775	79	77
Europe	140	150	15	13
North America	470	464	58	55
Japan, Australia, New Zealand	69	68	4	4
Subtotal	1,464	1,457	156	149
Latin America	550	329	94	54
Africa	188	150	39	31
Asia and Pacific LDCs	361	181	38	19
Subtotal (LDCs)	1,099	660	171	104
Total (world)	2,563	2,117	327	253

	Growing Stock per Capita (cu m biomass)	
Industrial countries	142	114
LDCs	57	21
Global	76	40

Source: Table 8–9 and forestry projections, Chapter 8, this volume.

of Africa and South Asia.[412] By the end of the century it may well have occurred throughout large areas of Africa, Asia, and Latin America.

Drastic reductions in global forest area, coupled with a simultaneous growth in demand for wood products, are sure to lead to efforts to intensify the management of the remaining forests to raise yields and to increased areas of timber plantations. These trends will have both positive and negative environmental impacts. Well-managed plantations and production forests (especially in temperate areas) can ease the cutting pressure on natural forests, but production forests are biologically less diverse, are poorer habitats for native animals,[413] and, in some instances, may be inferior to natural forests in soil and water conservation values.[414] Energy-intensive fertilizers, pesticides, and herbicides may be required, creating runoff and associated problems. Still, given the projected demands for forest products, intensified wood and fiber production will be absolutely necessary in many areas, especially in the tropics, if other large areas are to be preserved as natural forests.

In the discussion that follows, the environmental consequences of deforestation in the LDCs are examined first, then the effects of more intensive management in the remaining forests of both the LDCs and the industrialized nations, followed by a brief consideration of possible global effects of the expected changes in forest environments.

Deforestation in the LDCs

The world's forests are quite diverse, ranging from dense tropical rain forests to sparsely wooded savannas, from dwarf krummholz forests along alpine timberlines to thickets on semiarid chaparral land.[415] To simplify the discussion, however, all forests will be classified here into one of two broad categories: (1) closed forests, where dense tree canopies preclude the growth of grasses, or (2) open woodlands, where canopies are more open and ground cover includes grasses and forbs.

Closed Forests

Closed forests in the LDCs present difficult management challenges. Commercial timber cutters usually operate on a "cut-and-get-out" basis, making no effort to manage for perpetuity. The forest is "high-graded" of commercially valuable species, while much of the remaining vegetation is destroyed by the logging operations. Land for crops is often cleared (frequently by burning) with little or no use made of the wood,* and valuable

---

*Wood ashes do yield crop nutrients—until they are leached out, which is often quite quickly.

timber, such as teak, is sometimes used only for firewood. Although management regulations of some kind have now been established in almost every nation for public forests (and in some nations even for private forests), the ability to enforce such regulations is commonly limited, since the responsible agencies have insufficient personnel and inadequate budgets.[416] The need for land-use planning based on soil capabilities and site features is widely recognized, but the pace of planning is glacial, and land-use changes—forced by population growth and economic development— are proceeding rapidly.[417]

The disruption of water systems is the most certain environmental consequence of forest elimination. Deforestation is most rapid in the very region where water systems are most vulnerable: the equatorial (tropical) belt, lying between 15 degrees north and 15 degrees south latitude in Africa and America, and bulging up to 30 degrees north in Asia. The equatorial belt receives almost half the globe's total terrestrial rainfall. Many areas within this band receive over 3 meters of rainfall a year, and the rain is substantially more erosive than elsewhere in the world.[418] Until they are removed, the multistoried tropical forests buffer the force of torrential rains, absorb water, and slow runoff. Deforestation of this belt will have serious effects on the flows in the major river systems such as the Mekong, the Ganges, the Amazon, the Congo, and their tributaries; the shorter rivers of the equatorial island systems will also be affected. The effects will be felt in all zones of the equatorial-belt watersheds. Effects range from landslides in the mountains and siltation of reservoirs and irrigation areas to the smothering of marine life with silt in coastal areas.[419]

The extent to which populations in the Asian equitorial belt are dependent on indirect agricultural benefits from forests differs considerably from that of populations in the non-Asian areas of the belt. The Asian populations will be considered first.

The Asian Equatorial Belt. Most Asian forests lie above rich alluvial valleys and basins, the majority of which are intensively farmed and irrigated, and several of which support the largest, densest agricultural populations on earth. Almost one-fourth of humanity lives in these valleys and basins and depends for subsistence on critical irrigation water derived from forested watersheds. In India, Pakistan, and Bangladesh alone, about 500 million people depend on water running off the Himalayan watershed, and a similar number in East and Southeast Asia depend on water from the Himalayan and adjacent mountain systems.

Most of the humid Asian equatorial belt is subject to heavy rains during the monsoon and to relative drought during the rest of the year. Consequently, the intensive river basin farming depends on flood control and drainage for wet-season crops and on irrigation for any double-cropping. The loss of water control thus spells disaster.

Waterflows in the Asian river basins depend on what happens to the forests on the slopes of the Himalayan and other Asian mountain systems. How the millions of people living in these watersheds manage the land and forests will determine the stability of the streamflows available to the billion or so people living downstream. Unfortunately present land-use trends offer little hope that the forests will be conserved. The mountain people's populations are increasing by over two percent per year according to the projections in Chapter 2, and they perceive no alternative to clearing the forests to meet their needs. Many practice a combination of cropping and animal herding, and livestock populations are growing apace with the human populations.[420] Overgrazing is widespread and getting worse. Fire, routinely used to clear new croplands and to temporarily improve pastures, often gets out of control.[421] Commercial cutting has reduced the forest cover of the Himalayan watershed by as much as 40 percent in the past 30 years, and only an estimated 10 percent of the total area now under management by man in the East and West Himalayas of India (30,000 square kilometers) is still tree-covered.[422] Transformation of montane ecosystems into alpine deserts has become an immediate problem for large mountain populations; landslides and catastrophic floods are becoming annual disasters.[423]

The most severe consequences in the coming decades will occur downstream, across national boundaries in some cases. The potential for international disputes resulting from Himalayan deforestation was highlighted in several U.S. Embassy cables sent in response to Global 2000 Study queries (see appendix C). For example, the U.S. Embassy in Dacca cabled:

Should population pressures lead to large-scale removal of forest cover in Nepal and Assam, Bangladesh as a whole would be adversely affected by the increased runoff. Under present conditions the country is subject to periodic severe flooding, and the prospect of more frequent and damaging floods would threaten both the productivity of the land and large portions of the population. This may be the most significant environmental problem facing Bangladesh by the year 2000.

From the U.S. Embassy in New Delhi:

The combination of both overgrazing and stripping of trees for fuel is making a serious impact on the Himalayan watershed. Effects are seen in landslides, flooding on the Gangetic Plain, lowering of the ground-water table, and reservoir siltation. . . . Resolving the sociological problems of forestry management would appear to be as problematical as finding the resources for reforestation. Supplying an alternative means for the economic survival of the people currently using the forests for their livelihood must proceed simultaneously with good forestry practices.

And from the American Embassy in Islamabad, Pakistan:

The scale of the problem overwhelms scattered attempts to reverse the negative trends. Good forestry practices are not implemented, and no one really knows how much, if any, effective reforestation is taking place. Disruption of watershed cover is responsible for declining soil fertility, accelerated soil erosion, and increasingly severe flooding. . . . The forestry institutes, which direct the few programs, have proven to be inadequately financed and unable to meet either the immediate or the long-term needs of forest preservation.

Similar situations, where deforestation is undermining agriculture downstream, are reported (in the communications reproduced in Appendix C) from Thailand, Indonesia, and the Philippines, and are undoubtedly also occurring in Vietnam, Burma, Laos, and Malaysia.

The Non-Asian Equatorial Belt. Outside Asia, the dependency of the downstream populations on upstream forestry practices is less intense. The non-Asian portions of the equatorial belt are not so heavily populated and do not support a major portion of the earth's settled agriculture. However, even outside of Asia deforestation of watersheds will affect not only natural systems but also the downstream reservoirs, ports, cities, and transportation facilities, all of which will suffer from flooding, sedimentation, and decreased dry-season water levels.[424]

Events in Panama provide a microcosmic picture of what will occur on a much wider scale throughout tropical Africa and Latin America. All the water for operation of the Panama Canal comes from the watershed of Lake Gatun. Farmers have cleared forest from about half the watershed, and operation of the canal is already threatened by destabilization of water flows and by sedimentation of the lake and its reservoirs.

In May 1977, the surface of Lake Gatun dropped 3 feet below the level needed for full canal operation. Ships had to send part of their cargo across the isthmus by land, and some large carriers had to detour around the Horn. Such interruptions in the Canal's performance can be expected to become increasingly frequent if the trends in deforestation cannot be reversed.[425]

The highlands of Ethiopia and of the Peruvian, Equadorian and Bolivian Andes have long suffered from the effects of deforestation and are especially vulnerable to the consequent ecological deterioration. While their salubrious climates often attract more human settlements than the surrounding lowlands, the mountain terrain makes most soils prone to erosion whenever farming becomes intensive.[426] The hilly rainforest areas of West Africa are likewise subject to severe erosion, as population pressure forces shifting cultivators to shorten or eliminate fallow periods.[427] Consequently, some areas have already become useless badlands.

The elimination of tropical forests has several other damaging effects that are less dramatic than catastrophic floods. As regions are deforested, they lose much of the cooling effect of shade evapotranspiration and develop harsh microclimates.[428] Soil, fauna and flora are exposed to the full force of the sun, rain and wind. Plants that can survive are often vigorous weeds. Vain attempts are made to control the tough, inedible grasses that choke out other vegetation by more frequent burning, and the fires eat further into the remnant stands of trees, accelerating the decrease in life-support capacity.

Open Woodlands

Knowledge of open woodlands is fragmentary, as they are included in few resource inventories. They are thought to cover about 30 percent of the earth's total forest area, or about 1.2 billion hectares, but they contain less than 10 percent of the total global stock of wood. About half of the earth's total extent of this type of ecosystem is located in Africa, about 15 percent is in North America, and 12 percent in South America.[429]

Open woodlands in the tropics are found in semiarid zones, where rainfall is insufficient to support a dense closed forest. In these dry areas, fire is an effective tool for weed control and land-clearing. Being sparse, open woodland can supply only relatively small quantities of fuel for expanding populations and, in many countries (such as Sudan, Chad, Niger, Yemen, Iran, Afghanistan, Pakistan, India, and Nepal), have been nearly eliminated by wood gatherers.[430] Open

woodlands are most often used as rangeland, and their regeneration is inhibited by burning and overgrazing. Although most open forest species are fire-resistant, the trees in many regions have been decimated by too frequent or too severe burning in attempts to make short-term improvements.[431]

The transformation of open woodland to desert is well documented and has in many instances taken place within living memory. Where firewood gathering, overgrazing and uncontrolled burning occur, soil nutrients are leached beyond the reach of remnant plants, soil organic matter is depleted, erosion by wind and water becomes severe, and the ultimate consequence is often desertification. A large scale shift of vegetational belts is underway with desert encroaching into dry prairie, dry prairie into savanna, and savanna into forest.[432] By 2000 this succession will have sharply reduced the rangeland possibilities of the overused open woodlands.

Prospects for Amelioration

The demand for forest products, grazing land, and cropland will be high in the decades ahead, and the trends for both open woodlands and closed forests imply much tropical deforestation in the equatorial belt. Can these trends, and the associated environmental impacts, be reversed? The prospects are mixed. Many complex interacting factors are involved. No amelioration can be anticipated until there is awareness and, given awareness, explicit program ideas, then testing and demonstration. But forests are long-term resources, and economic considerations—especially during times of high discount rates—encourage short-term thinking. Finally, technologies are being developed which will make forest clearing quicker and less expensive. These factors all require examination.

There is a need for increased awareness both locally and within institutions. The Chipko Andolan "tree hugger" movement in northern India is an interesting example of growing awareness at the local level. The following passage is paraphrased from S.K. Chauhan's 1978 article[433] describing that movement:

Literally linking arms against indiscriminate deforestation by the lumber industry, these Himalayan villagers protectively hug the trees when lumberjacks approach to fell them! The Chipko movement's primary objective is to force the state government of Uttar Pradesh to change its antiquated forest policy. Most of the deforestation that takes place in this area is not because of wood collecting to meet basic energy needs but the result of the insatiable demand of the lumber industry.

After a serious flood and landslide five years ago, people of this region came to realize that their lives were intricately interwoven with the surrounding forest, and that official policy since colonial times had been tearing that web apart. As the thick, broad-leaf forests on the mountain tops were slowly sold away, the humus sponge that held the monsoon water back disappeared. Perennial streams now dry up soon after the monsoon season, and the collection of firewood has become a major preoccupation of the hill women. This deforestation has increased soil erosion and decreased local agricultural productivity.

The ecological usefulness of the government's afforestation programs in the region can be disputed. Under these programs, most of the felled oaks, rhododendron, and other broad-leaf trees are replaced with pine, because they grow faster and their wood is wanted in the market. But pine forests do not produce any humus to absorb water or increase soil fertility. Without urgent, proper management of these forests, the agricultural economy of a vast region of plains as well as hills will be threatened.

The Chipko leaders have organized large voluntary afforestation programs, planting broad-leaf trees in mountain areas and along riverbanks to halt erosion and provide a source of fuelwood. Yet the fact that the villagers themselves practice such conservation techniques, and feel impelled to bodily prevent the razing of trees, illustrates the failure of the country's development strategy. Instead of trying to link the life and economy of the local people, and thereby their development, with the rational exploitation of the only resource surrounding them (in this case, the forests) the government continues to support policies that regard these resources as things to be sold to the highest bidder.

Much more than local awareness is called for; institutional awareness and concern is imperative. In recent years there have been some encouraging signs of institutional awareness, at least at the international level. These developments include the establishment of the United Nations Environmental Program and the development of the World Bank policy for environmental as well as industrial forestry.[434] The U.S. Department of State and its Agency for International Development recently sponsored a strategy conference on tropical deforestation.[435] The papers presented at the Seventh World Forestry Congress, held in Buenos Aires in 1972, are probably the most comprehensive set of papers on silviculture as it is practiced today around the world.[436] Numerous LDC governments (including Malaysia, the Philippines, Thailand, India, China, and South Korea) are now showing serious concern over deforestation,[437] and these institutional devel-

opments may foreshadow increased financial support for forest management in the LDCs. However, forest conservation and reforestation projects will continue to face stiff competition for funds and institutional support. Industrial and agricultural projects that show a quick profit and give a more immediate response to the LDC's urgent need for economic growth are likely to continue to receive higher priority. Forestry projects that do receive priority and funding will still face formidable ecological, bureaucratic, and (perhaps even more formidable) sociological obstacles.

Several types of programs have been proposed to offset the adverse effects of deforestation in the LDCs. These proposals include:

• Better management of existing forest resources;
• Reforestation;
• Tree Plantations;
• Rangeland management with grazing controls and pasture improvement;
• Restriction of new land clearing, based on soil capability studies;
• Development of agro-forestry techniques for people who now have no alternative to planting annual crops on steep slopes;
• Dissemination of more efficient wood cooking stoves;
• Development of bio-gas and solar stoves to replace wood and charcoal burners; and
• Intensification of agriculture and other employment-creating forms of rural development in order to reduce the agricultural pressures on the remaining forest lands.

The *technical* feasibility of implementing some of these proposals in some less developed countries (especially those in the more temperate zones) has been tested in recent years. Agro-forestry projects (especially for palm oil) have been developed over the past decade in Malaysia,[438] and significant reforestation has been accomplished over the past two decades in the People's Republic of China.[439] Industrial wood plantations have been established in parts of Angola, Argentina, Brazil, Chile, India, Indonesia, Kenya, the Republic of Korea, Malawi, Morocco, Tanzania, and Zambia.[440] A village fuelwood plantation program is underway in the Republic of Korea.[441] Experiments with agroforestry are being carried out in the Philippines[442] and in Nigeria.[443] However, outside of the countries just named, few of these programs have gone beyond the demonstration stage.

Tropical deforestation is caused by a combination of (1) need for additional agricultural land, (2) need for additional fuelwood, and (3) a sustained world demand for tropical woods operating in the absence of effective and enforced programs for forest conservation and management. Synergisms are often involved. For example, although a growing population of subsistence farmers is clearing land to grow food, access to such land is possible in many cases only because commercial logging operations have opened the forests in response to growing domestic and foreign demand for wood products.[444] Access and transportation are also factors in the economics of clearing steep slopes. Even if the soil washes away after only one or two crops, farmers can support themselves over several seasons of clearing by selling firewood or charcoal on the regional market if transportation is available.[445] One of the causes of the growing world demand for forest products is, of course, population growth, but income is also a major factor, and the U.N. Food and Agriculture Organization (FAO) is well aware of both. Edouard Saouma, FAO Director General, stated recently that, based on projections of past trends:

Over the next 16 years it is expected that consumption of forestry products will rise by 75 percent to an annual roundwood equivalent of 4,000 million m^3. If international development strategies were to increase the buying power of the masses of people in the developing world, even by a small fraction, projected consumption figures would be far higher.[446]

In addition, possibilities for earning foreign exchange, needed by many LDCs to reduce large foreign debts, will continue to be a motivating factor in establishing tropical forest policy[447] and will therefore also influence the possibilities for ameliorating the tropical deforestation trends.

While techniques and technologies are being developed that will assist in protecting and expanding forests, other technical developments may affect the future of tropical forests adversely. A variety of faster, less costly technologies are being developed to replace cutting and burning, the traditional methods of clearing. For example, Agent Orange, the chemical defoliant used widely by U.S. armed forces in Vietnam, is reportedly available in farm supply stores in the Amazon basin, where it is used to clear land for cultivation.[448] The chemical 2,4,5-T, one of two herbicides contained in Agent Orange and invariably contaminated with the toxic compound dioxin, is now banned in the United States[449] because it has been linked with birth defects and miscarriages.*

Another innovative technique for efficient clearing of tropical forests in Brazil is the *correntao*.[450] This involves the use of very large anchor chains, roughly 100 meters in length and weighing up to 10 tons. Enormous tractors attached to each end drag them through the forest, uprooting trees and everything else in the path.† Still another technological development likely to significantly affect at least the Brazilian tropical forests is the "floating papermill." In 1978, industrialist Daniel Ludwig's floating papermill (longer than two football fields in size) was towed from its construction site in Japan through the Indian and Atlantic Oceans to its final destination along the Jari River, a tributary of the Amazon. *Time* magazine, reporting on the $250 million plant, commented that by 1981 the factory "will turn out 750 metric tons of bleached kraft pulp a day, enough to make a single strand of toilet paper stretching more than 6-½ times around the world. . . . To feed the mill's appetite, Ludwig's crews have cleared nearly 250,000 acres of jungle so far and planted 81 million fast-growing trees.[451] Eventually, Ludwig plans to "tame" an area of rain forest almost the size of Connecticut.

What then are the prospects for amelioration of the tropical deforestation trends in the LDC? While there are a number of important and encouraging demonstration projects, environmentally significant conservation and reforestation practices cannot be expected unless and until technically competent institutions are provided with more resources and authority.[452] Sociological research on community cooperation and institutions will also be necessary if village-level woodlots to meet woodlot and environmental needs are to be widely established.[453]

By the Year 2000

Assuming no change in policy (the standard policy assumption of the Global 2000 Study's projections), deforestation can be expected to continue as projected in Chapter 8. Deforestation will affect the rural segments of the LDC populations most severely. Small farmers in South and Southeast Asia, already among the world's poorest, will

---

*The Comptroller General of the United States has recommended that the Department of Defense conduct a survey of any long-term medical effects on military personnel who were

likely to have been exposed to herbicides in South Vietnam (*Health Effects of Exposure to Herbicide Orange in Vietnam Should Be Resolved*, Washington: U.S. General Accounting Office, Apr. 6, 1979.)
†This technique was used earlier (and may have been developed initially) in the United States, where it was used in aridzone range management. Undesirable woody vegetation was scraped from the land with heavy chains, after which preferred range grasses were sown. (John Valentine, *Range Development and Improvement*, Provo: Brigham Young Univ. Press, 1974, p. 516.)

face yet harder times as waterflows from the mountain watersheds become more erratic and as reservoirs essential for irrigation are filled with silt eroded from the deforested slopes. In Africa, herdsmen will find that rangeland will recover more slowly (where it does recover) from periodic droughts. Throughout the LDCs millions of farmers using shifting agriculture will experience sharply declining harvests as yields fall and the short fallow periods fail to restore soil fertility.

A consequence of deforestation and simultaneous population growth is that wood for fuel will be in short supply and more people will be forced to use grass, crop residues, and animal dung for cooking fuel, further endangering land productivity, since these organic materials are essential for the maintenance of soil quality. As prices for commercial fuel increase and gathered fuels become scarcer, the costs (both monetary and temporal) of boiling water and cooking food may become prohibitive for the poorest populations, especially in areas where fuelwood plantations have not been established.

Increased Intensity of Forest Management

As explained in Chapter 8, the real price of forest products is expected to rise in the coming two decades. The rising prices will enhance the profitability of investments in forest management, and forests can be expected to become increasingly subject to human control and manipulation through intensive silviculture and tree farming.

While it is not possible to know precisely how fast intensive silviculture will develop, the trend is clear. It is also clear that there will be both positive and negative environmental consequences. On the positive side, the higher yields resulting from faster growth of wood in the intensively managed stands and from more complete exploitation of accessible natural stands should take some pressure off the less accessible forest areas and thus allow the preservation of some forests in their natural state. Wood from intensively managed stands could certainly enhance the human environment for those who depend on firewood and charcoal for domestic fuel. On the negative side, a number of adverse environmental effects are anticipated, some of which raise questions about the basic viability of intensive silviculture, especially in the tropics.

The technological problems involved, are similar in many ways to those of intensive agriculture. Both intensive silviculture and intensive agricul-

ture involve high-yield strains and monocultures. Plant geneticists have been at work not only on grains but also on trees, and there are hopes that fast-growing supertree plantations[454] will be to forestry what Green Revolution methods have been to agriculture.* However, monocultures of genetically identical trees face essentially the same problems as monocultures of genetically identical grains. These basic problems were discussed at some length for the case of the Green Revolution in the food and agriculture section of this chapter; a few points particularly relevant to intensive silviculture and tree farming will be considered here.

A major, perhaps underestimated problem faced by both intensive silviculture and intensive agriculture is the increasing energy subsidies they require. The fossil fuel subsidies inherent in intensive agriculture have received much attention and have been discussed extensively in the literature (and earlier in this chapter), but the energy requirements of intensive silviculture have been examined relatively little. A 1970 study[455] found that fertilization and shorter rotation resulted in a 38 percent increase in Douglas fir production, while costs (excluding any costs of environmental protection) increased 64 percent. Still higher cost increases could be anticipated if the energy subsidies had been priced at the post-1973 level. Nonetheless it is certainly true that trees grow rapidly in the tropics, producing rotation times as short as 10 years. Attention is now being focused on nitrogen-fixing species that may not require fertilizer. More attention to and testing of indigenous species are needed, rather than further attempts to grow a few exotic species. But no matter what species are ultimately chosen, the energy subsidies inherent in intensive silviculture deserve closer examination before major commitments are made.

Another difficulty in applying the intensive Green Revolution methods to forests is that the time between harvests is so much longer for trees than for grains. A combination of genetics and management practices is expected to reduce temperate-zone growth cycles from 150 to 40 years for Douglas fir and from 60 to 35–40 years for southern pine.[456] Nonetheless, the exposure period for genetically identical monocultures of trees

---

*In 1975, the journal of the American Forest Institute looked forward to an increase of 100 percent in the productivity of land in the production of wood and an increase of 300 percent in fiber yields ("More Wood, Faster," *Green America*, Fall 1975).

(even in the tropics) will always be long compared with the corresponding exposure period for grains. As with grains, pests and pathogens may evolve ways to overcome the genetic defenses of single strains, producing plant epidemics comparable to the southern corn blight or the Dutch elm disease.[457]

As with the deforestation problem, the negative environmental impacts of intensive silviculture will probably be more severe in the tropics than in the temperate zones. Foresters and biologists have suspected for some time that the great ecological diversity of tropical forests, which makes them exceptionally stable under natural conditions, also makes them exceptionally vulnerable to permanent damage from logging operations and that natural forest stands degrade severely when subjected to intense use.[458]

Most silvicultural methods have been developed by foresters in the temperate zones and are of doubtful suitability or utility for forests of the humid tropics. A substantial research investment must be made to develop appropriate silvicultural methods for tropical environments. However, the time lag inherent in forestry research (a growth cycle measured in decades, as opposed to months for grains) delays the economic return from tropical forest research investments, making it difficult to obtain support for forestry research in the LDCs. In the absence of extensive tropical forestry research, technological breakthroughs are not likely, and the application of doubtful forest management methods can be expected to continue for at least several decades.

There are other reasons for environmental concern about increased silvicultural intensity: (1) In both the industrialized nations and the LDCs, the ability of many forest soils to sustain short-rotation tree cropping is doubtful. Recent U.S. research indicates that even in quickly recovering temperate-zone forests, the loss of soil nutrients following a clear-cutting operation is significant.[459] (2) There is some evidence that plantations of uniformly aged trees do not stabilize watersheds as well as the natural forests that preceded them. (3) Applications of pesticides and fertilizers are likely to affect ecosystem elements other than the trees they are intended for, reducing the diversity of both flora and fauna and threatening the health of forest lakes and streams. (4) In some places intensively managed forests may even become sources of pollution (from fertilizers and other applied chemicals), where they once functioned as filters of air and water.[460]

Given all these problems, how rapidly can the methods of intensive silviculture be applied? Even with the higher prices anticipated for forest products, there are serious difficulties in the way of rapid, global developments in intensive silviculture, and the pace of application promises to be slower than was the case for intensive agricultural methods.

To date, experience with intensive silviculture is limited to a very small number of complete planting-to-harvest cycles. Furthermore, as shown in Chapter 8, intensive silviculture is being practiced at present on a regional scale only in Europe, although significant local developments are taking place in Japan, North America, the People's Republic of China, Brazil, South Korea, and New Zealand. Less intensive techniques, such as regulation of livestock, pest control and reforestation are practiced on parts of the forests in most industrialized countries and on scattered sites in many LDCs. In most forests outside Europe and North America, however, the only management inputs are fire control and occasional cutting.

As a result of all of these present and potential problems, and because of limited planting-to-harvest experience, most businessmen and investors consider plantation forestry outside of the temperate zone an unproven technology.[461] Many decades will pass before the questions created by these problems have been answered. Investors will be slow to move into intensive silviculture, particularly in the tropics. Because of technical problems, most multinational forest product companies do not expect that the incentives* will warrant large-scale commercial planting before the 1990s.[462] It is even less certain when and if publicly sponsored and local commercial enterprises will undertake plantation forestry projects on a scale that would alleviate local and global firewood scarcities.

For all these reasons, major industrial wood harvests from manmade tropical forests are not likely to begin by the year 2000. Nonetheless, locally important harvests of wood for fuel and for village-level construction could be realized by 2000, and important watershed protection could be achieved in some areas where policies and attitudes are now changing and where fast-growing tree species are available.

---

*Several years ago, Brazil established strong tax incentives for reforestation, and a substantial amount of planting was done hastily by corporations and large landowners in the country's subtropical areas. Under these incentives, the area devoted annually to commercial planting was about three times the goal set by the Food and Agriculture Organization for all of Latin America. Brazil, however, has now reduced the tax incentives. (Gordon Fox, "Commercial Forestry," *Proceedings, U.S. Strategy Conference on Tropical Deforestation*, Washington: Department of State, Oct. 1978.)

Global-Scale Environmental Impacts

There are two global-scale environmental impacts to be anticipated from the forestry projections. First is a potential impact on the world's climate. Second is a significant reduction in the number of plant and animal species on the planet.

Changes in Climate

The anticipated change in global forest inventory may affect global climate patterns by increasing the amount of carbon dioxide in the atmosphere. Climatologists have been aware of a steady increase in atmospheric carbon dioxide (CO_2) for many years, and some, as already stated in Chapter 4, have expressed concern that a global warming trend may result. Until recently, it was assumed by most experts* that nearly all of the increase was coming from the burning of fossil fuels and that the earth's plants were absorbing some of the excess. However, recent calculations that take deforestation into account indicate that carbon stored in the biomass has been decreasing rather than increasing. One rough estimate indicates that as much as half the carbon in the earth's biomass may be stored in the forests, much of it in the tropics, and that current rates of forest clearing may be releasing amounts of carbon dioxide approximately equivalent to the amounts coming from fossil fuel consumption.[463] Others feel that these amounts and rates are probably lower. It is well known that not all of the CO_2 released to the atmosphere remains there, but there is still debate over the sinks. Some of the released CO_2 is stored in new forest growth, but the net decrease in wood volume projected in this study implies an acceleration of the CO_2 buildup that may have significance for climate as early as 2050.

Changes in Biological Diversity

The second global change implied by the forestry projections is a significant reduction in biotic diversity. The extent to which the diversity of the flora and fauna is maintained provides a basic index to the ecological health of the planet. Presently the world's biota contains an estimated 3–10 million species.[464] Until the present century, the number of species extinguished as a result of human activities was small, and the species so affected were regarded as curiosities. Between now and 2000, however, the number of extinctions caused by human activities will increase rapidly. Loss of wild habitat may be the single most important factor. The projected growth in human population and economic activity can be expected to create enormous economic and political pressure to convert the planet's remaining wild lands to other uses. As a consequence, the extinction rate will accelerate considerably.

The death of an individual is very different from the death of a species. A species is a natural biotic unit—a population or a series of populations of sufficient genetic similarity that successful reproduction between individuals can take place. The death of an individual of a particular species represents the loss of one of a series of similar individuals all capable of reproducing the basic form, while the death of a species represents both the loss of the basic form and its reproductive potential.

Extinction, then, is an irreversible process through which the potential contributions of biological resources are lost forever. In fact, plant and animal species are the only truly nonrenewable resources.[465] Most resources traditionally termed "nonrenewable"—minerals and fossil fuels—received that label because they lack the reproductive capability. Yet most nonbiological compounds and elements are, at least in theory, fully renewable. Given sufficient energy, nonbiological resources can be separated, transformed, and restored to any desired form. By contrast, biotic resources—species (not individuals) and ecosystems—are completely nonrenewable.* Once extinguished, species cannot be recreated. When extinct, biotic resources and their contributions are lost forever.

How many extinctions are implied by the Global 2000 Study's forestry projections? An estimate was prepared for the Global 2000 Study by Thomas E. Lovejoy of the World Wildlife Fund. Dr. Lovejoy's analysis, together with a tabular summary of the results, is presented on the next four pages. His figures, while admittedly rough, are frightening in magnitude. *If present trends continue—as they certainly will in many areas—hundreds of thousands of species can be expected to be lost by the year 2000.*

Extinction, of course, is the normal fate of virtually all species. The gradual processes of natural extinction will continue in the years ahead, but the *extinctions projected for the coming decades will be largely human-generated and on a scale that renders natural extinction trivial by comparison.*

---

*G. E. Hutchinson is an exception. In 1954 he estimated that the increase in atmospheric CO_2 from forest destruction was about equal to that from the burning of fossil fuels ("The Biochemistry of the Terrestrial Atmosphere," in G. P. Kuiper, ed., *The Solar System*, Chicago: Univ. of Chicago Press, 1954, vol. II, pp. 371–433).

---

*Also see the discussion of this point in Chapter 12.

A PROJECTION OF SPECIES EXTINCTIONS*

Virtually all of the Global 2000 Study's projections—especially the forestry, fisheries, population, and GNP projections—have implications for the extinction of species. Accepting these projections as correct, how many extinctions can be anticipated by 2000?

Probably the largest contribution to extinctions over the next two decades will come as a result of deforestation and forest disruption (e.g. cutting "high-grade" species), especially in the tropics. The forestry projections in Chapter 8 provide an estimate of the amount of tropical deforestation to be expected. The question then is: What fraction of the species now present will be extinguished as a result of that deforestation?

Possible answers are provided by the curves in Figure 13–8. The curves in this figure do not represent alternative scenarios but rather reflect the uncertainty in the percent of species lost as a result of a given amount of deforestation. The endpoints are known with more accuracy than other points on the curves. Clearly, at zero deforestation the resulting loss of species is zero—and for 100 percent deforestation, the loss approaches 100 percent. The reasons for the high losses at 100 percent deforestation are as follows.

The lush appearance of tropical rain forests masks the fact that these ecosystems are among the most diverse and fragile in the entire world. The diversity† of tropical forests stems in part from the tremendous variety of life zones created by altitude, temperature, and rainfall variations.[467] The fragility of tropical forests stems from the fact that, in general, tropical soils contain only a very limited stock of nutrients. Typically, the nutrients in tropical soils are only a small part of the total inventory of nutrients in the tropical ecosystem. Most of the nutrients are in the diverse flora and fauna of the forests themselves. Tropical forests sustain themselves through a rapid and highly efficient recycling of nutrients. Little nutrient is lost when an organism dies, but when extensive areas of forest are cleared, the nutrients are quickly leached out and lost.[468]

Studies have shown that there are a wide variety of tropical soils. Some (such as those in lowland swamps) are rich, but most are either thin, infertile, and highly acidic, or thick and highly leached of nutrients. Recent aerial surveys of the Amazon basin, for example, indicate that only 2 percent of the soils are suitable for sustained agriculture.[469] Once cleared, the recycling of nutrients is interrupted, often permanently. In the absence of the forest cover, the remaining vegetation and exposed soil cannot hold the rainfall and release the water slowly. The critical nutrients are quickly leached from the soils, and erosion sets in—first, sheet erosion, then gully erosion. In some areas only a few years are required for once dense forest lands to turn to virtual pavements of laterite, exposed rock, base soil, or coarse "weed" grasses. The Maryland-sized area of Bragantina in the Amazon basin is probably the largest and best-known area to have already undergone this process, becoming what has been called a "ghost landscape."[470]

With formerly recycled nutrients lost through deforestation and its aftereffects, the capacity of a tropical rain forest to regenerate itself is highly limited and much less than that of a temperate forest. The possibilities for regeneration are limited further by the fact that the reproductive biology of many of the tree species found in mature tropical forests is adapted to recolonizing small patches of disturbed forest rather than the large areas now being cleared.[471] As a result and in spite of rapid succession rates, the disruption and simplification from deforestation of tropical rain forests is, for the most part, irreversible, given the time scale necessary to preserve the present mature and diverse biota. While a few attempts at reforestation to natural tropical forest are being made, only limited success has yet been

---

*This projection was developed for the Global 2000 Study by Dr. Thomas E. Lovejoy of the World Wildlife Fund.
†Diversity here is used simply in the sense of numbers of species. Ecologists sometimes use more complex indices of ecological diversity.

Efforts to meet basic human needs and rising expectations are likely to lead to the extinction of between one-fifth and one-seventh of all species over the next two decades. A substantial fraction of the extinctions are expected to occur in the tropics.

The lost potential of the earth's biological resources is often neglected in considering the con-

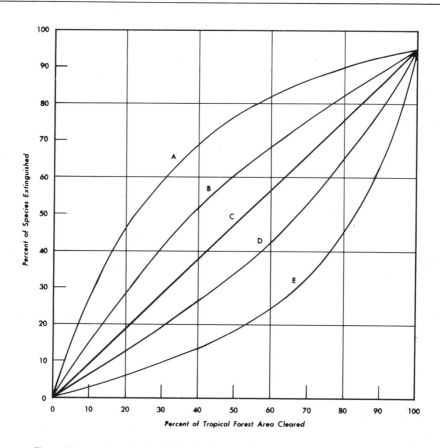

Figure 13-8. Loss of species through clearing of tropical forest areas—five projections.

achieved (e.g., in Puerto Rico). More typically, tropical forests are either cleared and abandoned, or (if the soil and economics permit) converted to plantation forests of high-growth species such as *Eucalyptus, Pinus,* and *Gmelina,* which are not suitable for the diverse local fauna found in mature tropical forests.

As a consequence (and for purposes of the rough calculations here) the rain forest areas modified by deforestation can be expected, with few exceptions, to include a negligible number of the species that were present in the virgin forests. The estimate used for the end-point of the curves in the figure for 100 percent deforestation is therefore a 95 percent loss of species. So much for the endpoints of the curves.

The general shape of the curves (convex, linear, or concave) depends in large part on the size of the areas needed to preserve the ecosystems on which the species depend. Unfortunately, little is known about the size of these areas.[472] Most tropical species occur at exceedingly low densities. Dispersal (to compensate for local extinctions) is probably an important part of their biology,[473] and this survival strat-

sequences of deforestation in the tropics. Tropical forests contain both the richest variety and the least well known flora and fauna in the world. It would be difficult to overstate the potential value of this huge stock of biological capital, which, if carefully managed, could be a rich, sustainable source of building materials and fuel, as well as medicinal plants, specialty woods, nuts, and fruits.

egy is impeded or precluded when forest areas are reduced to isolated reserves.

It is also known that only a limited amount of a rain forest region can be converted to nonforest before local (or regional) changes in climate will occur, endangering the remaining forest areas. For example, current estimates put the percent of precipitation in the Amazon basin generated by the forest (as opposed to the ocean) at slightly over 50 percent.[474] Although this contribution to the precipitation will not be eliminated entirely by deforestation, it will be reduced, and reductions in rainfall beyond a certain point could initiate an irreversible drying trend.

In the face of our limited knowledge, the concept of "refugia" provides one approach to estimating the areas needed to preserve tropical ecosystems and their species. During the Pleistocene glaciations, the climate in the equatorial regions was generally dryer and unable to support tropical rain forests. Rain forests did survive, however, in relatively small patches, now termed refugia.[475] It has been found that within the Amazon basin there are areas of concentration of species not occurring elsewhere (centers of endemism), and these areas of concentration are thought by many ecologists to represent vestiges of Pleistocene refugia. Refugia have now been identified in the basin for a few families of organisms (primarily small animals, including some insects and a few plants).[476] There is wide variation in size among the areas of concentration that have been measured, the smallest areas being for the class with the most species (i.e., insects). And, of course, the smaller the area of concentration, the more vulnerable the species are to extinction by reason of deforestation and loss of habitat.

How then should the curves in Figure 13–8 be drawn? Assuming that the refugia concept applies generally to all tropical forests, a convex curve (curve A or B) would result if the refugia turn out to be relatively small and if the refugia should happen to be cleared first. A linear curve (curve C) would result from random cutting if the refugia were not adjacent but overlapping, or were relatively small. (The limited data now available suggest that the re-

fugia are in fact relatively small for classes with the most numerous species.[477]) A concave curve (curve D or E) would result if the refugia should turn out to be small and highly overlapping, and (a) if efforts are made to identify and preserve the refugia, or (b) if the refugia are widely separated from one another.

While curve D is used in the following calculations,[478] it may underestimate the impacts of the projected deforestation.* Were it possible—which it is not—to create instantly a minimum system of biological reserves of adequate size and ideal location, the impacts of the projected deforestation would still be on the order of the effects of the Pleistocene glaciations.[479] Even so, such a system would not be secure because of local climatic effects and ever rising political and economic pressures. It is difficult to estimate how much of the world's tropical forest has been cleared and how such pressures will influence future cutting, but considering the amount of forest known to have already been destroyed, it is too late to achieve even the minimum system of reserves. Furthermore, present global conservation plans for rain forests are limited. For example, the *most ambitious proposal* for conservation in the Amazon basin would be site parks and reserves in the areas where refugia are thought to have occurred, but the total area of the parks and

---

*Even the deforestation projected in Chapter 8 may have been underestimated. Warwick Kerr predicts the loss of all Amazon forests (B. Dickson, "Brazil Learns Its Ecological Lessons the Hard Way," *Nature*, vol. 275, 1978, pp. 684–85), and P. W. Richards (op. cit.) predicts the loss of all untouched rain forests by the century's end. Very recently, however, some new information has become available for the tropical forests of the Amazon basin. According to Larry Rohter (op. cit.), Brazil's National Space Research Institute analyzed 32 photographs taken from a Landsat satellite and estimated in late 1978 that as much as one-tenth of the Brazilian Amazon forest has been razed. This is an area larger than the state of Texas and probably does not include areas that are now forested but are no longer diverse, virgin forest. On the matter of future cutting, the Brazilian Government is reported to be studying the use of "risk contracts" for the large-scale logging in the Amazon basin. The Superintendency for the Development of the Amazon (SUDAM) has identified approximately 100 million additional acres (between 5 and 10 percent of the total area of the Amazon basin) for timber exploitation.

However, if present trends continue, sustained benefits from this capital will never be realized. Unique local plants and animals will be unknowingly and carelessly destroyed. Particularly well-

adapted or fast-growing local trees will be cut before their fruits or seeds are collected. Predatory insects and plants with herbicidal or insecticidal properties will be lost for lack of observation and

TABLE 13–30

Extinctions of Species Implied by the Global 2000 Study's Projections

	Present Species[a] (in thousands)	Projected Deforestation[b]	Loss of Species[c]	Extinctions[d] (in thousands)
	LOW DEFORESTATION CASE[b]			
Tropical forests				
Latin America	300–1,000	50	33	100–333
Africa	150–500	20	13	20–65
S. and SE. Asia	300–1,000	60	43	129–430
Subtotal	759–2,500			249–828
All other habitats				
Oceans, fresh water, nontropical forests, islands, etc.	2,250–7,500	–	8[e]	188–625
Total	3,000–10,000			437–1,453
	HIGH DEFORESTATION CASE[b]			
Tropical Forests				
Latin America	300–1,000	67	50	150–500
Africa	150–500	67	50	75–250
S. and SE. Asia	300–1,000	67	50	150–500
Subtotal	750–2,500			375–1,250
All other habitats				
Oceans, fresh water, nontropical forests, islands, etc.	2,250–7,500	–	8[e]	188–625
Total	3,000–10,000			563–1,875

[a] The total of 3–10 million species (see reference 85) are assumed to be distributed roughly as follows: 10 percent in the virgin forests of the Amazon (P. H. Raven, personal communication to T. E. Lovejoy, 1974), 5 percent in African tropical forests, 10 percent in south and southeast Asian tropical forests, and 75 percent elsewhere (oceans, fresh water, nontropical forests, islands, etc.). It should be noted that the figures for the percentage of the world's biota in tropical rain forests are conservative. Many estimates (see Norman Myers, *The Sinking Ark*, London: Pergamon, forthcoming, 1979) place 30–40 percent of the total in the moist tropics and 70–80 percent in the tropics as a whole.
[b] See the forestry projections in Chapter 8.
[c] Derived from curve C in Figure 13–8.
[d] Calculated as the percent loss of species times the present number of species.
[e] The combined effects of loss of habitat, presence of toxic substances, eutrophication, desertification, simplification of forests in the temperate zones, acid rain, etc.—spread over five continents and the two-thirds of the planet's surface covered by the seas—are assumed to lead to a loss of one-twelfth of the planet's biota.

reserves would comprise only 5 percent of the total land area of the Amazon.[480] Such a system would mimic the distribution of forests at the height of the Pleistocene glaciations.[481]

What then is a reasonable estimate of global extinctions by 2000? Given the amount of tropical forest already lost (which is important but often ignored), the extinctions can be estimated as shown in Table 13–30. In the low deforestation case, approximately 15 percent of the planet's species can be expected to be lost. In the high deforestation case, perhaps as much as 20 percent will be lost. This means

that of the 3–10 million species[482] now present on the earth, at least 500,000–600,000 will be extinguished during the next two decades. The largest number of extinctions can be expected in the insect order—many of them beneficial species—simply because there are so very many species of insects. The next highest number of extinctions will be among plants. While the projected extinctions refer to all biota, they are *much* larger than the 1,000 bird and mammal species now recognized as endangered.[483] Clearly the extinctions caused by human activities will rise to unprecedented rates by 2000.

study. Diverse assemblies of gigantic trees, their understories, and their resident communities of mammals, birds, and insects—natural wonders every bit as unique and beautiful as the Grand

Canyon—will be irreparably lost. In short, the projected loss of tropical forests represents a massive expenditure of biological capital, an expenditure so sudden and so large that it will surely limit the future benefits that even careful management and husbanding can sustain from the remaining biotic resources of the earth.[466]

Conclusions

The Global 2000 Study's forestry projections have serious implications for the environment. In the Asian LDC's, deforestation will cause extensive erosion and will destabilize waterflows, adversely affecting the agriculture on which a quarter of the world's total human population depends. In the tropical zones of Africa and Latin America, deforestation will lead, in many cases, to the loss of the nutrients and to reduction of the soil quality essential for the recovery of the forests. Desert encroachment can be anticipated in parts of nearly every continent. Extinctions of species caused by human activities will explode to rates never before observed, perhaps on the same order as during the Pleistocene glaciations.[484]

The deforestation will be caused by a combination of population increase and economic growth. Currently the primary cause is agricultural expansion. By 2000, agriculture will have expanded about as far as it can, and fuelwood and forest product demands will become the primary causes. Populations needing firewood, charcoal, plots for agriculture, lands for grazing, and materials for village construction are projected to continue their rapid growth over the next two decades. In the industrialized nations, slower population growth coupled with economic growth and high per capita consumption of forest products will also have a large impact on world forests through increased demands for wood and paper products. The demand for commercial timber and paper in the less developed countries, while starting at a low base, is rising considerably faster than that in the industrialized countries, and as a result a rising number of LDCs are becoming dependent on forest-product imports.[485]

Prospects for amelioration of these trends are mixed, at best. On the one hand, there are a large number of difficulties. Silvicultural methods developed primarily in the temperate zones are of doubtful utility in the tropics, where most of the deforestation will occur. Intensive silviculture (tree plantations), patterned after Green Revolution agriculture, is a much-discussed hope but its methods face the same problems (including energy-intensiveness and genetic vulnerability of single-strain monocultures) as Green Revolution agriculture and over much longer planting-to-harvest periods. Experience with these methods (especially in the tropics) is limited to a few growth cycles at most. Investors are cautious, and major world plantings are not expected before the 1990s at the earliest because the economic incentives do not match the risks involved. On the other hand, the need for small-scale village woodlots is now recognized by international aid agencies and by many national governments, and many programs of this sort are now planned or underway.[486]

The tragedy of forests is that, like the commons,[487] they are another example of a common resource subject to misuse—but on a global scale. While forest lands are owned by individuals (or governments), forests provide community, national, and international benefits that go well beyond the benefits usually considered in forest management decisions. Moderation of temperatures, stabilization of waterflows, protection of soils, and provision of habitats for a wealth of unexamined biotic resources are some of the benefits of forests that accrue to society as a whole and do not enter into the normal calculus of forestry economics.

The difficulty—some would say, the impossibility—of managing common resources is well known. Garrett Hardin has written about the specific problem of managing and protecting commons-type biological resources.[488] He concludes that biotic resources cannot be preserved under commons management, and that socialism or private enterprise are the only workable alternatives, both of which have limitations. The socialism approach suffers from the problem of *quis custodiet ipsos custodes?* (who will watch the watchman himself?). The private enterprise approach, Hardin argues, has a serious weakness in the way it deals with time, the question being: Can conservation be accomplished over time solely as a result of economic self-interest?

Aldo Leopold, a wise and insightful observer of biotic resources and economic systems, considered this question and concluded:

A system of conservation based solely on economic self-interest is hopelessly lopsided. It tends to ignore, and thus eventually to eliminate, many elements in the land community that lack commercial value, but that are (as far as we know) essential to its healthy functioning. It assumes, falsely, I think, that the economic parts of the biotic clock will function without the uneconomic parts.[489]

More recently, economic analysis has provided further support for Leopold's conclusion.[490] A common approach to management decisions under private enterprise is to calculate the present value of the future stream of benefits to be obtained from alternative management strategies. Other things being equal, management strategies that maximize the present value of discounted future benefits are generally preferred.

What benefits are to be considered, and at what discount rate? Forest benefits to the entire watershed (e.g., water stabilization, erosion control, temperature moderation, species protection, recreation) are often not included in the calculations because they are "external" benefits, i.e., benefits not accruing to the self-interest of the forest landowner. Discount rates are also important because conservation by its very nature concerns itself with future values. As Hardin explains, "The higher the interest rate on money, the more difficult it is to conserve for the future. Or as economists put it: the higher the interest rate, the more heavily the purely rational man must discount the future. . . . Compound discounting, which increases as interest rates increase, diminishes and in the long pull virtually destroys [future values]."[491] And the Global 2000 Study's projections suggest that interest rates will remain high. Virtually every one of the projections is based on the assumption that large amounts of capital investment will be made in the sector; these investments of scarce capital can be expected to keep interest rates quite high.

Scott Overton and Larry Hunt of the University of Oregon have examined the implications of the present-value approach to forest management.

Their particular concern was whether this approach to management and conservation would keep the forest system in equilibrium at an optimal, sustainable yield. They concluded that the conventional economic analysis (ignoring the external costs and benefits of forests to the wider society) "must lead to a pattern of high cuts now and lower cuts later . . . to shorter and shorter rotations to the point of depletion of the resource, and to the conversion of forest lands to other uses until the relative price of forest products rises sufficiently high that the *economic* system is in equilibrium."[492]

It seems likely, therefore, that without basic changes in forest policy throughout much of the world, the environmental consequences of the Global 2000 Study's forestry projections are virtually inevitable. Even the bases for such policy changes are unclear. It is not at all obvious what should be done in each geographic area, and technology is certainly not the whole answer.[493] In general, localized approaches and solutions will probably be needed, but until all of the societal benefits of forests are taken into consideration in making forest policy and management decisions, societies around the world can expect that the forest-related environmental benefits that are taken for granted today will continue to slip away and will be sadly reduced in number and quality by the end of the century.

THE WATER PROJECTIONS AND THE ENVIRONMENT

The Projections

The Study's water resource projections, developed by the Department of the Interior and the Central Intelligence Agency, assume that water supply is constant and that demand increases with growth in population, expansion of irrigated agriculture, and increased industrial activity. The projections stress the severe limitations associated with supply-demand balance. But since regional or local quantitative data are lacking, global aggregates are presented (see Table 13–31).

The present global supply of fresh water (i.e., total runoff) is large relative to demand, at least in theory. Supply is now about 10 times demand but by the year 2000 is projected to be 3.5 times demand. This projection dramatizes the rapidity with which human demand is catching up with the world's theoretical availability of fresh water. However, even these figures are misleading because of the extreme seasonal and geographic unevenness in the distribution of water resources. Even now local and regional deficits occur on a seasonal and, increasingly, perennial basis.

Given present data limitations, the prospects for water in 2000 can be assessed only qualitatively. Based on examples from many areas, the projections anticipate serious water shortages in many nations or regions. Water development projects will be pursued, but severe shortfalls are expected in deficit areas. Areas noted as being particularly susceptible to water shortage include parts of Africa, North America, the Middle East, Latin America, and South Asia. Conflicts among competing water-demanding economic sectors and among nations drawing water from the same river systems are anticipated.

As a further complication, water supplies from streams and rivers may become less reliable in regions where deforestation is stripping watersheds bare. The projected decrease in the world's forests from 20 percent to 16 percent of the land surface by 2000 will take place largely in the LDCs, where needs for water already exceed supplies in some regions.

The water projections assume no climatic change. However, in the event of a cooling trend supplies would be adversely affected as a result of a more erratic pattern of rainfall. A warming trend, on the other hand, might reduce variability and increase supplies slightly, but in the central United States droughts might become more common.

Introduction

It is not possible to analyze the environmental implications of the water projections with precision because environmental impacts tend to apply to specific river basins or other hydrological units, and the water projections summarized in Table 13–31 could not achieve that level of detail. Nonetheless, five environmental topics related to the projections of water supply and to the consequences of water development and use are explored:

- Environmental developments affecting water supply (deteriorating catchments in river basins, acid rain, climatic change);
- Impacts of hydraulic works;
- Water pollution (of urban and industrial origin and of agricultural origin);
- Water-related diseases; and
- Extinction of freshwater species.

This range of topics reflects the multiplicity of characteristics, uses, and values of the water resource: Water is essential to human health and well-being; water is habitat for a diversity of aquatic life; water is a major component (and determinant) of the environment. In short, water is unique among resources in the diversity of its characteristics, uses, and values.

Environmental Developments Affecting Water Supply

Worldwide, two environmental developments are likely to have an impact on water supply by 2000: catchment and river basin deterioration and regional or global changes in climate. The trends in catchment and river basin deterioration are clearly discernible and accelerating. Climatic trends are less clear but just as important. Deteriorating catchment and river basin conditions will adversely affect water supplies by increasing variability. Climatic change could further increase variability.

Deterioration of Catchments and River Basins

From the standpoint of both water supply and water quality, the condition of a catchment or river basin is determined largely by the flora on the upper portions of the basin. The high, often steep portions of the basin usually receive a large proportion of the rainfall, and the flora on these slopes are critically important in determining the quality and flows of water throughout the basin.

A continuous mantle of vegetation in the upper portions of a basin has many benefits. The vegetation breaks the fall of the raindrops, absorbing the kinetic energy before it can dislodge soil particles. The vegetation also slows the runoff and enhances the absorptive properties of the soils. Where vegetation is present over the upper por-

TABLE 13–31

Projected Global Supply and Demand for Water by the Year 2000

Cubic kilometers per year

| | Projected Demand | | |
	With-drawn	Con-sumed[a]	Supply[b]
Irrigation	7,000	4,800	
Domestic	600	100	
Industrial	1,700	170	
Waste dilution	9,000		
Other	400	400	
Total	18,700	5,470	37,700

Source: The work of G. P. Kalinin, as presented in Chapter 9.
[a] Not returned to streams or rivers.
[b] Taken to be the mean annual discharge of all rivers.

tions of a river basin, the basin's water is generally relatively well regulated and clean.

In the absence of vegetative cover, rain flows off a basin's steep upper slopes as it would off a tin roof. The full kinetic energy of the raindrops is available to dislodge soil particles. A relatively unobstructed surface accelerates the runoff, producing greater flood peaks downstream.* The kinetic energy of the enhanced floods tears away riverbanks, broadens channels, and damages or destroys canals, bridges, and other hydrological developments. Canals and dams are rapidly filled with sediments eroded from upstream, and top-soils are carried far downstream to be deposited ultimately in estuaries and oceans, often adversely affecting biological productivity. Aquifers are not recharged, and in the dry season flows are low. As a result, the removal of vegetation—especially forests—from the upper portions of river basins and catchments increases erosion, reduces water quality, damages hydrologic developments, and reduces the water available during the dryer season.[494] On very steep (therefore unstable) slopes, removal of vegetation can trigger landslides and flows of debris. In the Cape Verde Islands, narrow, irrigated valleys have been buried meters deep by soil and debris swept down from denuded side slopes by intense rains.[495]

Deforestation, burning, overgrazing, and some cultivation practices all have potential for adversely affecting river basins and catchments. The Global 2000 forestry and agriculture projections both suggest that by 2000 such practices will have extended much further into the upper portions of river basins and catchments (see Chapters 6 and 8 and Appendix C).

Deforestation is one of the most serious causes of deterioration of catchments. In steep, high-rainfall zones such as the midslopes of the Andean and Himalayan mountains, forests are indispensable for protecting catchments and controlling runoff. Removal of trees, however, does not invariably jeopardize water supplies. In regions with moderate relief and low rainfall, removal of

forests and the substitution of other soil-binding vegetation that consumes less water (such as grasses) can improve lower-basin water supplies by increasing runoff—at the cost of tree growth. Scientifically controlled cutting of catchment vegetation has been employed in the United States and some other countries to increase runoff, or water yield, in dry regions.[496] To be successful this practice requires strong, enlightened institutional programs for careful land and water management over much of the affected basin. In most of the world there is as yet no such institutional capability, and as a result, the projected deforestation will in virtually all cases lead to adverse water impacts.

Burning, overgrazing, and cultivation practices that expose the soil for long periods can be expected to increase in many areas over the next two decades, contributing further to catchment deterioration. These practices intensify the extremes of flooding and aridity by reducing soil porosity and water storage capacity, by reducing organic matter, and by increasing compaction. In soils that are overgrazed, frequently burned, or continuously cultivated, organic matter (largely mulch from vegetative debris) can become sufficiently depleted to cause soil drought. Without the absorbent properties of these organic materials, soils are less able to retain moisture, and shifts in vegetation occur. The vegetation able to survive in such soils is typical of climates that are more arid than actual rainfall indicates. The intensification of soil drought is already in evidence in the African Sahel and other semiarid regions,[497] and much further deterioration of the water retaining properties of soils can be anticipated on the basis of the population and food projections.

Acid Rain

Acid rain is an environmental problem closely related to energy development. It deserves special note here because of its effects not only on water bodies over much of the world but also on many other parts of the biosphere.

While the Global 2000 energy projections are not specific enough to permit a detailed analysis of the future prospects for the acid rain problem, a few points can be made. First, increases in coal combustion in the magnitudes projected (13 percent by 1990) will significantly increase the production of the two primary causes of acid rain—sulfur oxides (SO_x) and oxides of nitrogen (NO_x). The 58 percent increase in oil combustion projected to occur by 1990 will also increase both SO_x and NO_x emissions; the 43 percent increase pro-

---

*The development of large urban areas can produce similar effects. Roofs, streets, and other impervious surfaces both increase the volume and shorten the duration of runoff, leading to flash floods and serious erosion downstream. In Arlington, Virginia, for example, the county's Environmental Improvement Commission has estimated that 50 percent of the land area in this suburban community as of 1972 had been covered over or in some way made impervious, and as a result damaging flash floods now occur in what were formerly small streams (*Arlington's Environmental Quality—1972*, County Planning Office, Arlington, Va., 1972). Since 1972 much more of the county has been made impervious, and an additional large highway is now under construction.

jected in natural gas combustion will also increase NO_x emissions. Technologies are available to remove sulfur oxides, but their removal is expensive and probably will not be required uniformly throughout the world. There is no practical technology for the removal of oxides of nitrogen from stack gases; the only control now available involves reduced combustion temperatures, which limit efficiencies. The water-quality consequences of increased emissions, especially increases of NO_x emissions, need to be considered carefully.

The immediate consequence of both SO_x and NO_x emissions is the acidification of precipitation. These gaseous compounds react in the atmosphere to form sulfuric acid and nitric acid, which, in turn, precipitate out of the atmosphere in both rain and snow. The acidified precipitation falls anywhere from a few hundred to a few thousand miles away from the source, depending on the strength of the prevailing winds.[498] As a result, the pH of rainfall is known to have fallen from a normal value of 5.7 to 4.5–4.2 (high acidic values) over large areas of southern Sweden, southern Norway, and the eastern U.S.[499] In the most extreme case yet recorded, a storm in Scotland in 1974, the rain was the acidic equivalent of vinegar (pH 2.4).[499a] Equivalent changes have almost certainly occurred elsewhere, for example, downwind of the German, Eastern European, and Soviet industrial regions. Effects of acid rain are only beginning to be understood but have now been observed in lakes, rivers, and forests, in agricultural crops, in nitrogen-fixing bacteria, and in soils.

The clearest ill effects of acid rainfall observed to date are on lake fisheries. A survey of over 1,500 lakes in southwestern Norway, which has acid rainfall problems similar to those of southern Sweden, showed that over 70 percent of the lakes with a pH below 4.3 contained no fish. This was true for less than 10 percent of the lakes in the normal pH range of 5.5–6.0.[500] Similar effects have been found in lakes in the Adirondack mountains of New York[501] and in some areas of Canada.[502] Acid rain appears to be the cause of both the low pH and the extinction of the fish (see also the discussion of fresh water extinctions in the fisheries section of this chapter). Within the last 20 years salmon disappeared from many Norwegian rivers, and trout soon followed. Measurement in such rivers almost always shows a decline in pH, usually attributable to acid rain. Similar occurrences have been observed in Sweden.[503]

Effects of acid rain on forest growth are only beginning to be understood. The effects on tree-seed germination are mixed.[504] Reductions in natural forest growth have been observed in both New England and Sweden.[505] One study tentatively attributed a 4 percent decline in annual forest growth in southern Sweden to acid rain.[506] Other observers feel that a decline in Scandinavian forest growth has not been conclusively demonstrated but suspect that the even more acidic rainfall expected in the future will cause slower growth.[507]

The effects of acid precipitation on leafy vegetation have been studied in the United States in the states of Maryland and West Virginia. While no major damage has yet occurred, one study concludes that current levels of acidity in rainfall present little margin of safety for foliar injury to susceptible plant species, but with the increasing emissions of pollutants that contribute to the formation of acid rain, there is substantial risk of surpassing the threshhold for foliar effects in the future.[508]

Little research has been undertaken on the effects of acid rain on large natural ecosystems, but one interesting study has now been done for the boundary-waters canoe area and the Voyageurs National Park (BWAS-VNP) wilderness areas in the north central United States. The findings are as follows:

Acid precipitation, by causing increased acidity in lakes, streams, pools and puddles, can cause slight to severe alteration in communities of aquatic organisms. . . . Bacterial decomposition is reduced and fungi dominate saprotrophic communities. Organic debris accumulates rapidly. Nutrient salts are taken up by plants tolerant of low pH (mosses, filamentous algae) and by fungi. Thick mats of these organisms and organic debris may develop which inhibit sediment-to-water nutrient and mineral exchange, and choke out other aquatic plants. Phytoplankton species diversity, biomass and production are reduced. Zooplankton and benthic invertebrate species diversity and biomass are reduced. Ultimately the remaining benthic fauna consists of tubificids and Chironomus (midge) larvae in the sediments. Some tolerant species of stoneflies and mayflies persist, as does the alderfly. Air breathing insects (water boatman, backswimmer, water strider) may become abundant. Fish populations are reduced or eliminated, with some of the most sought after species (brook trout, walleye, smallmouth bass) being the most sensitive and therefore among the first to be affected. Toxicity or elevated tissue concentrations of metals may result either from direct deposition or increased mobilization or both. Amphibian species may be eliminated. And finally, populations or activities of higher terrestrial vertebrates that utilize aquatic organisms for food or recreation are likely to be altered.[509]

The study concludes that "as more lakes are eventually impacted, the whole philosophy behind the wilderness experience that forms the basis of the establishment of the BWCA-VNP will be violated and the part of the BWCA which provides recreation will be reduced. Few people who utilize the BWCA-VNP could be expected to enjoy the areas made fishless by pollution from human activity."

The effects of acid rain on nonforest agricultural crops are under study and are beginning to be reported. Shoot and root growth of kidney bean and soybean plants have been found to be markedly reduced as a result of simulated acid rain of pH 3.2.[510] Similarly, nodulation by nitrogen-fixing bacteria on legumes is significantly reduced by simulated acid rain.[511] The growth of radish roots has been observed to decline by about 50 percent as the pH of rain falls from 5.7 to 3.0.[512]

The sensitivity of soils to acidification by acid rain varies widely from area to area, depending largely on the amount of calcium in the soil.[513] Calcium buffers the soil against acidification, but is leached out by acid rain; this leaching of calcium and soil nutrients has been found to increase with decreasing pH, and the pH of soils has been observed to decline more rapidly with more acidic rains.[514] The acidic soils that can result from acid rain could be expected to significantly reduce crop production in the affected areas unless large amounts of lime were applied.

In addition to damaging biota and soils, acid rain damages materials extensively over wide areas.[515] Even stone is being severely damaged. A dramatic example of the effects of acid rain and air pollution on stone is provided by the Egyptian obelisk moved from Egypt to New York in the 1890s (Fig. 13-9). While the inscription on the east face of the monument is still legible, the inscription on the west face has been destroyed by chemicals in the city's air, driven by New York's prevailing westerly winds.

The 13 percent increase in coal combustion by 1990 implies that large areas in and near industrial areas will continue to receive highly acidic rainfall. The rainfall in these areas is likely to become increasingly acidic as SO_x and NO_x emissions increase. The areas affected are likely to extend hundreds to thousands of miles downwind from the sources, a total geographic area large enough to include many lakes, watersheds and farmlands. The combined adverse effects in these areas on water quality (and indirectly on soil quality and plant growth) are likely to become increasingly severe.

Climatic Change

Water supplies and agriculture can be severely affected by climatic changes that are well within the range of historic experience. Changes in global temperatures could lead to either an increase or decrease in both the amount and variability of rainfall. The climate projections therefore have definite significance for water availability in the future.

The Global 2000 Study's climate projections provide little guidance, however, because of disagreement among climatologists on future trends. As discussed in Chapter 4 and in the Climate section of this chapter, the experts are more or less evenly divided over the prospects for warming or cooling, and most felt that the highest probability is for no change.[516] Faced with this uncertainty, the Global 2000 Study devised three climatic scenarios of roughly equal probability. There is considerable uncertainty as to the pattern of rainfall to be associated with these climate scenarios, but it is thought by many climatologists that global warming would lead to slight increases in precipitation in many areas and less year to year variation. (The central U.S., however, might experience more frequent drought.) A cooling trend is thought by many to be associated with less precipitation and increased year-to-year variation.

In short, there is much uncertainty about future global climate because of the present lack of agreement on causes, effects, and trends. Uncertainty over climate—and therefore also over water supplies and agricultural harvests—can be expected to lead to projects for the storage and regulation of water and to the development of food reserves in anticipation of unfavorable years.

Even if it were absolutely certain that the variability and amount of water supply would not deteriorate in the years ahead, there would still be reason to anticipate further projects to increase the storage and regulation of water and to develop food reserves. Population growth, urbanization, and the extension of both agriculture and forestry into more arid and variable regions has made the social and economic impacts of variability of water supplies greater than in the past. In the years ahead the impacts of even present variability can only become greater. As nations attempt to bring more marginal lands into production, fluctuations in water supply will quickly translate into social and economic vulnerability. Therefore, even in the absence of any climatic deterioration, incentives will be present to maintain food-grain reserves, accelerate water conservation efforts,

Figure 13–9. A monument to acid rain and air pollution—"Cleopatra's Needle," sent from Egypt to New York City in the 1890s. The inscription on the east face (*left*) is still legible; the inscription on the west face (*right*) has been erased by chemicals in the city's air, driven by the prevailing westerly winds. Ninety years in New York has done more damage to the stone than 3,500 years in Egypt. (*U.N. photo*)

modify macro- and microclimates, and develop hydraulic works to reduce the risk and uncertainty in water availability. What will be the environmental consequences of these efforts?

Impacts of Hydraulic Works

Both the prospect of destablizing deforestation in the upper portions of river basins and the certainty of continued (possibly even increased) climatic variability will encourage the development of hydraulic works for flow regulation, electrical generation, irrigation, and flood control. The Global 2000 Study's water projections assume increased withdrawals of water for all uses, but make no projections as to how additional water supplies will be developed or where supplies might fall short of future need. To meet the projected withdrawals a considerable expansion of engineering works for water regulation and dis-

tribution will be required, especially in regions with highly variable rainfall. By one estimate, 12,000 cubic kilometers of runoff will be controlled in the year 2000 by dams and reservoirs—30 percent of the total world runoff and three times the estimated 4,000 cubic kilometers now stored in the world's reservoirs.[517]

In the LDCs, where most of the world's untapped hydropower potential is located, river basin development schemes that integrate flood control, power production, and irrigation will be implemented for a number of reasons:

- The indispensable role of irrigation in increasing food production;
- The limited amounts of naturally fertile, well-drained, well-watered soils remaining to be brought into production;
- The need to control the floods of large rivers (e.g. Yellow River, Lower Mekong River)

where floods have been more or less tolerated in the past; and

• The need for electricity in economic development.

The environmental impacts of large river basin development schemes can be great. In the case of large dams, the impacts include:

• The inundation of farmland, settlements, roads, railroads, forests, historic and archeological sites, and mineral deposits;

• The creation of artificial lakes, which often become habitats for disease vectors such as the mosquitoes that transmit malaria and the snails which transmit schistosomiasis;

• The alteration of river regimes downstream of dams, ending the biologically significant annual flood cycle, increasing water temperature, and sometimes triggering riverbank erosion as a result of an increased sediment-carrying capacity of the water;

• The interruption of upstream spawning migrations of fish; and

• Water quality deterioration.

Irrigation systems have their own environmental problems:

• Danger of soil salinization and waterlogging in perennially irrigated areas;

• Water weeds, mosquitos, and snail infestation of drainage canals, with the danger of malarial and schistosomiastic infections spreading in areas where these diseases exist, especially in parts of Africa and Latin America; and

• Pollution of irrigation return water by a variety of agricultural chemicals, with negative consequences for aquatic life and for the human use of downstream waters.

While the benefits of dams and irrigation development may outweigh the costs, environmental impacts have a definite bearing on the benefit/cost ratios of river basin development schemes. Plans for the development of the Lower Mekong River Basin illustrate this point.

A series of engineering, economic, social, and environmental studies of the Lower Mekong Basin has been carried out under the aegis of the United Nations Committee for Coordination of Investigations. The development plan that has emerged from these studies calls for the construction over a 20-year period of a series of multi-purpose dams and associated irrigation works for the basin, which is shared by Thailand, Laos, Cambodia and Vietnam.[518] In 1974 the portion of the basin downstream from the People's Republic

of China supported about 33 million persons. Assuming the adoption of birth control methods at rates based on other South Asian experience, the U.N. studies project this population to grow ultimately to or beyond the Lower Mekong Basin's present food-production capacity, which is estimated to be potentially adequate for 123 million persons. To feed the expanded population by the end of the century, it will be necessary to expand paddy rice production from 1970s 12.7 million tons to 37 million tons. The studies suggest that this increase of nearly 200 percent cannot be achieved without flood control and new irrigation. It is estimated that multiple dams in the Lower Mekong River system could add up to 5 million hectares of land for double-cropping of rice and might provide enough food to support an additional 50 million persons in the basin.[519] The dams would generate badly needed power, and the reservoirs could, with proper management, become productive fisheries.

The proposed dams in the Lower Mekong Basin will involve significant social costs. For example, the reservoir behind the Pa Mong—the largest dam proposed for the Mekong River—would force the resettlement of 460,000 persons, mostly in Thailand. Land for resettlement en masse in large communities is not available, and Thailand is faced with the prospect of paying these people an estimated $626 million (approximately $1,400 each) to leave without a planned alternative, a situation euphemistically referred to as "self-settlement."[520]

The situation in the Mekong River Basin happens to be relatively well understood because 20 years of internationally coordinated studies have examined the entire river basin as a single planning unit. Other densely populated river basins in Asia, Africa, and Latin America are the focus of similarly ambitious schemes, but in most cases there are no coordinated studies or even adequate data. Consequently the full social and economic costs of these proposed projects can scarcely be estimated.

The environmental costs are just as hard to estimate. It is known that large dams produce very considerable ecological impacts on rivers and estuaries in temperate and subtropical areas. The Aswan Dam in Egypt is a case in point.

A considerable list of costly impacts are associated with the High Aswan Dam and the irrigation development that has subsequently taken place in the Nile Delta. They have been recently documented by Julian Rzoska[521] in a ten-years-later assessment, as well as by earlier researchers such as Kassas, George, and van der Schalie.[522] Here are some of their findings:

- 100,000 people had to be relocated from the reservoir site, which extends into Sudan. The people were mostly flood plain farmers of Nubian origin.
- The ancient Nubian temples were inundated (a considerable portion of them were salvaged intact in a UNESCO-organized emergency operation).
- The dam traps sediments that formerly enriched the flood plain as well as the Mediterranean Sea, with a loss in natural soil productivity and the collapse of the sardine fishery that once provided half of Egypt's fish.
- Waves and tides are now eroding the delta, which formerly was extending into the Mediterranean, and a reduction in the agriculturally important delta is slowly occurring.
- Year around irrigation in the delta, which represents 60 percent of Egypt's farmland, has elevated the water table and caused salinization, now being remedied through expensive drainage works financed by the World Bank.
- Schistosomiasis is rapidly spreading throughout the rural population as a consequence of the spread of the snail intermediate hosts in the irrigation canals, the lack of sanitary facilities and the continual exposure of the dense rural population.
- The water hyacinth spread almost uncontrollably throughout the canal systems, where it harbors snails and interferes with water flows.

This controversial project's benefits include an 8,000 megawatt electricity generating potential, and a doubling of agricultural potential on perennially irrigated soils.

While the extensive consequences of the Aswan Dam are reasonably well known and established, relatively little is known about the ecological effects of dams in tropical areas, where most of the need and potential is located. The animal species native to tropical rivers, estuaries, and oceans have frequently evolved life cycles that are linked to annual floods and the patterns of salinity and nutrient fluxes that accompany the floods. Regulation of river flows can therefore be expected to significantly affect large numbers of estuarine and oceanic organisms. Similar impacts can be anticipated in freshwater species. Their decline is not likely to be compensated by the development of aquaculture, especially if pollution seriously impairs water quality.

Water Pollution

The Global 2000 Study projections point to worldwide increases in urbanization and industrial growth and in the intensification of agriculture—

trends that, in turn, imply large increases in water pollution in many areas.

Water Pollution of Urban and Industrial Origin

By the year 2000, worldwide urban and industrial water withdrawals are projected to increase by a factor of about 5, reaching 1.8–2.3 trillion cubic meters (see Chapter 9). The higher figure is almost equal to the total annual runoff of 2.34 trillion cubic meters from the 50 United States. Most of the water withdrawn for urban and industrial use is returned (treated or untreated) to streams and rivers. If 90 percent is returned, the total combined discharge of water flowing through sewers and industrial outfalls by the year 2000 will be on the order of 1.6–2.1 trillion cubic meters.

Urban and industrial effluent will be concentrated in the rivers, bays, and coastal zones near the world's largest urban-industrial agglomerations. In the developing world—where 2 billion additional persons are projected to be living by 2000 and where rapid rates of urbanization continue—urban and industrial water pollution will become ever more serious because many developing economies will be unable or unwilling to afford the additional cost of water treatment.

Few LDCs have invested heavily in urban and industrial waste treatment facilities. As a result the waters below many LDC cities are often thick with sewage sludge and wastes from pulp and paper factories, tanneries, slaughterhouses, oil refineries, chemical plants, and other industries. One consequence of this pollution is declining fishing yields downstream from LDC cities. For example, the inland catch in the eastern province of Thailand, 696 tons in 1963, fell to 68 tons by 1968, and it is thought that water pollution, particularly from Bangkok, was the main cause of the decline.[523] Similar, though less extreme, declines have occurred around the world in freshwater systems, and in bays, lagoons, and estuaries. Frequently the changes are not measured but become apparent with the appearance of eutrophication, poisonous red tides, and the decline of inland fishing occupations.[524]

Efforts to control the effects of pollution from LDC cities can lead to international disputes. An example is the dispute that occurred in 1976 over India's withdrawal of water from the Ganges to flush out the port of Calcutta during the dry season when the water was needed in Bangladesh for irrigation.[525]

The reuse of urban and industrial waste water is likely to increase as urban populations expand rapidly in the water-short regions of West Asia and in arid portions of Mexico, Africa, and the U.S. Southwest. The use of waste water for irrigation will serve to recycle nutrients that would otherwise overload the absorptive capacity of rivers; however, a careful management and monitoring will be required to avoid pollution of ground-water and human exposure to disease pathogens, heavy metals, and other toxic substances.[526]

The use of water as the transport media for sewage is being questioned because of its high capital requirements, its potential for pollution, and its energy intensiveness. Composting toilets that avoid the water medium entirely have been developed and are being used more widely.[527]

Some water pollution problems are linked directly to air pollutants from urban and industrial areas, particularly from emissions of sulfur and nitrogen oxides from electric power plants burning fossil fuels (see "Acid Rain," above). The increased use of coal (a rich source of both sulfur and nitrogen oxides) promises a growing contribution of acid to rain water and to lakes. There is no known, economically practical method for controlling NO_x emissions. Control of SO_x emissions from coal is now technologically possible but is estimated to increase electricity costs by 6–15 percent. It seems that the price of "live" lakes will be high.[528]

Urbanization and industrial growth, in addition to increasing various forms of water pollution, will also increase the consumptive uses of water. Evaporative cooling for thermal-electric generating facilities is one of the fastest-growing consumptive uses of water.

Large amounts of water are used to remove waste heat from thermal-electric (primarily coal and nuclear) power plants, but until recently relatively little of this water has been consumed (i.e., evaporated). Until the early 1970s in the U.S. most of the waste heat from electricity generation—which amounts to approximately two-thirds of the total primary energy input to electrical generation*—was dissipated by means of once-through

---

* Nuclear plants typically convert roughly one-third of their primary energy input to electricity; the remaining two-thirds is usually lost as waste heat. Fossil-fuel-fired plants are only slightly more efficient. Over and above these losses, transmission-line losses are significant (A.L. Velikanov, *Hydrologic Problems Stemming from Energy Development*, U.N. Water Conference, Jan. 27, 1977, p. 6). The large amount of energy lost as waste heat is at the heart of some of the most intense criticism of energy policies that increase electrical generation for end uses that do not necessarily require electricity. See, for example, Amory B. Lovins, *Soft Energy Paths*, Cambridge, Mass.: Ballinger, 1977, and *Efficient Use of Energy*, American Institute of Physics Conference Proceedings no. 25, summarized in *Physics Today*, Aug. 1975.

cooling. With once-through cooling, large quantities of river, lake, or ocean water are pumped through condensers and returned to the natural water body approximately 10° C warmer. Between 1950 and 1972 annual water withdrawals in the U.S. for thermal-electric power plant cooling jumped from 50 billion to 275 billion cubic meters—2.5 times the average flow (110 billion cubic meters) of the lower Mississippi River—surpassing irrigation withdrawals in volume.[529]

Concern for biological and ecological damage caused by water intakes and by thermal pollution in the U.S. resulted in the promulgation in 1974 of standards for levels of thermal discharge to water bodies by power plants, but in 1976 the standards were remanded by court order. At present, thermal pollution has a low priority at the Environmental Protection Agency.[530] Thermal pollution impacts are numerous and generally deleterious in mid to low latitudes. In high latitudes waters are naturally so cold that aquatic life processes are slowed, and in these areas heated discharges from power plants can stimulate production of fish and other organisms. In the tropics, on the other hand, where waters are naturally warm and many species live near their upper temperature tolerance, thermal discharges are often lethal. At all latitudes increased temperature reduces the dissolved oxygen in the water, stressing aquatic fauna by speeding metabolic rates while at the same time depleting oxygen supplies.[531] Other impacts include:

- Destruction of small organisms such as fish larvae and plankton entrained in the cooling water intake and poisoned by antifouling biocides.
- Reduction of fish abundance, biomass, and species diversity in downstream thermal "plumes."
- Synergistic exacerbation of the stresses caused most organisms by other factors such as increased salinity, biological oxygen demand, and toxic substances.
- Shifting of the balance among algae species to favor blue-green algae, which create taste and odor problems in municipal water supplies.
- Sudden changes of temperature during startups and shutdowns, causing death of many sensitive species.[532]

The remanding of the 1974 Environmental Protection Agency regulations on thermal pollution left U.S. problems of thermal pollution unresolved. New plants tend to utilize evaporative cooling towers rather than once-through cooling because of insufficient volumes of water available rather than because of ecological considerations.[533] As a result, thermal water pollution in the U.S. may remain at about 1976 levels, while local atmospheric heat and humidity loadings in areas around new power plants increase. The U.S. Water Resources Council estimates that the consumptive use of water by the country's electrical generating facilities will increase rapidly (650 percent between 1975 and 2000).[534]

The net consumption (i.e., evaporation) of water can also be expected to continue increasing elsewhere in the world during the years ahead as thermal-electric generation grows and supply constraints and environmental considerations encourage shifts away from once-through cooling to evaporative cooling towers. A. L. Velikanov has estimated for the United Nations that waste heat discharged from thermal-electric plants throughout the world in 1973 was sufficient to evaporate 7–8 cubic kilometers (km³) of water if cooling towers had been in use everywhere.[535] This estimate may be low. European energy specialist Wolf Häfele calculates that if Europe had been using cooling towers exclusively in 1974, Europe alone would have been evaporating water at an annual rate of 16 km³.[536] Häfele expects this consumption to reach 30 km³ per year by 2000. Although this represents only about 1 percent of Europe's yearly runoff of 2800 km³, the additional consumptive demand on Europe's water resources would be significant.

Water Pollution of Agricultural Origin

Extensive pollution from fertilizer runoff can be expected, especially in developed, densely populated regions, if worldwide fertilizer usage increases from 55 kilograms per hectare (kg/ha)—the average 1971–75 rate—to around 145 kg/ha as projected. The U.S. Department of Agriculture projects fertilizer application rates in Japan, Western Europe, and Eastern Europe to reach 635, 355, and 440 kg/ha, respectively, by 2000 (see Table 6–15).* At these application rates it will be difficult to avoid at least some increase in the nitrogen pollution of water supplies and eutrophication of bodies of water.

The LDCs are likely to experience increasing water pollution by pesticides, especially chlorinated hydrocarbon insecticides used in irrigated rice culture and export crop production. The Food and Agriculture Organization expects that pesticide usage in the LDCs will grow at 10 percent per year for at least the near future. Should this

trend continue until 2000, the volume of pesticides used in the LDCs will have increased more than sevenfold.[537] Presently, about half the pesticides used in the LDCs are organochlorines, a trend that may continue because organochlorines are substantially less expensive than the more specific, less destructive and less persistent alternatives.

A sevenfold increase in the use of persistent pesticides in Asia would virtually eliminate the culturing of fish in irrigation canals, rice paddies, and ponds fed by irrigation water.[538] Organochlorine insecticides continue to collect in aquatic systems years after they have been applied and affect waters many miles downstream. At moderately high concentrations, they kill fish.[539] Already, many Asian farmers are reluctant to buy fry for their paddies or ponds for fear that pesticide pollution will kill the stock.[540] The amount of protein forfeited could be substantial. Per hectare yields of fish from well-tended ponds can be as high as the per hectare yields of rice, i.e., 2,500 kg/ha animal protein vs. 2,500 kg/ha carbohydrate.[541] Cage culture yields are extraordinarily high and show great commercial promise in several developing countries, as long as waters are not poisoned by pesticides. Projected pesticide increase seriously threatens both freshwater and brackish water aquaculture in much of Asia. If pesticide trends continue, aquaculture in Latin America and Africa will eventually face the same threat.

The protein that fish culture could provide is badly needed, especially in the humid tropics where aquaculture can thrive. Moreover, while alternative forms of producing animal protein tend to increase the pressures on already stressed soil systems, fish culture places no strain on terrestrial systems and is complementary to the careful water management schemes required for sustained agricultural production in many parts of the humid tropics. The FAO estimates that culture of fresh water and marine organisms could reach 20–30 million metric tons by 2000—between one-third and one-half of the present marine catch.[542] Further pesticide pollution will sharply diminish this promising prospect.

Increased pesticide use will also create water contamination problems in industrialized nations. To cite but one example: California health officials report that they have found dangerous levels of a pesticide—dibromochloropropane (DBCP)—in half of the irrigation and drinking water wells they have tested in one of the state's major agricultural areas, the San Joaquin valley. The U.S. Environmental Protection Agency banned the use of DBCP in 1977 on 19 fruit and vegetable crops

---

* The projection assumes that real energy prices remain constant to 2000; fertilizer projections were not reported for the Global 2000 standard case of rising energy prices.

after tests showed that the pesticide caused sterility in the workers who manufactured it and caused cancers in laboratory animals. Two years after the ban, California health officials found residues averaging 5 parts per billion (ppb) in the wells tested. The State has recommended that all wells showing more than 1 ppb of DBCP be closed to human consumption. At that level, one case of cancer is expected for every 2,500 persons who use the wells. Arizona health officials have tested 18 wells near Yuma and found 6 wells with concentrations of 4.6–18.6 ppb. of DBCP. The Environmental Protection Agency has allowed continued use of an estimated 10 million pounds of DBCP annually in the U.S. on crops such as soybeans, citrus fruits, grapes and nuts but is now considering restricting this amount.[543]

Other pesticides may not cause as many problems with water. California officials report that DBCP is the only pesticide they tested that shows a tendency to be absorbed into ground-water. Nonetheless, the projected increases in pesticide usage will create a variety of water contamination problems in the industrialized nations as well as in the less developed countries.

Irrigation will also add large amounts of salt contamination to the waters of many areas.[544] The water-use projections reveal that by the year 2000 between 4,600 and 7,000 billion cubic meters of water will be withdrawn for irrigation. Approximately 25–30 percent will be returned to streams carrying dissolved salts. In very arid areas return water is heavily contaminated with salts, concentrated by high rates of evaporation.

Salt pollution of arid-zone rivers draining away from irrigated lands will ultimately make the rivers unfit for further irrigation use in their lower reaches, as has already happened to the Shatt-al-Arab River, in Iraq and the Lower Colorado River in the U.S.[545] The Shatt-al-Arab was formed by the Tigris and Euphrates Rivers, whose delta soils were once covered with extensive date-palm and citrus orchards.

One remedy—a very costly and energy-intensive remedy—for the salt pollution of rivers is to desalinate the water. A 104 million gallon per day desalting facility will soon be in operation on the Lower Colorado River. Now under construction at Yuma, Arizona, this plant will be the largest desalting plant in the world, costing over $300 million. It is needed to fulfill a U.S. agreement with Mexico to deliver water in the Colorado River with a total dissolved solids content (including salts) of no more than 115 milligrams per liter (mg/l). Because of the leaching of salts from fields upstream, the dissolved-solids content had increased to 850 mg/l and was expected to reach 1,300 mg/l by 2000. Most plant species cannot tolerate water with more than 500 mg/l of dissolved solids.[546]

Water-Related Diseases

Water related diseases have been an unfortunate accessory to irrigation systems and dams as well as to pollution by human wastes and are virtually certain to become more prevalent during the rest of the century as more of the water environment becomes affected by human activities and wastes.

A wide variety of water developments can increase the incidence of water-related diseases. The creation of ponds, reservoirs, and irrigation and drainage canals in the course of water resource development, and the widespread inadequacy of waste water disposal systems in LDC cities, all favor the persistence or spread of a number of such diseases. In recent years new irrigation systems and reservoirs in Middle and North Africa and West Asia have provided ideal habitats for the intermediate snail host of schistosomiasis, which has spread dramatically among rural populations.[547] This debilitating disease of the intestinal and urinary tract now affects an estimated 250 million people throughout the world, approximately 7 percent of the entire human population. In some irrigation-project and reservoir areas, up to 80 percent of the population is affected.[548]

In addition to schistosomasis there are numbers of other serious water-related diseases. These include malaria, filariasis (elephantiasis), and yellow fever, all of which are transmitted by mosquitoes. Onchocerciasis, "river blindness" disease, is transmitted by flies. Paragonimiasis is a disease transmitted by a snail. Poorly managed water resource development projects, as well as the impact of urbanization on aquatic habitats and water quality, contribute to the spread of all of these diseases. Diseases typical of waste water contaminated by human feces—cholera, typhoid fever, amoebic infections, and bacillary dysentery— can become problems anywhere in the world. In LDCs today almost 1.5 billion persons are exposed to these diseases for lack of safe water supplies and human waste disposal facilities. Largely for this reason infant deaths resulting from diarrhea continue at a high rate. Every day 35,000 infants and children under five years of age die throughout the world; most of these deaths occur in LDCs.[549] Schistosomiasis afflicts 200 million people in 70 countries and elephantiasis is estimated to cripple 250 million more.[550] In parts of

Asia where night soil is extensively used as fertilizer, roundworm (*Ascaris*) infections will continue to be a threat because the roundworm's eggs are not easily killed.

Water-related diseases are not limited to countries that cannot afford sewage treatment. In industrialized countries the treatment of city waste waters with chlorine presents a different kind of water-related health problem—the possibility of cancer. When chlorine reacts with organic compounds in waste water, one of the resulting by-products is chloroform, a carcinogen. Elevated rates of fatal gastrointestinal and urinary cancer are reported by some scientists in communities that utilize water supplies contaminated with chloroform.[551] The U.S. National Academy of Sciences has recommended that strict criteria be applied in setting limits for chloroform in drinking water.[552]

Extinction of Freshwater Species

The International Union for Conservation of Nature and Natural Resources notes in the draft of its *World Conservation Strategy* that 274 fresh water vertebrate taxa are threatened by extinction as a result of habitat destruction. This number is larger than the number of similarly threatened vertebrate taxa in any other ecosystem group.[553]

It is not surprising that a large number of freshwater species are threatened with extinction through loss of habitat in view of the major changes that are occurring in freshwater systems. Damming, pollution, channelization, and siltation are causing massive alterations in freshwater ecosystems throughout the world. Fresh water species endemic to specific lakes, rivers, or upper reaches of river branches are particularly vulnerable because they are often easily extinguished by changes in water chemistry (the effects of acid rain for example), modification of streambed contours, alteration of water temperature, or the imposition of dams that prevent species from reaching their spawning grounds. Because of the anticipated increase in pollution and in manipulation of freshwater systems, many of the species now threatened may be extinct by 2000, and many now relatively common species may be on the way to extinction.

The trends in freshwater extinctions will be difficult if not impossible to reverse. In many areas political and social realities will stand in the way of installing expensive pollution control systems, of changing dam sites, or of reducing pesticide usage or coal combustion in order to save a fish or amphibian whose existence may be known to only a few people and whose value and impor-

tance may be perceived by fewer still. As a result, high rates of extinction among freshwater species are expected to continue.

Conclusion

Freshwater, once an abundant resource in most parts of the world, will become increasingly scarce in coming decades for two reasons. First, there will be greater net consumption, by cooling towers and, especially, by irrigation so that the total supply will decline. Second, pollution and the impacts of hydraulic works will effectively limit the uses of freshwater—and therefore, in effect, the supply. The deterioration of river basin catchments, especially as a result of deforestation, will increase the variability of supply, accelerate erosion, damage water development projects, and degrade water quality. It seems inevitable that the function of streams and rivers as habitat for aquatic life will steadily be sacrificed to the diversion of water for irrigation, for human consumption, and for power production, particularly in the LDCs.

The 1977 U.N. Water Conference served to focus global attention on the critical problems of managing the world's water resources in the coming decades. In the LDCs the development of water resources for irrigation and power is a key to providing for the economic needs of expanding populations. At the same time the ecological impacts of hydraulic works and of pollution from agricultural fields and urban industrial concentrations is greatly diminishing the capacity of water systems to support fish that are sorely needed to supplement meager diets. The lack of safe water supplies and of methods for sanitary disposal of human waste and waste water means that as many as 1.5 billion persons are exposed to fecally related disease pathogens in drinking water. These problems of water supply and quality in LDCs are so severe as to be matters of survival for millions of persons.

In industrial nations, water supply and quality will pose more subtle and therefore more complex questions of trade-offs and conflicts among users (or values) of freshwater. Water resources management in such nations is concerned not with human survival but with balancing demands for water resources against considerations of quality-of-life. But scarcities and conflicts are becoming more acute, and by the year 2000 economic, if not human, survival in many industrial regions may hinge upon water quality, or water supply, or both.

Perhaps the most underrated aspect of freshwater systems throughout the world is their function as aquatic habitat. At some point, high social and economic costs will follow the continued neglect of the water quality needed to maintain ecosystem health. This point may be marked by the failure of fish farms, or by a decline of the capacity of streams to accommodate wastes, or by the decline or disappearance of species that may possibly be of great future value. Given the criticality of the other uses of freshwater resources, the future integrity of aquatic habitats is by no means assured. In fact, since aquatic habitats are much more difficult to know and monitor than terrestrial ones, it is in serious doubt.

THE ENERGY PROJECTIONS AND THE ENVIRONMENT

The Projections

Assuming a 5 percent annual increase (starting in 1980) in the real price of oil, the Department of Energy, projects a growth in demand for commercial energy (i.e., energy from fossil fuels and from nuclear and hydro sources) of 3.0 percent per year for the 1975–90 period.* Total world commercial energy use (energy conversion) is projected to increase about 56 percent in 15 years—from 246 quadrillion (10^{15}) Btu to 384 quadrillion Btu in 1990.

The projected distribution of this increase among energy sources is illustrated in Table 13–32. The world's dependence on oil increases from 46 to 47 percent of total energy use. Annual oil consumption is projected to increase 66 quadrillion Btu (11.4×10^9 barrels), a 58 percent increase in oil use over 15 years. Coal's share is projected to increase 13 percent; by 1990, 20 percent of all the energy used is projected to come from coal. Natural gas usage is projected to grow by 43 percent, providing 17 percent of the world's commercial energy in 1990. Nuclear and hydroelectricity production† are projected to increase by 226 percent (more than tripling); by 1990 they account for about 16 percent of the world's *primary* energy uses, but (after subtracting losses of waste heat) provide only about 6 percent of the world's usable energy. Solar energy, other than conservation and hydroelectric, is not projected to be making a significant contribution to the world's energy production by 1990.

The distribution of the increased use of commercial energy forms among regions of the world is illustrated in Table 13–33. Energy consumption in the United States increases by 41 percent, less rapidly than the 87 percent increase in other industrialized countries. The LDCs increase their use of commercial energy forms by 64 percent, but because these countries use such a small amount of commercial energy now, the 15-year growth adds only one percentage point to their fraction of the world total. The OPEC countries use a relatively small, but rapidly growing (more than 6 percent per year), fraction of the world's primary energy. The centrally planned economies increase their annual energy use by 34 percent, but their share of the world total declines from 31 to 27 percent. Overall, the global use of primary energy increases by 56 percent.

Projected changes in per capita use of primary energy are illustrated in Table 13–34. U.S. per capita energy use increases by 27 percent over 15 years, from 553 percent of the world average to 586 percent. The other industrialized countries increase their per capita energy use more rapidly (72 percent) to reach 325 percent of the world average by 1990. The LDCs (including OPEC countries) increase their per capita consumption by 27

---

*Because of the complexities of the world energy situation, the Department of Energy did not feel its projections could be extended beyond 1990. See chapters 10 and 20 for further details.

†The Department of Energy projections lump together nuclear and hydroelectric generation; most of the increase must be in nuclear generation because most of the large undeveloped hydroelectric sites are in the LDCs, and few of these will be developed over the next 15 years.

percent, to reach 19 percent of the world average. (The OPEC countries, even though their populations are relatively small, account for 36 percent of the combined LDC-OPEC increase in energy use.) The centrally planned economies increase their per capita energy use by 12 percent but decline relative to the world average from 97 percent to 90 percent. For the world as a whole, per capita annual energy use increases 20 percent from 60 million to 72 million Btu. The world average oil consumption in 1990 will be the equivalent of approximately 12 barrels of oil per person per year. The global variation ranges from about 73 barrels per person per year in the U.S. to about 2.4 barrels per person in the LDCs (including the OPEC countries).*

Introduction

The DOE energy projections are based largely on an industrialized country perspective. The projections in Tables 13–32, 13–33, and 13–34 focus exclusively on what might be termed the commercial energy sources—oil, coal, natural gas, and nuclear and hydro sources—used primarily in industrialized economies. Important as these commercial energy sources and their environmental impacts are, they provide an incomplete picture of energy development and use and of environmental impacts over the next two decades.

In the less developed countries, noncommercial, organic fuels—wood, crop wastes, charcoal, and dung—are collected and burned daily by an estimated 1.5 billion persons, approximately 40 percent of the total human population. These energy sources are used extensively throughout rural regions and even in cities, but because of their low energy content both per unit weight and per unit volume, they are not commonly traded in international commerce. Nevertheless, these organic fuels are traded locally and are vitally important to the economies in which they are used. Furthermore, their use has environmental implications of a significance comparable to that of commercial energy sources.

Two other categories of energy need to be mentioned briefly. One might be termed traditional sources; the other high-technology sources. The traditional sources involve well-established techniques and technologies for converting solar, wind, and water power into useful work. Examples include sailing ships, windmills, water mills and wheels, hydraulic rams, solar drying and distilling, charcoal-fired smelters and forges, and human and draft animal power. Not much importance has been assigned to these traditional sources of energy over the last several decades in the industrialized nations until recently, when "intermediate" and "appropriate" technologies[554]

---

* These projections were made by DOE in 1978, and DOE has revised its estimates since. See, for example, *National Energy Plan II*, Washington: Department of Energy, May 1979.

TABLE 13–32

Global Primary[a] Energy Use, 1975 and 1990, by Energy Type

	1975		1990		Percent Increase (1975–90)	Average Annual Percent Increase
	10^{15} Btu	Percent of Total	10^{15} Btu[b]	Percent of Total		
Oil	113	46	179	47	58	3.1
Coal	68	28	77	20	13	0.8
Natural gas	46	19	66	17	43	2.4
Nuclear and hydro	19	8[c]	62	16[c]	226	7.9
Solar (other than conservation and hydro)[d]	–	–	–	–	–	–
Total	246	100	384	100	56	3.0

Source: The 1990 figures are from the Department of Energy's projections in Chapter 10 and note b, below. The 1975 figures for the centrally planned economies were taken by DOE from K. A. D. Inglis, *BP Statistical Review of World Oil Industry, 1976*, London: British Petroleum Company, Ltd., 1976; the other 1975 figures are from DOE's own sources.

[a] All of the nuclear and much of the coal primary (i.e., input) energy is used thermally to generate electricity. In the process, approximately two-thirds of the primary energy is lost as waste heat. The figures given here are primary energy.
[b] The conversions from the DOE projections in Table 10–8 were made as follows: *Oil:* 84.8 × 10^6 bbl/day × 365 days × 5.8 × 10^6 Btu/bbl = 179 × 10^6 Btu. *Coal:* 5,424 × 10^6 short tons/yr × 14.1 × 10^6 Btu/short ton [DOE figure for world average grade coal] = 77 × 10^{15} Btu. *Natural gas:* 64.4 × 10^{12} ft³/yr × 1,032 Btu/ft³ = 66 × 10^{15} Btu. *Nuclear and Hydro:* 6,009 × 10^{12} Wh [output]/yr × 3.412 Btu/Wh × 3 input Btu/output Btu = 62 × 10^{12} Btu.
[c] After deductions for lost (waste) heat (see note a), the corresponding figures for output energy are 2.7 percent in 1975 and 6.0 in 1990.
[d] The IIES projection model is able to include solar only as conservation or hydro.

TABLE 13–33

Regional Distribution of Global Primary Energy Use, 1975 and 1990

	1975 Annual Use		1990 Annual Use		Percent Increase (1975–90)	Average Annual Percent Increase
	10^{15} Btu	Percent of Total	10^{15} Btu	Percent of Total		
United States	71	29	100	26	41	2.3
Other industrialized countries	67	27	125	33	87	4.2
Less developed countries	25	10	41	11	64	3.3
OPEC countries	6	2	15	4	150	6.1
Centrally planned economies	77	31	103	27	34	1.9
World	246	100	384	100	56	3.0

Source: The 1990 figures are from Department of Energy's projections in Chapter 10. The 1975 figures for the centrally Planned Economies were taken by DOE from K. A. D. Ingles, *BP Statistical Review of World Oil Industry, 1976*, London: British Petroleum Company, Ltd., 1976; the other 1975 figures are from DOS's own sources.

TABLE 13–34

Per Capita Global Primary Energy Use, Annually 1975 and 1990

	1975		1990		Percent Increase (1975–90)	Average Annual Percent Increase
	10^{6} Btu	Percent of World Average	10^{6} Btu	Percent of World Average		
United States	332	553	422	586	27	1.6
Other industrialized countries	136	227	234	325	72	3.6
Less developed countries*	11	18	14	19	27	1.6
Centrally planned economies	58	97	65	90	12	0.8
World	60	100	72	100	20	1.2

Source: The energy figures are from the Department of Energy (see Chapter 10 and Table 13–33). The population figures were obtained from the Bureau of the Census (see Chapter 2).

* Since population projections were not made separately for the OPEC countries, those countries have been included here in the LDC category.

began to attract attention. Now these and related technologies are being reexamined by many groups, including the National Academy of Sciences, and it is generally agreed that many traditional technologies and techniques and their modern elaborations (e.g., methane generation) show great promise for rural development applications.[555] A major advantage of the modernized traditional sources is their small-scale, decentralized nature, which allows a wide range of applications especially in poor rural areas.

The high-technology category of energy sources includes a number of technologies now being researched or undergoing development. There are many examples: large-scale synthetic fuel production from coal, nuclear fusion, nuclear fission breeder reactors, hydrogen fuel, solar photovoltaic cells for direct electrical generation, large wind turbines for electrical generation, and large scale geothermal and ocean thermal energy con-

version. Most of these high technologies are very large-scale approaches to energy supply and are beyond the reach of the poorest regions of the world.

In the discussion that follows, the environmental impacts of the Department of Energy (DOE) projections for commercial energy in industrialized society are considered first. The Brookhaven National Laboratory (BNL), under contract with DOE, analyzed the environmental implications of the DOE projections, but the analysis, as will be explained more fully below, does not provide an adequate basis for assessing the environmental consequences of future energy developments, largely because of technological uncertainties. Technology is then discussed in terms of the spectrum of alternatives and the various environmental consequences implied by these alternatives. The environmental implications of possible future high technologies are not discussed because these technologies are not projected by DOE as making significant contributions to the world's energy economy by 1990.

The environmental impacts of noncommercial organic fuels used in the LDCs is considered next, together with two "intermediate" or "appropriate" technologies that are becoming commercialized to a degree in some LDCs: methane gas and charcoal. Since the DOE projections did not include noncommercial energy sources, the discussion of organic fuels, charcoal, and methane is based largely on projections and estimates developed by the United Nations.

Commercial Energy in Industrial Societies

The environmental implications of the DOE energy projections cannot be analyzed in detail for two reasons. First, the analytical tools needed for the assessment of the environmental consequences of even national (let alone global) energy projections are still being developed. Second, the DOE energy projections for the Global 2000 Study are not sufficiently detailed to permit the full application of even the presently available tools for environmental analysis. Consider first the limitations in available tools for environmental analysis.

Much has been written, and continues to be written, about the environmental aspects of energy development. Probably the largest portion of this work in the U.S. is being conducted or sponsored by one agency or another of the federal government.* Most of the analyses and reports are highly detailed and lack both the breadth and synthesis required for policy analysis and for the Global 2000 Study.

In spite of the large numbers of energy-environment studies, the information and analytical framework needed to systematically, comprehensively, and objectively compare the impacts of

alternative energy strategies do not exist. Recently, however John P. Holdren has proposed a framework for such analysis.[556] The framework, in its barest outline, involves the following sequence:

1. Identification of the *sources* of effects on the environment, in the form of specific technological systems and activities;
2. Identification and characterization of the *inputs* to the immediate environment that are produced by these sources, where "input" is taken to encompass what is put into, taken out of, or done to the surroundings;
3. Analysis of the *pathways* by which the inputs lead to stresses on the components of the environment at risk;
4. Characterization and quantification of these *stresses*;
5. Analysis of the *responses* of the components at risk to the stresses imposed;
6. Identification and quantification of the *costs* to human well-being associated with these responses.[557]

At present, the six steps of this sequence cannot be completed systematically for any nation, let alone for the world. *Sources* can now be identified in terms of specific technological systems and activities, but most national (and all global) energy projections and scenarios do not provide the basic source information in the detail needed for a comprehensive environmental analysis. Large volumes of data of mixed quality on pollution and residual *inputs* into the environment are being gathered in "data bases." However, the assembling and synthesizing of this data into a coherent, readily usable form is proceeding only relatively slowly. (Basic environmental input data are now being summarized in a large data book[558] by the office of the Assistant Secretary for the Environment, DOE. When complete, this volume will provide an important and useful source of data on the amounts of pollutants various energy

---

*The volume of energy-environment research and analysis sponsored by the government is staggering. The Environmental Protection Agency has developed a directory just to assist government personnel and other interested persons in locating the principal government officials involved in the program ("Who's Who in the Interagency Energy/Environment R&D Program," June 1978). In April 1977, the Energy Research and Development Administration published a 4-volume *Inventory of Federal Energy-Related Environment and Safety Research for FY 76*, totaling approximately 1,500 pages.

Debate surrounds the energy-environment research agenda. The Department of Energy has obtained research recommendations from consultants (e.g., METREK Division of the MITRE Corporation *International Aspects of Energy and the Environment: Status and Recommendations*, Apr. 1978).

Congressional committees and the Council on Environmental Quality have developed their own views (see Congressional Research Service, "Research and Development Needs to Merge Environmental and Energy Objectives," prepared for the House Subcommittee on Environment and the Atmosphere, Mar. 1978; and the Council's "Environment and Conservation and Energy Research and Development: Assessing the Adequacy of Federal Programs," Government Printing Office, Sept. 1976). The following two books by INFORM, a nonprofit environmental research group in New York City, provide an excellent overview of industrial research on new energy technologies: Stewart W. Herman and James S. Cannon, *Energy Futures: Industry and the New Technologies*, 1976; Walter C. Patterson and Richard Griffin, *Fluidized-Bed Energy Technology: Coming to a Boil*, 1978.

TABLE 13-35

U.S. Source Documents on the Effects of Pollutants

Subject	Title	Source[a]	Year
Air pollution	*Air Quality Criteria for Nitrogen Oxides*	EPA	1971
	Nitrogen Oxides	NAS	1977
	Air Quality Criteria for Hydrocarbons	HEW	1970
	Air Quality Criteria for Sulphur Oxides	HEW	no date
	Sulfur Oxides	NAS	1978
	Air Quality Criteria for Photo Chemical Oxidants	HEW	1970
	Ozone and Other Photo Chemical Oxidants	NAS	1977
	Air Quality for Particulate Matter	HEW	1969
	Particulate Polycyclic Organic Matter	NAS	1972
	Air Quality Criteria for Carbon Monoxide	HEW	1970
	Carbon Monoxide	NAS	1977
Water pollution	*Quality Criteria for Water*	EPA	1976
	Drinking Water and Health	NAS	1977
Climate	*Energy and Climate*	NAS	1977
Land disruption	*Permanent Regulatory Program Implementing Section (501)(b) of the Surface Mining Control and Reclamation Act of 1977*	DOI	1979
	Rehabilitation Potential of Western Coal Fields	NAS	1974
Thermal pollution	*The Environmental Effects of Thermal Discharges*	EPA	1974
	Biological Effects of Once-Through Cooling	UWAG	1978
Low-probability, high-risk events	*Reactor Safety: Assessment of Accident Risks in U.S. Commercial Nuclear Power Plants*	NRC	1975
	The Risks of Nuclear Power Reactors: A Review of the NRC Reactor Safety Study	UCS	1977
	Risk Assessment Review Group Report to the U.S. Nuclear Regulatory Commission	NRC	1978
	Liquefied Energy Gases Safety	GAO	1978
Radioactive pollution	*The Effects on Population of Exposure to Low Levels of Ionizing Radiation*	NAS	1972
	Radiological Quality of the Environment in the U.S., 1977	EPA	1977
	Report of the Interagency Task Force on Ionizing Radiation	HEW	1978
	The Effects on Populations of Exposure to Low Levels of Ionizing radiation	NAS	1979
Synthesis of U.S. energy-related environmental impacts	*The Strategic Environmental Assessment System*[b]	DOE	1978

[a] In the order in which the abbreviations appear in the table: U.S. Environmental Protection Agency; National Academy of Sciences; U.S. Department of Health, Education, and Welfare; U.S. Department of the Interior; Utility Water Act Group, Richmond, Va.; U.S. Nuclear Regulatory Commission; Union of Concerned Scientists, Cambridge, Mass.; U.S. General Accounting Office; U.S. Department of Energy.
[b] The U.S. Government does not have a model capable of a synthesis of all energy-related environmental impacts along the lines of Holdren's 6-step sequence discussed in the text, but the Strategic Environmental Assesssment System (SEAS) is used by DOE for its environmental analysis (see. for example. DOE's Office of the Assistant Secretary for Environment. *National Energy Plan II. Appendix: Environmental Trends and Impacts,* May 1979. p. 2). Also. there is no single source of documentation for the SEAS model. but Richard J. Kalagher et al. indicate in a recent DOE-sponsored report that "documentation on the SEAS methodology. data bases, and other detailed information on the system" may be found in the 31 references listed on page 95 of the report (*National Environmental Impact Projection No. 1.* McLean. Va.: MITRE Corp.. Dec. 1978).

sources put into the environment.) Information on *pathways, stresses, responses,* and *costs* is still incomplete and fragmented (see Table 13-35). Given the fragmentary information available for many of the six steps in the sequence, it is not surprising that at present adequate analytical models do not exist for translating environmental inputs from even a national energy projection or scenario through the pathways, stresses, and responses to the costs to human well-being,* and

* The model now being used by the Department of Energy—the Strategic Environmental Assessment System (SEAS)

considering the complexities involved, time will be needed to improve the models.

In view of the present limitations in capabilities for the analysis of environmental consequences of energy projections, the most that could be hoped for in the Global 2000 Study's analysis was a clear indication of inputs only—the environmental inputs from world energy developments out to the year 2000. However, even this relatively

model—is more integrated than many national energy models. Some results from the SEAS model are discussed later in this section.

modest goal proved impossible for several reasons. First, the DOE projections do not extend to 2000. Because of technical, political, economic, and policy uncertainties (see Chapters 10 and 20 for further details), the DOE was unable to extend its projections beyond 1990. Second, the DOE energy projections are not sufficiently detailed to permit anything but the broadest of environmental assessments. The fraction of coal to be strip-mined is not projected; the percent sulfur in the coal to be burned is not specified; nuclear and hydroelectric generation—technologies with quite different environmental effects—are lumped together.

Given the incomplete and tentative nature of the energy projections, a detailed and systematic environmental analysis could not be expected. However, DOE was asked to provide at least a general analysis of the environmental implications of its projections, and the Department contracted this work to the Brookhaven National Laboratory (BNL).

Environmental Analysis—The Brookhaven National Laboratory Projections

The DOE–BNL environmental projections include energy-related air pollutant emissions (carbon dioxide, carbon monoxide, sulfur dioxide, oxides of nitrogen, particulates, and hydrocarbons), radioactive emissions (tritium, population exposure to radiation, and solid high-level waste), land-use requirements, and solid-waste generation. Unfortunately, the simplifying assumptions underlying the DOE–BNL environmental projections severely limit the usefulness of the results. These assumptions are: (1) that by 1985 all energy facilities throughout the world will be retrofitted to meet U.S. new-source performance standards* for sulfur dioxide, oxides of nitrogen, particulates, and hydrocarbons; and (2) that for other environmental emissions and effects, emissions per fuel unit produced and consumed will remain at presently estimated values. The DOE–BNL land-use and solid-waste estimates pertained only to those aspects of the energy system for which DOE was able to supply Brookhaven with projections (unfortunately this excluded strip-mining). The estimates thus give only a partial picture of en-

---

* See *Clean Air Act*, 42 U.S.C. 1857 et seq. In its *Eighth Annual Report—1977* (p. 26), the Council on Environmental Quality writes—concerning the 1977 amendments to the Act— that "sections of the Amendments provide a more vigorous definition of new-source performance standards requiring performance at least as good as that which could be obtained by using the 'best technological system of continuous emission reduction.' "

ergy-related effects. No base-year (1975) residual emission figures could be provided because the DOE energy projections did not include base-year figures.* Given these assumptions and limitations, the DOE–BNL figures must be regarded at best as lower bounds on the expected environmental impacts.

The DOE–BNL environmental projections are presented in Tables 10–16, 10–17, and 10–18 of Chapter 10 for three cases in which oil prices are assumed to remain constant out to 1990. The Global 2000 Study's base case—oil prices increasing at 5 percent per year starting in 1980—was not analyzed. However, the low-growth case leads to a total world energy consumption similar to that in the Global 2000 Study's base case, but the mix of technologies is of course different. The DOE–BNL residuals projections for the low-growth case are shown in Table 13–36. The DOE–BNL environmental projections are discussed in detail in Chapter 10 and will not be discussed here. Because of fundamental limitations in the DOE–BNL approach, remedial efforts would be insufficient. Another approach is needed.

Environmental Analysis—Another Approach

The energy problem has several dimensions—political, economic, resource, technological, environmental, social—and difficult decisions will be required of each nation in each of these areas. The basic difficulty in developing projections of the environmental consequences of energy development is that few nations have yet made these difficult decisions. As a result, there is much uncertainty as to the approaches and technologies that will be used.

In the discussion that follows, the resource and economic aspects of the energy problem are examined briefly to establish a framework for the spectrum of technological alternatives various nations are now considering. The environmental consequences of the technological options at the ends of the spectrum are then discussed and compared. This comparison, based on U.S. national studies, provides a range of possible environmental consequences. Finally, the comparison is extended globally, with particular attention to environmental impacts of energy development that could have significant implications for some of the other Global 2000 Study projections.

The Resource Problem. Essentially, the resource aspects of the commercial energy problem

---

* Late in the study, DOE did provide a limited amount of base-year data, which have been used in Tables 13–32, 13–33, and 13–34.

TABLE 13–36

Projected Annual Emissions: 1985 and 1990, Low-Growth Case[a]

	European OECD Countries	U.S. and Canada	Japan	Less Developed Countries	OPEC Countries	Centrally Planned Economies	World
1985							
Carbon dioxide							
(*billions of short tons*)	4.78	6.85	1.51	2.57	0.80	7.52	24.0
Carbon monoxide							
(*millions of short tons*)	22.5	13.4	6.68	15.7	5.50	22.4	86.1
Sulfur dioxide							
(*millions of short tons*)	11.8	13.0	4.52	7.07	1.33	29.8	67.4
Oxides of nitrogen							
(*milliions of short tons*)	13.5	15.7	4.71	8.21	2.38	19.7	64.1
Particulates							
(*millions of short tons*)	6.3	9.02	2.03	6.56	0.54	30.6	55.0
Hydrocarbons							
(*millions of short tons*)	2.56	1.84	0.79	1.73	0.59	2.99	10.5
Land use							
(*millions of acres*)	13.7	18.7	3.37	11.9	0.004	15.1	61.2
Solid wastes							
(*millions of short tons*)	80.1	218	7.43	45.6	0.58	149	500
Tritium							
(*thousands of curies*)	103	142	22.9	34.6	3.64	47.9	354
Population exposure							
(*thousands of man-rems*)	3.98	5.44	0.88	1.33	0.14	1.84	13.6
Solid high-level wastes							
(*billions of curies*)	11.0	15.1	2.44	3.69	0.39	5.10	37.6
1990							
Carbon dioxide							
(*billions of short tons*)	5.20	7.31	1.62	3.05	0.97	8.42	26.6
Carbon monoxide							
(*millions of short tons*)	26.2	13.1	8.44	19.6	6.96	25.0	99.2
Sulfur dioxide							
(*millions of short tons*)	12.7	13.8	4.68	8.42	1.56	33.4	74.6
Oxides of nitrogen							
(*millions of short tons*)	14.8	16.2	4.44	9.74	2.88	22.0	70.7
Particulates							
(*millions of short tons*)	6.66	9.73	2.15	7.81	0.63	34.2	61.2
Hydrocarbons							
(*millions of short tons*)	2.94	1.85	0.38	2.14	0.73	3.35	12.0
Land use							
(*millions of acres*)	15.7	21.6	4.43	15.7	0.007	21.6	79.0
Solid waste							
(*millions of short tons*)	75.1	243	7.49	50.2	1.02	168	545
Tritium							
(*thousands of curies*)	178	214	42.4	74.6	12.0	118	639
Population exposure							
(*thousands of man-rems*)	6.83	8.23	1.63	2.87	0.46	4.53	24.6
Solid high-level wastes							
(*billions of curies*)	18.9	22.9	4.52	7.95	1.28	12.6	68.1

Source: Department of Energy–Brookhaven National Laboratory projections.

[a] The important assumptions behind the figures in this table are discussed briefly in the text of this chapter and. more fully. in Chapter 10.

facing the world is that convenient, easily transported, relatively clean-burning petroleum and natural gas resources are being depleted. As these resources become increasingly scarce, a transition to other forms of energy must be made. How quickly the transition must be made depends upon how much oil will ultimately be recovered and how rapidly the oil is used.

While there is still uncertainty and debate over how much oil will ultimately be recovered, estimates are becoming more refined. The lack of consensus on estimates of ultimately recoverable conventional world oil resources stems (1) from several economic, technical, and geologic uncertainties that are not likely to be resolved soon, and (2) from a failure to fully utilize existing public

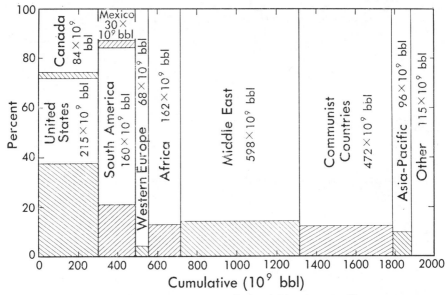

Figure 13–10. Distribution and present production of ultimately recoverable conventional crude oil resources of the world. Shaded areas represent cumulative production to date. (*M. King Hubbert, in Congressional Research Service*, Project Interdependence: U.S. and World Energy Outlook Through 1990, *Washington, 1977, p. 644*)

information about world oil resources. A recent report prepared for the Central Intelligence Agency by Richard Nehring of the Rand Corporation provides a detailed, publicly available description of the known recoverable crude oil resources of the world and an explicitly reasoned estimated range of ultimately recoverable conventional crude oil resources.[559]

The Nehring report focuses on the relatively small number of giant oil fields, defined as fields having an ultimate recovery of 500 million barrels or more. These giant oil fields contain more than 75 percent of the known recoverable oil resources of the world. Their comprehensive examination provides an efficient means of assessing world oil resources.

After a lengthy and detailed analysis, Nehring concludes[560] that the ultimate recoverable conventional crude oil resources of the world are somewhere between 1,700 and 2,300 billion barrels.* Nehrings "best estimate" of the ultimately

recoverable conventional crude oil resources of the world (i.e., the middle of his range) is 2,000 billion barrels. The global distribution of this resource is illustrated in Figure 13–10, in which the shaded areas indicate the fractions of the ultimately recoverable crude oil resources that have already been produced. The United States has produced the largest fraction of its crude oil resources (approximately 50 percent); Canada, Mexico, and Western Europe have produced relatively small fractions of theirs.

How fast will the world's crude oil resources be consumed? This question cannot be answered with precision. As Nehring notes, the future depletion rate will depend on (1) the production policies of OPEC, (2) the development of technology for offshore Arctic and deepwater exploration and production, and (3) the existence of the necessary economic incentives to producers and refiners. However, it is possible to estimate roughly how long the world's crude oil resources will last.

* These figures were estimated prior to the recent reports of a major oil province in Mexico. The Mexican find, therefore, may be considered to be one of "the two to four major oil provinces" that Nehring expects to be discovered and developed. The Mexican find is large, probably on the order of 50–60 billion barrels of petroleum (as opposed to "oil equiva-

lent"). This amount is roughly equal to 10 percent of the petroleum ultimately recoverable in the Middle East or 50 percent of the oil yet to be produced in the United States—or about 3 percent of the ultimately recoverable crude oil resources of the world.

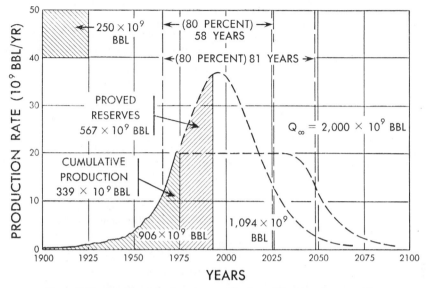

Figure 13–11. Possible production rate curves for the world's ultimately recoverable crude oil resources. (*M. King Hubbert in Congressional Research Service*, Project Interdependence: U.S. and World Energy Outlook Through 1990, *Washington, 1977, p. 642*)

The production rate curve for any finite resource—including crude oil—has a bell shape. The production rate starts at zero when the resource was first tapped. The curve then rises as the production rate increases. Ultimately, the curve must peak and return to zero as the oil resource is exhausted. On such a curve, a steep rise in the real costs of discovery and production can be anticipated. The total area under the curve must equal the total oil ultimately economically recoverable.[561]

Using 2,000 billion barrels (Nehring's best estimate) for the ultimately recoverable resource, Figure 13–11 illustrates two possible shapes of the future crude oil production rate curve for the world. In both cases, the total area under the curves is equal to the total ultimately recoverable conventional crude oil resource of the world (2,000 billion barrels), and the initial portion of the curves corresponds to historic experience. The symmetric curve rises to a peak about 1990, declining thereafter. The second curve shows that if petroleum production were held at about 1975 rates, the decline in production could be postponed for about two decades. The symmetric curve assumes that 80 percent of the world's total ultimately recoverable conventional resources are consumed over a 58-year period; with production

limited to the 1975 rate, 80 percent of the resources are consumed over an 81-year period.

The resource aspect of the world's commercial energy problem is, in essence, that crude oil (and natural gas) cannot continue to grow at historical rates. Figure 13–12 illustrates the problem for crude oil. The rapidly rising curve continues the growth trend experienced in the 1950s, 60s, and early 70s. The lower curve is the symmetric production curve (from Fig. 13–11) for the world's ultimately recoverable conventional crude oil resources. The rapidly growing gap is an indication of the resource aspect of the world's commercial energy problem.

The Economic Problem. The economic aspect of the world's commercial energy problem stems largely from the observation[562] that GNP and energy growth have been correlated in the past, as illustrated in Figure 13–13 for the U.S. The concern is that (1) if GNP measures social welfare and (2) if growth in GNP is both correlated with and caused by energy growth, reduced energy growth would necessarily affect social welfare adversely. However, there are many reasons to doubt these two suppositions. It is well known that GNP is not an adequate or satisfactory measure of social welfare. Furthermore, there is wide variation among nations and regions in the amount

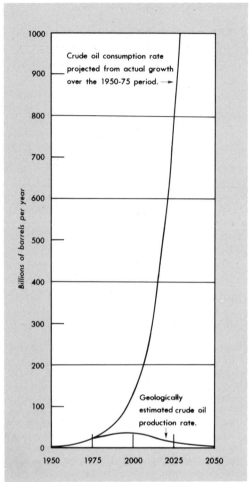

Figure 13-12. Geologically estimated global crude oil production rates compared with consumption rates projected from actual growth over the 1950-75 period. The production curve is from Figure 13-11; the consumption curve is projected from historic consumption rates over the 1900-75 period.

of GNP (and welfare) produced per unit of energy used,* and the hypothesized causal linkages between energy use and GNP (and welfare) are clearly subject to varying degrees of efficiency.[563]

---

* A study prepared by the MITRE Corporation for the Department of Energy (Richard J. Kalagher et al., "National Environmental Projection No. 1," Dec. 1978, p. 83) forecasts that by 1990 the U.S. economy will generate $19 billion of GNP per quad (10^{15} Btu) of energy supply, up about 19 percent from the 1975 performance of $16 billion GNP per quad of energy supply.

Since GNP figures include the value of services performed in cleaning up the environment as well as economic activities that create pollution, social welfare could actually increase as a result of reduced GNP, at least to the extent that more efficient use of energy could reduce the polluting component of GNP without reducing the beneficial component.* While all of the future consequences are still not entirely clear, the social, economic, and environmental consequences of alternative energy paths are important considerations in projecting an energy future.

The Technological Options. There are many ideas as to how the United States and other nations might best respond to the resource and economic aspects of the world energy problem. The most widely discussed ideas are based on the use of increased amounts of energy derived from five primary energy sources: coal, oil, natural gas, nuclear fission, and solar. Increased use of each of these primary sources has environmental impacts. These impacts are described briefly in the following paragraphs.

• Coal production and use involve serious environmental problems, most of which can be limited through control measures.

Worker health and safety is a special concern with coal. Coal mining is a hazardous occupation, even when careful attention is given to maintaining a safe and healthy workplace. Without such attention, frequent accidents and a high incidence of black-lung disease would be the norm.

Adverse land and water impacts are also a prime concern. Without proper controls, surface mines can lead to large-scale land disruptions. Natural habitats can be largely destroyed, and farmlands can be rendered unproductive. The physiological and ecological character of the affected regions can be markedly changed. Land subsidence is a common occurrence with deep mines. Water pollution, especially acid mine drainage, is associated with both surface and underground mines.

Without adequate controls, coal combustion can release considerable amounts of air pollutants, including sulfur dioxide, nitrogen oxides, particulates, and trace metals. These pollutants

---

* Further support for this point is provided by the forthcoming report of the Demand and Conservation Panel of the National Academy of Sciences' Committee on Nuclear and Alternative Energy Systems (discussed in part in "U.S. Energy Demand: Some Low Energy Futures," *Science*, Apr. 14, 1978, pp. 142–52), and in the report of the Energy Project at the Harvard Business School (Robert Stogaugh and David Yergin, eds., *Energy Future*, New York: Random House, 1979).

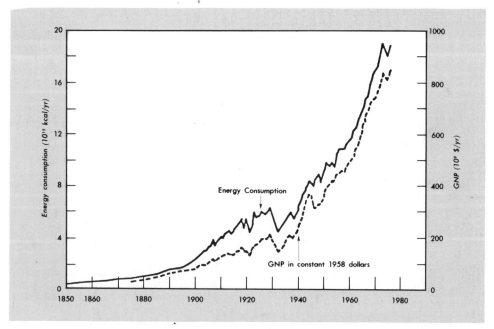

Figure 13-13. Historical growth of GNP and commercial energy use in the United States, 1850-1976. (*U.S. Statistical Abstracts*)

can produce health or ecological concerns on a local, regional, national, and sometimes even international scale.

The ecological effects associated with acid rains have only recently become of widespread concern. The combustion of coal and other fossil fuels produces oxides of sulfur and nitrogen that acidify rain over wide areas. (The acid rain problem is discussed extensively in the water section of this chapter.)

The combustion of coal and other fossil fuels releases carbon dioxide, contributing to the problem of its accumulation in the atmosphere. Global atmosphere CO_2 levels have already increased by about 10 percent above pre-industrial concentrations. The global consequences of continued CO_2 buildup are not well understood, but there is concern that a gradual, irreversible, and potentially dangerous change in the world's climate could occur over the next century as a result of the "greenhouse effect." (The CO_2 problem is discussed extensively in the climate section of this chapter.)

• Oil produces environmental impacts that are both similar to and different from those produced

by coal. The environmental impacts associated with the combustion of oil and coal are generally similar, but on a per unit energy basis tend to be less severe with oil. The comparison, however, is not completely straightforward because some of the impacts are not fully commensurable. (The problem of comparability becomes more acute with energy sources that are even more dissimilar—e.g., coal versus nuclear energy.)

The most prominent generic environmental difference between coal and oil concern production and transportation. The problems of production and transportation of oil include the likely disruption of some pristine areas (such as the arctic and antarctic regions), the possibility of blowouts during the exploration and drilling phases, and the likelihood of major spills due to transportation accidents. Ocean transportation by supertanker is of particular concern. Over the last decade, large oil spills from supertankers have become a global problem. Chronic oil pollution from many sources, land- and marine-based, also remains a serious concern.

• Natural gas produces substantially less air pollution per unit of energy than either oil or coal.

Being gaseous under normal conditions, it poses less risks to land and water during overland transport. Natural gas, however, is increasingly being liquefied and transported via ocean tankers. In the event of a serious accident near a major population center, a tanker filled with highly volatile liquefied natural gas poses the risk of a disastrous fire or explosion.

• Nuclear energy raises a set of environmental concerns that are largely different from those associated with fossil fuels. Electrical energy generation at a nuclear power plant does not, for example, directly produce conventional air pollution. Also, due to the comparatively high energy content of uranium ores that are presently available, much less land is disrupted to produce a unit of energy from uranium than from coal.

Nuclear power, however, does have several important societal and environmental problems associated with its widespread use. These include concerns related to reactor safety, nuclear waste disposal, and international security.

Nuclear reactor safety is a continuing issue. The possibility of a truly catastrophic accident, involving a reactor meltdown that releases considerable amounts of radiation and could lead potentially to thousands of deaths and billions of dollars of property damage, has been a concern since the beginning of the technology. Elaborate safety measures with several levels of redundancy have been developed to prevent such an event. Even though the likelihood of a major accident at a carefully designed, maintained, and managed reactor is small, its precise value is uncertain and nonzero. The actual degree of risks under various conditions of design, maintenance, and management continues to be the subject of intensive analysis. Needless to say, if nuclear power plants are not subject to careful design, maintenance, and management, these facilities pose far greater risks to public health and welfare.

The total global amounts of nuclear waste generated by reactor operations have grown steadily. Nuclear waste products are toxic, highly radioactive, and long-lived. Some of the radioactive isotopes in nuclear wastes remain dangerously radioactive for hundreds of thousands of years, a period many times longer than recorded history. Safe disposal will require extended containment in sites that are stable over geological periods of time. Many disposal techniques have been proposed but none has yet been established as fully satisfactory. Research aimed at resolving this problem must receive greater attention than in the past.

Nuclear power may also increase the risk to world security, both through the possibility of added vulnerability to terrorist actions and through its potential for accelerating the proliferation of nuclear weapons. Acts of vandalism and sabotage to nuclear power plants have been reported in several countries. While no radioactive releases due to such attacks have been reported so far, this possibility remains a serious concern. Nuclear power may also accelerate weapons proliferation. The spread of sensitive facilities (e.g., enrichment and reprocessing plants) can result in direct access to weapons-usable materials. To date, the technology for enriching uranium and separating plutonium from spent fuel has been tightly controlled and limited almost exclusively to those nations already possessing nuclear weapons. However, this situation may change in the future if more nations seek to acquire enrichment and reprocessing facilities. The widespread use of plutonium and highly enriched uranium would increase the availability of both, and thereby also increase the risk of further proliferation of nuclear weapons throughout the world while offering no substantial advantage over the continued use of low-enriched uranium in the nuclear energy facilities of those nations that do not now have nuclear weapons. Furthermore, a substantial disadvantage could occur in that a proliferation of nuclear weapons capability would diminish world security and in turn threaten the energy security of all nations.

• Solar energy is available in several forms, including hydropower, wind power, organic material (biomass), ocean thermal energy conversion, and direct sunlight. Its environmental problems vary markedly both in kind and in degree from one technology to another. Even for a given technology, the environmental implications depend on the scale of the facility and on site-specific factors.

Hydro facilities that generate electricity usually generate from a few kilowatts to thousands of megawatts. Environmental concerns associated with hydropower include the disruption of river flows and aquatic life, flooding of land and wetland habitats, potential public health problems related to ecosystem changes, and possible long-term effects on agricultural production at those locations where the reservoir is used for irrigation.

Energy production via large and small wind systems also raises a number of minor but consequential environmental concerns. These include safety problems associated with blade or tower failure, worker and neighborhood exposure to noise, electromagnetic interference, and windmill aesthetics.

The potential environmental problems associated with increased reliance on biomass could be severe. As noted elsewhere in this Study, LDCs have been particularly subject to the overuse of biomass for basic energy needs. The problems in some LDCs include widespread deforestation and the loss of essential nutrients due to the use of animal wastes to meet domestic energy requirements. These problems are already very critical in some countries and may become even more critical in the future.

By comparison, the use of bioenergy in industrialized countries appears to pose problems of considerably smaller magnitude. These include the possibility of small- to moderate-scale ecological effects due to the development of intensive biomass "farms," air pollution associated with the increased use of fuelwood, and air and water pollution associated with the production of liquid or gaseous fuels from biomass.

Ocean thermal energy conversion (OTEC) systems pose several environmental problems (see "The Projections and the Marine Environment" above), whose nature, magnitude, and effects are still somewhat uncertain. Three unexplored areas provide the source of this uncertainty. First, the technology is evolving rapidly and is subject to substantial modifications. Second, the specific nature of the impact of OTEC facilities in an ocean environment is not well understood. Third, the aggregate environmental impact of an OTEC "farm" is unknown. The most important concerns identified so far include: the need to avoid ecology sensitive areas by proper site selection; displacement of sufficient oceanic water to alter the temperature and chemical characteristics of the marine environment; entrainment and possible destruction of marine organisms; and corrosion of metallic surfaces, which could lead to the buildup of toxic substances in the marine food chain.

The potential methods of harnessing direct solar radiation range from large-scale electrical generating installations to small-scale applications for home space heating, hot water, and electricity. The vast majority of the applications appear to be relatively benign environmentally. Most of the environmental impacts are typically associated with the production of equipment rather than operation. Large-scale solar "power towers" and solar cells in space to generate microwave power beamed to earth are possible exceptions. Ongoing research is aimed at the better identification of the environmental effects associated with these and other systems.

Given these primary sources of energy—coal, oil, natural gas, nuclear fission and solar—there are a wide spectrum of mixes under consideration by nations around the world as possible solutions to their energy problems. The spectrum ranges from heavy dependence on nuclear energy and nonrenewable fossil fuels (especially coal) with minimal attention to the productivity and efficiency of energy use on the one hand, to heavy emphasis of renewable resources (especially the various forms of solar energy), increased productivity (i.e., end-use conservation), and increased efficiency in the energy sector (i.e., thermodynamic matching of energy source to end-use requirements*) on the other. These two extremes of the solution spectrum are now widely referenced to as the "hard" and the "soft" paths.[564]

The hard path/soft path dichotomy is a convenient means of capsulizing the *range* of environmental impacts that may be expected from energy development in the decade ahead. While both the hard path and the soft path have environmental impacts, their relative difference in emphasis on conservation, productivity, efficiency and renewable/nonrenewable sources leads to very different environmental impacts. For a time, the most complete comparisons of hard and soft path scenarios were provided by the writings of Amory Lovins[565] and his critics,[566] but a number of additional studies are now available. Most of the new studies are not strictly hard path or soft path studies, but are definitely closer to one end of the spectrum or the other. The discussion that follows relates these studies to the hard and soft path concepts and compares environmental consequences. Finally, the range of energy-related environmental impacts that might be experienced globally in 2000 is considered briefly in light of the comparison.

The Hard Path

Studies of hard path options abound. The discussion here is limited to two. The first is the work of the World Energy Conference (WEC), which

---

* The degree to which the energy industry requires primary energy to deliver end-use energy for the needs of society is illustrated by the example of converting coal to another form of energy, namely electricity. If three lumps of coal are burned in a thermal power plant to generate electricity, *the energy sector of the economy loses the energy from two lumps of coal as waste heat.* Similar losses occur in the conversion of coal to synthetic fuels. Such inefficiencies in the energy sector can be minimized by matching thermodynamically the quality of the energy delivered to the quality of the energy needed for the performance of particular end uses.

provides what is probably the most complete global hard path scenario yet developed, but has only a very limited environmental analysis.* The second is U.S. national energy scenario developed by the U.S. Department of Energy. The environmental implications of the DOE scenario have been analyzed much more fully than the WEC scenario.

The World Energy Conference Study. The relatively hard path scenarios developed by the WEC anticipate significant growth in both coal and nuclear. The WEC analysis,† noting that ultimately production regulates demand, projects potential world primary energy production in 2000 at 690 exajoules (EJ).§ The potential production mix is as follows: coal, 170 EJ; oil, 195 EJ; gas, 143 EJ; nuclear, 88 EJ; hydraulic, 34 EJ; unconventional oil and gas, 4 EJ; renewable solar, geothermal, and biomass, 56 EJ.[567]

The WEC presents a range of energy demand projections for 2000. All of the projections are based on assumed rates of economic growth and assumed elasticities of energy use relative to income and price. High growth ("H") cases and low growth ("L") cases were developed using the following assumed annual economic growth rates:

	OECD Nations	Centrally Planned Economies	Less Developed Countries	World
High growth	3.7	4.5	5.3	4.1
Low growth	2.8	3.2	3.8	3.0

The income and price elasticities vary from case to case. The high-growth case H3 includes only the impact of a significant price response and results in a demand of about 680 EJ (646 quad) in 2000—an increase of a factor of two over energy use in 1972 (the study's base year). The H5 scenario includes not only the high price response, but also oil utilization constraints and vigorous conservation measures, which exceed the normally expected consumer response to higher energy prices. The H5 assumptions result in a demand of about 560 EJ (532 quad) in 2000—an increase of about a factor of 1.7 over 1972 use. The low-growth case L4 assumes a high price response, further oil constraints, further conservation meas-

ures, and the use of oil primarily for premium uses. The L4 assumptions result in a demand of about 520 EJ (494 quad)—an increase of about 1.5 times over 1972 use.[568]

The World Energy Conference's consideration of environmental constraints is confined to one page in its current work.[569] This brief discussion recalls for the reader the assumption in the WEC analysis that current environmental and antipollution standards will remain unchanged. The discussion continues by noting that of course standards will change; and because "in the case of an emergency an ample supply of energy is given a higher priority than at least the more marginal concern for the environment, . . . we believe that proper measures to prevent energy shortages should form a part of a comprehensive and responsible environmental policy."[570]

The WEC environmental assessment continues, "It is often said that the least-polluting joule is the one never produced. This is not necessarily true. In fact many antipollution measures, adopted, or proposed, require the use of more energy rather than less.[571]

The WEC concludes its environmental discussion with a call for more environmental analysis. It should be noted that environmental considerations are one of the three major topics on the program of the next WEC conference.[572]

The DOE hard path scenario. The Department of Energy recently contracted with the MITRE Corporation to analyze the environmental implications of a DOE scenario that lies close to the hard end of the spectrum of energy paths. The scenario, known as Projection Series C, is one of a set developed by DOE's Energy Information Administration and reported in the Administration's annual report.[573] In Table 13–37, Projection Series C* is compared with the original definition of the hard path. While there is a close correspondence between the scenario and the definition, this is not the "hardest" of the scenarios being considered by DOE. The DOE-sponsored MITRE analysis[574] describes this scenario as a "business-as-usual" scenario, characterizing "a middle range of energy futures likely to result if

---

* The scenarios developed by Workshop on Alternative Energy Strategies (WAES) might also have been considered here, but they exclude nations having centrally planned economies and have no more environmental analysis than the WEC work.
† The WEC projections extend to 2020, but to facilitate comparison with other figures in this report, the WEC figures presented here are the ones for 2000.
§ 1 EJ = 10^{18} joules = 0.95×10^{15} Btu = 0.95 quad.

*Since the above was written, DOE has published a similar environmental analysis of National Energy Plan II (NEP-II). The NEP-II scenario for low-priced oil ($21/bbl in 2000) is based on the identical average annual growth rate in primary energy conversion—2.82 percent per year. The NEP-II scenario for high-priced oil ($38/bbl in 2000) has a slightly slower average annual growth rate in primary energy conversion—2.60 percent per year.

policies in existence prior to the passage of the National Energy Act* are continued.

The DOE-MITRE analysis of Projection Series C is based on present and anticipated environmental regulations, many of which are under attack or in question. Among these regulations, the air and water quality regulations are particularly important.†

Based on these and other assumptions, the DOE-MITRE report presents a mixed and incomplete picture through 1990 of the U.S. environmental future implied by the Projection Series C

---

*Deregulation provided for in the National Energy Act will gradually raise the cost of domestic oil and gas to world price levels, but will not significantly alter the basic strategy characteristic of Projection Series C.

†The MITRE analysis (pp. 19, 59–60) describes its assumptions about these regulations as follows:

"The 1970 Clean Air Act Amendments to the Air Quality Act of 1967 ('Clean Air Act') provide the legislative basis for most environmental regulations and assumptions used in this section of the report. The Clean Air Act stipulated that the federal government set National Ambient Air Quality Standards (NAAQS) for five pollutants: total suspended particulates, sulfur dioxide, nitrogen dioxide, hydrocarbons, and carbon monoxide. Each state was then required to develop and submit a State Implementation Plan (SIP) to the Environmental Protection Agency (EPA) Administrator. The SIP specifies strategies to achieve the level of air quality established by the NAAQS for individual polluting categories in all regions of the state. EPA also set New Source Performance Standards (NSPS) for selected industrial categories. Compliance with both the SIP and NSPS is assumed in the environmental forecasts of this report, although full compliance with SIP standards is not assumed until 1985. It is assumed that new sources coming on line after 1975 meet EPA's original NSPS standards until the revised NSPS regulations of the Clean Air Act Amendments of 1977 become effective.

". . .The revised NSPS regulations require the use of the 'Best Available Control Technology' (BACT) for new major emitting facilities. This BACT requirement has been simulated for new coal-fired electric utilities (projected to be operational in 1984 or later) and new industrial boilers (initiated in 1981) or later). . . .

"Title II of the Clean Air Act (as amended in August 1977) specifies emission limits (in grams of pollutant per vehicle mile traveled over the lifetime of a vehicle) for mobile pollution sources. These emission limits have been translated by EPA into emission factors (also expressed in grams per mile) which account for increasing pollutant emissions as the vehicle ages. In several cases, the emission factors for new vehicles are lower than the emission limits set because increasing emissions due to vehicle deterioration are accounted for by increasing emission factors over time. . . . The Federal Water Pollution Control Act stipulated that the Environmental Protection Agency (EPA) develop industry-specific guidelines limiting releases of major pollutants. . . . The effluent limitations developed by EPA set two levels of guidelines: 'Best Practicable Technology' (BPT) currently available, to be met by July 1, 1977; and 'Best Available Technology' (BAT) economically achievable, to be met by July 1, 1983. This DOE-MITRE study assumes that 100 percent industrial compliance with BPT standards will be achieved in 1979, and with BAT standards by 1985."

---

hard path scenario. The treatment of air pollution covers most of major energy related pollutants: sulfur oxides, hydrocarbons, carbon monoxide, nitrogen oxides, hydrocarbons and particulates, but omits carbon dioxide.* The discussion of water pollution covers total dissolved solids and nitrogen discharges. Water consumption is projected, but no indications of land disruption and loss by mining (especially coal strip-mining and uranium mining) are provided. Solid wastes (especially scrubber sludge and ash) are projected, but nuclear wastes and radiation associated with the nuclear fuel cycle are not. Despite its limitations, this is one of the broadest and most complete environmental assessments yet provided by DOE in its energy scenarios and strategies.† The principal findings are exerpted briefly below.

According to the DOE-MITRE report, the en-

---

* The major importance of carbon dioxide to the formulation of energy policy is discussed in a recent report sent by four scientists to the Council on Environmental Quality (George M. Woodwell, Gordon J. MacDonald, Roger Revelle, and C. David Keeling, "The Carbon Dioxide Problem: Implications for Policy in the Management of Energy and Other Resources," Washington: Council on Environmental Quality, July 1979).

† There is wide variation in the extent to which environmental considerations have been included in major domestic and world energy studies. In the U.S., for example, the Federal Energy Administration's 1974 Project Independence Report included a brief 15-page environment assessment (Chapter 4), addressing a wide range of environmental impacts associated with six scenarios for $7 and $11 oil, but without much integration and synthesis. The 1974 report of the Ford Foundation's Energy Policy Project (A Time to Choose, by S. David Freeman et al., Ballinger, 1974) anticipated higher oil prices and included a reasonably thorough environmental assessment in its analysis of alternative energy policies (p. 179). The 1977 Congressional Research Service report Project Interdependence discussed briefly the environmental constraints associated with various possible energy sources. The National Academy of Science's Implications of Environmental Regulations for Energy Production and Consumption (1977) is very detailed on those environmental impacts now being regulated in the U.S.

The National Energy Plan (Executive Office of the President, 1977) integrates general environmental considerations at many points, but specifics are limited. The Department of Energy did not prepare an environmental impact statement for the plan, but an "environmental assessment statement" is expected to be released in 1979 (John Pearson, Energy Information Administration, personal communication, 1979). In May 1979, DOE submitted a revised National Energy Plan (NEP II) to Congress, containing an appendix, Environmental Trends and Impacts, that addresses the environmental consequences of the revised plan and its energy-pricing proposals, similar in scope to the DOE-MITRE report discussed in the text above.

Outside the U.S., there is also wide variation in the ways in which energy and environment are considered. The Secretariat for Future Studies in Sweden has produced two reports on energy that contain extensive and integrated consideration

TABLE 13–37

Comparison of the Hard Path Definition and the Energy Information Administration's Projection Series C

Hard Path Definition	Projection Series
Twin goals: sustaining growth in energy consumption (assumed to be closely and causally linked to GNP and to social welfare) and	The Projection Series C scenario projects the following trends in macroeconomic and energy consumption:
minimizing oil imports	Increased petroleum imports. The costs of production and distribution for all energy sources except oil and gas were held constant by the Energy Information Administration. Changes in oil and gas costs, however, are induced through alternative assumptions regarding their physical availability. The Projection Series C case postulates a constant real price of imported oil of $15.32 per barrel in 1978 dollars.
Rapid expansion of the coal sector (mainly coal strip-mined and converted into electricity or synthetic fuels).	Coal production, particularly in the West, will increase dramatically, reflecting increased demand brought about by higher (post-1973) prices of oil and gas, particularly for electricity generation. Electricity sales will grow at 4.8 percent per year, rather than the historic 7 percent, reflecting saturation of air conditioning and major appliances that included high rates of penetration during the 1960s. This is consistent with the 5 percent growth from 1970 to 1976 and 4.2 percent from 1976 to 1977.
Rapid expansion of the oil and gas sectors (increasingly from arctic and offshore wells).	Increased oil imports. Domestic oil production will increase slightly over current levels because of the development of Alaskan oil fields and the outer continental shelf. Lower 48 production of natural gas will continue to decline, although less rapidly, after Alaskan North Slope gas distribution systems are completed. Fuel shares in the industrial economic sector indicate a shift from gas to oil and, to a lesser extent, to electricity, reflecting declining gas supplies.
Rapid expansion of the nuclear fission sector (especially in fast breeder reactors).	Large increases in nuclear power.
Limited or no use of solar and conservation technologies.	Solar technologies are not expected to contribute significantly to total energy supply through 1990. The key elements in supply-demand patterns through 1990 are assumptions about the degree of energy conservation in general and of oil and gas in particular, as a result of economic presssures and mandatory conservation measures introduced 1973. One example of such measures is the imposition of fuel efficiency standards for automobiles.

The inset within the first row reads:

	1975	1985	1990
GNP (*billions of 1972 dollars*)	1,202	1,803	2,017
Energy consumption (*quadrillion Btus*)	70.6	94.6	108.5[a]

Source: Hard path definition—Amory B. Lovins. *Soft Energy Paths: Toward a Durable Peace.* Cambridge. Mass.: Ballinger, 1977. p. 26. Projection Series C—Richard J. Kalagher et al., "National Environmental Impact Projection No. 1." McLean. Va.: MITRE Corp.. Dec. 1978. pp. 1, 150.
[a] Compare the Department of Energy's projection for the Global 2000 Study, which has the U.S. consuming 100 quadrillion Btus in 1990 (Table 13–33).

of environmental impacts ("Energy and Society: Conceptual Outline Introducing a Futures Study," Dec. 1975; and Måans Lönnroth et al., *Energy in Transition: A Report on Energy Policy and Future Options,* Mar. 1977). The 1977 *World Energy Outlook: A Reassessment of Long-Term Energy Developments and Related Policies,* prepared for the Organization for Economic Cooperation and Development, does not explicitly consider the environmental dimension of energy prospects. The lengthy report of the Workshop on Energy Strategies (*Energy: Global Prospects 1985–2000,* McGraw-Hill, 1977) concludes its consideration of environment in less than two pages (p. 41). The global energy analysis work of the International Institute of Applied Systems Analysis is oriented primarily toward economic and resource considerations but does contain a limited environmental dimension (see, for example, W. Häfele, "Energy Options Open to Mankind Beyond the Turn of the Century," International Conference on Nuclear Power and Its Fuel Cycle, Schlossburg, Austria, May 1977; and Häfele and W. Sassin, "The Global Energy System," *Annual Review of Energy,* vol. 2, 1977).

The international environmental group Friends of the Earth has published books on world energy strategies (Amory B. Lovins, *World Energy Strategies: Facts, Issues and Options,* Ballinger, 1975) non-nuclear energy options (Lovins and John H. Price, *Non-Nuclear Futures: The Case for an Ethical Energy Strategy,* Ballinger, 1975), and soft energy paths (Lovins, *Soft Energy Paths: Toward a Durable Peace,* Ballinger 1977), all of which contain general but not highly detailed considerations of social, political, and physical environments. The Rockefeller Foundation sponsored *World Energy Survey* by Ruth Leger Sivard (World Priorities, Leesburg, Va., 1979) contains a brief environmental discussion. The various reports of the World Energy Conference (WEC) contain nothing on the environmental aspects of energy (Robert J. Raudebaugh, Executive Director of WEC's U.S. National Committee, personal communication, Feb. 15, 1979). The WEC, however, plans to include environmental considerations in two of the four major program divisions at its 1980 meeting (11th World Energy Conference, 1980, "Energy for Our World," Technical Program with Instructions for Authors, 1979).

vironmental implications of the Projection Series C hard path scenario are as follows:

- Little or no improvement is shown for sulfur oxide (SO_x) emissions. All improvements occur by 1985 when it is assumed that standards for existing sources will have been met. If SO_x emissions are to be reduced by 1990, the retirement of old plants must be accelerated or the standards tightened.
- Large increases in nitrogen oxide (NO_x) emissions are anticipated. Throughout the forecast period, combustion activity (primarily by electric utilities) is responsible for the majority of SO_x and NO_x releases.
- Significant national reductions are expected by 1990 in the emissions of particulates, hydrocarbons, and carbon monoxide.
- Large increases in dissolved solids (especially sulfates, creating acid problems) are anticipated.
- Little or no improvement is shown for point-source nitrogen releases to water.
- Significant national reductions are expected by 1990 in point-source discharges of major water pollutants such as biochemical oxygen demand, suspended solids, total phosphorus, and numerous metals.
- Large increases in ash and scrubber sludge are anticipated.
- High-Btu gasification of coal is expected to produce major increases in cyanide releases in regions with gasification plants unless zero discharge regulations are imposed.
- Thermal discharges are not calculated, but large increases in water consumption for evaporative cooling are anticipated. Both utilities and other manufacturing industries contribute substantially to increased water consumption by 1990. The increasing role of nuclear-powered generation is a factor in this increase. Development of both energy and manufacturing activity may be seriously limited by existing or anticipated water shortages in several regions of the country.

The DOE-MITRE report does not address the following energy-related environmental considerations:

- Land losses to facilities development, uranium mining, and strip-mining are not calculated or discussed.
- Nuclear wastes and radiation from the nuclear fuel cycles are not calculated or discussed.
- Occupational safety and health issues are not addressed.

When the environmental trends are viewed at the regional and local levels, the picture reveals impacts that are otherwise masked by the national trends. Figure 13–14 summarizes the most significant energy-related regional impacts.

The DOE-MITRE report describes the environmental trends from the Projection Series C hard path scenario as "a middle ground of likely environmental futures" for the U.S. How typical might such impacts be for other industrial economies?

Serious as many of the DOE-MITRE environmental trends are, they may underestimate the impacts that would follow in many nations from a hard path energy policy. This is because the degree of environmental protection assumed in the DOE-MITRE report requires significant national commitments of capital, resources, and labor. The report notes that

Total pollution control costs (capital plus operating and maintenance expenditures) will increase at an annual rate of 3.1 percent between 1975 and 1990, but will decline relative to GNP.

Direct and indirect energy requirements for pollution control are projected to increase by 50 percent between 1975 and 1990, but will account for no more than 3.7 percent of total U.S. energy use in any one year. . . . The number of persons in 1990 that will be employed directly or indirectly in pollution control-related activities is estimated to be 1.8 million, or 1.6 percent of total U.S. employment.

It is not clear that all industrial nations (perhaps even including the U.S.) will be able or willing to commit as much of their capital, resources, and labor to environmental protection as is assumed in the DOE-MITRE report.

There are a number of variations of the hard path. The most significant differences among these variations concern the major sources of additional primary energy. Some variations involve a large growth in nuclear energy; others involve large increases in coal combustion. The environmental implications of these two variations are significantly different, and their economic advantages and disadvantages differ from region to region.

The primary argument for nuclear power in the U.S., for example, has been that it would produce cheaper electricity than alternative energy sources. Early advocates suggested that fission would produce electricity "too cheap to meter." Nuclear power has certainly no prospect of becoming too cheap to meter. As a result, the basic argument of its cost advantage over alternative sources has been questioned frequently with the charge that if all costs were properly accounted for, and sub-

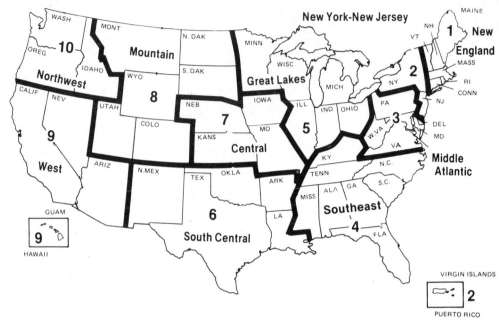

Region 1

TDS discharges double due primarily to electric utilities. Slight increase in particulate emissions. Moderate increase in SO_x emission due to conversion to coal.

Region 2

Arsenic discharges double due to pharmaceuticals industry. Moderate increase in SO_x emission due to conversion to coal. High amounts of sludge generated by 1990.

Region 3

Sulfate discharges increase by 1/5 due to coal mining activities. Substantial decline in SO_x and particulate emissions by 1990. High sludge and NCSW volumes from electric utilities and industrial boilers burning coal by 1990.

Region 4

· TDS releases triple due to electric utilities and chemical industry. Several non-ferrous metals and chlorides discharges double by 1990. High particulate emissions in 1975 with substantial decline by 1990. High sludge and NCSW volumes by 1990.

Region 5

TDS discharges increase by 1/2 due to electric utilities and chemical industry. High sludge and NCSW volumes by 1990 primarily to electric utilities and industrial boilers burning coal.

Region 6

Projected increases in energy related water consumption by 1990 may face strong competition from other sources. TDS and chloride discharges more than double by 1990 due to organic chemicals industry. Cyanide releases increase by 1/2 due to high BTU coal gasification. Largest projected increase in SO_x emissions. Regional increases in SO_x from new coal burning electric utilities and industrial boilers.

Region 7

Large portion of national cyanide discharges in 1990 due to high BTU coal gasification. Regional increases in SO_x due to new coal combustion. Increases in sludge and NCSW generation due to new coal burning facilities.

Region 8

Projected increases in energy related water consumption may face strong competition from other uses. Cyanide releases more than double due to high BTU coal gasification. Substantial sulfate releases from coal mining and electric utilities activities. Large increases in NCSW generation by 1990 due to oil shale activities.

Region 9

Large increases in NCSW volumes by 1990 primarily in California. SO_x emissions decline.

Region 10

TDS discharges double due to electric utilities. Potassium releases doubles due to smelting.

Figure 13–14. Major regional trends associated with the DOE-MITRE Projection Series C (Hard Path) Energy Development Scenario. In the regional analyses, TDS stands for total dissolved solids; NCSW stands for noncombustible solid wastes. (*National Environmental Impact Project No. 1, MITRE Corp., Dec. 1978*)

sidies stripped away, nuclear power would not be competitive with alternative energy sources.[575] The Ford Foundation's nuclear energy policy study group addressed this question and concluded in 1977, before the Three Mile Island nuclear reactor accident in Pennsylvania, that in the United States nuclear energy based on uranium, but not plutonium, is somewhat less costly than coal, but that in much of the country "the choice is so close and the uncertainties sufficiently large that the balance could easily shift either to increase or eliminate the small average advantage that nuclear power presently enjoys."[576]

For Japan and Western Europe, the Ford study concludes that

a shift to heavy reliance on coal would require increasing dependence on imports from the United States and Eastern Europe. The political acceptability of such dependence is not clear. There is also a question as to how large a foreign market [for coal the United States] could supply and still meet its own growing domestic demand. For these reasons, a greater preference for nuclear power should be expected in these countries than in the United States.[577]

For the LDCs, the Ford study concludes that the demand for nuclear power is "very uncertain":

Nuclear power may be competitive in some twenty developing countries by the year 2000, and others may install it for noneconomic reasons. As a practical matter, the large, 1,000 MWe nuclear power plants now being built [by commercial manufacturers] to achieve economies of scale are not matched to the small power grids of most developing countries. More suitable, smaller plants (less than 600 MWe) would have significantly higher capital cost per kilowatt and, in the absence of demand, are no longer being built. For these reasons, nuclear power may be ruled out as an economic energy option for many developing nations.[578]

In the U.S. and many other countries, decisions on major electric power facilities are made by utility executives based on costs to the utilities (after government subsidy) rather than on costs to the nation as a whole. The costs of decommissioning old plants and disposing of nuclear wastes are minimized because of the uncertainty of those costs. Recent accidents—such as occurred at Three Mile Island in Pennsylvania[579] have raised interest rates, and underwriters point to the possible need for further costly regulations, designs, and plant shutdowns.[580] As a result, the costs of nuclear power—including those costs perceived

by utilities and banks—may become increasingly comparable with coal.*

While there are many factors beyond purely economic ones involved in the choice of national energy policy beyond the purely economy factors. Nonetheless, a number of recent decisions seem to support the conclusions of the Ford study. In the U.S., the states of California and Montana have limited the construction of new nuclear facilities until the federal government will have demonstrated a capacity to safely dispose of the nuclear wastes.[581] Sites for nuclear plants and disposal areas continue to present a problem; only the states of Washington, New Mexico, and Nevada are still sympathetic to locating new waste disposal sites within their boundaries.[582] The governors of the only three states now willing to accept even low-level nuclear wastes recently wrote to the Nuclear Regulatory Commission and the Department of Transportation demanding tightened enforcement of safety rules on the shipment of nuclear wastes if their states are to continue receiving radioactive materials. The Governor of South Carolina cut off shipments from the damaged reactor at Three Mile Island.[583] In Europe, antinuclear sentiments significantly contributed to a change of government in Sweden,[584] and voters elected to terminate work on a nearly complete nuclear plant in Austria in 1978.[585] In the Federal Republic of Germany, the construction of a nuclear reprocessing plant considered essential to Germany's energy program for the next two decades was recently "postponed indefinitely."[586] European expectations for nuclear energy can be seen in the history of OECD projections for 1985 nuclear-generating capacities shown in Figure 13–15. It seems likely, therefore, that at least until 2000, the hard path option will include some nuclear power (primarily existing plants) but will emphasize coal.

The Soft Path

There are many ideas about the technologies most appropriate to a soft path future. These technologies were originally defined in terms of five characteristics:

---

*The costs of the Three Mile Island accident are now thought to be higher than the first estimates. Repairing the damaged reactor (unit 2) will cost not $140 million, but $240–320 million; in addition, the cost of replacing the reactor core is estimated at $60–85 million; the utility will not be permitted to restart the undamaged reactor (unit 1) for 18 months to 2 years, leading to costs—over and above those directly attributable to the accident—of $14 million per month. ("Costs Still Climbing at Three Mile Island," *Science*, Aug. 3, 1979, p. 475)

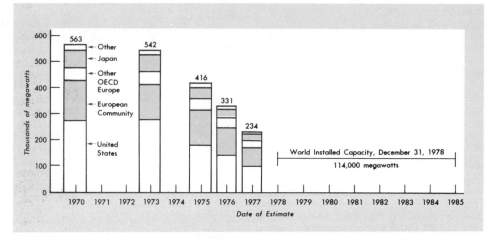

Figure 13-15. OECD countries' projections of 1985 nuclear generating capacity for the world, by dates of estimates. (*From "Nuclear Energy," Central Intelligence Agency, Aug. 1977, p. 39; world installed capacity data from U.S. Department of Energy, Energy Information Administration.*)

1. They rely on renewable energy flows that are always there whether we use them or not, such as sun and wind and vegetation: on energy income, not on depletable energy capital.

2. They are diverse, so that as a national treasury runs on many small tax contributions, so national energy supply is an aggregate of very many individually modest contributions, each designed for maximum effectiveness in particular circumstances.

3. They are flexible and relatively low technology—which does not mean unsophisticated, but rather, easy to understand and use without esoteric skills, accessible rather than arcane.

4. They are matched in scale and in geographic distribution to end-use needs, taking advantage of the free distribution of most natural energy flows.

5. They are matched in *energy quality* to end-use needs [thus increasing the productivity of the primary energy used].[587]

The number of national soft path and low-energy studies from around the world has increased rapidly in the last few years. Several of these studies for some of the nations having energy-intensive economies are discussed in the following pages.*

The Solar Sweden Study. One of the most thorough national soft path studies now available is

the *Solar Sweden* report produced by the Secretariat for Future Studies in Stockholm.[588] This report addresses the feasibility of basing the Swedish energy supply *completely* on solar energy (solar radiation, hydro power, wind power, and wave power) in the not too distant future. (Complete dependence on solar energy would be difficult for Sweden since it is quite far north and receives only about 40 percent of the solar energy per unit area that is received by countries in North Africa.) While the report does not advocate that Sweden turn solely to solar energy, the report concludes that *by 2015 Sweden could shift entirely to solar energy without prohibitive costs and without major changes in life styles.*

The *Solar Sweden* analysis is based on a number of assumptions. The goods and services produced are assumed to double relative to 1975. The efficiency with which energy is used to produce the goods and services is assumed to increase as illustrated in Table 13–38. Care is taken to match the quality of an energy source with the quality required for particular end uses, as described in Table 13–39. The quality of the energy delivered remains essentially unchanged. The resulting energy system is illustrated in Figure 13–16. The final value for energy use in 2015 is not quite 500 × 10^{12} watt hours (WH), compared with 390 × 10^{12} WH in 1975. (The corresponding figures in quads are 1.7 and 1.3, respectively.)

The *Solar Sweden* energy system is very diversified. Production and use of biomass dominates and includes energy plantations on land and in

---

*Readers interested in a more complete inventory and continuing reporting of national soft-path studies are referred to the journal *Soft Energy Notes* (San Francisco, Friends of the Earth).

TABLE 13-38

Solar Sweden **Assumed Production of Goods and Services and Specific Energy Use, 1975 and 2015**

	Energy		Goods and Services Produced in 2015 Relative to 1975	
	1975	2015	Production	Specific Energy Need[a]
	TWH[b]		*Percent*	
Production of goods	165	264	+ 100	− 20
Production of services				
Transport	75	75	+ 100	− 50
Other	70[c]	70[d]	+ 100	− 50
Housing, including domestic electricity	80	80	+ 40	− 30
Total end use	390	489		
Conversion losses	25[e]	79[f]		
Total supply	415	568		

Source: Thomas B. Johansson and Peter Steen, *Solar Sweden*, Stockholm: Secretariat for Futures Studies, 1978, p. 26.

[a] Energy required to produce a unit of goods or services.
[b] 1 TWH = 10^{12} watt hours = 3.41×10^{-3} quads.
[c] Of which space heating is approximately 40 TWH.
[d] Of which space heating is approximately 31 TWH.
[e] Losses in electricity distribution and refineries.
[f] Losses occur mainly in domestic methanol production.

the sea and the use of straw, reeds, and logging waste. Solar heating is used for space heating together with district heating based on plants fueled with biomass for combined generation of electricity and heat. The electricity sector becomes relatively large and the proportion of electricity larger than today. Electricity is produced from hydro power, wind power, and solar cells and in fuel cells and plants for combined generation. By making the latter into relatively small units, they can be located to minimize energy waste, e.g., by using the waste heat for space heating. Methanol, from biomass, is introduced into the transport sector.

In making its economic calculations, the *Solar Sweden* report assumes that the costs for the renewable energy system are and remain those that can be foreseen for the 1980s. The calculations show that building up such a system is compatible with the assumed doubling of the production of goods and services, implying an increase of approximately 2 percent annually. Of this annual increase approximately one-eighth goes to the new energy system, and the remaining seven-eighths are necessary to increase the production of goods and services. Thus, the report concludes, a renewable energy system does not demand a lower standard of living, but merely requires that part of the increase in goods and services is utilized to create such a system.

In discussing the advantage of a solar Sweden, the report notes that the energy system it sketches is domestic, and that as a result, uncertainties concerning the possibilities of importing various energy raw materials do not exist. Balance of payment is not to any large extent influenced. The use of many different dispersed energy sources makes the system relatively invulnerable. The system is preferable from the environmental point of view because it limits emissions and does not increase the risk of catastrophic occurrences.

But the environmental implications of the solar Sweden energy system are not completely beneficial. The report notes that the demand on land

TABLE 13-39

Solar Sweden **Percent Distribution of Energy, by Energy-Quality Categories A–I, 1971 and 2015[a]**

	1971			2015		
	Industry	Transport	Other	Industry	Transport	Other
A Lighting, small motors	2		15	5		40
B Electricity for chemical processes	3			3		
C Stationary motors	15			17		
D Transports	3	100		2	100	
E Process heat (> 1000°C)	22			23		
F Process heat (500–1000°C)	9			9		
G Process heat (100–500°C)	26			26		
H Process heat (< 100°C)	9			9		
I Low temperature heat (space heating)	11		85	6		60
Total	100	100	100	100	100	100
Percent of total energy use	41	17	42	54	15	31

Source: Thomas B. Johansson and Peter Steen, *Solar Sweden*, Stockholm: Secretariat for Futures Studies, 1978, p. 26.

[a] The quality classification A–I are not strictly thermodynamic but are user oriented.

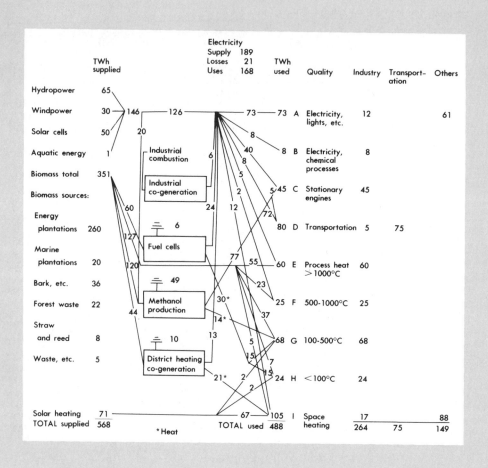

Figure 13-16. The Solar Sweden energy system for the year 2015. The supply from renewable sources and the amounts from each are given on the left. The end use of energy is divided into energy quality categories A through I on the right. The linkage between supply and use is shown in the center of the figure. Numbers indicate the energy (in TWh=10^{12} watt-hours) represented by each line. *(From "Solar Sweden," Stockholm, 1978, p. 32)*

is great because of the low intensity of solar radiation in Sweden. It is estimated that approximately 3 million hectares would be needed, mainly for energy plantations. As now conceived, the plantations would need to be heavily fertilized, particularly with nitrogen. Methods of controlling damage from game animals, rodents, fungi, and insects would also be needed. The environmental problems of managing large-scale energy plantations—and ecologically acceptable management techniques—are discussed in two related Swedish reports.[589]

Finally, the *Solar Sweden* report acknowledges conflicts of interest concerning the 3 million hectares that would be needed for energy plantations. The other sectors most interested in utilizing the same areas would probably be the forest industry and recreation. The forest industry in Sweden currently uses approximately 23 million hectares. Wind power, etc., might meet with resistance from those who own recreational houses near the plants. Therefore, an important question is how Swedish society should balance the interests of forest industry, recreation, and energy production in the future. The report concludes that these interests can be balanced and conflicts resolved with farsighted planning.[590]

Soft Energy Studies in Canada. Canada has also given thought to soft energy scenarios for its future[591] and has examined the possibilities for energy plantations. The Canadian Ministry of Energy, Mines, and Resources, in its *Tree Power* report,[592] assessed the energy potential of forest biomass in Canada for three technologies: (1) direct electricity generation or cogeneration, (2) conversion to methanol, and (3) low Btu gasification. Costs were established, where possible. The Canadian forest resources are large, and the report notes that data on the extent of Canadian forest resources are "severely lacking." Using various estimates of the resource, the report estimates that the total annual productivity of the forest is about 400×10^6 ODt (oven-dried metric tons), equivalent in energy to 8×10^{18} joules. The present Canadian wood harvest of 51×10^6 ODt for all purposes has an energy content of about 1×10^{18} joules. The report concludes:

The medium term to 1990 will realize more forest energy but will require changes in harvesting technology and forest management practice as well as development of conversion and end use technologies.
Over the longer term to 2025, the extensive forest and energy plantations could provide a large fraction of the carbon based fuel requirements. However a development program including extensive environmental assessment of the impacts of such large scale use will be needed. For example, the effect of collecting forest residue in the medium term and of plantations in the longer term could be to strip the soil of nutrients.[593]

U.S. Studies. In the U.S., the Department of Energy has indicated its interest* in consideration

of soft path options by establishing a Standing Committee on Soft Technology under the R&D Coordinating Council† and by initiating a small-grants program for several studies. These studies are listed and described briefly in Table 13–40.

The DOE-sponsored California Distributed Energy Study[594] is probably the most detailed and thorough soft path analysis now available. The study analyzes hypothetical future energy systems for the State of California in the year 2025. Assuming a doubling of population, a tripling of total economic activity, and a quadrupling of energy prices by 2025, the study reaches four important conclusions for the State:

1. It is possible to achieve a balance between energy demand and energy supply only through strict attention to conservation for buildings, improved efficiencies of end-use appliances, and improved efficiencies in industry.[595]
2. It is possible, in purely technical terms, to come quite close to operating the postulated advanced, post-industrial society in California using indigenous, sustainable resources.[596]
3. The environmental impacts of certain "soft" technologies—notably increased end-use efficiency, active and passive solar heating and cooling with individual building or neighborhood units, fuel production from biomass in the form of wastes, and dispersed on-site wind generators—will prove markedly smaller than those of virtually all of the traditional "hard" technologies, as well as smaller than those of the more centralized technologies for harvesting renewables.[597]
4. To achieve a distributed [soft] energy outcome which is approximately that described [in the California study] by a time close to 2025 requires that implementation begin almost at once.[598]

While the California Distributed Energy Study is the only detailed soft path study now available, a number of studies have examined aspects of a soft path for the whole of the U.S. The findings and conclusions of approximately 40 related studies have been drawn together by the Council on Environmental Quality (CEQ) in a recent report that compares the hard and soft paths for the United States.[599] Some of the major findings reported by CEQ are as follows:

• There is now clear evidence that the United States can maintain a healthy economy without the massive increases in primary energy called for under the hard path.
• Recent macroeconomic analyses indicate that there is a more loose and flexible linkage be-

*The DOE interest in what it terms "small-scale, appropriately distributed technology" was expressed most clearly at a public briefing on January 26, 1978, in Washington. The official transcript of this briefing (published as *DOE Role in Support of Small-Scale Appropriately Distributed Technology,* DOE Office of Consumer Affairs, Aug. 1978) is available from the National Technical Information Service. The specific programmatic efforts reported in the briefing are summarized in Table 13–4.
†As of August 1978, it was established that the Standing Committee would be chaired by the Assistant Secretary for Conservation and Solar Applications, and that the Committee would have representatives from the DOE Offices of Energy Technology, Energy Research, Environment, and Policy and Evaluation (p. 144 of the briefing cited in the previous note). As of this writing (March 1979), no Committee members had been appointed, and the Committee's purpose had not been resolved.

THE PROJECTIONS

TABLE 13–40

U.S. Department of Energy Studies Underway as of August 1978 to Examine "Soft Path" Options

Subject or Title	Responsible DOE Office	Budget	Description
Small-Grants Program	Conservation and Solar	$3 million (FY 78) $8 million (FY 79)	This program provides small grants (up to $50,000) for conservation and solar efforts. The $3 million pilot program started in Region 9 and was heavily over subscribed. Approximately 1,100 grant requests were received; approximately 100 were funded. The budget has now been increased to $8 million for all 10 federal regions. A preliminary report on the effectiveness of the grants has been prepared.[a]
Appropriate Technology Characterization	Policy and Evaluation	$250,000	Contract to Arthur D. Little, Inc., Cambridge, Mass., for an engineering notebook describing the technical and economic aspects of "appropriate," "soft," and "transitional" technologies. A draft has been circulated for review at DOE, but as of March 1979, the report was not publicly available.[b]
"California Case Study: Decentralized Energy Systems"	Policy and Evaluation	$700,000	This study, conducted jointly by the Lawrence Berkeley Laboratory and the Lawrence Livermore Laboratory, is probably the most thorough and detailed examination of a "soft path" option for a specfic region—California. The DOE preface to the study indicates that it was undertaken largely as a response to "Energy Strategy: The Road Not Taken," by Amory B. Lovins (*Foreign Affairs*, Oct. 1976). Two reports and many supporting documents have been produced.[c] Further work on this topic has been proposed by the two laboratories involved, but DOE, as of March 1979, was not willing to fund additional work.
"Any Town USA"	Policy and Evaluation	$240,000	SRI International was to provide a study on how a "typical" American town might look under a soft path solar future. The study was completed in 1977 but was never published or publicly released by DOE. A limited number of copies of the report are available directly from SRI International.[d]
Energy Futures: Solar and Nuclear Alternatives	Policy and Evaluation	$500,000	This study at the Institute for Energy Analysis, Oak Ridge Associated Universities, has two objectives: (1) to project the contribution that solar energy might make by the year 2020; (2) to investigate how far nuclear development could continue if all additional reactors were located on sites where nuclear reactors are already located or under construction. DOE representatives report that the contractor was unable to develop the solar portion of the study to any extent; the contractor reports that DOE lost interest in the solar portion of the study. In any event, as of March 1979, a nuclear report was available, but the solar report was incomplete.[e]
Overview of Soft Energy Paths and Decentralized Energy Systems in the United States	Environment	Not applicable	This subject was ultimately subsumed under "Alternative Energy Futures" below.
Development of Community Level Technology Assessments	Energy Technology	$500,000 (FY 78) $250,000 (FY 79)	As a part of a longer study, contractors were to work with local communities to develop "self-assessments of solar futures." As of March 1979, one contractor had started work, and Requests for Proposals (RFPs) are pending. No report was publicly available at that time, but one report prepared under the program may be obtained from another source.[f]
Alternatives Energy Futures	Environment	$179,000	This work was contracted to the Argone National Laboratories and in turn subcontracted to the Center for Energy Studies in the Department of Industrial Engineering. The work was done by faculty and students as a part of Industrial Engineering Course 235 at Stanford University. As of March 1979, no report was publicly available from DOE, but a report was expected to be available from Stanford.[g]

TABLE 13–40 (cont.)

Subject or Title	Responsible DOE Office	Budget	Description
Less Developed Countries	International Affairs	$1,600,000	This joint DOE/State Department program of cooperative assistance to selected developing countries is intended to provide a complete and objective energy assessment, including all the basic data and information needed for the development of an energy plan for the country being analyzed. A wide range of energy options—both nuclear and nonnuclear—are considered with emphasis given to employing indigenous resources. An assessment of Egyptian energy options is now complete and has been very well received by Egypt and international development and lending institutions.[h] A report on Peru is in progress, and five other reports are being considered.

Source: U.S. Department of Energy, Office of Consumer Affairs. *DOE Role in Support of Small-Scale Appropriately Distributed Technology,* Official Transcript of Public Briefing and Addendum on Jan. 26, 1978, CONF–780132, Washington: National Technical Information Service, Aug. 1978, p. 144. Budgets and descriptions of studies are based on information provided by the responsible DOE offices and DOE contractors.

[a] DOE San Francisco Operations Office, Appropriate Energy Technology Program, *Summary of Projects: Appropriate Energy Technology, Pilot Regional Program,* 1978 (available from Appropriate Energy Technology, DOE, 1333 Broadway, Oakland, Calif. 94612); DOE Div. of Buildings and Community Systems, Assistant Secretary for Conservation and Solar Applications, "Appropriate Technology: A Fact Sheet," Washington, 1977; "Report to Congress on Appropriate Technology Pilot Regional Program," undated, unpublished (available from, Jerry D. Duane, DOE, Office of the Assistant Secretary for Conservation and Solar Applications).
[b] Edward Blum, DOE, Office of the Assistant Secretary for Policy and Evaluation, personal communication, Mar. 1979.
[c] Paul P. Craig and M. D. Levine, "Distributed Energy Systems in California's Future: Issues in Transition," Lawrence Berkeley Laboratory, Jan. 16, 1979 (draft).
[d] John Reuyl et al., *Solar Energy in America's Future: A Preliminary Assessment,* Menlo Park, Calif.: SRI International, Mar. 1977.

[e] The nuclear report is M. J. Ohanian et al., *Feasibility of a Nuclear Citing Policy Based on Existing Cites,* Oak Ridge: Institute for Energy Analysis, Nov. 1979. As of May 1979, the Institute was still planning seven topical reports on solar energy: two were final, three were being revised following review, one was under a new review, one was still being written. The final reports are as follows: R. W. Gilmer and R. E. Meunier, "Electric Utilities and Solar Energy: The Service Contract in a New Social Context," Oak Ridge Associated Universities. Apr. 1979; final reports being revised at Oak Ridge Associated Universities are (with dates of draft): R. W. Gilmer "The Social Control of Energy: A Case for the Promise of Decentralized Solar Technologies," Apr. 2, 1979; W. D. Devine, Jr., "Energy Accounting for Solar and Alternative Energy Sources," Jan. 1979; D. B. Reister and W. D. Devine, Jr., "Total Costs of Energy Services," Mar. 1979. The following draft is being reviewed: D. A. Boyd, "The Stochastic Sun: Identifying the Recoverable Resource," Mar. 1979.
[f] C. T. Donovan et al., *Energy Self-Sufficiency in Northampton, Massachusetts,* Jan. 3, 1979 (available from A. S. Krass, School of Natural Science, Hampshire College, Amherst, Mass. 01002).
[g] Grant Ireson et al., *Alternative Energy Futures: An Assessment of Options for U.S. Society to 2025,* Institute for Energy Studies, Stanford University, forthcoming, 1979.
[h] DOE Developing Countries Energy Program, *Egypt-United States Cooperative Energy Assessment,* Washington, 1978, 5 vols.

tween energy use and the economy than previously thought.

- These studies generally conclude that low energy growth is not only consistent with continued economic expansion and a high standard of living but can also have a positive effect on employment and can provide an important weapon in the fight against inflation.

- Much of the energy saved by a departure from the hard path would be realized in the form of reduced imports of oil and natural gas for which Americans pay a high price both economically and in terms of national security. Improvements in U.S. balance of payments can be anticipated principally due to reduced dollar outflows for direct purchases of foreign fuels.

The CEQ conclusion, in short, is that the United States can do well, indeed prosper, on much less energy than has been commonly supposed.

But what about the environmental impacts of a departure from the hard path? The CEQ report also provides one of the more complete national comparison now available of scenarios related to the hard and soft path environmental impacts. This comparison is made on the basis of two energy supply futures[600] (see Table 13–41).* Future I, with a total demand of 85 quads (1 quad = 10^{15} Btu) reflects a strong, sustained commitment to conservation (higher energy productivity) and the use of renewable energy sources. In Future II, energy demand grows by 1.9 percent per year reaching 120 quads by 2000.

The CEQ report compares the environmental impact of these two energy futures as follows:

The most important difference in energy supply between the two futures described above arise from the need to place great emphasis on coal and nuclear in Future II. In the high-growth future these two sources collectively supply 2.1 times as much energy (an additional 34 quads) in the year 2000 as they would in the low-energy future. Although it is not feasible to describe completely

---

*The CEQ report is not a true comparison of hard and soft paths for the U.S. because both of the energy supply futures contains the same solar component (19 quads). For a true hard/soft comparison for the U.S., it would be necessary to replace the 19 quads of solar in Future II with an additional 19 quads of coal or nuclear.

TABLE 13–41

Energy Supply in 1977 and Two Supply Scenarios for the Year 2000

Quads (10^{15} Btu) of Primary Fuels

	1975	2000 Future I	2000 Future II
Oil and gas	56.5	40	46
Solar[a]	4.2	19	19
Nuclear	2.7	8	18
Coal	14.1	18	37
Total	77.5	85	120

Source: Council on Environmental Quality. *The Good News About Energy*. Washington: Government Printing Office. 1979. p. 20.

[a] The solar category includes all renewable energy sources. The 4.2 quads includes 1.8 quads from biomass. which is usually not included in national energy statistics.

the details of these two futures, specific, important environmental impacts related to the additional use of coal and nuclear energy in Future II have been estimated and presented in Table [13–42]. . . . Although the total impacts of all these trends is highly uncertain, it is nonetheless clear that a national—indeed, global—policy emphasizing energy conservation [(i.e., increased productivity in the energy sector) and benign sources] will allow the world more flexibility and time to maneuver in the event of incipient, adverse developments.[602]

Low Energy Study for Denmark. Domestic nonrenewable energy sources are limited in Denmark. In the face of rapidly rising energy costs, the country has been considering a variety of options for reducing its needs for foreign oil. Much of the energy analysis in Denmark has assumed that little departure from traditional energy growth rates could be accomplished without serious economic implications. A 1976 study, sponsored jointly by the Niels Bohr Institute and the International Federation of Institutes for Advanced Study,[603] found much more flexibility in the GNP-energy relationship than had been assumed in the past.

The Danish study examines the economic consequences of two scenarios out to 2005. One scenario assumes a continuation of the traditional growth in energy use (3–5 per cent per year); the other assumes a reduced growth (under 1.5 per cent per year). In the traditional-growth scenario, energy is used more or less traditionally. In the reduced-growth scenario, major efforts are made to increase the thermodynamic efficiency with which the energy is used.

The study found that over a 15-year period Denmark could make major reductions in its energy requirements without harm to general economic development. The energy savings for the two cases are illustrated in Figures 13–17 and 13–18. Overall, the study concluded that the reduced energy growth, while requiring somewhat larger investments over the next 15 years, produced a

TABLE 13–42

Relative Environmental Impacts of Low- and High-Energy Growth Futures

	1977	2000 Future I	2000 Future II
Coal production (*millions of tons/year*)[a]	613	782	1,609
Cumulative coal mined, 1977–2000 (*millions of tons*)[b]	—	16,000	25,500
Cumulative area strip-mined, 1977–2000 (*square miles*)[c]	—	1,200[l]	2,000[m]
Cumulative area affected by subsidence (*square miles*)[d]	—	1,400–3,300[n]	2,300–5,300[o]
Number of coal power plants (*nominal 1,100 MW*)[e]	200	243	500
Number of nuclear power plants (*nominal, 1,100 MW*)[f]	43	135	304
Area required for transmission lines for new coal and nuclear plants (*square miles*)[g]	—	3,900	16,500
Radioactive tailings to supply uranium for 1977–2000 (*million tons*)[h]	—	400	800
Volume of low-level radioactive wastes generated, 1977–2000 (*millions of cubic feet*)[i]	—	34	66
Spent fuel generated, 1977–2000 (*thousands of tons*)[j]	—	61	120
Total spent fuel generated over lifetimes of plants constructed through the year 2000 (*thousands of tons*)[k]	—	121	274

Source: Council on Environmental Quality. *The Good News About Energy*. Washington: Government Printing Office. 1979. pp. 23–24.

[a] Nominal tons at 23 million Btu each.

[b] Assuming linear growth in production.

[c] Assuming (1) one-half of coal is mined in the West. one-half in the Midwest and East; and (2) all of Western coal and one-half of rest is strip-mined. Area disturbed: 50 acres per million tons in the West and 100 acres elsewhere. See *Energy/Environment Fact Book*, DOE/EPA. Dec. 1977. p. 60.

[d] Assuming 230 to 529 acres affected per ton of coal mined. depending on mining techniques. See *Energy Alternatives: A Comparative Analysis*. University of Oklahoma. Science and Public Policy Program. May 1975. pp. 1–56.

[e] Assumes 70 percent of coal will continue to be used by electric utilities, capacity factors will average 55 percent and individual plant efficiencies 35 percent.

[f] Assumes capacity factors of 60 percent and average efficiencies of 33 percent.

[g] Based on an average value of 17,188 acres per gigawatt of capacity. See *Energy and the Environment: Electric Power*, CEQ. Aug. 1973. p. 42, note 8.

[h] Assuming 0.1 percent uranium ore. 0.25 percent tailings assay. and annual loading of 30 tons of fuel per reactor per year.

[i] Based on an annual volume of 16,500 cubic feet per plant-year. See "Report to the President by the Interagency Review Group on Nuclear Waste Management." Oct. 1978, p. D–6 (draft).

[j] Assuming 30 tons discharged per reactor per year.

[k] Assuming 30 tons discharged per reactor per year and 30-year plant lifetimes.

[l] 3,108 sq km.

[m] 5,180 sq km.

[n] 3,626–8,547 sq km.

[o] 5,957–13,727 sq km.

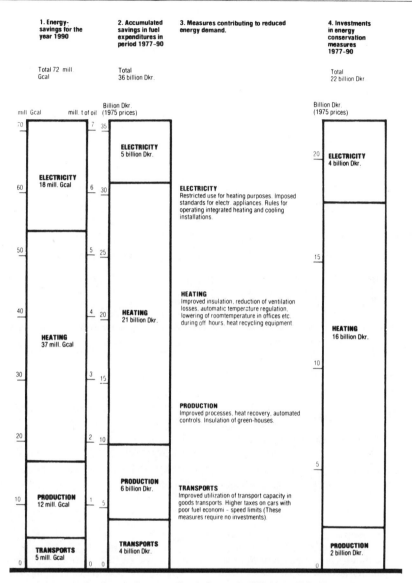

1. Energy-
savings for the
year 1990

2. Accumulated
savings in fuel
expenditures in
period 1977–90

3. Measures contributing to reduced
energy demand.

4. Investments
in energy
conservation
measures
1977–90

Total 72 mill.
Gcal

Total
36 billion Dkr.

Total
22 billion Dkr.

Figure 13–17. Survey of energy savings in Denmark, 1977–90; "mill Gcal" = millions of gigacalories = 10^{15} calories; Dkr = Danish kroner. (*Sven Bjørnholm*, Energy in Denmark, 1990 and 2005, *Neils Bohr Institute, 1976, p. 34*)

considerable overall advantage to the economy—also to the reliability of Danish energy supplies and to the environment.

Low-Energy Study for the United Kingdom. In London, the International Institute for Environment and Development has studied the potential

for energy conservation in the U.K.[604] The Institute's study uses the official U.K. Department of Energy estimates of GNP growth* and examines

* For the next 10–15 years GNP is assumed to grow as fast as, or faster than during the 1960s. By 2025 GNP roughly doubles in one case; it trebles in another.

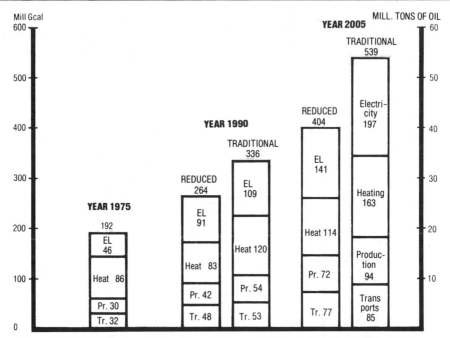

Figure 13–18. Traditional and reduced demand for energy in Denmark, 1990 and 2005, showing quantities of fuel by type of demand. Fuel consumption is calculated by assuming the losses in the fuel conversion and distribution system that applied in 1975. (*Sven Bjørnholm*, Energy in Denmark, 1990 and 2005, *Neils Bohr Institute, 1976, p. 35*)

alternative strategies for supplying the needed energy. The study assumes a series of policies encouraging efficient use of energy. These include:

- Improved thermal performance of new residential dwellings, offices, public-sector buildings, such as schools and hospitals, and industrial buildings (by tightening the building regulations);
- Energy performance standards for cars (and possibly also light-goods vehicles) to accelerate and ensure the timely implementation of technical developments already under way in the motor industry;
- Energy performance standards for major household electrical goods and cooking stoves to ensure the introduction of relatively simple, low cost improvements (such as better insulation) and similar standards for lighting;
- Possible legislation to reduce the use of oil in heating homes, offices, and public-sector buildings, as well as in industrialized boilers ("possible legislation," because the authors believe

that the gradual reduction assumed may occur without legislation).

The study's conclusions (in the authors' words) are as follows:

- In 2000 the U.K. could be entirely self-sufficient on North Sea oil and gas even on central estimates of reserves.
- Coal production need be only some 120 million [metric tons] a year, far below the 170 million target in the [U.K.] "Plan for Coal."
- From 1976–2000 we have assumed the construction of only 4.5–6.5 GW [gigawatts] of nuclear capacity, or three to five average-sized stations, compared to 30 GW in the current Department of Energy reference forecast. If more were built there would be such a surplus of generating capacity that a choice would have to be made between leaving nuclear stations idle and reducing coal production to uncomfortable low levels.
- Over the same period, only 26–30 GW of generating capacity of all kinds need be built (most of it replacing existing plant) compared to 83 GW in the Energy Department's reference fore-

cast. The saving in capital investment would be around £26–30,000 million for the plant alone, or well over £1,000 million a year. We would be most surprised if this did not greatly exceed the costs of all the energy conservation measures we have assumed for all sectors and fuels.

- After 2000 the only significant fuel shortfalls are in North Sea oil, taking the central estimate of reserves. This "gap" reaches an annual 36–47 million [metric tons] of oil by 2025 in the Low and High cases respectively, or roughly half recent levels of oil imports. It could be filled from several sources, either from the large quantities of crude oil that should even then be flowing in world trade or by the import of liquid fuels made from crops grown in the tropical belts. . . .
- Coal production need be only 128–148 million [metric tons] in 2025, or well below the present target for 2000.
- Electricity output can be met by building only 6 GW of nuclear capacity in the first quarter of the next century. Nuclear power in our projections thus becomes a peripheral issue and could be abandoned as an option if—for whatever reason—it became prudent to do so. We have, however, assumed a continuing nuclear programme at a "tick over" level sufficient to keep the industry alive as an insurance measure.
- The fast breeder reactor and the plutonium fuel cycle, with all their risks of nuclear weapon proliferation and public opposition, could be shelved indefinitely. [605]

Commercial Energy in Industrial Societies— Environmental Prospects

The DOE projections and the hard and soft path studies reviewed here all suggest that major—perhaps even massive—changes in the world's commercial energy economy will inevitably be in progress well before 2000 and that these changes in the energy economy could well bring with them major environmental consequences throughout the world. The type and magnitude of the environmental impacts depends largely on the choice of technologies to be employed in the energy sector of the economy to provide energy for end-use needs, i.e., the production of goals and services.

As already noted, there is a spectrum of technological options open for the future of the energy sector. The spectrum ranges from the soft path (emphasizing both efficient use of energy in the energy sector itself and renewable forms of energy, especially solar, for primary sources) to the hard path (emphasizing large increases in primary energy production, especially coal and nuclear generation of electricity and the production of synthetic fuels). Options at the soft path end of the spectrum lead to a relatively efficient energy sector, capable of meeting end-use needs with less primary energy imputs than possible with options near the hard end of the spectrum. Every option along the hard-soft spectrum produces social and environmental side effects. While most studies suggest that options toward the soft end of the spectrum produce impacts less serious than options toward the hard end, the soft options too have their effects. The *Solar Sweden* report discussed above candidly acknowledges concern over intensive energy plantations, and the brief mention in the report of the International Institute for Environment and Development of "the import of liquid fuels made from crops grown in the tropical belts" might involve some significant environmental implications outside the U.K.

It is now widely recognized and accepted that the largely undesirable side effects of energy-sector development must be taken into account in the selection and development of energy futures, but it is not yet widely understood that these side effects—rather than resource or narrow economic considerations—define the energy dilemma in the long term. As noted in the DOE-sponsored California Distributed Energy Study:

The energy problem resides fundamentally in the fact that the relation between energy and well-being is two-sided. The application of energy as a productive input to the economy, yielding desired goods and services, contributes to well being; the environmental and social costs of getting and using energy subtract from it. At some level of energy use, and for a given mix of technologies of energy supply, further increases in energy supply will produce incremental social and environmental costs greater than the incremental economic benefits—that is growth [in energy consumption] begins to do more harm than good. This level can be said to define a rational "limit to growth," as distinct from a strictly physical one.

That such a level, beyond which energy growth no longer pays, exists in principle for any mix of technologies of supply and end-use is easily shown from basic economics and physical science; predicting its magnitude exactly is much harder, the more so because social costs even less quantifiable than environmental ones may dominate. Lovins[606] evidently believes that the United States is already near or beyond the point, given the "hard" energy technologies on which it relies, where further growth hurts more than it helps. Whether he is right or wrong about exactly where we are now, however, or in specific judgments about the merits of "hard" versus "soft" technologies, it is clear that energy policy for the long term should be shaped by awareness that social-environmental costs, not exhaustion of resources, will limit the amount of human well-being derivable from energy. Maximizing this quantity will require striving for technologies of energy supply with low social and environmental costs per unit of energy delivered, and fostering patterns and technologies of energy end-use that squeeze from each such unit the maximum contribution to human well-being.

This perspective, then, elevates environmental and social characteristics to the top of the list of criteria used to select supply technologies from the menu of genuinely long-term options—fission breeder reactors, fusion, direct and indirect harnessing of solar flows, and possibly some forms of geothermal energy. It rationalizes the possibility that society will choose to pay more (in economic terms) for a more benign energy source than for a less benign one. And it argues for using, as a criterion for selecting short-term and transition energy sources, the extent to which these promote and facilitate the transition to a longer term energy future built on more benign sources and efficient end-use.

Given a perspective that places environmental and social impacts at the heart of the energy predicament rather than on the periphery, it becomes essential to compare the impacts produced by alternative energy options systematically, comprehensively, and objectively.[607]

The environmental and social impacts of alternative energy options for the next two decades have not been compared "systematically, comprehensively, and objectively" for the U.S., let alone the world. While these ideas will never be fully achieved, progress is being made and should continue. For the U.S., the DOE-MITRE study,* DOE-sponsored California Distributed Energy Study, and the CEQ comparison of alternative energy futures—all three summarized above—are the most current (but still highly inadequate) efforts. On the world level, the primary analyses now available that address energy-related environmental and social impacts are a few very brief reports by the U.N. Environment Programme[608] and the works by Lovins already cited.† On the

basis of the analyses now available, only two things can be said. The first is that the more efficient energy sector produced by soft path options leads to a need for less primary energy. The second is that, to the extent that primary energy production leads to undesirable social and environmental impacts and to the extent that soft path technologies are less damaging to the environment, a shift toward the soft path options can be expected to reduce these impacts.*

Systematic, comprehensive and objective analyses of alternative energy options are urgently needed. These studies will not be done easily or quickly, but in their absence it may be difficult to obtain public support of any choice of energy policy. As time goes on, the situation (as Fig. 13–12 suggests) will only become more urgent, and options may become more restricted. Lovins, for example, argues that some options will be effectively foreclosed by delay.[609] (There have been sharp exchanges between Lovins and his critics on this point.[610]) It is clear, however, that the world's remaining petroleum resources need to be invested wisely in infrastructure, and capital needs to be well matched to genuinely long-term energy options. The choice of both the long-term options and the transitional approaches can be facilitated by further attention to, and analysis of, the associated social and environmental impacts.

Noncommercial Fuels

The preeminent noncommercial fuel throughout the world is wood. (Charcoal, also important,

---

*Since this text was drafted, DOE released its second National Energy Plan (NEP-II), which includes an appendix on environmental impacts (DOE Office of the Assistant Secretary for Environment, *National Energy Plan II, Appendix: Environmental Trends and Impacts*, Washington, May 1979). The appendix contains information quite similar to the DOE-MITRE study, plus an analysis of the environmental implications of specific NEP-II initiatives.

†Several persons reviewing the manuscript of this Study suggested adding to these the report of the Workshop on Alternative Energy Strategies (*Energy: Global Prospects 1985–2000*,

New York: McGraw-Hill, 1977) and the works of the World Energy Conference (see especially World Energy Commission of the World Energy Conference, *World Energy: Looking Ahead to 2000*, New York: IPC Science and Technology Press, 1978). Neither is appropriate. The WAES report deals with only a part of the world and concludes its treatment of the environment in less than two pages. The WEC, as noted earlier, is only now beginning to consider the environmental implications of energy sector development (Robert J. Raudebaugh, Executive Director of the WEC's U.S. National Committee, personal communication, Feb. 15, 1979).

*Additional analyses on these points are becoming available. These include the report of the Energy Project at the Harvard Business School (Robert Stobaugh and David Yergin, eds., *Energy Future*, New York: Random House, 1979) and the forthcoming report of the Demand and Conservation Panel of the National Academy of Sciences' Committee on Nuclear and Alternative Energy Systems (discussed in part in "U.S. Energy Demand: Some Low Energy Futures," *Science*, Apr. 14, 1978, pp. 142–52). Both reports point to the advantages of an efficient energy sector of the economy and to the economies of conservation. This last point is made effectively in *Energy: The Case for Conservation* by Denis Hayes (Worldwatch Paper 4, Washington: Worldwatch Institute, Jan. 1976). All three reports support the general points made in the text above.

is derived from wood.) Only in the developing countries, however, does firewood continue to be a major fuel; 90 percent of the worlds fuelwood consumption is in the LDCs.[611] Worldwide, the energy derived from wood amounted to 13.3 × 10^{15} Btu in 1974, roughly the same amount as the total from hydroelectric sources.[612] Dried dung (providing an estimated 1.7 × 10^{15} Btu in 1974) and crop residues (providing an estimated 1 × 10^{15} Btu in 1974) are the other major noncommercial fuels.[613] They are important in densely populated regions, such as northern India's Gangetic Plain, and in the treeless Andean mountains in South America. Thus the noncommercial fuels—wood, charcoal, dried dung, and crop residues—are all organic fuels.

Statistics concerning noncommercial, organic fuels are incomplete, due to the inherent difficulties in collecting such data, and to the relative lack of attention given these forms of energy by governments and world organizations. The United Nations Food and Agriculture Organization (FAO) has attempted over the past decade to survey these fuels even partially.

It is not possible to make a precise distinction between commercial and noncommercial fuels. Large quantities of firewood are marketed commercially, and the statistics now available on wood consumption include wood converted to commercial charcoal (estimated at 5 percent of the total fuelwood consumption) along with noncommercial firewood. Dung is also sold to some extent, so that its noncommercial designation is not entirely accurate. Furthermore, crop residues are increasingly being used along with animal manure in the production of methane gas on a commercial basis, so that the noncommercial category is not precise in this case either. Although the discussion that follows focuses on the noncommercial uses of these organic fuels, there is a discernible trend toward commercialization.

Wood, dung, and crop wastes are used throughout the LDCs as a source of energy for the preparation of meals and for heating. An estimated 1.0–1.5 billion persons[614] (more than a quarter of the total world population) use fuelwood as their primary energy source for cooking. Most of these persons are located in rural areas where firewood has traditionally been a free good. An additional 100 million or more persons use dried dung and crop wastes for the same purpose.[615]

Global estimates of the share of noncommercial energy in the total energy picture in developing countries vary widely from a high of 70 percent to a low of 30 percent.[616] It is known that these fuels (wood, dung, and crop wastes) account for

approximately 56 percent of the total energy consumption in India and 58 percent of the total in Africa. Commercial energy—coal, gas, oil, electricity, and charcoal—is used almost exclusively by the wealthiest 20 percent of the people in poor countries.[617]

It was once hoped that fossil fuels (especially kerosene) would reduce fuelwood and charcoal use, thereby decreasing deforestation pressures. The rapid increases in fossil fuel prices since 1973, however, have largely eliminated this hope. The rate of growth in LDC kerosene consumption has been slowed significantly, and the demand for fuelwood and charcoal is thought to be rising rapidly, in spite of percentage increases in the prices of these fuels that are as large or larger than the percentage increases in the price of fossil fuels. Switching from kerosene to fuelwood has been reported in parts of Africa[618] and is probably occurring in many other poor LDC areas where fuelwood is still relatively plentiful. As a result, the demand for fuelwood and charcoal in the years ahead may grow as fast as—or even faster than—LDC populations.

The primary environmental consequences of fuelwood consumption are those associated with deforestation, described earlier in this chapter. In the paragraphs that follow, a few additional energy-specific impacts associated with fuelwood are presented. The discussion then turns to the impacts of the use of dung and organic residues for fuel impacts which are serious for soil productivity. The discussion concludes with a consideration of the prospects for controlling the environmental impacts of noncommercial fuels.

Fuelwood

Today there is an inverse relationship between the level of economic development and the use of fuelwood. The poorest countries or regions use the most fuelwood; it is the principal source of fuel for the poorest families in these regions. Domestic energy requirements in developing countries range from a low of 0.2 m^3 (cubic meters) of wood per person per year burned in open cookfires in tree-short South Asia,[619] to a medium of 0.5 m^3 in the warm tropics and to a high of over 2 m^3 per person per year in the colder uplands, where wood is burned for both cooking and warmth.[620] The average annual per capita consumption where wood is abundant is about 1 m^3 (approximately 450 kg of wood),* but it drops to

---

*For comparison, a cord of wood (a common measure in the U.S.) is a pile measuring 4 × 4 × 8 feet (128 ft^3 or 3.6 m^3). Therefore, 1 m^3 of wood is less than 0.3 cord.

less than 0.5 m³ in wood-poor areas such as China, India, the Near East, and North Africa.[621]

The demand for fuelwood in developing countries is estimated (largely on the basis of data collected before the major oil price increases started in 1973) to have been growing 1–2 percent per year. Based on this growth rate, the FAO projected in 1976 that consumption would reach 2 billion cubic meters annually by the year 2000.[622] In contrast, fuelwood consumption in developed nations was falling at the rate of 6 percent per year in 1975 and represented less than 1 percent of the total energy consumed by these countries.[623] (This downward trend, however, may now have been reversed as a result of the recent rapid increases in the cost of fossil fuels.) In 1977 the FAO revised its estimate upwards to a 2.2 percent annual increase in demand in LDCs and predicted that by 1994, there would be a fuelwood shortage of 650 million cubic meters annually in wood-poor countries.[624] For comparison, this figure is roughly one quarter of the year 2000 fuelwood consumption projected by the FAO.

Wood is the only household fuel for most of the rural families in the developing world, and even urban families meet as much as 25 percent of their fuel needs with fuelwood.[625] However, because of its high weight per unit fuel value, wood is seldom collected from farther away than 10 kilometers and ordinarily is not transported by road from beyond 50 kilometers. Therefore scarcities tend to be local. Still, as scattered rural populations deplete local wood resources, entire regions become treeless, and an increasing effort must be exerted to find and carry wood to the home. In the arid Sahel of Africa, the gathering of fuelwood has become a full-time job, requiring in places 360 person-days per year per household.[626] Urban families, too far from collectible wood, spend 20–30 percent of their income on wood in some West African cities. Large industries involving trucks or animal carts exist to bring fuelwood into cities.[627] When demand is concentrated in large towns or cities, the surrounding areas become barren to a distance of as much as 50–100 kilometers.[628]

FAO's annual shortfall of 650 million cubic meters of fuelwood by 1994 is an alarming projection. It implies the reduction of essential fuel consumption, expanded deforestation, increased wood prices and growing amounts of dung shifted from field to fireplace.[629] The fuelwood problem is every bit as great for the poor LDC rural dweller as is the problem of increased petroleum costs for the more affluent citizen of the developed world.

There are no panaceas or quick fixes for the fuelwood problem. Tree plantations established today will require at least 10 years of growth prior to harvest, and growth rates are slow in the semi-arid regions where scarcities are already critical. In the Sahel, annual production of wood in native scrub forests, on a continuous basis, ranges from less than 0.5 m³ per hectare at the desert's edge—or enough for only one person's fuel needs—to up to 5 m³ per hectare in the less arid belt adjacent to the wooded savanna.[630] Near the wooden savanna, a hectare of well-tended forest could satisfy the fuel needs of a family of six or more.[631] Since the region's remaining forest stock has not yet been measured, the extent of the present fuelwood supply is not known, but local scarcities are evidenced by the treeless landscapes around towns. The Club du Sahel* notes that where populations exceed 25 persons per square kilometer, total deforestation is inevitable, and many areas of the Sahel have already surpassed this population density.[632] By the year 2000, the Club estimates that total firewood consumption will increase from the 1975 figure of 16 million to 33.5 million cubic meters, including 9.8 million burned in cities.[633] To meet this demand it is calculated that 150,000 hectares per year of forest plantations would have to be established—50 times the present rate of 3,000 hectares per year.[634]

The picture is not all bleak, however. Wood can be conserved through the use of more efficient stoves. In many areas the potential for conservation exists for ample village woodlots. The constraints in most areas are more sociological than technical, though the difficulty of sociological constraints is not to be underestimated.[635]

Charcoal

The manufacture and commercial use of charcoal appears to be increasing in the LDCs, where it is used primarily for cooking and heating in rural and urban areas. Much of the increase is in urban areas. The increasing use of charcoal in cities is explained by a combination of factors: increases in prices of kerosene, liquid gas, and electricity; lack of fuelwood as deforestation extends beyond distances from which it can be economically transported; and increasing urbanization of LDC populations.[636]

Information on the production and use of charcoal is not routinely collected by many nations, and as a result the data now available are not sufficient for making detailed projections. However, the information that is available from sev-

---

* An international voluntary association of nations, organized to mobilize assistance to drought stricken Sahelian states.

eral countries indicates increases in both the rate of consumption and the price of charcoal in LDCs.[637] In Ghana, which has desert scrub, savanna woodlands, and humid evergreen forests, charcoal consumption in 1975 was estimated at over 280,000 tons, and use was growing at an estimated 2.7 percent per year.[638] Kenya's consumption in 1972 was 310,000 tons, half of it in cities, and demand was growing at 7 percent per year.[639] For the poor communities that ring cities in Kenya, charcoal is now the major fuel. In Mozambique, 6,000 families earn their livelihood by supplying charcoal to the capital city Maputo.[640] Even in rural areas of East Africa, up to 50 percent of the people buy their charcoal.[641] In Sudan and Thailand, charcoal represents over 40 percent of the wood consumed for fuel; in India, however, its use is relatively small.[642] In general, the pattern appears to be one of an increasing trade in charcoal in urban markets, particularly in low-income quarters, and an increasing amount of charcoal manufacture.

While most charcoal is used for domestic cooking and heating, Brazil, the world's largest charcoal producer, uses most of its production for smelting pig iron, 45 percent of which is smelted with charcoal. Brazil burned 3.6 million tons of charcoal in smelters during 1978 and this figure is expected to increase at 10 percent per year, doubling every 7 years.[643] In the State of Minas Gerais, where 56 smelters supply 85 percent of Brazil's pig iron, virtually all of the original 55 million hectares of forest have been removed, largely for charcoal production. At present rates of cutting, there will be no more savanna forest in Minas Gerais by 1982.[644] To ensure a continuing supply of wood and charcoal, the Brazilian government enacted a law in 1967 requiring wood-using industries to be self-sufficient in wood by 1982. A successful program of fiscal incentives (now reduced) resulted in the establishment of over 1.5 million hectares of eucalyptus by late 1978.[645]

The actual combustion of charcoal fuel has minimal direct environmental impact. It is cleaner-burning than wood or coal. Its sulfur content is roughly one tenth that of even coking coal, making it an ideal smelting fuel.[646] It has twice the caloric value of most air-dried wood, at less than half the weight, and as a result it can be transported from much greater distances than wood. The carbonization process used to make charcoal consumes some energy to drive off water and other volatile substances, but if wood is used as the energy source, it is energy that otherwise probably would not be used or sold because of local surpluses or the cost of transporting the wood.

The indirect environmental effects of charcoal use are more significant. Because charcoal is such an attractive alternative fuel for urban uses, and because its manufacture is a simple and universally known technology, future conversion of forests and other vegetation to charcoal will continue to be an important and probably increasing activity in LDCs. Uncontrolled deforestation and its consequences (described earlier in this chapter) will therefore be a parallel and increasing result of intensified charcoal trade and manufacture. A related social consequence will be a decline in self-sufficiency among rural dwellers who will lose the natural vegetation they now exploit for multiple purposes—medicine, construction materials, tool woods, food, livestock forage, vegetable gums, etc.[647] The establishment of fast-growing fuelwood plantations of such species as eucalyptus will ensure a continuing supply of fuelwood, but will not replace the numerous other uses of native vegetation. These environmental and related socioeconomic consequences will be particularly noticeable in the areas around large cities, out to a distance of perhaps as much as 200 kilometers, depending upon the cost of transport. If the land is available and plantings can be encouraged and protected, large blocks of eucalyptus (or other fast-growing species such as pines or the acacia *Leucaena*) can be expected to replace the diverse, slower-growing native forests in the vicinity of large cities. Otherwise, the native forests near cities may simply be removed and not replanted.

Dung and Crop Residues as Fuel

Once fuelwood demands exceed forest production, a variety of stresses and changes begin. Arid regions have virtually no alternatives to fuelwood, and after it is gone desertification is speeded. In more humid agricultural regions that have become deforested, the alternative open to poor people is to turn to burning dung and crop residues (stalks, hulls, etc.) for cooking and warmth.

The shift to dung and crop residues is already well advanced in the treeless Gangetic Plain of India, Nepal, other parts of Asia, and the Andes of South America.[648] The FAO reports that in 1970 India burned 68 million tons of cow dung and 39 million tons of vegetable waste, representing 35 percent of her total noncommercial energy consumption.[649] Worldwide, an estimated 150–400 million tons of dung are burned for fuel, the lower estimate being equivalent to 13 percent of the amount of energy provided by firewood.

Dry dung has about the same caloric value as wood per unit weight.[650]

The burning of dung and crop residues is a disastrous loss. For the world's poor, these organic materials are the only sources of the nutrients needed to maintain the productivity of farmlands. It is the poorest people—the ones least able to afford chemical fertilizers—who are now being forced to burn their organic fertilizers. The combustion of dung and crop residues is equivalent to burning food. One ton of cow dung contains enough nutrients to produce 50 kilograms of food grain, which in turn can feed one person for four months.[651] The burning of almost 70 million tons of cow dung in India wastes nutrients equal to more than one-third of India's chemical fertilizer use.[652]

In the LDCs the potential contribution of organic materials (including human wastes) to soil fertility is enormous. The Food and Agriculture Organization reports that in a study done by J. C. C. van Voorhoeve for the World Bank the amount of nitrogen, potassium, and phosphorus potentially available to the LDCs from organic sources in 1971 was 7.8 times the amount actually applied that year as chemical fertilizer, worth $16 billion at 1973 prices. For 1980, the van Voorhoeve study found that at least 80 million metric tons of organic nutrients—worth $21 billion— could be supplied from organic sources.[653] If the amount of dung burned increases in proportion to population growth (the same assumption made for fuelwood consumption), 250–670 million tons per year would be burned annually by 2000, representing a loss of approximately 5–13 million metric tons of nitrogen (assuming 2 percent nitrogen dry weight). In monetary terms, these lost nutrients would be worth roughly $2 billion annually.

It is essential to understand that while inorganic substitutes exist for organic sources of nitrogen, potassium, and phosphorus, there is no substitute for organic matter itself. The proteins, cellulose, and lignins that comprise plant residues increase the porosity and water-holding capacity of soils, thereby serving to prevent erosion and provide the conditions needed for good root development.[654] Organic matter is also the food for the soil's microbiological life, which slowly converts and releases nutrients (and trace elements) in forms and at rates that plants can assimilate.[655]

Bio-Gas

Methane gas, also known as marsh gas, can be obtained from organic wastes by means of a relatively straightforward technology.[656] Manure and plant wastes are fed into enclosed chambers of brick, concrete, or steel construction. Anaerobic bacterial digestion of the organic matter produces methane (CH_4) and carbon dioxide (CO_2), the products of bacterial respiration. The environmental consequences of this growing form of energy production are generally quite positive. The resulting sludge retains all of the mineral salts and nitrogen (although little of the cellulose or carbohydrates) in the original material. Thus, the fertilizing benefits of the organic wastes are retained in the sludge* while the energy value of the manure and crop residues is captured in the form of methane gas. The energy value of the gas produced ranges from 18,630 to 26,080 kilojoules (500–700 Btu/ft^3) per cubic meter. In small farm applications the gas is piped directly to the kitchen for cooking.

Small-scale bio-gas plants have been the subject of intensive research and development in recent years, especially in India and the People's Republic of China. A major focus of this research has been on family-size plants (2–3 m^3 of gas per day). The offal from at least five cows (or an equivalent amount from other animals or humans) is needed to produce this amount of methane. Since many rural poor do not have so many animals, this source of energy is not accessible individually to the poorest rural people. India and China are developing larger bio-gas plants (10 m^3 of gas per day) that show considerable promise for community use.[657]

Both China and India have begun developing bio-gas production facilities. China has already built 7 million bio-gas plants and a total of 70 million are targetted for 1985.[658] India plans to build 100,000 bio-gas plants per year for the next decade. This rather modest number would affect only 1–2 percent of India's people; it would process the manure of only 2–4 percent of India's cows and recover only 100,000 metric tons per year of nitrogen fertilizer.[659] Presently, India has only 7,000 bio-gas plants.[660] Taiwan, South Korea, and Thailand are also promoting this form of energy development.

Problems of operation and maintenance, initial cost, and social equity have impeded rapid diffusion of this promising technology,[661] but the many benefits of bio-gas technology assure it an important role in the decades ahead.

---

* There is another advantage. The digestion process kills many pathogens affecting both plants and humans, thus improving human health and reducing the transfer of crop diseases from year to year. This advantage is particularly important in those areas where night soil is used as fertilizer.

Noncommercial Fuels—Environmental Prospects

Growing populations and increasing prices of commercial fuels (especially fossil fuels) can be expected to lead to rapidly increasing demands for organic noncommercial fuels. This increasing demand will lead to many environmental impacts.

The environmental impacts of deforestation have been discussed earlier in this chapter ("The Forestry Projections and the Environment") and will not be repeated here. One general outcome of deforestation is, of course, a shift to other sources of fuel, such as organic matter. A single and disastrous consequence can readily be predicted: decline in soil productivity and the decline, therefore, in the production of food for humans and animals. More specifically, a number of physical and environmental effects of diminished levels, or disappearance of, organic matter in soils can be determined:

• Diminished capacity of soils to hold water, therefore greater susceptibility to drought during dry periods, exacerbated by loss of lignin by-products.
• Decreased porosity, therefore poorer aeration and absorption of water and more difficult tilling plus a tendency to become compacted and, during rains, waterlogged, leading to erosion and fast runoff.
• Less adhesion between soil particles and greater susceptibility to erosion by wind or water.
• Reduced reservoir of plant nutrients (and therefore reduced fertility) and greater loss of nutrients to leaching action of soil water.
• Overall loss in productivity of the land.

These effects have long been known[662]; avoiding them through husbandry of soil organic matter has been a hallmark of wise farming for thousands of years.

In regions with scarce fuel supplies, it is not likely that cattle populations will grow and compensate for the increased burning of dried dung. As noted in Tables 13–2 and 13–4, cattle populations will increase in many areas but on overgrazed lands; the animals will eat less and produce less dung as land productivity declines. The situation may lead to a self-accelerating downward trend in soil productivity, driven by efforts of increasing populations to survive on decreasing quantities of plant production.

In regions with steep slopes erosion may be the *coup de grace* for lands which have been deprived of organic matter, reducing them in extreme cases to bare rock and in wide areas to infertile soils, which will require decades or more of careful management and conservation if they are to be returned to productivity. Such severe hillside erosion has already been documented in Central America, the Andean region of Latin America, the East African Highlands, and the Himalayan hills.[663] In less steep landscapes, the land will simply produce less food and plant matter, and both animals and people will go hungry or starve—or migrate if the alternative exists. Adverse climatic developments aggravate declining productivity, as experience in the Sahel has shown.

A reversal of these alarming trends is being sought by the World Bank, the Food and Agricultural Organization of the United Nations, and U.S. Agency for International Development,[664] and other organizations that have studied the problem.[665] Reduction in the use of wood, dung, and plant residues for fuel could be achieved by several means:

• *Use of kerosene.* This is judged to be too expensive for the poorest people.*
• *Improved efficiencies in the technologies used in the production of charcoal.*
• *Improved efficienty of fuel use.* This is the most promising option. Open fires waste over 90 percent of the heat generated. Improved stoves, of which a number of designs exist suited to different cultures, can reduce wood consumption by 70 percent.[666]
• *Utilization of methane digesters.* This process holds much promise, but requires an initial capital outlay of several hundred dollars, and the possession of livestock. Thus, it holds little promise for the dilemma of the poorest people (no free fuel and no ability to purchase an alternative), but the process does save the value of organic matter while also exploiting its energy.[667]
• *Development of fuelwood plantations.* This is a promising solution after a few years to a decade for growth, but is beset by lack of institutional capabilities for large scale plantation programs, as well as social and economic problems at the local level (see Chapter 8).
• *Solar and wind energy.* There is increasing interest in the use of solar energy for cooking and for irrigation pumping and of wind for pumping and other energy needs.

---

* The World Bank is concerned about the effects of increasing world oil prices on non-OPEC developing economies and has initiated a new program to accelerate petroleum exploration and production in the non-OPEC developing countries. (See *A Program to Accelerate Petroleum Production in the Developing Countries*, Washington: World Bank, January 1979.

What then are the prospects for noncommercial, organic fuels by the year 2000? The answer—to the extent that it can be given—depends largely on which geographic region is being considered. Potentials for organic matter production vary among regions by a factor of 10 or more, as do population densities. Awareness of the importance of organic fuels is growing rapidly in some areas, less rapidly in others. The role of cattle husbandry and traditional methods of cooking and disposing of organic wastes also show cultural variations, which not only influence the practice of using organic fuels but also the potentials for socially and economically feasible alternatives. However, further increases in population and further increases in the costs of fossil fuels imply substantially increased pressures on organic fuel resources virtually everywhere by the year 2000.

Conclusion

How the many nations of the world will respond to the rapidly changing energy situation is uncertain, and as a result it has not been possible for the Department of Energy to develop energy projections that extend to the year 2000. While DOE did prepare projections that extend to 1990, the information required to analyze the environmental implications of these projections is not available. As a result, it has been necessary to limit the discussion of environmental impacts to a qualitative consideration of a range of energy development options bounded by the hard and soft paths. From this qualitative consideration it is clear that all energy sources have environmental impacts associated with their development and use. The energy challenge to each nation over the next two decades is to develop an energy economy that balances the advantages of more energy with the disadvantage of the environmental and social impacts. While the situation is still very uncertain, trends are emerging for both the commercial and the noncommercial energy economies.

At present, the world's commercial energy sector (fossil fuels, nuclear energy, and hydropower) is developing a structure that is much nearer the hard path end of the spectrum of options than the soft path end. If the overall, primary-energy growth rate projected by the Department of Energy out to 1990 were to continue to 2000, the result would be a commerical energy economy consuming 517 quads (517×10^{15} Btu) annually, more than double the 1975 figure. If, in addition, this commerical energy were to be supplied by a global energy sector similar in composition of that described in Table 13–41 for the United States, the consequences might be expected to include the following proportionate increases in the environmental impacts described in Table 13–42:

- Several thousand million tons of coal production per year by 2000.
- Approximately one hundred thousand million tons of coal mined cumulatively, 1975–2000.
- Many thousands of square kilometers of land strip-mined cumulatively.
- Many thousands of square kilometers of land affected by subsidence cumulatively.
- Approximately one thousand (nominally 1,100 Mw) coal power plants.
- Several hundred (nominally 1,100 Mw) nuclear power plants.
- Several tens of thousands square kilometers required for transmission lines for electricity generated by new coal and nuclear plants.
- Approximately 1,000 million tons of radioactive tailings from supplying uranium, 1977–2000.
- Approximately ten million cubic meters of low-level radioactive wastes.
- A few 100,000 tons of spent nuclear fuel, 1977–2000.
- Several 100,000 tons of spent nuclear fuel generated over the lifetimes of the plants constructed through the year 2000.

While these estimates are highly uncertain, they are the best estimates that can be made with the projections and data currently available, and they do indicate the order of magnitude of the cumulative impacts of a global hard path over the decades ahead.

In addition to its environmental impacts, the global hard path option will maintain and increase thermodynamic inefficiencies in the energy sector itself. Large amounts of energy will be used in converting one form of energy to another, and the resulting energy forms will not in many cases be efficiently matched thermodynamically to end-use requirements.

As the soft path studies illustrate, requirements for nonrenewable primary energy (and the associated environmental impacts) could be reduced by increasing the thermodynamic efficiency in the energy sector, by increasing the contribution of renewable sources of primary energy, and by increasing end-use conservation. However, the DOE energy projections show only relatively small shifts in these directions through 1990.

Trends in the world's noncommercial energy economy lead to environmental consequences that are quite different from those implied by the commercial economy. The FAO projection of a 650 million cubic meter annual shortage of firewood in the LDCs means that approximately a quarter of the needed fuelwood in the LDCs may not be available. The shortfall implies increased deforestation and shifts to alternative fuels (dung and crop residues). Both the deforestation and the shift to alternative fuels will have adverse affects. The deforestation will enhance erosion and destabilize stream flows. The combustion of dung and crop residues will deprive the soil of needed nutrients and organic matter.

The most serious environmental impacts implied by the noncommercial energy trends could be reduced significantly by extensive development of village woodlots and the use of methane generators. Encouraging initiatives in both areas have been noted above. Nevertheless, if present trends continue, the organic fuel needs of increased LDC populations can be expected to seriously affect forestry and agriculture in large parts of Africa, Asia, and Latin America by the year 2000.

By then, the commercial and noncommercial energy sectors may be having increasing effects on each other. Higher costs of kerosene can be expected to expand the use of organic fuels in LDCs, increasing further the pressures on LDC forests. The resulting deforestation and wood combustion will contribute potentially significant amounts of carbon dioxide to the atmosphere and will reduce the amount of vegetation available globally to absorb CO_2—developments that, in turn, will increase concerns in the world's commercial energy economy over the climatological consequences of continued and expanded fossil fuel combustion.

THE NONFUEL MINERALS PROJECTIONS AND THE ENVIRONMENT

The Projections

Collectively, the demand for the 18 nonfuel minerals considered in the projections prepared by the Department of the Interior, was expected to grow at around 3 percent per year, slightly more than doubling between 1975 and 2000. In most cases it appears possible to accommodate the projected growth of mineral demand, but there are a number of unanswered questions concerning the price at which demand will be met, especially if energy prices increase significantly above their present levels. As higher-grade resources in accessible locations are exhausted, new mining ventures will tend to exploit lower-grade deposits and deposits in less accessible parts of the world with more fragile environments. Some of the projected increases in supply are large and will require contributions of both virgin and recycled materials. The industrialized nations will continue to depend heavily on resources imported from LDCs and are projected to absorb over three-fourths of the world's nonfuel mineral production until at least the year 2000.

Introduction

The Global 2000 Study projections indicate that in the decades ahead there will be increasing needs both for mineral resources and for environmental conditions beneficial to biological resources. These two resource needs, at least in the context of present policy and practice, are to a degree in conflict. Thus tensions between materials demand and environmental quality can be expected to continue. In the past—and even to a greater degree now—mineral resource policy has been based on the assumption that mining is the most appropriate use for mineral-bearing land. Not long ago in the United States, however, the Study Team on Environmental Problems Associated with Metallic and Nonmetallic Mineral Resources, working under the sponsorship of the National Academy of Sciences, advised against making the assumption that mining is necessarily the most appropriate use of mineral-bearing land.[668] The goal recommended by the U.S. Secretary of Interior is a proper balance between mineral extraction and environmental protection.[669] Achieving that balance in the U.S. and elsewhere will require significant changes of policy and practice, as well as significant expenditures. According to a United Nations estimate, the cost of abating all world pollution due to mining by the year 2000 would be about $200 billion, or 1–2 percent of the product value.[670]

Richard A. Carpenter, Executive Director of the National Academy of Sciences' Commission on Natural Resources, has summarized the situation as follows:

The tensions between availability of materials and quality of the environment will increase with economic growth and the appreciation of environmental values. These tensions can be relieved to an extent by internalizing the costs of environmental protection so that they are reflected in the price of materials. . . .

Environmental protection regulations will result in (i) increased costs for many materials; (ii) disruptive changes in uses of materials, due to environmental characteristics and revised cost of effectiveness calculations; (iii) restrictions on the siting of processing and manufacturing installations; (iv) preemption of access and surface rights to some mineral bearing lands, particularly those that are federally controlled; (v) diversion of capital from new production facilities; and (vi) frustrating delays in decisions, such as those affecting leasing and plant siting.

In return for these generally undesirable disruptions in the continued development and supply of materials, society will obtain: (i) improved quality of air and water; (ii) long-term protection of the natural ecosystems of which man is a part; (iii) more efficient allocation of natural resources on the basis of more accurate and complete accounting of costs; (iv) improved human health through decreased contamination of the environment with toxic substances; and (v) conservation of materials through a closing of the production, use, and disposal cycle.

Ingenuity and a more complete understanding of the parts and interactions of the energy, materials, and environmental system can do much to reduce the tensions in these conflicts and bring about equitable trade-offs among societal goals.[671]

Significant environmental damage can be anticipated from the projected increases in mineral production and utilization. These impacts will be felt as a continuation of both the direct and the indirect consequences of mining on land. Mining the seabed will present new and unique environmental impacts. The three types of impacts are discussed below.

Direct Environmental Effects of Mining on Land

As shown in Table 13–43, mines, quarries, and wells yielded about 21 billion short tons of refined mineral materials worldwide in 1976 (25 billion if oil and gas are included). Of the quantity produced, roughly 16 billion tons were nonmetallic minerals, mainly stone, sand, and gravel; 8 billion tons were fuels; and nearly 1 billion tons were metals.

Most mineral resource production now occurs in the industrialized countries. About 14 billion tons of refined mineral materials were produced in Japan, Canada, Australia, South Africa, and the industrialized countries of Europe in 1976; 4 billion tons were produced in the United States, and 7 billion tons in the less developed countries. This marketed mineral output amounted to 2 tons per person annually in the LDCs, 20 tons per person in the United States, and 16 tons per person in the other industrialized countries (Fig. 13–19).

Direct effects of mining on the landscape, such as surface disturbance, deposition of overburden and tailings, and generation and disposal of pollutants, tend to be roughly proportional to the quantity of minerals extracted. Such effects, in the absence of measured data, can therefore be roughly estimated by applying conversion coefficients to estimates of future production. Estimates of utilized land areas and generated mining wastes derived in this manner are presented below, after which their implications for air and water resources are discussed briefly.

Land Use in Mineral Production

The extent of the earth's surface disturbed by worldwide mining operations has never been measured accurately. It is estimated in Table 13–43 at roughly 1.5 million acres per year in 1976, growing to 3 million acres per year by 2000 (excluding surface disturbed by oil and gas operations). The land area that will be directly disturbed during the 1976–2000 period is approximately 60 million acres, or 94,000 square miles—an area roughly equal to West Germany, or 0.2 percent of the earth's total land surface. By comparison, the southern border of the Sahara Desert, by moving steadily southward during the last 50 years, is believed to have encompassed some 250,000 square miles of land once suitable for agriculture or grazing.[672] and it is expected that the closed forests of the world will be reduced by 1.72 million square miles between 1978 and 2000.[673]

However, the projected figure (94,000 square miles of land expected to be directly disturbed by mining over the next quarter century) is misleadingly small. The mines themselves are not the only areas disturbed by mining operations. It has been said that the least of the problems is "the hole in the ground." Mining operations are responsible for water and air pollution, for destruction of fish and wildlife habitats, for erosion, and the impairment of natural beauty many miles from the mine sites. The extensive areas indirectly affected by mining are not included in the 94,000 square mile figure, and virtually no data are available

TABLE 13–43

Estimated Land Area Utilized for World Mineral Production Compared with Annual Production, 1976–2000

Mineral Commodity	Ratio of Mineral Production (in millions of short tons) to Acres of Land Utilized in the U.S. in 1971[a]	1976 Production (billions of short tons)	1976 Land Utilized (thousands of acres)	1985 Production (billions of short tons)	1985 Land Utilized (thousands of acres)	2000 Production (billions of short tons)	2000 Land Utilized (thousands of acres)
Stone	30	7.7	231	8.2	246	14.8	444
Sand and gravel	50	6.9	345	10.5	525	17.3	865
Commodities not elsewhere specified[b]	60[c]	1.5	90	2.2[c]	132	3.5[c]	210
Clays	120	0.6	72	0.8	96	1.1	132
Bituminous coal[d]	130	3.5	455	4.0	520	4.8	624
Iron (in ore)	170	0.5	85	0.8	136	1.1	187
Phosphate rock	260	0.1	26	0.2	52	0.5	130
Copper	12,670	0.008	101	0.013	165	0.022	279
Uranium[e]	200,000	0.000025	5	0.000107	21	0.000193	39
World total (excluding petroleum and natural gas)		20.8	1,410	26.7	1,893	43.1	2,910

Note: Production figures assume U.S. 1971 ratio of marketable production to land utilized (column 1). Production figures for 1985 and 2000 are U.S. Bureau of Mines projections for demand, which is assumed to be matched by production.
[a] Millions of short tons produced : acres of land utilized.
[b] Mainly cement, anthracite coal, salt, and other nonmetallic minerals, but excluding petroleum and natural gas.
[c] Estimated figure, based on the relative contributions of cement, anthracite coal, salt, and other nonmetallic minerals.
[d] This fuel mineral is included here for purposes of comparison.
[e] Figures do not include centrally planned economies; data was not available.
Sources: Ratios calculated from U.S. Bureau of Mines, Land Utilization and Reclamation in the Mining Industry, 1930–71, 1974. Production data for 1976 from U.S. Bureau of Mines, Mineral Commodity Summaries, 1978. Production estimates for 1985 and 2000 from U.S. Bureau Mines, Mineral Trends and Forecasts, 1976.

on the overall amounts of land disturbed by mining.

Mining directly disturbs land in a number of ways. According to United States experience over the 1930–71 period, 59 percent of such land was utilized for excavation and 38 percent for disposal of mine and mill waste; the remaining 3 percent either subsided or was otherwise disturbed by underground workings.[674]

Large areas have been directly disturbed by surface mining for certain metals—in Malaysia for tin, in New Caledonia for nickel, in Australia for titanium, and on various Pacific islands for phosphate.[675] Work has begun near Hambach, West Germany, on an open-pit lignite mine that will cover 30 square miles of what are (or were) farms, forests, and villages.[676] A proposed bauxite mine in Western Australia will destroy the only forest in a million square mile area. The mining company answers critics that it believes most of the trees have an incurable root disease. The company has also offered to attempt reforestation.[677]

By 1977, land directly disturbed by surface mining in the United States totaled 5.7 million acres.[678] The strip mining of bituminous coal accounted for the largest part of this. The thinner the coal seam, the greater the area disturbed for a certain quantity of coal. In the western United States, for example, the mining of 30-foot seams of Wyoming coal disturbs 25 acres of land for every million tons produced, whereas mining 10-foot seams of Washington, Arizona, Colorado, or Utah coal disrupts 72–80 acres per million tons of coal recovered.[679] There is 12 times as much coal available by deep mining in the United States as by stripping,[680] but although deep mining appears to cause less land degradation than surface mining, it entails greater occupational hazard and discomfort and greater cost.

The nonfuel minerals commodities principally responsible for direct land disturbance during mining are sand and gravel, stone, copper, iron, clays, and phosphate rock ore. Table 13–43 provides estimates and projections of the areas disturbed worldwide during the mining of these commodities in the years 1976, 1985, and 2000.

ABOUT 40,000 POUNDS OF NEW MINERAL MATERIALS ARE REQUIRED ANNUALLY FOR EACH U.S. CITIZEN

| 8000 LBS. STONE | 8000 LBS. SAND AND GRAVEL | 660 LBS. CEMENT | 450 LBS. CLAYS | 430 LBS. SALT | 1400 LBS. OTHER NONMETALS |

| 1000 LBS. IRON AND STEEL | 46 LBS. ALUMINUM | 16 LBS. COPPER | 14 LBS. ZINC | 11 LBS. LEAD | 31 LBS. OTHER METALS |

PLUS

| 7650 LBS. PETROLEUM | 5200 LBS. COAL | 4200 LBS. NATURAL GAS | 1/7 LB. URANIUM |

TO GENERATE:

ENERGY EQUIVALENT TO 300 PERSONS WORKING AROUND-THE-CLOCK FOR EACH U.S. CITIZEN

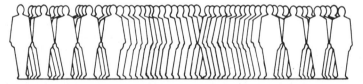

U.S. TOTAL USE OF NEW MINERAL SUPPLIES IN 1975 WAS ABOUT 4 BILLION TONS !

Figure 13–19. Consumption of new mineral materials per person in the United States in 1975. (*U.S. Bureau of Mines,* Status of the Mineral Industries 1976)

The figures, admittedly approximate, were derived for each commodity by observing the ratio of production tonnages to land acreages disturbed and utilized in the United States in 1971 (as reported in a Bureau of Mines study[681]) and applying these ratios to the Bureau's projections of world mineral demand (which were equated with production).

There are several factors influencing the accuracy of the area estimates in the table. The mix of mining methods used in the United States, es-

pecially the ratio of surface to underground mining, differs from that of the world as a whole. The United States is also atypical in that it exploits much low-grade ore deep beneath the surface. It should also be remembered that as miners everywhere deplete the world's high-grade, accessible ores, they will be turning to deposits requiring even more surface disturbance. Some new production processes (such as leaching ores in place) show promise for reducing the land requirements of mining, but it is doubtful that these processes will be in widespread use before 2000. Lastly, it should be noted that the projected production figures have a wide range of uncertainty, which carries over into the land utilization figures.

In addition to land disrupted by "the hole in the ground," other land is affected by mining wastes. Furthermore, dust and toxic materials from the wastes generated in mining and refining often spreads to surrounding areas, reducing their ability to support life.

The wastes from mining and the early stages of refining are usually bulky, and sometimes toxic. For many deposits, the tons of earth that must be moved to expose the ore body exceed the tonnage of ore ultimately recovered from the site. This surface material removed (the "overburden") and the residue left after processing (the "tailings") are usually discarded in open piles.

Accurate data on the worldwide magnitude of mining waste generated annually are not available, but it is known that in industrialized countries the mining and cleaning of coal produces more waste than the extraction of any nonfuel mineral. According to the Organization for Economic Cooperation and Development, annual accumulations of coal mining waste are 90 million metric tons in the United States, 60 million tons in West Germany, and 56 million tons in the United Kingdom.[682] Uranium is also responsible for large amounts of mining waste. Nonfuel mineral commodities whose extraction is accompanied by considerable waste include (in descending order of apparent magnitude of waste) copper, iron ore, phosphate rock, stone, and clays.

Table 13–44 gives estimates of the amount of waste generated by the world output of six mineral commodities.* The estimates are rough approximations, derived by multiplying world production or projected demand by the ratio of marketable product to waste experienced in the United States in 1975.[683] While these estimates suffer from the same kinds of limitations as the estimates in Table 13–43, they do suggest that world production of the six commodities (totaling 9 billion tons) generated approximately 14 billion tons of waste in 1976. The projection for 2000 is 18 billion tons of commodities produced and 34 billion tons of waste. Future mining and milling wastes are expected to increase faster than the output of mineral commodities, partly because the demand for minerals with high ratios of waste to marketable product (phosphate rock, copper, and uranium)

is projected to increase faster than the demand for minerals with low waste to product ratios (stone and clays). The actual increase of waste will probably be greater than the increase in Table 13–44, which does not take into account the fact that, as time goes on, the average grade of ores worked will generally be lower.

Several countries are now seeking ways to protect agricultural land, forests, and waterways from pollution from mine wastes. In the Philippines, where mines discharge 140,000 tons of waste daily, the country's Bureau of Mines is investigating potential uses of some of the mine waste as material for cement, ceramics, and construction.[684] There is plenty of waste to work with. For example, nonfuel mining operations in the United States in 1975 moved 4.2 billion tons of material, of which 2.6 billion tons represented crude ore and 1.6 billion tons mining waste; 94 percent of the crude ore and 99 percent of the mining waste was from surface mines.[685]

What happens to mined-out land after operations move on or cease? When nothing is done, the abandoned and useless sites usually remain an ugly, hazardous area and a major source of water pollution, air pollution, and soil erosion. Vegetation is slow to regenerate naturally because of displaced soil, steep slopes, and drainage, which usually is acid, alkaline, or saline. These problems are particularly acute in areas where coal has been strip mined.[686]

According to the Environmental Protection Agency,[687] representative annual rates of erosion from various land uses are as follows:

Land Use	Metric Tons per Square Kilometer	Short Tons per Square Mile	Relative Rate (Forest = 1)
Forest	8.5	24	1
Grassland	85	240	10
Abandoned surface mine	850	2,400	100
Cropland	1,700	4,800	200
Active surface mine	17,000	48,000	2,000
Construction	17,000	48,000	2,000

Reclamation efforts can reduce the environmental damage caused by mining wastes. Mining companies—at least in some nations—are increasing the incidence and degree of reclamation of mined lands. These efforts are largely in response to conservation movements and more stringent legislation.

Although world data on the extent of reclamation of mined-out lands are not available, some information for the United States is available. Of U.S. land used for mining in the 1930–71 period, 40 percent has been designated "reclaimed."[688]

---

* As indicated above, coal generates an enormous quantity of mining waste, but data corresponding to that presented in Table 13–44 could not be obtained for coal.

TABLE 13-44

Estimates of Solid Wastes Generated Annually by World Production of Selected Mineral Products, 1976–2000

Mineral Product	Ratio of Tons of Waste to Tons of Marketable Product (U.S. 1975)		1976			1985			2000		
	Mining Waste	Milling Waste	Marketed Production	Mining Wastes	Milling Wastes	Marketed Production	Mining Wastes	Milling Wastes	Marketed Production	Mining Wastes	Milling Wastes
			Millions of short tons								
Stone	0.073	0.008	7,700	600	100	8,192	600	100	14,849	1,100	100
Clays	0.85	Negligible	580	500	-*	761	600	-*	1,061	900	-*
Iron ore	3.46	2.13	987	3,400	2,100	1,293	4,500	2,800	1,947	6,700	4,100
Phosphate rock	4.45	2.84	118	500	300	207	900	600	456	2,000	1,300
Copper	501	188	8	4,000	1,500	13	6,500	2,400	22	1,100	4,100
Uranium	14,235	673	0.04	600	30	0.1	1,400	100	0.2	2,800	140
Total (all six commodities)			9,393	9,600	4,000	10,466	14,500	6,000	18,335	24,500	9,800

Note: Figures for mining and milling wastes assume U.S. 1975 ratios of marketable production to waste (columns 1 and 2), usually rounded to the nearest 100 million tons. Production figures for 1985 and 2000 are U.S. Bureau of Mines projections for demand, which is assumed to be matched by production.

* Less than 500,000 tons.

Source: U.S. Bureau of Mines, "Mining and Quarrying Trends in the Metal and Nonmetal Industries," in *Minerals Yearbook 1975; Mineral Commodity Summaries 1978;* and *Mineral Trends and Forecasts, 1976.*

However, the quality of the reclamation varies considerably. In some cases the effort has been minimal; in others serious difficulties are presented by hilly terrain and limited rainfall.

Land reclamation success stories are heard from many other nations. For example, in Ostrava, Czechoslovakia, red oak has started to grow on coal dumps characterized by steep slopes and very limited soil.[689] American Metal Climax, Inc. of New York conducts a project to farm its acquired coal lands (at Sullivan, Indiana) before strip mining and plans to develop the land's most productive resources after mining.[690] A cement plant at Bamburi, on Kenya's Indian Ocean coast, has rehabilitated hundreds of acres of land from which it quarried coral limestone; the area now has a forest of 30,000 trees, a productive farm, and fish ponds.[691]

As of mid-1977, 70 percent of the land disturbed by surface mining and needing reclamation in the United States was not under any legal requirement to be reclaimed.[692] This situation led to the Surface Mining Control and Reclamation Act of 1977. The law, which applies only to coal lands, stipulates that mined-over areas be returned approximately to their original contours. A tax on currently produced surface coal will be used to finance the reclamation of "orphaned" lands left from earlier operations. Slopes of more than 20 degrees on waste dumps are prohibited.[693]

Compliance with the new reclamation law is estimated to add from 50 cents to $4.00 to the cost of producing a ton of surface-mined coal in the United States.[694] Rehabilitating coal fields in the western United States, parts of which have a dry climate, would cost an estimated $925 to $2,750 per acre.[695] According to an Argonne National Laboratory study, reclamation of mined land in some localities (such as certain phosphate rock sites in Florida) may be a profitable endeavor if proper land use planning and marketing strategies are employed.[696]

Under present policy in most nations, the mining of a particular piece of land is usually permitted even when mining operations conflict with other uses of the land. However, stipulations and conditions are increasingly being made that take other potential land uses into consideration. In a few cases, mining has even been prohibited for environmental reasons. For example, the Rio Tinto Zinc Corporation was prohibited from mining in the Snowdonia National Park, Wales.[697] The Swedish Government has assured environmental groups and local authorities it will refuse to issue requested permits for strip mining mineral-bearing slate deposits in the Naerke area of southern Sweden.[698] In a region of Western Australia recently experiencing a diamond rush, the government set aside as off limits to mining a 440 square mile park near Cape Londonderry.[699] Ecological (as well as economic) factors figured significantly in the decision of the Puerto Rican Department of Natural Resources to not allow Kennecott Copper Corporation and American Metal Climax to mine an estimated 243 million tons of copper reserves on the island.[700] The United States has largely closed its national parks to mining; it has also prohibited surface mining of coal on prime farmlands unless they can later be restored to their original productivity and has prohibited mining that damages water supply.[701] Trends such as these may reduce to a degree the land disruption caused by mining, but they will also increase somewhat the cost of mineral products.

Impact of Mineral Production on Air Quality

Air pollution generated from mining and processing activities (particularly high-temperature metallurgical operations) produces serious environmental and health problems. Air pollutants of particular concern are sulfur oxides, particulates, asbestos, radionuclides (radium and radon), coke oven emissions, arsenic, lead, and fluorides.[702]

Most sulfur oxide contamination of the atmosphere is caused by the combustion of fossil fuels, especially coal, but in addition, sulfur oxides go up the stacks of smelters treating sulfide ores of metals such as copper, nickel, lead, and zinc.

In 1974 U.S. copper smelters emitted 8,214 tons of sulfur oxides daily, 10 percent of the nation's total. However, smelter emissions are being reduced. The 1974 emissions were 33 percent below previous highs and the 1986 emissions are expected to be 90 percent below the earlier peak.[703] Unfortunately, such reductions are not the trend everywhere. The Cuajone copper mining and smelting project in Peru will soon double emissions and effluents from the site; it is expected that 60,000 tons of sulfur oxides will be released into the air and 30 million tons of tailings discharged into the sea annually. The World Bank, one of the project's lenders, has persuaded the borrower to accept, in principle, the incorporation of a number of environmental safeguards in project design.[704] The copper-nickel smelters of the Sudbury district of Ontario, Canada, emit 2.7 million tons of surfur oxides annually, causing losses of timber with a value of $117,000 per year in a 720 square mile zone of severe damage.[705] Such sulfur oxides contribute more widely, of course, to the problems of acid rain discussed in

this chapter in the section entitled "Water Projections and the Environment." They are also known to increase the incidence of asthma, chronic bronchitis, and emphysema.[706]

Uranium-mill tailings present a radioactive air pollution problem. The radium in the tailings decays to the radioactive gas radon, whose decay products are responsible for the high incidence of lung cancer among uranium miners in Europe and the United States.[707] Piles of uranium tailings in the United States total 140 million tons and could reach a billion tons by the year 2000.[708] Lyman J. Olsen, director of the Utah State Division of Health, reports that thousands of people work and live in close proximity to the tailings pile of an inactive uranium-mill site in Salt Lake City and are exposed to radioactive dust, radon gas and its decay products, and gamma radiation.[709] An active uranium mill near Grants, New Mexico, has dumped 23 million tons of tailings on 265 acres; the pile rises to a height of 100 feet. Covering such dumps with 8–12 feet of clay would reduce the radon eminations to twice background levels.[710] The cost of safe disposal of all uranium tailings in the United States is conservatively estimated at $140 million.[711]

Although radiation at phosphate rock mines is apparently a somewhat lesser problem,[712] the Global 2000 Study projections of a doubling to quadrupling of fertilizer use by the year 2000 imply an increase in the amount of radioactive phosphate waste. In Florida radiation from phosphate wastes is already an issue. According to a preliminary report by the U.S. Bureau of Mines, there could be a twofold increase in the incidence of lung cancer among persons living in structures built on reclaimed phosphate lands in Florida.[713]

Impact of Mineral Production on Water Quality

Surface and underground water is frequently polluted by effluents of mining and milling operations and by rainfall or stream action on solid mine and mill wastes. Thirty-four percent of waste water discharged by all major U.S. industrial groups in 1973 was from production of primary metals, 8 percent from petroleum and coal products, and 1 percent from stone, glass, and clay products.[714]

One example of water pollution from mining is acid mine drainage, which is caused by the reaction of water and air with sulfur-bearing minerals in coal or metal mines and dumps. The sulfuric acid produced in this reaction enters streams, lakes, and rivers where it lowers the pH, killing many forms of life.

Another notable example of water pollution by

mining wastes is the dumping of salt wastes by East German potash mining companies into the Werra River. The Werra, which weaves across the border between East and West Germany, flows into the Weser River, which is now so salty that the city of Bremen can draw on it for only 20 percent of its water supply.[715] In addition, wastes from potash mines in France have long been implicated as one of the primary sources of contamination of the Rhine River.

In 1978, a series of earthquakes affecting Japan's Izu Peninsula caused the collapse of earthen dams holding mine wastes containing poisonous sodium cyanide. Fish were killed not only in the Mochikoshi and Kano Rivers but as far away as Suruga Bay.[716]

The Philippine Inter-Agency Committee on Environmental Protection has reported the discharge of about 100,000 tons of mine tailings per day in eight major river systems in the country, affecting an estimated 130,000 hectares of agricultural land.[717] The Japan International Cooperation Agency is expected to study the feasibility of a project for collecting tailings from at least four of the six major copper mines in the Baguio district of the Philippines and transporting them by pipeline for discharge into the Lingayen Gulf.[718]

In Peru, tailings from copper mines are polluting the San Juan, Mantaro, Locumba, and Moche rivers with iron, acid, magnesium, and other metals. The World Bank recommends a Mantaro cleanup project to be completed by 1980 to bring the iron content of the waste outflow down to 0.1 gram per liter and to reduce the acidity by 99.9 percent.[719]

As part of the opening of a molybdenum mine at Urad, Colorado, American Metal Climax constructed diversion structures and two miles of underground pipeline so that streams will flow around and under the mill and tailings areas and emerge from the property uncontaminated. The streams involved are part of the water supply for Golden, Colorado. A reservoir, holding water for mining and milling the ore, will be open to the public for camping, fishing, and the enjoyment of the surroundings.[720]

The Reserve Mining Company, a subsidiary of Armco Steel and Republic Steel Corporations has dumped approximately 67,000 tons of iron ore waste (taconite tailings) daily into Lake Superior for the past 23 years. The wastes contain microscopic asbestos fibers from a mine at Babbitt, Minnesota, and an ore-processing plant at Silver Bay, Minnesota.[721] Asbestos fibers are now present in the drinking water of Duluth and other communities that draw water from the lake. Airborne asbestos fibers are known to cause serious lung diseases, including a particularly dangerous form of cancer. Whether similar problems arise from the drinking of water containing asbestos has not been established. Nevertheless, state and federal courts have determined that a potential health hazard exists[722] and have ruled that Reserve must change to on-land disposal. It is estimated that the required pollution control facilities will cost $370 million.

The increased mining that follows from the Global 2000 Study's projected demand for fuel and nonfuel minerals could easily increase the amount of water pollution from mining activities. Present policies may limit the effects somewhat, but the quality of water used for drinking, irrigation, and fish culture can be expected to be adversely affected in at least some areas.

Indirect Effects of Mining on Land

The direct effects of most mining operations on land, while not negligible, are localized and relatively small compared to many other forms of human economic activity such as farming, forestry, and urbanization. By contrast, the indirect effects of mining can be quite large, especially since the infrastructure developed for mining operations often permits a large number of other activities that would be very difficult or impossible to carry on without it. Among the many indirect effects of mining on land are the boom-and-bust cycle, access roads, demand for renewable resources, and energy requirements. Each will be briefly considered here.

The boom-and-bust cycle of communities near mining and refining centers is a virtually inevitable consequence of the nonrenewable nature of mineral resources. Demographic and economic instabilities usually result.* In the short run, small communities may be unable to supply the community services needed by the overwhelmingly large numbers of new citizens drawn to a new

---

* The U.S. Department of Housing and Urban Development has prepared a report suggesting how to manage growth when an area is suddenly affected by the rapid growth accompanying resource exploitation. The report focuses primarily on growth associated with energy development but applies equally to growth associated with the exploitation of nonfuel minerals. It includes brief case studies of the impacts of growth associated with the Jim Bridger Power Plant in Sweetwater County, Wyoming, the nuclear power plant in Calvert County, Maryland, and oil production and coal mining in Campbell County, Wyoming; the effects of North Sea oil and gas production on Scotland are also examined. (*Rapid Growth from Energy Projects—Ideas for State and Local Action—A Program Guide*, Washington: Department of Housing and Urban Development, 1976.)

mining operation. In the long run (of a decade or two), these services may not be needed at all.

D. B. Brooks and P. W. Andrews, in reviewing the problem of boom-and-bust cycles on a global basis for a 1973 United Nations Symposium on Population, Resources and Environment, noted that:

Even if mining communities are more carefully planned today, their inherent tendency to deplete their reason for existence cannot be ignored, because the result is often a depressed region with high unemployment and few services. Such problems are intensified by the cyclical nature of investment in minerals, so that there tend to be cycles, every 20 to 40 years, during which a nation is faced with waves of mine closures.[723]

This type of local economic instability is exacerbated by the relative isolation of mining from the rest of the economy. Mining generally does not spawn significant amounts of associated industrial or manufacturing activities, especially if carried out in remote areas.

Mining activities, especially in remote areas, require improved access roads. The access roads built to mines often lead to other forms of natural resource exploitation that are undesirable if uncontrolled. As happened in coal mining regions of Southern Appalachia and in the copper and silver mining regions of Chile, forests are often removed from a wide area around the mine, either to provide timber for mining operations, housing construction, railroad ties, and fuel, or simply because improved transportation makes previously inaccessible forests exploitable.

The excessive production, use, and marketing of charcoal is a case in point. A few countries still use charcoal to smelt and refine ores, among them Brazil, Argentina, Malaysia, Australia, and India.[724] The consequences of this practice are illustrated by what is happening in Brazil. The once extensive, mixed-hardwood open woodlands of the Brazilian plateau are being rapidly consumed. In the state of Minas Gerais, it is estimated that by 1982, 45 million hectares of forest will have been cut down, largely for conversion to charcoal to smelt pig iron.[725] The destabilizing impact of this deforestation on soils and the hydrological cycle is discussed in more detail in the energy section of this chapter.

Not all energy for mining and processing comes from renewable sources. Most energy for the mining and metals industries comes from nonrenewable sources, and these energy requirements lead to yet another indirect consequence of the projected increases in mining activities.

Like the technologies of the Green Revolution in agriculture and the intensive silviculture discussed elsewhere in this chapter, the technologies of mining and processing are energy-intensive and are becoming more so. The worldwide energy dependence of mining and processing has not been studied carefully, but the linkages between energy and minerals in the U.S. has been examined to some extent. The reason for concern over the energy-intensiveness of mining and processing is that lower-grade ores generally require more energy for extraction, processing, and refining at a time when energy costs are projected to increase significantly in the years ahead. As Earl Hayes notes,

Each material has a fixed lower bound of ore grade, below which energy costs make processing uneconomic. . . . Energy costs [in general] rise rapidly as ore grade decreases. At some lower limit, say 0.25%, the energy expenditures dominate the whole recovery picture. Technological improvements in rock disintegration, transportation and concentration will have to be made if such low-grade ores are to be considered reserves—that is, resources that can be processed economically.[726]

Hayes also notes that in 1971 the energy inputs for processing metallic and nonmetallic minerals totaled 69×10^{15} Btu. The net energy output was 57×10^{15} Btu. The U.S. materials industry uses over 20 percent of the nation's energy to process materials: 8 percent for metals, 7.8 percent for chemicals and allied products, 4 percent for petroleum refining, and 2 percent for nonmetallics. Steel, aluminum, plastics, cement, and gasoline account for half of the 20 percent.[727]

As these figures make clear, the projected worldwide increases in minerals production can be expected to have a number of indirect environmental consequences through the associated demands for energy.

Effects of Mining the Seabed

As mentioned in Chapter 12, if the politics of the ocean floor are adequately resolved and if manganese nodules prove economically competitive with the ores for which they would substitute, large-scale mining of the ocean floor may commence before the year 2000. The environmental implications of mining the seabed have already been discussed in detail in this chapter in the section on "The Projections and the Marine Environment."

Conclusions

The environmental consequences of an approximate doubling of the global mining of nonfuel

TABLE 13–45

Apparent Opportunities for Further Mineral Development

Country	Mineral	Value of World Output, 1968 (in millions of 1968 dollars)	Percent of World Reserves	Percent of World Output
Zambia	copper	7,740	10	Quite small
Chile	copper	7,740	19	12
Thailand	tin	750	32	9
Indonesia	tin	750	12	Quite small
U.S.	zinc	1,450	27	12
U.S.	lead	775	37	14
Cuba	nickel	1,100	24	Quite small
Morocco	phosphorus	835	42	13
Guinea	bauxite	340	34	Quite small
Australia	bauxite	340	34	15

Source: Rex Bosson and Bension Varon. *The Mining Industry and the Developing Countries.* New York: Oxford, 1977. App. G.

minerals between now and 2000 are difficult to assess. Possibilities for considerably expanded production seem to exist in countries having large portions of the world's reserves of critical, high-value minerals (Table 13–45). Major new resource discoveries have been reported in ecologically fragile areas such as the seabed, the Amazon basin, Oceania, Siberia, and south central Africa. A disproportionate fraction of resource development is expected to take place in the LDCs, where environmental protection measures may be limited.

Smelting, refining, and milling usually occur in major industrial centers rather than at the mine site, but mineral exploitation and processing can have devastating impacts on extraction and concentration sites and their adjoining communities. Although the mining and concentration operations may continue for only a decade or two, they leave permanent scars on the landscape, especially in the case of open pit mines, which can be very deep.[728] Superficial mining of ores such as bauxite that are the result of weathering or are found in sedimentary formations may be less destructive of the land, which can be restored to productive forests, to pasture, or even to farmland if precautions and ecological conditions are adequate. The recovery of such sites will take many more years in arid or cold (tundra) regions than in hot humid regions, however. How long it will take for mining scars to heal in the oceans is still highly uncertain.

The indirect effects of boomtowns, new transportation systems, and other infrastructures associated with mining operations may be more lasting and significant than the direct effects. Land and water for mining and refining will in many cases be in direct competition with agriculture, forestry, urban water supplies and other uses. Conflicts with local populations over the use of land and water resources can be expected to increase. In West Germany opposition was encountered when an entire village was relocated recently to make room for a coal mine.[729] In central Florida, opposition has been raised to phosphate mining because of competition for the water used in beneficiating the ore.

These and other environmentally related conflicts will increase in the years ahead as the minerals industry is forced to turn to poorer, less accessible, more energy-demanding ores than those presently being exploited. As a result, the environmental damage done by mining is likely to increase markedly unless policies change and production technologies and practices improve significantly.

CLOSING THE LOOPS

Introduction

The previous 10 sections of this chapter have considered the Global 2000 Study's projections for population, GNP, climate, technology, food and agriculture, forestry, marine and coastal resources, water, energy, and nonfuel minerals for the purpose of determining what impact those projections will have *on the environment* between now and the year 2000. In the final sections of this chapter, however, the perspective will be reversed. The focus will shift to the impact that the environmental developments presented in the preceding 10 sections would have *on the population, economic, and resource projections* of Chapters 2–12.

Figure 13–1 at the beginning of this chapter illustrates a reversed—ecological—perspective, showing first how population, economic, and resource factors affect environment (as presented in the preceding 10 sections of this chapter) and how, in turn, the environment feeds back upon (affects) population, economy, and resources. While Figure 13–1 illustrates, at least conceptually, how the feedback loops are closed in nature, it must be emphasized that in the discussion that follows the feedback loops are not actually closed analytically, and that they cannot be closed with the government's current models.

The problem is that the government's present analytical tools for making population, GNP, and resource projections are not designed to accept explicit environmental feedback. Most of these models simply assume implicitly that the environment will do what it has done in the past, only more so; and this assumption leads to discrepancies between the environmental assumptions of the population, GNP, and resource projections and the environmental conditions implied by these projections. Put simply, the environment cannot do what some of the projections assume it will do.

Although there is no way in which revised, more realistic environmental assumptions can be entered into the projection models, it is possible to (1) compare each model's environmental assumptions with the environmental conditions implied by the population, GNP, and resource projections, (2) note the discrepancies (which would not exist if the environmental feedback effects were actually present in the models), and (3) consider how the discrepancies might affect the population, GNP, and resource projections *if* it were possible to alter the environmental assumptions to eliminate the discrepancies. Since it is not possible to alter the environmental assumptions in the population, GNP, and resource projections, the discrepancies remain, and the projections retain their basically open-loop, linear

character.* Nonetheless, the examination of the discrepancies and their implications provides a step toward a more ecological perspective.

As a preparation for shifting to this more ecological perspective on the future world environment, it is helpful to review the impacts upon the environment already presented in this chapter. Because, from the environmental point of view, economic and political boundaries are of very limited relevance, it is necessary to organize the information around major environmental classifications—terrestrial, atmospheric, aquatic—rather than around the economic and political jurisdictions considered heretofore. This is essential as a first step in closing the feedback loops because, for instance, many of the projections imply changes in the aquatic environment, and all of these changes need to be considered in comparing the future aquatic environment with the water assumptions in the various projections. Similarly, several of the projections imply changes in soil conditions, and it is the overall soil conditions that result from all the changes that need to be compared with the projections' implicit assumptions about soils. In such cases, how is the whole ecological perspective to be determined on the basis of fragmented projections—and then again how is the whole environmental future to be made relevant to fragmented projection models?

The approach used here is to gather the implications of the fragmented projections into one extensive table—Table 13–46. This table is organized *primarily* by the earth's major environments: terrestrial, atmospheric, aquatic. This primary organization establishes the holistic perspective characteristic of the environment. The *secondary* organization of the table is by major geographic groupings: global, regional (i.e., continental or more than one nation state), and local (i.e., subcontinental, individual nation states, or smaller economic or political units). The "local" category is further subdivided into "rural" and "urban." This organization of the table demonstrates the relationship of economic and geopolitical areas.

In the text that follows Table 13–46, the future world environment is discussed first in terms of the three major environments (still in the original perspective of projections impacting on the environment) so that the overall ecological description of the future world environment can finally

---

*These missing feedback loops and many other deficiencies in the government's current analytical capabilities are discussed in Chapter 14 and succeeding chapters of Parts II and III.

TABLE 13-46

Summary of Impacts on the Environment Implied by the Global 2000 Study's Population, GNP, and Resource Projections, by Major Environments

A. TERRESTRIAL ENVIRONMENTS

	Global	Regional (continental or more than one nation state)	Local (subcontinental, individual nation states, or smaller)	
			Urban	Rural
Population	No impact projected.	No impact projected.	Arable land lost to new or expanding human settlements by the year 2000 is projected to be 25 million hectares.	Increased numbers of subsistence farmers in LDCs will result in deterioration in land productivity, overgrazing, and deforestation.
GNP	No impact projected.	Slow economic growth rates in densely populated LDCs will increase the pressures of people and domestic animals on land.	Continued terrestrial disposal of toxic industrial and urban wastes will create potential health hazards in both industrialized countries and LDCs.	No impact projected.
Climate	No impact projected.	No impact projected.	No impact projected.	No impact projected.
Technology	No impact projected.	No impact projected.	No impact projected.	No impact projected.
Agriculture and food	Land productivity is declining in many industrialized countries as well as LDCs. Losses of range and farmland to desertification by 2000 could total 2,800 million hectares, primarily in Africa and Asia. One half the total irrigated land is already damaged by waterlogging, salinization, and alkalinization. By 2000, an additional 2.75 million hectares could be lost or damaged.	Regional germ plasm in traditional crops is being lost as increasingly marginal lands are being brought under cultivation and local varieties are replaced by high-yield varieties.	No impact projected.	Soil erosion and compaction will be a continuing—perhaps intensifying—problem for intensively-cropped, clean-tilled land in both industrialized countries and LDCs. Heavy dependence on pesticides will further deplete insect predator populations, reducing the crop protection offered through insect ecology, but the trend toward integrated pest management may compensate or even rehabilitate some areas.
Fisheries and marine developments	No impact projected.	No impact projected.	No impact projected.	No impact projected.
Forest exploitation	Hundreds of thousands of species of plants and animals will be extinct by 2000—a major reduction of a global genetic resource.	Between 1975 and 2000, 446 million hectares of forests will be removed to meet global demands for forest products, fuelwood, and ag-	No impact projected.	Critical catchment areas and inherently unstable land will become destabilized by deforestation leading to erosion and land slippage.

	ricultural land. The deforestation will occur primarily in the LDCs and will: (1) cause irreparable or long term damage to the land by exposing the soil to sun and rain; (2) render up to 600,000 species of plants and animals globally extinct; (3) destabilize slopes of catchments, especially in the Himalayan range and other mountains of Asia and in Latin American ranges.	Deforestation rates are relatively slow in industrialized countries, balanced by plantations.	No impact projected.	Habitats for wildlife (including predators of agricultural pests) will be destroyed in large amounts.
Water resource development and regulation	No impact projected.	No impact projected.	No impact projected.	Large impoundments will inundate agricultural lands, forests, mineral deposits, human settlements, roads, etc., especially in densely populated LDC areas.
Energy	No impact projected.	In industrialized regions (North America, Eastern and Western Europe, Japan, U.S.S.R., South Africa, and Australia) energy development by 2000 will result in: • Thousands of millions of tons of coal mined annually. • Approximately one hundred thousand million tons of coal mined cumulatively over the 1975–2000 period. • Many thousands of square kilometers of land strip-mined cumulatively. • Many thousands of square kilometers (collectively) of land adversely affected by subsidence. • Land for approximately 1,000 coal power plants (nominal 1,100 Mw). • Land for several hundred nuclear power plants (nominal 1,100 Mw).	Where LDC urban poor rely on charcoal or firewood, urban demand will result in total denudement of surrounding countryside to as great a distance as 100 kilometers.	Strip mining of coal and uranium will cause land disturbance, and mine tailings will pose radiation danger.

A. Terrestrial Environments (cont.)

Global	Regional (*continental or more than one nation state*)	Local (*subcontinental, individual nation states, or smaller*)	
		Urban	Rural
	• Several tens of thousands of square kilometers of land for transmission lines for new coal and nuclear plants.		
	• Approximately 1,000 million tons of radioactive tailings from supplying uranium for the 1975–2000 period.		
	• Approximately 10 million cubic meters of low-level radioactive wastes.		
	• A few 100,000 tons of spent nuclear fuel.		
	• Several 100,000 tons of spent nuclear fuel over the lifetimes of the plants constructed through the year 2000.		
	Coal development can be expected to be most intense in those areas with large coal deposits (U.S. and Eastern Europe); nuclear development most intense in those areas with limited coal resources (Western Europe. Japan).		
	In the less developed regions (North and Middle Africa. parts of the Middle East. much of Asia. parts of Latin America). the energy impacts will be primarily in organic fuels leading to:		
	• A 650 million cubic meter annual shortfall in fuelwood before 2000. causing (1) combustion of even small bushes and aggravated erosion and desertification. and (2) increased use of dung and crop residues for fuel.		

Nonfuel minerals	Annual combustion of 250–670 million tons of dung by 2000, depriving the soils of the equivalent of $2 billion in chemical fertilizer.	No impact projected.	No impact projected.	The mining of quarries of bauxite, sand, gravel, and limestone, as well as the mining of metallic minerals from hard rock, will result in long-term—sometimes permanent—local land disturbance and loss.

B. ATMOSPHERIC ENVIRONMENTS

Population	No impact projected.	No impact projected.	No impact projected.	No impact projected.
GNP	Some spray-can propellants and some high-altitude aircraft flights may contribute to the depletion of the ozone layer.	No impact projected.	LDC air pollution—especially by toxic substances—will increase if polluting industries move from areas with strong environmental standards to areas with limited or no standards.	
Climate	No impact projected.	No impact projected.	No impact projected.	No impact projected.
Technology	No impact projected.	No impact projected.	No impact projected.	No impact projected.
Agriculture and food	Nitrous oxide release to air from bacterial conversion and nitrogen fertilizer may contribute to depletion of the ozone layer. DDT and other organochlorines enter the atmosphere where they accumulate and are precipitated out in rain, which ultimately will contaminate the oceans.	No impact projected.	No impact projected.	Pesticides sprayed from aircraft may create local air quality problems and poison people and animals. Smoke and dust will create local air quality problems. Land clearing will cause greater weather and microclimate extremes.
Fisheries and marine developments	No impact projected.	No impact projected.	No impact projected.	No impact projected.

A. ATMOSPHERIC ENVIRONMENTS (cont.)

	Global	Regional (continental or more than one nation state)	Local (subcontinental, individual nation states, or smaller)	
			Urban	Rural
Forest exploitation	446 million hectares of forest will be lost as an absorber of atmospheric carbon dioxide (CO_2). CO_2 will be added to the atmosphere as a result of burning a portion of the trees that were on the 446 million hectares cleared.	No impact projected.	No impact projected.	Noticeable increase in humidity will occur near reservoirs and irrigation systems.
Water resource development and regulation	No impact projected.	No impact projected.	No impact projected.	Slight increase in humidity near reservoirs and irrigation systems.
Energy	CO_2 emissions will increase to 26–34 billion short tons per year, roughly double the CO_2 emissions of the mid-1970s. 446 million hectares of CO_2-absorbing forests will be lost. Burning of much of the wood on 446 million hectares will produce more CO_2. Decomposition of much soil humus will release more CO_2. Establishment of trends in fossil fuel combustion and deforestation, which will lead inevitably to significantly larger concentrations of CO_2 in the earth's atmosphere during the 21st century. A doubling of the CO_2 concentration by 2050 could increase the average temperature of the earth by about 3°C, melting much of the polar ice over an estimated period of 200 years and flooding large	In industrialized regions of the world (North America, Eastern and Western Europe, Japan, U.S.S.R., South Africa, and Australia) the annual production and combustion of several thousand million tons of coal will produce regionally significant emissions of particulates, carbon monoxide, nitrogen oxides, sulfur oxides, and toxic heavy metals. In some areas, emission control standards will limit or reduce some emissions. In the U.S., for example, the Department of Energy estimates that under present standards, national emissions of sulfur oxides will decline until 1985 and increase thereafter. In the less developed regions, increased combustion of wood, dung, and coal is not expected to result in multinational or continental air quality problems.	Coal combustion will result in 5 to 20 times more air pollutants (CO, NO_x, SO_2, hydrocarbons, smoke, smog) than at present and higher temperatures than surrounding countryside. LDC cities will probably not demand emission controls on coal power and heating plants, and as a result will experience large increases in many air pollutants, especially sulfur oxides and particulates.	Hotter local weather will occur where forests have been removed for fuelwood or charcoal.

Nonfuel minerals	No impact projected.	...amounts of coastal land.	Increased emissions of sulfur and nitrogen oxides will acidify the rain over wide areas.		No impact projected.

C. Aquatic Environments

Population	No impact projected.	No impact projected.	Human wastes create increasingly severe water pollution problems in many LDC urban areas.		No impact projected.
GNP	No impact projected.	Pollution by toxic wastes from petrochemical, metallurgical, and other industries will accumulate in regional seas and gulfs with slow or restricted water circulation (e.g., Red Sea, Caspian Sea, Persian Gulf, Mediterranean).	In or near large cities—especially in the middle-income LDCs—serious water pollution by organic and inorganic wastes, some highly toxic, can be expected from areas of industrial concentration and ports. Construction on coastal and wetland habitats will reduce spawning and breeding habitats and damage reefs.		
Climate	Climate change of sufficient magnitude to influence global water supplies are thought possible by 2000, but there is no consensus on either the climate change or the associated change in water supply.	Climate change of sufficient magnitude to influence regional water supplies is thought possible by 2000, but there is no consensus on either the climate change or the associated change in water supply.	Climate change of sufficient magnitude to influence local water supplies are thought possible by 2000, but there is no consensus on either the climate change or the associated change in water supply.		No impact projected.
Technology	No impact projected.	No impact projected.	No impact projected.		No impact projected.
Food and agriculture	No impact projected.	Consumptive (evaporative) use of water for irrigation will increase. Surface waters will contain increased amounts of salts, fertilizers, and pesticides. Persistent pesticides and their degradation products, especially the organochlorine group, will accumulate in marine sediments and bioaccumulate in marine food chains.	Pesticide, fertilizer and other chemical manufacturing plants may pollute local waters with effluents.	Streams receiving runoff from farmlands, especially irrigated lands, will receive increased quantities of pesticides, herbicides, sediments, nitrites, and nitrates. Persistent pesticides in runoff will contaminate sediments and near-shore waters and damage spawning and breeding waters. Feedlots and food-processing plants will pollute local waters with organic wastes, depressing dissolved oxygen levels and killing fish.	No impact projected.

C. AQUATIC ENVIRONMENTS (cont.)

	Global	Regional (continental or more than one nation state)	Local (subcontinental, individual nation states, or smaller) — Urban	Local — Rural
Fisheries and marine development	Intensive commercial fishing will continue to deplete oceanic stocks of tuna and other traditionally preferred species.	Populations of preferred fish species may decline in some regional seas (e.g., the Mediterranean) as a result of intensive fishing and pollution. The 200-mile economic zone, on the other hand, may lead to improved management of some regional and national fisheries.	Fishing in heavily polluted rivers, coastal waters, and estuaries will decline or become restricted due to health hazards of toxic chemicals and pathogens.	
Forest exploitation	No impact projected.	Extensive deforestation and land-clearing will alter the hydrology of major rivers, exaggerating extreme high and low flows.	Local streamflow and seasonal floods will increase in basins with deforested watersheds.	Aquifer recharge will diminish following deforestation, reducing ground-water supplies and increasing vulnerability to drought. Intensive tree-farming will add fertilizers and pesticides to local waters.
Water resource development and regulation	No impact projected.	Large-scale dams, impoundments, and modifications of river flows will significantly alter salinity, temperature, and flows of nutrients in estuaries, disrupting the life cycles of many organisms and adversely affecting biological productivity in the affected waters.	Hazards of schistosomiasis, malaria, and other water-borne diseases will be increased significantly through irrigation projects that create and expand habitats for the vectors and hosts of these diseases. Increasing consumptive use of water will diminish the capacity of streams and rivers to carry and degrade wastes, including soil salts. Impoundments on smaller rivers to store water, control floods, and generate electricity will alter hydrologic regimes to the detriment of aquatic productivity, only partially compensated for by still-water fisheries in reservoirs.	
Energy	Open oceans will be polluted by oil from tankers and by atmospheric fallout from the combustion of fossil fuels.	In the industrialized regions of the world (North America, Eastern and Western Europe, Japan, U.S.S.R., South Africa, and Australia), there will be several aquatic	Oil pollution of ports, coastal waters, and estuaries from accidental losses occurring during transfers, or from groundings or collisions. Local waters will experience thermal and other kinds of pollution as a result of coal and nuclear generating plants with once-through cooling,	

impacts of energy development: Acidic drainage from approximately one thousand million tons of coal mined annually will affect water quality and aquatic life over large areas.

Lakes in southern Scandinavia and eastern North America will become acidified as a result of acid rain and snow.

Oil from offshore wells and tankers (operational discharges and accidental spills), and terrestrial runoff will pollute coastal and open ocean areas.

Large increases in the number of coal and nuclear power plants will create a large impact on the aquatic environment through once-through cooling or consumptive, evaporative cooling.

In the less developed regions, two aquatic impacts of energy development can be expected: Stream and river flows will be destabilized as a result of deforestation for fuelwood; oil development and export in petroleum exporting countries will adversely affect water quality and aquatic resources.

which alters aquatic ecology, lowers dissolved oxygen, kills fish eggs, and may cause fish kills.

Consumptive use of water for evaporative cooling in generating plants may be large enough to affect stream flows in some areas, potentially reducing the ability of streams to absorb wastes and degrading water quality locally.

Local streams and rivers will be polluted by acidic drainage from mines.

| Nonfuel minerals | No impact projected. | Deep-sea mining is not expected to produce seriously adverse effects in the short run (years) but the long-term, ultimate effects of bottom disruption, turbidity in the deep ocean waters, and the processing of wastes are still very uncertain. | Deep-sea mining will produce silt and processing wastes that may be locally damaging to marine ecosystems. |

TABLE 13-46 (cont.)

D. Low Probability, High-Risk Events Affecting All Environments

	Global	Regional (continental or more than one nation state)	Local (subcontinental, individual nation states, or smaller)	
			Urban	Rural
Climate	As populations grow, forcing the use of more marginal and arid lands, world food production will become more vulnerable even to (relatively) high-probability variations in climate.	Regional manifestations of the global problem will be significant, especially for South Asia, the United States, the U.S.S.R., and the Sahel region of Africa.	Vulnerability, large increases in prices, and supply interruptions will be especially high in urban areas.	Vulnerability is less in rural areas but, locally, will be severe, as in the African Sahel.
Food and agriculture	Habitat for the wild progenitors of major food crops will continue to be lost while single-variety monocultures expand. As a result, there would be an increased probability of plant epidemics (e.g., the U.S. problem with corn blight in the early 1970s), which could significantly affect world food supplies and markets.	Regional manifestations of the global problem will be experienced.	Urban areas will be more vulnerable to increased prices and supply interruptions.	Rural areas will be less vulnerable than urban areas to supply interruptions and increased prices.
	Increased dependence of agriculture on fossil fuel intensive inputs increases the vulnerability of crop production to disruptions of energy supplies.			
Energy	The increased use of nuclear energy increases the probability of further nuclear proliferation and of nuclear terrorism.	A 226 percent increase in nuclear and hydroelectric (mostly nuclear) generation by 1990 (several hundreds of plants by 2000), will increase the probability of a serious accident in a nuclear reactor or in some other portion of the nuclear cycle.	Local manifestations of the global and regional impacts will be experienced. Increased marine transport of liquefied energy gases will increase the risks of fires or explosions in ports.	No impact projected.

Note: Throughout Table 13-46 the word "will" is used in the sense that an impact will follow if the population, GNP, and resource projections are fulfilled and if there is no change in current environmental projection policies.

be related back to the environmental assumptions in projection models for the discussion of discrepancies and their implications in the section entitled, "Assumptions, Discrepancies, and Feedback."

It should be emphasized here once again that the entries in Table 13–46 and in the following section ("The Global Environment in 2000") summarize impacts *on the environment* implied by the Global 2000 Study's population, GNP, and resource projections. Where an entry in the table indicates "No impact projected," it means simply that the Global 2000 Study's projections for population, GNP, and resources do not imply an impact in this particular area. For example, although there are many indirect implications of the projected increase in human population, the projected increase is not expected to have a direct, global effect on the world's soils. As a result, the first entry in Table 13–46 under Terrestrial Environment is "No impact projected."

The Global Environment in 2000

Most aspects of environmental deterioration are not global in scale, but those that are are serious and troubling indeed. They are serious not only because they develop slowly on a massive scale but also because they are usually not subject to any quick technological fixes. They are troubling not only because data and knowledge on their development and causes are often only sketchy, but also because the institutions studying and addressing these problems are underfunded and understaffed. Furthermore, solutions to many global environmental problems are related directly or indirectly to economic development and population stabilization efforts, and therefore programs to address global environmental problems must inevitably become involved in some of the world's most difficult and complex social, political, and economic problems.

Serious environmental developments on a global scale are clearly in evidence—on the land, in the atmosphere, and in the water. The global problems of the terrestrial environment are considered first.

The World's Terrestrial Environment in 2000. The world has only recently begun to take measure of the universal and momentous nature of trends in the condition of the terrestrial environment. The data now available are largely a result of a series of specialized international conferences and studies sponsored by the United Nations. The general picture is that of a decline in soil quality and productive capacity over much of the planet,

but especially in the difficult or marginal environments, such as mountains, arid lands, and very humid regions. The most massive losses or damages to the world's lands, forests, and genetic wealth have been taking place and will continue to take place in the less developed regions of Africa, Latin America and Asia, but the industrialized countries are also being affected.

Some reference figures are helpful in adding perspective to the discussion of the future of the terrestrial environment. The most basic of these figures is the earth's total area: 51,000 million hectares (510 million square kilometers) or 197 million square miles. Of the earth's total surface, more than 70 percent is ocean (361 million sq km). About 25 percent (132 million sq km) is ice-free land. About 5 percent (26 million sq km) is closed forest and 2 percent (12 million sq km) is open forest and range land. Deserts now cover about 2 percent of the surface area (7.9 million sq km). About 3 percent (15 million sq km) is arable land. Irrigated land amounts to less than 1 percent of the arable total, as does the total urban area.

Table 13–47 presents the major trends in the world's terrestrial environment. In geographic terms, desertification is the most sweeping change. If unchecked, the process of desertification that is claiming range land and some crop land, especially in Africa and Asia, will more than triple the present 7,922 thousand square kilometers of desert in the world, possibly by 2000. Twenty one

TABLE 13–47

Projected Changes in Global Vegetation and Land Resources, 1975–2000

	1975	2000	Change	Percent Change
	millions of hectares			
Deserts	792	1,284	+ 492	+ 62
Closed forests	2,563	2,117	− 446	− 17
Irrigated area	223	273	+ 50	+ 22
Irrigated area damaged by salinization and related problems[a]	111.5	114.6	+ 3.1	+ 3
Arable land	1,477	1,539	+ 62	+ 4

Source: Global 2000 Study projections.

a. Estimated as follows. In Chapter 9 it is estimated that half of the world's total irrigated area is already damaged; thus the 1975 figure is approximately 111.5 million ha. The U.N. estimates (*Desertification: An Overview,* U.N. Conference on Desertification, 1977, p. 12.) that approximately 125,000 ha are degraded annually due to waterlogging, salinization, and alkalinization. Assuming that this annual figure remains constant to the year 2000, a total of 3.1 million ha. would be added to the damaged area, bringing the total to 114.6 million ha.

percent of the earth's ice-free surface would then be desert.

At the other climatic extreme—the humid tropics—deforestation is projected to remove 446 million hectares of closed forest by 2000, thus reducing the amount of the earth's surface covered with closed forests from one-fifth to one-sixth of the total. Because of the low fertility of many soils in the humid tropics, the removal of tropical forests may represent a onetime exploitation with high long-term costs, especially for the survival of local flora and fauna.

At no time in recorded history has the specter of species extinction loomed so ominously. Largely a consequence of deforestation and the "taming" of wild areas, the projected loss over two decades of approximately one-fifth of all species on the planet (at a minimum, roughly 500,000 species of plants and animals) is a prospective loss to the world that is literally beyond evaluation. The genetic and ecological values of wild or newly identified species continue to be discovered. They represent an irreplaceable evolutionary legacy whose value, particularly the value of the many expected to be lost in the tropics, will certainly increase especially if the earth's climate becomes warmer. The fact that humankind derives most of its food from no more than 15 species of plants masks to some extent the importance of genetic extinction, but not for the plant breeders who rely on the traits of wild progenitors of domestic plants in their continuing battle against pests and disease and in efforts to increase yields.

Arable land for agriculture is projected to increase by about 4 percent over the next two decades to a total of 15.4 million square kilometers. This global projection, however, hides a number of important considerations. In some areas the amount of arable land is actually projected to decline. Where arable land is projected to increase, the projection is based on the assumption that capital will be available to bring the land into cultivation at two to three times the present cost per hectare. Furthermore, overall basic land productivity is declining in many areas.

Irrigated lands, a part of the productivity problem, are projected to increase by about 28 percent, again assuming that large amounts of capital will be available for water regulation and irrigation projects. However, one-half of the world's irrigated soils are presently suffering the effects of salinization and alkalinization resulting from inadequate drainage and poor water management. The amount affected will increase during the rest of the century. Barring unprecedented improvements in water and soils management, the

historic and present intractability of this problem does not bode well for irrigation in arid zones. While the areas affected are relatively small, irrigated lands generally have exceptionally high yields, and their loss, or even their reduced productivity, is therefore very important. In the U.S., for example, the extremely productive San Joaquin Valley in California is experiencing increasing problems of salinization.

Worldwide, the productivity of arable, unirrigated land is declining in many areas due to overintensive use. While in the industrialized countries, a loss in natural productivity is partially obscured by heavy use of increasingly expensive, petroleum-based chemical fertilizers, that is not the case in the LDCs. While lack of comprehensive data limits appreciation of the phenomenon, observations in Africa and in India and elsewhere in Asia point to continuing erosion, loss of organic matter, shortened fallow periods, and declining soil quality in the decades ahead.

The prospect of declining soil quality can be seen to be very serious when viewed against a backdrop of increasing population densities on arable lands. The trends in arable hectares per capita throughout the world are illustrated in Figure 13–20. With less than 2000 square meters (one-fifth of a hectare, or one-half acre) of arable land per capita projected for the year 2000 in the LDCs, continuation of the deterioration in soil quality and natural productivity would be disastrous. Nonetheless, since birth rates are not projected to decline to replacement levels anytime soon and since little additional land will be brought into cultivation, very intensive use—and abuse—of land can be expected to continue well into the 21st century.

While there are definite global trends toward soil loss, soil deterioration, and species extinctions, these terrestrial trends are generally subject to remedial action on a national or even local scale. By contrast, the atmosphere and the oceans are examples of global resources held in common, and all nations must inevitably participate in the resolution of problems in these areas. *Institutionally,* therefore, the problems of the atmospheric and aquatic environments are even more difficult of solution than those of the terrestrial environment.*

---

*It can be reasonably argued that terrestrial resources are also, in effect, a global commons problem. Foreign economic assistance and international trade in oil, grain, and forest products involve many nations directly or indirectly in the fate of other nations' terrestrial environments. Nonetheless, each nation does have significantly more control over its soils, forests, and fresh water resources than it does over its share of the world's atmosphere and oceans.

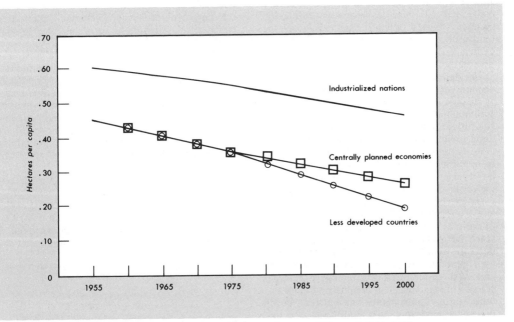

Figure 13-20. Arable land per capita, 1955, 1975, and 2000. (*From Chapter 6, Table 6-13*)

The World's Atmospheric Environment in 2000.
Two global atmospheric changes resulting from anthropogenic pollutants are of great consequence over the long term: the increase in concentrations of carbon dioxide (CO_2) and the depletion of the ozone layer in the stratosphere.

Most climatologists expect a general, global warming as a consequence of increased atmospheric concentrations of CO_2, but the timetable for significant global warming is not agreed upon. The National Academy of Sciences projected a 6° C warming by the latter half of the 22nd century, but it appears very likely that significant global climatic warming could occur long before that time. A panel of scientists assembled by the Department of Energy anticipates that a doubling of atmospheric CO_2 would result in a 2–3° C warming as early as the year 2050.[730]

U.S. analyses of early warming trends are supported by World Meteorological Organization (WMO) reports on atmospheric carbon dioxide. The WMO also suggests that with a doubling of CO_2 the global average temperature would increase by almost 3° C above its present level[731] and that gradual warming of the lower atmosphere, expecially at high altitudes, would create global and regional climatic effects detectable before the end of this century and significant before the end of the next.[732] The Declaration of the 1979 World Climate Conference of the WMO states that the burning of fossil fuels, deforestation, and changes of land use have increased the CO_2 content in the atmosphere by about 15 per cent during the last century and are continuing to increase CO_2 concentrations by about 0.4 per cent per year.[733]

Most recently, four scientists reported to the Council on Environmental Quality on the CO_2 problem, noting—among other things—that the time is at hand when industrialized nations must begin careful consideration of the implications of their energy policies for the CO_2 balance of the atmosphere. The scientists concluded: "If we wait to prove that the climate is warming before we take steps to alleviate the CO_2 build-up, the effects will be well underway and still more difficult to control. The earth will be committed to appreciable changes in climate with unpredictable consequences. The potential disruptions are sufficiently great to warrant the incorporation of the CO_2 problem into all considerations of policy in the development of energy.[734]

A global warming would mean more rain and a melting of polar ice, with a consequent rise in sea level. Temperature increases in polar regions would be 3 or 4 times greater than global averages. If the West Antarctic ice sheets were to melt,* it could raise sea levels worldwide by 5 meters.[735] Even if only a 1° C increase in average temperature were experienced, it would make the earth's climate warmer than it has been at any time in the last 1,000 years.[736]

The date at which significant depletion of the ozone layer could take place is at least as uncertain as the date for significant effects of carbon dioxide accumulation. It is thought that continued use of chlorofluoromethanes at the 1974 rate would reduce global ozone by 14 percent over 50 years. Gases emitted from high-altitude aircraft and from nitrogen fertilizers, thought to have a similar, if lesser, effect on ozone, would also contribute to the depletion.

Ozone absorbs ultraviolet and cosmic radiation, and as a result its depletion allows greater amounts of these biologically potent forms of radiation to reach the earth. It is estimated that a 1 percent decrease in ozone increases ultraviolet radiation by 2 percent. The known consequences of increased ultraviolet radiation include a greater incidence of skin cancer in humans and damage to other species (both plants and animals), but the biological impacts of increased ultraviolet radiation have not been studied extensively.

The World's Aquatic Environment in 2000. Over the next two decades, changes in the world's aquatic environment are expected to occur primarily on or near land. Freshwater will be affected most, followed by changes in coastal marine waters and habitats. The deep open-ocean waters interact only very slowly with surface and coastal waters and are not expected to change significantly by 2000.

The precise nature of freshwater pollution is highly localized, but the general problem of water quality deterioration is global in scope. In the less developed regions, pollution of water supplies by disease pathogens or parasites is perhaps the major problem. In industrialized and urbanized regions, pollution of waterways and ground water by municipal sewage and industrial wastes (toxic chemicals and heavy metals) are principal concerns. In rural areas, nonpoint pollutants—fertilizers, pesticides, salt-laden irrigation drainage, and other contaminants emitted from sources that are difficult or impossible to pinpoint—are of universal concern.

Ultimately, rivers carry many freshwater pollutants to the oceans, and over the next two dec-

_____
*Scientists believe that with a 6° C increase in the earth's average temperature, the melting would require about 200 years.

ades coastal waters will be steadily polluted by oil, persistent chemicals (including organochlorine pesticides), and by heavy metals, even though discharges of these pollutants are controlled in a number of nations. The U.S. alone now discharges 50 million tons of waste per year into the ocean—80 percent of it dredge spoils, 10 percent industrial waste, 9 percent sewage sludge, and 1 percent miscellaneous.[737] In addition, increased offshore oil and gas drilling, a projected 7 percent increase in ocean traffic (including the transport of oil), the mining of the seabed, and the urbanization and industrialization of coastal areas will all contribute to ocean pollution.

Continuing heavy exploitation of coastal fisheries and upwellings, as well as pollution and loss of estuarine habitats, will deplete preferred stocks of fish (e.g., tuna) worldwide. The following trends for fish and shellfish populations are based on the Global 2000 Study projections:

	Annual Harvest (in millions of metric tons)	Trend
Marine species	60	Peak, 1970
Freshwater species	10	Peak, 1975
Marine aquaculture	3	Increasing, 1979
Freshwater aquaculture	3	Increasing, 1979
Total	76	
Demand in year 2000	83.5	

The 200-mile economic zone may lead to improved management of marine fisheries, but the pressures on these resources are expected to continue to increase.

Low-Probability, High-Risk Events Affecting All Environments. By 2000 the world will be more vulnerable to several low-probability high-risk events. Food production will be more vulnerable to fluctuations in climate and to disruptions in energy supplies for fertilizer production, farm machinery fuel, and irrigation. Loss of wild progenitors of major food crops could lead to increased difficulty in maintaining pest and pathogen resistance in high-yield hybrids. A major shift to nuclear power could make the energy sector vulnerable, should a major nuclear accident occur. And a *major* shift to coal could make the energy sector vulnerable, should a serious problem develop with CO_2. While it may be that none of these difficulties will occur, the disruptive potential of such events will increase significantly by 2000.

Special Regional Problems

In addition to the worldwide environmental developments just described, Table 13–46 includes a large number of regional developments involving continents or more than one nation state. Six regional developments are discussed here: (1) the increasing use of coal combustion by industrial regions; (2) their increasing use of nuclear power; (3) fuelwood shortages in rural LDC areas; and developments in (4) regional seas, (5) transnational river basins, and (6) wet tropical regions.

Industrial Regions Turning to Coal. Two large industrial regions are rich in coal resources—the United States and Eastern Europe. It is likely that the coal resources of these regions will be developed much more extensively over the next two decades. While it is not possible to anticipate the environmental consequences in detail, there are broad implications for the land, air, and water of these regions.

The land impacts are primarily associated with coal mining, power plant facilities, and transmission lines. Worldwide, over the 1977–2000 period, approximately 100,000 million tons of coal can be expected to be mined, reaching the rate of several thousand million tons per year by 2000. Strip-mined land would total tens of thousands of square kilometers, and subsidence would affect an additional tens of thousands of square kilometers. Land for more than 1,000 coal-fired power plants would be needed. Additional transmission lines would require many tens of thousands of square kilometers. Much of the affected land would be in the United States and Eastern Europe.

The atmospheric impacts would include significant increases in combustion residuals—particulates, heavy metals, carbon monoxide, nitrogen oxides, and sulfur oxides. Emissions of most of these residuals would depend on the control measures applied, but no economically practical technology is available to control the release of oxides of nitrogen.

The aquatic impacts of increased coal combustion include thermal discharges, increased consumptive uses, and acid drainage. Once-through cooling kills many small organisms and young fish, causes damaging variations in water temperatures and reduces dissolved oxygen concentrations. Evaporative cooling towers are projected to cause the second largest increase in consumptive use of water, and in parts of water-scarce Europe, water for cooling towers may be subject to limiting constraints until other needs have been met. In the

U.S., water for coal processing and the production of synthetic fuels may pose constraints in the arid West. Increased deep- and surface-mining could easily lead to much water pollution in the U.S. and Europe, especially with silt and acid. The U.S. has recently passed strip-mining legislation, but it remains to be seen how effectively the legislation can be enforced.

Increased emissions of oxides of nitrogen and sulfur will aggravate another aquatic effect of increased coal combustion—the acidification of rain. Acid rain is already a problem not only for northeastern Europe and the U.S. but also for neighboring states. Weather patterns carry the emissions and contaminated water vapor north of the industrial centers in northern Europe and the northeastern U.S. Thousands of lakes and streams in southern Sweden and Norway, in the U.S. Adirondacks, and in adjacent areas in Canada have been damaged—perhaps irreparably—by acid rain. These waters normally yield abundant arctic char, salmon, and trout, but are losing much of their aquatic life as the acidity increases. Lower forms of aquatic life and juvenile life forms are extinguished by the excessive acidity caused by the rain. Evidence has now been presented suggesting that the emissions that cause acid rain may travel more than 10,000 kilometers to contribute to atmospheric haze in the Arctic.[738] The shift to more coal use will aggravate future acid rain problems.

Industrialized Regions Turning to Nuclear Power. Neither Western Europe nor Japan have large coal resources and may, as a result, turn increasingly to nuclear power in the decades ahead. A shift toward nuclear power would bring its own environmental impacts, starting with the mining of uranium. In addition to the land disturbed, thousands of millions of tons of radioactive tailings will result from supplying uranium for the world over the 1977–2000 period.

The nuclear plants and transmission lines themselves require large amounts of land. The projected 226 percent increase in nuclear and hydroelectric generation by 1990 (most of it nuclear) will require hundreds of additional nuclear power plants. By the year 2000, the spent nuclear fuel will accumulate in amounts measured in hundreds of thousands of tons. There will also be more than 10 million cubic meters of low-level wastes that will have to be stored somewhere. In view of local opposition to locating such plants in many areas and of even more widespread opposition to storing radioactive wastes in most localities, it is not at all clear where these plants will be located or where the radioactive materials will eventually be stored.

The reactor accident and its aftermath at Three Mile Island, Pennsylvania, in March and April 1979, dramatized the hazards of nuclear power. Subsequent reviews and investigations are sharpening the basis for assessing and reducing the risks of nuclear power, but it is now virtually certain—at least in the United States—that the development of nuclear power will be delayed. It will be more closely regulated and, as a result, will become more expensive.

Fuelwood Shortages in the LDCs. By 1994, there will be a 650 million cubic meter shortfall in fuelwood in the LDCs, according to the Food and Agriculture Organization. This shortfall is about one-half the present fuelwood consumption in LDCs and would furnish the cooking and heating needs of approximately 650 million persons. Today, by comparison, an estimated 1.5 billion persons warm themselves and cook with wood. The numbers will surely increase as long as the price of alternative fuels continues to increase more rapidly than income.

The fuelwood shortage will be felt throughout the world, especially in the semiarid regions. These same semiarid regions are threatened by desertification, and of course fuelwood exploitation of the slow-growing trees in open woodlands and "bush" of Africa and Asia is one of the primary causes of desertification. Fuelwood shortages will also affect the populations of high mountains in LDCs where tree growth is slow and human numbers are high—the Himalayas, the Hindu Kush range, the Andes of South America, and other, lesser massifs.

Statistical data on the open woodlands of the world and the woody vegetation of semiarid regions are limited, but it is known that approximately 50 percent of the world's total open woodlands are in Africa and 12 percent in South America. The fuelwood crisis has already afflicted Africa seriously and shows no sign of easing soon. Firewood and charcoal production account for 90 percent of the total forest exploitation on that continent. In the Sahel, the present rate of reforestation, an inconsequential 3,000 hectares per year, is far, far below the 150,000 hectares that needs to be planted there each year if future demands are to be met.

To reverse the fuelwood shortage trend, truly dramatic increases in the establishment of fuelwood plantations will have to be made worldwide. If the trend is not reversed, all other vegetation (and dung as well) will be used for fuel in the

affected areas, as is already the case in parts of India, Nepal, Sahelian Africa, and South America. Most of the people living in semiarid zones threatened by desertification are pastoralists and herdsmen, and the resulting disappearance of soil organic matter will have disastrous effects on their ability to feed themselves and their animals. The carrying capacity of the land will decline as soils lose the fertility and water-holding capacity provided by organic matter. Outmigration or starvation (or both) will accompany this scenario of land degradation. As many as 600 million people now living in the zones threatened by desertification would cause (and would ultimately be victimized by) this process.

Pollution of Regional Seas. Many regional seas, or gulfs with relatively poor circulation, are suffering from land-based pollution introduced by rivers or directly by sewage pipes from cities and industrial sites. The Mediterranean Sea, the Persian Gulf, and the Caspian Sea exemplify this problem.

The threat to the Persian Gulf is growing rapidly. Sixty percent of all the oil carried by ships throughout the world moves through the shallow Persian Gulf. There are 20 existing or planned major industrial centers along the coast. Heavy pollution of the Persian Gulf as well as the Mediterranean has resulted in international, antipollution agreements and action plans, sponsored by the United Nations Environment Program. These plans, a first step toward cleanup, are also intended to prevent further deterioration and to improve documentation concerning pollution levels and the resources affected.[739]

Transnational River Basin Development. Of the world's 200 large rivers, 148 are shared by two states and 52 by 3–10 countries each. Examples include the Nile, shared by Ethiopia, Uganda, Sudan, and Egypt; the lower Mekong River, shared by Laos, Thailand, Vietnam, and Cambodia; the Plata, shared by Brazil, Bolivia, Uruguay, Paraguay, and Argentina; and the Ganges shared by Nepal, India, and Bangladesh.

Large-scale development in transnational river basins often have environmental impacts that extend across national borders. Difficult political problems of international equity result from the ecological and socioeconomic impacts that follow from urgently needed dams and by flood-control, drainage, and irrigation projects. Downstream states may experience costs while upstream states enjoy the benefits. Reduced flows, sudden changes in flows (related to generation of peak power), dislocation of populations from reservoir sites, water-related diseases (such as malaria and schistosomiasis) associated with man-made lakes and irrigation projects, and water quality problems resulting from agricultural runoff—all are problems of river development with the potential to stir up international conflicts. Rivers, such as the Euphrates and the Jordan, running through water-short regions will be especially susceptible to development conflicts.

The LDCs in particular will have to grapple with these difficult problems, since their hydroelectric power generating potential is relatively undeveloped. Increased petroleum prices have greatly enhanced the economics of hydroelectric power in the LDCs, and the needs for flood control and increased irrigation (assumed in the food projections) are similarly compelling.

Wet Tropical Regions. Forty percent of the remaining 1,680 million hectares of "closed" tropical forest will have been destroyed by 2000, according to the forestry projections in Chapter 8. Much or most of this destruction will occur in the Amazon Basin, in the Indonesian territories of Sumatra, Kalimantan, and West Irian, and in Papua New Guniea. Equatorial Africa's small amount of closed tropical forest (approximately 40 million hectares) will be all but gone by 2000. Increases in firewood gathering, shifting agriculture, permanent agriculture, and industrial forestry will all contribute to this destruction of the world's tropical forests.

The fate of these deforested areas remains in doubt. The intensification of shifting agriculture through shortened fallow periods will degrade large areas or force their conversion to grazing land. Relatively little of the forested land is projected to have been converted to permanent agriculture. Portions may succumb to laterization while other areas will be invaded by cogon grass (*Imperata cylindrica*) or other vigorous weed species that will be virtually impossible to exclude as soil fertility declines. Regions with almost sterile soils will become useless, covered with grass too coarse for cattle. This case is exemplified by the quartzite sands of the Gran Sabana regions of Venezuela, once forested by broadleafed trees, now covered only by short grass. There has been no natural regeneration of the trees. Large areas will be degraded forest—devoid of commercially valuable species—but will still be heavily vegetated.

In addition to the loss of productivity, deforestation of these humid regions will render extinct as much as one-half of their genetic heritage, representing anywhere from 375,000 species to well over a million. The loss is incalcuable since most of the tropical gene pool has not been identified and studied, but if the wet tropics contain one-third of the world's species, as scientists have estimated, the projected losses will be truly momentous.

Deterioration of Urban Environments

A general worsening of urban environments in the less developed countries is a virtual certainty, with population growth and poverty as the most important factors. As illustrated in Table 13–48, the population of LDC cities is projected to grow at the extraordinary rate of 4.3 percent per year, almost tripling over the 1975–2000 period. Of the 2.2 billion total world increase in population between 1975 and 2000, almost half—930 million additional persons—will live in LDC cities. The *increase* in LDC urban populations is projected to be larger than the entire 1975 urban population of the world. Although LDC economic growth is expected to be concentrated in urban areas, it is doubtful that LDC cities will have the resources necessary to keep pace with the increasing needs for public services and facilities.

To keep pace with the projected increases in needs during the next two decades, LDC cities would have to essentially triple all of the facilities and services that have been built up over the past centuries. The chances of this happening are unlikely at best. Water supplies and sanitation services in most LDC cities and surrounding slums are already being rendered obsolete by rapid population influxes. Almost 1.5 billion persons in LDCs—more than one-third of the world's total population—presently lack safe water and waste disposal facilities. LDC cities will also be hard pressed to provide food and the sanitary conditions for safe food distribution. Most LDC cities have only very limited sewage systems, or none at all. Noise, congestion, and air pollution are as bad—or worse—in many LDC cities as they are in industrialized nation cities. Infant mortality

TABLE 13–48

Urban Population in All Cities of 100,000 or More

	1950	1975	2000
	millions		
World	392	983	2,167
Industrialized countries	262	503	756
Less developed countries	130	480	1,411

Source: Trends and Prospects in the Populations of Urban Agglomerations 1950–2000, as Assessed in 1973–1975, New York: United Nations, 1975.

continues to be high in LDC urban slums and uncontrolled settlements partly because of diseases (such as diarrhea) related to poor sanitation and contaminated water and because of inadequate diets, which increase susceptibility to diseases. Already most of the 35,000 infants and children under the age of 5 who die throughout the world each day were born and died in the LDCs, and the proportion is likely to increase in the years ahead.

Urban populations in industrialized countries are also projected to increase over the next two decades, but at a relatively manageable 1.6 percent per year. However, even this growth rate leads to a 50 percent increase over the 1975–2000 period.

Urban areas in industrialized countries are likely to be most adversely affected by deteriorating air quality resulting from a large increase in coal combustion and from the possibility that some nations will relax emission standards so as to reduce the economic costs of emission control. While national energy plans are by no means firm, and while the energy projections anticipate only a modest 13 percent increase in coal combustion by 1990, many observers anticipate large increases. The health and environmental consequences of an increased use of coal will be determined by the stringency of environmental controls. If there is no change of policy (the Global 2000 Study's standard assumption) emissions can be expected to begin increasing in at least some parts of the world. In the U.S., for example, a middle-range energy scenario developed by the Department of Energy shows sulfur oxide emissions decreasing through 1985 but increasing thereafter as a result of increased coal combustion and the slow retirement of old power plants. Similar trends can be expected elsewhere. In fact, in some areas there may even be efforts to relax present emission standards because of the economic costs entailed.

However, the human health consequences of exposure to air pollutants may be more serious in LDC cities than in the cities of industrialized nations. Emissions from increased coal combustion in LDC cities are not likely to be tightly regulated, and some highly polluting industries (including some emitting toxic substances) are avoiding regulations in industrialized nations by locating plants in LDCs, where there are far fewer regulations.[740] Furthermore, the health impacts of air pollutants in LDC cities are likely to be complicated—especially in the poorer sections— by poverty, disease, and poor nutrition.

Assumptions, Discrepancies, and Feedback

With completion of the description of the future world environment as it is implied by the population, GNP, and resource projections of Global 2000, the shift can now be made to an examination of the effect the environment will have *on* these population, GNP, and resource projections. As illustrated in Figure 13–1 earlier in this chapter, this is the point at which the closing of the feedback loops can begin. As already noted, the loops cannot actually be closed analytically here, but the implications of the lack of closure can be analyzed to a degree. The basic process to be used is (1) to identify the environmental assumptions, both implicit and explicit, that were made in developing the population, GNP, and resource projections, (2) to compare these assumptions wth the future world environment (terrestrial, atmospheric, and aquatic), as treated in the preceding section and in Table 13–46, (3) to note the differences (discrepancies) between the assumptions and the environmental perspective, and (4) to consider how these discrepancies would feed back to and alter the population, GNP, and resource projections.

The actual tracing through of the assumptions, discrepancies, and effects becomes quite complicated because of the number of feedback loops involved. The two loops shown in Figure 13–1 linking back to the two driving-force projections (population, and GNP) and the resource projections are highly simplified representations of the myriad ways the environment influences the prospects for future developments in populations, GNP, and resources. Analysis of these influences on the population and GNP projections is particularly complex because many of the environmental influences from these projections come indirectly through the resource projections.

As an aid to systematic discussion of these many influences, Figure 13–21 presents a conceptual model of the major feedbacks linking the environmental projections back to the other projections. This conceptual model underlies the discussion that follows. The Global 2000 population, GNP, and resource projections imply a future world environment (summarized in Table 13–46). When this world environment is compared with the assumptions that are inherent in the population, GNP, and resource projections, a number of significant discrepancies appear. The discrepancies generally result from unrealistic assumptions in the population, GNP, and resource projections about the ability of the environment

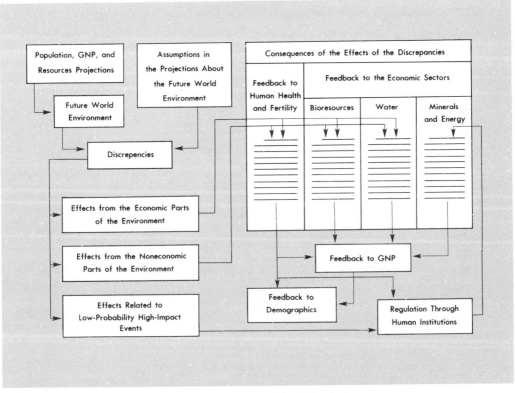

Figure 13-21. Conceptual model for closing the loops.

to supply increased goods and services. The effects of the discrepancies are traced through the environment to consequences which feed back to human health and the economic sectors. The collective consequences are subsequently traced on through the human health and the economic sectors for their secondary consequences and their feedback to the GNP and demographic projections. The discussion of the feedback to the economic sectors includes illustrative economic impacts that are referred to later in the discussion of feedbacks to GNP.

Developments in the environment have virtually no *direct* effect on the mineral and energy sectors of industrialized economies. (Fuel and nonfuel deposits and mining operations are not affected directly by, for example, water pollution, air pollution, and species extinctions.) However, there are significant indirect effects. These indirect effects arise largely through human health effects and low-probability high-impact events that lead (through human institutions) to tighter

environmental (and safety and health) regulation of the mineral and energy sectors.

The effects of the discrepancies that feed back onto human health and the economic sectors are disaggregated into two categories in Figure 13–21: effects from the "economic" and effects from the "noneconomic" parts of the environment. The distinction is between those aspects of the environment on which markets place economic value (e.g., land, water, forests, fish stocks) and those aspects of the environment on which markets place relatively little—or no—economic value (e.g., population of insect predators, pollinating insects, decomposer organisms, and nitrogen-fixing bacteria; spawning habits; and a variety of biological and ecological *processes*, such as the annual flooding or drying cycles that trigger reproductive behavior in fish and other species). This distinction is made to emphasize a point made years ago by Aldo Leopold, namely, that one cannot expect the "economic" parts of the

TABLE 13–49

Environmental Assumptions Inherent in the Population, GNP, and Resource Projections

Population	The population projections anticipate declines in fertility and mortality, partly because of an assumption that environmental conditions affecting human populations will improve significantly over the next two decades. The lack of consideration of migration assumes implicitly that differences in environmental conditions will not lead to significant migration.
GNP	The GNP projections make no explicit environmental assumptions. Implicitly, however, they assume that over the next two decades the environment will supply goods and services free (or at no increase in cost), in vastly increased amounts and without breakdown or interruption.
Food and agriculture	The food and agriculture projections take into account losses of arable land due to urbanization and assume (1) that other losses and deterioration of soil will occur at about the same rate as in the past, (2) that losses of soil and soil fertility can be made up through the application of increased amounts of fertilizers, pesticides, and irrigation water, and (3) that losses to insects and plant diseases will not increase significantly.
Forestry	The forestry projections assume that the adverse effects of deforestation and forest simplification will not reduce the rapid rate of large amounts of deforestation, especially in the tropics. The projections assume, further, that serious deterioration of soils will follow much of the anticipated deforestation but that there is potential for applying intensive methods of silviculture through the use of rapidly growing species and, possibly, the use of fertilizers.
Water	The water projections do not specfically address environmental developments that may affect water supplies and quality; they assume implicitly that environmental developments will not significantly alter future water supplies.
Marine	The marine projections note that pollution of the ocean will ultimately, if continued, adversely affect fish stocks and catches but significant effects are not expected by 2000.
Energy	The energy projections make no explicit environmental assumptions and assume implicitly that environmental considerations and regulations will not interfere with achieving the 56 percent increase in the use of fossil fuel and nuclear energy projected for 1990. The projections also assume that there will be no significant increase in the cost of pollution control.
Minerals	The minerals projections include no explicit environmental assumptions and assume implicitly that the environmental implications of mining and refining will not lead to further regulation and increased costs, and that lands now containing mineral resources or reserves will not be protected in any way that would make the mineral resources unavailable for exploitation.

environment to function without the "noneconomic" parts.

The environmental assumptions inherent in the population, GNP and resource projections are summarized in Table 13–49. With few exceptions, the models do not have provisions for explicit environmental assumptions, and as a result, the environmental assumptions tend to be implicit and, in some cases, quite vague.

Before discussing the assumptions of the individual projections, a point concerning time lags must be stressed. The population, GNP, and resource projections imply a number of environmental impacts that will not nearly have run their courses by 2000. The continued flow of long-lived, toxic organochlorines (e.g., PCBs and DDT) into the world's oceans is but one example. In these cases, time lags occur between the causal action (the developments implied by the population, GNP, and resource projections) and the ultimate feedback, through the environment, back to the projection.

In many cases (such as soil deterioration, species extinctions, and CO_2 accumulations) the projections lead to environmental feedbacks that will not have produced their total effect until well beyond 2000.

Feedback to the Forestry Projections

Of all the resource projections, the forestry projections may have the most significance for the future world environment. Feedback to these projections is therefore taken up first.

The forestry projections are based on only a few environmental assumptions: (1) that the adverse effects of deforestation will not lead to regulation and control of deforestation, especially in the tropics; (2) that serious deterioration of soils will follow much of the anticipated deforestation in the tropics; and (3) that in most of the areas to be deforested there is potential for intensive methods of silviculture using fast-growing species and, possibly, fertilizers. The projections themselves, being extrapolations of historic trends, assume that the 18–20 million hectare annual net deforestation rate will remain constant despite growth in population and economic activity.

There are relatively few discrepancies between the environmental assumptions underlying the forestry projections and the future world environment implied by all of the projections. Serious soil deterioration is expected. In some tropical areas there may be potential for intensive silvicultural methods with pesticides, fertilizers, and fast-growing species. However, this potential certainly does not extend to all of the areas expected to be deforested, and where the potential does exist, it will be reduced by the extinction of both locally adapted, fast-growing tree species and insect predators, especially birds and predatory insects.

The environment projections summarized in Table 13–46 imply a significant increase in the acidity and extent of acid rain. This development may reduce forest growth in some areas, especially in northern Europe, the northeastern U.S., southern Canada, and parts of the U.S.S.R. Acidification of soil may also occur over a period of years. The acid rain phenomena will probably reduce rates of growth and increase the difficulty of reforestation efforts.

The environment projections also imply that significant forest areas will be inundated by water development projects. For the most part the affected areas will be deforested before flooding; so the primary effect on the forestry projections would be to reduce the area available for reforestation.

The most significant environmental assumption in the forestry projections is that the adverse effects of deforestation will not lead to regulation and control. The adverse effects of deforestation—deterioration of soils (permanent in some cases), the extinction of hundreds of thousands of species, the destabilization of hydrologic flows, the increase in atmospheric carbon dioxide (CO_2), the loss of large amounts of CO_2-absorbing vegetation—are all of such significance as to raise the possibility of a major change in forest policy throughout the world, especially in the LDCs. Although there are some small encouraging signs in individual countries (as noted in Chapter 8 and in the forestry section of this chapter), large, rapidly growing populations of the rural poor in many LDCs make careful management of forests for timber production and other uses increasingly difficult. The forests of mountain regions, so essential to soil protection and runoff control, are particularly endangered by encroaching populations of land-hungry rural poor. The slow-growing

trees of the open forests of the world's arid lands are similarly vulnerable to expanding rural populations and their needs for wood for fuel and construction. And finally, it must be remembered that the forestry projections assume that the net rate of deforestation will *not* increase with increasing populations.

All things considered, the environmental assumptions underlying the forestry projections are generally consistent with the environment projections, and environmental feedback is not likely to alter the forestry projections significantly. If anything (as the forestry projections also conclude), the anticipated loss of only one-fifth of the world's remaining forests over the next two decades "represents a mildly optimistic scenario."

Feedback to the Water Projections

As noted in the water projections, meaningful statements describing water supply can be made only for relatively small areas, and then only after detailed on-site investigations of the water resources available. Unfortunately, data are not forthcoming for assessing global water resources and their future on an area by area basis, and as a result the water projections are presented on the basis of national and world averages.

The averaging process vastly overstates available water resources. Virtually every area as large as a nation has areas with substantial surpluses of water as well as areas of water shortage. The U.S. is an example. The Pacific Northwest as a region has ample—even surplus—water, whereas the Southwest has severe water limitations. The aggregation of the water resources of these two regions into average figures for the U.S. implicitly assumes that water from surplus areas can be made available to water-limited areas. In reality, however, surplus water throughout the world goes unused. Some of it will continue to go unused unless large numbers of very large, very expensive hydraulic works are constructed. Some of it will remain unused because of the energy and economic costs of lifting water considerable heights.

The projections focus on rates of replenishment of water resources. The rates of replenishment are assumed to be measured approximately by the total surface drainage from an area. This assumption overestimates water resource replenishment in some areas and underestimates it in others. The assumption overestimates replenishment in areas drawing on fossil waters because here the replenishment is essentially zero. In other areas the assumption underestimates replenishment (or at least the availability of water of altered quality) because it neglects reuse possibilities.

The projections address both withdrawals of water (water that is potentially available for reuse) and consumptive use of water (largely evaporative uses that preclude reuse) but do not consider in-stream uses. Issues relating to transportation, aquatic habitats, water as an energy resource, flood-plain agriculture, and water quality are not considered.

In addition to the assumptions and emphases mentioned above, the water resource projections are based on several other important assumptions.

The projections assume that an approximate 50 percent increase in world population and a 146 percent increase in economic activities will roughly double the demand for water in nearly half of the countries of the world by the year 2000. They recognize that arid regions will experience water shortages long before 2000 but do not address the shortages that will be entailed by the need to preserve river flows for carrying away wastes. Existing water quality problems for irrigation (i.e, salt) and potable water supplies (pathogens and toxic substances) are noted but are not related quantitatively to the water shortages already occurring in many localities. The projections set forth various ways to deal with water shortages: augmentation of supplies (storage and reuse), reduction of water use (pricing policy, regulation, technological innovation), and allocation. The influence of possible climate changes and of anticipated land-use changes on supplies are not considered. Interrelationships between water quality and flow on the one hand and the living resources of streams, lakes, and the oceans on the other are not taken into account.

A comparison of the assumptions underlying the water projections with the environmental projections brings out a number of discrepancies. These discrepancies relate to the effects of (1) land-use changes, (2) possible climate changes, (3) changes in consumptive uses, (4) changes in water quality, and (5) habitat changes.

Effects of Land-Use Changes. Perhaps the most significant land-use change projected for 2000 is extensive deforestation, which has dramatic implications for water availability. Lacking the regulating effect of forests in the upper elevations of river basins, water flows will become more extreme during both the high and low flow periods. Water supplies will be reduced in both quantity and quality. The reduction in quantity will be a result of rapid runoff, which cannot be retained for later use. The reduction in quality will be a result of the increased silt loads that accompany increased erosion.

The LDC forests will be most affected. The tropical rivers of Africa and Latin America carry enormous quantities of water and will become highly destructive if their peak flows are augmented. Similar problems can be anticipated in parts of Africa and in Asia. The remaining forests of the Himalayan range are particularly important since the waters of the range feed a number of large rivers that supply the needs of millions of persons. It is estimated that by the year 2000 the Ganges Basin alone will contain 500 million persons, who will be dependent on that river for agricultural, industrial, and drinking water.

The steep and rugged terrain of the Himalayas and the Andean ranges prohibit the construction of the large dams that might tame their rivers and regulate their flows. Consequently only vegetative cover and special land management can be employed to control runoff. The denuding of catchments will exaggerate high flows and high sediment loads, and will reduce dry-season flows. These changes will in turn lead to extreme problems in the management of irrigation systems and impoundments throughout the affected regions.

A world survey has yet to be made of the economic impact on water projects of the sedimentation, greater fluctuations in flow, and more frequent flood peaks that result from vegetative changes in steep catchments. It was expected that large impoundments such as Volta Lake in Ghana or Lake Nasser behind the Aswan Dam would have useful "lives" of 100 years or more, but these and other lakes and dams will have much shorter lives if sedimentation increases. Wherever major denuding occurs upstream of a large reservoir, accelerated filling by sediments is likely to become evident by the year 2000, and in small rivers with high sediment loads, impoundments may become economically infeasible because of the short time it would take them to fill with sediment.

Deforestation would also affect ground-water recharge and, ultimately, flows from springs. This effect is well established, but the extent of its impact across the world is undocumented and difficult to assess because subsurface water movements can only be determined by carefully executed surveys using radioactive isotopes or dyes.

Effects of Possible Changes in Climate. In addition to the effects of deforestation, potential changes in climate would certainly affect water supplies. There is not full agreement among climatologists either as to the climate changes anticipated or as to their consequences for water supplies, but many climatologists associate increased variability and reduced rainfall with a cooling trend, and increased rainfall (except perhaps in the south central area—dustbowl of the 1930s—of the U.S.) with an increase in temperature.

Effects of Changes in Consumptive Uses. Over and above the effects of deforestation and possible climatic change, water availability will be influenced by increased consumptive uses of water for irrigation and for the discharge of waste heat through evaporative cooling towers. Thermal electric (coal and nuclear) power plants discharge approximately two-thirds of their input energy as waste heat; increasingly these discharges are through evaporative cooling towers. By 2000 the consumptive use of water for waste heat discharges is expected to be regionally significant in the U.S., Europe and Japan.

The biggest increase in consumptive (evaporative) use of water will come about as a result of the growth in irrigated agriculture.

Irrigation is already the largest consumptive use of water, and although the agricultural projections are not specific as to the amount of additional irrigation implied, it is clearly large. The projections suggest that the pressure on water resources due to irrigation of arid lands is likely to increase even more rapidly than pressures on arable land resources, which will increase by only about 4 percent in area by the year 2000 over the 1971–75 average figure. The increased consumptive use of water in agriculture will decrease the supply of water available for other uses, especially for energy applications.

Effects of Changes in Water Quality. Irrigation will decrease water availability in yet another way. Salts washed out of the soils will enter streams and rivers, contributing to a general decrease in water quality and in some areas effectively reducing water supplies by rendering water unfit for reuse.

There is an important linkage between the environmental implications of the agricultural and water projections. The agricultural projections anticipate both increases in irrigated land and a net increase in arable land over and above land losses. To achieve the increase in arable and irrigated land anticipated, marginal arid lands will be brought into cultivation, in some areas through irrigation and the removal of soil salts. However, the problems of salinization in irrigated soils are resolved only by flushing salts out of the soil with water. The rivers and streams that receive the salt-laden drain water become increasingly salty. As the water projections note, the buildup of concentrations of salts in rivers flowing through irrigated lands in arid regions is inevitable. The result downstream is water unfit for irrigation. This phenomenon has no solution other than the removal of salts.

Desalting rivers is expensive. A 104-million gallon per day desalting plant under construction at Yuma, Arizona, will cost an estimated $315 million. It will reduce the salinity of the Colorado River as it passes from the U.S. into Mexico from 850 milligrams per liter (mg/l) to 115 mg/l in accordance with a 1973 agreement. Without the plant, the Bureau of Reclamation projected that salinity levels would climb to 1,300 mg/l milligrams per liter by 2000, and that every additional milligram per liter of salt would cause an equivalent of $230,000 in damages annually to water users in the lower reaches of the river.[741]

Desalting rivers also requires energy. The Yuma plant will require 4.3 megawatts of hydroelectric energy to run the pumps that supply pressure for reversed osmotic desalinization. The electric generative use of the water, therefore, also competes with irrigation use. Of the plant's input waters, 70 percent emerge at 250 parts per million (ppm) salt concentration and flow back into the river; 30 percent emerge at 9,000 ppm and flow into a briny lagoon. Wind and solar generation methods are being considered to reduce the hydroelectric demands of the plant.

If the assumption in the food and agriculture projections is correct—namely that there will be significant increases in the agricultural use of arid lands through irrigation—large water losses (through evaporation) from the supplying streams and rivers are inevitable. At the same time, salts will be flushed out of the soils. More salt and less water means higher salt concentrations downstream. Accordingly, one of two results will follow: Irrigated farming costs will either increase significantly so as to include the cost of salt removal, or the salts from the fields of farmers upstream will be added to those in the fields of farmers downstream.

Salts are not the only way in which the environmental implications of the food projections impact on water quality. The use of fertilizers, pesticides, and herbicides is projected to double on a global average but to quadruple in the LDCs. The fertilizer runoff will lead to the eutrophication of many lakes and streams especially in the LDCs. Contamination with pesticides will reduce the possibilities for aquaculture, reducing the availability of badly needed fish protein. Probably the net effect in the LDCs will be to reduce the amount of water that is safely available for fish culture and for human consumption.

Other decreases in water quality will also occur. In addition to salts and pesticides, increasing amounts of fertilizers, toxic substances, oil, disease pathogens, acids (from mine drainage and acid rain), and sediments can be expected to enter the world's waters, especially in the LDCs. The net effect will again be either a reduction in the safety of the water available for various uses or increased costs of protecting water supplies.

The economic costs of water protection are significant. In the U.S., for example, a predecessor of EPA—the Federal Water Pollution Control Administration (FWPCA)—attempted to estimate the ultimate costs of water protection in 1970 as this nation was beginning seriously to clean up its waters. The FWPCA concluded that it would cost $4.4 billion to bring municipal water treatment systems up to desired standards, and that additional needs related to urban and suburban growth would bring the total to $10 billion for the 1970–75 period.[742] The total public expenditures in the U.S. on water-pollution control for the 1977–86 period is now estimated to be on the order of $200 billion,[743] and the portion of these costs associated with potable water may go still higher.

Habitat Changes. Both the water and the food projections explicitly or implicitly assume the development of many more water-regulation projects—dams, dikes, canals, etc. The severe ecological consequences of many of these projects are beginning to be examined more carefully during the planning process. As a result, some planned projects can be expected to be delayed, redesigned, or dropped in the years ahead.

The LDCs can anticipate the largest ecological impacts as a result of future water development for two reasons. First, the industrialized nations have already developed most of their water resources, and while some further development will occur, it will probably proceed with caution informed by the ecological results of earlier, less cautious developments. Water resources in the LDCs are less developed and more likely to proceed with relatively less careful consideration of the ecological consequences.

The second reason is that water development leads to a number of severe ecological changes in the LDCs that do not occur (or occur to a much lesser degree) in the industrialized nations. Probably the most significant of these ecological changes is the spread of habitat for disease vectors and hosts. The implications of large dams and irrigation projects for the spread of malaria, schistosomiasis, and river blindness will be of increas-

ing concern to water planners throughout the world, and it is likely that a number of large water developments now planned in LDCs will be delayed or abandoned in the years ahead when their ecological implications are better understood. In this way ecological and habitat considerations will feed back to influence the water projections.

The preceding comparisons of the assumptions underlying the water projections with the environmental projections bring out a number of discrepancies relating to changes in land use, climate (possibly), consumptive uses, water quality, ecology, and habitat. These discrepancies cannot be related quantitatively to the water projections, but they all support the general conclusion of the water projections, namely that throughout the world, even before the year 2000, shortages of water of usable quality can be expected to become more frequent, more extensive, and more severe than those being experienced today.

Feedback to the Food and Agriculture Projections

The environmental assumptions in the food and agriculture projections take into account some, but not all, of the influences that follow from the environmental projections. The major environmental assumptions underlying the food and agriculture projections are as follows:

- Weather variability (but not global climate change) is analyzed as the principal variable in the three alternative projections of food production, and as a result climate overall is assumed to remain favorable over the next two decades.

- Some land is assumed to be lost to urbanization (and perhaps other causes), but the amounts assumed lost to specific causes are not indicated. Trends in *net* arable area provide some clues and are given in Chapter 6 in Table 6–12. By 2000, the amounts of arable land in North Africa, the Middle East, and South Asia are projected to *decline* (relative to areas under cultivation in 1985) as the "economic and environmental costs of maintaining cultivated areas near physical maxima become prohibitive."

- The projections assume that increasing inputs of fertilizer and irrigation and other energy-intensive inputs will compensate for erosion and the other forms of land deterioration now being experienced throughout the world.

- Deterioration of range lands is not specifically addressed in the projections and is assumed implicitly not to be a constraining factor on the projected livestock production.

- The projections assume that substantially increased amounts of water will be available for irrigation, but the specific water assumptions are unclear. The text of Chapter 6 indicates that water management for irrigation could become the single most important constraint to increasing yields in the LDCs, but the quantitative implications of water constraints are not analyzed. Also, the extent to which irrigation is leading to the salinization of soils is not discussed.

- The continuing losses of diverse local (and wild) crop strains is implicitly assumed not to adversely affect the success of plant breeders in developing still higher-yielding varieties and protecting food crops against pests and pathogens. Yields are assumed to continue increasing at essentially the same rates as in the past two decades.

- Pollution by pesticides and fertilizers is assumed not to constrain the use of pesticides and fertilizers. Pollution is mentioned in Chapter 6 as a potential problem particularly in the LDCs, but it is also implied that these countries will have neither the capacity nor the motivation to control fertilizer and pesticide pollution, especially if controls would reduce yields.

It is notable that the projections foresee only a small increase (about 4 percent) in arable land over the last quarter of this century, and after 1985 decreases are projected in some regions. Land limitations and production constraints, especially water shortages, lead to a decline in per capita food production relative to 1970 levels in North Africa, the Middle East, and the Central African LDCs, and only slight increases in South Asia. In other words, over the period of the projections there will be no major improvement in the food supply for the world's poorest populations, and what improvements do occur will require an increase of 95 percent in the real price of food.

Against this sobering outlook, a comparison of the environmental assumptions in the food projections with the environmental projections gives little reason for optimism. Discrepancies are apparent in connection with land deterioration, losses of genetic resources, pest and disease management problems, water problems, and the effects of air pollution.

Effects of Land Deterioration. Erosion, salinization, alkalinization, waterlogging, compaction, and loss of organic matter are all aspects of the soil deterioration processes at work throughout the world. While soil deterioration is a less easily quantified phenomenon than land lost to urban sprawl, its effects are being felt in both LDCs and industrialized nations.

In the industrialized nations, the primary forms of land deterioration are erosion, compaction, and salinization. The projections assume that continued and increasing quantities of energy-intensive inputs (especially chemical fertilizers, but also irrigation water, herbicides, and pesticides) will compensate for basic declines in soil conditions and productivity. This assumption is supported by past experience. In the U.S., for example, almost two-thirds of the crop land needs treatment for erosion and compaction, but as a result of increasing energy-intensive inputs, yields continue to increase and many large farms continue to make a profit.[744]

The discrepancy between the assumptions of the food projections for industrialized countries and the environmental projection involves the feasibility of continued increases in energy-intensive inputs over the next two decades. Diminishing returns are experienced; input costs are increasing rapidly with energy prices; adverse externalities (such as the effects of toxic pesticides on human and animal health* and ground-water pollution) are becoming matters of concern.

Although there are admittedly some significant exceptions, the issue in most industrialized nations is not irreparable soil damage but the increasing vulnerability of the agricultural sector of the economy to disruption. Present practices lead to three forms of vulnerability. First, present farming practices with energy-intensive inputs and cost-cutting methods lead to soils that are less able to absorb and retain water; rain and irrigation are both of less help to crops, and the soils are more vulnerable to wind erosion during a drought or a shift to a period of dryer climate. Second, diminishing returns on increasingly expensive energy-intensive inputs can be sustained only to a

---

*Many workers in LDC countries use pesticides without adequate training or protection. In Central America, for example, there were 19,300 medically certified pesticide poisonings over the 5-year period 1971–76. Most of the poisonings (17,-000) occurred in El Salvador and Guatemala where there are about 360 cases per year for each 100,000 persons. By comparison, in the U.S. there are only about 0.17 cases per 100,000 persons. In Central America pesticides have also contaminated animals. In 1976 about 500,000 pounds of beef imported to the U.S. from El Salvador were rejected for levels of up to 95 parts per million of DDT; the U.S. threshold level is 5 ("Toxic chemicals: How More than 50 Nations on Five Continents Handle Their Most Deadly Pollutants," *World Environment Report,* June 18, 1979, p. 2).

point, and along the way further soil damage (especially erosion and compaction leading to hardpan soils) will accumulate. When damage is far enough advanced, productivity drops regardless of added fertilizers. Some U.S. soils have reached and passed that point. [745] Third, the food needs of an increasing world population combined with rapid increases in energy prices could lead either to a very rapid increase in the cost of food (effectively pricing a much larger portion of the world's population out of the market) or to a relatively sudden and disruptive shift away from energy-intensive methods of agriculture. Restoration of mildly damaged soils could be accomplished over a decade with fallowing and green manuring with leguminous cover crops, but restoration of severely damaged land would require much longer, and a disruptive effect on production could be expected during the restorative period. The food projections in Chapter 6 note that there are a variety of cultural practices and management techniques available to reduce agricultural dependence on energy-intensive inputs, but the projections question the ability of farmers to maintain or expand production levels while shifting away from energy-intensive inputs.

There is little question, however, that rising input costs and further diminishing returns are in prospect and that a careful and objective analysis of scientific and public policy options for reorientating trends in agriculture is needed. Evidence is accumulating that present research and policy priorities are in need of reorientation, [746] but short-term and institutional interests are also involved. In this connection, David Vail of Bowdoin College asks a very relevant question about agriculture in the industrialized nations: "In view of the power, objectives, and past behavior of the industries (and government agencies) that have shaped and promoted [energy-]intensive technology, is it reasonable to expect a transformation of priorities just because it would be in society's long-run interest?"[747]

For the LDCs, the food projections assume that land deterioration will not be more serious than in past decades because farmers will be aware of the problems, will institute practices preventing more extensive deterioration, and will charge more for their crops to cover increased costs. There is a significant discrepancy between these assumptions and the environmental projections.

Basically, the environmental projections anticipate significant increases in the intensity of use of agriculture lands in the LDCs and very few preventive or remedial measures. The primary LDC remedial measures implied by the food pro-

jections are a fourfold increase in the use of fertilizers, herbicides, and pesticides and a large increase in irrigation. With the projected increase in energy costs, and with the environmental (and political) implications of the implied water development, it seems unlikely that remedial or preventive measures will be able to counter the pressures for overuse. Furthermore, the environmental projections suggest that deforestation will increase the degradation of the LDC agricultural lands, both through more erratic streamflows and increased erosion and through a fuelwood shortage, which will result in an increase in the burning of dung that would otherwise have been returned to the soil as nutrients.

The economic consequences of land deterioration are more immediate in the LDCs than in the industrialized countries. Overgrazing, desertification, and salinization are major problems. Harold E. Dregne, chief of the U.N. Environment Programme's working groups on desertification, finds the total annual production losses due to desertification and salinization (an estimated $15.6 billion[748]) to be distributed as follows: $3.3 billion due to waterlogging and salinization of irrigated land; $6.7 billion due to range deterioration; $5.6 billion due to deterioration of rainfed crop land. Most of these losses would be borne by the LDCs. Dregne computed the production loss potential at 40 percent of production on irrigated lands (due to salinization), 60 percent on ranged land, and 25 percent on rainfed crop land. Average gross incomes per hectare from lands not affected by desertification or salinization were estimated at $400 for irrigated land, $90 for rainfed crop land and $3.50 for range land.

Another measure of the economic impact of land deterioration is the estimated cost of remedial measures. According to the Committee on Problems of the Environment of the International Council of Scientific Unions (SCOPE), it would cost $25 billion to rehabilitate 50 million hectares with the heaviest salt damage. [749] The U.N. Environment Program estimates that it will cost $400 million a year to combat desertification. [750] So far no global price tag has been placed on halting erosion or overgrazing.

Effects of Genetic Resource Losses. The food and agriculture projections assume that yields will continue to increase at essentially the same rate as over the past two decades. The yield increases come in part from distribution of technologies already demonstrated in field experiments and in part from further experimental improvements, especially in seed. Improvements in seed involve both increased plant productivity and increased (or at least maintained) resistance to plant pests and pathogens. To achieve these ends, local strains of crop species are needed, and these are being lost rapidly.

The projected extinction of one-fifth of all species—plants and animals—on the planet is an indication of the overall pressure on genetic resources. Most of these extinctions will occur as a result of tropical deforestation. The genetic losses of most concern to agriculture are not so much located in tropical forests as in dry and marginal lands where local strains of important food grains have evolved high-yield or disease-resistant traits. These local strains are being lost in two ways. First, local strains are lost as more and more farm lands are put into production with commercial rather than local seed. Second, land-clearing is destroying habitat for many local wild varieties. [751]

Concerned plant scientists are increasing their efforts to collect varieties of crops from all over the world before they are lost. The International Rice Research Institute has a collection of 45,000 rice strains in Los Banos, Philippines but considers that its collection is only a fraction of the world's known rice germ plasm. [752] There is little doubt that large numbers of local strains will be lost in the decades ahead. Without new genetic materials to work with, there are very real limits to what plant breeders can accomplish.

Although the genetic losses most significant to present-day agriculture are far more likely to occur in the fields of subsistence cultivators than in tropical forests, the extinctions in tropical forests also have implications for future agriculture. Tropical forests contain wild progenitors of many important crops—cocoa, rubber, oil palm, pineapple, and many nuts and fruits, as well as medicinal plant species and many plants of unexplored food and medical potential. Should the world's climate become warmer and wetter, as many climatologists believe likely, these and other tropical species could become exceedingly important.

Finally, it should be mentioned that, livestock genetic resources are also being lost at a rapid rate and without extensive efforts at preservation. Livestock, especially ruminants, are important in the world's food future because of their capacity to convert cellulose plant materials (indigestible to humans) into high-quality protein.

Effects of Pest and Disease Management Problems. The food projections assume that agricultural pests and diseases will not present more difficult problems in the future than they have in the past. The projections anticipate that these problems will be managed through a global doubling in the use of pesticides. A still larger increase in pesticides is anticipated for the LDCs.

By contrast, the environmental projections suggest that pest and disease problems will increase, especially if reliance continues to be placed primarily on pesticides. The methods of integrated pest management* may offer a more effective alternative, but continued dependence on pesticides will enhance resistance in pests and decimate predator populations. Extensive monocultures of genetically identical plants will further increase vulnerability.

The economic impact of pest management problems will be felt particularly in cash and export crops. The problems caused by heavy applications of pesticides have been well demonstrated in cotton fields of the world [753] as well as on plantations of tea, oil palm, vegetables, and fruits. [754] In Northeastern Mexico 250,000 hectares of cotton were totally destroyed by the bollworm *Heliothis* when it became resistant to all of the pesticides used against it. [755] Similar problems of resistance were experienced in Texas where the costs of protecting cotton in the Rio Grande Valley were higher than anywhere else—11 percent of the total production costs. In 1966 cotton farmers in the U.S. were using 47 percent of all pesticides used by U.S. farmers, [756] and pest control costs had become inordinately high.

Although many cotton farmers, especially in the U.S., Mexico, and Peru, are shifting to integrated pest management techniques for cotton, pesticides applied to cotton elsewhere in the world continue to represent a large share of the total pesticide chemical usage. In fact, in LDCs export corps (including cotton) receive most of the pesticides now used. [757]

The projected 100 percent increase in food production by 2000 is weakened to the extent that it assumes that a doubling of the world average application rate of pesticides to food crops (and a quadrupling of the application rate in the LDCs) will enhance production. Modest applications of pesticides in conjunction with the ecological and cultural techniques of integrated pest management generally contribute to increased yields in the short run, but massive increases in the use of pesticides alone will definitely increase the chances of major increases in pest resistance over the next two decades, as has happened already in cotton.

---

*"Integrated pest management" applies to a wide array of pest management techniques that greatly reduce the use of pesticides and rely more on biological controls and cultural techniques.

The assumption in the food projection that further adoption of existing high-yield technology will occur is in essence an assumption that larger monocultures of genetically identical strains will increase. This assumption implies increased vulnerability of food staples. The establishment of still larger monocultures of rice, wheat, and corn propagated from an excessively narrow genetic base enhances the probability of crop epidemics on a scale even larger than the 1972 corn blight epidemic in the U.S. The potential economic impact of such an epidemic is enormous. While a useful quantification of this potential is not possible, the possibility is real and is increased by the trends assumed in the food projections.

Effects of Air Pollution. The food projections assume that the adverse effects of air pollutants on agricultural production will not increase over the next two decades, but the environmental projections point to a number of potential increases in air pollution, some of which can be expected to affect agriculture adversely.

The increased combustion of coal will produce at least three combustion products of potential significance to agriculture, namely, sulfur oxides (SO_x), nitrogen oxides (NO_x) and carbon dioxide (CO_2). Increased CO_2 in the air could increase plant growth, but SO_x and NO_x emissions are known to have adverse effects on plants. SO_x emissions can be controlled with the technology now available, so the extent of emissions depends on national pollution control standards. In the U.S., for example, present standards would reduce SO_x emissions until about 1985, when emissions would start increasing again. NO_x emissions cannot be controlled with existing pollution control technologies. The energy projections are not sufficiently detailed or precise to permit an estimate of the areas that will be exposed to increased concentrations of SO_x and NO_x.

Air pollution already causes significant damage to agricultural crops. In the U.S., air pollution damage to crops in Southern California alone cost farmers $14.8 million per year during the 1972–76 period. The losses amounted to 2 percent of the crop categories affected. Celery, potatoes, and tomatoes were especially hard hit.

Over the next two decades the impact of air pollutants on agriculture can be expected to increase, especially for farmers downwind of industrial centers. The effects may be particularly severe near industrial centers in LDCs.[758]

Effects of Aquatic Changes. The food projections assume that water resources will be available to effectively utilize a doubling in the application of fertilizers. (The twofold increase is a world average; a quadrupling of fertilizer use is anticipated in the LDCs.) The projections note that water management could become the single most important constraint on increasing yields in the developing world.

The environmental projections lend strong support to the concern over water constraints not only in the developing world, but also in industrialized nations. Competition with energy development will be intense in parts of many industrialized nations (e.g., the Western U.S.). While neither the water assumptions in the food projections nor the water projections themselves are sufficiently detailed to permit a close comparison, much examination of regional water supplies would be needed to determine if the water assumptions of the food projections are fully justified.

In addition to water supply, the environmental projections point to two other aquatic developments that will affect the food projections. One concerns the acidity of rain water, the other, variations in supply.

The increased emissions of sulfur oxides and nitrogen oxides from coal combustion are causing rainfall over wide areas to become more acidic. Much of the eastern half of the United States and parts of southern Canada, northern Europe, and southern Scandinavia have all been affected. The effects of acid rain on crops and soils are only beginning to be investigated, but it is already known that simulated acid rain adversely affects the growth of some food crops, including soybeans and kidney beans. It is also known that over a period of 3–5 years simulated acid rain begins to acidify soils. Most food crops do not grow well in acid soils. The extent to which acid rain will adversely affect food production is still unknown, but over the next 20 years it will probably have much more effect than is assumed in the food and agriculture projections in Chapter 6.

The implications of the anticipated deforestation for streamflows also apply to agriculture in large portions of the developing world. The absence of forest cover in the upper reaches of river basins tends to exaggerate both peak and minimum flows. As a result, flooding and erosion will be increased during rainy periods, and irrigation potentials will be reduced during dry periods. This effect is not considered in the development of the food projections.

As the preceding paragraphs have indicated, there are apparently many discrepancies between the environmental assumptions underlying the food projections and the environmental projections made in the food and agriculture section of this chapter. Land deterioration is likely to be more extensive than assumed. The assumed primary reliance on chemical fertilizers to maintain soil fertility will lead to further soil deterioration as well as to increased costs and economic vulnerability. Lost genetic resources will reduce the prospects for additional decades of yield increases. The assumed primary reliance on pesticides as a pest management strategy implies further pesticide resistance in pest populations and decreased populations of pest predators. Air pollution will have adverse effects, as will acid rain. Although the water assumptions are not explicit, the adverse effects of deforestation on water supplies will further complicate an already difficult situation.

If these apparent discrepancies could be taken into account, the feedback from the environmental projection would alter the food projection in several ways. Most basically, per capita food consumption might well be less than that projected in Alternative III in Chapter 6, namely, a 4 percent increase worldwide, a decline of 20 percent in Africa and the Middle East, and increases only in the U.S., the U.S.S.R., and in Eastern and Western Europe. The real cost of food might increase more than the 100 percent projected, and even before 2000 those LDC economies that are largely agrarian may experience a decline in the growth of their GNP.

Feedback to the Fisheries Projections

The fisheries projections make several environmentally related assumptions concerning marine fisheries, freshwater fisheries, and aquaculture.

For marine fisheries, the projections assume that:

- Increasing demand for marine fish will not lead to overfishing so severe that it depletes fish stocks.
- Continuing pollution of coastal waters with oil, pesticides, heavy metals, and other toxic substances will have an overall negative effect on the quality or quantity of marine fish catches. However, the projections implicitly assume that such pollution will not be severe by the year 2000.
- Continuing losses of estuaries and coastal wetlands will not significantly reduce natural marine productivity by 2000.
- Improved fishing technologies will not be used in ways that threaten fisheries.
- The present world harvest of marine fish of about 60 million metric tons (mmt) will not increase on a sustained basis; careful planning and management could, in theory, raise the harvest of natural marine production to 100 mmt by 2000; and economic model projections based on continued population and GNP growth lead to a fish demand in 2000 of 81–83 mmt.

For freshwater fisheries, the projections assume that:

- Natural freshwater fisheries are fully exploited at the present 10 mmt catch.
- Environmental deterioration will not adversely affect this natural freshwater catch.

For aquaculture (fresh- and saltwater), the projections assume that:

- There is a significant potential for expanding the present 6 mmt harvest of largely high-unit-value species.
- This potential will not be seriously affected by environmental developments over the next two decades.

The environmental projections show developments that will adversely affect natural production of fish, both marine and freshwater, and that will reduce the potential for both freshwater and marine aquaculture. The only question is how soon will the adverse effects be felt.

Feedback from both continued pollution of coastal waters and the loss of coastal habitat could significantly affect the marine fisheries projections. Discharges of oil, pesticides, heavy metals, and other toxic substances are expected to continue to increase, especially in LDC coastal waters. By 2000, the impact on fisheries may not be universal, but many areas will experience continuing or increasing contamination by long-lived pollutants that may decrease production regionally or severely contaminate marine resources.

The continuing losses of coastal habitats—estuaries, salt marshes, mangrove communities, etc.—may not lead to a significant global decline in marine fisheries by 2000. Nonetheless, it is known that most important marine species are dependent at some point in their life cycles on such habitats, and continued loss of these habitats must ultimately have significant impacts on marine fisheries—impacts that could begin to be felt before 2000.

An example illustrates the economic significance of coastal marine habitats in the U.S.: Estimates made in the northeastern United States and the Gulf of Mexico demonstrate that fish production alone on an acre of submerged coastal wetlands has an annual value (in 1970 dollars) of $380, which over even a relatively short 20-year life period represents $7,980 at a 5 percent discount rate. However, for every acre of coastal wetlands dredged or filled, the production of two additional acres is lost because of the resulting disruption by siltation and other impacts. As a result, a single acre of coastal wetlands lost to dredge and fill operations represents $23,940 in lost seafood production potential alone,* and coastal wetlands provide many other ecological benefits that have not been included in this estimate.[759]

Marine fish production will also be affected by hydrologic developments on the land. The productivity of coastal waters is enhanced by the normal flows of rivers and the sediments and organic matter they bring to the ocean food chain. This function of rivers is being increasingly impaired by large dams which control floods, regulate flows, and trap sediments and organic matter. The food and the water projections implicitly assume that a large number of dams and reservoirs will be constructed by 2000. The importance, magnitude, and timing of the resulting impact on ocean fisheries can be deduced from examples but cannot be projected in any detail. (In some cases the impact on marine fish production may be offset to some degree by new fish production in the reservoirs.) The effect of the Aswan Dam on the Mediterranean's sardine fishery is a well-known example of this phenomenon.

The effects of irrigation development, increased sewage discharge from LDC cities, and increased use of pesticides and fertilizers could seriously affect both the projected freshwater catch and aquaculture. Irrigation development often adversely affects habitats for freshwater fish by increasing temperatures, reducing the oxygen content of the water and increasing salinity. The projected increase in the use of fertilizers will enhance algal blooms, eutrophication, and depletion of dissolved oxygen in reservoirs and lakes. Acid rain from increased coal combustion will acidify lakes in many industrialized nations, eliminating the use of the lakes for aquaculture or the natural production of fish. Pesticide residues from a doubling to a quadrupling of pesticide applications will pollute streams, rivers, reservoirs, and lakes, killing small fish.

---

*These figures are not intended to establish a precise value for coastal wetlands. Estimated values vary widely and are hard to estimate (See "The Value of Wetlands" in Elinor Lander Horwitz, *Our Nation's Wetlands: An Interagency Task Force Report*, GPO stock no. 041–011–00045–9, Washington: U.S. Government Printing Office, 1978, pp. 28–29). The figures are used here only as an indication of real, non-zero value for coastal wetlands.

Coastal and estuarine breeding and spawning waters for many oceanic fish will also be affected, especially in regional seas. In the Mediterranean, for example, coastal aquaculture, which now yields 165,000 tons of fish each year, is seriously threatened by land-based pollution, as are the 700,000 tons caught annually in the open Mediterranean. The $5.0 billion price tag on the cleanup of the Mediterranean Sea is well justified by the benefits of conserving these fisheries resources as well as the 100 million visitor per year tourist industry and the 100 wetland sanctuaries for birds and marine life.[760]

Brackish-water fish ponds line the coasts of many Asian countries and yield highly prized Chinese milkfish and shrimp. They too are seriously threatened by pollution, particularly pesticides in runoff but also by toxic substances in municipal and industrial effluents.[761] Paddy rice *cum* fish culture operations are also jeopardized by pesticides in water and an important nutritional impact results, since snails, crabs, and small fish which normally inhabit flooded rice paddies are a major source of protein for farm families throughout Asia.[762]

As the preceding paragraphs have indicated, there are a number of potential and apparent discrepancies between the assumptions of the fisheries projections and the environmental projections. If the apparent discrepancies could be eliminated in the analysis, the accumulative effects of the environmental trends, in conjunction with increasing demands for fishery products, could lead to a decrease in the world's total fishery resources. The anticipated environmental developments will certainly have a negative effect on these resources because the trends are largely disruptive and poisoning. When these effects would be felt is open to speculation, but there is a distinct possibility that the adverse effects of continued environmental deterioration will have noticeably affected many fishery resources before 2000.

Feedback to the Minerals Projections

The environmental projections are not likely to have significant direct feedbacks to the nonfuel minerals/projections because mineral production is not particularly sensitive to environmental conditions. A change in air quality, for example, has little direct effect on mining.

There are indirect feedbacks, however, that may be significant. As land disruption, water pollution, and air pollution affect human health and the nonmining sectors of the economy, human institutions (e.g., governments, insurance companies, etc.) may impose further regulations that will reduce the environmental impacts of mining and increase mining costs.

The nonfuel mineral projections are not based on any explicit environmental assumptions. Implicitly, they assume that environmental regulations will not significantly constrain world mining activities over the next two decades. They assume further than the nonfuel minerals sector will receive all of the water and energy needed for the projected growth. All of these assumptions are somewhat questionable.

Water, for example, is needed in the mining and processing of both fuel-mineral and nonfuel-mineral ores, and water availability could be an important constraint. While the amounts needed for mining are relatively small (in the U.S. they amount to only about 2 percent of total withdrawals), and while the water-quality requirements are relatively low, water resources will become increasingly constrained everywhere. Competition for water between agriculture, minerals development, and energy production will become much more intense in the years ahead.

The use of energy in mining and refining may be more troubling. The energy requirements of declining ore grades has not yet been examined carefully, and the economics of mining will certainly be affected by further increases in energy costs. The economic recoverability of some resources now classed as (economically recoverable) reserves may even be affected if energy prices continue to rise sharply.

Finally, laws and regulations to preserve environmental quality may be tightened in the future as the projected increases in mining and refining activities impact on land, air, and water resources. However, the assumptions underlying the projections—no tightening of the laws and regulations controlling the environmental impacts of mining—are consistent with the Global 2000 Study's overall assumption of no policy changes between the present and the year 2000.

Feedback to the Energy Projections

Like the nonfuel minerals projection, little or no direct environmental feedback is expected to commercial energy production (coal, oil, gas, plus nuclear and hydro generation) in the industrialized nations, but significant feedback may be involved in the LDCs' use of organic fuels.

The energy and fuel mineral projections do not make explicit assumptions about the future environment but implicitly assume that environmental laws and regulations will not limit development or significantly increase costs over the next two decades. The energy projections assume further that there will be no constraints on the water or energy needed for energy development.

Large amounts of water are needed for coal mining, synthetic fuel production, and oil-shale production, and at least in the arid west, these water needs will conflict with mining and agricultural needs. In 1978, the U.S. Water Resource Council anticipated increasing pressures on water resources in the Missouri and Upper Colorado River basins, where coal and oil-shale mining are developing, but beyond those areas, the Council foresaw no other major conflicts between the water needs of the coal industry and of other water users.[763] The water picture in the U.S. may change, however, if there is a significant increase in the production of synthetic fuels, which require large amounts of water.

Water for evaporative cooling at nuclear and coal-powered electric generating plants may also present problems in some areas. In Western Europe, for example, withdrawals for evaporative cooling may present a constraint when added to all other water demands. In the U.S., consumptive cooling water withdrawals are expected to be the fastest-growing component of water use over the 1975–2000 period, increasing from 1.3 to 7.8 percent of total water consumption. Overall, water can be expected to become more of a constraint than is assumed in the energy, agriculture, and nonfuel minerals projections.

Like water, energy itself is a critical input in energy development. The energy projections implicitly assume that adequate energy will be available for energy development, conversion, and delivery. In fact, the energy efficiency of the energy sector (end-use energy supplied per unit of primary energy used) may decrease as a result of the projected increases in primary energy conversion to secondary energy forms, especially electricity and (perhaps) synthetic fuels. This means that the energy sector itself will require increasing amounts of primary energy in order to supply a given amount of end-use energy need in the economy. Net energy analysis and energy efficiency are not a part of the current energy projections, and its seems likely that the energy efficiency of the energy sector will be examined more extensively in the years ahead. Ultimately, some of the assumptions underlying the energy projections may be brought into question.

Energy development in the industrialized nations will produce significant environmental impacts over the next two decades, and the laws and regulations relating to its development may change significantly. The energy projections, however, assume no change in environmental regulations and no significant increases in the cost of environmental protection. This assumption is consistent with the Global 2000 Study's overall assumption of no policy change.

In the LDCs, there will be feedback from the environmental projections to the energy projections in two ways. First, deforestation from all causes will contribute to the growing shortages of fuelwood. Second, deteriorating range conditions may reduce the amount of dung available for fuel.

Feedback to the GNP Projections

The feedback of the evironmental projections to the GNP projections (and also to the population projections, which are considered next) is more complex than the feedbacks considered so far. The complexities arise both from the several linkages through which environmental feedback influences GNP and from the indirect nature of the feedbacks.

Environmental developments influence GNP in at least three different ways. One way is through the influence that environmental developments have on individual economic sectors, which in turn influence the total GNP. Another is through the influence that human health has on GNP. Finally, the economic activity associated with environmental protection efforts also influences GNP.

These three linkages from the environment to GNP are not easily discerned in the assumptions that underly the GNP projections. While there are no explicit environmental assumptions in those projections, they seem to assume implicitly that the environment will continue to provide each economic sector with the same goods and services as in the past, but in substantially increased amounts, without interruption and without increase in cost (generally taken to be zero). The discrepancies that follow from this assumption are, of course, somewhat different for the industrialized countries than for the LDCs.

Feedback to the Industrialized Economies. Feedback from the environment through the various sectors of the economy have been discussed in the preceding sections on forestry, water, food, fisheries, nonfuel minerals, and energy. These feedbacks involve parts of the environment that are economically valued (e.g., land and forests), as well as parts that are not valued economically (e.g., populations of predator insects). An attempt has been made to include in these discussions a few indications of the costs of lost environmental goods and services. (The estimated

loss of seafood production totaling—by one estimate—nearly $24,000 for each acre of dredged coastal wetlands is but one example.*) Unfortunately, available data on such losses are so incomplete that the cost figures cannot even be termed spotty, but they make a basic point: The goods and services provided by the environment—from the decomposition of wastes to the absorption of carbon dioxide—contribute substantially but subtly to the GNP in each economic sector. Projected losses in environmental goods and services will significantly affect every economic sector, but especially—but not exclusively—those involving renewable resources.

There will also be feedback from the nonrenewable resource sectors. For example, different energy strategies allow for comparable degrees of environmental protection with very different capital (and GNP) implications. All of the projections are based on the assumption of no capital constraints. In actual fact, capital is scarce and expensive, and intense competition among the sectors can be expected over the next two decades as efforts are made to develop a new energy economy, raise food production, increase water availability, increase mineral production, *and* protect the environment. Increasing costs of obtaining many resources can be expected to contribute to inflation and capital scarcity, thus indirectly affecting GNP.

Feedback from environmental protection efforts to GNP is also subtle and complex. No studies have yet been done of this feedback for industrialized economies as a group, but the issue has been examined for the U.S. economy.

The U.S. study, recently done by Data Resources, Inc. (DRI) for the Environmental Protection Agency (EPA), analyzes the economic effects of federal air and water pollution control programs over the 1970–86 period. The DRI study arrived at the following conclusions:

- The extra investment required for the federal air and water pollution control programs has a positive economic effect until 1981, after which it turns slightly negative due to inflation and reduced productivity. As a result the real GNP would be 1.0 percent lower at the end of the period than if there has been no incremental pollution control expenditures.

---

*The figures used here are only illustrative. Estimates vary widely. (See "The Value of Wetlands," in Elinor Lander Horwitz, *Our Nation's Wetlands: An Interagency Task Forced Report*, GPO Stock No. 041–011–00045–9, Washington: U.S. Government Printing Office, 1978, pp. 28–29.

- The federal air and water pollution control programs are slightly inflationary, adding 0.3 percent to the overall rate of inflation each year through 1986.
- Employment benefits remain constant, even after construction ends, due to the labor needed in operation and maintenance of pollution control equipment and installations.[764]

At the time of the DRI study's release, EPA's administrator pointed out that the DRI study did not measure many of the benefits of cleaner air and water, and as a result depicted the worst possible economic impact. Had the study been more complete, the negative impacts might have been largely counterbalanced or outweighed by consideration of benefits such as enhanced agricultural production, greater fish harvests, lower maintenance and depreciation costs for materials and processes affected by air and water pollution, and improved health.[765]

The EPA administrator's comments on the DRI study refer to the third type of feedback from the environment to GNP, namely the linkage through human health. While again no studies for the industralized nations as a group have been done, the impacts of air pollution on human health in the U.S. have been studied in a report, also prepared for EPA, by a group of resource economists at the University of Wyoming. Completed in 1979, the study documents a very significant linkage between environment, health, and GNP. It concludes that the health benefits from a 60 percent reduction in air pollution would amount to a total annual savings of $40 billion ($185 per person)—$36 billion representing a decrease in illnesses and $4 billion, a decrease in mortality rates.[766] The major health benefits associated with the reduction in air pollution particulates were more on-the-job time for everyone and increased productivity of those people suffering from chronic illnesses associated with air pollution. The Environmental Protection Agency estimated on the basis of the figures above that the 12 percent decrease *in particulates alone* that has been achieved between 1970 and 1977 provides $8 billion in health benefits each year compared to the total 1977 expenditures on *all air pollutants* from stationary sources (the primary sources of particulates) of $6.7 billion.[767]

The linkages between the environment and GNP involve a number of subtleties; the linkages through human health and soil conditions provide two interesting examples. In the case of human health, improvements in air quality increase productivity and time on the job, both of which contribute to increased GNP. But these are not the only effects. An improvement in health *reduces* the goods and services delivered by the medical sector of the economy, thus *diminishing* GNP. Similar subtleties occur in the case of soil health. Declines in soil quality due to compaction and erosion are known to be occuring widely in the U.S., but by replacing lost fertility with energy-intensive inputs, declining soil productivity may actually increase GNP—but at the cost of (among other things) increased dependence on foreign sources of energy. These two examples suggest that in industrialized countries the linkages between environmental developments and GNP may be quite different from the linkages between environmental developments and national welfare.

Feedback to the LDC Economies. The model used to develop GNP projections for the LDCs makes environmental assumptions that are similar to those contained in the GNP models of industrial economies. Neither of the GNP models makes explicit assumptions about goods and services provided by the environment; both assume implicitly that environmental goods and services will be available without interruption in much larger quantities and at no increase in cost. Furthermore, in the case of the model of the LDC economies, it is assumed that environmental considerations are relatively unimportant compared with trade with developed nations. This last assumption is inherent in the model's structure, under which the LDC economies are assumed to expand only through trade with industrialized countries, and as a consequence, can grow only when industrial economies are growing. This last assumption has been questioned both as to its necessity and its desirability for the LDCs.

Actually, the same three types of linkages relate environmental developments to GNP in the industrialized countries as in the LDCs. The three linkages—through the economic sectors, through human health and productivity, and through expenditures on environmental protection—are probably even more important in determining GNP (and welfare) in the LDCs than in the industrialized nations.

Linkages through the economic sectors illustrate this last point. In the LDCs, the industrial sectors (such as oil, chemicals, steel, and manufacturing) are by definition less developed (i.e., industrialized), and the economic sectors based on renewable resources (forestry, fisheries, agriculture) are the economic mainstays of the domestic economy. Environmental deterioration strongly affects the renewable resource sectors. Deforestation is, simply put, a matter of living from biological capital, not from its dividends, and the LDCs' tropical forest capital will largely be spent by 2000. Fuelwood shortages will increase the use of dung for fuel, reducing the recycling of nutrients to the soil, and so will adversely affect the agricultural sector. Deforestation will exaggerate peak and minimum streamflows, which will increase erosion, degrade water quality, and reduce productivity in the agricultural and fisheries sectors. Overgrazing will deplete grass and range land resources, which will speed up desertification and adversely affect the agricultural sector. Efforts to increase agricultural production with pesticides, fertilizers, and irrigation will require increasingly expensive energy-intensive inputs, which may in turn intensify balance of payment problems to a greater extent than they increase domestic GNP. The projected quadrupling of agricultural chemical usage would also adversely affect the fisheries sector. In short, projected environmental developments in the LDCs can be expected to have pervasive adverse effects on GNP through the vitally important agricultural, forestry, and fisheries sectors of the economies.

The effects of environmental developments on GNP via human health and productivity are equally strong. The projected increases in urbanization in the absence of adequate sewage and potable water facilities can only lead to significant increases in the incidence of fecally related contagious disease and morbidity generally. The quadrupled use of pesticides will (and already has) lead to major increases in worker illness and poisoning. The water development projects implied by the food projections will expand habitats for disease vectors, increasing the incidence of schistosomiasis, river blindness, and malaria. Widespread malnutrition will complicate the increased morbidity. The combined effects of the projected environmental developments can be expected to significantly reduce human productivity and GNP in the LDCs.

To date many of the LDCs have not made major investments in industrial pollution control technologies, and the GNP projections assume that laws and regulations affecting industrial pollution control expenditures in the LDCs will not be increased significantly over the next two decades. This assumption is consistent with the Global 2000 Study's overall assumption of no policy change.

In the absence of stringent pollution control laws and regulations, multinational corporations engaged in highly polluting industrial processes may find the LDCs increasingly attractive sites for their plants. Industries involved in the production of toxic substances may become especially interested in LDC locations.[767a] Increased industrial activity, even of the highly polluting sort, may increase the GNP of LDC economies—and perhaps even national welfare—but before this possibility is accepted as valid, the adverse effects of the pollution on other economic sectors and on human productivity need to be examined carefully.*

In both LDCs and industrialized countries, environmental developments influence GNP directly through economic sectors, indirectly through human health and productivity, and, subtly, through expenditures on environmental protection. The Global 2000 Study's projections of GNP make no explicit assumptions about the environment but implicitly assume that environmental developments will not reduce GNP growth in either developed or developing countries. A comparison of this assumption with the preceding paragraphs reveals many discrepancies. While it is not possible to modify the GNP projections to eliminate these discrepancies, a more adequate consideration of environmental developments in the GNP projections would probably lead to lower estimates of GNP growth, especially in the LDCs. In any case, environmental deterioration will impair the quality of life in both industrialized and developing countries, and "additions" to GNP required to offset pollution or health damages might more properly be substituted since they do not involve a net increase in *desired* goods and services.

Feedback to the Population Projections

Feedback from the environmental projections to future population levels occurs through the effects of environmental changes on health, mortality, fertility, and migration. The feedback through health, mortality, and fertility will be most significant for the LDC population projec-

---

*M. Greg Bloche, a Yale medical student, has recently interviewed the minister of health in the People's Republic of China on the subject of the environmental and health impacts of industrialization. He reports that China is having the same difficulties as industrialized nations in coping with rapid increases (a doubling over two decades) in the illnesses of industrialization—cancer, hypertension, and heart diseases. He also reports familiar tensions in carefully and objectively examining the merits of environmental standards and quotes the minister of health as remarking tersely: "Of course the Ministry of Health wants high standards and the Ministry of Industry wants low standards. You can spend less money on low standards." (M. Greg Bloche, "China Discovers Health Perils Accompany Modernization," *Washington Post*, Aug. 19, 1979, p. A21.)

tions. The feedback through migration will also affect LDC demographics to a small extent and will have a relatively long-lasting effect on populations in some industrialized nations.

Feedback to the Population Projections for the LDCs. The environmental assumptions underlying the LDC population projections are largely subassumptions of the fertility and mortality rate assumptions. Fertility rates and mortality rates are not projected by the population model, but rather are fed into the model as a large number of time-series assumptions/projections. The environmental assumptions underlying the externally developed fertility and mortality projections are the assumptions that need examining here.

To understand how environmental assumptions enter into the fertility and mortality assumptions/ projections, the methods by which these projections were developed must first be reviewed briefly (a more detailed explanation will be found in Chapters 2 and 15). The process is basically this: The fertility rate (or mortality rate) for the base year is estimated on the basis of available data and is then projected forward in time, using one or two methods—either a general continuation of past trends or the establishment of a "target" figure for the final year of the projection. Under both approaches, the projected fertility rate (or mortality rate) is adjusted upward or downward to take into account assumed influences of the environment and other factors, such as the availability of family planning services.*
There are two environmentally related assumptions used in developing and adjusting the projections of the LDC fertility rates: (1) continued moderate social and economic progress in all LDCs throughout the projection period and (2) a more or less continuous decline in fertility rates throughout LDC societies caused in part by the assumed continuation of social and economic progress. The environmentally related assumption underlying the mortality rate assumption/projection is basically that, to the extent that improved sanitation, nutrition and environmental conditions have led to decreased mortality rates in the past, continued improvements will lead to similar decreases in mortality rates in the future.

There appear to be a number of discrepancies between the Global 2000 Study's low-fertility, low-mortality population assumptions/projections and the Study's environmental projections. The population projections assume continued improvements in human welfare throughout LDC societies. Discrepancies between this assumption and the environmental projections can be seen for large aggregate areas of the LDC nations, for large rural LDC areas, and increasingly for LDC urban areas.

The assumed continued moderate social and economic progress throughout the LDCs appear to be contradicted by trends in GNP, food, and energy. The per capita GNP projections—even without correction for decreased goods and services from the environment—do not show moderate increases throughout the LDCs. In the medium case, growth in per capita GNP slows to 0.1 percent per year for parts of South Asia for the 1985–2000 period. Per capita GNP growth for the entire African continent slows to less than 1.4 percent per year for the same period, and although figures for the poorest countries in Africa are not available separately, they are certain to be much lower than the continental average. Food consumption per capita does not show moderate increases throughout the LDCs. For the LDCs overall, per capita daily caloric consumption—again, with no reductions for anticipated environmental problems—increases only slightly, from 93 percent of FAO minimum standards for the 1973–74 period to 94 percent in 2000. This single percentage point increase masks declines for the poorest LDC nations and for the poorest classes in all LDC societies. Per capita daily calorie consumption in the Central African LDCs falls from 90 percent of FAO minimum standards for the 1973–74 period to 77 percent in 2000.* The energy sector will also affect health. The projected doubling of world energy prices will force the LDCs, chronically short of foreign exchange, to depend increasingly on domestic organic fuels. But the Food and Agriculture Organization projects that by 1994 there will be a fuelwood shortfall of 650 million cubic meters annually, approximately one quarter of the fuelwood consumption projected by FAO for the year 2000. The health hazards associated with undercooked foods and inadequate heat are well known. In short, the aggregate

---

*At the request of the U.S. Agency for International Development, two sets of demographic projections were developed for the Global 2000 Study. One set was developed by the U.S. Bureau of the Census, the other by the Community and Family Study Center (CFSC) of the University of Chicago. The two projections use basically the same environmental assumptions but differ significantly in their assumptions concerning the effectiveness of family planning progams. Further details on the differences between the two sets of projections is provided in Chapters 2 and 15 and in Paul Demeny, "On the End of the Population Explosion," *Population and Development Review,* Mar. 1979, pp. 141–62, and in Donald J. Bogue and Amy Ong Tsui, "A Rejoinder to Paul Demeny's Critique," May 1979 (draft submitted to *Population and Development Review*).

---

*The figures for per capita daily calorie consumption are from Alternative III of the food and agriculture projections in Chapter 6—the only alternative that includes increasing energy costs.

projections of GNP, food, and energy—even without any correction for environmental deterioration—do not suggest continued moderate progress for all segments of the populations throughout the LDCs.

Beyond the broad, aggregate trends, rural LDC areas will experience problems uniquely their own. The pressure on all agricultural lands will increase enormously. The number of persons that will have to be supported per arable hectare will increase from 2.9 in the 1970–75 period to 5.3 by 2000. The expansion of irrigation facilities implicitly assumed in the food projections will substantially increase habitats for disease vectors. Malaria-carrying mosquitos are developing progressively greater resistance to the major pesticides used to control them. The quadrupled use of pesticides assumed in the food and agriculture projections will lead to increased pesticide pollution and poisonings.

The largest impacts on LDC health, however, may occur in the urban areas. Over the last quarter of this century the urban population of the world is projected to increase from 39 percent to almost 50 percent. The largest increases will occur in LDC cities. Mexico City is projected to increase from 10.9 million in 1975 to 31.6 million in 2000, roughly three times the present population of metropolitan New York City. Calcutta is projected to reach nearly twice New York's present population by 2000. Jakarta's population more than triples to reach 16.9 million. Altogether, it is projected that 1.2 billion additional persons—roughly a quarter of the present total world population—will be added to LDC cities, and the most rapid growth will be in uncontrolled settlements, where populations are now doubling every 5–7 years. Financial resources are not likely to be available to the poor in uncontrolled settlements or to their city governments, even for providing safe water. Sewage facilities will be limited at best. Fecally related diseases can be expected to increase. The forestry and energy projections suggest that warm, dry, uncrowded housing will be even less available than now—a condition that will foster the transmission of contagious diseases. Pathogen resistance to the least expensive antibiotics and other drugs is becoming more common in the treating of many diseases, including malaria, typhoid, dysentery, and the venereal diseases. This increased resistance, along with continued malnutrition, will make epidemics more frequent and harder to control.

Overall, there appear to be significant discrepancies between the environmental projections and the assumptions underlying the population projections for the LDCs. If it were possible to correct these discrepancies by incorporating feedback from environmental projections into the demographic projections for the LDCs, some significant numerical changes would probably occur. The projections for Pakistan are a case in point.

The environmental and other projections for Pakistan do not support the general assumption underlying the population projections, namely, continued moderate increases in social and economic welfare. Even before any environmental considerations are taken into account, growth in Pakistan's per capita GNP is projected essentially to come to a halt during the 1985–2000 period, and there are many environmental considerations to be taken into account in Pakistan. Virtually every environmental feedback discussed in the past few paragraphs applies to Pakistan. Therefore, to the extent that the fertility and mortality rates for Pakistan were assumed to be lowered by continued moderate increases in social and economic welfare, the rates are too low. If environmental feedbacks had been explicitly taken into account, life expectancies might have been projected to remain about the same or to increase only slightly rather than to rise by an average of nine years.* Similarly, something less than a 28 percent decline in the crude birth rate (from 44.54 to 32.12) might have been anticipated, even with a fairly strong family planning program.

If environmental feedback were to be explicitly considered throughout the population projections, analogous adjustments would be necessary in the projections for many other LDC countries, including Haiti, Thailand, Mexico, India, Indonesia, Bolivia, Bangladesh, and the countries of sub-Saharan Africa.

Feedback to the Population Projections for the Industrialized Countries. The feedbacks to the population projections for the industrialized nations are relatively few compared to those for the LDC population. The linkages are primarily through the health implications of energy development and through migration.

The energy projections show clearly that by 2000 a transition away from petroleum must be well in progress for most industrialized nations. The choices lie along a spectrum that ranges from the soft path (a highly efficient energy sector using a minimal amount of primary energy drawn as much as possible from solar and other renewable sources) to the hard path (a relatively inefficient energy sector using relatively large amounts of primary energy drawn from coal and nuclear

---

*For females, the projected increase over the 1975–2000 period is from 53.63 to 63.95 years (19 percent) in the medium series of the Bureau of Census projections; for males the increase is from 54.50 to 62.30 years (14 percent).

sources). Most nations have yet to choose among their options, but when the choice is made, it will have significant health implications. The hard path coal option implies increasing problems with particulates, oxides of sulfur, and oxides of nitrogen, all of which have health adverse effects. The hard path nuclear option implies increasing problems of disposal of radioactive wastes from uranium mining, from low-level nuclear wastes, and from spent nuclear fuel, and radiation problems as well. The soft-path renewable-resource options also present a number of health problems. The energy projections do not extend to 2000, and it is not possible to predict how nations will make their energy choices. Whatever the choices are, however, they can be expected to have significant and varied health implications, but are unlikely to significantly affect population growth.

The other major feedback from the environmental projections to the population projections for the industrialized nations involves migration. International migration is a difficult subject from many perspectives, including that of the demographer. The demographer's problem is that migrants are often in violation of immigration laws, and as a result avoid being counted in a census.

Difficult as the problem is for demographers, the projected LDC population growth coupled with the projected LDC environmental trends suggests that there will be increasing pressures from international migration. Although the flows cannot be quantified and projected precisely, increased migration can be anticipated from North Africa to Europe, from South Asia to the oil-rich nations of the Middle East, and from Central to North America (Mexico City, for example, is only about 500 miles from the Mexican-U.S. border).

Even the limited statistics available for the United States illustrate the demographic significance of migration. The so-called natural increase (excess of births over deaths) for the U.S. is now roughly 1.3 million per year. Approximately 400,000 foreign visitors per year remain in the country illegally, and in addition approximately 800,000 successfully enter the country illegally each year, adding about 1.2 million persons to the U.S. population annually, an amount almost identical with the natural increase of about 0.6 percent per year.* As a result, the population growth rate for the U.S. is probably closer to 1.2 percent per year than the 0.6 percent per year estimate given in Table 2–12 in Chapter 2. Similar (and probably

increasing) immigration can also be expected for parts of Europe and the Middle East.

It is thus clear that feedback from the environmental projections to the population projections has implications for the population estimates for both LDC and industrialized nations. For the industrialized nations, migration may increase growth rates in some cases by one half of a percentage point or so. For the LDCs, the effects are more complex and dependent on the situation in individual countries. If environmental factors could have been taken into account explicitly throughout the Global 2000 Study population projections, the total world estimates for 2000 might well have been about the same as the present projection—a 46–64 percent increase to a total world population of 5.9–6.8 billion in 2000—but for somewhat different reasons: Birth rates would have generally been somewhat higher and life expectancies lower .

Summing Up

The foregoing analysis of the environmental feedbacks to the Global 2000 projections reveals numerous and serious differences (discrepancies) between the projected future world environment and the assumptions that were used in the population, GNP, and resource projections of Chapters 2–12. Many of the study projections assume implicitly that terrestrial, aquatic, and atmospheric resources will continue to provide goods and services in ever increasing amounts without maintenance, moderation, or protection.† Such

---

*These estimates were obtained in 1976 by Justin Blackwelder, president of the Environmental Fund, Washington, from the U.S. Immigration and Naturalization Service (INS) and were published by the Environmental Fund in 1976 in "U.S. Population Larger Than Official Census Figures." The INS has since stopped making such estimates, and will not now confirm or deny the estimates (E. Collison, INS Staff Investigator,

personal communication, 1979). Anne Ehrlich suggests that the figures are too high (personal communication, 1979). *The Golden Door*, a recent book on migration between Mexico and the United States attempts to trace the history of the 800,000 estimate (Paul R. Ehrlich, Loy Bilderback, and Anne Ehrlich, New York: Ballantine, 1979, p. 180). INS Staff Investigator E. Collison suggests the recent work of Clarice Lancaster of the U.S. Department of HEW and Frederick Scheuern of the U.S. Social Security Administration as a widely accepted estimate. Clarice Lancaster and Frederick Scheuern estimate that in 1970 there were between 2.9 and 5.7 million illegal aliens in the U.S. ("Counting the Uncountable: Some Initial Statistical Speculations Employing Capture-Recapture Technique," paper presented at the American Statistical Association Annual Meeting, 1977).

†In the U.S., this and related assumptions have been questioned with increasing frequency by many groups. The relationship between the environment and human economic institutions is highly complex, and many environmental leaders believe that some basic value changes will be needed before a sustainable relationship can develop. Several feminist writers have drawn interesting parallels between the values underlying the relationship between humankind and Mother Nature on the one hand and values underlying relationships between men and women. See, for example: Susan Griffin, *Woman and Nature: The Roaring Inside Her*, New York: Harper, 1978; Mary Daly, *GYN/ECOLOGY: The Metaphysics of Radical Feminism*, Boston: Beacon, 1978; and Dorothy Dinnerstein, *The Mermaid and the Minotaur: Sexual Arrangements and Human Malaise*, New York: Harper, 1978.

assumptions are unrealistic. The Global 2000 Study's environmental analyses point to many areas where the capacity of the environment to provide goods and services can no longer be taken for granted. There are two reasons. First, the demand for environmental goods and services is outstripping the capacity of the environment to provide, as both population and per capita consumption expand. Second, in many areas the ecological systems that provide the goods and services are being undermined, extinguished, and poisoned. While informed and careful management of the environment might still increase the goods and services it provides in some areas, in other areas the demands placed on the environment are approaching, and in some areas have exceeded, its sustainable carrying capacity.

Added insight into the meaning of the Global 2000 Study's projections can be obtained by comparing them with a National Academy of Sciences estimate of the ultimate carrying capacity of the global environment. The Academy's 1969 report, *Resources and Man*, concluded that the world population must be stabilized at levels considerably lower than 10 billion, if human life is to be comfortably sustained within the resource limits of the earth.[768] The Academy also concluded that, even by sacrificing individual comfort and choice, the human population is unlikely ever to exceed 30 billion persons.

Information that has become available since 1969 tends not only to confirm the Academy's findings but to point to even more severe limits. For example, the Academy based its conclusion as to the earth's carrying capacity on the assumed availability of 61 million hectares more arable land than was projected by the U.S. Department of Agriculture for the Global 2000 Study. The Academy's report assumed a sustainable fish catch 40 million tons per year higher than the National Oceanic and Atmospheric Administration has estimated for the Global 2000 Study.* In its estimates, the Academy had assumed that one-half of the world's potentially arable land was under cultivation so that a twofold increase in production could be expected by developing the other half, and two additional twofold increases could be obtained by increased productivity and innovation respectively, leading to an eightfold potential increase in food production. Its study made no mention of the productivity losses re-

sulting from salinization (which now affects half of the world's irrigated soils), or of the soil losses and hydraulic destabilization that will accompany the projected deforestation. Nor did the Academy anticipate the rapid rise in the cost of energy-intensive fertilizers and pesticides. In short, the vast majority of the information that has become available over the past decade suggests that the Academy's estimate is reasonable, perhaps even optimistic: The earth's carrying capacity, under intensive management is about 10 billion persons "with some degree of comfort and individual choice," and about 30 billion otherwise.

The world's population picture has, of course, changed since the Academy's report in 1969, when there were about 3.6 billion persons and the total was increasing at about 2 percent per year. In 1979, there are approximately 4.3 billion persons, and the number is increasing at about 1.8 percent per year. The Global 2000 Study's projections suggest that by 2000 there will be about 6.35 billion persons, and that the number will increase at about 1.7 percent per year. Clearly, if present demographic trends continue, population growth will not stop—i.e., the annual percentage increase will not fall to zero—until well into the 21st century. If a net reproductive rate of 1.0 (replacement fertility) could somehow be achieved in 2000, the world's population would peak at approximately 8.4 billion by about the year 2100.[769] If it were to continue growing at the rate projected for 2000 (1.7 per unit per year), the world population would reach 10 billion in 2027, and 30 billion in 2091.

As of 1980, the year 2027 is 47 years away. To put it another way, a child born in 1980 will be 47 years old in 2027. Persons now under the age of 24 years can expect to live to 2027 (assuming a 70-year life expectancy). They may be living in a world whose population is approaching the maximum number that an intensively managed earth can sustain with, as the National Academy puts it, "some degree of comfort and individual choice." What are the major environmental developments that these persons may observe?

The Global 2000 Study's environmental projections, based on the assumption of no changes in policy, point to major changes in all three of the earth's major environments—terrestrial, aquatic, and atmospheric. The projections also point to a group of emerging environmental problems, some of which are global in scope, some of which involve vicious circles of causality, and some, increased societal vulnerability. By and large, these environmental problems will be difficult to resolve, even with major policy changes.

---

*It is perhaps notable that the historically steep upward trend in marine fish catch peaked at 60 million tons just as the National Academy of Sciences made its estimate of a 100 million ton potential.

In the terrestrial environment, the basic change to be anticipated is a general deterioration of soil quality over most of the earth. The immediate causes vary from one area to another, but generally involve demands on local ecosystems and soils and population growth that will be impossible to sustain. Desertification will claim large areas in the LDCs of Africa, Asia, and Latin America, as will erosion following shortened fallow cycles and tropical deforestation. Erosion, compaction, and hardpanning will affect increasingly large areas in the industrialized nations, as will salinization, alkalinization, and waterlogging of irrigated lands everywhere. Farm land will continue to be lost to urban and village expansion.

The global aquatic environment will also deteriorate generally, both in its saltwater and freshwater portions. Freshwater will be slowed by dams and irrigation works, warmed by waste heat from energy facilities (thus reducing the oxygen content), reduced in flow by more consumptive (i.e., evaporative) uses such as irrigation and evaporative cooling for energy facilities, salted by irrigation drainage, eutrophied by fertilizer runoff and sewage, acidified by acid mine drainage and acid rain, destablized by deforestation, and polluted by silt, pesticides, and other toxic substances. Freshwater habitats for disease vectors will increase. Habitats for species that require swift, clean, cool water (like salmon in the U.S.) will decline. Coastal marine waters will suffer from loss of important habitats—estuaries, salt marshes, mangroves, reefs—as well as from heavy pressure on fish and mammal populations, continued pollution by crude oil from offshore extraction, marine transport, and terrestrial runoff, and an influx of toxic materials, the effects of which will continue to be experienced for decades, at a minimum.

The atmosphere will—again, under the assumption of no change in present policies—receive increasing amounts of effluents from coal combustion. Oxides of nitrogen and sulfur will cause increased health problems and will produce acid rain. Particulates will increase health problems. Carbon dioxide emissions resulting from deforestation and from all forms of fossil fuel combustion (especially increased use of coal and synthetic fuels) will continue to increase the global concentration of CO_2 in the atmosphere, creating conditions that many scientists believe could raise the average temperature of the earth, melt polar ice, raise sea levels, and flood coastal areas during the 21st or 22nd century. Some spray-can propellents and refrigerants, some high-altitude aircraft flights, and nitrogen fertilizers will release chemicals in varying amounts that tend to reduce concentrations of ozone in the upper atmosphere, potentially increasing the amount of ultraviolet radiation, which is damaging to plants, animals, and humans.

Several developments are anticipated that will affect all three major environments (air, water, land). The release of toxic substances, including pesticides, is being controlled increasingly in industrialized nations, but under present policies growing amounts of these substances can be expected to enter the air, land, and water in LDCs. Materials emitting low-level radiation will be released in increased amounts into all three environments. Oxides of nitrogen and sulfur from fossil fuel combustion will increase atmospheric concentrations, acidify rain, and ultimately alter chemical balances in surface waters and soils over wide areas. The rate of extinctions of species in all three environments will increase dramatically, leading to the loss of perhaps one-fifth of all plant and animal species by 2000.

Some new classes of environmental problems will become more evident and more important— among them: problems that require global cooperation; problems that are very long-lived; problems that lead to increasing social vulnerability; and problems that originate in vicious-circle types of causations.

Problems of the global commons—the earth's atmosphere and oceans—can be expected to become more important and urgent in the years ahead. Management of global CO_2 and ozone concentrations are probably the most important and difficult issues of the global commons, but the protection of marine mammal populations (a global-commons problem on which some progress has already been achieved) will continue to be a concern. Institutional mechanisms for dealing with these issues are limited. The International Maritime Consultative Organization (IMCO) has made significant progress in dealing with oil pollution from tankers, but has made little progress in reducing the flow of toxic substances into the oceans. The U.N.-sponsored Law of the Sea Conference constitutes one of the broadest efforts made so far to deal with such problems, but the slowness of the progress made by this conference and related follow-up activities illustrates the extreme difficulties involved in achieving the necessary cooperation on issues related to the global commons. Efforts to manage CO_2 and ozone concentrations on a global scale are just beginning, and considering the issues involved—fossil fuel combustion, deforestation, high-altitude flight, perhaps even the rate of use of nitrogen fertilizers—agreements can be expected to be at least as difficult to reach as in the case of the Law of the Sea.

Multilateral cooperation on only a somewhat smaller scale will be required to deal with a number of terrestrial, coastal, and freshwater environmental issues. Desertification problems often cross national boundaries, as do some of the herding populations involved. Deforestation is being driven not only by domestic needs, but also by multinational markets and corporations. Protection of regional seas will be impossible without multilateral cooperation, and the protection and management of many river basins will require cooperation among two or more nations as well. Since the needs of upstream and downstream users often conflict, river development and management may become an increasing source of conflict among nations as water resources become still more heavily committed.

Long-lived toxic pollutants also present a new class of environmental problems. Many toxic substances—heavy metals, radioactive materials, and some toxic chemicals—have very long lives, and their release or mobilization into the environment creates changes for which there is no apparent remedial action. Mercury, lead, high-level radioactive wastes, dioxin, and PCBs are examples. Many metals, some of which bioaccumulate, are highly toxic, and once mobilized by mining, refining, dredging, or industrial processes, are expected to produce adverse effects for decades— or centuries—to come, especially in the oceans. The consequences are many and varied. It is well known, for example, that the utility of biological resources (e.g., fish and shellfish) has been degraded or destroyed by heavy metals, but it is less well known that some bacteria have developed resistance to mercury poisoning and as a consequence also to several antibiotics. (Research with the genus *Vibrio* and the genus *Bacillus* have led to the conclusion that the antibiotic and mercury resistances are genetically linked and caused by the mercury exposure.[770]) High-level radioactive wastes are extremely toxic and must be kept safely separated from the environment for tens of thousands of years, a period that exceeds the stable life of any civilization in history, and even exceeds the period of recorded history. Long-lived toxic chemicals present similar problems. While several industrial nations are now tightening regulations for the use and disposal of toxic chemicals, the controls are far from adequate. Even determining which individual chemicals are toxic will be difficult, and the problem of synergistic toxicity of two or more chemicals presently lacks a feasible solution.[771] Furthermore, old chemical dumps

(such as the Love Canal dumpsite in New York State),[772] contaminated river bottoms (such as those of the Hudson River in New York[773] and the James in Virginia),[774] and contaminated lands (such as the environs of Seveso, Italy)[775] will continue to pose threats to animals—and human life—for many years to come.

Another class of environmental pressures is leading to increased vulnerability, especially in the world's food production and energy systems. Food production around the world is leading to various forms of soil deterioration. Fertility is being maintained, pests controlled, and yields enhanced through energy-intensive (or more specifically, fossil fuel-intensive) inputs of fertilizers, chemicals, and fuels for tractors and irrigation motors. The food needed to feed the population projected for 2000 can be produced only through the continued and increased dependence of agriculture on fossil fuels. The increased vulnerability that this trend implies is illustrated by the disruption in energy supplies caused recently by the change of government in a single nation— Iran, by no means the largest of the world's energy suppliers. The vulnerability of energy-intensive agriculture is increased further by expanded areas of genetically similar (or identical) monocultures, by expansion of agriculture into increasingly arid and marginal lands, and by the projected deforestation (which exaggerates seasonal variations in water availability and thus increases vulnerability to drought).

In the energy area, increased reliance on nuclear energy will create another environmentally related vulnerability. The accident at Three Mile Island in Pennsylvania demonstrated dramatically that nuclear accidents, whatever their probability, can and do happen. In the Three Mile Island accident, relatively little damage was done to the environment, but radioactive gases were released, and the governor of Pennsylvania felt it necessary to partially evacuate an area within five miles of the stricken plant. As a result of the accident, and of concern over the safety of a second reactor at the same site built by the same manufacturer, a significant fraction of the electric energy supply for Pennsylvania has been lost for a period of years. Public concern is now such that another serious accident or a terrorist attack* could lead to a significant curtailment in nuclear generation in many countries. The projected 226 percent increase in nuclear generation by 1990 will increase this vulnerability.

---

*There have been a significant number of attacks on nuclear installations. See Michael Flood, "Nuclear Sabotage," *Bulletin of the Atomic Scientists,* Oct. 1976, pp. 29–36.

Finally, there is a growing class of environmental problems that will be extremely difficult to resolve because of a vicious circle of causes and effects. This class of problems is particularly acute in the land-deterioration/population-growth phenomenon in some of the poorest rural areas in the LDCs: Environmental deterioration is accelerated by further population growth; human reproduction rates are kept up by poor living conditions (and other social welfare problems);[776] and living conditions decline further as the environmental resources deteriorate.

The important linkages between the population, welfare, and resource demands have long been recognized and included in development plans and projection models, but the linkages from the environment back to population, welfare, and resources have often been neglected. So it is with the Global 2000 Sudy's projections. As illustrated in Figure 13–1, the linkages from the population and GNP projections to resource demands are well established. This chapter has analyzed the environmental implications of the population, GNP, and resource projections and has attempted to close the feedback loops linking the projected future world environment back to the other projections. While the feedback loops could not actually be closed, the environmental assumptions underlying the population, GNP, and resource projections were identified and compared with the environmental future these projections imply. The environmental assumptions implicit in the population, GNP, and resource projections amount in many cases to an assumption that the environment will provide its goods and services in much larger amounts, without interruption, and without increase in cost. The environmental analysis suggests that this assumption is, in many cases, unrealistically optimistic. The analysis also shows that the goods and services provided by the environment can no longer be taken for granted.

REFERENCES

Population Section

1. Wendell Berry, *Unsettling of America,* San Francisco: Sierra Club, 1977, pp. 210–17.
2. See, for example, Colin M. Turnbull, *The Forest People: A Study of the Pygmies of the Congo,* New York: Simon and Schuster, 1962.
3. Raymond F. Dasmann et al., *Ecological Principles for Economic Development,* New York: Wiley, 1973, p. 82.
4. *Conservation and Rational Use of the Environment,* UNESCO and FAO report to the U.N. Economic and Social Council, Mar. 12, 1968.
5. Garrett Hardin and John Baden, eds., *Managing the Commons,* San Francisco: Freeman, 1977.
6. Garrett Hardin, "The Tragedy of the Commons," *Science,* Dec. 13, 1968, pp. 1243–48.
7. For two particularly interesting examples, see the story of the Tasaday in John Nance, *The Gentle Tasaday: A Stone Age People in the Philippine Rain Forest,* New York: Harcourt, 1975; and the story of the decline of the Mayan civilization as told in Harold M. Schmecht, Jr., "Study Depicts Mayan Decline," *New York Times,* Oct. 23, 1979, p. C1, and in E. S. Deevey et al., Mayan Urbanism: Impact on a Tropical Karst Environment," *Science,* Oct. 19, 1979, pp. 298–306.
8. See, for example, Colin M. Turnbull, *The Mountain People,* New York, Simon and Schuster, 1972. This phenomenon extends beyond herding societies. See, for example: D. A. Schanche, "King, Cripple-Makers Rule Cairo's Army of Beggars," *Washington Post,* Sept. 2, 1978, p. A–11; Abdell Atti Hamed, *Adventures of a Journalist at the Bottom of Egyptian Society,* Cairo: Akbar al Yom Publishing House, 1974.
9. *Arid Lands in Transition,* Harold E. Dregne, ed., Washington: American Association for the Advancement of Science, 1970.
10. Ibid.
11. *The State of Food and Agriculture.* Rome: Food and Agriculture Organization, Nov. 1977 (draft), ch. 3, pp. 3–16.
12. Ibid.

13. T. C. Byerly et al., *The Role of Ruminants in Support of Man,* Morrilton, Ark.: Winrock International Livestock Research and Training Center, Apr. 1978; T. D. Nguyen and H. A. Fitzhugh, *WINROCK MODEL for Simulating Ruminant Production Systems,* Morrilton: Winrock, Dec. 1977.
14. Robert B. Batchelder and Howard F. Hirt, "Fire in Tropical Forests and Grasslands," U.S. Army Natick Laboratories, June 1966, pp. 136, 168 (this excellent report is available from the National Technical Information Service).
15. *Tropical Forest Ecosystems: A State of Knowledge Report,* Natural Resources Research XIV, Paris: UNESCO/UNEP/FAO, 1978, pp. 467–81.
16. Ibid., p. 475.
17. Dasmann et al., op. cit.
18. P. H. Nye and D. J. Greenland, *The Soil Under Shifting Cultivation,* Technical Communication No. 51, Bucks, England: Commonwealth Agricultural Bureaux, 1960.
19. *Tropical Forest Ecosystems,* op. cit., pp. 470–76.
20. R. F. Watters, *Shifting Agriculture in Latin America,* Rome: Food and Agriculture Organization, 1971.
21. Lester R. Brown, *The Worldwide Loss of Cropland,* Washington: Worldwatch Institute, Oct. 1978; "Desertification: An Overview," U.N. Conference on Desertification, 1977; Erik P. Eckholm, *Losing Ground: Environmental Stress and World Food Prospects,* New York: Norton, 1976.
22. For further details, see the forestry section of this chapter, also Chapter 8 and App. C, and "Proceedings of the U.S. Strategy Conference on Tropical Deforestation," Washington: U.S. Agency for International Development, 1978.
23. U.N. Conference on Desertification, Earthscan Press Briefing Document No. 6, Aug. 1977.
24. Eckholm, *Losing Ground,* op. cit.; App. C of this volume; "Desertification: An Overview," op. cit.
25. *Environmental Quality 1978,* annual report of the Council on Environmental Quality, Washington: Government Printing Office, 1979, ch. 3.

26. Ibid.
27. Ibid.
28. Ibid.
29. Ibid.
30. Denis Hayes, *Repairs, Reuse, Recycling–First Steps Toward a Sustainable Society*, Washington: Worldwatch Institute, Sept. 1978.
31. *Environmental Quality 1973*, annual report of the Council on Environmental Quality, Washington: Government Printing Office, 1974, p. 204.
32. The obscuring of environmental impacts that results from trade and commerce is brought out in Edward Goldsmith and John P. Milton, eds., "The Future of America," *The Ecologist*, Aug./Sept. 1977, pp. 245–340.
33. Hardin, "Tragedy of the Commons," op. cit.
34. Garrett Hardin, "Political Requirements for Preserving Our Common Heritage," Ch. 20 in Council on Environmental Quality, *Wildlife and America*, Washington: Government Printing Office, 1979.
35. Thane Gustafson, "The New Soviet Environmental Program: Do The Soviets Really Mean Business?" *Public Policy*, Summer 1978, pp. 455–76; Marshall I. Goldman, *The Spoils of Progress: Environmental Pollution in the Soviet Union*, Cambridge, Mass., MIT, 1972.; Donald R. Kelly et al., *Economic Superpowers and the Environment: United States, Soviet Union and Japan*, San Francisco; Freeman, 1976.
36. Susan Swannack-Nunn et al., *State-of-the-Environment Profile for the People's Republic of China*, Washington: National Council for U.S.–China Trade, Apr. 1979. Also see B. J. Culliton, "China Adopts New Law for Environmental Protection," *Science*, Oct. 26, 1979, p. 429.
37. An excellent history of U.S. efforts to protect its environment will be found in J. Clarence Davies III and Barbara Davies, *The Politics of Pollution*, 2d ed., Indianapolis: Bobbs-Merrill, 1975; also see P. R. Portney, ed., *Current Issues in U.S. Environmental Policy*, Baltimore: Johns Hopkins, 1978.
38. Talbot Page, *Conservation and Economic Efficiency: An Approach to Materials Policy*, Baltimore: Johns Hopkins, 1977, ch. 7; Kenneth J. Arrow, "The Rate of Discount for Long-Term Public Investment," in Holt Ashley et al., *Energy and the Environment: A Risk Benefit Approach*, New York: Pergamon, 1976, pp. 113–41.
39. Ibid.
40. *The Determinants and Consequences of Population Trends*, vol. 1, New York: U.N. Dept. of Economic and Social Affairs, 1973.
41. "Trends and Prospects in Urban and Rural Population, 1950–2000, as Assessed in 1973–74," New York: Population Div., U.N. Dept. of Economic and Social Affairs, Apr. 25, 1975, p. 10.
42. Ibid.
43. An excellent introduction to this topic, prepared for the U.N. Conference on Human Settlements, is Barbara Ward, *The Home of Man*, New York: Norton, 1976.
44. "Trends and Prospects in Urban and Rural Population, 1950–2000," op. cit., p. 11.
45. "Third World Urban Sprawl," *ILO Information* (U.S. ed.), vol. 6, no. 4, 1978, pp. 1, 9.
46. Ibid.
47. "Trends and Prospects in the Populations of Urban Agglomerations, 1950–2000, as Assessed in 1973–1975," ESA/P/WP.58, New York: Population Div., U.N. Dept. of Economic and Social Affairs, Nov. 21, 1975.
48. Peter H. Freeman, "The Environmental Impact of Rapid Urbanization: Guidelines for Policy and Planning,"

Washington: Office of International and Environmental Programs, Smithsonion Institution, 1974, table 12, p. 42.
49. Peter H. Freeman, ed., *The Urban Environment of Seoul, Korea: A Case Study of Rapid Urbanization*, Washington: U.S. Agency for International Development, Nov., 1974.
50. "World Population: The Silent Explosion," *Department of State Bulletin*, Fall 1978, pp. 17–18.
51. Ward, op. cit., p. 193.
52. World Health Organization, "Community Water Supply and Wastewater Disposal," May 6, 1976, p.4.
53. Ibid., p. 5.
54. J. R. Simpson and R. M. Bradley, "The Environmental Impact of Water Reclamation in Overseas Countries," *Water Pollution Control*, vol. 77, no. 2, 1978, p. 223.
55. Ibid.
56. Bruce McCallum, *Environmentally Appropriate Technology*, Dept. of Fisheries and Environment, Canada, Apr. 1977, pp. 109–11; Lane deMoll, ed., *Rainbook: Resources for Appropriate Technology*, New York: Schocken, 1977, pp. 191–94.
57. World Health Organization, "Disposal of Community Wastewater," Technical Report Service no. 541, 1974.
58. Elaine de Steinheil and Hilary Branch, "Enforcing Environmental Law in Venezuela," *World Environment Report*, Feb. 27, 1978, p. 3.
59. William F. Hunt et al., *Guideline for Public Reporting of Daily Air Quality: Pollutant Standards Index*, U.S. Environmental Protection Agency, Aug. 1976.
60. Loretta McLaughlan, "Peruvian Ecologist Urges Lima to Enact Air Pollution Law," *World Environment Report*, Aug. 14, 1978, p. 5.
61. Sam Cohen, "Sulphur Dioxide in Ankara's Air Found Twice that of WHO Standard," *World Environment Report*, Dec. 19, 1977, p. 5.
62. R. Murali Manohar, "Massive Air Pollution in Bombay Cause of Respiratory Ailments," *World Environment Report*, May 8, 1978, p. 5.
63. Ibid.
64. Ibid.
65. Erick Eckholm, *The Other Energy Crisis: Firewood*, Washington: Worldwatch Institute, 1975.
66. *State of Food and Agriculture*, op. cit., p. 25.
67. "Third World Urban Sprawl," op. cit.
68. Lester R. Brown, *The Twenty-Ninth Day*, New York: Norton 1978.
69. "Trends and Prospects in Urban and Rural Population, 1950–2000," op. cit.
70. Council on Environmental Quality, U.S. Dept. of Housing and Urban Development, and U.S. Environmental Protection Agency, "The Costs of Sprawl: Environmental and Economic Costs of Alternative Residential Development Patterns at the Urban Fringe," Washington: Government Printing Office, Apr. 1974; also see the Council's "The Quiet Revolution in Land Use Control" and "The Growth Shapers," Washington: Government Printing Office, 1971, 1976.
71. Hayes, op. cit.
72. Executive Office of the President, "The National Energy Plan," Washington: Government Printing Office, Apr. 1977.
73. Ibid., p. VII.
74. Ibid., pp. VIII, X.
75. Office of Technology Assessment, "Analysis of the Proposed National Energy Plan," Washington: Government Printing Office, Aug. 1977, pp. 197–80.
75a. *The Journey to Work in the United States: 1975*, Washington: Government Printing Office, July 1977; Spencer

Rich, "Auto Data Reflect an Abiding Passion," *Washington Post*, July 22, 1979, p. A20.

75b. L. R. Brown, C. Flavin, and C. Norman, *Running on Empty: The Future of the Automobile in an Oil Short World*, New York: Norton, 1979.

76. *Environmental Quality 1978*, op. cit. p. 220; also see U.S. Bureau of the Census, *Geographic Mobility: March 1975 to March 1978* and *Social and Economic Characteristics of the Metropolitan and Nonmetropolitan Population: 1977 and 1970*. Washington: Government Printing Office, Nov. 1978.

77. *Environmental Quality 1978*, op. cit., p. 227.

78. George J. Beier, "Can Third World Cities Cope?" Washington: Population Reference Bureau, Dec. 1976.

79. Eckholm, *Losing Ground*, op. cit.; Dasmann et al., op. cit.; *Tropical Forest Ecosystems*, op. cit.

80. *Canada as a Conserver Society: Resource Uncertainties and the Need for New Technologies*, Ottawa: Science Council of Canada, Sept. 1977.

81. U.N. Dept. of Economic and Social Affairs, *The Determinants and Consequences of Population Trends: New Summary of Findings on Interaction of Demographic, Economic and Social Factors*, vol. 1, New York, 1973.

82. N. R. E. Fendall, "Medical Care in the Developing Nations," in John Fry and W. A. J. Farndale, eds., *International Medical Care*, Wallingford, Pa.: Washington Square East, 1972, p. 220.

83. World Bank, "Health," Sector Policy Paper, Washington, Mar. 1975, annex 2, pp. 72–73; also see M. E. McHale et al., *Children in the World*, Washington: Population Reference Bureau, 1979, pp. 30–34.

84. World Bank, op. cit.

85. Ibid., p. 7.

86. Tim Dyson, "Levels, Trends, Differential and Causes of Child Mortality—A survey," *World Health Statistics Report*, vol. 30, no. 4, 1977, pp. 289–90.

87. John Bryant, *Health and the Developing World*, Ithaca, N.Y.: Cornell, 1969, p. 39.

88. W. J. van Zijl, "Studies on Diarrhoeal Diseases in Seven Countries by the WHO Diarrhoeal Diseases Advisory Team," *Bulletin of the World Health Organization*, vol. 35, no. 2, 1966, pp. 249–61.

89. Ibid.

90. Lester R. Brown, *World Population Trends: Signs of Hope, Signs of Stress*, Washington: Worldwatch Institute, Oct. 1976, pp. 15–25.

91. Sheldon M. Wolff and John V. Bennetts, "Gram-Negative Rod Bacteremia," *New England Journal of Medicine*, Oct. 3, 1974, pp. 733–34; Henry E. Simmons and Paul D. Stolley, "This is Medical Progress? Trends and Consequences of Antibiotic Use in the United States," *Journal of the American Medical Association*, Mar. 4, 1974, pp. 1023–28; LaVerne C. Harold, "Transferable Drug Resistance and the Ecologic Effects of Antibiotics," in M. Taghi Farvar and John P. Milton, eds., *The Careless Technology, Ecology and International Development*, Garden City: Natural History Press/Doubleday, 1972, pp. 35–46.

92. Wolff and Bennett, op. cit.

93. Eugene J. Gangarosa et. al., "An Epidemic-Associated Episome?," *Journal of Infectious Diseases*, Aug. 1972, pp. 215–18.

94. Ibid.

95. J. Olarte and E. Galindo, "Factores de resistencia a los antibióticos encontrados en bacterias enteropatógenas aisladas en la Ciudad de· México," *Reviews of Latin American Microbiology*, vol. 12, 1970, pp. 173–79.

96. Pan American Sanitary Bureau, Regional Office of the

World Health Organization, *Weekly Epidemiological Report*, no. 22, 1972, pp. 129–30.

97. World Health Organization, *Weekly Epidemiological Record*, Oct. 14–Nov. 11, 1977. pp. 325–70; June 23–30, 1978, pp. 181–96.

98. Marietta Whittlesey, "The Runaway Use of Antibiotics," *New York Times Magazine*, May 6, 1979, p. 122.

99. Ibid.

100. Ibid; Janice Crossland, "Power to Resist," *Environment*, Mar. 1975, pp. 6–11.

101. Office of Technology Assessment, *Drugs in Livestock Feed*, vol. I, *Technical Report*, Washington: Government Printing Office, 1979.

102. Whittlesey, op. cit.

103. Ibid.

104. Davidson R. Gwatkin, "The Sad News About the Death Rate," *Washington Post*, Dec. 2, 1978, op ed page; and his "The End of an Era: A Review of the Literature and Data Concerning Third World Mortality Trends," Washington: Overseas Development Council, forthcoming.

105. U.S. Public Health Service, National Center for Health Statistics, *Vital Statistics of the United States*, vol. 2, sec. 5, *Life Tables*, Hyattsville, Md., 1977, pp. 5–15.

106. There is a very extensive literature on this topic. For a small sample, see Michael J. Hill, "Metabolic Epidemiology of Dietary Factors in Large Bowel Cancer," *Cancer Research*, Nov. 1975, pp. 3398–3402; F. R. Lemon and T. T. Walden, "Death from Respiratory System Disease Among SDA Men," *Journal of the American Medical Association*, vol. 198, 1966, p. 117; Roland L. Phillips, "Role of Life-Style and Dietary Habits in Risk of Cancer Among Seventh-Day Adventists," *Cancer Research*, Nov. 1975, pp. 3513–22; Denis P. Burkitt, "Epidemiology of Cancer of the Colon and Rectum," *Cancer*, July 1971, pp. 3–13; "Statement of Dr. D. M. Hegsted," in U.S. Senate Select Committee on Nutrition and Human Needs, *Dietary Goals for the United States*, Washington: Government Printing Office, Feb. 1975, p. 3; Jacqueline Verrett and Jean Carper, *Eating May Be Hazardous to Your Health: How Your Government Fails to Protect You from the Dangers in Your Food*, New York: Simon and Schuster, 1974; Erik P. Eckholm, *The Picture of Health: Environmental Sources of Disease*, New York: Norton, 1977.

107. U.S. Public Health Service, *Health, United States 1978*, Washington: Dept. of Health, Education, and Welfare, 1978, pp. 220–21.

108. "Report to the President by the Toxic Substances Strategy Committee," Washington: Council on Environmental Quality, Aug. 1979 (public review draft).

109. Richard Doll, "Introduction," and J. W. Berg, "Worldwide Variations in Cancer Incidence as Clues to Cancer Origins," in H. H. Hiatt et al., eds, *Origins of Human Cancer*, Cold Spring Harbor, New York: Cold Spring Harbor Laboratory, 1977. Also see Thomas H. Maugh II, "Cancer and Environment: Higginson Speaks Out," *Science*, vol. 205, 1979, pp. 1363–66.

110. U.S. Public Health Service, *Annual Summary for the United States, 1977: Births, Deaths, Marriages, and Divorces*, pp. 28–29, and *Monthly Statistics Report—Provisional Statistics*, Washington: Dept. of Health, Education, and Welfare, 1977, 1979.

111. Ibid.

GNP Section

112. Commission on Population Growth and the American Future, *Population and the American Future*, Washington: Government Printing Office, Mar. 27, 1972, p. 48.

113. Lester R. Brown, *The Global Economic Prospect: New Sources of Economic Stress,* Washington: Worldwatch Institute, May 1978, p. 6.
114. J. Krieger et al., "Facts and Figures for the U.S. Chemical Industry," *Chemical and Engineering News,* vol. 57, 1979, pp. 32–68.
115. U.N. Environment Programme, *State of the Environment 1978,* United Nations, Nairobi, 1978.
116. Organization for Economic Cooperation and Development, Chemicals Committee, *Chemicals in the Environment,* Paris, 1977.
117. U.S. Dept. of Labor, Occupational Safety and Health Administration, "Occupational Exposure to 1,2-Dibromo-3-chloropropane (DBCP) Occupational Safety and Health Standards," *Federal Register,* Mar. 17, 1978, pp. 11514–33.
118. Thomas H. Milby, ed. *Vinyl Chloride: An Information Resource,* Washington: National Institutes of Health, Mar. 1978.
119. U.S. Senate Committee on Commerce, Science, and Transportation, *Hazardous Materials Transportation: A Review and Analysis of the Department of Transportation's Regulatory Program,* Washington: Government Printing Office, 1979, pp. 13–14.
120. Environmental Defense Fund and the New York Public Interest Research Group, *Troubled Waters: Toxic Chemicals in the Hudson River,* New York, 1977.
121. *Environmental Quality 1977,* annual report of the Council on Environmental Quality, Washington: Government Printing Office, 1977, pp. 15–16.
122. US Environmental Protection Agency, *EPA Activities Under the Resource Conservation and Recovery Act—Fiscal Year 1978,* Washington: Government Printing Office, 1979, pp. 1–3.
123. Dick Kirschten, "The New War on Pollution is Over the Land," *National Journal,* 1979, pp. 603–6; John Walsh, "Seveso: The Questions Persist Where Dioxin Created a Wasteland," *Science,* Sept. 9, 1977, pp. 1064–67; John C. Fuller, *The Poison that Fell From the Sky,* New York: Random House, 1977, p. 94; Thomas Whiteside, "A Reporter at Large: Contaminated," *New Yorker,* Sept. 4, 1978, pp. 34–81 (published also as *The Pendulum and the Toxic Cloud,* New Haven: Yale, 1979).
124. Report of the Governing Council of the United Nations Environment Programme on the Work of its Fifth Session, Governing Council Decision 85(v), Nairobi, May, 1977.
125. World Bank, *Sociological Planning and Political Aspects,* Aug. 1978, ch. 7.
126. Study Group on Unintended Occurrence of Pesticides, *The Problems of Persistent Chemicals: Implications of Pesticides and Other Chemicals in the Environment,* Paris: Organization for Economic Cooperation and Development, 1971.

Climate Section

127. "Climate Change to the Year 2000: A Survey of Expert Opinion," Washington: National Defense University, 1978.
128. Ibid.
129. P. R. Crow, *Concepts in Climatology,* New York: St. Martin's, 1971, p. 480 ff.; C. E. P. Brooks, *Climate through the Ages,* New York: Dover, 1949.
130. *Climate and Food: Climatic Fluctuation and U.S. Agricultural Production,* Washington: National Academy of Sciences, 1976.
131. Well-developed introductions to the issues of climatic change are provided in Paul R. Ehrlich et al., *Ecoscience:*

Population, Resources, Environment, San Francisco: Freeman, 1977, pp. 672–94; Ralph M. Rotty, "Energy and the Climate," Oak Ridge: Institute for Energy Analysis, Sept. 1976; Bert Bolin, "Energy and Climate," Stockholm: Secretariat for Future Studies, Nov. 1975. More detailed information is provided in U.S. Committee for the Global Atmospheric Research Program, *Understanding Climatic Change: A Program for Action,* Washington: National Academy of Sciences, 1975; Study of Man's Impact on Climate, *Inadvertent Climate Modification,* Cambridge, Mass.: MIT, 1971; Study of Critical Environmental Problems (SCEP) *Man's Impact on the Global Environment,* Cambridge, Mass.: MIT, 1970; Geophysics Study Committee, *Energy and Climate,* Washington: National Academy of Sciences, 1977.
132. "Crop Yields and Climate Change: The Year 2000," Washington: National Defense University, Dec. 1978, (draft abstract of Task II final report).
133. Ibid.
134. Rotty, op. cit.
135. U. Siegenthaler and H. Oeschger, "Predicting Future Atmospheric Carbon Dioxide Levels," *Science,* vol. 199, 1978, pp. 388–95.
136. Geophysics Study Committee, op. cit.
137. For a relatively simple discussion of the phenomena, see G. M. Woodwell, "The Carbon Dioxide Question," *Scientific American,* Jan. 1978, pp. 34–43. Also see G. M. Woodwell et al., "The Biota and the World Carbon Budget," *Science,* Jan. 13, 1978, pp. 141–46; G. E. Hutchinson, "The Biochemistry of the Terrestrial Atmosphere," in G. P. Kuiper, ed., *The Solar System,* Chicago: University of Chicago, 1954, vol. 2, pp. 371–433. For a recent counteropinion, see W. S. Broecker et al., "Fate of Fossil Fuel Carbon Dioxide and the Global Carbon Budget," *Science,* vol. 206, 1979, pp. 409–18.
138. Siegenthaler and Oeschger, op. cit.
139. Ibid.
140. Peter G. Brewer, "Carbon Dioxide and Climate," *Oceanus,* Fall 1978, pp. 13–17.
141. Siegenthaler and Oeschger, op. cit.
142. For an especially clear introduction, see the short report by Gordon J. F. MacDonald: *An Overview of the Impact of Carbon Dioxide on Climate,* McLean Va.: MITRE Corp., Dec. 1978; also see U.S. Office of Technology Assessment, *The Direct Use of Coal,* Washington: Government Printing Office, Apr. 1979, pp. 226–30; *Carbon Dioxide Emissions from Synthetic Fuels Energy Sources,* Washington: Dept. of Energy, August 8, 1979.
143. Geophysics Study Committee, op. cit., p. 4.
144. George D. Robinson, "Effluents of Energy Production: Particulates," in Geophysics Study Committee, op. cit.
145. Ibid.
146. A Miller and J. C. Thompson, *Elements of Meteorology,* Columbus, Ohio: Merrill, 1970; A. G. Borne, "Birth of An Island," *Discovery,* vol. 25, no. 4, 1964, p. 16.
147. J. Ernst, "African Dust Layer Sweeps into SW North Atlantic Area," *Bulletin of the American Meteorological Society,* vol. 55, no. 11, 1974, pp. 1352–53; J. B. Lushine, "A Dust Layer in the Eastern Caribbean," *Monthly Weather Review,* vol. 103, no. 5, 1975, pp. 454–55.
148. R. A. Bryson and T. J. Murray, *Climates of Hunger: Mankind and the World's Changing Weather,* Madison: University of Wisconsin, 1977.
149. Robinson, op. cit., p. 70.
150. Rotty, op. cit., p. 19.
151. A. Kh. Khrgian, *The Physics of Atmospheric Ozone,* Leningrad: Hydrometeorological Institute, 1973 (English translation, 1975), pp. 31–32.

152. *Environmental Impact of Stratospheric Flight: Biological and Climatic Effects of Aircraft Emissions in the Stratosphere,* Washington: National Academy of Sciences, 1975, pp. 5–7, 9–10.
153. "Response to the Ozone Protection Sections of the Clean Air Act Amendments of 1977: An Interim Report," Washington: National Academy of Sciences, 1977.
154. *Halocarbons: Environmental Effects of Chlorofluoromethane Release,* Washington: National Academy of Sciences, 1976.
155. *Environmental Impact of Stratospheric Flight,* op. cit.
156. *Nitrates: An Environmental Assessment,* Washington: National Academy of Sciences, 1978; W. C. Wang et al., "Greenhouse Effects due to Man-Made Perturbations of Trace Gases," *Science,* Nov. 12, 1976, pp. 685–90. Also see G. L. Hutchinson, A. R. Mosier, "Nitrous Oxide Emissions from an Irrigated Cornfield," *Science,* Sept. 14, 1979, pp. 1125–27.
157. A. J. Grobecker et al., "The Effects of Stratospheric Pollution by Aircraft," report of the Climatic Impact Assessment Program, Washington: Department of Transportation, 1975; *Environmental Impact of Stratospheric Flight,* op. cit.
158. *Nitrates,* op. cit. pp. 362–63.
159. *Halocarbons,* op. cit.; Council on Environmental Quality and Federal Council for Science and Technology, "Fluorocarbons and the Environment," Washington: Government Printing Office, 1975.
160. *Nitrates,* op. cit., p. 364.
161. Ibid., especially ch. 7.
162. Ibid., p. 362.
163. Ibid. p. 361.
164. Ibid., p. 363.
165. R. P. Turco et al., "SSTs, Nitrogen Fertilizer and Stratospheric Ozone," *Nature,* Dec. 28, 1978, pp. 805–7; Paul J. Crutzen and Carleton J. Howard, "The Effect of the HO_2 + NO Reaction Rate Constant on One-Dimensional Model Calculations of Stratospheric Ozone Perturbations," *Pure and Applied Geophysics* (Milan), vol. 116, 1978, pp. 497–510.
166. *Environmental Impact of Stratospheric Flight,* op. cit., p. 7; Geophysics Study Committee, op. cit., p. 4.
167. *Environmental Impact of Stratospheric Flight,* op. cit., p. 45.
168. Ibid., p. 49.
169. Ibid., pp. 177–221.
170. Ibid., p. 13.
171. Ibid., pp. 222–31.
172. Ibid., p. 11.
173. Ibid., p. 47; *Results of Research Related to Stratospheric Ozone Protection,* U.S. Environmental Protection Agency, Jan. 1978.
174. *Environmental Impact of Stratospheric Flight,* op. cit., p. 47.
175. *Results of Research Related to Stratospheric Ozone Protection,* op. cit.
176. Section 153 of the Clean Air Act, as amended.
177. *Nitrates,* op. cit., ch. 11.
178. Ibid., p. 18.
179. Geophysics Study Committee, op. cit., p. 97.
180. Weather Modification Board, "A U.S. Policy to Enhance the Atmospheric Environment," Washington: Department of Commerce, Oct. 21, 1977; "Desertification: An Overview," op. cit.
181. Rotty, op. cit., p. 15.
182. Ibid.
183. SCEP, *Man's Impact on the Global Environment,* op. cit.
184. S. F. Singer, "The Environmental Effects of Energy Pro-

duction," in S. F. Singer, ed., *The Changing Global Environment,* Dordrecht; Netherlands: Reidel, 1975, pp. 25–44.
185. A. H. Murphy et al., "The Impact of Waste Heat Release on Simulated Global Climate," Laxenburg, Austria: International Institute of Applied Systems Analysis, Dec. 1976, p. 23.
186. Geophysics Study Committee, op. cit., p. 4.
187. Ibid.
188. See especially George M. Woodwell et al., *The Carbon Dioxide Problem: Implications for Policy in the Management of Energy and Other Resources,* Washington: Council on Environmental Quality, July 1979; also see references cited in Reference 142.
189. Woodwell et al., *The Carbon Dioxide Problem,* op. cit.

Technology Section

190. Cynthia Gorney, "University Is Sued Over Development of Sophisticated Harvesting Machines," *Washington Post,* Jan. 18, 1979, p. A11.
191. See, for example, the case histories in M. Taghi Farvar and John P. Milton, eds., *The Careless Technology: Ecology and International Development,* New York: Doubleday, 1972.
192. Raymond F. Dasmann et al., *Ecological Principles for Economic Development,* New York: Wiley, 1973, pp. 182–235.
193. E. F. Schumacher, *Small is Beautiful: Economics as if People Mattered,* New York: Harper, 1973, p. 165.
194. A thoughtful discussion of some of the options for a postindustrial technological society is provided in Willis W. Harman, *An Incomplete Guide to the Future,* Stanford, Calif.: Stanford Alumni Association, 1976.
195. Colin Norman, "Soft Technologies, Hard Choices," Washington: Worldwatch Institute, June 1978.

Food and Agriculture Section

196. "Demand for Food Production Reduces Land's Capacity to Produce," Council on Environmental Quality news release, Mar. 13, 1977, announcing publication by the Council on Mar. 14, 1977, of Paul F. Bente, Jr., "The Food People Problem: Can the Land's Capacity to Produce Food Be Sustained?"
197. Joint FAO/WHO ad hoc Expert Committee, "Energy and Protein Requirements," Rome: Food and Agriculture Organization, 1973.
198. See, for example, Erik Eckholm and Frank Record, *The Two Faces of Malnutrition,* Washington: Worldwatch Institute, 1976; *World Food and Nutrition Study,* interim report, Washington: National Academy of Sciences, 1975.
199. U.S. Department of Agriculture, Economics, Statistics, and Cooperative Service, "Report Assessing Global Food Production and Needs as of March 31, 1978," Washington, Mar. 1978.
200. S. Reutlinger and M. Selowsky, *Malnutrition and Poverty,* World Bank Occasional Paper 23, Washington, 1976.
201. Robert McNamara, "Address to the 1978 Annual Meeting of the World Bank–International Monetary Fund Board of Governors," Washington, Sept. 1978.
202. Philip Handler, "On the State of Man," address to the annual convocation of Markle Scholars, National Academy of Sciences, Sept. 29, 1974.
203. An excellent listing of the literature available in this area will be found in Lester R. Brown, *The Worldwide Loss of Cropland,* Washington: Worldwatch Institute, Oct.

1978; for U.S. data, see U.S. Department of Agriculture, Economic Research Service, "American Agriculture: Its Capacity to Produce," Washington, Feb. 1974.

204. Erik P. Eckholm, *Losing Ground: Environmental Stress and World Food Prospects* New York: Norton, 1976.

205. "Desertification: An Overview," U.N. Conference on Desertification, Aug. 1977, p. 11.

206. *The State of Food and Agriculture 1977*, Rome: Food and Agriculture Organization (draft), calculated from table 3–28.

207. "Desertification: An Overview," op. cit., pp. 5–6; *Desertification: Environmental Degradation in and Around Arid Lands*, Boulder: Westview Press, 1977.

208. Erik Eckholm and Lester R. Brown, *Spreading Deserts— The Hand of Man*, Washington: Worldwatch Institute, Aug. 1977; *State of Food and Agriculture 1977*, op. cit., table 3–14.

209. Ibid., p. 13; "Case Study on Desertification—Luni Development Block, India," U.N. Conference on Desertification, Aug. 1977, especially pp. 39ff.

210. F. Kenneth Hare, "Climate and Desertification: Background Document," U.N. Conference on Desertification, Aug. 1977, p. 36.

211. "Population, Society and Desertification," U.N. Conference on Desertification, Aug. 1977.

212. "Desertification: An Overview," op. cit., pp. 7–8; "Synthesis of Case Studies of Desertification," U.N. Conference on Desertification, Aug. 1977.

213. "Desertification: An Overview," op. cit., p. 12.

214. Calculated from data in ibid. and *Production Yearbook 1975*, Rome: Food and Agriculture Organization, 1976.

215. "Case Study on Desertification: Mona Reclamation Experimental Project, Pakistan," U.N. Conference on Desertification, Aug. 1977.

216. "Transnational Project to Monitor Desertification Processes and Related Natural Resources in Arid and Semi-Arid Areas of Southwest Asia," U.N. Conference on Desertification, Aug. 1977.

217. "Transnational Project to Monitor Desertification Processes and Related Natural Resources in Arid and Semi-Arid Areas of South America," U.N. Conference on Desertification, Aug. 1977, p. 8.

218. Ibid., p. 12.

219. U.S. Bureau of Reclamation, California Dept. of Water Resources, and California State Water Resources Control Board, *Agricultural Drainage and Salt Management in the San Joaquin Valley*, Fresno, Jan. 1979.

220. "Ecological Change and Desertification" and "Technology and Desertification," U.N. Conference on Desertification, Aug. 1977.

221. "Haiti: A Study in Environmental Destruction," *Conservation Foundation Letter*, Nov. 1977, pp. 1–7.

222. Walter Parham, "LDC Deforestation Problem: A Preliminary Data Base," U.S. Agency for International Development, Technical Assistance Bureau, Mar. 8, 1978 (manuscript).

223. U.S. General Accounting Office, "To Protect Tomorrow's Food Supply, Soil Conservation Needs *Priority* Attention," report to the Congress by the U.S. Comptroller General, Feb. 14, 1977.

224. See, for example, Luther J. Carter, "Soil Erosion: The Problem Persists Despite the Billions Spent on It," *Science*, Apr. 22, 1977, pp. 409–411; D. Pimentel et al., "Land Degradation: Effects on Food and Energy Resources," *Science*, Oct. 8, 1976, pp. 149–155; R. Blobaum, "Loss of Agricultural Land," Washington: Council on Environmental Quality, 1974; R. A. Brink, "Soil Deterioration and the Growing World Demand for

Food," *Science*, Aug. 12, 1977, pp. 625–30; Brown, *Worldwide Loss of Cropland*, op. cit.

225. Approximated from table 9.7 in Harry O. Buchman and Nyle C. Brady, *The Nature and Properties of Soils*, 6th ed., New York: Macmillan, 1960.

226. Calculated from data in ibid. and Pimentel et al., "Land Degradation," op. cit., table 1.

227. F. H. King, *Farmers of Forty Centuries: Permanent Agriculture in China, Korea, and Japan*, Emmaus, Pa.: Rodale, 1973, and New York: Gordon Press, 1977 (reprints of the original 1911 ed.).

228. "Physical Environment," ch. 13 in Organization for Economic Cooperation and Development, *Interfutures*, Paris, May 16, 1977 (draft).

229. Brown, *Worldwide Loss of Cropland*, op. cit.

230. Organization for Economic Cooperation and Development, op. cit.

231. Ibid.

232. Brown, *Worldwide Loss of Cropland*, op. cit.

233. Luther J. Carter, "Soil Erosion: The Problem Persists Despite the Billions Spent on It," *Science*, Apr. 22, 1977, pp. 409–11.

234. U.S. General Accounting Office, op. cit.

235. See, for example, *Environmental Quality 1970*, p. 41, and *1971*, pp. 107–8, annual reports of the Council on Environmental Quality, Washington: Government Printing Office, 1970, 1971; U.N. Environment Programme, "Overviews in the Priority Subject Area—Land, Water and Desertification," Feb. 1975; "Technology and Desertification," op. cit.

236. An excellent introduction with extensive additional references is provided in the short Council on Environmental Quality (CEQ) report by R. Blobaum, already cited, especially pp. 7–11. Also see CEQ's *Environmental Quality 1970*, op. cit., pp. 173–75; *1971*, p. 63; *1973*, pp. 215, 306; *1974*, p. 343; *1975*, pp. 163, 179–80, 451; *1977*, pp. 90–91; and CEQ, *The Costs of Sprawl*, Washington: Government Printing Office, Apr. 1974.

237. U.S. Department of Agriculture, Soil Conservation Service, "Cropland Erosion," Washington, June 1977.

238. Brown, "Worldwide Loss of Cropland," op. cit.

239. R. Soderlund and B. H. Svensson, "The Global Nitrogen Cycle," in Svensson and Soderlund, eds., *Nitrogen, Phosphorus, and Sulphur—Global Cycles*, Stockholm: Ecological Bulletin, 1976, p. 66.

239a Martin Alexander, *Soil Microbiology*, New York: Wiley, 1961, pp. 263–66.

239b F. E. Allison, *Soil Organic Matter and its Role in Crop Production*, New York: Elsevier, 1973.

239c Frank J. Stevenson, Chapter 1 in W.V. Bartholomew and Francis E. Clark, eds., *Soil Nitrogen*, Madison, Wis.: American Society of Agronomy, 1965, p. 33.

239d V. W. Meints et al, "Long Term Trends in Total Soil N as Influenced by Certain Management Practices," *Soil Science*, vol. 124, 1977, pp. 110–16.

239e Daniel Kohl, Washington University, St. Louis, Mo, personal communication, 1979.

240. *Eutrophication: Causes, Consequences, Correctives*, Washington: National Academy of Sciences, 1969; Programme on Man and the Biosphere, "Consultative Group on Project 9: Ecological Assessment of Pest Management and Fertilizer Use on Terrestrial and Aquatic Ecosystems (Part on Fertilizers)," Rome: UNESCO, Jan. 1974.

241. *Drinking Water and Health*, Washington: National Academy of Sciences, 1977, pp. 411–25.

242. *Nitrates: An Environmental Assessment*, Washington: National Academy of Sciences, 1978, pp. 5–15.

243. Ibid.

244. "Pesticide Requirements in Developing Countries: Summary of Replies to FAO Questionnaire," Food and Agriculture Organization, 1975.

245. For but one small example, see P. Lernoux, "Crop Spraying in Northern Colombia Causing Ecological Disaster," World Environment Report, New York: Center for International Environment Information, Sept. 1978.

246. There is a growing literature on integrated pest management. See for example: Council on Environmental Quality, *Integrated Pest Management*, Washington, Nov. 1972 and *Integrated Pest Management: Status and Prospects in the United States* (forthcoming, 1979); "Integrated Pest Management," *California Agriculture* (special issue), Feb. 1978; *Pest Control: Strategies for the Future*, Washington: National Academy of Sciences, 1972; Committee on Scholarly Communication with the People's Republic of China, *Insect Control in the People's Republic of China*, Washington: National Academy of Sciences, 1972; D. Pimental, ed., *World Food, Pest Losses, and the Environment*, Boulder: Westview Press, 1978, pp. 17–38, 163–84.

247. See H. L. Harrison et. al., "Systems Study of DDT Transport," *Science*, Oct. 30, 1970, pp. 503–8; G. M. Woodwell et. al., "DDT in the Biosphere: Where Does It Go?," *Science*, Dec. 10, 1971, pp. 1101–7; Programme on Man and the Biosphere, "Expert Consultations on Project 9: Ecological Assessment of Pest Management and Fertilizer Use on Terrestrial and Aquatic Ecosystems (Part on Pesticides)," UNESCO, 1974.

248. *Environmental Quality 1975*, op. cit., pp. 368–76.

249. A detailed discussion of the role of pesticides and predators in the control of plant-eating mites is provided in C. B. Huffaker et. al., "The Ecology of Tetranychid Mites and Their Natural Control," *Annual Review of Entomology*, 1969, pp. 125–74; J. A. McMurty et al., "Ecology of Tetranychid Mites and their Natural Enemies: A Review, Pt. 1, Tetranychid Enemies: Their Biological Characters and the Impact of Spray Practices," *Hilgardia*, 1970, pp. 331–90.

250. Robert F. Luck et al., "Chemical Insect Control—A Troubled Pest Management Strategy," *BioScience*, Sept. 1977, p. 608.

251. "Pest Control and Public Health, in *Pest Control: An Assessment of Present and Alternative Technologies*, Washington: National Academy of Sciences, 1976, vol. 5, p. 219.

252. Ibid.

253. Council on Environmental Quality, *Integrated Pest Management* 1972, op. cit., p. 4.

254. Ray F. Smith and Harold T. Reynolds, "Some Economic Implications of Pesticide Overuse in Cotton," in California Dept. of Food and Agriculture, *New Frontiers in Pest Management: Conference Proceedings*, Sacramento, Dec. 1977, pp. 25–34.

255. See reference 246, above.

256. See Paul R. Ehrlich et al., *Ecoscience: Population, Resources, and Environment*, San Francisco: Freeman, 1977, ch. 11; Luck et al., op. cit., pp. 606–11.

257. See, for example, F. W. Plapp and D. L. Bull, "Toxicity and Selectivity of Some Insecticides to *Chrysopa carnea*, a Predator of the Tobacco and Bud Worm," *Environmental Entomology*, June 1978, pp. 431–34; F. W. Plapp and S. B. Vinson, "Comparative Toxicities of Some Insecticides to the Tobacco Bud Worm and Its Ichneumonid Parasite, *Compoletis sonorensis*," *Experimental Entomology*, June 1977, pp. 381–84.

258. Normal Myers, *The Sinking Ark*, New York: Pergamon, 1979.

259. Jack R. Harland, "Genetics of Disaster," *Journal of Environmental Quality*, 1972, pp. 212–15.

260. Judith Miller, "Genetic Erosion: Crop Plants Threatened by Government Neglect," *Science*, Dec. 21, 1973, p. 1232; G. L. Carefoot and E. R. Sprott, *Famine on the Wind: Man's Battle Against Plant Disease*, Chicago: Rand McNally, 1967, p. 81.

261. Carefoot and Sprott, op. cit., pp. 53, 54, 98, 117, 119, 130–32, 138, 139.

262. Miller, "Genetic Erosion," op. cit., p. 1232.

263. *Genetic Vulnerability of Major Crops*, Washington: National Academy of Sciences, 1972, pp. 13, 14.

264. Carefoot and Sprott, op. cit., pp. 194–201.

265. A. J. Ullstrop, "The Impacts of the Southern Corn Leaf Blight Epidemic of 1970 and 1971, *Annual Review of Phytopathology*, 1972, pp. 37–50; L. A. Tatum, "The Southern Corn Leaf Blight Epidemic," *Science*, Mar. 19, 1971, pp. 1113–16; A. L. Hooker, "Southern Leaf Blight of Corn—Present Status and Future Prospects," *Journal of Environmental Quality*, 1972, pp. 244–49.

266. Tatum, op. cit.

267. U.S. Department of Agriculture, Agricultural Marketing Service, unpublished data.

268. M. W. Adams et al., "Biological Uniformity and Disease Epidemics," *BioScience*, Nov. 1, 1971, pp. 1067–70.

269. C. E. Yarwood, "Man-Made Plant Diseases," *Science*, Apr. 10, 1970, pp. 218–20.

270. W. C. Snyder et al., *California Agriculture*, vol. 19, no. 5, 1963, p. 11.

271. A good overview of these problems is provided in *Genetic Vulnerability of Major Crops*, Washington: National Academy of Sciences, 1972.

272. A readable introduction to the problems of preserving genetic resources is provided in Erik Eckholm, *Disappearing Species: The Social Challenge*, Washington: Worldwatch Institute, July 1978; also see Marc Reisner, "Garden of Eden to Weed Patch," *Natural Resources Defense Council Newsletter*, Jan.-Feb. 1977; *Conservation of Germplasm Resources: An Imperative*, Washington: National Academy of Sciences, 1978; *Genetic Improvement of Seed Proteins*, Washington: National Academy of Sciences, 1976; Programme on Man and the Biosphere, "Expert Panel on Project 8: Conservation of Natural Areas and of the Genetic Material They Contain," Morges, Switzerland: UNESCO, Sept. 1973; Myers, op. cit.; Commission on International Relations, *Underexploited Tropical Plants with Promising Economic Value*, Washington: National Academy of Sciences, 1975; Grenville Lucas and A. H. M. Synge, "The IUCN Threatened Plants Committee and Its Work Throughout the World," *Environmental Conservation*, Autumn 1977; International Union for Conservation of Nature and Natural Resources Threatened Plants Committee, *List of Rare, Threatened and Endemic Plants in Europe*, Strasbourg, 1977.

273. Hugh H. Iltis et al., "*Zea diploperennis* (Gramineae): A New Teosinte from Mexico," *Science*, Jan. 12, 1979, pp. 186–88; also see Walter Sullivan, "Hope of Creating Perennial Corn Raised by a New Plant Discovery," *New York Times*, Feb. 5, 1979; Richard Orr, " 'Mexico Connection' May Improve Corn," *Chicago Tribune*, Feb. 18, 1979; "Maize Seeds Plant Hope," *Milwaukee Sentinel*, Jan. 30, 1979.

274. Hugh H. Iltis, personal communication, Mar. 5, 1979.

275. "Maize Seeds Plant Hope," op. cit.

276. Erik Eckholm, "Disappearing Species," op. cit.

276a "Seeds of Trouble," editorial, *Washington Post*, Nov. 10, 1979, p. A22.

277. Harlan, op. cit., p. 214.

278. *The State of Food and Agriculture 1977*, op. cit., pp. 3-40-3-43.

279. *CIMMYT Review 1974*, Centro Internacional de Mejoramiento de Maiz y Trigo (International Maize and Wheat Improvement Center), Mexico, 1974, p. 7.

280. Ibid.

281. O. H. Frankel and J. G. Hawkes, eds., *Crop Genetic Resources for Today and Tomorrow*, New York: Cambridge Univ. Press, 1975.

282. Ibid.

283. *Genetic Vulnerability of Major Crops*, Washington: National Academy of Sciences, 1972, ch. 5.

284. P. S. Carlson and J. C. Polacco, "Plant Cell Cultures: Genetic Aspects of Crop Improvement," *Science*, May 9, 1975, pp. 622–25.

285. Handler, op. cit.

286. *Production Yearbook 1974*, Rome: Food and Agriculture Organization, 1974.

287. Lester R. Brown, *The Twenty-Ninth Day*, New York: Norton, 1978, p. 145.

288. D. Pimentel et al., "Food Production and the Energy Crisis," *Science*, Nov. 2, 1973, pp. 447–48.

289. *The State of Food and Agriculture 1976*, Rome: Food and Agriculture Organization, 1977, p. 93.

290. See, for example, ibid., ch. 3; Pimentel et al., "Food Production," op. cit.; Arjun Makhijani and Alan Poole, *Energy and Third World Agriculture*, Cambridge, Mass.: Ballinger, 1975; G. Leach, "Energy and Food Production," *Food Policy*, Nov. 1975, pp. 62–73.

291. Pimentel et al., "Food Production," op. cit., p. 448.

292. See, for example: U.S. Department of Agriculture, Economic Research Service, "The One-Man Farm," Washington, Aug. 1973; Makhijani and Poole, op. cit.; William Lockeretz et al., "A Comparison of Production, Economic Returns, and Energy Intensiveness of Corn Belt Farms that Do and Do Not Use Inorganic Fertilizers and Pesticides," St. Louis: Center for the Biology of Natural Systems, Washington Univ., July 1975; *The Journal of the New Alchemists*, vols. 1–4, 1973–77; W. Berry, *The Unsettling of America: Culture and Agriculture*, San Francisco: Sierra Club, 1977.

293. E. F. Schumacher, *Small is Beautiful: Economics as if People Mattered*, New York: Harper, 1973. For an introduction to the technical issues associated with technology transfer for agricultural development, see: D. Goulet, *The Uncertain Promise: Value Conflicts in Technology Transfer*, New York: IDOC/North America, 1977.

294. U.S. Department of Agriculture, Economic Research Service, "The One-Man Farm," op. cit., p. V.

295. See reference 292, above.

296. Henry J. Groen and James A. Kilpatrick, "China's Agricultural Production," in U.S. Congress, *Chinese Economy Post-Mao: A Compendium of Papers Submitted to the Joint Economic Committee*, vol. 1 *Policy and Performance*, Washington, Nov. 9, 1978, pp. 632–34.

297. Erik Eckholm, *The Dispossessed of the Earth: Land Reform and Sustainable Development*, Washington: Worldwatch Institute, June 1979.

Marine Environment Section

298. Bert Bolin, "The Carbon Cycle," *Scientific American*, Sept. 1970, pp. 126, 131.

299. Paul R. Ehrlich et al., *Ecoscience: Population, Resources, Environment*, San Francisco: Freeman, 1977, pp. 352, 354.

300. Edward D. Goldberg, *The Health of the Oceans*, Paris: UNESCO, 1976, p. 17.

301. Ibid., p. 19.

302. Goldberg, op. cit., p. 17.

303. "Marine Overview," op. cit., pp. 8, 9.

303a *The International Conference on Tanker Safety and Pollution Prevention*, London: Inter-Governmental Maritime Consultative Organization, 1978.

303b Walter R. Courtenay, Jr. and C. R. Robins, "Exotic Organisms: An Unsolved, Complex Problem," *BioScience*, vol. 25, June 23, 1975, pp. 306–13.

304. Ivan Valiela and Susan Vince, "Green Borders of the Sea," *Oceanus*, Fall 1976, p. 10; Charles B. Officer, "Physical Oceanography of Estuaries," *Oceanus*, Fall 1976, pp. 3, 4; SCEP Work Group on Ecological Effects, "Phosphorus and Eutrophication," in William H. Matthews et al., eds., *Man's Impact on Terrestrial and Oceanic Ecosystems*, Cambridge, Mass.: MIT, 1971, p. 321; R. Eugene Turner, "Intertidal Vegetation and Commercial Yields of Penaeid Shrimp," *Transactions of the American Fisheries Society*, vol. 106, no. 5, 1977, pp. 411–16.

305. Valiela and Vince, op. cit., p. 100.

306. Eugene P. Odum and Armando de la Cruz, "Particulate Organic Detritus in a Georgia Salt Marsh–Estuarine System", in *Estuaries*, George Lauff, ed., Washington: American Association for the Advancement of Science, 1957.

307. Paul J. Godfrey, "Barrier Beaches of the East Coast," *Oceanus*, vol. 19, no. 5, Fall 1976, p. 31.

308. Valiela and Vince, op. cit., p. 14.

309. UNESCO, Div. of Marine Sciences, "Human Uses and Management of the Mangrove Environment in South and Southeast Asia, September—October 1977," Paris, Oct. 12, 1978, pp. 1, 2; Scientific Committee on Oceanic Research (SCOR), "Minutes—SCOR Working Group 60 on Mangrove Ecology, May 16–18, 1978, San José, Costa Rica," p. 2; Lawrence E. Jerome, "Mangroves," *Oceans*, Sept.-Oct. 1977, p. 42.

310. Ibid.

311. "Marine Overview," op. cit., p. 31; B. J. Copeland et al., "Water Quantity for Preservation of Estuarine Ecology," in Ernest F. Gloyna and William S. Butcher, eds., *Conflicts in Water Resources Planning*, Center for Research in Water Resources, Univ. of Texas at Austin, 1972, pp. 107–26.

312. Valiela and Vince, op. cit., p. 11.

313. Elinor Lander Horwitz, *Out Nation's Wetlands: An Interagency Task Force Report*, Washington: Government Printing Office, 1978, p. 44.

314. Godfrey, op. cit., p. 37.

314a W. N. Lindall, Jr. et al., "Fishes, Macroinvertebrates, and Hydrological Conditions of Upland Canals in Tampa Bay, Florida," *Fishery Bulletin*, (National Oceanic and Atmospheric Administration), vol. 71, no. 1, 1973, pp. 155–63.

315. Horwitz, op, cit., p. 46.

315a M. Grant Gross, "Waste-Solid Disposal in Coastal Waters of North America," in William H. Matthews, Frederick E. Smith and Edward D. Goldberg, eds., *Man's Impact on Terrestrial and Oceanic Ecosystems*, Cambridge, MA: The MIT Press, 1971, p. 258.

316. Valiela and Vince, op. cit., p. 13.

317. Ibid., p. 12.

318. UNESCO, Div. of Marine Sciences, op. cit., p. 1; Jerome, op. cit., p. 44.

319. UNESCO, Div. of Marine Sciences, op. cit., p. 2.

320. Ibid.; Scientific Committee on Ocean Research, op. cit., pp. 8, 9; Dr. Samuel Snedacker, University of Miami Rosensteil School of Marine and Atmospheric Sciences, personal communication to Dr. Elliott A. Norse, Council on Environmental Quality, 1979.

321. R. E. Johannes, "Pollution and Degradation of Coral Reef Communities," in E. J. Ferguson Wood and R. E. Johannes, eds., *Tropical Marine Pollution*, Amsterdam: Elsevier, 1975.

322. P.R. Ehrlich, "Population Biology of Coral Reef Fishes," *Annual Review of Ecology and Systematics*, Sept. 1975, pp. 211–47.

323. Robert E. Johannes, "Life and Death of the Reef," *Audubon*, Sept. 1976, pp. 45, 46; Johannes, "Pollution and Degradation," op. cit., p. 13.

324. "Life and Death of the Reef," op. cit., p. 50.

325. V. J. Chapman, ed., *Ecosystems of the World*, vol. 1, *Wet Coastal Ecosystems*, Amsterdam: Elsevier, 1977, p. 1.

326. Michael Waldichuk, *Global Marine Pollution: An Overview*, Paris: UNESCO, 1977, p. 32; E. D. Goldberg, "Atmospheric Transport" in Donald W. Hood, ed., *Impingement of Man on the Oceans*, New York: Wiley, Interscience, 1971, pp. 75–88.

327. Carl J. Sindermann, "Environmentally Related Diseases of Marine Fish and Shellfish," *Marine Fisheries Review*, Oct. 1978, p. 43; *New York Bight Project: Annual Report for FY 1976*, Marine Ecosystems Analysis Program, Boulder: NOAA Environmental Research Laboratories, Dec. 1977.

328. *New York Bight Project*, op. cit., p. 25.

329. *Environmental Quality, 1978*, annual report of the Council on Environmental Quality, Washington: Government Printing Office, 1978, p. 178.

330. American Chemical Society, *Cleaning Our Environment: A Chemical Perspective*, Washington, Oct. 1978, pp. 2, 4.

331. *Environmental Quality 1978*, op. cit., p. 183; John C. Fuller, *The Poison that Fell from the Sky*, New York: Random House, 1977.

332. Robert H. Boyle, "Getting Rid of PCBs," *Audubon*, Nov. 1978, p. 150.

333. Ibid.; "N.Y. Plan to Remove PCBs," *Science News*, July 15, 1978, p. 39.

334. Waldichuk, op. cit., p. 22.

335. Goldberg, op. cit., p. 47.

336. Waldichuk, op. cit., p. 22.

337. John Todd, personal communication, 1979, concerning research done at San Diego State University in 1969 in 18 ecosystems with 9 species of fish.

338. Waldichuk, op. cit., pp. 22.

339. *New York Bight Project*, op. cit., pp. 25, 26; Goldberg, op, cit., p. 61.

340. Goldberg, op. cit., p. 66.

341. *Assessing Potential Ocean Pollutants*, Washington: National Academy of Sciences, 1975, pp. 190, 202.

342. Ibid. pp. 191–202; Goldberg, op. cit., p. 66.

343. Waldichuk, op. cit., p. 22.

344. Goldberg, op. cit., p. 48.

345. *Assessing Potential Ocean Pollutants*, op. cit., p. 122.

346. George M. Woodwell et al., "DDT in the Biosphere: Where Does It Go?" *Science*, Dec. 10, 1971, pp. 1101–7.

347. Paul R. Spitzer et al., "Productivity of Ospreys in Connecticut—Long Island Increases as DDT Residues Decline," *Science*, Oct. 20, 1978, pp. 333–34; Daniel W. Anderson et al., "Brown Pelicans: Improved Reproduction off the Southern California Coast," *Science*, Nov. 21, 1975, pp. 806–8.

348. Waldichuk, op. cit., p. 17; Goldberg, op. cit., p. 114.

349. Waldichuk, op. cit., p. 17.

350. Richard A. Greig and Douglas R. Wenzloff, "Trace Metals in Finfish from the New York Bight and Long Island Sound," *Marine Pollution Bulletin*, Sept. 1977, pp. 198–200; R. A. Greig et al., "Trace Metals in Sea Scallops *Placopecten magellanicus*, from Eastern United States," *Bulletin of Environmental Contamination and Toxicology*, New York: Springer, 1978, pp. 326–34.

351. Goldberg, op. cit., p. 99.

352. Ibid., p.112.

353. *Assessing Potential Ocean Pollutants*, op. cit., p. 333.

354. Ibid., p. 301.

355. Goldberg, op. cit., pp. 113, 114.

356. Waldichuk, op. cit., p. 20; T. Chow and C. Patterson, "The Occurrence and Significance of Lead Isotopes in Pelagic Sediments", *Geochemica et Cosmochemica*, vol. 26, 1962, pp. 263–306; M. Rama and E. Goldberg, "Lead-210 in Natural Waters", *Science*, vol.13, 1961, pp. 98–99.

357. Goldberg, op. cit., p. 109.

358. Ibid., p. 114.

359. Ibid.

360. E. Goldberg et al., "A Pollution History of Chesapeake Bay," *Geochemica et Cosmochemica*, vol. 42, 1978 pp. 413–25.

361. Richard A. Greig and Richard A. McGrath, "Trace Metals in Sediments of Raritan Bay," *Marine Pollution Bulletin*, Aug. 1977, pp. 188–192; Ruth Waldhauer et al., "Lead and Cooper in the Waters of Raritan and Lower New York Bays," *Marine Pollution Bulletin*, Feb. 1978, pp. 38–42.

362. Goldberg, *Health of the Oceans*, op. cit., p. 112.

363. Ibid., pp. 79–97.

364. Ibid.

365. Ibid.

366. Ibid.

367. Council on Environmental Quality, *OCS Oil and Gas: An Environmental Assessment*, vol. 1, Washington, Apr. 1974, p. 112.

368. *Petroleum in the Marine Environment*, Washington: National Academy of Sciences, 1975, pp. 83–84.

369. John H. Vandermeulen, "The Chedabucto Bay Spill—Arrow, 1970," *Oceanus*, Fall 1977, pp. 31–39.

370. Howard L. Sanders, "The West Falmouth Spill—*Florida*, 1969," *Oceanus*, Fall 1977, pp. 15–24.

371. George R. Hampson and Edwin T. Moul, "Salt Marsh Grasses and #2 Fuel Oil," *Oceanus*, Fall 1977, pp. 25–30.

372. *Petroleum in the Marine Environment*, op. cit., pp. 52–53; A Crosby Longwell, "A Genetic Look at Fish Eggs and Oil," *Oceanus*, Fall 1977, pp. 46–58.

373. Council on Environmental Quality, *OCS Oil and Gas*, op. cit., pp. 106–111; Goldberg, *Health of the Oceans*, op. cit., p. 134; Donald F. Boesch et al., *Oil Spills and the Marine Environment*, Cambridge, Mass.: Ballinger, 1974, pp. 8–9; Frederick P. Thurberg, et al., "Some Physiological Effects of the *Argo Merchant* Oil Spill on Several Marine Teleosts and Bivalve Molluscs," from *In the Wake of the* Argo Merchant, Center for Ocean Management Studies, University of Rhode Island, Kingston, 1978; George R. Gardner, "A Review of Histopathological Effects of Selected Contaminants on Some Marine Organisms," *Marine Fisheries Review*, Oct. 1978, pp. 51–52; John J. Stegeman, "Fate and Effects of Oil in Marine Animals," and Jelle Atema, "The Effects of Oil on Lobsters," *Oceanus*, Fall 1977, pp. 59–73.

374. John W. Farrington, "The Biogeochemistry of Oil in the Ocean," *Oceanus*, Fall 1977, p. 9.
375. Douglas Pimlott et al., *Oil Under the Ice: Offshore Drilling in the Canadian Arctic*, Canadian Arctic Resources Committee, Ottawa, 1976.
376. Valiela and Vince, op. cit., pp. 14, 16.
377. William E. Odum and R. E. Johannes, "The Response of Mangroves to Man-Induced Environmental Stress," in *Tropical Marine Pollution*, op.. cit.; Valiela and Vince, op. cit., pp. 14, 16.
378. Johannes, "Pollution and Degradation," op. cit., pp. 14–17; Johannes, "Life and Death of the Reef," op. cit., pp. 48–50.
379. Burrell, op. cit.
380. Johannes, "Pollution and Degradation," op. cit., pp. 14–15; Johannes, "Life and Death of the Reef," op. cit., pp. 48–50.
381. Ibid.
382. Johannes, "Pollution and Degradation," op. cit., pp. 19, 20; Johannes, "Life and Death of the Reef," op. cit., p. 50; "Marine Overview," op. cit., pp. 8, 40.
383. Johannes, "Pollution and Degradation," op. cit., pp. 21–22.
384. Goldberg, *Health of the Oceans*, op. cit., p. 19; J. B. Coltron, Jr., "Plastics in the Ocean," *Oceanus*, vol. 18, no. 1, 1974, pp. 61–64; Edwin Carpenter et al., "Polystyrene Spherules in Coastal Waters," *Science*, vol. 178, 1972 p. 749.
385. Waldichuk, op. cit., pp. 31, 32; Carpenter et al., op. cit.; Gardner, op. cit., pp. 51, 52.
386. Goldberg, *Health of the Oceans*, op. cit., p. 17.
387. "Marine Overview," op. cit., p. 11.
388. John Gulland, "The Harvest of the Sea," in W. W. Murdoch, ed., *Environment: Resources, Pollution, and Society*, Sunderland, Maine: Sinauer Press, 1975, pp. 167–89; C. P. Idyll, "The Anchovy Crisis," *Scientific American*, June 1973, pp. 22–29.
389. Ehrlich et al., *Ecoscience*, op. cit., pp. 354–55.
390. Kenneth S. Norris, "Marine Mammals and Man," in Howard P. Brokaw, ed., *Wildlife and America*, Washington: Government Printing Office, 1978, pp. 320–21.
391. Sidney J., Hold and Lee M Talbot, ed., "The Conservation of Wild Living Resources," final report, Airlie House (Va.) Workshops, Feb., Apr. 1975, p. 4; Lee M. Talbot, "History, Status and Conservation Problems of the Great Whale Populations," Symposium on Endangered Species, American Association for the Advancement of Science annual meeting, Feb. 28, 1974, p. 24.
392. Holt and Talbot, op. cit., p. 11.
393. Ehrlich et al., op. cit., pp. 360–61.
394. Public Law 92–522, 92nd Congress, H.R. 10420, Oct. 21, 1972, 86 Stat. 1027.
395. J. Frederick Grassle, "Diversity and Population Dynamics of Benthic Organisms," *Oceanus*, Winter 1978, pp. 42, 43, 45.
395a Susumu Honjo and Michael R. Roman, "Marine Copepod Fecal Pellets: Production, Preservation and Sedimentation," *Journal of Marine Research*, vol. 36, 1978, pp. 45–57.
395b K. L. Smith, Jr., "Benthic Community Respiration in the NW Atlantic Ocean: *In Situ* Measurements from 40 to 5200 m," *Marine Biology*, vol. 47, 1978, pp. 337–47.
395c Howard L. Sanders, "Evolutionary Ecology and the Deep Sea Benthos," in *The Changing Scenes in Natural Sciences 1776–1976*, Academy of Natural Sciences, 1977, pp. 223–43.
396. Goldberg, *Health of the Oceans*, op. cit., pp. 19.
397. Ibid.
398. Robert E. Burns, "Effect of a Deep Ocean Mining Test,"
NOAA Pacific Marine Environmental Laboratory, Seattle, Aug. 1978.
399. "Deep Ocean Mining Environmental Study—Phase I," progress report, *National Oceanic and Atmospheric Administration*, Boulder, Aug. 1976, pp. xii–xiv, 152–54.
400. Burns, op. cit.
401. Ibid.
402. Ibid.
403. "Marine Overview." op. cit., p. 41.
404. Richard A. Frank, *Deepsea Mining and the Environment*, Report to the Working Group on Environmental Regulation of Deepsea Mining, American Society of International Law, St. Paul: West, 1976, p. 2.
405. Goldberg, *Health of the Oceans*, op. cit., pp. 50, 51.
406. Waldichuk, op. cit., p. 38.
407. Ibid.
408. U.N. Environment Programme, "Report of the Executive Director," Feb. 20, 1978, pp. 139–66; Baruch Boxer, "Mediterranean Action Plan: An Interim Evaluation", *Science*, Nov. 10, 1978, pp. 585–90.
409. Goldberg, *Health of the Oceans*, op, cit., p. 19.

Forestry Section

410. For a recent insightful analysis of the implications of tropical forest losses, see Norman Myers, *The Sinking Ark*, Elmsford, N.Y.: Pergamon, 1979.
411. Peter Sartorius, "Sociological and Environmental Consequences of the Reduction or Elimination of Primary Tropical Forests," in *Technical Conference on the Tropical Moist Forests*, Rome: Food and Agriculture Organization, 1977; Eneas Salati et al., "Origem e Distribucão das Chuvas na Amazônia," *Interciencia*, July-Aug. 1978, pp. 200–05.
412. George P. Marsh, *The Earth as Modified by Human Action*, New York: Scribner, 1885; Erik Eckholm, *Losing Ground: Environmental Stress and World Food Prospects*, New York: Norton, 1976.
413. See, for example, the discussion of the poor habitat value of eucalyptus plantations, which are replacing millions of hectares of native forest in Minas Gerais, Brazil in *Planoroeste II*, 3 vols. Belo Horizonte: Secretaria de Estado de Planejamento e Coordenação Geral, Secretaria de Agricultura, Secretario de Estado de Ciência e Tecnologia, 1978.
414. Samuel H. Kunkle, "Forestry Support for Agriculture Through Watershed Management, Windbreaks, and Other Conservation Measures," Washington: U.S. Forest Service, Oct. 1978.
415. Betty J. Meggers et al., eds., *Tropical Forest Ecosystems in Africa and South America: A Comparative Review*, Washington: Smithsonian Institution Press, 1973, pp. 313, 324. For more detailed studies of shifting agriculture/forest systems, see: P. H. Nye and D. J. Greenland, *The Soil Under Shifting Cultivation*, Burks, England: Commonwealth Agricultural Bureaux, 1960, 156 pp.; R. F. Watters, *Shifting Cultivation in Latin Ameria*, Forestry Development Paper No. 17, Rome: Food and Agriculture Organization, 1971.
416. Douglas R. Shane, "A Latin American Dilemma: Current Efforts to Develop the Tropical Forest Areas of Thirteen Latin American Nations," U.S. Strategy Conference on Tropical Deforestation, Washington, June 12–14, 1978 (manuscript).
417. *Tropical Forest Ecosystems: A State-of-Knowledge Report*, Natural Resources Research XIV, Paris: UNESCO, 1978, pp. 317–553; also *Conservation and Rational Use of the Environment*, U.N. ECOSOC, 44th Session, Agenda Item 5(d), 1968; Raymond F. Dasmann et al.,

Ecological Principles for Economic Development, New York: Wiley, 1973, pp. 51–75.

418. M. L'voich, *Global Water Resources and their Future,* Moscow, 1974; and *Tropical Forest Ecosystems,* op. cit., pp 35–56; Joseph A. Tosi, Jr., and Robert F. Voertman, "Some Environmental Factors in the Economic Development of the Tropics," *Economic Geography,* vol. 40, no. 3, 1964; Norman Hudson, *Soil Conservation,* Ithaca: Cornell University Press, 1971, pp. 179–95.

419. Raymond F. Dasmann et al., op cit., pp. 208–12; Robert N. Allen, "The Anchicaya Hydroelectric Project in Colombia: Design and Sedimentation Problems," in M. Toghi Farrar and John P. Milton, eds., *The Careless Technology: Ecology and International Development,* New York: Doubleday, 1962, pp. 318–42. For coastal sedimentation from interior erosion, see Carleton Ray, *Marine Parks for Tanzania,* Washington: Conservation Foundation, Oct. 1968, pp. 11, 17.

420. *The State of Food and Agriculture 1977,* Rome: Food and Agriculture Organization, Nov. 1977 (draft), pp. 3-4-3-19, Lester R. Brown, *The Global Economic Prospect: New Sources of Economic Stress,* Washington: Worldwatch Institute, May 1978, p. 9; also see the "Population" section of this chapter.

421. Robert B. Batchelder, "Spatial and Temporal Patterns of Fire in the Tropical World", in *Proceedings, Tall Timbers Fire Ecology Conference, No. 6,* Tallahasse, 1967, pp. 171–90.

422. "Mountains," in *A World Conservation Strategy,* Morges, Switzerland: International Union for Conservation of Nature and Natural Resources, Jan. 1978 (draft), p. 8.

423. Ibid., pp. 8–9; also see Appendix C, especially the cables from Dacca and New Delhi.

424. Dasmann et al., op. cit.

425. Frank Wadsworth, "Deforestation—Death to the Panama Canal," in U.S. Agency for International Development, *Proceedings of the U.S. Strategy Conference on Tropical Deforestation,* Washington, Oct. 1978.

426. Edward G. Farnworth and Frank B. Golley, eds., *Fragile Ecosystems: Evaluation of Research and Applications in the Neotropics,* New York: Springer, 1974.

427. "Shifting Cultivation and Soil Conservation in Africa," *Soils Bulletin 24,* Rome: Food and Agriculture Organization, 1974; R. Persson, *Forest Resources of Africa,* Stockholm: Royal College of Forestry, 1977.

428. Duncan Poore, "The Value of Tropical Moist Forest Ecosystems and Environmental Consequences of their Removal," *Unasylva,* vol. 28, nos. 112–13, 1976 pp. 127–43.

429. Calculated from Reidar Persson, "The Need for a Continuous Assessment of the Forest Resources of the World," Eighth World Forestry Congress, Jakarta, Oct. 16–28, 1978.

430. For a general introduction to these problems, see Erik Eckholm, "The Other Energy Crisis: Firewood," Washington: Worldwatch Institute, 1975; Eckholm, *Losing Ground,* op. cit.; Erik Eckholm and Lester R. Brown, "Spreading Deserts—The Hand of Man," Washington: Worldwatch Institute, July 1978. Also see "Arvores por Ferro," *Veja* (Brazil), Nov. 8, 1978, pp. 77–78.

431. Water Deshler, "An Examination of the Extent of Fire in the Grassland and Savanna of Africa Along the Southern Side of the Sahara," in *Proceedings of the Ninth International Symposium on Remote Sensing of Environment,* Environmental Research Institute of Michigan, Ann Arbor, 1974, pp. 23–29. Also see Batchelder, op. cit.; Robert B. Batchelder and Howard F. Hirt, *Fire in Tropical Forests and Grasslands,* U.S. Army Natick Laboratories, 1966; R. Rose Innes, "Fire in West African Vegetation," in *Proceedings, Tall Timbers Fire Ecology Conference, No. 11,* Tallahassee: 1972, pp. 147–73; O. C. Stewart, "Fire as the First Great Force Employed by Man," in W. L. Thomas, Jr., *Man's Role in Changing the Face of the Earth,* Chicago: Univ. of Chicago, 1956, pp. 115–33.

432. M. Kassas, "Desertification versus Potential for Recovery in Circum-Sahara Territories," in Harold E. Dregne, ed., *Arid Lands in Transition,* Washington: American Association for the Advancement of Science, 1970, p. 124.

433. S. K. Chauhan, "Tree Huggers Save Forests", *Development Forum,* Sept. 1978, p. 6.

434. "Forestry: A Sector Policy Paper," Washington: World Bank, Feb. 1978.

435. U.S. Department of State and U.S. Agency for International Development, *Proceedings of the U.S. Strategy Conference on Tropical Deforestation,* Washington, Oct. 1978.

436. A summary of the Seventh World Forestry Congress and a list of the 142 papers is in "Commission I: The Silviculturists," *Unasylva,* Special Issue, no. 104, 1972, pp. 15–30; individual papers are available from the authors or on microfiche from the Food and Agriculture Organization, Rome. The proceedings of the Eighth Congress (Jakarta, 1978) should provide a comprehensive updated overview when available.

437. Erik Eckholm, *Planting for the Future: Forestry for Human Needs,* Washington: Worldwatch Institute, February 1979.

438. Chapter 8, this volume.

439. Jack Westoby, "Forestry in China," *Unasylva,* no. 108, 1975, pp. 20–28; Jack Westoby, "Making Trees Serve People," *Commonwealth Forestry Review,* vol. 54, no. 3–4, 1975; S. D. Richardson, *Forestry in Communist China,* Baltimore: Johns Hopkins University Press, 1966; William K. Kapp, *Environmental Policies and Development Planning in Contemporary China and Other Essays,* Paris: Mouton, 1974; For an illuminating discussion of the extent to which China has extinguished species to provide more land for "useful" plants, see Anita Thorhaug, ed., *Botany in China,* Stanford: Stanford Univ., forthcoming, 1980; and *Plant Species in the Peoples' Republic of China,* Washington: National Academy of Sciences, 1978.

440. Eckholm, *Planting for the Future,* op. cit.; pp. 11, 37; *Forestry: A Sector Policy Paper,* op. cit., p. 28.

441. Hans Gregersen, "Appraisal of Village Fuelwood Plantations in Korea," U.N./FAO, SIDA Project Case Study No. 2, St. Paul, Minn., 1977 (draft).

442. N. Vietmeyer and B. Cottom, "Leucaena: Promising Forage and Tree Crop for the Tropics," Washington: National Academy of Sciences, 1977; Michael D. Benge, "Banyani: A Source of Fertilizer, Feed and Energy for the Philippines," USAID Agricultural Development Series, Manila, 1977.

443. R. M. Lawton, "The Management and Regeneration of Some Nigerian High Forest Ecosystems," in: *Tropical Forest Ecosystems,* op. cit., pp. 580–88; and H. Ray Grinnell, "A Study of Agri-Silviculture Potential in West Africa," Ottawa: International Development Research Centre, Oct. 1977.

444. Willem Meijer, *Indonesian Forest and Land Use Planning,* Lexington: Univ. of Kentucky, Botany Department, 1975.

445. Ibid.; T. E. Lovejoy, "The Transamazonica: Highway to Extinction," *Frontiers,* Spring 1973.

446. Edouard Saouma, "Statement by the Director-General of FAO," Eighth World Forestry Congress, Jakarta, Oct. 16–28, 1978.
447. Larry Rohter, "Amazon Basin's Forests Going Up in Smoke," *Washington Post*, Jan. 5, 1978, p. A14.
448. Ibid.
449. Clive Cookson, "Emergency Ban on 2,4,5-T Herbicide in U.S.", and Alistair Hay, "Dioxin: The 10 Year Battle that Began with Agent Orange," *Nature*, Mar. 8, 1979, pp. 108–09.
450. Rohter, op. cit.
451. "Daniel Ludwig's Floating Factory: A Giant Pulp Mill for the Amazon Wilderness," *Time*, June 19, 1978, p. 75.
452. J. G. Bene et al., "Trees, Food and People," Ottawa: International Development Research Centre, 1977; Robert O. Blake, "Response to Date—Institutions," in *Proceedings of the U.S. Strategy Conference on Tropical Deforestation*, U.S. Dept. of State, Oct. 1978, pp.25–30; "Forestry: A Sector Policy Paper," op. cit.; Jack C. Westoby, "Forest Industries for Socio-Economic Development," Eighth World Forestry Congress, Jakarta, Oct. 1978.
453. Eckholm, "Planting for the Future," op. cit.
454. Norman E. Johnson, "Biological Opportunities and Risks Associated with Fast Growing Plantations in the Tropics," *Journal of Forestry*, Apr. 1976.
455. A. E. Lugo, "Ecological Role of Fertilizers in Relation to Forest Productivity and Dollar Subsidy by Man," in *Proceedings of the Florida Section*, Society of American Foresters, Gainesville, Fla., 1970, pp. 21–33.
456. "Watching the Trees Grow—From Space," *Nation's Business*, Jan. 1979, p. 57.
457. J. L. Keas, and J. V. Hatton, "The Implication of Full-Forest Utilization on Worldwide Supplies of Wood by Year 2000," *Pulp and Paper International*, vol. 17, no. 6, 1975, pp. 49–52.
458. A. Gomez-Pompa et al., "The Tropical Rain Forest: A Nonrenewable Resource," *Science* vol. 177, 1972, pp. 762–65; Duncan Poore, "The Value of Tropical Moist Forest Ecosystems and the Environmental Consequences of Their Removal," *Unasylva* vol 28, no. 112, 1976, pp. 127–43; J. Ewel and C. Conde, "Potential Ecological Impact of Increased Intensity of Tropical Forest Utilization," Madison, Wis.: U.S. Department of Agriculture, Forest Service Forest Products Research Laboratory, 1976 (manuscript).
459. G. E. Likens et al., "Recovery of a Deforested Ecosystem," *Science*, vol. 199, 1978, pp. 492–96.
460. Carl Olof Tamm et al., "Leaching of Plant Nutrients from Soil as a Consequence of Forestry operations," *Ambio*, vol. 3, no. 6, 1974, pp. 211–21.
461. William Gladstone, Manager, Tropical Forestry Research, Weyerhaeuser Company, personal communication, June 1978.
462. Ibid.
463. G. M. Woodwell et al., "The Biota and the World Carbon Budget," *Science*, Jan. 13, 1978, pp. 141–146.
464. P. H. Raven et al., "The Origins of Taxonomy," *Science*, vol. 174, 1971, pp. 1210–13; "Trends, Priorities and Needs in Systematic and Evolutionary Biology," *Systematic Zoology*, vol. 23, 1974, pp. 416–39.
465. *Environmental Quality 1978*, annual report of the Council on Environmental Quality, Washington: Government Printing Office, Dec. 1978, pp. 328–30.
466. For discussions of these points, see *Underexploited Tropical Plants with Promising Economic Value* and *Conservation of Germplasm Resources: An Imperative*,

Washington: National Academy of Sciences, 1975 and 1978; Erik Eckholm, *Disappearing Species: The Social Challenge*, Washington: Worldwatch Institute, July 1978.
467. Joseph A. Tosi, Jr., "Climatic Control of Terrestrial Ecosystems: A Report on the Holdridge Model," *Economic Geography*, Apr. 1964, pp. 173–81, especially p. 178.
468. National Research Council. *Soils of the Humid Tropics*, Washington: National Academy of Sciences, 1972; Tamm et al., op. cit; P. W. Richards, "The Tropical Rain Forest," *Scientific American*, vol. 169, no. 6, 1973, pp. 58–67.
469. Rohter, op. cit.
470. Ibid.
471. Tamm et al., op. cit.; Richards, op. cit.; Gomez-Pompa et al., op. cit.
472. See D. S. Simberloff and L. B. Abele, "Island Biogeography Theory and Conservation Practice," *Science*, vol. 171, 1976, pp. 285–86; J. Terborgh, "Island Biogeography and Limitations" (response to Simberloff and Abele), *Science*, vol. 193, 1976, pp. 1028–29; T. E. Lovejoy and D. C. Oren, "Minimum Critical Size of Ecosystems," in R. L. Burgess and D. M. Sharpe, eds., *Forest Island Dynamics in Man-Dominated Landscapes*, New York: Springer, 1979; J. M. Diamond and R. M. May, "Island Biogeography and the Design of Natural Reserves," in R. M. May, ed., *Theoretical Ecology: Principles and Applications*, Oxford: Blackwell, 1976, pp. 163–86; E. O. Wilson and E. O. Willis, "Applied Biogeography," in M. L. Cody and J. M. Diamond, eds., *Ecology and Evolution of Communities*, Cambridge, Mass: Harvard University Press, 1975, pp. 522–34.
473. T. E. Lovejoy, "Bird Diversity and Abundance in Amazon Forest Communities," *Living Bird*, vol. 13, 1975, pp. 127–91; C. S. Elton, "Conservation and the Low Population Density of Invertebrates Inside Neotropical Rain Forest," *Biological Conservation*, vol. 7, 1975, pp. 3–15; G. E. Hutchinson, *Principles of Population Ecology*, New Haven: Yale Univ. 1978.
474. E. Salati et al., "Origem e Distribuiçã das Chuvas na Amazônia," *Interciencia*, vol. 3, 1978, pp. 200–5; and N. A. Villa Nova et al., "Estimativa da Evapotranspiração na Bacia Amazônica," *Acta Amazônica*, vol. 6, 1976, pp. 215–28.
475. J. Haffer, "Speciation in Amazonian Forest Birds," *Science*, vol. 165, 1969, pp. 131–37.
476. Ibid.; J. Haffer, *Avian Speciation in Tropical South America, with a systematic Survey of the Toucans* (Ramphastidae) *and Jacamars* (Galbulidae)," Cambridge, Mass.: Nuttall Ornithological Club, 1974; P. E. Vanzolini, "Paleoclimates, Relief, and Species Multiplication in Equatorial Forests," in Meggers et al., op. cit., pp. 255–58; G. T. Prance, "Phytogeographic Support for the Theory of Pleistocene Forest Refuges in the Amazon Basin, Based on Evidence From Distribution Patterns in *Caryocaraceae, Chrysobalanaceae, Dichapetalaceae,* and *Lecythidaceae*," *Acta Amazônica*, vol. 3, 1973, pp. 5–28; K. S. Brown, Jr., "Centros de Evolução, Refúgios Quaternários e Conservação de Patrimônios Genéticos na Região Neotropical: Padrões de Diferenciação na Ithomiinae (*Lipidoptera: Nymphalidae*)", *Acta Amazônica*, vol. 7, 1977, pp. 75–137.
477. Brown, op. cit.
478. Support for a curve of this sort is suggested in A. Sommer, "Attempt at an Assessment of the World's Tropical Forests," *Unasylva*, vol. 28, 1976, pp. 5–25.
479. T. E. Lovejoy, "Refugia, Refuges and Minimum Critical

Size: Problems in the Conservation of the Neotropical Herpetofauna", in W. E. Duellman, ed., *South American Herpetofauna: Its Origin, Evolution and Dispersal,* Lawrence, Kan.: Museum of Natural History, Univ. of Kansas, 1979.

480. G. B. Wetterberg, et al., "Umma Anális de Prioridades em Conservação da Natureza na Amazônia," Seria Tecnica No. 8, Brasilia: Ministerio da Agricultura, 1977.

481. Lovejoy, "Refugia," op. cit. The concept of Pleistocene refugia in present tropical forest areas and the applicability of this concept to conservation will be explored during meetings to be held in Caracas, Venezuela, Feb. 8–13, 1979, under the auspices of the Association for Tropical Biology.

482. Raven et al., op. cit.; "Trends, Priorities and Needs," op. cit.

483. *Red Data Book,* Morges, Switzerland: International Union for Conservation of Nature, vol. 1, *Mammalia,* in press; vol. 2, *Aves,* by W. B. King, 1978

484. Lovejoy, "Refugia," op. cit.

485. Eckholm, "Planting for the Future," op. cit.

486. Ibid.

487. Garrett Hardin, "The Tragedy of the Commons," *Science,* vol. 162, 1968, pp. 13–18.

488. Garrett Hardin, "Political Requirements for Preserving Our Common Heritage," in Council on Environmental Quality, *Wildlife and America,* forthcoming, 1979, pp. 310–16.

489. Aldo Leopold, *A Sand County Almanac,* New York: Ballantine, p. 251 (originally published by Oxford University Press, 1949).

490. See especially Scott Overton and Larry Hunt, "A View of Current Forest Policy, with Questions Regarding the Future State of Forests and Criteria of Management," in *Transactions of the Thirty-Ninth North American Wildlife and Natural Resources Conference,* Washington; Wildlife Management Institute,1974, pp. 334–53, Also see John Maynard Keynes, *Essays in Biography,* New York: Meridian, 1956; Daniel Fife, "Killing the Goose," *Environment,* vol. 13, no. 3, 1971, pp. 20–27.

491. Hardin, "Political Requirements," op. cit., p. 315.

492. Overton and Hunt, op. cit.

493. Hardin, "Political Requirements," op. cit., p. 316.

Water Section

494. Food and Agriculture Organization, *Soil Conservation and Management in Developing Countries,* FAO Soils Bulletin 33. Rome, 1977; *Guidelines for Watershed Management,* FAO Conservation Guide 1, Rome, 1977; E. Eckholm, *Losing Ground,* New York: Norton, 1976.

495. P. H. Freeman, et al., *Cape Verde: Assessment of the Agricultural Sector,* report submitted to the Agency for International Development, McLean, Va.: General Research Corporation, 1978.

496. H. W. Anderson et al., *Forests and Water: Effects of Forest Management on Floods, Sedimentation and Water Supply,* Pacific Southwest Forest and Range Experiment Station report, Washington: U.S. Forest Service, 1976.

497. M. Kassas, "Desertification versus Potential for Recovery in Circum-Saharan Territories," in H. E. Dregne, ed., *Arid Lands in Transition,* Washington: American Association for the Advancement of Science, pp. 123–142; "Status of Desertification in the Hot Arid Regions; Climate Aridity Index Map; Experimental World Scheme of Aridity and Drought Probability," U.N. Conference on Desertification, 1977.

498. A. P. Altschuller, "Transport and Fate of Sulfur and Nitrogen Containing Pollutants Related to Acid Precipitation," unpublished report to the Environmental Protection Agency; George M. Hidy et al., "International Aspects of the Long Range Transport of Air Pollutants," report prepared for the U.S. Department of State, Westlake Village, Calif.: Environmental Research and Technology, Inc., Sept. 1978.

499. Commission on Natural Resources, National Research Council, *Implications of Environmental Regulations for Energy Production and Consumption: A Report to the U.S. Environmental Protection Agency from the Committee on Energy and the Environment,* Washington: National Academy of Science, 1977, vol. 6, p. 68; Northrop Services, Inc., "Interim Report: Acid Precipitation in the United States—History, Extent, Sources, Prognosis," a report to the Environmental Protection Agency, Corvallis, Ore.: Environmental Research Laboratory, Dec. 18, 1978; J. N. Galloway et al., "Acid Precipitation in the Northeastern United States," *Science,* vol. 194, 1976, pp. 722–24; G. E. Likens, "Acid Precipitation" *Chemical Engineering News,* vol. 54, 1976, pp. 29–44.

499a G. E. Likens, et al., "Acid Rain," *Scientific American,* Oct. 1977, pp. 43–51.

500. George R. Hendrey et al., "Acid Precipitation: Some Hydrobiological Changes," *Ambio,* vol. 5, no. 5–6, 1976, pp. 224–27. For a good general overview of the impact of acid precipitation in Norway, see Finn H. Braekke, *Impact of Acid Precipitation on Forest and Freshwater Ecosystems in Norway,* SNSF-Project, NISK, 1432 Aas-NHL, Norway, Mar. 1976.

501. C. L. Schofield, "Acid Precipitation: Our Understanding of the Ecological Effects," in *Proceedings of the Conference on Emerging Environmental Problems: Acid Precipitation,* U.S. Environmental Protection Agency Region II, New York, 1975.

502. D. M. Whelpdale, "Large Scale Atmospheric Sulphur Studies in Canada", *Atmospheric Environment,* vol. 12, 1978, pp. 661–670; Roderick W. Shaw, "Acid Precipitation in Atlantic Canada", *Environmental Science and Technology,* vol. 13, no. 4, Apr. 1979, pp. 406–11; Ross Howard, "48,000 Lakes Dying As Ontario Stalls", *Toronto Star,* Mar. 10, 1979, p. C4.

503. Arild Holt-Jensen, "Acid Rains in Scandinavia," *Ecologist,* Oct. 1973, pp. 380–81.

504. Jeffrey J. Lee and David E. Webber, "The Effect of Simulated Acid Rain on Seedling Emergence and Growth of Eleven Woody Species," unpublished report, Corvallis Environmental Research Laboratory, U.S. Environmental Protection Agency, Corvallis, Ore.; Braekke, op. cit., pp. 53–59.

505. National Academy of Sciences, *Implications of Environmental Regulations for Energy Production and Consumption,* Washington, 1977, p. 66.

506. Leon S. Dochinger and Thomas A. Seliga, "Acid Precipitation and the Forest Ecosystem," *Journal of the Air Pollution Control Association,* Nov. 1975, p. 1105.

507. Holt-Jensen, "Acid Rains in Scandinavia," op. cit., pp. 381–82; Carl Olof Tamm, "Acid Precipitation: Biological Effects in Soil and on Forest Vegetation," *Ambio,* vol. V. no. 5–6, 1976, pp. 235–38; Braekke, op. cit., pp. 53–59.

508. J. S. Jacobson and P. Van Leuken, "Effects of Acidic Precipitation on Vegetation" in S. Kasuga et al., eds., *Proceedings of the Fourth International Clean Air Congress,* Tokyo: Japanese Union of Air Pollution Prevention Associations, 1977, pp. 124–27.

509. Gary E. Glass, "Impacts of Air Pollutants on Wilderness Areas of Northern Minnesota," Environmental Research

Laboratory–Duluth, U.S. Environmental Protection Agency, Mar. 5, 1979, pp. 129–30 (draft).

510. Stephan Gage, assistant administrator, research and development, U.S. Environmental Protection Agency, personal communication, 1979.

511. D. S. Shriner, "Effects of Simulated Rain Acidified with Sufuric Acid on Host-Parasite Interactions," *Journal of Water and Soil Pollution,* vol. 8, no. 1, 1976, pp. 9–14.

512. Norman Glass, U.S. Environmental Protection Agency, Corvallis, Ore., Environmental Research Laboratory, personal communication, 1979.

513. W. H. Allaway, "pH, Soil Acidity, and Plant Growth," and N. T. Coleman and A. Mehlich, "The Chemistry of Soil, pH," in *Soil: The 1957 Yearbook of Agriculture,* Washington: Government Printing office, pp. 67–71 and 72–79.

514. John O. Reuss, "Chemical/Biological Relationships Relevant to Ecological Effects of Acid Rainfall," Corvallis, Ore.: National Environment Research Center, U.S. Environmental Protection Agency, June 1975; Dale W. Johnson and Dale W. Cole, "Anion Mobility and Soils: Relevance to Nutrient Transport from Terrestrial to Aquatic Ecosystems," U.S. Environmental Protection Agency, June 1977.

515. Environmental Protection Agency, Air Pollution Control Office, *Air Quality Criteria for Nitrogen Oxides,* Washington: Government Printing Office, Jan. 1971; National Research Council, Committee on Medical and Biologic Effects of Environmental Pollutance, *Nitrogen Oxides,* Washington: National Academy of Sciences, 1977; U.S. Department of Health, Education, and Welfare, National Air Pollution Control Administration, *Air Quality Criteria for Hydrocarbons,* Mar. 1970, and *Air Quality Criteria for Sulphur Oxides,* undated. Washington: Government Printing Office.

516. "Climate Change to the Year 2000," Washington: National Defense University, 1978.

517. K. Szesztay, "Summary: Hydrology and Man-Made Lakes," in William C. Ackermann et al., eds., *Man-Made Lakes: Their Problems and Environmental Effects,* Washington: American Geophysical Union, 1973.

518. Committee for Coordination of Investigations of the Lower Mekong Basin, *Pa Mong Optimization and Downstream Effects Study: Environmental Effects of Pa Mong,* Bangkok: Mekong Secretariat, 1976.

519. Ibid.

520. Ibid.

521. Julian Rzoska, "A Controversy Reviewed," *Nature,* June 10, 1976, pp. 444–45.

522. Mohammed Abdul-Fatah Kassas et al., "Impact of River Control Schemes on the Shoreline of the Nile Delta"; Carl George, "The Role of the Aswan High Dam in Changing the Fisheries in the Southeastern Mediterranean"; Henry van der Schalie, "World Health Organization Project Egypt 10: A Case History of a Schistosomiasis Control Project," all in T. Farvar and J. P. Milton, eds., *The Careless Technology: Ecology and International Development,* New York: Doubleday, 1972.

523. *The State of Food and Agriculture 1971,* Rome: Food and Agriculture Organization, 1971, p. 152.

524. Ibid., pp. 152–53.

525. A. T. Abbas, "Problems of Water Resource Development in Bangladesh," U.N. Water Conference, 1976.

526. Office of Water Program Operations, "Application of Sewage Sludge to Cropland: Appraisal of Potential Hazards of Heavy Metals to Plants and Animals," Washington: U.S. Environmental Protection Agency, No. 15, 1976; Bernard P. Sagik and Charles A. Sorber, eds., *Risk Assessment and Health Effects of Land Application of Municipal Wastewater and Sludges,* conference proceedings, San Antonio: Center for Applied Research and Technology, University of Texas, Dec. 1977; G. W. Leeper, *Managing the Heavy Metals on the Land,* New York: Marcel Dekker, 1978.

527. Bruce McCallum, *Environmentally Appropriate Technology,* Ottawa: Ministry of Fisheries and Environment, Mar. 1975, p. 115; Lane de Moll, ed., *Rainbook: Resources for Appropriate Technology,* New York: Schocken, 1977, pp. 191–94.

528. J. T. Dunham et al., "High Sulfur Coal for Generating Electricity," in P. H. Abelson, ed., *Energy: Use, Conservation and Supply,* Washington: American Association for the Advancement of Science, 1974, pp. 83–88.

529. G. H. Davis and L. A. Wood, "Water Demands for Expanding Energy Development," USGS Circular 703, Washington: U.S. Geological Survey, 1974.

530. John Lun, U.S. Environmental Protection Agency, personal communication, 1979.

531. P. R. Ehrlich et al., *Ecoscience: Population, Resources, Environment,* San Francisco: Freeman, 1977, p. 670.

532. Ibid.; and C.C. Coutant and S.S. Talmadge, "Thermal Effects," *Journal of Water Pollution Control Federation,* June 1977, pp. 1369–1425.

533. John Lun, op. cit.

534. U.S. Water Resources Council, *The Nation's Water Resources: 1975–2000,* Washington: Government Printing Office, Dec. 1978.

535. Velikanov, op. cit.

536. Wolf Häfele, "Energy Choices that Europe Faces: A European View of Energy," in Abelson, op. cit. pp. 97–104.

537. U.S. Agency for International Development, *Environmental Impact Statement on the AID Pest Management Program,* vols. 1 and 2, Washington, May 13, 1979; also its *Environmental and Natural Resource Management in Developing Countries: A Report to Congress,* vols. 1 and 2, Washington, Feb. 1979.

538. R. Pantulu, *Role of Aquaculture in Water Resource Development: A Case Study of the Mekong Project,* Bangkok Secretariat, 1974 (manuscript).

539. Environmental Protection Agency, *Quality Criteria for Water,* Washington, 1976

540. Pantulu, op. cit.

541. Ibid. Also see Barbara J. Culliton, "Aquaculture: Appropriate Technology in China," *Science,* Nov. 2, 1979, p. 539; and R. Zweig and W. O. McLarney, "Aquaculture," *Journal of the New Alchemists,* (Woods Hole, The New Alchemy Institute), 1977, pp. 63–82.

542. Food and Agriculture Organization, "The Potential of Fisheries to Developing Countries and the Requirements for Investment," FAO Fisheries Circular 343, Rome, 1977.

543. Bill Richards, "Toxic Chemical Found in California Wells," *Washington Post,* June 15, 1979, p. A2.

544. "Desertification: An Overview," U.N. Conference on Desertification, 1977.

545. Farvar and Milton, op. cit.

546. U.S. Bureau of Land Reclamation, "Increasing Available Water Supplies Through Weather Modification and Desalination," U.N. Water Conference, New York, 1976.

547. Farvar and Milton, op. cit.

548. Jane Stein, *Water: Life or Death,* Washington: International Institute for Environment and Development, June 1977; *Environmental Aspects of a Large Tropical Reservoir: A Case Study of the Volta Lake, Ghana,* Wash-

ington: Office of International and Environmental Programs, Smithsonian Institution, 1974.

549. Erik Eckholm, *The Picture of Health*, New York: Norton, 1977.

550. Letitia Obeng, "Water and Health," in International Institute for Environment and Development, *Clean Water for All*, Washington, 1976, pp. 13–18.

551. Talbot Page et al., "Drinking Water and Cancer Mortality in Louisiana," *Science*, July 2, 1976, pp. 55–57.

552. *Drinking Water and Health*, Washington: National Academy of Sciences, 1977.

553. *World Conservation Strategy*, Morges, Switzerland: International Union for Conservation of Nature and Natural Resources, Jan. 1978 (draft), p. WCS/Strategy/4.

Energy Section

554. E. F. Schumaker, in *Small Is Beautiful: Economics as if People Mattered* (New York: Harper, 1973), is one of those who drew attention to the importance of intermediate or appropriate technology.

555. National Research Council, *Energy for Rural Development* and *Methane Generation from Human, Animal and Agricultural Wastes*, Washington: National Academy of Sciences, 1976, 1977.

556. John P. Holdren, "Environmental Impacts of Alternative Energy Technologies for California," in *Distributed Energy Systems in California's Future*, vol. 2, Washington: Government Printing Office, May 1978.

557. Ibid., p. 4.

558. Richard J. Kalagher et al., *Environmental Data for Energy Technology Policy Analysis*, Office of the Assistant Secretary for Environment, Department of Energy, Mar. 10, 1978 (draft).

559. Richard Nehring, "Giant Oil Fields and World Oil Resources," Santa Monica, Calif.: Rand Corp., June 1978.

560. Ibid., p. 85.

561. M. King Hubbert, "World Oil and Natural Gas Reserves and Resources," in Congressional Research Service, *Project Interdependence: U.S. and World Energy Outlook Through 1990.* Washington: Government Printing Office, Nov. 1977, pp. 632–44.

562. See, for example, Edison Electric Institute, *Economic Growth in the Future: The Growth Debate in National and Global Perspective*, New York: McGraw-Hill, 1976; Workshop on Alternative Energy Strategies, *Energy: Global Prospectives 1985–2000*, New York: McGraw-Hill, 1977.

563. Amory B. Lovins, "Energy Strategy: The Road Not Taken,"*Foreign Affairs*, Oct. 1976; Amory B. Lovins, *Soft Energy Paths: Toward a Durable Peace*, Cambridge, Mass.: Ballinger, 1977; Hugh Nash, ed., *Progress as if Survival Mattered*, San Francisco: Friends of the Earth, 1977. For further details on the relationship between energy and GNP, see Sam H. Schurr and Joel Darmstader, "Some Observations on Energy and Economic Growth," in *Future Strategies for Energy Development: A Question of Scale*, proceedings of a conference at Oak Ridge, Tenn., Oak Ridge Association Universities, 1977, pp. 280–97.

564. Lovins, "Energy Strategy" and *Soft Energy Paths*, op. cit. Also see P. R. Ehrlich et al., *Ecoscience: Population, Resources, Environment*, San Francisco: Freeman, 1977, Ch. 8, 14, and 15.

565. Lovins, "Energy Strategy" and *Soft Energy Paths*, op. cit.

566. All major criticisms of Lovins' work have been collected by the Senate Select Committee on Small Business and Committee on Interior and Insular Affairs and published in a report of more than 2,000 pages: *Alternative Long-Range Energy Strategies: Additional Appendixes—1977*, Washington: Government Printing Office, Dec. 9, 1976.

567. World Energy Commission of the World Energy Conference, *World Energies: Looking Ahead to 2020*, New York: IPC Science and Technology Press, 1978.

568. Ibid.

569. Ibid., p. 228.

570. Ibid.

571. Ibid.

572. Robert J. Raudebaugh, executive director of WEC's U.S. National Committee, personal communication, Feb. 15, 1979.

573. DOE Energy Information Administration, "Projections of Energy Supply and Demand and Their Impacts," in *Administrator's Annual Report to Congress, 1977*, Washington, Apr. 1978, vol. 2.

574. Richard J. Kalagher et al., *National Environmental Impact Projection No. 1*, McLean, Va.: MITRE Corp., Dec. 1978.

575. Ford Foundation Nuclear Energy Policy Study Group, *Nuclear Power Issues and Choices*, Cambridge, Mass.: Ballinger, 1977, p. 7.

576. Ibid., p. 8.

577. Ibid., p. 11.

578. Ibid.

579. Eliot Marshall, "H₂ Bubble Is Unexpected Source of Trouble," and "A Preliminary Report on Three Mile Island," *Science*, Apr. 13 and 20, 1979, pp. 152–53 and 280–281.

580. Tim Metz, "Financial Fallout: Post Accident Costs May Be Biggest Hurdle for Nuclear Expansion," *Wall Street Journal*, Apr. 24, 1979, p. 1; "Assessing the Damage at Three Mile Island," *Science*, May 11, 1979, pp. 594–96.

581. "Montana Passes a Nuclear Initiative,". *Science*, Nov. 24, 1978, p. 850.

582. Luther J. Carter, "Nuclear Wastes: Popular Antipathy Narrows Search for Disposal Sites," *Science*, Sept. 23, 1977, p. 1265–66.

583. David S. Broder, "U.S. Gets Ultimatum on Nuclear Waste," *Washington Post*, July 11, 1979, p. A2.

584. "European Doubts About Nuclear Power", *Science*, Oct. 8, 1976, p. 164; Robert Skole, "Sweden's Nuclear Election," *The Nation*, Oct. 9, 1976, pp. 334–37.

585. "Austria Declines to Start a Nuclear Power Program," *Science*, Nov. 24, 1978, p. 850; "Austrians Turn Down Nuclear Power Plant in Close Referendum," *Washington Post*, Nov. 6, 1978, p. A24.

586. John Vinocer, "West Germany Postpones Building a Key Atom Plant," *New York Times*, May 17, 1979, A7.

587. Lovins, *Soft Energy Paths*, op. cit. pp. 38–39.

588. Thomas B. Johansson and Peter Steen, *Solar Sweden: An Outline to a Renewable Energy System*, Stockholm: Secretarial for Futures Studies, 1978.

589. Lars Emmelin and Bo Wiman, *The Environmental Problems of Energy Production*, Stockholm: Secretariat for Future Studies, 1978 (Swedish); Lars Emmelin and Bo Wiman, "Environmental Report," in *Preliminary Report from the Energy Commission, Group A, Safety and Environment*, Stockholm: Ministry of Industry, Oct. 1977 (Swedish).

590. Johansson and Steen, op. cit.

591. W. R. Derrick Sewell and Harold D. Foster, *Images of Canadian Futures: The role of Conservation and Renewable Resources*, Ottawa: Environment Canada, 1976.

592. Peter Love and Ralph Overend, *Tree Power: An Assessment of the Energy Potential of Forest Biomass in*

Canada, Ottawa: Ministry of Energy, Mines and Resources, 1978.
593. Ibid., p. ix.
594. *Distrbuted Energy Systems in California's Future,* Interim Report, Washington: Government Printing Office, May 1978. 2 vol.
595. Ibid., vol. 1, p. vi.
596. Ibid.
597. Ibid., vol. 2, p. 60
598. Ibid., vol. 1, p. ix.
599. Council on Environmental Quality, *The Good News About Energy,* Washington: Government Printing Office, 1979.
600. Ibid, p. 23.
601. Department of Energy Impacts Panel, *Domestic Policy Review of Solar Energy,* Washington, Oct. 1978.
602. Council on Environmental Quality, op. cit.
603. Sven Björnholm, *Energy in Denmark, 1990 and 2005: A Case Study,* Copenhagen: The Niels Bohr Institute, Sept. 1976.
604. Gerald Leach et al., *A Low Energy Strategy for the United Kingdom,* Cambridge, England: J. W. Larman, 1979.
605. Ibid., pp. 18, 19.
606. Lovins, *Soft Energy Paths,* op. cit., p. 26.
607. Holdren, op. cit., pp. 1–3.
608. "Regional Information on Industry and Environment," in *Industry and Environment,* Nairobi: U.N. Environment Programme (UNEP), 1979; *National Energy Policies: An Overview,* Nairobi: UNEP, 1979; *Solar 2000,* Nairobi: UNEP, 1979.
609. Lovins, *Soft Energy Paths,* op. cit., pp. 59–60.
610. *Alternative Long-Range Energy Strategies,* op. cit.
611. Food and Agriculture Organization, *The State of Food and Agriculture, 1976,* Rome, 1976, Ch. 3.
612. Ibid.
613. Ibid.
614. Ibid.
615. Ibid.
616. Food and Agriculture Organization, *The State of Food and Agriculture,* op. cit. p. 89; also see Arjun Makhijani and Allan Poole, *Energy and Agriculture in the Third World: A Report to the Energy Policy Project of the Ford Foundation,* Cambidge, Mass.: Ballinger, 1975, p. 19.
617. Arjun Makhijani, *Energy Policy for the Rural Third World,* London: International Institute for Environment and Development, 1976.
618. D. Brokensha and B. Riley, "Forest, Foraging, Fences and Fuel in a Marginal Area of Kenya," Univ. of Calif., Santa Barbara, prepared for the Firewood Workshop, sponsored by USAID's Africa Bureau, June 1978; "The Double Problem of Charcoal," *"The Center Report* (Nairobi, Environmental Liaison Center) vol. 3, no. 3, Aug. 1978.
619. Erik Eckholm, Personal communication, 1979.
620. J. E. M. Arnold and J. Jongma, "Fuelwood and Charcoal in Developing Countries," *Unasylva,* vol. 29, no. 118, 1978, pp. 2–9.
621. Ibid.
622. Food and Agriculture Organization, *The State of Food and Agriculture,* 1976, op. cit.
623. World Bank, *Forestry Sector Policy Paper,* Washington, 1978.
624. FAO Committee on Forestry, "A Forecast of Wood Consumption," *Unasylva,* vol. 29, no. 118, 1978, pp. 33–34.
625. Arnold and Jongma, op. cit.
626. Food and Agriculture Organization, *The State of Food and Agriculture,* op. cit.

627. Erik Eckholm, personal communication, 1979.
628. Arnold and Jongma, op. cit.
629. Erik Eckholm, *Planting for the Future: Forestry for Human Needs,* Washington: Worldwatch Institute, Feb. 1979, p. 30.
630. F. R. Weber, "Economic and Ecologic Criteria of Forestry and Conservation Projects in the Sahel," prepared for the USAID Sahel Development Program, Boise, Idaho: International Resource Development and Conservation Services, 1977.
631. Ibid.
632. Club du Sahel, and Comité Permanent Inter-Etats de Lutte contre la Sécheresse dans le Sahel, *Energy in the Development Strategy of the Sahel: Situation, Perspectives, Recommendations,* Paris: Club du Sahel, 1978.
633. Ibid.
634. Ibid.
635. Erik Eckholm, *Planting for the Future,* op. cit.
636. Weber, op. cit. Brokensha and Riley, op cit.; "The Double Problem of Charcoal," op. cit.
637. Brokensha and Riley, op. cit.; W. M. Floor, "Energy Options in Rural Areas of the Third World," 8th World Forestry Conference, Jarkarta, Oct. 1978.
638. Tze I. Chiang, et al., *Pyrolytic Conversion of Agricultural and Forestry Wastes in Ghana: A Feasibility Study,* prepared for USAID, Atlanta: Georgia Institute of Technology, 1976.
639. "The Double Problem of Charcoal," op. cit.
640. Clark University Program for International Development, *Fuelwood and Energy in Eastern Africa,* Worcester, Mass.: Clark Univ., 1978.
641. Ibid.
642. J. E. M. Arnold, "Wood Energy and Rural Communities," 8th World Forestry Congress, Jakarta, Oct. 1978.
643. "Arvores por Ferro," *Veja* (Brazil), Nov. 8, 1978, pp. 77–78.
644. Ibid.
645. Peter H. Freeman, "Environmental Aspects of Development in the Paracatu River Basin, Brazil," submitted to the Organization of American States, Washington: Threshold Inc., 1978.
646. D. E. Earl, *A Report on Charcoal,* Rome: Food and Agriculture Organization, 1974.
647. Brokersha and Riley, op. cit.
648. Makhijani, *Energy Policy, op. cit.;* Food and Agriculture Organization, op. cit.; Erik Eckholm, *The Other Energy Crisis: Firewood,* Washington: Worldwatch Institute, 1975.
649. Food and Agriculture Organization, op. cit.
650. Ibid.; Arnold and Jongma, op. cit.
651. Lester Brown, Personal communication, 1979.
652. Arnold and Jongma, op. cit.; Eckholm, *The Other Energy Crisis,* op. cit.; Erik Eckholm, personal communication, 1979.
653. Food and Agriculture Organization, *Organic Materials in Soil Productivity,* FAO Soils Bulletin 35, Rome, 1977, pp. 94–95; see also J. J. C. van Voorhoeve, *Organic Fertilizer Problems and Potential for Developing Countries,* Washington: World Bank Fertilizer Study, Background Paper 4, 1974.
654. U.S. Department of Agriculture, *Soil: The 1957 Yearbook of Agriculture,* Washington: Government Printing Office, 1957.
655. Food and Agriculture Organization, *Organic Materials,* op. cit.
656. National Research Council, *Methane Generation,* op. cit.
657. Food and Agriculture Organization, *Organic Materials,* op. cit.

658. D. Thery and Van Giap Dang, "The Chinese Biogas Phenomenon" *Ecodevelopment News*, Dec. 1978, pp. 15–16.
659. Makhijani and Poole, op. cit.
660. W. M. Floor, "Energy Options in Rural Areas of the Third World," 8th World Forestry Conference, Jarkarta, Oct. 1978.
661. Ibid.; National Research Council, *Energy for Rural Development*, op. cit., and *Methane Generation*, op. cit.
662. U.S. Department of Agriculture, *Soil*, op. cit.; Food and Agriculture Organization, *Organic Materials*, op. cit.
663. Erik Eckholm, *Losing Ground*, New York: Norton, 1976; also see the observations on environmental deterioration woven into Peter Matthiessen, *The Snow Leopard*, New York: Viking, 1978.
664. D. French, "Firewood in Africa," Firewood Workshop, USAID Africa Bureau, Washington, June 1978.
665. Makhijani, *Energy Policy*, op. cit.
666. Arnold and Jongma, op. cit.
667. Makhijani, *Energy Policy*, op. cit.; National Research Council, *Methane Generation*, op. cit.; Food and Agriculture Organization, *China: Recycling of Organic Wastes in Agriculture*, FAO Soils Bulletin No. 40, Rome, 1977; Thery and Dang, op. cit.

Nonfuel Minerals Section

668. National Academy of Sciences and National Academy of Engineering, *Man, Materials and Environment*, Cambridge, Mass.: MIT, 1973, p. 88.
669. U.S. Department of the Interior, "Environmental Issues and the Mineral Industry," in *Mining and Minerals Policy*, Washington: Government Printing Office, July 1976, Ch. 7, pp. 95–105.
670. United Nations, *Environmental Impacts on the Growth and Structure of the World Economy*, E/AC.54/L.76, 1975.
671. Richard A. Carpenter, "Tensions Between Materials and Environmental Quality," *Science*, Feb. 20, 1976, pp. 665–68.
672. U.S. Agency for International Development, *Desert Encroachment on Arable Lands: Significance, Causes and Control*, Washington, Aug. 1972.
673. See the forestry projections in Chapter 8.
674. James Paone et al., *Land Utilization and Reclamation in the Mining Industry, 1930–71*, Bureau of Mines Information Circular 8642, Washington: Government Printing Office, 1974.
675. Raymond F. Dasmann, *Environmental Conservation*, New York: Wiley, 1976, p. 356.
676. J. M. Bradley, "W. Germany to Develop World's Largest Open Pit Lignite Mine," *World Environment Report*, July 4, 1977, p. 5.
677. Don Lipscombe, "Australian Conservationists Lose to Giant Alumina and Gas Projects," *World Environment Report*, Sept. 11, 1978, p. 3.
678. U.S. Soil Conservation Service, *Status of Land Disturbed by Surface Mining in the United States as of July 1, 1977, by States*, Advisory CONS–5, Washington, Feb. 9, 1978.
679. *Rehabilitation Potential of Western Coal Fields*, Washington: National Academy of Sciences, 1974.
680. Energy Policy Project of the Ford Foundation, *Exploring Energy Choices: A Preliminary Report*, New York: Ford Foundation, 1974.
681. Paone et al., op. cit.
682. Peter Dewhirst, "OECD Reports on Waste Material Use in Road Construction," *World Environment Report*, July 3, 1978, p. 5.
683. John L. Morning, "Mining and Quarrying Trends in the Metal and Nonmental Industries," in Bureau of Mines, *Minerals Yearbook 1975*, Washington: Government Printing Office, 1977.
684. Arthur Miller, "Philippines Seeking to Recycle, Reduce Waste in Mining Operations," *World Environment Report*, Oct. 24, 1977, p. 5.
685. Morning, op. cit.
686. Argonne National Laboratory, *Land Reclamation Program Annual Report July 1976-October 1977*, ANL/LRP–2, Argonne, Ill., 1978, p. 7.
687. *Methods for Identifying and Evaluating the Nature and Extent of Non-Point Sources of Pollutants*, EPA–430/9–73–014, Washington: Environmental Protection Agency, Oct. 1973, p. 6.
688. Paone et al., op. cit.
689. "Czechs Reclaim Coal Strip Mines by Planting Acorns," *World Environment Report*, Aug. 15, 1977, p. 8.
690. Human Resources Network, *The Handbook of Corporate Social Responsibility-Profiles of Involvement*, Radnor, Pa.: Chilton; 1975, p. 179.
691. Charles Harrison, "UNEP Hails Rehabilitation Of Limestone Quarry in Kenya," *World Environment Report*, Feb. 27, 1978, p. 1.
692. U.S. Soil Conservation Service, op. cit.
693. *Environmental Quality 1977*, annual report of the Council on Environmental Quality, Washington: Government Printing Office, 1977, pp. 87–89.
694. Ibid., p. 331.
695. David Sheridan, "A Second Coal Age Promises to Slow Our Dependence on Imported Oil," *Smithsonian*, Aug. 1977, p. 35.
696. J. R. LaFevers, et al., "A Case Study of Surface Mining and Reclamation Planning, International Minerals, and Chemical Corp. Phosphate Operations, Polk County, Fla.", *Integrated Mined-Area Reclamation and Land Use Planning*, vol. 3B, Argonne, Ill.: Argonne National Laboratory, 1977.
697. Dasmann, op. cit.
698. "Sweden Refuses Permits For Strip Mining of Slate," *World Environment Report*, Feb. 14, 1977, p. 6.
699. "Create Land Reserve at Scene of Diamond Boom," *World Environment Report*, Aug. 28, 1978, p. 8.
700. Ariel Lugo, Council on Environmental Quality, personal communication, 1979.
701. *Environmental Quality 1977*, op. cit., pp. 87, 89, 90.
702. *Asbestos: The Need for and Feasibility of Air Pollution Controls*, Washington: National Academy of Sciences, 1971; *Relationship Between Environmental Quality, Health, and Safety and the Availability and Price of Minerals*, Washington: Environmental Protection Agency, Nov. 17, 1978.
703. Ibid.
704. *Environment and Development*, Washington: World Bank, June 1975, pp. 17–18.
705. S. N. Linzon, "Effects of Sulfur Oxides on Vegetation," *Canadian Forestry Chronicle*, vol. 48, no. 4, 1972, pp. 1–5.
706. Carl M. Shy, "Health Hazards of Sulfur Oxides," *American Lung Association Bulletin*, Mar. 1977, pp. 2–7.
707. Luther J. Carter, "Uranium Mill Tailings: Congress Addresses a Long-Neglected Problem," *Science*, Oct. 13, 1978, pp. 191–95.
708. Ibid.
709. Ibid.
710. Ibid.
711. Ibid.
712. *Preliminary Findings, Radon Daughter Levels in Structures Constructed on Reclaimed Florida Phosphate Land,*

Washington: Environmental Protection Agency, Oct. 1975.

713. *Phosphate—1977,* Mineral Commodity Profiles MCP–2, Washington: Bureau of Mines, May 1977, p. 14.

714. *Relationship Between Environmental Quality, Health, and Safety,* op. cit.

715. J. M. Bradley, "East and West Germany Squabble Over Polluted Werra River," *World Environment Report,* Oct. 24. 1977, p. 2.

716. A. E. Cullinson, "Collapse of Slag Yard Dams in Japan Pollutes Two Rivers," *World Environment Report,* June 5, 1978, p. 5.

717. "Environmental Protection Unit Established in Philippines," *World Environment Report,* June 20, 1977, p. 8.

718. "Japanese Agency Studies Filippino Mine Wastes," *World Environment Report,* May 22, 1978, p. 8.

719. Loretta McLaughlan, "Chemical Congress in Peru Indicts Copper Mine Pollution of Rivers," *World Environment Report,* Dec. 5, 1977, p. 6; "New Peruvian Method Recovers Copper From Water," *World Environment Report,* July 4, 1977, p. 6.

720. Human Resources Network, op. cit., p. 180.

721. "Reserve Mining Company to Remain in Minnesota," *New York Times,* July 8, 1978, p. 35; M. Howard Gelfan, "Mining Firm Wins a Round in Dumping Fight With State," *Washington Post,* Feb. 1, 1977, p. 43.

722. Irving J. Selikoff, "Asbestos in Water," in *Water—Its Effect on Life Quality,* Seventh International Water Quality Symposium Proceedings, Lombard, Ill.: Water Quality Research Council, 1974.

723. D. B. Brooks and P. W. Andrews, "Mineral Resources, Economic Growth and World Population," in P. H. Abelson and A. L. Hammond, eds., *Materials: Renewable and Nonrenewable Resources,* Washington: American Association for the Advancement of Science, 1976, pp. 41–47.

724. D. E. Earl, "A Report on Charcoal," Rome: Food and Agriculture Organization, 1974.

725. "Arvores por Ferro," *Veja* (Brazil), Nov. 8, 1978, pp. 77–78.

726. Earl T. Hayes, "Energy Implications of Materials Processing," in Abelson and Hammond, op. cit., pp. 33–37.

727. Ibid.

728. Harry M. Caudill, *Night Comes to the Cumberlands: Biography of a Depressed Area,* Boston: Little, Brown, 1963.

729. Bradley op. cit.

Closing the Loops

730. William P. Elliot and Lester Machta, eds., *Workshop on the Global Effects of Carbon Dioxide from Fossil Fuels, 1977,* Washington: U.S. Department of Energy, May 1979, p. 24.

731. *Report of the Scientific Workshop on Atmospheric Carbon Dioxide, 1976* Geneva: World Meteorological Organization, 1977, p. 13.

732. *World Climate Conference: Declaration and Supporting Documents,* Geneva: World Meteorological Organization, Feb. 1979, p. 4.

733. Ibid., p. 4.

734. George M. Woodwell, et al., "The Carbon Dioxide Problem: Implications for Policy in the Management of Energy and Other Resources," Washington: Council on Environmental Quality, July 1979.

735. "Making the Most of the CO$_2$ Problem" *Science News,* Apr. 14, 1979, p. 244. Op. cit.

736. William W. Kellog, "Facing Up to Climatic Change," *Ceres,* vol. 11, 1978, pp. 13–17. Kellog, op. cit.

737. Committee on Environmental Improvement, *Cleaning Our Environment: A Chemical Perspective,* Washington: American Chemical Society, 1978, p. 209.

738. Richard A. Kerr, "Global Pollution: Is the Arctic Haze Actually Industrial Smog?," *Science,* July 20, 1979, pp. 290–93.

739. "Gulf States to Attend Kuwait Conference," U.N. Environment Program, press release, Nairobi, Apr. 14, 1978.

740. Barry Castleman, "The Export of Hazardous Factories to Developing Nations," *International Journal of Health Services,* forthcoming, 1979; "Trouble for Export," *Washington Post,* Aug. 27, 1979, p. A26. In addition, the Health Hazard Export Study Group of the University of Connecticut Health Center will sponsor a conference on the Exportation of Hazardous Industries to Developing Countries on Nov. 2 and 3, 1979 at Hunter College, New York City. The conference will be held in conjunction with the annual meeting of the American Public Health Association. Conference proceedings will be available in Jan. 1980 from ABT Associates, Cambridge, Mass.

741. "Increasing Available Water Supplies Through Weather Modification and Desalination," New York: U.N. Water Resources Branch, 1976.

742. Clyde LaMotte, "The U.S. Plan to Control Water Pollutions," *Ocean Industry,* June 1970. pp. 39–45.

743. *Environmental Quality 1978,* annual report of the Council on Environmental Quality, Washington: Government Printing Office, 1978, p. 446.

744. David Pimentel et al., "Land Degradation: Effects on Food and Energy Resources," *Science,* vol. 194. 1976, pp. 149–55.

745. See *Conservation Foundation Newsletter,* Dec 1978.

746. Robert C. Oelhaf, *Organic Agriculture,* New York: Wiley, 1979; also see William Tucker, "The Next American Dust Bowl," *Atlantic Monthly,* July 1979, pp. 38–49.

747. David Vail, "The Case for Organic Farming." *Science,* July 13, 1979, pp. 180–81.

748. Harold E. Dregne, cited in "Desertification: What is it? Where is it? Who has it? Is it expensive? How does it happen?" *IUCN Bulletin,* (International Union for the Conservation of Nature and Natural Resources), Aug./Sept., 1977, p. 45.

749. Scientific Committee on Problems of the Environment, "Arid Lands in Developing Countries: Environmental Effects," Paris: International Council of Scientific Unions, 1976.

750. United Nations Environment Program press release, Nairobi, Sept. 14, 1977.

751. "Perennial Corn Hope," *Development Forum,* Mar. 1979, p. 5.

752. "Riceless World?" *Development Forum,* Mar. 1979, p. 5.

753. O. Beingolea Guerrero, "Integrated Pest Control, Latin America," Conference on Environmental Sciences in Developing Countries, Nairobi, Feb. 1974.

754. Lim Guan Soon, "Integrated Pest Control, Asia," Conference on Environmental Sciences in Developing Countries, Nairobi, Feb. 1975.

755. Guerrero, op. cit.

756. Ray Smith, "Economic Aspects of Pest Control," Univ. of Calif., Berkeley, 1970 (unpublished paper).

757. *The State of Food and Agriculture, 1976,* Rome: Food and Agriculture Organization, 1976.

758. Richard M. Adams et al., *Methods Development for Assessing Air Pollution Control Benefits,* vol. 3, *A Preliminary Assessment of Air Pollution Damages for Se-*

lected Crops Within Southern California, Washington: Environmental Protection Agency, Feb. 1979.

759. Anne K. Robas, *South Florida's Mangrove-Bordered Estuaries: Their Role in Sport and Commercial Fish Production,* Sea Grant Information Bulletin no. 4, Univ. of Miami, 1970.

760. United Nations Environment Programme, *The Mediterranean Action Plan,* Nairobi, 1977; also see the program's 1977 press releases nos. 85, 147, and 162.

761. *Coastal Zone Pollution in Indonesia with Emphasis on Oil: A Reconnaissance Survey,* Washington: Smithsonian Institution, 1974.

762. Asia Bureau, U.S. Agency for International Development, "Environmental Assessment of the Small Farm Systems in the Phillipines," Washington, 1978.

763. U.S. Water Resource Council, *The Nation's Water Resource, 1975–2000,* vol. 1, *Summary,* Washington: Government Printing Office, 1978.

764. "The Macroeconomic Impact of Federal Pollution Control Programs: 1978 Assessment," report submitted to the Environmental Protection Agency and the Council on Environmental Quality by Data Resources, Inc., Cambridge, Mass; Jan. 11, 1979.

765. D. M. Costle, "The Benefits of a Cleaner Environmental," *EPA Journal,* Jan. 1979, pp. 2–3.

766. Thomas D. Crocker et al., *Methods Development for Assessing Air Pollution Control Benefits,* vol. 1., *Experiments in the Economics of Air Pollution Epidemiology,* Washington: Environmental Protection Agency, Feb. 1979.

767. "Health Benefits from Stationary Air Pollution Control Appear Substantially More than Costs," Environmental Protection Agency, press release, Mar. 29, 1979.

767a Castleman, op. cit.

768. National Academy of Sciences, Committee on Resources and Man, *Resources and Man,* San Francisco: Freeman, 1969, p. 5.

769. There is an extensive literature on this general subject. For a short introduction, see Lester R. Brown et al., *Twenty-Two Dimensions of the Population Problem,* Washington: Worldwatch Institute, Mar. 1976. For a well articulated Marxist perspective on this subject, see Mahmood Mamdani, *The Myth of Population Control,* New York: Monthly Review Press, 1972.

770. National Oceanic and Atmospheric Administration, *New York Bight Project Annual Report for FY 1976–76T,* Boulder: Marine Ecosystems Analysis Program, Dec. 1977, p. 28.

771. Council on Environmental Quality, *Report to the President by the Toxic Substances Strategy Committee: Public Review Draft,* Washington, Aug. 1979.

772. Dennis Hanson, "Earthlog," *Audubon,* Nov. 1978, pp. 14, 16–17; "A Nightmare in Niagara," *Time,* Aug. 14, 1978, p. 46.

773. Robert H. Boyle, "Getting Rid of the PCBs," *Audubon,* Nov. 1978, p. 150; "N.Y. Plan to Remove PCBs" *Science News,* July 15, 1978, p. 39.

774. *Environmental Quality 1978,* op. cit., p. 183; John C. Fuller, *The Poison that Fell from the Sky,* New York: Random House, 1977, p. 94.

775. John Walsh, "Seveso: The Questions Persist Where Dioxin Created a Wasteland," *Science,* Sept. 9, 1977, pp. 1064–67; Fuller, op. cit.; Thomas Whiteside, "A Reporter at Large: Contaminated," *New Yorker,* Sept. 4, 1978, pp. 34–81 (published also as *The Pendulum and the Toxic Cloud,* New Haven: Yale, 1979).

776. See references 769.

3 The Government's Global Model: The Present Foundation

This chapter introduces Part II of the Global 2000 Study's *Technical Supplement*. Part I (Chapters 1–13) responded to the first aspect of the President's directive establishing the Study: to make a "study of the probable changes in the world's population, natural resources, and environment to the end of the century." Part II (Chapters 14–23) responds to the second aspect of the President's directive: that "this study will serve as the foundation of our longer-term planning."*

Specifically, Part II describes and analyzes the set of formal computer-based models and less formal computational procedures used to develop the projections presented in Part I. It is these models and procedures, rather than the projections themselves, that constitute the real "present foundation" for the government's longer-term planning. This is because:

- These models and procedures embody—in an outward and visible form—many of the assumptions present in the minds of those responsible for the government's longer-term planning.

- These models and procedures are actually used by Government planners to help delineate the implications of those assumptions, to test and revise those assumptions where appropriate, and more generally to provide analytic support for long-term policy decisions.

A presentation of the government's present foundation for longer-term planning requires both a holistic overview of the entire set of models and procedures underlying the projections and a detailed examination of each model and procedure. This first chapter of Part II provides the holistic overview, while Chapters 15–23, which follow,

---

*Part III of this volume (Ch. 24–31) also responds to the second aspect of the President's directive by describing, analyzing, and comparing several highly integrated, long-term, global models not currently in extensive use by the U.S. government. These models and their projections provide important additional insights for use in analyzing the Global 2000 Study's projections and otherwise strengthening the present foundation for the government's longer-term planning.

describe and analyze each element of the set individually. This chapter can be thought of as primarily examining the external relationships among a set of "black boxes," whereas Chapters 15–23 explore the internal contents of each black box in detail. For the reader's convenience, a summary description of each "element" (or black box) is provided at the end of this chapter.

The "Government's Global Model"

Throughout Part II of this volume, the set of formal models and the less formal computational procedures used to develop the Study's projections are referred to, collectively, as the "government's global model" (for projecting probable changes in the world's population, natural resources, and environment to the end of the century).* Of course, the U.S. Government does not presently have an integrated computer model of the world. In fact, it may at first seem inappro-

---

*Additional specialized terms and phrases used in Part II:

Computer-based model—For the purposes of the Global 2000 Study, a computer program which simulates the behavior of some real-world phenomenon (for example, population growth or the patterns of world food trade) by using mathematical equations to make projections.

Input—Data (including assumptions) required before use can be made of a computer-based model or other computational procedure.

Output—Data created as a result of making use of a computer-based model or other computational procedure.

Endogenous calculations—Calculations performed by a computer-based model or other computational procedure.

Exogenous calculations—Calculations performed either in preparing input before making use of a computer-based model or other computational procedure, or in preparing output after making use of a computer-based model or other computational procedure.

Dynamically calculated projections—For the purposes of the Global 2000 Study, projections made endogenously for a future year that are dependent in part on projections (also made endogenously) for a preceding year or years.

Statically calculated projections—For the purposes of the Global 2000 Study, projections made endogenously for a future year that are independent of projections made endogenously for a preceding year or years. Exogenous changes in the input determine the year for which the projections are being calculated.

priate for this report to make reference to this collection of analytic procedures as though it were a fully integrated entity—with a food sector maintained by the Department of Agriculture, an energy sector maintained by the Department of Energy, an environmental sector scattered through many agencies, and so forth.

Instead, each agency has its own idiosyncratic way of projecting the future, based on its own responsibilities and interests. These different approaches were never designed to be used as part of an integrated, self-consistent system like the "government's global model." They were designed by different people, at different times, using different perspectives and methodologies, to meet different needs. While many are widely recognized as making outstanding use of state-of-the-art analytic procedures appropriate to their respective sectors, they produce projections that are mutually inconsistent in important ways.

Nevertheless, there are at least three compelling reasons for describing and evaluating these different approaches as a collective whole:

1. The various sectoral models and calculation procedures (arbitrarily aggregated in this discussion into a set of 11 "elements") have, to a limited degree, actually been developed and maintained in ways that involve mutual interactions via an informal, almost glacial process.
2. Projections developed using these elements have generally been used by the government and others as though they had been calculated on a mutually consistent basis.
3. These elements should be capable of being used on a mutually consistent basis—regardless of how they have actually been developed and maintained, and regardless of how their projections have generally been used. In fact, the President implicitly directed that the elements be used and evaluated in this way when he commissioned the Global 2000 Study.

The U.S. Government has a large collection of analytic procedures for anticipating future trends in a wide range of areas. The Global 2000 Study asked the federal agencies to develop projections using the methodologies that they routinely use for this purpose.

These methodologies—or tools—can be considered collectively as elements of the government's overall global model. Normally these elements are not employed in ways that ensure that the assumptions they use are mutually consistent. For the purposes of this study, ensuring consistency became a high priority, and every effort was made to enhance interactions and consistency among elements.

But in spite of the discipline established by the Study to ensure consistency, a number of internal contradictions were inherent in the analysis and, unavoidably, they remain. To put it more simply, the analysis shows that the executive agencies of the U.S. Government are not now capable of presenting the President with internally consistent projections of world trends in population, resources, and the environment for the next two decades.

These contradictions do not completely invalidate the overall results of the Study—in fact, the Study's projections are the most consistent such set the government has ever produced—but they do suggest that the results of the projections understate the severity of potential future problems. The analysis also points to ways in which the quality of the government's long-term analytic tools can be improved.

One of the most important findings of the Study is that the sectoral trends projected in Part I interact with each other in the real world in ways that are not represented in the government's global model—essentially because of the institutional context in which the elements of the model were developed and are being used. This context emphasizes sectoral concerns at the expense of interactions among sectors and leads to distorted and mutually inconsistent projections. Important decisions—involving billion-dollar federal programs and even the national security—are partially based on these projections.

In the discussion that follows, the "present foundation" (the government's global model) is first described in terms of its scope and in terms of the linkages between its elements. With this overall description to work from, the operation of the elements as a collective whole is analyzed. The implications of this analysis are then examined with regard to (1) interpreting the projections and (2) strengthening the present foundation. Finally, the 11 elements of the government's global model are summarized, using a fixed format to facilitate comparisons.

The remainder of this chapter is divided into five sections and several subsections, as follows:

Description of the Present Foundation
    Scope of the Global 2000 Study
    Linkages Prior to the Global 2000 Study
    Linkages Under the Limited Discipline of the Global 2000 Study
Analysis of the Present Foundation
    Inconsistent Variable Values
    Use of Diverse Sources of Information
    Absence of Feedback
    Structural Incompatibilities
    Institutional Factors Underlying the Discrepancies

Description of the Present Foundation

The government's present foundation for longer-term planning—the government's global model, as previously defined—is more than the sum of its parts. It is the sum both of its 11 elements and of the linkages among them. For the reader's convenience, the projections and detailed discussions in this volume related to each of the 11 elements are cross-referenced in Table 14–1.

The discussion that follows first reviews the decisions made in defining the scope of the Global 2000 Study, then describes the linkages that existed prior to the President's directive establishing

TABLE 14–1

Index to Projections and Detailed Discussions Related to Each of the 11 Elements of the Government's Global Model

Element	Projections Developed Using the Element	Detailed Description of the Element
In the order presented in the last section of this chapter	*Part I, Chapter*	*Part II, Chapter*
1. Population	2	15
2. GNP	3	16
3. Climate	4	17
4. Technology*	5	23
5. Food	6	18
6. Fisheries, Forestry, Water	7,8,9	19
7. Energy	10	20
8. Energy residuals	10	20
9. Fuel minerals	11	21
10. Nonfuel minerals	12	22
11. Environment	13	19

* A composite element, bringing together under a single heading the various assumptions and approaches related to the technological innovations used by the different elements, together with their deployments and impacts.

the Study, and, finally, describes the linkages established under the limited discipline imposed by the Study.

Scope of the Global 2000 Study

Within the scope of the President's directive, several decisions were made that played a major role in determining the ultimate shape of the Global 2000 Study by alternately selecting and excluding factors and considerations related to long-term global analysis:

1. The mandate of the Global 2000 Study was to focus on trends and changes rather than on goals. The Study was to look ahead, primarily to the year 2000 but not much beyond. It was concerned with biophysical matters, as opposed to social, political, and economic developments. While economic considerations were introduced in a limited way to help tie the projections together, economic, political, and social, considerations were essentially outside the scope of the Study.

2. Analytic methods were used wherever possible, to the exclusion of more normative or qualitatively descriptive approaches that might have been used to gather ideas and opinions from country and sectoral experts.* Naturally, the government makes use of many computational procedures for policy analysis other than those used by the Global 2000 Study, and many organizational units make use of sources other than those relied on by the Study. But, in general, those other procedures produce projections that are either not global and long-term, (i.e., to the end of the century, as defined by the President's directive) or not generally used by the governmental unit with primary responsibility for developing the type of projections required for this Study. Hence, such procedures were not included among the 11 elements comprising the government's global model appropriate for meeting the objectives of this Study.†

3. Wherever possible, use was made of the tools, data, and capabilities available within the federal government. This choice was made to fa-

---

*For example, the field anomaly relaxation method for projecting whole-body future patterns, developed by the Stanford Research Institute.
† Broad surveys of other models used by the U.S. Government are provided in *A Guide to Models in Governmental Planning and Operations,* Washington: Environmental Protection Agency, Aug. 1974, and in G. Fromm et al., *Federally Supported Mathematical Models: Survey and Analysis,* Washington: National Science Foundation, June 1975. A discussion of the evolving role of models in governmental processes is provided in M. Greenberger et al., *Models in the Policy Process,* New York: Russell Sage Foundation, 1976.

cilitate an evaluation of the present foundation for longer-range planning—but as a result of this decision, the contributions of many tools available in universities, the private sector, and other institutions were omitted. A further consequence of this choice is that individual agency views were not cross-evaluated with other perspectives from the private sector, except to the extent that these may have been incorporated in the views and criticisms of the Study's advisers.

4. Among the tools available in the federal government, it was necessary to pick and choose specific topical areas within the broader categories of population, natural resources, and the environment. Some of these choices were voluntary, others were not. For example, grasslands are a resource that could not be evaluated in the time available. While mineral consumption is projected, mineral demand, supply, and price are not projected because the government has no capability to project these on a global basis. The long-term global environmental analysis was assembled from a large number of sources, most of them outside the government, since the government has no capacity for such analysis that could be brought to bear on the Study.

5. Among the many variables selected for projection, some basic disaggregations were made, but disaggregation was not possible in every case or, necessarily, in even the most significant cases. For example, the number, age, and sex of the world's human populations were considered, but other factors (for example, educational, rural-urban, racial, religious, income, and other socioeconomic distributions) were not. Total energy consumption was considered, but not in terms of the end-use requirements for low-grade versus high-grade forms of energy; no net energy considerations were included. Out of nearly 100 resources traded internationally, only 12 were considered. Competition among crops for arable land was not specifically considered. Also, the environmental projections could not be geographically disaggregated in many cases because of the limitations of available data.

Linkages Prior to the Global 2000 Study

Each of the various agencies and departments of the executive branch of the federal government has always had some capacity to make long-term assessments of global trends related to population, natural resources, and the environment— such as the assessments discussed in Appendix A. Recent examples include *World Population: 1977* by the Bureau of the Census, *World Food Situation and Prospects to 1985* by the Department of Agriculture, *Mineral Facts and Problems* by the Bureau of Mines, and *World Energy Prospects* by the Department of Energy's predecessor, the Federal Energy Administration.

Prior to the Global 2000 Study, such reports were generally prepared largely independently of each other.* Little formal attempt was made to ensure that the assumptions used by one agency were consistent with those used by another. Little consideration was given to mutual interactions and feedback over time. Little heed was paid to intersectoral problem areas and concerns that were not the immediate responsibility or a special interest of that particular agency. Instead, it was implicitly assumed that long-term issues relating to population, natural resources, and the environment could be studied and analyzed on a largely independent basis.

Interaction among various elements of the government's global model still tends to occur very infrequently. Even the activities of the interagency task forces cited in Chapter 1 and discussed at greater length in Appendix A have done little to improve coordination among the government's numerous computational procedures. This is due largely to the relatively narrow focus and brief life span of most of those procedures. They tend to focus on a single set of narrowly conceived factors directly relevant to specialized sectoral concerns and to give priority to more pressing and parochial short-term tasks.

While it is true that the individual reports discussed in Appendix A have been independently prepared, there has always been some interaction between the agencies as they proceeded to formulate their projections. But most interactions occur as part of a relatively slow process. In general, one agency completes and publishes a study report, which, when read by other agencies, informs the future study efforts of those agencies.

Those individual studies have not all been undertaken at the same time, of course, nor have they necessarily made use of mutually consistent assumptions. Thus, while some feedback (and some interaction) does occur, as manifested in the process just described (and occasionally in formal and informal task force collaborations), such feedback tends to be extremely limited. Nevertheless, when viewed from this perspective, a quasi-integrated governmental global model can be seen

---

*The extent to which formal collaborative joint task force efforts were undertaken is discussed in Appendix A. The trend has been increasing, but the Global 2000 Study is the first official study to use all 11 elements concurrently.

that is more than the sum of a set of independent elements and their respective projections.

A signal indication of the relative lack of direct interaction among the elements and associated experts (prior to the Global 2000 Study) was provided when the Global 2000 staff met with the agency experts responsible for the maintenance and operation of the 11 elements of the government's global model. With one or two exceptions at the most, none of the agency experts had met each other previously, and none knew anything about the assumptions, structures, requirements, and uses of the others' calculation procedures—although on occasion they were required to make use of projections developed by the other elements.

Linkages Under the Limited Discipline of the Global 2000 Study

The various agencies' miscellaneous published projections could have been used as the Global 2000 Study's projections, but while this would have addressed the first aspect of the President's directive establishing the Study, it would not have addressed the second. The foundation thus established would have been of unknown reliability, making interpretation of the projections uncertain. Moreover, no basis would have been established for strengthening the present foundation.

Therefore, a special limited discipline was established for the Global 2000 Study—that is, a conscious choice was made (1) to employ, wherever possible, the very tools and data used within the federal government, and (2) to employ those tools and data on the most coordinated basis feasible within the constraints of the Study. In keeping with this decision, the Global 2000 Study's central staff established three criteria to be followed in developing the Study's projections, namely, that the projections be developed using analytical procedures, wherever possible, which were essentially (1) long-term, (2) global, and (3) in general use by the agencies primarily responsible for the type of projections required by the Study.

It was also clear that the normal linkages and mode of operation of the government's global model were not adequate for the Global 2000 Study, and so a special effort was made to increase linkages between the elements and to improve the consistency of these assumptions by:

- Using the output from one element as the input to another whenever this was readily feasible within the time and resource constraints of the Study.

- Providing special opportunities for relevant agency experts to exchange views with each other in order to encourage them to make their elements (and derived projections) more mutually consistent.

- Providing special opportunities for the various agency experts to exchange views with and receive comments from various experts not directly affiliated with the participating agencies. This also was done to encourage the agency experts to make the elements (and their derived projections) more mutually consistent.

The initial assignments of responsibility to the appropriate agencies have already been presented in Chapter 1. The agencies identified experts, both inside and outside the agencies, whom the agencies considered most appropriate for discharging the responsibility of preparing the projections requested by the Study's central staff. These "agency experts" (identified in the Acknowledgment section of the Preface) then became responsible for selecting and utilizing analytical procedures that they felt best met the Study's criteria.

The agency experts were asked to produce a first draft of their projection in just six weeks, at which time they, the Study staff, and a small group of outside experts* met for a weekend synthesis meeting. The purpose of the meeting was to improve the consistency of the projections and to begin—at least subjectively—to consider the implications of the natural resource and environmental projections for the independently derived projections of gross national product (GNP) and population. A certain amount of difficulty was anticipated in this preliminary meeting, and, in fact, many inconsistencies were revealed. The experts then decided collectively how best to adjust and modify the projections to improve the internal consistency of the whole set. The final projections were prepared during the following two months.

The projections had to be undertaken as part of a sequential process, since the structures of the elements themselves precluded their being used simultaneously. This process is illustrated in Figure 14–1.

While this sequential process permitted some interaction among the various elements of the government's global model, many important linkages could not be included at all. In particular, the population and GNP projections that were

---

*These experts are also identified in the Acknowledgments section of the Preface to this volume. A discussion of their activities, together with a summary of their views, is presented in Appendix B.

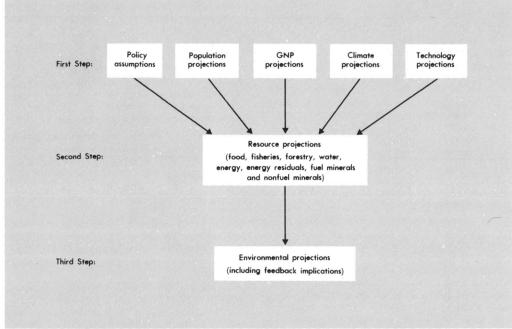

Figure 14-1. Sequential steps followed in linking elements of the government's global model.

prepared during the first step were based largely on extrapolations of past trends and were uninformed by interactive feedback from the resource and environmental projections or from each other. The resource and environmental analyses also projected developments that could significantly feed back to and influence each other, but these feedbacks were also not represented by explicit linkages.

Although an attempt was made to develop projections of resource consumption and environmental impacts using a single source for population projections and GNP projections, this effort was only partially successful.* While projections provided by these single sources were used in preparing the Study's food and energy projections,

they were not used in preparing the climate, technology, fisheries, forestry, water, fuel minerals, and nonfuel minerals projections. Nor were they used explicitly in preparing the environmental projections derived from the other projections.†

The limited extent to which both vertical and horizontal linkages were actually established for the Study is indicated in Figure 14-2. Additional steps were taken by the Study in order to obtain some indication of the extent to which the environmental impacts projected by the Study would have influenced the Study's other projections—had they been available and taken into account when those projections were made. These steps were discussed previously in the "Closing the Loops" section of Chapter 13 and are therefore

---

*Another initial objective was to examine the implications of the projections as they applied to a specific geographic region. This examination would have provided another test of the consistency of the projections and would also have given the global (sometimes nebulous) projections a more specific geographic reference for policy analysis. Unfortunately this examination could not be completed within the time and resource constraints of the Study because of the major differences in the ways that the various models represent geographic regions. Nonetheless, an effort was made in the preparation of Chapters

15–23 to provide the reader with as much detailed numeric information as possible on one arbitrarily selected region—North Africa. The interested reader may wish to examine further the additional problems and inconsistencies exposed by drawing this information together for purposes of comparison.

† Similarly, it was not possible to ensure that the assumption of no significant policy change was followed in developing the various projections (as shown later, in Table 14-2 and summarized in the element descriptions at the end of this chapter).

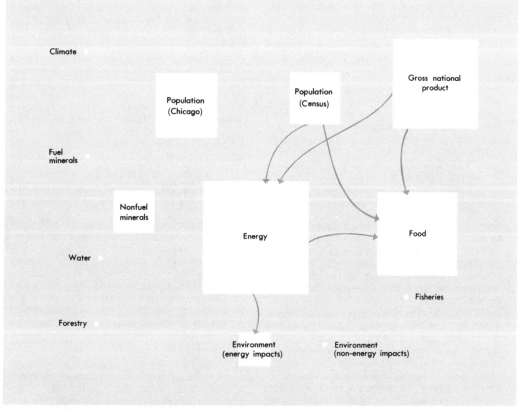

Figure 14–2. Linkages achieved between elements of the government's global model. Areas are proportional to the complexity of explicit quantitative relationships. The small squares represent negligible complexity.

not discussed further in this chapter, nor included in Figure 14–2.

Attempts by the Study to link together the elements of the government's global model focused entirely on linking the outputs of one element with the inputs of another. Because of the severe difficulties encountered in meeting even this limited objective, no attempt was made to evaluate deeper linkage opportunities or the challenges related to melding the various structures and paradigms.

A crude measure of uncertainty surrounding the projections was obtained as part of the limited discipline of the Global 2000 Study by requesting all participants to provide high, medium, and low variations of their projections wherever feasible. In practice, the high, medium, and low variations

that were prepared in making the resource and environmental projections were largely obtained by varying the population and GNP assumptions on which they were based. Most of the participating agency experts were reluctant to assign either statistical or subjective estimates of relative probability to these variations.

Even under the limited discipline of the Global 2000 Study, multiple sources for population and GNP projections were used in developing many of the Study's other projections. For this reason, inconsistencies unavoidably abound in the Study's collected set of projections—as well as for other reasons which will be discussed later in this chapter. Nevertheless, under the discipline of the Study, more consistency was achieved regarding linkages as basic as the use of consistent population and GNP projections than in any previous official governmental projections related to long-term, global trends in population, natural resources, and the environment.*

Analysis of the Present Foundation

The tacit assumption underlying the development and use of each separate element of the government's global model has been that long-term global trends in population, natural resources, and the environment can be projected separately in an essentially consistent and accurate manner. This assumption is false. As will be seen in the following analysis, projections from the government's global model fail to meet the most fundamental test of consistency—that the basic conclusions of an analysis shall not contradict its basic premises. And because the conclusions are not mutually consistent, they cannot be accurate.†

While consistency is a necessary prerequisite for accuracy, consistency alone does not ensure accuracy. Projections which should be and are consistent can nevertheless be wrong. Moreover, certain real-world phenomena in a state of dynamic disequilibrium (for example, markets where supply and demand are not in balance) would be inaccurately represented by projections in which supply and demand were statically balanced in accordance with a foolish consistency.

Nor does accuracy ensure usefulness. The ultimate usefulness of a projection (and, in a sense, its accuracy) can only be judged relative to its intended purpose. And it is likely that different criteria should be used to evaluate different projections, depending on the purposes for which the projections were developed. For example, some projections are best evaluated in terms of how well the underlying equations are fitted to past data. Others are best evaluated in terms of how well the equations can be defended as logically representing relationships existing in the real world. Some projections are best evaluated in terms of how accurately and precisely they predict (1) the timing of events in the real world or (2) the particular values pertaining to certain variables at particular times. Others are best evaluated in terms of how well they illuminate possible future patterns of behavior, even if the timings and magnitudes of the patterns they project are not precisely accurate.

The various elements of the government's global model were not designed to be used on a fully mutually consistent basis, even though projections developed using them are often treated as though they were. Therefore, it is in a sense unfair to the designers of these elements to analyze them on a holistic basis—even though a holistic perspective is, as discussed in the previous section, a basic requirement of the President's directive creating the Study. Moreover, it would have been more unfair to the designers of the elements to note that the elements are capable of performing a number of agency-specific functions not required under the mandate of the Global 2000 Study.

Despite the numerous inconsistencies which are about to be analyzed, the projections developed for this Study using the government's global model are the most complete and internally consistent ever developed by the executive agencies of the government. The central staff of the Global 2000 Study concluded, as have many of the Study's advisers, that the overall findings are

---

*The projections reported in this Study are based on the collective judgment of the agency experts who participated in the effort. In an effort to ensure internal consistency, several adjustments were required in individual agency projections. As a result, the projections may not agree completely with projections previously published by the participating agencies. Since the manuscript has not been subjected to formal interagency clearance procedures, the agencies are not responsible for any errors in fact or judgment that may have occurred in making these adjustments.

† One of the problems in analyzing models (and one of the strengths of models) is that models change over time. The models analyzed here are the models used to develop the Global 2000 Study projections. Since the projections were developed, several of these models have been modified, improved, or expanded, in some cases in response to problems and issues identified in the course of this study. The Department of Agriculture has established links to the International Institute for Applied Systems Analysis in Vienna and with the Mesarovic-Pestel World Integrated Model. The Department

of Energy is exploring feedback relationships to GNP. The Central Intelligence Agency is developing an expanded capability for nonfuel minerals analysis and projections. The World Bank has developed a new economic model which, Bank analysts report, eliminates many of the problems identified in this report. New projections also differ from those prepared for the Global 2000 study. The World Bank is projecting lower growth rates. The Department of Energy now expects oil price increases to occur sooner than projected and to have more impact on economic growth. The Department of Agriculture anticipates increases in the real price of food to occur sooner. The Bureau of the Census now expects life expectancies to increase more slowly than projected in some countries. While there have been changes in both individual models and projections, nothing has changed fundamentally concerning the problems of inconsistency and internal contradiction that occur when an effort is made to integrate the projections from the various elements of the government's global model. The basic problem addressed by this chapter has not changed and is not soon likely to change significantly.

valid, for reasons that will be discussed later in this chapter in the section entitled "Interpreting the Projections."

The essential problem with the current elements of the government's global model (and the projections derived from them) is, of course, the fact that they were designed to simulate sectoral aspects of long-term global trends largely to the exclusion of interactions between and among sectors. This design is no institutional accident but is in conformity with the bureaucratic division of responsibility within the executive agencies.* But real-world phenomena interact—especially in the longer term—in ways that do not conform to the bureaucratic division of responsibility or to narrowly focused sectoral models. Hence, the government's global model in its present form can only imperfectly project the consequences of these interactions. Furthermore, in the absence of ongoing institutional incentives to address cross-sectional interactions, the present form of the government's global model is not likely to change significantly in the foreseeable future.

The following analysis of the government's global model addresses six subjects: (1) the ubiquitous and important inconsistencies in the government's global model; (2) the extent to which the inconsistencies result from the use of diverse sources of information; (3) the extent to which the inconsistencies are due to the absence of important feedback relationships; (4) the various structural differences between the elements that make calibration difficult; (5) some of the institutional factors that underlie the discrepancies—including the use of the elements to develop projections intended primarily for advocacy purposes.

Inconsistent Variable Values

The 11 elements of the government's global model make use of many of the same variables—for example, population growth rates. Some assumed values are assigned to these variables prior to making use of an element, while other values are calculated as an intermediate or final step in developing an element's projections.

In many cases, the values assigned to the same variables by different elements are inconsistent

with each other.* For example, one set of projections assumed that population growth rates in the less developed countries (LDCs) would decline significantly, while another calculated that they would not. One set of projections assumed that per capita gross national product (GNP) in the LDCs would increase significantly, while another calculated it would not.

In order to help the reader understand the collective implications of these numerous inconsistencies, the following discussion is divided into four subsections, each of which addresses an important set of inconsistent variable values (the overwhelming number of environmental projection findings—discussed at length in Chapter 13—which explicitly contradict major variable values involving virtually all the other elements, are not included). The first subsection concerns population and GNP growth rates; the second and third, commodity trade prices and volumes; the fourth, capital and resource utilization. Each subsection consists of a paragraph providing a brief perspective on a set of inconsistencies, a diagram visually summarizing the set, and an itemization of specific inconsistencies.† The inconsistencies presented are representative but not exhaustive; nor are the four aggregates into which they have been grouped exhaustive. Other aggregates could have been assembled to make other points, but these four seemed sufficient to establish the ubiquity and seriousness of the inconsistencies.

Inconsistent Population and GNP Growth Rates

The Global 2000 Study population and GNP projections were developed independently of each other and appear to be mutually inconsistent. Because these projections were used to calibrate several of the Study's other projections, the distortions created by their inconsistencies have skewed those other projections. Additional dis-

---

*This fragmented approach is not unique to the executive branch. The U.S. Congress, through its committee structure, faces similar (but somewhat different) difficulties in systematically analyzing interrelated issues.

---

*The variables described here as inconsistent are not always precisely or even approximately commensurable. Therefore, the "inconsistencies" cited in this discussion should be understood as apparent only and subject to further verification. It was not possible to reconcile them more closely with each other within the time and budget constraints of the Global 2000 Study.

† In these somewhat technical itemizations, many methodologies and reports are referred to by short names or abbreviations—for example, the "cohort-component methodology" or the "WAES study." Providing even a brief explanation of these terms in this context would have distracted the reader's attention from the inconsistencies that are the focus of the immediate discussion. The reader is referred to the final section of this chapter for a brief explanation of these terms and to Chapters 15–23, where each is described at greater length.

crepancies were created when still other projections in the preceding chapters utilized population and GNP projections developed independently of the Study.

Figure 14–3 illustrates some of the inconsistencies regarding population and GNP growth rates. Four of the 11 numbered "elements"* considered in this chapter are involved: population (1), GNP (2), food (5), and nonfuel minerals (10). Four apparent inconsistencies are discussed below: (A) LDC social and economic development, (B) LDC population growth, (C) world population growth, and (D) GNP growth in LDCs. The arrows represent linkages that should or did occur. The broad end of the arrow is attached to the source of a particular type of information; the arrowhead indicates where the information is required as an input. The plus and minus symbols locate points of apparent inconsistency in the linkages.

A. *LDC Social and Economic Development.* The food element (5), the GNP element (2), and the population element (1), of the government's global model appear to have posited different rates of LDC social and economic development. Specifically, the Department of Agriculture's GOL (Grain, Oilseed, Livestock) model projected (in the medium-growth case, over the 1970–2000 period) that global per capita food consumption will increase only slightly and that this increase will not be evenly distributed, so that declines will be experienced in some LDCs. Similarly, the WAES (Workshop on Alternative Energy Sources) study, which is an integral part of the GNP element (2), projected (in the medium-growth case, which averages the two WAES cases, over the 1985–2000 period) that in some countries (e.g., Brazil, Mexico, Bangladesh) real per capita GNP (calculated using the Global 2000 Study's population projections) is likely to increase only marginally and that in others (e.g., Pakistan) real per capital GNP is likely to decline. In contrast, the Census Bureau's cohort-component methodology assumed (in all three cases, over the 1975–2000 period) that all LDCs will continue to make moderate progress in social and economic development.

B. *LDC Population Growth.* The population element (1) and the GNP element (2) appear to have posited different population growth rates in the LDCs. Specifically, the Census Bureau's co-hort-component methodology projected (in the medium-growth case, over the 1975–2000 period) that the LDCs will not experience significantly lower total population growth rates over the 1985–2000 period relative to the 1975–85 period—that is, the average annual growth rate over the 1985–2000 period (2.09 percent) was projected to be only 0.07 percentage points lower than the average annual growth rate over the 1975–85 period (2.16 percent).* In contrast, the WAES study arbitrarily reduced all GNP growth rates (including those of the LDCs) by roughly 10–30 percent (in both WAES cases, over the 1985–2000 period) to reflect the projected impact of assumed declining population growth rates on GNP growth.

C. *World Population Growth.* The population element (1) and the nonfuel minerals element (10) appear to have posited different population growth rates for the industrialized nations relative to world population growth rates. Specifically, the Census Bureau's cohort-component methodology projected (in the medium-growth case, over the 1975–2000 period) that average annual U.S. and U.S.S.R. population growth (0.6 and 0.8 percent, respectively) will be significantly lower than average annual world population growth (1.8 percent)—despite, for example, a projected 20 percent increase in U.S. fertility rates over the same period. In contrast, the 1977 Malenbaum Report relied upon by the Department of the Interior assumed (in the one case presented, over the 1973–2000 period) that average annual U.S. and U.S.S.R. population growth (1.0 and 1.3 percent, respectively) will be less dramatically lower than average annual world population growth (1.9 percent).

D. *GNP Growth in LDCs.* The GNP element (2) and the nonfuel minerals element (10) appear to have posited different GNP growth rates in the LDCs. Specifically, the WAES study projected (in the medium-growth case, which averages the two WAES cases, over the 1975–2000 period) that collectively African, Asian, and Latin American GNP will increase roughly 5 percent per year. In contrast, the IOU (Intensity of Use) methodology relied upon by the Department of the Interior assumed (in the one case presented, over the 1973–2000 period) that collectively African, Asian and Latin American GNP will increase roughly 3.5 percent per year.

---

*The number following each element is the sequence number arbitrarily assigned to that element in the last section of this chapter.

*In the Bureau of the Census high-growth series, the average annual population growth rate in the LDCs actually increases from 2.32 percent per year over the 1975–85 period to 2.39 percent per year over the 1985–2000 period.

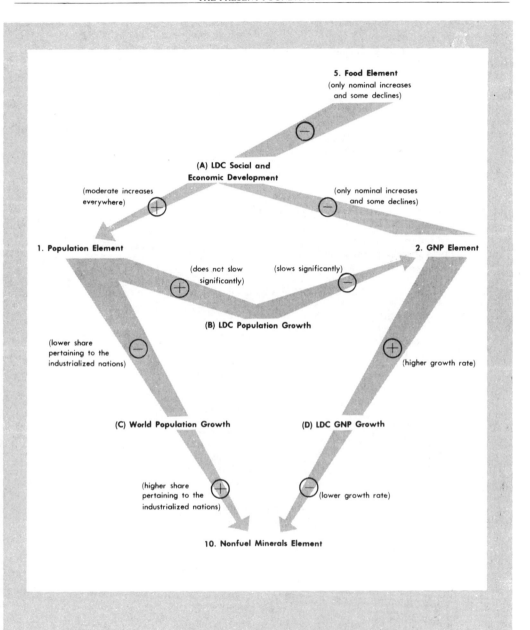

Figure 14-3. Inconsistent population and GNP growth rates.

Inconsistent Commodity Trade Prices

Major disparities exist among many of the elements of the government's global model regarding commodity price projections. Not merely the extent of real-price changes, but even the direction of such changes, is inconsistently projected with regard to fundamental price variables involving fertilizer, nonfuel minerals, food, and energy.

Figure 14–4 illustrates major inconsistencies regarding commodity price projections. Five elements of the government's global model are involved: GNP (2), food (5), energy (7), fuel minerals (8), and nonfuel minerals (10). Four inconsistencies in commodity trade prices are discussed below: (A) fertilizer prices, (B) mineral prices, (C) food prices and (D) energy prices.

A. *Fertilizer Prices*. The nonfuel minerals element (10) and the food element (5) of the government's global model appear to have posited different growth rates in real fertilizer prices. Specifically, the 1977 Malenbaum Report relied on by the Department of the Interior projected "a gradual weakening of demand forces relative to supply forces" and concluded, therefore, that "the long-term tendency, 1985 and 2000, may thus be for lower materials prices [including those involved in the production of fertilizers] relative to prices of the final products in which they are used." In contrast, the Department of Agriculture's GOL model assumed that fertilizer prices will increase in response to rising energy prices (in the rising-energy-price case and the pessimistic case, over the 1970–2000 period), though the exact assumed fertilizer price increases are not explicitly disaggregated from other cost assumptions.

B. *Mineral Prices*. The nonfuel minerals element (10), the GNP element (2), and the energy element (7) appear to have posited different growth rates in mineral prices—at least, with respect to copper and tin. Specifically, the 1977 Malenbaum Report relied on by the Department of the Interior projected "a gradual weakening of demand forces relative to supply forces" and concluded, therefore, that "the long-term tendency, 1985 and 2000, may thus be for lower materials prices relative to prices of the final products in which they are used." In contrast, the World Bank's SIMLINK (SIMulated trade LINKages) model assumed growth in average real prices for copper and tin (in all three cases, over the 1975–85 period) to be roughly 5.2 and 2.5 percent per year, respectively. Also in contrast, the Energy Department's IEES (International Energy Evaluation System) model assumed (in all four cases,

over the 1975–90 period) that the various resources indirectly required to produce energy (e.g., nonfuel minerals) will be available in unlimited supply at current real prices.

C. *Food Prices*. The food element (5) and the GNP element (2) appear to have posited different growth rates in real-world food prices—at least, with respect to wheat. Specifically, the Agriculture Department's GOL model projected that the real price of wheat (in the medium-growth case, over the 1970–85 period) will increase 2.1 percent per year. In contrast, the World Bank's SIMLINK model assumed that the real price of wheat (in all three cases, over the 1975–85 period) will decline at roughly 0.6 percent per year.

D. *Energy Prices*. The energy element (7), the GNP element (2), and the fuel minerals element (9) appear to have posited different growth rates in energy prices—at least, with respect to petroleum prices. Specifically, preliminary projections made by the Energy Department's IEES model for the Study showed that the world demand for petroleum is likely to exceed world supply (at constant real 1978 prices) well before the year 2000; therefore, new projections were developed arbitrarily assuming a 5 percent per year increase (in the rising-energy-price case, over the 1980–1990 period), which showed that equilibrium conditions for supply-and-demand quantity and prices would be likely to be achieved under this assumption. In contrast, the World Bank's SIMLINK model assumed that real petroleum prices (in all three cases, over the 1975–85 period) will remain constant at 1975 levels. Also in contrast, U.S. Geological Survey Circular 725 (from which the Study's U.S. oil and gas resource and reserve estimates were derived) assumed a continuation of 1974 prices and of price-cost relationships and technological trends generally prevailing a few years prior to 1974.

Inconsistent Commodity Trade Volumes

As in the case of commodity prices, major disparities exist among many of the elements of the government's global model regarding commodity trade volume projections. The GNP projections, for example, assumed lower growth rates in world food trade than projected by the food element and higher growth rates in world minerals trade than projected by the nonfuel minerals element.

Figure 14–5 illustrates some of the major inconsistencies regarding commodity trade volumes. Four elements of the government's global model are involved: GNP (2), food (5), fisheries

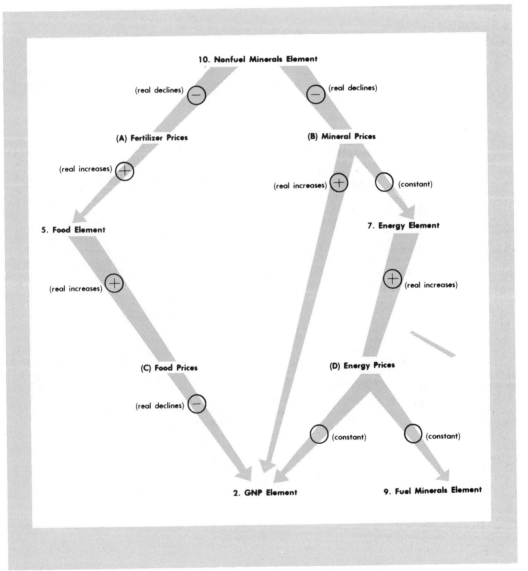

Figure 14-4. Inconsistent commodity trade prices.

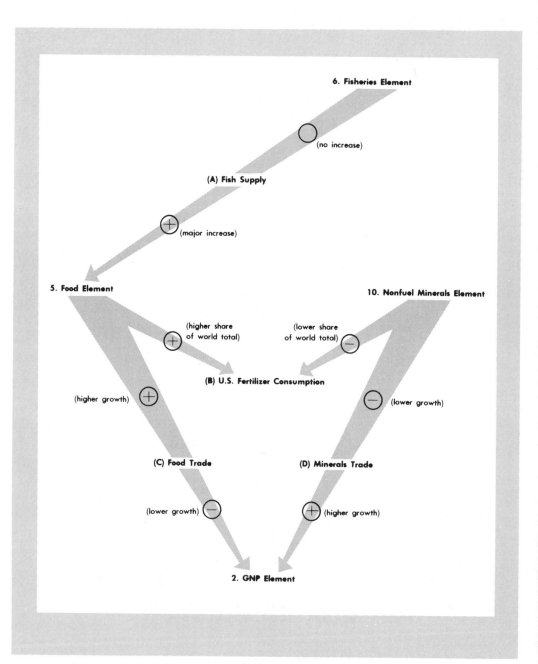

Figure 14-5. Inconsistent commodity trade volumes.

(6), and nonfuel minerals (10). Four inconsistencies are discussed below: (A) fish supply, (B) U.S. fertilizer consumption, (C) food trade, and (D) minerals trade.

A. *Fish Supply.* The fisheries element (6) and the food element (5) of the government's global model appear to have posited different growth rates in world fish catches. Specifically, the Commerce Department's judgmental forecasting procedures projected (in the medium case, the only case projected, over the 1975–2000 period) that while catches of some species may increase, others are likely to decrease, keeping the total annual fish catch essentially constant. In contrast, the Agriculture Department's total food submodel assumed in essence that the size of each country's fish catch (except in the case of Japan) will provide a constant percentage of the food needs of each country (in all four cases, over the 1975–2000 period), implicitly requiring that the annual fish catch for each country (except Japan) increase at essentially the same rate as population.

B. *U.S. Fertilizer Consumption.* The food element (5) and the nonfuel minerals element (10) appear to have projected different growth rates in U.S. fertilizer consumption relative to growth rates in the rest of the world—at least, with respect to phosphate rock (which is used primarily for fertilizer). Specifically, the Agriculture Department's fertilizer submodel projected growth in U.S. fertilizer consumption (in the medium, constant-energy-price case, the only case projected, over the 1973–2000 period) to be somewhat lower (3.2 percent per year) than in the rest of the world (4.0 percent per year). In contrast, the Interior Department's calculations (loosely based on the 1972 Malenbaum Report) projected growth in U.S. consumption of phosphate rock (in the most probable case, over the 1973–2000 period) to be significantly lower (2.6 percent per year) than in the rest of the world (5.9 percent per year).

C. *Food Trade.* The food element (5) and the GNP element (2) appear to have posited different growth rates in world food trade—at least, with respect to wheat. Specifically, the Agriculture Department's GOL model projected growth in trade in wheat between all countries (in the medium-growth case, over the 1970–85 period) to be 4.1 percent per year. In contrast, the World Bank's SIMLINK model assumed growth in trade in wheat between the industrailized nations and the LDCs (in all three cases, over the 1975–85 period) to be 2.5 percent per year.

D. *Minerals Trade.* The nonfuel minerals element (10) and the GNP element (2) appear to have posited different growth rates in quantities of minerals traded in world markets—at least with respect to aluminum and zinc. Specifically, the IOU methodology relied upon by the Department of the Interior projected growth in world consumption of primary aluminum and zinc (in the one case presented, over the 1973–85 period) to be 4.2 and 3.3 percent per year, respectively. In contrast, the World Bank's SIMLINK model assumed growth in trade in a collective category of certain key minerals (namely, bauxite, lead, phosphate rock, silver, and zinc) between the industrialized nations and the LDCs (in all three cases, over the 1975–85 period) to be 6.3 percent per year.

Inconsistent Capital and Resource Utilization

No consistent accounting was made of capital and resource allocations among the eleven elements of the government's global model. Thus, significant omissions or double-counting may have been implied in projected levels of water availability and some forms of capital investment. Significant omissions or double-counting may also be involved in assumptions regarding the future allocation of land and labor. But it is impossible to compare these assumptions in this discussion, since they were completely inexplicit in almost all elements and could not be inferred without extensive analysis beyond the scope and resources of the Global 2000 Study.

Figure 14–6 illustrates some of the significant omissions or double-counting that may have occurred regarding capital and resource utilization. Six elements of the government's global model are involved: GNP (2), food (5), water (6), energy (7), energy residuals (8), and nonfuel minerals (10). Four inconsistencies are discussed below: (A) water availability, (B) investment in agricultural inprovement, (C) investment in pollution control, and (D) LDC resource consumption.

A. *Water Availability.* The water element (6), the food element (5), the GNP element (2), the energy element (7), and the nonfuel minerals element (10) appear to have posited different levels of water availability. Specifically, the judgmental forecasting procedures used by the Study's water consultants projected (in the medium case, the only case presented, over the 1975–2000 period) that problems of water shortage will be more widespread and severe by 2000 than they are now—in part as a result of extensive deforesta-

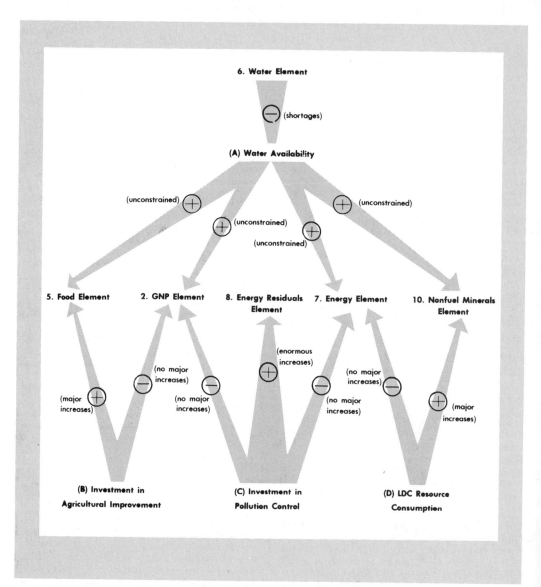

Figure 14-6. Inconsistent capital and resource utilization.

tion. In contrast, the Agriculture Department's GOL model assumed (in all four cases, over the 1970–2000 period) no explicit limitations on water availability (at current real prices), although limitations on arable land were explicitly considered. Also in contrast, the World Bank's SIMLINK model assumed (in all three cases, over the 1975–85 period) that foreign exchange earnings rather than savings, capital, or labor will constrain GNP growth in the LDCs; resource availability (e.g., water) was not assumed to be a binding constraint. Also in contrast, the Energy Department's IEES model assumed (in all four cases, over the 1975–90 period) that the various resources indirectly required to produce energy (e.g., water) will be available in unlimited supply at current real prices. Also in contrast, the IOU methodology relied upon by the Department of the Interior assumed (in the one case presented, over the 1973–2000 period) that long-term growth in minerals and materials consumption will not be governed by supply limitations (e.g., water).

B. *Investment in Agricultural Improvement.* The food element (5) and the GNP element (2) appear to have assumed different growth rates in investment for agricultural improvement. Specifically, the Agriculture Department's GOL model assumed (in all four cases, over the 1970–2000 period) that major increases in public and private investment will be made throughout the world to increase cropped areas. In contrast, the World Bank's SIMLINK model assumed (in all three cases, over the 1975–85 period) that the proportion of an LDC's GNP allocated for agricultural improvement will not vary markedly from recent historic experience.

C. *Investment in Pollution Control.* The energy residuals element (8), the GNP element (2), and the energy element (7) appear to have assumed different growth rates in investment for pollution control. Specifically, the Energy Department's IEES–ESNS (International Energy Evaluation System–Energy System Network Simulator) model assumed (in all three cases, 1975–90) that an extremely large investment in pollution control technologies will be made by all countries by 1985 so that by that time all energy conversion facilities throughout the world will meet or will have been retrofitted to meet 1978 U.S. new source performance standards for carbon monoxide, sulfur dioxide, nitrous oxides, and particulates. In contrast, the World Bank's SIMLINK model assumed (in all three cases, over the 1975–85 period) that the proportion of an LDC's GNP allocated for environmental protection will not vary markedly

from recent historic experience. Also in contrast, the Energy Department's IEES model assumed (in all four cases, over the 1975–90 period) that the real cost of applying technology to protect the environment will not significantly increase the real cost of building or operating energy facilities in the future.

D. *LDC Resource Consumption.* The energy element (7) and the nonfuel minerals element (10) appear to have assumed different growth rates in LDC resource consumption, although comparisons are not easily made. Specifically, the Energy Department's IEES model implicitly assumed (in all four cases, over the 1975–90 period) that industrialization within the LDCs will not cause LDC resource consumption (energy, in this case) to increase faster than the LDCs growth in GNP. In contrast, the IOU methodology relied upon by the Interior Department assumed (in one case presented, over the 1973–2000 period) that industrialization within the LDCs will require them to consume increasing amounts of resources (in this case, minerals and materials) per unit of per capita GNP as industrialization proceeds.

Use of Diverse Sources of Information

There are a number of inconsistencies among the elements of the government's global model due to the different elements making use of different sources of information for the same sets of assumptions.

For example, many federal agencies, including the Departments of Agriculture, Energy, and the Interior have customarily made use of international population estimates and projections developed by organizations other than the Bureau of the Census. These estimates vary widely, as may be seen in the following recent estimates of the average annual rate of LDC population growth in 1975:

	Percent
U.S. Agency for International Development	1.88
U.S. Bureau of the Census	2.25
U.N. Secretariat, Population Division	2.34
Environmental Fund (privately sponsored)	2.55

Projections of future population growth rates are usually even more divergent than these estimates of past population growth rates.

Many federal agencies have also often made use of divergent international GNP projections developed by organizations other than the World Bank's Economic Analysis and Projections Department. The State Department's Agency for International Development, for example, has cus-

THE GOVERNMENT'S GLOBAL MODEL

TABLE 14–2

Selected Contrasting Assumptions of the 11 Elements of the Government's Global Model

The 11 Elements of the Government's Global Model	Cases Presented	Selected Policy Assumptions	Selected Population Assumptions	Selected GNP Assumptions	Selected Climate Assumptions	Selected Technology Assumptions
1. Population	a. High-growth case b. Medium-growth case. c. Low-growth case	Major extension of family planning throughout the world	Zero net migration between regions	Moderate social and economic progress throughout the world over the 1975–2000 period	Not considered	No major technology breakthroughs or setbacks affecting fertility or mortality rates
2. GNP	a. High-growth case b. Medium-growth case c. Low-growth case	Continuation or implementation of prudent policies to maximize export earnings	Major reduction in population growth rates in all countries over the 1985–2000 period	GNP growth in LDCs largely dependent on industrial nation GNP growth	Not considered	Major increasing returns on most LDC gross capital investment
3. Climate	a. Warming case b. Constant temperature case c. Cooling case	Deliberate human efforts to modify climate excluded	Not explicitly considered	Not explicitly considered	Extreme climatic change not considered	Deliberate human efforts to modify climate excluded
4. Technology	The same technology assumptions usually applied to all cases pertaining to a given element; no coordination of assumptions among different elements	Extensive deployment of family planning, nuclear-power and air pollution-abatement technologies (some of which may require significant policy changes in some countries)	No major technical breakthroughs or setbacks affecting fertility or mortality rates	Major increasing returns on most LDC capital investment	Deliberate human efforts to modify climate excluded	Major technological progress in almost all projections; no technological setbacks or adverse side effects anticipated
5. Food	a. Optimistic case b. Middle case c. Pessimistic case d. Rising-energy-price case	Major public and private investment in agricultural land development continued; worldwide shift toward more fossil-fuel-intensive agricultural techniques	a. Global 2000 low-growth case b. Global 2000 medium-growth case c. Global 2000 high-growth case d. Global 2000 medium-growth case	a. Global 2000 high-growth case b. Global 2000 medium-growth case c. Global 2000 low-growth case d. Global 2000 medium-growth case	Explicit assumption of no climatic change	Widespread deployment of fertilizer and other yield-enhancing inputs, producing steadily increasing yields—comparable to the increases experienced over the past two decades.

Selected Food Assumptions	Selected Fisheries, Forestry, and Water Assumptions	Selected Energy Assumptions	Selected Energy Residuals Assumptions	Selected Fuel Minerals Assumptions	Selected Nonfuel Minerals Assumptions	Selected Environmental Assumptions
Not explicitly considered (except as noted under "Selected GNP Assumptions")	Not explicitly considered (except as noted under "Selected GNP Assumptions")	Not explicitly considered (except as noted under "Selected GNP Assumptions")	Not explicitly considered (except as noted under "Selected GNP Assumptions")	Not explicitly considered (except as noted under "Selected GNP Assumptions")	Not explicitly considered (except as noted under "Selected GNP Assumptions")	Not explicitly considered (except as noted under "Selected GNP Assumptions")
Lower trade volumes at lower prices than Global 2000 food projections	Not explicitly considered	Unlimited energy at constant real prices	Not considered	Unlimited energy at constant real prices	Higher trade volumes at higher prices than Global 2000 nonfuel minerals projections	Not explicitly considered
Not explicitly considered	Not explicitly considered	Not explicitly considered	Not explicitly considered	Not explicitly considered	Not explicitly considered	Not explicitly considered
Widespread deployment of fertilizer and other yield-enhancing inputs, producing steadily increasing yields comparable to the increases experienced over the past two decades.	Development of less wasteful methods for harvesting nontraditional fish species; development of less wasteful methods and of methods for exploiting nontraditional forestry species; water assumptions unknown	Widespread deployment of light-water nuclear electric power plants	By 1985, all countries' energy facilities retrofitted to meet U.S. new source performance standards for CO, SO_x, NO_x, and particulates	Continuation of the price-cost relationships and technical trends generally prevailing in years prior to 1974 assumed in all U.S. oil and gas resource and reserve estimates	Increasingly less intensive mineral use in highly industrialized countries; increasingly more intensive mineral use in LDCs.	Side effects of technology, coupled with institutional and social problems, appear to be the root cause of many of the world's most serious environmental problems; but technology can also solve many problems
No major increase in meat share of LDC diets	Major increases in fish catches implicitly assumed; adverse impacts of deforestation not considered; explicit assumption of unlimited water at constant real prices	a. Constant energy price b. Constant energy price c. Global 2000 rising-energy-price case d. Global 2000 rising-energy-price case (In all cases, unlimited energy supply assumed at cited costs)	Not considered	No fuel resource constraints (other than price)	No nonfuel minerals resource constraints (except energy price effects)	No large scale land degradation due to environmental or human factors (other than urbanization) and no increased pest resistance.

Table 14–2 (cont.)

The 11 Elements of the Government's Global Model	Cases Presented	Selected Policy Assumptions	Selected Population Assumptions	Selected GNP Assumptions	Selected Climate Assumptions	Selected Technology Assumptions
6. Fisheries	A single medium case.	Improved management of fisheries and protection of the marine environment on a worldwide basis	Assumptions not explicit	Assumptions not explicit	Not considered	Development of methods for harvesting nontraditional fish species
Forestry	A single medium case	Some policy changes throughout the world regarding current deforestation practices	Assumptions not explicit	Assumptions not explicit	Not considered	Development of less wasteful production techniques and of methods for exploiting nontraditional forestry species
Water	a. Higher case b. Lower case	Unknown	Unknown	Unknown	Unknown	Unknown
7. Energy	a. Optimistic case b. Middle case c. Pessimistic case d. Rising-energy-price case	Implementation of more effective energy conservation programs within the OECD countries; OPEC countries to supply oil to meet residual demand up to their maximum production capacity	a. Global 2000 low-growth case b. Global 2000 medium-growth case c. Global 2000 high-growth case d. Global 2000 medium-growth case	a. Global 2000 high-growth case b. Global 2000 medium-growth case c. Global 2000 low-growth case d. Global 2000 medium-growth case	Not considered	Widespread deployment of light-water nuclear electric power plants
8. Energy residuals	a. Optimistic case b. Middle case c. Pessimistic case	Major public and private investment in air pollution abatement technologies by all countries	Not explicitly considered (except as derived from preceding energy projections)	Not explicitly considered (except as derived from preceding energy projections)	Not considered	By 1985, all countries' energy facilities retrofitted to meet U.S. new source performance standards for CO_x, SO_x, NO_x, and particulates
9. Fuel minerals	A single medium case	Continuation of 1974 prices assumed in all U.S. oil and gas resource and reserve estimates	Not considered	Not considered	Not considered	Continuation of the price-cost relationships and technical trends generally prevailing in years prior to 1974 assumed in all U.S. oil and gas resource and reserve estimates

Selected Food Assumptions	Selected Fisheries, Forestry, and Water Assumptions	Selected Energy Assumptions	Selected Energy Residuals Assumptions	Selected Fuel Minerals Assumptions	Selected Nonfuel Minerals Assumptions	Selected Environmental Assumptions
Not considered	Water projections not considered	Not considered	Not considered	Not considered	Not considered	No significant pollution affecting growth of fishery stocks; no significant losses of estuarian areas
Not considered	Water projections not considered	Not considered	Not considered	Not considered	Not considered	No significant impacts affecting forest growth (e.g., acid rain, increased UV radiation, or increased pest resistance)
Unknown	Unknown	Unknown	Unknown	Unknown	Unknown	Unknown
Not considered	No nonfuel resource constraints in the industrialized countries (except as limited by GNP); bio-energy resource constraints in the LDCs	Net energy not explicitly considered	Not considered	Not directly related to the Study's fuel minerals projections	No nonfuel resource constraints (except as limited by GNP)	Not explicitly considered
Not considered	No resource constraints	a. Global 2000 optimistic case b. Global 2000 middle case c. Global 2000 pessimistic case	No capital investment constraints	Not considered	Not considered	By 1985, all countries' energy facilities retrofitted to meet U.S. new source performance standards for CO, SO_x, NO_x, and particulates
Not considered	Not explicitly considered	Not directly related to Study's energy projections	Not considered	Net energy not explicitly considered	Not explicitly considered	Not explicitly considered

Table 14–2 (cont.)

The 11 Elements of the Government's Global Model	Cases Presented	Selected Policy Assumptions	Selected Population Assumptions	Selected GNP Assumptions	Selected Climate Assumptions Selected	Selected Technology Assumptions
10. Nonfuel minerals	A single medium case	No changes	Single set of projections derived from U.N. projections	Single set of projections based on Malenbaum's personal judgment	Not considered	Increasingly less intensive mineral use in highly industrialized countries; increasingly more intensive mineral use in LDCs
11. Environment	Same cases as provided for each element, but generally only medium cases analyzed	No policy changes (except as derived from preceding projections)	Global 2000 medium case	Global 2000 medium case	Several environmental developments assumed potentially capable of influencing global climate	Technologies are generally available to address the world's most serious environmental problems (e.g., soil erosion and deterioration); social and institutional problems (not technological problems) are often the primary impediment to environmental protection

tomarily relied on the World Bank's generally more optimistic individual country analyses. The Department of Agriculture's Economics, Statistics, and Cooperatives Service has customarily used projections developed by the U.N. Food and Agriculture Organization (FAO). The Department of Energy's Energy Information Administration has used projections made by the intergovernmental Organization for Economic Cooperation and Development (OECD). The Interior Department's Bureau of Mines has relied on international economic projections developed by Professor Wilfred Malenbaum of the University of Pennslyvania.*

Under the limited discipline achieved by the Global 2000 Study, much more consistent use than heretofore was made of the projections developed using the population and GNP elements by other elements of the government's global model. Nevertheless, inconsistent assumptions abound, as shown in Table 14–2, which provides a cross-index of selected, diverse assumptions used by the elements. Many of these inconsistent assumptions are described in greater detail in the summaries of the various elements presented in the last section of this chapter and in Chapters 15–23.

Even a single set of assumptions may contain internal inconsistencies as a result of being compiled from diverse sources. For example, the U.S. government does not maintain its own single, consistent source of GNP projections. The GNP projections most frequently used pertaining to the

*The FAO and OECD projections have tended to be significantly higher than those of the World Bank and Professor Malenbaum. Moreover, these projection differences have tended to be significantly greater on a regional or country by country basis than on a global basis.

Selected Food Assumptions	Selected Fisheries, Forestry, and Water Assumptions	Selected Energy Assumptions	Selected Energy Residuals Assumptions	Selected Fuel Minerals Assumptions	Selected Nonfuel Minerals Assumptions	Selected Environmental Assumptions
Not considered	Explicit assumption of no resource constraints	Explicit assumption of no resource constraints	Explicit assumption of no environmental constraints	Explicit assumption of no resource constraints	Explicit assumption of no resource constraints	Explicit assumption of no environmental constraints
Global 2000 rising-energy-price case	Global 2000 medium case	Global 2000 rising-energy-price case	Global 2000 medium case	Global 2000 medium case	Global 2000 medium case	Considered extensively on a comprehensive, interrelated basis

OECD countries* are those assembled by the headquarters staff of the OECD. The most frequently used GNP projections for the LDCs are those developed by the World Bank. The most frequently used GNP projections for the centrally planned economies are those developed by the U.S. Central Intelligence Agency.

Each of these sources prepares its projections using different statistical conventions and independently developed assumptions regarding the future. Such GNP projections are therefore not internally consistent, as noted in Chapter 3. Because they are not collectively maintained by the

U.S. government, it was not possible within the mandate and constraints of the Global 2000 Study to examine in any detail the assumptions underlying the GNP projections routinely used by the government.* What information is available suggests that population, resources, and the environment are not taken into account through any explicit functional relationships and are included only judgmentally, if at all.

Three further problems related to the use of diverse sources for GNP projections are noted below. They are representative of the types of problems encountered when diverse sources are also used for population, food, energy, and other projections:

---

*The Organization for Economic Cooperation and Development includes the following countries: Australia, Austria, Belgium, Canada, Denmark, Finland, France, the Federal Republic of Germany, Greece, Iceland, Ireland, Italy, Japan, Luxembourg, the Netherlands, New Zealand, Norway, Portugal, Spain, Sweden, Switzerland, Turkey, the United Kingdom, and the United States.

---

*However, one important computer model used to develop GNP projections (the World Bank's SIMLINK model) is discussed in some detail in Chapter 16.

1. The GNP projections published by the OECD for its member nations are widely regarded as "pious hopes." To obtain a measure of realism, the World Bank has routinely adjusted the OECD projections substantially downward before using them. Further downward adjustments were made by the WAES study* (and recommended for Global 2000 Study use by World Bank analysts) to account for the fact that those GNP projections have in the past been based on the assumption made by individual OECD nations that they will be able in the future to import unrealistically large amounts of OPEC oil.

2. The World Bank's projections of LDC growth rates assume that the primary force driving LDC economic progress is growth in the economies of the industrialized countries. As yet, neither the theory nor the specific numbers involved in this assumption have been adequately validated. The theoretical and numeric basis underlying the GNP projections for the centrally planned economies are subject to even less general agreement.

3. The Global 2000 Study's per capita GNP figures come directly from combining the population and GNP projections, which were developed independently of each other and have been shown previously in this chapter to be mutually inconsistent. Moreover, in projecting beyond about 10 years, all the Study's GNP projections have been based on a simple exponential growth model involving an assumed percentage of annual compound growth. This exponential growth assumption produces absurd results in the long run† and assumes implicitly that no resources or environmental constraints will be encountered that cannot be overcome by unspecified technological developments (which themselves are further assumed to create no constraining resource or environmental problems). To the extent that the GNP projections include any consideration of population, natural resources, or the environment, that consideration is exogenous, judgmental, and not open to examination or verification.

---

*The World Alternative Energy Strategies study sponsored by the Massachusetts Institute of Technology, which is discussed in Chapter 16. The GNP projections for LDCs developed for that study are presented as part of the Global 2000 Study's GNP projections in Chapter 3.

† World Bank analysts note that their official GNP projections rarely extend more than 10 years into the future. The exponential growth rates mentioned above were developed as a special accommodation to the needs of the WAES study and were never intended to be applicable beyond the year 2000.

Absence of Feedback

A second critical factor accounting for the inconsistencies previously presented is the general lack of feedback between elements of the government's global model. Under the limited discipline (described earlier in this chapter) established by the Global 2000 Study, only a few basic linkages were made between the elements, as shown schematically in Figure 14–2. But even if a much more strict and comprehensive discipline had been possible (for example, the use of single sources of information for related input assumptions required by the elements), two fundamental structural problems related to feedback would have been encountered in attempting to link the elements together on a consistent basis:

• The elements have been designed to accommodate only the sequential unidirectional linkages previously shown in Figure 14–1—that is, the population and resource projections must precede the resource projections, which must precede the environmental projections.

• The sets of assumptions which are made prior to using many of the elements are "frozen" in the sense of not being responsive to changed conditions in the course of projection computations.

These two problems are actually two dimensions of the same feedback issue. The first problem, regarding sequential unidirectional linkages, focuses on intersectoral distortions—the fact that certain sectors are represented in the government's global model as influencing others, but as not themselves being influenced by others. The second problem, regarding "frozen" sets of assumptions, focuses on temporal distortions—the fact that the general absence of feedback produces increasingly severe inconsistencies the further into the future the projections are extended.

Sequential Unidirectional Linkages. In most of the elements of the government's global model, population and GNP are conceived as "driving forces." Given assumed levels of population and GNP, the various elements calculate the consumption of food, energy, minerals, and other resources. But no calculations are made regarding the influence of the scarcity or abundance of food, energy, minerals, and other resources—as projected by their respective elements—on population or GNP. Similarly, no calculations are made regarding the influence of environmental factors—as projected by the environmental element—on population, GNP, or the various natural resources.*

In the case of the population projections, for example, certain extremely general assumptions are made regarding social and economic development, and in many cases these are inconsistent with the projections developed by other elements. But there is little or no provision in the population element itself that would allow precise, explicit, quantitative adjustments in the element's calculations to be made in response to the precise, explicit, quantitative calculations made by the other elements.

In short, the issue is not merely that the reverse linkages have not been made (for example, from per capita food consumption to population) but that the current structural design of the elements generally precludes their being made. The population and GNP elements are essentially incapable of taking precise account of the results of the natural resource projections. And the population, GNP, and natural resource elements are incapable of taking precise account of the results of the environmental projections. In actuality, of course, they take little or no account of them at all—precise or imprecise. While the environmental element is not capable of taking the results of the population, GNP, and resource elements precisely into account, it does at least consider them qualitatively.

It should also be noted here that even if the models were structured so as to facilitate the establishment of the needed reverse linkages, many of the linkages would have to be established conjecturally because the empirical evidence presently available is limited. However, even a conjectural linkage would, in most cases, be far preferable to the assumption of no linkage when such an assumption is known to be significantly in error. Furthermore, if sensitivity tests show the linkage to be a critical and sensitive linkage, priority can thus be established for the collection of needed empirical data.

"Frozen" Sets of Assumptions. Each element of the government's global model makes use of sets of assumptions (i.e., time-series inputs) which may be thought of as "frozen." They are frozen in the sense that they are determined prior to

_____
*The very significant effects that the environmental projections could be expected to have on the population, GNP, and resource projections are discussed under "Closing the Loops" in Chapter 13. However, as pointed out in that chapter, all of the projections retain their basically open-loop character because none of the missing feedback linkages could actually be established through direct dynamic effects on the elements' calculations.

using the element and are not altered in response to changed conditions implied by calculations made by the element and by the other elements. In other words, there is no feedback from the element's computations to the original set of frozen assumptions.

For example, as already shown in Figure 14–2:

• The population projections were developed with fixed assumptions regarding social and economic progress.

• The gross national product projections were developed with fixed assumptions regarding population growth.

• The energy projections were developed with fixed assumptions regarding population and GNP growth.

• The food projections were developed with fixed assumptions regarding increases in population, GNP, and energy prices.

• The population, GNP, and resource projections were developed with fixed assumptions concerning the environment.

• The environmental projections were developed with fixed assumptions concerning the population, GNP, and resource projections.

In some cases, the set of fixed or frozen assumptions used by one element may summarize the projections developed through the complex calculations of another element. Often these complex calculations are summarized in the form of simple time-series data or fitted equations. In other cases, the set of frozen assumptions may come from a source entirely outside the government's global model and may explicitly contradict calculations made by another element of that model. Often these frozen assumptions are not explicitly stated in quantitative terms, but may nevertheless be inferred—for example, in terms of some commodity being available in unlimited supply or at constant real prices, or both.

The government's long-term global projections implicitly assume either (1) that the use of frozen sets of assumptions would produce logically consistent projections or (2) that any inconsistencies would be relatively inconsequential in view of simplifications made in the overall representation of the global system and data uncertainty. These assumptions tend to be valid for short-term (i.e., 1–2 year) projections—where, in the absence of major dislocations, major trends generally tend to perpetrate themselves forward smoothly—but are increasingly dubious when the projections extend for 5, 10, 20, or more years. As projections are extended further into the future, feedback interactions become increasingly important as major trends collide with one another and are deflected from their original paths in complex ways. The elements of the government's global model are generally not structured and linked together in a way that allows such deflections to occur. As a result, the trends override one another and produce increasingly serious inconsistencies as the projections move further into the future.

Structural Incompatibilities

Any model of reality necessarily selects and excludes relationships and data in order to clarify the issues it is intended to simulate. Thus, the 11 elements of the government's global model naturally embody simplifications, limitations, and omissions that may well have been entirely appropriate for the purposes for which the elements were originally designed, but which make effective coordination between elements extremely difficult. The inability or failure to transfer information represented in one element according to one set of structural conventions to a different element utilizing a different set of structural conventions provides a third explanation for the inconsistencies previously presented.

Most elements, for example, make use of different conventions for representing the world geographically, which makes coordination difficult. Some elements provide great detail on the Western industrialized nations and little detail on the LDCs, or vice versa, while most provide almost no detail on the centrally planned economies. Some elements are fundamentally incapable of simulating interactions among separate geographic regions except through changes in exogenous assumptions (so that interregional adjustments cannot be taken into account by them). Other elements are fundamentally interregional, that is, their basic purpose is to project future interregional trade balances, based on the assumption that static economic equilibrium conditions will obtain in the future in a way that maximizes total world economic efficiency for the sector for which the projection is developed.

A perspective on the geographic differences among those elements with the most complex explicit quantitative relationships is presented in the first five maps in the colored map section. These maps illustrate the extent to which each element (1) aggregates (or disaggregates) the various regions of the world and (2) makes independent (or interdependent) projections for those regions. The maps also show the level of detail represented in each aggregate.

Most elements make use of different conventions for representing temporal change, which also adds to the difficulties of coordination. Some elements are theoretically capable of projecting well beyond the year 2000, others were not designed to project beyond 1985 or 1990. Some elements were designed to calculate equilibrium balances between supply and demand at equilibrating prices and are fundamentally incapable of simulating change over time, except through changes in exogenous assumptions. This means that they cannot take into account dynamic disequilibria. Other elements are fundamentally dynamic—that is, their basic purpose is to display trends and modes of behavior over time.

Other major structural differences and limitations include:

- Many elements are based on analytic methods that require crucial interdependent variables to be projected independently in advance.
- Many require these variables not to exceed historial ranges or rates of growth.
- Most are incapable of simulating fundamental structural change.
- Many have limited capacity to integrate inconsistent inputs developed using other analytical methods.

Many of these differences are summarized on an element by element basis in Table 14–3. A more complex account of them is provided in the last section of this chapter and in Chapters 15–23.

Institutional Factors Underlying the Discrepancies

Many institutional factors underlie the inconsistencies. As Table 14–3 shows, each of the 11 elements of the government's global model was developed in a different bureaucratic context. It would be surprising indeed if the elements did not significantly differ from each other since each was developed

- by different people (even experts differ among themselves),
- at different times (the real world changes over time),
- using different perspectives and methodologies (which use different simplifying assumptions and different computational techniques),
- to meet different needs (affecting the selection of assumptions and the validation of calculations).

Moreover, it would be naive not to recognize that projections and the procedures used to pro-

TABLE 14–3

Selected Institutional and Structural Differences Among the Elements of the Government's Global Model

Element	Primary Source of Projections	Primary Computational Procedures	First Major Use	Major Geographic Representation	Temporal Representation	Number of Cases Examined
1. Population	Census Bureau; University of Chicago	Cohort-component methodology	Early 1930s	The world in 23 independent regions	1975–2000 (dynamically calculated)	3
2. GNP	WAES Study (MIT) and World Bank	SIMLINK model; judgmental extrapolation	1974	Primarily 6 LDC aggregates, with limited interaction	1975–85 (dynamically calculated) 1985–2000 (informally extrapolated)	3
3. Climate	National Defense University study (CIA)	Weighted expert opinion	1977	The world in 8 regions	1977–80, 1981–90, 1991–2000, (discontinuously calculated)	3
4. Technology	Diverse independent sources	Diverse unrelated methodologies	Diverse	Usually global only	No consistent representation	1 per element
5. Food	Department of Agriculture	GOL model	1974	The world in 28 interrelated regions	1985 2000 (discontinuously calculated)	4
6. Fisheries, forestry, and water	NOAA; CIA; Department of the Interior	No explicit quantitative model	Diverse	Typically by interrelated ecosystem	2000 (informally extrapolated)	1,1,2
7. Energy	Department of Energy	IEES model	1977	The world in 5 interrelated regions	1985 1990 (essentially discontinuously calculated)	4
8. Energy residuals	Department of Energy	IEES-ESNS model	1978	The world in 5 independent regions	1985 1990 (discontinuously calculated)	3
9. Fuel minerals	Independent expert (affiliated with the Departments of Energy and the Interior)	Ecletic (based on many previous studies)	Diverse	No consistent representation	No temporal dimension	In general, 1
10. Nonfuel minerals	Professor Malenbaum (University of Pennsylvania)	IOU methodology	1972	The world in 10 independent regions	1985 2000 (discontinuously calculated)	1
11. Environment	Multiple sources coordinated by Study staff	No explicit quantitative model	Diverse	The industrial and developing economies and selected ecosystems, on an interrelated basis.	Generally 2000 (informally extrapolated)	No consistent selection of cases

duce them have frequently been criticized by Congressional committees and others as subject to influences not purely analytical in origin. Each agency has its own responsibilities and interests, its own constituencies, and its own pet projects. Often, an agency finds it helpful to use advanced analytic techniques (and associated projections) as weapons in the adversary process of initiating, justifying, and defending its programs. As a result, there have been many occasions in which the elements (and associated projections) of the government's global model have been used in support of (or in opposition to) highly controversial programs, and the credibility of the projections has become a subject for debate. This has been especially true in recent times, as both the issues and the advanced analytic procedures used for examining the issues have become increasingly complex and, in a sense, incomprehensible to many nonexperts.

Under these conditions, government agencies have occasionally been accused of falsifying the data on which their projections are based or of adding "fudge factors" to equations to produce desired results. While these accusations are relatively infrequent, agencies have often been accused of carefully tailoring the assumptions underlying their analyses so as to ensure that desired results are attained in a way that is analytically defensible. To the extent that these circumstances occur, they contribute to the inconsistencies previously presented.

Interpreting the Projections

The preceding analysis has identified inconsistencies, incompatibilities, and other problems, which must inevitably raise questions regarding the validity of the projections presented in Part I, Chapters 2–13. Some of these problematic issues are discussed below.

Validity of the Basic Findings

Before discussing the implications of the problems identified in the preceding section of this chapter, it is important to point out that the projections presented in Part I nevertheless represent the most consistent set of projections ever developed making use of the set of elements that constitute the government's global model. No alternative governmental projections currently available provide a more logically coherent foundation for the government's longer-term planning. This is, of course, because the Global 2000 Study represents the first occasion in which even an effort (regardless of its deficiencies) has been made to apply—collectively and consistently—the global, longer-term methodologies routinely used by the government to project trends regarding population, natural resources, and the environment.

With this in mind, it may be helpful for the reader to review some of the most basic findings of Part I. Only the most fundamental adjustments to the elements of the government's global model would change the basic thrust of the following findings.

Population. Total world population growth rates will not decline significantly by the year 2000. Instead, roughly twice as many additional new people will be added to the world's population over the 1975–2000 period (on a net basis) as were added over the 1950–1975 period. A very large proportion of this population growth will occur in the LDCs, particularly in South Asia, Africa, and Latin America.

GNP. Per capita GNP Increases about 55 percent worldwide, but increases only marginally in several LDCs. The problems leading to the decline in the growth of per capita GNP will become more intense over the 1985–2000 period.

Climate. Should any climate change occur, its most adverse effects (largely involving changes in average temperature, precipitation patterns, and weather variability) are likely to be felt in the temperate regions, where most of the world's major food-exporting nations are located.

Food. Global per capita food consumption will not increase significantly, despite major increases in real food prices and in agricultural investment. Declines in per capita food consumption will occur in many of the poorest LDCs, with the most rapid declines occurring over the 1985–2000 period.

Resource Prices. The real prices of food, fish, lumber, water, and energy will increase significantly, with the steepest increases occurring over the 1985–2000 period.*

The Environment. Major strains will be placed on ecological systems throughout the world and, as a result, the goods and services that have heretofore been provided by the environment can no longer be simply taken for granted. The significant deterioration in terrestrial, aquatic, and atmospheric environments projected to occur around the world will inevitably impact adversely on agricultural productivity, human morbidity and mortality, overall economic development, and perhaps even on climate—among other factors. These strains are likely to be felt most strongly in the LDCs toward the end of the century, though there is much current evidence of their existence.

---

* This particular finding raises several important economic questions. If the real prices of these commodities increase as projected, for what corresponding commodities will real prices decrease? If no compensating real-price decreases are projected, what do these "real" price increases mean theoretically—or even semantically? Unfortunately, even attempting to develop answers to these difficult questions would have exceeded the time and resource constraints of the study.

In short, increasingly severe stresses will be felt on a global basis toward the end of the century. These stresses will be most severe in the world's poorest nations, but the industrialized countries will also feel their effects.

It is the conclusion of the staff of the Global 2000 Study and many of the Study's advisers that these basic findings are qualitatively correct, even taking into account the many current deficiencies of the government's global model. There are three major reasons for holding this view:

1. They represent no radical departures, for the most part, from projections published over many years by their respective sources.
2. They are supported collaterally, for the most part, by alternative projections developed by numerous organizations with similar sets of sectoral concerns.
3. They are supported (in terms of many of their most basic thrusts) by projections developed using a set of less complex but more highly integrated global models.*

If anything, the severity of the effects of these basic trends may be understated, due to the very limited feedback between the elements of the government's global model. This view is largely corroborated by projections developed using more highly integrated models.

It is also the conclusion of the staff of the Global 2000 Study and many of the Study's advisers—in view of the preceding analysis in the government's global model—that it is impossible to assign a high probability to any of the specific numeric projections presented in the preceding chapters.

Biases Due to Inconsistent Variable Values

The complex patterns of bias caused by the inconsistent variable values used by different elements of the government's global model make adjustment extremely difficult. In particular, a chicken-and-egg problem is encountered in attempting to make simple quantitative adjustments to any single set of projections developed by a single element of the model.

For example, the assumptions about GNP that were made in order to develop the population projections are contradicted by the GNP projections. Specifically, the population projections were based on the assumption that significant reductions in fertility will occur because of improved social and economic conditions throughout the world. But the projections of per capita GNP do not show significant improvements in economic

---

* These nongovernmental projections are described, analyzed, and compared in considerable detail in Part III of this volume.

conditions in many parts of the world, especially those with the most rapidly growing populations.*

Similarly, the assumptions about population that were made in order to develop the GNP projections are contradicted by the population projections. Specifically, the GNP projections were adjusted downward for the 1985–2000 period because of an assumption that population growth rates will have declined by that time. But the population projections show the world population growth rate continuing at an essentially constant 1.8 percent per year.

If one begins by adjusting the GNP projections (to resolve the obvious inconsistency regarding population), then they are adjusted upward (to take into account the lack of decline in population rates). Potentially, this makes the GNP projections consistent with the population projections (leaving the population projections unchanged).

If, on the other hand, one begins by adjusting the population projections (to resolve the obvious inconsistency regarding GNP), then they are adjusted upward (to take into account the lack of improvement in social and economic conditions). If the per capita GNP figures are then recalculated, social and economic conditions are seen to be even worse than before and another upward adjustment to the population figures is required, and so on until a limit perhaps is reached (greatly increasing the population projections). Conversely, if the second step is to readjust the GNP projections, a balance may then be struck making the population projections consistent with the GNP projections (by significantly increasing both the population and GNP projections).

Does one begin, then, by assuming the GNP projections to be correct and adjusting the population projections, or vice versa (or something in between)? Where is the lever and where is the fulcrum?

These problems are compounded as more elements and relationships are taken into consideration—such as the following:

• For example, the food projections show that in certain regions of the world (notably North Africa and the Middle East) there will be some declines in food per capita (even using the apparently too low population projections). This finding reinforces the finding of the per capita

---

* It should be noted, however, that these per capita GNP projections do not take into account possible shifts in patterns of distribution that could either increase or decrease the per capita incomes of different economic groups within a given population, even assuming a fixed level of overall per capita GNP.

GNP projections that social and economic conditions will not improve throughout the world.

- The food projections also assume that there will be no constraints on water development for agriculture. But this is contradicted by the water, forestry, and environmental projections, implying that a downward adjustment should be made to the food projections. This in turn would lead to a downward adjustment to the per capita food projections.

- The food projections also assume that land deterioration from intensive use will not occur. But this is contradicted by the environmental projections,* implying the need for further downward adjustments to the food projections and per capita food projections.

- Downward adjustments to the per capita food projections would necessitate increases in the population projections, lowering further the per capita food projections and requiring yet another round of adjustments.

- Higher population projections would in turn probably increase the severity of water problems (due to more pressures from fuelwood demand and increased deforestation) and the rate of land deterioration (due to more intensive farming practices), further lowering the food projections and the per capita food projections. Thus, the adjustment process would have to continue until a limit was reached (if ever).

Again, if one wanted to adjust the food, GNP, or population projections for consistency (as opposed to attempting to actually adjust and rerun the elements themselves on some more integrated basis), where is one to begin—or end? Where is the lever and where is the fulcrum?

---

* Because the environmental projections show that the combined environmental impacts of all other projections have the potential to alter almost all the other projections in generally adverse ways, there is some justification for concluding that the Global 2000 Study's projections are by and large "optimistically" biased and in need of a "pessimistic" correction. But before projections can be meaningfully described as optimistic or pessimistic, the values by which they are being judged must be made clear. For whom, where, and at what time are projections optimistic or pessimistic? Are projections of extensive firewood combustion optimistic or pessimistic for those who need heat now? Are the same projections optimistic or pessimistic for their children, or for plant breeders needing genetic resources? Projections and models are not value free, and hence relative optimism or pessimism is very much in the eye of the beholder. The perspectives and values of an American farmer and an improverished citizen from an LDC in evaluating the prospect of future food price increases by the year 2000 might be very different, so that it is not necessarily helpful to attempt to characterize the projections as biased favorably or unfavorably without careful qualifications.

Strengthening the Present Foundation

While few concrete, quantitative steps can be taken to adjust the projections presented in Chapters 2–13 in order to improve their reliability (for reasons just discussed), several options exist for improving the current form of the government's global model itself, so that subsequent projections will become significantly more reliable. In view of the fact that billions of dollars in federal funds are currently expended based on decisions using projections developed by the various agencies, it should not be difficult to develop cost justifications for appropriate improvements. Several minor improvements to the government's global model have already been made in the course of executing the present Study, and further minor improvements are possible in the near future if a moderate commitment of the necessary resources is made. But it should also be recognized that major improvements will require (1) a new institutional commitment to the development of long-term, global analytic procedures throughout the government, and (2) a much greater investment in time and resources than was available to the Global 2000 Study.

Need for an Ongoing Institutional Mechanism

The numerous problems currently associated with the government's global model are primarily symptoms of a deeper, more fundamental problem. The dubious assumptions, omissions, inconsistencies, and incompatibilities are only technical manifestations of a severe institutional problem: The executive branch of the government currently has no ongoing institutional entity with the explicit responsibility and authority necessary for resolving such technical and philosophical problems. In the absence of such an entity, it is difficult to imagine how the government's capabilities for longer-term analysis and planning can improve significantly.

The Study's agency experts are generally aware of the limitations in the present elements of the government's global model. With few exceptions, the agencies are planning to develop new computational procedures that will eventually replace those used now. But unless some coordination is provided, there is little reason to think that the new procedures will be any more compatible, consistent, or interactive than the present ones. A priority task, therefore, is to survey the development plans related to long-term, global analysis of all of the relevant agencies—with the objective of coordinating the modification of existing sectoral elements (or, where appropriate, the development of new sectoral elements) and of coordinating the specific needs of the agencies.

Discussions with the Study's agency experts already indicate that several additional analyses are needed if the completed Global 2000 Study is to be of maximum benefit to the agencies. Finding answers to the following questions deserves the highest priority:

1. What are the strategic and economic implications of the trends now foreseen?
2. What policy changes might be pursued to alter the trends in a desirable manner?
3. What technologies might contribute most significantly to the evolution of a more desirable future?

Fortunately, the Study has already provided a basis for initiating an increased level of interagency cooperation and coordination on data exchange and model formulation.

Potential Technical Improvements

The extent to which relatively modest incremental modifications of the government's existing models could permit more synergistic interaction and feedback than was achieved in the Global 2000 Study is clearly an important area for early investigation. Simple modifications (e.g., developing projections in which all elements use the Study's population and GNP projections) would be relatively inexpensive and could be made relatively rapidly. Similarly, somewhat more consistent projections could be achieved simply through the imposition of a somewhat more extensive amount of coordination and arbitration. In many instances the agencies' choices of different data sources and different simplifying assumptions may be inadvertent. The pressure of short-term tasks often requires the agencies' modeling experts to make expeditious simplifications, which are rarely reviewed in depth and which are difficult to revise once made. Other discrepancies may reflect real differences of opinion among the agencies responsible. But whether inadvertent or substantive, these discrepancies should be amenable to resolution through interagency negotiation and arbitration—if a suitable institutional mechanism could be held responsible for identifying the discrepancies and encouraging the negotiation and arbitration.

Iterative adjustments might further improve the projections. For example, the results of all the Global 2000 Study's projections could be used as the basis for a new set of assumptions in the existing models for the development of new GNP and population projections. These new GNP and population projections could then be used to develop new resource and environmental projections. If this cycle were repeated one or more times, it might provide a stronger degree of temporal and intersectoral interaction and consistency. But such cycles could only be executed on a block-recursive basis—that is, a full set of projections would have to be obtained from one element before making projections for another element that required the former element's projections. At best, the procedure is likely to be clumsy, time-consuming, and expensive, and there is no assurance that closure (or even moderate convergence) would be possible. Even if a major attempt had been made to resolve many of the more obvious inconsistencies and incompatibilities among the elements, major structural inconsistencies would remain, making convergences and the verification of convergences problematic.

As Chapters 15–23 demonstrate, the present elements of the government's global model are sufficiently dissimilar that incremental improvements of the kinds discussed above would be of only limited utility. Put simply, there is no possibility that the present sectoral elements of the government's global model could be used on a fully integrated, simultaneous, and interactive basis. Severe structural and computational differences among the elements preclude their being operated in this manner. Furthermore, to achieve even a modest degree of consistent, simultaneous interlinkage would require such extensive modifications of the present elements that the creation of an entirely new family of elements might well be more cost-effective.

It is doubtful, however, that the government will find it convenient anytime soon to work with a single large computer model of the world. In fact, attempting to develop and maintain a single all-purpose model might not be well advised, even in the long run. On the one hand, the departments and agencies have individual and unique projection needs that could not be satisfied easily with a single large global model. On the other hand, one model is not likely to ever be capable of providing the diverse perspectives on issues essential to the sound formulation of policy. A more pluralistic approach would therefore appear to be both desirable and necessary.

Such a pluralistic approach could incorporate several of the following principles:

• All major development and use of analytic procedures related to long-term global projecting in a government agency would continue to be undertaken by the agency or under its sponsorship—using funds and personnel allocated specifically for this purpose.

- A major effort would be made to encourage much more extensive development and use of existing and new long-term global models.
- A major effort would also be made to ensure that governmentwide protocols were established and enforced regarding documentation standards, access, reproducibility, and comparisons with standard series projections, together with other steps to facilitate public understanding of the elements of the government's global model and derived projections.

Incorporating Broader Perspectives

Several important steps could be taken to ensure that a broader range of perspectives is drawn upon than is currently the case in developing and making use of the government's global model. For example:

1. *A coordinating body to improve understanding of models.* At present, information related to the Study projections and their underlying methodologies is not easily examined by even the policymakers and members of Congress, let alone the private sector and general public. The basic documentation on the elements of the government's global model is incomplete and of mixed quality and is only now being made available to the public as the third volume of the Global 2000 Study. If the government's computer-based tools and models are to achieve their potential for benefiting policy analysis, ways must be found to facilitate understanding of the assumptions on which they are based. One or more coordinating bodies might give attention to this problem, representing both the perspectives of analytic expertise and social, political, and economic experience.

2. *Increased interaction with the private sector, educational institutions, other national efforts, and international agencies.* Since all models are simplifications of reality, one basic purpose of a model is to provide a basis for its own improvement. An important part of any process for improving the sectors of the government's global model is increased interaction with individuals and organizations that could help to improve the government models. The private sector has much data and much familiarity with particular economic sectors. Therefore, an organized private sector review of the assumptions and structures of the government's longer-term models could both improve the models and reduce the number of unanticipated changes in government policy.

Modeling in educational institutions needs to be encouraged to provide both new techniques and diversity of perspectives in the available models. Since other nations and international agencies face similar analytical problems, more extensive and penetrating interaction among professionals would be helpful in extending techniques and information around the world.

3. *A more useful and internally consistent capability for longer-range analysis and planning.* This must start with an improved exchange of information. At present, even the agency experts responsible for the development, use, and maintenance of the individual sectoral elements of the government's global model have little knowledge of the assumptions, methodologies, and requirements of the other sectoral elements. The third volume of the Global 2000 Study will provide a reference manual on the various sectoral models, but much more is needed. Opportunity should be provided not only for the agencies' modeling experts, but also for experts from congressional staffs, the private sector, educational institutions, and the general public to learn about these models and to gain experience in their use. Increased understanding and ideas for improvements are sure to result from such information exchanges.

4. *Improved documentation of the elements of the government's global model.* Better documentation is badly needed. The third volume of the Global 2000 Study provides an initial attempt to draw the pieces together, but the basic reference documents should be available from a single source. Furthermore, the quality of the documentation—especially regarding descriptions of assumptions underlying the projections—needs to be improved. Impartial validation should also occur.

Summary Descriptions of the 11 Elements

Each of the 11 elements of the government's global model is described here in terms of nine topics of particular relevance to the analysis presented earlier in this chapter.

Source of the designated projections
Explicit linkages to other elements of the government's global model
Critical policy and technology assumptions
Analytic methodology used to develop the projections
Brief description of the methodology
First major use of the methodology

Geographic representation within the methodology

Temporal representation within the methodology

Cases analyzed for the Global 2000 Study using the methodology

The 11 elements are described in the order in which they appear in Table 14–1. Much of the material presented below is encapsulated in Tables 14–2 and 14–3.

1. Population Element

Source. At the suggestion of the Agency for International Development (AID) of the U.S. Department of State, two independently developed sets of population projections were prepared for the Study. The Bureau of the Census of the U.S. Department of Commerce developed the projections that were subsequently used in preparing the Study's energy and food projections and its per capita GNP projections. The Community and Family Study Center at the University of Chicago developed alternative projections, which highlight the potential impact of family planning programs on population size and structure.

Explicit Linkages to Other Elements of the Government's Global Model. The Census and Chicago population projections were not developed taking into explicit account any of the Study's other projections. However, the Census projections were subsequently used in developing the Study's food and energy projections (and the derived energy-residual and environmental-impact projections).

Critical Policy and Technology Assumptions. With regard to policy, all population cases assumed that almost all countries that do not already do so will make family planning services available to an appreciable portion of the population during the 1975–2000 period, and that countries with family planning programs now in operation will extend coverage, particularly in rural areas. This meant, for example, that in the Census projections for Bangladesh (in the medium-growth case; over the 1975–2000 period) fertility rates were exogenously projected to decline 40 percent, as discussed in Chapter 15.

With regard to technology, no major breakthroughs or setbacks affecting fertility or mortality rates (e.g., regarding birth control devices or medical discoveries) were assumed.

Analytic Methodology. Both the Census and Chicago projections make use of the cohort-component methodology. The name of this methodology refers to the fact that each "cohort" of a given population (each group of males or females born in the same year) is treated separately and explicitly with respect to each major demographic "component" (mortality, fertility, and net migration). Each set of projections was prepared using somewhat different versions of a FORTRAN computer program of about 1,000 lines (including extensive comments).

Chicago's exogenous fertility projections also make use of an additional, explicit quantitative methodology. Given a population's 1975 fertility rate and the "strength" in 1975 of its family planning programs, Chicago's computer-based methodology projects future fertility rates, relying entirely on explicitly defined assumptions regarding the future development and efficacy of family planning programs; no other factors are considered in making these projections.

Brief Description. The cohort-component methodology projects population size and structure based on exogenous projections of mortality, fertility, and net migration rates.

Only demographic variables are considered in developing the population projections. No explicit mathematical relationships are used at any point that involve nondemographic factors—such as the size and distribution of per capita income; requirements for food, housing, schools, jobs, or medical facilities; likely welfare expenditures; educational opportunities; work roles and opportunities for women or men; or the influence of environmental factors on health. Internal migration (for example, between rural and urban areas or between social classes) is not represented, nor are differential growth rates for separate ethnic, racial, or religious groups.

First Major Use. Although the cohort-component methodology, developed in the 1930s, has been used extensively by demographers for decades, it was not until the late 1960s that the Bureau of the Census began making major use of it to develop international population projections, at the request of AID. At that time, AID asked Census to develop a model that would avoid what appeared to be biases contained in U.N. population estimates and projections, and subsequently to perform various policy analyses.

Several years later, in August 1977, AID asked the University of Chicago to develop a new projection methodology and undertake projections which would take more explicit account of the likely future impact of family planning programs (which AID was encouraging) on population size and structure. The Chicago population projections presented in the Study, developed in response to this request, emphasize the potential efficacy of AID's programs. Thus, the Chicago high, medium, and low world population projections for the year 2000 are 3 to 12 percent lower than the Census projections.

Geographic Representation. The cohort-component methodology can be used to develop projections for any appropriately defined population. Separate projections were prepared for 23 countries and subregions for the Global 2000 Study, at the request of the Study's central staff. These 23 areas include collectively all the world's population; moreover, the 12 less developed countries for which individual projections were made represent 75 percent of the current total population of the LDCs.

In the case of the Global 2000 Study, projections for each of the 23 countries or subregions were made independently of each other, and summed as appropriate. Migration between countries or subregions was assumed to be zero, for analytic reasons explained in Chapter 15.

Temporal Representation. Projections of a given population's size and structure were made dynamically—on a year by year, sequential basis. These projections were based on exogenous projections of mortality and fertility. For the Global 2000 Study, projections were presented in Chapter 2 for each 5-year interval of the 1975–2000 period.

Cases Analyzed. Three sets of projections were developed by both Census and Chicago: a high-growth, a medium-growth, and a low-growth case. In general, Census and Chicago used different estimates of current population sizes and structures and different mortality and fertility projections. Within both the Census and Chicago projections, variations among the high-growth, medium-growth, and low-growth cases were based entirely on different fertility rate projections (and in the Census projections, in the case of China, on different estimates of actual population size in 1975). Mortality assumptions and the zero net migration assumption did not vary within either the Census set of projections or within the Chicago set of projections.

2. Gross National Product Element

Source. No U.S. agency is responsible for developing a consistent set of long-term GNP projections for all the world's nations. Therefore, on the recommendation of the U.S. Agency for International Development of the U.S. Department of State, the Global 2000 Study turned to the office within the World Bank Group responsible for estimating consistent GNP projections for the Western industrialized nations and less developed

countries through 1985.* On the recommendation of Bank staff members, the Global 2000 Study supplemented the Bank's projections with GNP growth rates to the year 2000 developed for the 1977 Workshop on Alternative Energy Strategies (WAES), sponsored by the Massachusetts Institute of Technology.

The WAES group had first developed its own projections for the Western industrialized nations, and then—with the assistance of World Bank staff members—developed a consistent set of LDC projections using World Bank analytic tools. The World Bank and WAES projections were subsequently supplemented for the Global 2000 Study with projections for the centrally planned economies (CPEs), developed by the U.S. Central Intelligence Agency. Unfortunately, the GNP projections for the CPEs presented in this volume are considered unrealistically low by the CIA, when viewed together with the Study's other GNP projections (due to statistical differences discussed briefly in Chapter 3). However, it should be noted that the CPE growth rates used by the World Bank in developing the LDC growth rates for the WAES Study are much higher than those reported in this volume.

Explicit Linkages to Other Elements of the Government's Global Model. The GNP projections were not developed taking into explicit account any of the Study's other projections, except that the per capita GNP projections were subsequently calculated using the Study's population projections (developed by the Bureau of the Census). However, the GNP projections were subsequently used in developing the Study's food and energy projections and the derived energy-residual and environmental-impact projections.

Critical Policy and Technology Assumptions. No major policy changes were assumed. With regard to technology, however, all the GNP projections for the LDCs assumed that the productivity of capital in almost all of the LDCs will increase significantly over the 1975–85 period. This meant, for example, that in the other-South-Asia LDC group, a given investment could be thought of as producing 60 percent more incremental GNP in 1985 than in 1977 (in constant dollars), as discussed in Chapter 16.

Analytic Methodology. Most of the GNP projections (those for the LDCs) were developed making use of a dynamic, block-recursive computer model known as SIMLINK (SIMulated trade LINKages). The model contains over 200

_____

*The World Bank Group is an international organization affiliated with the United Nations.

econometric structural equations and is written in approximately 1,500 lines of FORTRAN.

Brief Description. SIMLINK simulates world trade between the industrialized nations and the LDCs. Its purpose is to aggregate and adjust, as appropriate, the economic growth projections developed for individual LDC nations by World Bank analysts, so as to take account explicitly and consistently of likely limitations in the worldwide availability of foreign trade earnings and foreign investment capital. If these adjustments were not made, projections made by both the individual LDCs and World Bank analysts would sum to implausible levels of world trade and foreign investment.

Trade between industrialized nations or between LDCs is not explicitly represented in SIM-LINK, nor is primary commodity trade between the LDCs and the CPEs. Current debt levels and growth trends in these levels are also not explicitly accounted for.

No explicit account is taken by SIMLINK of future population sizes and structures or of potential environmental impacts. Resources are represented primarily on the basis of historic cost-price relationships and past trends in growth of production.

First Major Use. An early version of SIMLINK began to be applied in 1974. One of the first applications examined the potential direct effect of recent and potential changes in the international price of oil on LDC economic growth rates (which are of crucial financial importance to the World Bank). The model supported the Bank's view that the direct impact of changes in the price of oil on LDC economic growth would be minor. However, the model also showed that changes in the growth rates of the industrialized nations, which might also be affected by changes in the price of oil, would have major direct impact on LDC economic growth.

Geographic Representation. SIMLINK treats the Western industrialized and socialist nations exogenously as four aggregates, each with its own GNP growth rate and elasticity of demand for LDC exports of manufactured goods. The LDCs are selectively represented by six aggregates: India, other-South-Asia countries, low-income Africa, lower-middle-income countries, middle-income-countries, and upper-middle-income countries. Each aggregate is treated at the same level of detail. SIMLINK simulates trade between each of the six LDC aggregates and (1) the Western industrialized nations and (2) the CPEs. Trade among the six LDC aggregates is not simulated,

nor is trade between the industrialized nations and the CPEs.

Several simplifying assumptions were made in developing the SIMLINK model. Within each of the six LDC aggregates, geographically and socioeconomically diverse LDCs—such as (1) Argentina, Jamaica, and Yugoslavia, or (2) Bolivia, Thailand, and Morocco—are treated as if they were single entities because they have roughly the same levels of per capita income. Many LDCs are not included in the model. For example, the OPEC income-surplus nations were not explicitly represented in the version of SIMLINK used for the WAES Study. However, those LDCs that are specifically included are said by Bank analysts to represent most of the population and national income of the LDCs.

Temporal Representation. Projections of world trade directly affecting the LDCs are based on exogenous projections of (1) Western industrial and CPE growth rates, trade volumes, and prices for many major commodities and (2) inflation rates for all years to be covered by the projection. After these exogenous projections are completed, SIMLINK projects LDC economic growth rates sequentially, year by year.

Bank analysts note that SIMLINK was not constructed to make projections beyond 1985, that they have little confidence in using it to develop longer-term projections, and that they have recently replaced it with a more comprehensive system of models. For the WAES Study, SIM-LINK projections were developed for the 1975–90 period and extrapolated judgmentally to 2000.

Cases Analyzed. High, medium, and low GNP projections were used in the Global 2000 Study. The high and medium projections derive largely from figures developed for the WAES Study. The high-growth case generally projects a continuation of 1960–72 growth patterns, whereas the low-growth case projects a continuation of the patterns characteristic of the 1973–75 period—just sufficiently above that period's population growth to allow an advance in real global GNP per capita. The third (medium-growth) set of projections was developed by averaging the growth rates used in the high and low projections.

3. Climate Element

Source. The Global 2000 Study's climate projections were developed by the Central Intelligence Agency (CIA), based on an interagency research project on climate conducted by the National Defense University (NDU), with participation by the U.S. Department of Defense, the

U.S. Department of Agriculture, and the National Oceanic and Atmospheric Administration of the U.S. Department of Commerce. The first of the NDU project's four tasks—to define and estimate the likelihood of changes in climate during the next 25 years and to construct climate scenarios for the year 2000—was completed in February 1978, and the results were published in the National Defense University report entitled *Climate Change to the Year 2000.** The remaining three tasks of the NDU project included (1) estimating the likely effects of possible climatic changes on selected crops in specific countries, (2) evaluating the domestic and international implications of these specific climate-crop cases, and (3) transmitting the research results to individuals and organizations concerned with the consequences of climatic changes in fields other than agriculture.

Explicit Linkages to Other Elements of the Government's Global Model. The climate cases were not developed taking into direct account any of the Study's other projections, nor were they used in developing any of those projections, since, as it turned out, none of the other elements used to develop the Study's other projections was capable of directly taking into account any climatic variation from patterns established over the past 2–3 decades.

Critical Policy and Technology Assumptions. With regard to both policy and technology, deliberate human efforts to modify climate were excluded from the analysis.

Analytic Methodology. A special survey methodology devised by the Institute for the Future (hereafter referred to as the NDU methodology) was used to gather, weigh, and consolidate the views of numerous experts on climate. The purpose of the NDU project was not to forecast climate change or reach a consensus on how climate will change, but rather to synthesize reasonable, coherent, and consistent possibilities for world climate to the end of the century, and to put plausible bounds on the likelihood of each of these possibilities occurring.

Brief Description. The CIA developed three simplified cases for the Global 2000 Study, based primarily on the more complex and highly qualified findings of the NDU report. The approach

used in developing the NDU report was to seek and weigh a wide range of expert opinion. This synthesized survey approach seemed likely to yield the most meaningful results obtainable, in view of the fact that there is currently no single well-accepted quantitative model of the causal forces thought to determine climate.

In the first of the NDU project's four tasks, a questionnaire defining five future climate possibilities was prepared and completed by a diverse group of climatological experts. The emphasis of the project was placed primarily on assessing probabilities related to (1) average global temperature, (2) average latitudinal temperature, (3) carbon dioxide and turbidity (including particulates), (4) precipitation change, (5) precipitation variability, (6) midlatitude drought, (7) Asian monsoons, (8) Sahel drought, and (9) the length of the growing season.

Individual responses were weighted by each participant's expertise, as evaluated by self and peers, and responses to this questionnaire were then used to calculate complex topographical probability functions associated with each specified case.

First Major Use. The NDU methodology was first developed and used in connection with this particular NDU study in the mid-1970s, although it is related to Delphi-survey techniques developed over the past two decades.

Geographic Representation. The NDU study developed separate probability functions primarily with regard to each of eight regions (polar, higher midlatitude, lower midlatitude, and subtropical regions in both Northern and Southern Hemispheres). Geographic causal linkages between the phenomena occurring in these regions were informally assessed on an individual, undocumented basis by each of the participants in the study.

Temporal Representation. Probability functions were assessed for three time periods: 1977–80, 1981–90, and 1991–2000. Temporal causal linkages between the phenomena occurring in these time periods were informally assessed on an individual, undocumented basis by each of the participants.

Cases Analyzed. The three climate cases developed for the Global 2000 Study represent simplifications of three of the five NDU cases, namely, they approximate the three more moderate cases projected by the report as most probable. However, it should be kept in mind that in excluding the more extreme, large-scale changes, the Global 2000 Study has omitted consideration of climatological developments that could have an

---

* These climate "projections" are actually scenarios (in the sense of being internally consistent statements of possible future developments), rather than "projections" (in the sense of being foreseeable consequences of present trends). In order to facilitate comparisons with the other element descriptions in this chapter, they will henceforth be referred to as "cases" in this discussion.

extremely pronounced effect on the Study's other projections.

The following three world-climate cases were developed for the 1975–2000 period. They differ primarily with regard to assumed future global temperature and precipitation patterns.

Case	Temperature	Precipitation
No change	Similar to 1941–70 period (i.e., less variability than over the past 100–200 years).	Similar to 1941–70 period (i.e., less severe drought in the Sahel and less monsoon failure in India than recently experienced).
Warming	Global temperatures increase by 1° C, with only slight warming in the tropics.	Annual precipitation increases 5–10 percent and becomes less variable; probability of U.S. drought increases.
Cooling	Global temperatures decrease by 0.5° C, with only slight cooling in the tropics.	Precipitation amounts decline and variability increases; probability of U.S. drought increases.

4. Technology Element

Source. This section brings together under one heading (as a major element of the government's global model) the disparate methods used by the other elements of the government's global model to project rates of technological innovation, deployment, and impact. The fact is that no government agency has unique responsibility for projecting future rates of technological change for use in other official projections and forecasts. As a result, each agency develops its own technological projections and forecasts on a virtually independent basis.

This practice was also followed in developing the Global 2000 Study's projections. The Study's assumptions concerning future rates of technological change were determined independently by the various agencies for their individual contributions to the Study.

Explicit Linkages to Other Elements of the Government's Global Model. No explicit linkages were made between any of the other 10 elements of the government's global model with respect to technology. Those elements from which projections were developed using projections developed by other elements, however, could be thought of as incorporating implicitly the technology as-

sumptions of those other elements (often inconsistently).

Critical Policy and Technology Assumptions. No explicit, consistent policy assumptions were made with regard to technological innovation, deployment, or impact. However, some representative critical technological assumptions are cited below, under "Cases Analyzed." In general, technological progress is assumed, potential setbacks are not considered, and adverse side effects are not considered.

Analytic Methodology. Over the years, government agencies have developed a wide variety of diverse methodologies for projecting (often implicitly) technological assumptions. These technological projections are then incorporated in projections and forecasts of other variables of interest. In some cases, these technological projections are made in advance of making use of the methodologies which comprise the other elements of the government's global model; in other cases, they are calculated concurrently with other calculations made using the methodology. The actual techniques used by the various elements to project technological innovation, deployment, and impact are so idiosyncratic that a more explicit overall description (such as that provided in Chapter 23) is not feasible here.

Brief Description. Most technologies were projected to yield increasing benefits over time at exponential rates corresponding to recent historical experience. In some cases, the deployment of existing technology was projected to occur at rates faster than recent historical experience (e.g., in the population projections and energy-residual projections). The potential adverse and dysfunctional consequences of technological innovation and deployment were almost never explicitly considered, except in the environmental projections.

First Major Use. The agencies' overall projection methodologies generally have unique ways of incorporating the underlying technology assumptions. Therefore, the first major use of the diverse methodologies for technological projections tended to coincide with the first major use of the overall projection methodologies of which they are a part. Little or no consistency was imposed regarding the rate at which technological advance is projected in various fields (e.g., in response to allocations of federal research budgets), and the Global 2000 Study represents the first time the government's various approaches to longer-term, global technological projection have even been cursorily examined on a collective basis in an official executive branch report.

Geographic Representation. Most projections assumed that all regions of the world will be culturally and physically capable of accepting technological change to approximately the same extent and at approximately the same rates.

Temporal Representation. No systematic attempt was made by the Study to assure the use of consistent assumptions regarding likely future rates of technological innovation, deployment, and impact collectively in the Study's projections. Therefore, it is unlikely that the temporal representation of technological change among the various elements is to any degree consistent, although the inexplicit character of the way technology is represented in many elements of the government's global model makes this virtually impossible to assess.

Cases Analyzed. No consistent, systematic projections of technology per se were made for the Study, but diverse technological assumptions were incorporated in all of the other projections developed for the Study. Some key examples are provided below:

- All the population projections assumed that almost all countries that do not already do so will make family planning technologies and services available to an appreciable portion of the population during the 1975–2000 period, and countries with family planning programs now in operation will extend coverage, particularly in rural areas. This meant, for example, that in the Census projections for Bangladesh (in the medium-growth case), fertility rates were exogenously projected to decline 40 percent over the 1975–2000 period, as discussed in Chapter 15.

- Almost all the GNP projections for the LDCs assumed that the productivity of capital in the LDCs will increase significantly over the 1975–85 period. This meant, for example, that in the other-South-Asia LDC group, a given investment could be thought of as producing 60 percent more incremental GNP in 1985 than in 1977 (in constant dollars), as discussed in Chapter 16.

- All the food projections assumed that the widespread deployment of fertilizer and other yield-augmenting inputs (together with other factors) will lead to further increased yields comparable to the increases experienced over the past two decades (the period of the Green Revolution). This meant, for example, that annual LDC grain production was projected to increase 125 percent over the 1975–2000 period (in the medium case), as discussed in Chapter 5.

- All the energy projections assumed the widespread deployment of light-water nuclear electric power plants. This meant, for example, that electrical generation from nuclear and hydro-power sources was projected to increase about 200 percent over the 1975–90 period (in the medium case), as discussed in Chapter 5.

- All the energy-residual projections (i.e., projections of residuals such as pollutants or waste heat from energy conversion processes) assumed implicitly that major public and private investment will be made in pollution abatement technologies so that by 1985 all energy facilities in all countries will have met or have been retrofitted to meet 1978 U.S. new source performance standards for various emissions, as discussed in Chapter 10.

5. Food Element

Source. The Study's food projections were developed by the U.S. Department of Agriculture's Economics, Statistics, and Cooperatives Service.

Explicit Linkages to Other Elements of the Government's Global Model. The projections are based on the Study's population projections (developed by the Bureau of the Census) and GNP projections. In addition, the Study's rising-energy-price projections were used in developing the two food cases (which assume increasing petroleum prices) and the Study's associated environmental projections. However, no Study projections (other than population, GNP, and energy) were directly used in developing the Study's food projections (i.e., no use was made of the Study's projections involving climate, fisheries, forestry, water, energy residuals, fuel minerals, nonfuel minerals, or the environment).

Critical Policy and Technology Assumptions. With regard to policy, the projections all assumed that major public and private investment in agricultural land development will be made. With regard to technology, they assumed that widespread deployment and use of fertilizer and other yield-augmenting inputs (together with other factors) will lead to further increased yields comparable to the increases experienced over the past two decades (the period of the Green Revolution). This meant, for example, that annual LDC grain production (in the medium case, over the 1975–2000 period) was projected to increase 125 percent.

Analytic Methodology. A computer-based static-equilibrium model known as the GOL (Grain, Oilseed, Livestock) model was the primary tool used in developing the food projections. The

GOL model consists of approximately 930 econometric equations, which are solved simultaneously.

Three additional procedures were used to make projections of arable area, total food production and consumption, and fertilizer use. They were developed since the fall of 1977 specifically for the Study, and were based on the application of comparatively simple computational procedures to some of the results of the GOL calculations. These additional calculations were made without the use of a computer-based model.

Brief Description. The GOL model projects world production, consumption, and trade quantities and prices in grains, oilseeds, and livestock products based on exogenous projections of population, GNP, growth in crop yields due to the deployment of more efficient yield-enhancing technology, and other variables. The model's structure is most detailed for grain; other food products are represented in less detail. Collectively, the relationships incorporated in the model are said to represent approximately 70–80 percent of total world food production, consumption, and trade. No environmental considerations (other than land scarcity and weather) are explicitly represented in the model. Similarly the public and social costs associated with developing and maintaining the productive capacity required by 2000 are not explicitly represented in the model.

First Major Use. Along with other analyses, the model was initially used in 1974 to generate projections supporting the U.S. position paper for the Rome Food Conference sponsored by the Food and Agriculture Organization. The model's initial projections showed that over the next decade the world could produce enough grain (at real prices above the relatively low prices of the late 1960s) to meet the demands of (1) a largely cereal diet in the developing world and (2) a moderately rising grain-feed meat diet (based in part on grain-fed livestock) in the industrial nations. The U.S. position paper prepared for the conference made use of these projections to support policy views favoring, in general, the limiting of government intervention in domestic and world food markets, and questioning, in particular, the need for an extensive international system of government-owned food reserves.

Geographic Representation. A total of 28 closely interrelated regions are represented at varying levels of detail. The 28 regions consist of 8 regions of Western industrial nations, 3 regions of centrally planned economies, and 17 regions of less developed countries (LDCs). All regions have crop equations, but not all regions have full livestock sectors. The centrally planned regions are represented solely by collapsed international trade equations (that is, area yield and production projections are generated by "satellite" models, while consumption is calculated as production plus or minus trade).

Temporal Representation. The GOL model is a static equilibrium model. It is described as static in that it does not dynamically develop projections on a year by year basis. Instead, its projections are derived from estimated values for an initial base period, directly adjusted to correspond to anticipated equilibrium conditions in a final year, without calculating successive values for the intervening years. This process of one-step projecting is based on the assumption that the world's grain-oilseed-livestock production and trade system was in rough equilibrium (supply equaled demand at the reported market price) in the base period and that the solution calculated for any single future year will also be in rough equilibrium. The GOL model is thus extremely limited in its capacity to simulate the many important aspects of agricultural market behavior that are in a state of dynamic disequilibrium over periods exceeding one year.

GOL projections for 1985 and 2000 were developed for the Global 2000 Study starting with 1969–71 (average) base-line conditions (adjusted somewhat using data through 1976) and projecting to 1985 and 2000.

Cases Analyzed. Four projections of world food production, consumption, and trade were developed for the Study, based on different assumptions for population growth, GNP growth, weather, and the real price of petroleum. The four food cases* are summarized below:

Cases	Population Growth	GNP Growth	Weather	Real-Price of Petroleum
Medium	Medium	Medium	Same as last three decades	Constant ($13/ bbl., 1978 dollars)
Optimistic	Low	High	More favorable than last three decades.	Constant ($13/ bbl., 1978 dollars)
Pessimistic	High	Low	Less favorable than last three decades	Increasing (5 percent per year in real terms, 1980–2000)
Rising energy price	Medium	Medium	Same as last three decades	Increasing (5 percent per year in real terms, 1980–2000)

*The "cases" are referred to as "alternatives" and "scenarios" in Chapters 6 and 18. Alternative I of Chapter 6 embodies both the medium and the rising-energy-price cases; Alternative II is the optimistic case; Alternative III is the pessimistic case. In these cases, the changes in assumptions regarding weather (a term used to refer to relatively short-term variations within historic norms) are not considered equivalent to changes in assumptions regarding climate (a term used to refer to fundamental long-term change).

6. Fisheries, Forestry, Water Element

Source. Because of their methodological similarities, the fisheries, forestry, and water projections are described together here as if they were one element in the government's global model. The fisheries projections were developed by the National Oceanic and Atmospheric Administration of the U.S. Department of Commerce and by outside consultants. The forestry projections were developed by the Central Intelligence Agency, with assistance from the Department of Agriculture and the Department of State (and its Agency for International Development). The water projections were developed by the Department of the Interior, with assistance from the CIA and outside consultants.

Explicit Linkages to Other Elements of the Government's Global Model. The fisheries, forestry, and water projections were not developed taking into direct account any of the Study's other projections or each other, nor were they used in developing any of the Study's other projections, except the environmental impact projections.

Critical Policy and Technology Assumptions. With regard to policy, the fisheries projections assume, on a worldwide basis, good management of fisheries and protection of the marine environment; the forestry projections assume some policy changes throughout the world regarding current deforestation practices; the water projections' policy assumptions are unknown. With regard to technology, the fisheries projections assume the invention of methods for harvesting nontraditional species; the forestry projections assume the invention of both less wasteful production techniques and methods for exploiting nontraditional species; the water projections' technology assumptions are unknown.

Analytic Methodology. Descriptive and judgmental analyses (rather than elaborate mathematical models) were used in developing the fisheries, forestry, and water projections.

Brief Description. The fisheries production (supply) projections were based on empirical evidence and ecological theory. The fisheries consumption (demand) projections were based on broadly generalized assumptions about the relationships between population, income growth, and income elasticities of demand for marine products. Together, these projections suggest that future fish consumption will be constrained by production and price.

The forestry projections were based on a review of the literature of forest economics and ecology, combined with informed judgment. In cases where sources were in conflict (for example, when ecological and anthropological projections came to different conclusions regarding the sustainability of slash-and-burn agriculture), the source with the stronger empirical evidence was preferred.

Two sets of projections of water availability were presented by the Department of the Interior and the CIA: (1) the lower projection of increases in the "consumption" (withdrawal) of "water controlled by man" over the 1975–2000 period was developed by C. A. Doxiadis; (2) the higher projection of global water requirements by the year 2000 was developed by Russian hydrologist G. P. Kalinin. The projections were apparently not chosen by the Department of the Interior for their excellence, but because other global water projections could not be found or developed.

First Major Use. The fisheries and forestry projections were developed specifically for the Global 2000 Study. In the case of the water projections, the Doxiadis projections were originally published in the report, "Water for Peace," prepared for the International Conference on Water for Peace held in Washington, D.C., in 1967. The Kalinin projections were originally published in UNESCO's *Impact of Science in Society*, April–June 1969.

Geographic Representation. Projections involving fisheries, forestry, and water resources are severely complicated by the fact that the boundaries of the political jurisdictions responsible for gathering information on them and for managing them do not coincide with the natural boundaries of the ecological systems involved. These complications are greatest in the case of the fisheries projections, which had to be made largely on the basis of species rather than geographic region. In the case of the forestry projections, the supply, demand, and price of forest products were considered separately for each of the major forest regions of the world. A separate section was devoted to the problems of the humid tropics.

In the Study's water projections, the point is made that there is no such thing as a global water economy in the same sense as, for example, a global economy for minerals and fuels. Since the cost of transporting water tends to be high when large distances are involved, water problems tend to be local or regional, rather than global.

Temporal Representation. The fisheries, forestry, and water projections are either based on straight-line (linear) or exponential (nonlinear) extrapolations of past trends.

Cases Analyzed. Only a single medium case was evaluated for the fisheries and forestry projections; both a lower and a higher set of water projections were presented. The specific assumptions behind these cases (to the extent they are known) are reported in Chapters 7, 8, and 9.

7. Energy Element

Source. The Study's energy projections were developed by the Energy Information Administration of the U.S. Department of Energy.

Explicit Linkages to Other Elements of the Government's Global Model. The Study's population projections (developed by the Bureau of the Census) and GNP projections were used in developing the energy projections. None of the Study's other projections were used, but the energy projections were used in developing the Study's food, energy residuals, and environmental projections (but not in developing the climate, fisheries, forestry, water, fuel minerals, or nonfuel minerals projections).

Critical Policy and Technology Assumptions. With regard to policy, all the energy projections assumed the implementation of more effective energy conservation policies within the member countries of the Organization for Economic Co-operation and Development (OECD). With regard to technology, all the energy projections assumed the widespread deployment of light-water nuclear electric power plants. This meant that electrical generation from nuclear and hydropower sources was projected (in the medium case, over the 1975–2000 period) to increase more than 200 percent, as discussed in Chapter 5.

Analytic Methodology. The energy projections were made with a computer-based static-equilibrium model known as the International Energy Evaluation System (IEES). IEES is a family of complex supply, demand, and production models, integrated by means of a large linear-programming-matrix representation of approximately 2,-000 rows and 6,000 columns. The data quantifying world energy supply and demand, and production and transportation costs necessary for these integrating calculations, are supplied by six IEES submodels. These submodels have been assembled independently of one another, and are executed sequentially, drawing on their own outside data sources.

Brief Description. The IEES model projects world energy production, consumption, and trade, based on exogenous projections of population, GNP, trends in the international price of petroleum, and other variables. The model emphasizes the fossil fuel sector by providing elaborate detail for petroleum (and related fuels) and coal while incorporating significantly less detail for nuclear energy, solar energy, energy conservation programs, firewood, and emerging technologies. For example, solar energy is not explicitly represented and can be included in the projections only by an exogenous assumption of a given solar contribution to electrical generation or to conservation. Supply of nuclear facilities is determined largely outside of the model by exogenous projections and assumptions.

The IEES system of models is structured around a single large integrating linear-programming matrix representation. According to the model's theory, the world energy market operates as a free market whose equilibrium minimizes the total cost of meeting the world's energy demands at a specific, assumed price of oil.* Demand and supply are balanced through a price mechanism that adjusts marginal costs of supply and demand to equal values through iterative adjustments. The Organization of Petroleum Exporting Countries (OPEC) is assumed to provide as much oil as might be wanted (up to its maximum production capacity), independent of the price of oil assumed for the model run.

There are several important assumptions implicit in the operation of the IEES price mechanism. In each year projected, energy production outside of OPEC is assumed to respond within limits to prevailing energy prices, with little or no time lag. Oil production outside of OPEC generally does not meet demand, and IEES achieves supply-demand balance by assuming OPEC meets the residual demand (which in some runs exceeds the OPEC maximum production capacity) at whatever oil price prevails in the year in question. The energy production alternatives are assumed to be selected solely on the basis of meeting projected demand at the lowest possible global cost. In general, only gross energy production figures are presented; net energy production figures (i.e., gross energy production less the energy consumed in obtaining the gross energy production) are not calculated. Forms of energy supply which are not generally traded internationally (except hydropower and geothermal energy) are not represented in the model.

---

* In the analyses performed for the Global 2000 Study, the OPEC oil price scenario (constant at $13 per barrel in 1975 dollars until 1980, then increasing at 5 percent per year) was assumed. However, the Department of Energy does have an Oil Market Simulator (OMS) model with which the Department makes medium term forecasts of OPEC oil prices. OMS is calibrated to ILES and in forecasting runs annually equilibrated oil supply with the oil demand projected by ILES.

Since OPEC currently provides such a significant share of the oil used by the U.S. and other nations, the IEES model's assumptions about OPEC are of critical importance. IEES assumes (in all cases analyzed for this Study) that OPEC will provide as much oil as can be consumed independent of the exogenously projected price. However, if projected OPEC production exceeds OPEC capacity, an oil price increase is implied.

Generally, IEES is used to study the world balance of energy supply and consumption for specifically assumed oil prices—given essentially exogenous supply estimates for all energy sources. Interfuel trade-offs in consumption and conservation are the key results calculated.

The social or environmental effects of the energy sector are not evaluated by IEES, nor is resource depletion explicitly represented in the model. While gross national product is included as one of the major determinants of energy demand, IEES implicitly assumes that GNP growth is independent of energy availability and price.

First Major Use. IEES is based on the same analytic structure as the Project Independence Evaluation System (PIES), the initial computer-based model developed to analyze U.S. energy-policy options following the 1973–74 oil embargo.* IEES makes international projections that are consistent with the PIES domestic projections. Thus, IEES is essentially a copy of the PIES structure (a few deviations were necessary) using international data. The first major public analysis performed by IEES was released for distribution in 1978 (and previously circulated in 1977 in a form intended for limited distribution). It supports the view that petroleum demand is likely to exceed the production capacity of the OPEC nations in the mid-1980s, assuming real petroleum prices do not increase significantly above 1975 (real) prices in the near future.

Geographic Representation. IEES simulates a modern competitive energy market that deals primarily in fossil fuels. Four groups of countries are represented in the model at varying levels of detail: member countries of OECD, the OPEC countries, the CPEs, and the less developed countries. The OECD countries, which consume 80 percent of the world's oil production and are generally the world's most industrialized nations, are treated most extensively in the demand submodel

_____

* PIES was originally used to analyze ways of achieving President Nixon's goal of energy independence for the United States by 1980. While the results showed that such a goal was unachievable by 1980, the model suggested that the goal could be attained by 1985, if the Administration's proposed energy policies were adopted.

analyses, although all of the submodels produce data for every part of the world. In contrast, the energy economies of the LDCs are not treated in detail and in fact contain significant omissions. For example, the large proportion of LDC energy economies based on firewood and other biofuels is not represented.

Temporal Representation. Although some of its submodels exhibit dynamic behavior, IEES is essentially a static-equilibrium model. Like the GOL model used to develop the Study's food projections, IEES is "static" in that it does not dynamically develop its projections year by year with developments in one year influencing opportunities and difficulties in succeeding years. The IEES projections are made in a one-step process that starts in a base year (e.g., 1975) and progresses directly to the final year (e.g., 1990) under the assumption that the international energy system is in equilibrium and optimally efficient during the intervening years.

The time-dependent characteristics of the IEES projections derive entirely from exogenous projections used as driving inputs to the IEES model. In the main part of the IEES system, variables change over time only in direct response to changes in exogenously projected variables.

The model's static equilibrium projections for a given year are internally independent of its projections for all other years and may well be inconsistent with projections for other years. However, the demand submodel (which serves as the basis for the initial demand estimates) is an annual dynamic model which imposes some intertemporal consistency. The model develops its projections for a given year based on exogenously projected economic and resource conditions for that one year only, without explicitly considering developments that might be anticipated beyond the year in question. The model therefore operates as if the planners' goals were to optimize for just that year, without any further planning for successive years. One exception is that demand data can be (and are) exogenously adjusted to reflect energy conservation measures expected to be implemented by the OECD countries.

Projections for the Study were made for 1985 and 1990, but not for 2000. IEES was not constructed to project beyond 1990, and at this time Department of Energy analysts have little confidence in using it to develop longer-term projections or in extrapolating such projections judgmentally.

Cases Analyzed. Four projections of world energy production, consumption, and trade were developed for the Study. These projections were primarily based on different assumptions regarding population growth, GNP growth, and the real price of petroleum, as summarized below*:

Case	Population Growth	GNP Growth	Real Price of Petroleum
Medium	Medium	Medium	Constant ($13/bbl., 1978 dollars)
High	High	Low	Constant ($13/bbl., 1978 dollars)
Low	Low	High	Constant ($13/bbl., 1978 dollars)
Rising energy price	Medium	Medium	Increasing (5% per year in real terms, 1980–90)

8. Energy Residuals Element

Source. The projections of energy residuals were developed by the Brookhaven National Laboratory, under contract to the Department of Energy's Office of Technology Impacts.

Explicit Linkages to Other Elements of the Government's Global Model. Like the Study's energy projections, the study's energy residuals projections are derived (via the energy projections) from the Study's population and GNP projections. However, they neither influenced any of the Study's other projections (other than the environmental projections) nor were they influenced by any of the Study's other projections (i.e., climate, food, fisheries, forestry, water, fuel minerals, or nonfuel minerals projections).

Critical Policy and Technology Assumptions. With regard to policy and technology, all the energy residuals projections (i.e., projections of residuals such as pollutants or waste heat from energy conversion processes) assumed implicitly that major public and private investment will be made in pollution abatement technologies so that by 1985 all energy conversion facilities throughout the world will have been retrofitted to meet the 1978 U.S. new source emission standards for carbon monoxide, sulfur dioxide, oxides of nitrogen and particulates.

Analytic Methodology. The energy residuals projections were developed using a highly simplified version of a computer-based network model or accounting tool known as the Energy Systems Network Simulator (ESNS). ESNS is currently capable of calculating the emissions of 435 energy-conversion processes, using 69 exogenously derived coefficients to transform energy consumption figures into estimates of residuals.

* The "cases" are referred to as "scenarios" in Chapters 10 and 20.

Brief Description. The simplified version of ESNS used in the Study makes repeated use of the following equation, summed across end-use (sectoral) categories and across fuel-type categories:

Total regional residuals generated (by emissions type)
= Total regional energy conversion (by fuel type)
× residuals generated (by emission type) per unit of energy conversion.

The national (i.e., U.S.) ESNS model was modified for use in this Study by adapting it to accept (as input) the results of the International Energy Evaluation System (IEES)—the model used to develop the Study's energy projections. The adaptation was difficult since (1) the international version could not be developed without making assumptions about emissions control standards on a worldwide basis, (2) the output from the IEES model (particularly the estimates of fuel consumption by end uses for the LDCs, the OPEC regions, and the centrally planned economies) were too aggregated for use in the ESNS model, and (3) the IEES projections for the Global 2000 Study do not include a base case—such as 1975—to which residuals in later years can be compared.

The adapted ESNS model is therefore severely limited by the capability of IEES, and the resulting model is best thought of as the IEES-ESNS model. An especially critical limitation to the value of the IEES-ESNS analysis is the assumption that by 1985 all countries will have met the U.S. new source performance standards discussed above.

First Major Use. ESNS itself was first developed in 1975 to assist the U.S. Energy Research and Development Agency (a predecessor agency of the U.S. Department of Energy) in analyzing the residuals implicit in the energy developmental programs it was advocating. The present Study marks the first time the ESNS model has been used to make long-term global projections.

Geographic Representation. The geographic representation in ESNS is necessarily the same as in the IEES energy projections—that is, the world is represented as four major regions or groups of nations: OECD Countries (also represented separately), the OPEC countries, the centrally planned economies, and the LDCs.

Temporal Representation. The temporal representation is necessarily the same as in the case of the energy projections—i.e., projections were developed for 1985 and 1990 and not for previous or subsequent years.

Cases Analyzed. The three cases analyzed are

necessarily the same as those analyzed in the energy projections—the low, medium, and high cases—except that the fourth (rising-energy-price) case was not analyzed.

9. Fuel Minerals Element

Source. The Study's estimates of fuel minerals reserves and resources were developed from a variety of sources since no one federal agency has exclusive responsibility for producing such estimates. These sources included the U.S. Geological Survey (USGS) of the Department of the Interior, the Department of Energy (DOE), and some private organizations, most notably the World Energy Conference (WEC). A consistent set of estimates was compiled, compared, and interpreted for the Study by a government expert who had worked with both DOE and Department of the Interior's Bureau of Mines.

Explicit Linkages to Other Elements of the Government's Global Model. The fuel minerals projections were not derived from any of the Study's other projections—including the Study's energy projections—nor were they used in developing any of the Study's additional projections other than the environmental projections.

Critical Policy and Technology Assumptions. With regard to policy, the U.S. oil and gas resource and reserve estimates assume a continuation of 1974 energy prices. With regard to technology, the U.S. oil and gas resource and reserve estimates assume a continuation of price-cost relationships and technological trends generally prevailing in years prior to 1974.

Analytic Methodology. The methods used to derive fuel resource and reserve estimates vary, to some extent, with the organization that gathered the estimates. In general, the organizations cited above made use of secondary rather than primary sources of information—that is, they queried corporations and other organizations and totaled these various estimates, or they adapted estimates that other organizations had derived previously from similar sources.

Brief Description. While field surveys and explorations are the best primary source of information, it has been necessary in this Study to rely primarily on secondary or tertiary sources. For example, the resource figures for solid fuels used in this Study are based on WEC estimates. The WEC sends questionnaires to the participating countries, requesting information on reserves, resources, maximum depth of deposit, minimum seam thickness, and other critical factors. In many cases, methods of estimating reserves and re-

sources differ significantly from country to country. As a result, it has not been possible to describe a consistent systematic methodological approach, even for individual fuel minerals.

First Major Use. The USGS, in addition to reviewing other sources of information, has been doing its own field geological research for decades to support its U.S. resource and reserve estimates. However, in 1974, the USGS reported new oil and gas estimates based on new techniques, which are discussed briefly in Chapter 21. The new oil and gas estimates are significantly lower than previous estimates, so the present USGS estimates may be thought of as dating from 1974. WEC started using its survey techniques to estimate reserves and resources prior to World War II and has published estimates periodically ever since. DOE develops its own estimates of U.S. coal reserves using techniques developed by its various predecessor agencies. For oil and natural gas reserve figures, DOE relies largely on estimates made by the U.S. Geological Survey, updated by DOE's own survey's and augmented for the most current months by data published by the American Petroleum Institute and the American Gas Association, trade associations of the oil and gas industries.

Geographic Representation. No consistent pattern of geographic representation has been followed in developing the fuel minerals projections.

Temporal Representation. Both resource and reserve estimates are dynamic concepts. Exploration shifts resources from the undiscovered category to the identified category. Economic and technological developments move resources between the economic and subeconomic categories. Reserves are those resources that are identified as economic and have not yet been depleted.

The Global 2000 Study's resource and reserve estimates do not have a dynamic perspective. The estimates presented are based on a static concept; they are applicable to a particular year but have no other time dimension. In general, they are based on the assumption that there will be a continuation of current price-cost relationships and technological trends, although the U.S. oil and gas resource and reserve estimates (derived from USGS Circular 725) assume a continuation of 1974 prices and of generally prevailing pre-1974 price-cost relationships and technological trends.

Cases Analyzed. Only one set of estimates was developed for the Study, but in many instances the probabilities associated with different measures of statistical variance have also been indicated.

10. Nonfuel Minerals Element

Source. The Study's nonfuel mineral-consumption projections were assembled by the Study's central staff, with assistance from the U.S. Department of the Interior's Bureau of Mines and outside consultants. Since the Bureau does not have and could not produce the disaggregated international projections needed for this Study, the Study's projections were based in large part (at the suggestion of the Bureau) on projections developed in 1972 by Wilfred Malenbaum for the National Commission on Materials Policy and were supplemented by projections prepared in 1977 by Malenbaum for the National Science Foundation. Malenbaum's projections cover 12 minerals and materials, said to account for 80–90 percent of the value of the total world mineral production. Consumption projections for an additional 75 minerals and materials have also been developed by the Bureau of Mines, making use of Malenbaum's analysis.

To facilitate review and comparison with the other trends presented in this Study, only a representative subset of these consumption projections is presented in Chapter 12. This subset consists of 10 minerals and materials projected by Malenbaum and 9 additional minerals projected by the Bureau of Mines.

Explicit price projections are not available from either the Department of the Interior or from Malenbaum's published analyses.

Explicit Linkages to Other Elements of the Government's Global Model. The nonfuel minerals projections were not derived from any of the Study's other projections, nor were they used in developing any of the Study's additional projections (other than the environmental impact projections).

Critical Policy and Technology Assumptions. With regard to policy, no significant changes are assumed. With regard to technology, the projections assume increasingly less intensive mineral use in highly industrialized countries and increasingly more intensive mineral use in the LDCs.

Analytic Methodology. Both the 1972 and 1977 Malenbaum projections were developed using a methodology known as the Intensity of Use (IOU) analysis. This methodology utilizes simple arithmetic procedures based on the relative intensity with which a given commodity is projected to be consumed per unit of per capita gross domestic product (GDP). This relative intensity of use is referred to as the material's IOU statistic. A relatively high IOU statistic indicates that a relatively large quantity of a given commodity is projected to be consumed per unit of per capita GDP.

Brief Description. In the 1977 Malenbaum Report (which was the report relied upon primarily by the Study) consumption projections for 12 minerals and materials were developed independently of each other, using the IOU methodology. They were based on exogenous projections of GDP and population, in combination with an extrapolation of historic relationships between mineral consumption and per capita GDP (developed according to IOU theory).

IOU theory assumes that as less developed countries industrialize, they use increasing quantities of minerals per unit of per capita GDP; conversely, it assumes that as industrial countries move toward postindustrial status, they use decreasing quantities of minerals per unit of per capita GDP. Malenbaum's use of IOU methodology also assumes explicitly that long-term growth in minerals and materials consumption will not be governed by supply limitations—whether due to depletion, environmental constraints, price increases, or other factors. In particular, it assumes explicitly that future consumption of minerals and materials will be largely independent of price, though Malenbaum notes that—to the vague and imprecise degree that prices are considered—they are projected to decline.

First Major Use. The IOU methodology is said to have been developed by the International Iron and Steel Institute in 1972 and tends to produce lower consumption projections than other methodologies (since it assumes that increasing economic growth in the industrial countries requires increasingly less consumption of minerals and materials per unit of per capita economic growth). Malenbaum's studies based on this particular methodology were used by the National Commission on Materials Policy to demonstrate the feasibility of striking a balance between the national need to produce goods on the one hand and to protect the environment on the other.

Geographic Representation. In the Malenbaum mineral-consumption projections the world is divided into 10 countries or groups of countries, treated independently and at the same level of detail. The Bureau of Mine's projections are disaggregated geographically into only two parts: the United States and the rest of the world.

Temporal Representation. The IOU methodology involves no endogenous dynamic calculations. Projections for any given year are based entirely on exogenous population and GDP projections and IOU assumptions. The exogenous population and GDP assumptions must be aggregated in the same way as the data used to project future trends in the IOU statistics and must be consistent with the historical data used to develop the IOU relationships. The 1977 Malenbaum Report presented historical estimates for the 1971–75 period and earlier, and projections for 1985 and 2000.

Cases Analyzed. For a variety of reasons it was not possible to obtain nonfuel minerals projections specifically for the Global 2000 Study. As a result it was necessary to rely entirely on previously published projections—namely, the 1977 Malenbaum Report—which presents only one set of consumption projections: the medium one. This set of projections is based on Malenbaum's population and GDP projections, which differ in complex ways from those of this Study (see Chapter 22).

The Bureau of Mines' projections for an additional 75 minerals and materials are made for three cases: a probable, high, and low case. However, the Bureau's assumptions are not sufficiently explicit or documented to determine exactly how these assumptions relate to those of the Study, and so only the Bureau's probable case projections have been presented in Chapter 12.

11. Environment Element

Source. The environmental projections were prepared by the Study's central staff, with assistance from the Environmental Protection Agency, the Agency for International Development of the U.S. Department of State, the Council on Environmental Quality, and outside consultants. In particular, the Council on Environmental Quality and the Environmental Protection Agency conducted extensive reviews of the drafts of Chapter 13. On the basis of the first of these reviews, the Study's central staff rewrote the environmental chapter over a period of about six months. The primary contributions to the final draft came from several persons: Gerald O. Barney, Study Director; Jennifer Robinson, a member of the Study's central staff; Peter Freeman, a free-lance environmental and development consultant; Jeffrey Maclure, a member of the Study's central staff; Allan Matthews, a retired foreign service officer; Bruce Ross, an ecologist on the staff of the Central Intelligence Agency; Thomas Lovejoy of the World Wildlife Fund, Washington, D.C.; Paul Lehr, a Washington-area writer specializing in climatological issues; and Richard Hennemuth, Assistant Director of the Northeast Marine Fisheries Laboratory, National Oceanic and Atmospheric Administration, Woods Hole, Massachusetts.

Explicit Linkages to Other Elements of the Government's Global Model. The Study's environmental projections were based primarily on the medium cases of all of the Study's other projections. Although they were directly used by none of the Study's other projections, a serious attempt was made to assess how feedback from the combined influence of all of the environmental impacts would feed back to influence the population, GNP, and resource projections. The basic conclusion of this analysis was that feedback from the environmental projections would have significantly altered the population, GNP, and resource projections if it had been possible to include this feedback explicitly.

Critical Policy and Technology Assumptions. With regard to policy and technology, no major changes were assumed other than those implicitly carried forward from the other study projections from which the environmental impact projections were derived.

Brief Description. The original plan of the Study called for each participating agency to analyze the environmental implications of its own projections. It was assumed that in responding to the requirements of the National Environmental Policy Act, each of the agencies would have developed a capacity to analyze the environmental implications of its trend projections. As it turned out, most do now have some capacity for environmental analysis, but only rarely is the capability available for examining the environmental implications of long-range global projections. As a result, the environmental analyses that came appended to the agencies' projections, with some exceptions, were minimal or nonexistent. Confronted with this situation, the Study's central staff was forced to strengthen the contributions that had been made and to prepare environmental analyses in those cases where none had been contributed. A number of consultants assisted to accelerate the work, but the extended environmental analysis unavoidably delayed the Study. Along the way it became clear that the government presently has only a very limited analytical capacity for integrated, long-term projections of global environmental trends.

Analytic Methodology. The environmental projections were made using the descriptive, deductive, and inductive methods of scholarly and scientific research. Whenever possible, the environmental analyses emphasized the qualititative and quantitative aspects of the ability of the environment to support human life and to provide goods and services. Particular attention was given to situations in which the goods and services provided by healthy environmental systems are threatened for large portions of the world's population or over large geographical areas. Special attention was given to situations where widespread or irreversible damage to the environmental systems now threatens to occur. Uncertainties were unavoidable in the environmental analysis because there are still many gaps in scientific knowledge and data in this field.

The environmental projections or analyses were made from two different perspectives. One perspective started with each of the other (nonenvironmental) projections reported in the Study and analyzed the implications of that projection for the environment. This perspective is analogous to that involved in the preparation of the environmental impact statements required by the National Environmental Policy Act. The other perspective started with the overall environmental impacts of all the projected trends and analyzed the feedback implications of all these environmental impacts collectively on each of the other (nonenvironmental) projections. The government does not routinely perform analysis from this second (feedback) perspective, but parts of the annual *Environmental Quality* reports of the Council on Environmental Quality are analogous in intent.

First Major Use. The environmental analyses were necessarily developed specifically for this Study; however, they are based on techniques that have been in widespread use for decades.

Geographic Representation. Like the fisheries, forestry, and water projections, the environmental projections are complicated by the fact that the boundaries of the political jurisdictions responsible for management and data collection do not coincide with the natural boundaries of ecological systems. Whenever possible, the environmental analysis is presented in terms of geographical subdivisions that correspond to the areas of particular ecological systems (e.g., a river basin or watershed). In many cases, data limitations made it necessary to use national subdivisions in discussing specific examples of problems, when ecological boundaries would have been more appropriate.

Temporal Representation. In most cases environmental impacts are projected to the year 2000. They are developed generally from straight-line (linear) and from exponential (nonlinear) extrapolations of past trends, and from inference from ecological theory.

Cases Analyzed. As previously noted, the environmental projections were based primarily on the medium cases of the Study's other projections. Although they themselves were not used in developing any of the Study's other projections, a special analysis was subsequently prepared discussing many of the implications of the environmental projections with regard to the other (nonenvironmental) projections of the Study. This special analysis is presented as part of Chapter 13.

Appendix A

Lessons from the Past*

A survey of some of the commissions, studies, and task forces of the past 70 years whose experiences might be helpful to those now attempting to provide methods and instructions in support of decision-making for international efforts in population, resources, and the environment.

Introduction

A study of the world's population, natural resources, and environment, made at this juncture, must be viewed in historical perspective. If the study is to serve as a foundation for the nation's longer-term planning, as directed by the President, it must take cognizance of the similar major efforts that have gone before and consider their strengths and weaknesses. Experiences of the past have much to teach us about what arrangements will and will not lead to quality analysis, decisions, and actions addressed to important long-term issues. This appendix will briefly examine studies, commissions, and institutional efforts conducted during this century on population, natural resources, environment, and related subjects to see what lessons can be learned from these experiences that might be applicable today. Commissions reviewed in this appendix have in common high-level governmental connections and include for the most part presidentially appointed or designated groups looking into national and international issues concerned with population, natural resources, or the environment.

There has never been an organized, continuing effort in the federal government to take a holistic approach toward consideration of probable changes in population, natural resources, and the environment. Yet a number of attempts to tackle parts of the problem have been undertaken during the last 70 years. Starting with the second Theodore Roosevelt Administration, continuing through 10 years of Franklin D. Roosevelt's Administration, and during the 25 years from Truman to Ford, temporary presidential and congressional

*As noted in the acknowledgments, this appendix is the commissioned work of Robert Cahn and Patricia L. Cahn. The opinions expressed are those of the authors and are not necessarily endorsed by the participating agencies or their representatives.

committees, commissions, and boards have flowered and wilted from time to time. For the most part, this futures work covered the nation's natural resources and materials and produced results that have proved helpful in some measure. Rarely, however, did such groups consider global potentials and problems, and then only superficially.

Over the years, government has tended to wait until crises occur and then has reacted to them— rather than study and analyze issues beforehand. On those occasions when groups have addressed problems with an eye to the future, a President— and others who initiate such studies—have seldom sustained the original level of interest, although much valuable data has been developed, alternative choices have been explored, and options have been presented in the form of recommendations. In most cases, suggestions or recommendations have been made for the formation of an institution to carry on the work of looking at future problems, but none of the recommendations has led to establishing a permanent group. Thus decision-makers and the public have never had the benefits that would accrue if a long-range study group at a high level of government, free from pressures for immediate results, had been in existence to offer alternatives that might help avert or solve future difficulties.

Historical Perspective, 1908–1967

The Theodore Roosevelt Administration

National Conservation Commission (1908). Even as far back as the first decade of the 20th century, when natural resources seemed virtually inexhaustible, a few conscientious conservationists were looking into the future to a time of scarcities and shortages. "The Nation is in the position of a man, who, bequeathed a fortune, has gone on spending it recklessly, never taking the trouble to ask the amount of his inheritance, or how long it is likely to last." That picture, probably overly grim for its time, was painted at the initial meeting in 1908 of the executive committee of the newly appointed National Conservation Commission. The group promptly agreed to have a study made to estimate the existing available natural resources, the proportion that had already been used or exhausted, the rate of increase in their consumption, and the length of time these resources would last if the present rate of use was to continue. Thus began the first national inventory of natural resources.

President Theodore Roosevelt created the Commission as an outgrowth of the May 1908 White House Conference on Natural Resources. He appointed 49 members, with about equal representation among scientists, industry leaders, and public officials, but when the President requested funds of Congress to carry out the inventory, the Senate voted down the bill. Nevertheless, by presidential order Roosevelt directed the heads of several bureaus to make investigations as requested by the Commission in the areas of minerals, water resources, forests, and soils.

The full Commission met on December 1, 1908, to hear the reports of experts, which were later transmitted to the President in three volumes. This first inventory of the nation's natural resources was "but an approximation to the truth," wrote resource expert Charles Richard Van Hise in 1911. "But it is an immense advance over guesses as the natural wealth of the nation . . . [and] furnishes a basis for quantitative and therefore scientific discussion of the future of our resources." The Commission's report was published as a Senate document in a limited edition. (The Commission's recommendation for a popular edition had been turned down by the House Committee on Printing.)

Before leaving office, President Theodore Roosevelt sought to broaden interest in the conservation of resources beyond U.S. boundaries. He invited the governors of Canada and Newfoundland and the President of Mexico to appoint Natural Resource Commissioners and send representatives to a meeting with his National Conservation Commission. At this first North American Conservation Conference, held in Washington, D.C., in February 1909, a Declaration of Principles was issued, and the founding of permanent conservation commissions in each country was recommended.

In a separate action, President Roosevelt requested all the world powers to meet at The Hague for the purpose of considering the conservation of the natural resources of the entire globe. Efforts to institutionalize concern for preservation of natural resources faded, however, after William Howard Taft became President in March 1909, and the international conference was never held.

The intense congressional opposition accorded these efforts resulted not so much from objections to the subject matter as from reaction to what the legislators regarded as the President's attempt to bypass Congress by appointing too many presidential commissions. The opposition prevented the National Conservation Commission and its inventory of resources from becoming a congressionally mandated effort. Gifford Pinchot, whom Roosevelt had appointed as head of the National Conservation Commission, did keep the Commission alive, but without President Taft's approval and at his own expense, and the Commission evolved into a kind of private lobby for conservation.

The Hoover Administration

President's Research Committee on Social Trends (1929). The first organized effort in the area of social reporting was made in the autumn of 1929, when President Herbert Hoover appointed a President's Research Committee on Social Trends. The six-member committee, chaired by Wesley C. Mitchell, included Charles E. Merriam (who, with Mitchell, was to become a member of Franklin D. Roosevelt's original three-man National Planning Board) and William F. Ogburn, who was designated director of research. The Committee was called upon "to examine and report upon recent social trends in the United States with a view to providing such a review as might supply a basis for the formulation of large national policies looking to the next phase in the Nation's development." The Committee issued annual reports, under the editorship of Ogburn, for five years—until the end of the Hoover Administration in 1933.

Ogburn then published a book, *Recent Social Trends,* comprising a report by the Committee, to which a group of papers by experts had been added. In a Foreword, dated October 1932, Hoover wrote: "It should serve to help all of us to see where social stresses are occurring and where major efforts should be undertaken to deal with them constructively." The Committee claimed that the importance of their reports and of the book was in the effort to interrelate the disjointed factors and elements in the social life of America and to view the situation as a whole.

Many government organizations and private citizens contributed to the study, but the work received its major funding from the Rockefeller Foundation. The book did not take up war, peace, or foreign policy, nor did it mention the economic situation that was developing into the Great Depression, and there was no chapter devoted to social science research itself. The topics discussed were population, utilization of natural wealth, the influence of invention and discovery, communication, shifting occupational patterns, the rise of metropolitan communities, the status of racial and ethnic groups, the family and its functions, the activity of women outside the home, childhood and youth, the people as consumers, health and medical practice, public welfare activities, and government and society.

In a 1969 article, social scientist Daniel Bell, harking back to *Recent Social Trends*, commented on the report's chapter on medicine, which dealt with the rise of specialized medical practice, the divergence between research and general practice, and the consequences of geographical concentration. If the signposts in that chapter had been heeded, he wrote, they "would have gone far to avert the present crisis in the delivery of health care." Bell also claimed that the chapter on metropolitan communities was an accurate foreshadowing of postwar suburban problems.

The Franklin D. Roosevelt Administration

National Planning Board; National Resources Board; National Resources Planning Board 1933–43. For the first 10 years of Franklin D. Roosevelt's Presidency, the availability of natural resources to meet future needs for at least six years ahead was a primary consideration of the National Resources Planning Board and its two predecessor organizations. Two special commitments of the President—conservation of natural resources and government planning to achieve social goals—were linked in Roosevelt's use of this Board.

The effort started in 1933 when a National Planning Board was established under Interior Secretary Harold Ickes' Public Works Administration to coordinate the planning of public works projects. The President's uncle, Frederick Delano,* was a Board member along with political

* Delano had been chairman of a privately funded citizens study of the Joint Committee on Bases of Sound Land Policy, which in 1929 issued a 168-page report *What About the Year 2000?* This was an economic summary of answers to the questions: "Will our land area in the United States meet the demands of our future population?" and "How are we to determine the best use of our land resources?"

scientist Charles Merriam and economist Wesley Mitchell. The following year, when Congress by joint resolution asked the President for a comprehensive plan for the development of the nation's rivers, Roosevelt sought to make the Planning Board a part of the White House and to give it the lead role in the river-planning project. Ickes, aided by other Cabinet officers, fought the President's idea, and a compromise resulted in the so-called National Resources Board, its six Cabinet officers under Ickes, as Chairman, outnumbering the three members of the former Planning Board.

In December 1934, the new Board produced an extensive report. Its almost 500 pages, the Board claimed, "brings together for the first time in our history, exhaustive studies by highly competent inquirers of land use, water use, minerals, and related public works in their relation to each other and to national planning." The report addressed itself to such problems as "Maladjustments in Land Use and in the Relation of Our Population to Land, and Proposed Lines of Action." It also included an inventory of water resources, a discussion of policies for their use and control, recommendations for a national mineral policy and a discussion of its international aspects.

The December 1934 report to the President pointed to the significance of the recommendations from the two technical committees that had assisted in preparing the report—one on land-use planning and one on water planning. Both committees recommended the need for a permanent planning organization. The report repeated a recommendation of the former Planning Board that a permanent national planning agency be established. In defense of planning, the report stated:

It is not necessary or desirable that a central system of planning actually cover all lines of activity or forms of behavior. Such planning overreaches itself. Over-centralized planning must soon begin to plan its own decentralization, for good management is local self-government under a central supervision. Thus wise planning provides for the encouragement of local and personal initiative.

Bills to institutionalize a national planning agency were defeated in Congress during the next four years, with opposition coming from antiplanners in Congress, from within the Administration (notably the Army Corps of Engineers, the Forest Service, the Tennessee Valley Authority, and the Bureau of Reclamation), and from a powerful lobbying group known as the Rivers and Harbors Congress.

Finally, in 1939, after Roosevelt had succeeded in getting his executive reorganization plan through Congress and establishing an Executive Office of the President (without the planning agency, of which Congress unrelentingly disapproved), he reconstituted his planning group into the National Resources Planning Board and placed it in his Executive Office by presidential order. Although this action was unpopular with Congress, Roosevelt used his personal influence to get about $1 million a year appropriated for the Board's activities.

From 1934 to 1939, Delano, Merriam, and Mitchell had continued to serve as a planning board and as planning advisers to the President. As members of the revised National Resources Planning Board, the three established a number of technical committees and a field organization. By 1943 the Board had 150 full-time Washington employees, 72 field employees, and 35 per diem consultants. As its staff proliferated, however, it lost much of the influence it had gained as a coordinating body and became merely one agency among many. It met formally with the President more than 50 times, and held many informal meetings for discussion of long-range problems. Its proposals, however, did not ordinarily include detailed recommendations for implementation, and the Board did not strive for action. In 1939, when World War II began, the Board shifted its priority to postwar planning. After the 1940 election, President Roosevelt instructed the Board "to collect, analyze, and collate all constructive plans for significant public and private action in the post-defense period insofar as these have to do with the natural and human resources of the Nation."

Although Roosevelt had been the Board's chief (and sometimes its only) power base, he finally became resigned to the fact that it could not be permanently established and in 1943 signed an appropriations bill directing that the National Resources Planning Board be abolished and that its functions not be transferred to any other agency.

During the 10 years of their existence, the Board and its predecessors issued numerous research publications, including extensive data collections and studies of many national problems. They conducted statistical and analytical studies on subjects such as river basin development and frequently aided some federal agencies in getting their ideas up to the President. More than 300 publications reveal how Roosevelt's boards had expanded from natural resource studies and plan-

ning into other futures efforts and subjects that had largely been neglected.*

Part of the Roosevelt boards' poor relations with Congress derived from the members' belief that as a staff arm of the President they should not develop close relationships with Congress. The National Resources Planning Board gave little encouragement to members of Congress who were sympathetic, and its work (some Congressmen thought) enhanced the power of the Presidency unduly and contributed to loss of power by Congress.

The Truman Administration

President's Materials Policy Commission (1951). After the high rate of consumption of natural resources, especially minerals, during World War II, potential scarcities of industrial materials threatened the nation. Then the Korean War caused prices of materials to rise sharply, and the fact that the nation's resources strength was indeed limited became increasingly recognized. On the recommendation of W. Stuart Symington, then chairman of the National Security Resources Board, President Harry S. Truman created the President's Materials Policy Commission in January 1951. He charged the new Commission to "make an objective enquiry into all major aspects of the problem of assuring an adequate supply of production materials for our long-range needs and to make recommendations which will assist me in formulating a comprehensive policy on such materials." In a letter to Commission Chairman William S. Paley (Columbia Broadcasting System Board Chairman), President Truman wrote: "We cannot allow shortages of materials to jeopardize our national security nor to become a bottleneck to our economic expansion."

When the President called Mr. Paley and the four other members of the blue-ribbon citizen Commission to his office late in January 1951, he included in his directions the need to make their study international in scope and to consider the needs and resources of friendly nations. The 18-month study was the most comprehensive of its

---

* Significant titles include: *Economics of Planning of Public Works; Human Resources; Trends in Urban Government; Rural Zoning; Our Cities, Their Role in the National Economy; Technology and Planning; Consumer Incomes; Problems of a Changing Population; A Plan for New England Airports; Urban Planning and Land Policies; Housing Progress and Problems; War-Time Planning in Germany; Rates and Rate Structure; Transportation Coordination; Railroad Financing; After Defense—What?; The Future of Transportation; The Framework of an Economy of Plenty;* and *Post-War Problems of the Aircraft Industry.*

type ever done. Seven Cabinet departments and 25 federal agencies or commissions made special investigations, loaned personnel, and gave consulting help. Research assistance was provided by 20 universities, as well as by experts from more than 40 industries, the International Materials Conference, the International Bank for Reconstruction and Development, and the International Monetary Fund.

The resulting 5-volume report, *Resources for Freedom,* published in June 1952, contained some far-reaching recommendations, but it did not create any great public splash, nor did it have an immediate effect on national policy. It was, however, the first major study to perceive the resources situation as a problem not of absolute shortages but of dealing with rising "real costs," which would be at least as pernicious than shortages. In retrospect, it is easy to see that the Commission neglected several areas now perceived as vital, such as population trends and environmental factors relating to the new technological developments that the Commission assumed would alleviate many future shortage problems. While the report emphasized the danger of increased U.S. dependence on foreign sources of raw materials, it saw as the main problem the technical difficulties of obtaining materials from less developed countries without first considering the trade or political factors that might block access to the resources.

The Commission's inventory of resources, its studies, and its projections for the ensuing 25 years were extremely valuable, and a number of its recommendations were prescient. In projecting materials availability a quarter of a century ahead, it proved remarkably accurate in several areas. The Commission recommended that the nation should have "a comprehensive energy policy and program which embraces all the narrower and more specific policies and programs relating to each type of energy and which welds these pieces together into a consistent and mutually supporting pattern with unified direction."

The concluding chapter of the Commission's first volume addressed the problem of "Preparing for Future Policy." It stated that no single study by a temporary group can deal adequately with the immensely complicated situation "cutting across the entire economy, persisting indefinitely, and changing from year to year."

The report recommended that a single agency—not an operating agency—should survey the total pattern of activities in the materials and energy field, make periodic reports to industry, the public, and to the legislative as well as executive branches of government and be an advisory body located in the Executive Office of the President, framing recommendations for long-range policy (as much as 25 years ahead). The Commission somewhat perfunctorily recommended as a possible solution that the existing National Security Resources Board (NSRB) in the Executive Office of the President serve this function. The NSRB could, if given funds and authority, collect in one place the facts, analyses and program plans of other agencies on materials and energy problems. The Board could also evaluate materials programs and policies in all these fields; it could recommend appropriate action for the guidance of the President, the Congress, and the Executive agencies, and report annually to the President on the long-term outlook for materials, with emphasis on significant new problems, major changes in outlook, and necessary modifications of policy or program. The Paley Commission suggested that to the fullest extent consistent with national security, the annual reports should be made public.

The Paley Commission report reached President Truman in June 1952. By then the resources scarcity issue had lost its political priority and failed to arouse public's concern. Truman took the logical step of directing the NSRB to review the report and its recommendations and to advise him of follow-up actions deemed appropriate. He wrote to NSRB Chairman Jack Gorrie on July 9, 1952, asking the Security Resources Board to

initiate a continuing review of materials (including energy) policies and programs within the executive branch, along the lines recommended by the Commission, and report annually to the President on the progress of materials programs and policies and the long-term outlook for materials, with emphasis on significant new programs.

The NSRB had been established within the Executive Office of the President under the National Security Act of 1947, and its function was to advise the President on the coordination of military, industrial, and civilian mobilization. Thus, many of its activities were concerned with materials. Serving on the Board were the Secretaries of Agriculture, Commerce, Interior, and Labor and the heads of the National Security Agency, the Defense Materials Procurement Agency, and the Defense Production Administration.

NSRB Chairman Gorrie submitted his report to President Truman in 1953, six weeks before Truman left office. It included a recommendation for the President to "ask the Congress to provide the NSRB with adequate funds to enable the Board to develop policy designed to improve the national position with respect to resources affecting the Nation's security, and to carry out the directives in the President's memorandum of July 9, 1952.''

Truman left office without taking any action on this recommendation. The new Eisenhower Administration, committed in the election campaign to a lessening of federal intervention and a cutting back of government agencies, ignored the Commission's recommendations, and NSRB eventually faded out of existence.

Resources for the Future (*1952*). William Paley, foreseeing the problem posed by lack of a continuing body to carry out recommendations of the President's Materials Policy Commission, set up an office with his own funds to respond to questions about the Commission's report, to keep some of the statistics up to date, and to keep public interest alive. He established his small office in 1952 as a nonprofit corporation with the name Resources for the Future.

About this time, a group of conservationists, led by former National Park Service Director Horace M. Albright (who was also prominent in the mining industry) were trying to interest the Ford Foundation in establishing a fund to provide financial assistance to conservation organizations. Among Albright's 25 cosponsors was Paley, who also served on a Ford Foundation program development committee on natural resources. This committee recommended establishment of an independent resources center to provide up-to-date information in conservation and natural resources and a continuous evaluation of the long-range programs of the federal government. The committee also recommended a White House National Resources Conference, patterned after Theodore Roosevelt's 1908 Conference on Natural Resources.

As a result of these recommendations, the Ford Foundation agreed to back the conference and to set up a research center—for which purpose Paley then turned over his nonprofit corporation, Resources for the Future. At a December 1952 meeting in New York, Albright succeeded in getting President-Elect Dwight D. Eisenhower to agree to sponsor the White House Conference. But shortly after inauguration, the President's Chief of Staff Sherman Adams sought to kill the Conference because, according to Albright, Adams thought he detected a strong odor of "ex-New Dealers," idealists, and planners on the staff and board of directors of Resources for the Future. After Albright and Paley persuaded Lewis W. Douglas, former director of the Bureau of the

Budget and a conservative critic of the New Deal, to serve as Conference chairman, Adams compromised. He agreed that Eisenhower would be the Conference keynote speaker but insisted that the Conference should not be sponsored by the White House. The resulting 3-day Mid-Century Conference on Resources for the Future drew 1,600 participants in December 1953. Although it endorsed no legislative or political proposals, the Conference did call attention to the need for policy changes and continuing research in resources management.

Resources for the Future carried on some of the work of the Paley Commission. Although it could not directly influence government policy and was not ordinarily international in scope, it continued to make long-range projections of the national economy based on population, the labor force, productivity, and other factors. It then tried to predict from these findings the probable resource requirements, and match them against possible supply, with attention to prices. Paley continued to serve on the board of directors and was partly responsible for the inauguration of a major study, published in 1963, *Resources in America's Future, 1960–2000*.

The Eisenhower Administration

Outdoor Recreation Resources Review Commission (*1958*). One of the most successful presidential commissions in recent times—in terms of getting its major recommendations implemented—was the Outdoor Recreation Resources Review Commission, which spanned two administrations. Congress passed the Act establishing the Commission in June 1958 after many years of lobbying by conservation groups. Although the Commission was not established by presidential request, Eisenhower readily signed the law and, after a delay of several months, appointed the respected philanthropist and conservationist Laurance S. Rockefeller Chairman. Eight congressmen and six public figures representing widespread interests in outdoor recreation rounded out the Commission.

Although the timing of the Commission's report of its study violated one of the basic axioms of presidential commissions (don't start a study in one Administration and present the results to a new Administration—especially an Administration of the other political party), almost everything else about the Commission was a perfect example of how a presidential commission can operate to achieve its ends. The law establishing the Commission was carefully drawn so as to involve members of Congress who could later sponsor legislation to carry out the Commission's recommendations. The law provided for the appointment of two majority and two minority members of both the Senate and House Interior Committees. This provision ensured stability in case of changes in congressional assignments.

The law also provided for an Advisory Council composed of the Secretaries of federal departments and the heads of independent agencies with a direct interest and responsibility in outdoor recreation, as well as 25 citizen members covering most interests and geographic areas.

Chairman Rockefeller had national stature and an aptitude for working with Congress, the executive branch, and citizen groups. He attracted a bright, capable staff with administrative abilities (it included the future Governor of Massachusetts and the first head of the National Endowment for the Arts).

The research undertaken by the Commission gave a solid base to its recommendations and was valuable as well as newsworthy. The recommendations included an institution through which Commission goals could be carried out. A follow-on citizen lobbying and information activity was organized by the Commission chairman to stimulate continuous press and public interest and to work for implementation of the recommendations.

The Act creating the Commission set forth three basic goals. They were to determine: (1) the outdoor recreation wants and needs of the American people at that time and for the years 1976 and 2000; (2) the recreation resources of the nation available to satisfy those needs—for the same three periods; and (3) policies and programs that would ensure that present and future needs would be adequately met.

The Commission staff, working with federal agencies and private groups, devised a system of classifying outdoor recreation resources so as to provide a common framework and serve as a tool in recreation management. Particular types of resources and areas would be managed for specific uses such as high density recreation, unique natural areas, wilderness, or historic and cultural sites.

Five joint two-day meetings were held by the Commission with the Advisory Council, during which they made on-site inspections of the various types of federal and state recreation areas, including some where they camped out overnight. When the Commission adopted a draft of its recommendations, they submitted the recommendations to the Advisory Council for additions or changes.

The major items among the 53 recommendations of the Commission were:

- Establishment of a Bureau of Outdoor Recreation in the Department of the Interior to coordinate the recreation activities of the federal agencies, to assist state and local governments with technical aid, to administer a grants-in-aid program for acquisition planning for development and acquisition of needed areas, and to act as a clearinghouse for information.
- Development of a federal grants-in-aid program with initial grants to states of up to 75 percent of the total costs for planning and 40–50 percent of acquisition costs.
- Provision of guidelines for managing areas, with a common system of classifying recreation lands.

When the Commission report was submitted to President Kennedy by Chairman Rockefeller in January 1962, it had the unanimous approval of the 15 commissioners. The timing of its release was propitious. The popularity of outdoor recreation was booming. Federal and state land-management agencies were finding it difficult to cope with the growing numbers of visitors, and Congress welcomed help in devising solutions.

Rockefeller did not leave implementation of the recommendations to chance or political whim. With private funds and the cooperation of the other citizen members of the Commission, he immediately established the Citizens Committee for the Outdoor Recreation Resources Review Commission Report. Two full-time coordinators were hired, both experienced conservationists familiar with congressional procedures. Working principally through citizen groups, the organization concentrated in 1963–64 on acquainting citizens with the Commission's report and stimulating discussion and resolution of public policy issues in the light of its findings and recommendations. A booklet, "Action for Outdoor Recreation for Americans," was widely circulated and served as a follow-up to the report. Leaders of the Senate and House Interior Committees who had served on the Commission introduced legislation to implement its major recommendations.

Congress created the Bureau of Outdoor Recreation in the Department of the Interior to serve as a focal point for outdoor recreation at the federal level and as a liaison point for similar state and local agencies. A Land and Water Conservation Fund was established by Congress to assist states and local governments and federal agencies to acquire land for recreation. The fund was generously endowed with a share of the income from federal offshore oil revenues. In 1964, Congress passed the National Wilderness Act, providing for a national wilderness system, as recommended by the Commission.

President's Commission on National Goals (1960). A year before leaving office, President Eisenhower appointed the President's Commission on National Goals "to develop a broad outline of coordinated policy and programs to set up a series of goals in various areas of national activity." This privately financed activity was sponsored by the American Assembly (Eisenhower had requested that the effort be nonpartisan and have no connection with the government). The 10 members of the Commission were all from the private sector; Henry M. Wriston served as chairman and William P. Bundy as director of the Commission's staff. Approximately 100 people took part in discussions sponsored by the Commission, and 14 individuals submitted essays, which were subsequently published in 1960, just before Eisenhower left office.

The publication's two major sections covered U.S. domestic goals and the U.S. role in the world. There were chapters on education, science, the quality of American culture, and technological change, but there were no formal recommendations, and no follow-up activity took place.

The Kennedy Administration

National Academy of Sciences Committee on Natural Resources (1963). At the suggestion of Presidential Science Adviser Jerome Weisner, President John F. Kennedy announced in a Special Message on Natural Resources, February 1961, that he would be asking the National Academy of Sciences to undertake

a thorough and broadly based study and evaluation of the present state of research underlying the conservation, development, and use of natural resources, how they are formed, replenished and may be substituted for, and giving particular attention to needs for basic research and to projects that will provide a better basis for natural resources planning and policy formulation.

Since Detlev W. Bronk, then President of the National Academy of Sciences, lacked a background in natural resources, he appointed a Committee on Natural Resources to lead the study. The Committee consisted of 13 Academy members, one of whom also represented government, Roger Revelle, then Science Adviser to the Secretary of the Interior. Bronk did not appoint a Committee chairman but convened the organizing sessions himself and gave most of the responsibility for preparing the summary report to John S. Coleman of the Academy staff.

The Committee held a number of seminars led by members of the Committee and each bringing together 20 to 30 experts from government, industry, and academia to discuss issues to be covered in seven reports: Renewable Resources, Water Resources, Environmental Resources (never completed), Mineral Resources, Energy Resources, Marine Resources, and Social and Economic Aspects of Natural Resources. After each seminar, the Committee convened for a week to revise its papers and discuss preparation of a summary document. Although Frank Notestein of the Population Council was a Committee member, no major population-related studies were undertaken. Two of the six completed reports are of special interest here. "Energy Resources" by M. King Hubbert, then employed by the Shell Development Company, estimated the nation's crude oil reserves at about 175 billion barrels. He predicted that production would peak in the late 1960s and that thereafter domestic production and reserves would decline (an estimate that has proved highly accurate). However, Interior's then Assistant Chief Geologist Vincent E. McKelvey, had authored a study for the U.S. Geological Survey which estimated that total domestic oil reserves were on the order of 590 billion barrels. McKelvey predicted that production would not peak for many years and that scarcities would not occur for 30 years or so. As a result of this disagreement, the committee's summary report did not base its recommendations on Hubbert's projections and did not present the oil-depletion issue in a form that made clear the consequences and the course of action that should be taken if Hubbert was correct.

Gilbert White's report "Social and Economic Aspects of Natural Resources" considered the worldwide effects of population growth and distribution on natural resources and also identified the many natural resource areas that required coordination between resource development and the overall welfare of society. White stressed the need to compare demand with supply in both energy and mineral production, to determine who would bear the costs of meeting future energy requirements.

The Committee's summary report to the President made 11 major recommendations, of which the last stressed the need for a small central natural resources group within the federal government. Such a group should be capable of conducting a continuing overall evaluation of research problems related to resources, of bringing to public attention evaluations of natural resources research needs, and of initiating and supporting research that falls outside the interests and competencies of existing agencies. The group should also provide support for international cooperation in resources research.

Submitted to the President in November 1962, the Academy report was referred to Presidential Science Adviser Wiesner, who in turn referred it to the President's Science Advisory Council and the Federal Council for Science and Technology. Whatever interest Wiesner had been able to generate at the presidential level at the beginning of the project had evaporated by the time the report was completed. Although the Academy was eventually asked to design specific programs to implement two of the 11 recommendations, no new research programs were undertaken, and no continuing institution was established.

In the opinion of John Coleman, who was responsible for the summary report, a temporary body such as the Academy's Committee on Natural Resources had little opportunity to build a constituency for its recommendations in Congress or among the public. And without supporters in positions of power or influence, there was no way to implement the findings. The Academy did, however, involve more than one hundred experts in the course of preparing the reports, and Coleman suggests that uncounted benefits came from the attention given to future research problems by these experts.

The Johnson Administration

National Commission on Technology, Automation, and Economic Progress (1964). In the course of its work, the National Commission on Technology, Automation, and Economic Progress (established by Congress in 1964 with 14 members appointed by President Lyndon B. Johnson) considered national goals and a system of social reporting. The Commission's report to the President early in 1966 stated that formation of a national body of distinguished citizens representing diverse interests and constituencies and devoted to a continuing discussion of national goals would be valuable. "Such a body would be concerned with 'monitoring' social change, forecasting possible social trends, and suggesting policy alternatives to deal with them," the report stated. "Its role would not be to plan the future, but to point out what alternatives are achievable and at what cost." Five of the Commission members insisted on including a footnote expressing regret that the report did not explicitly recommend establishing such a national body, but nothing was done about the matter by the President or by Congress.

Public Land Law Review Commission (1965). Many observers believe that inclusion of powerful members of Congress on a commission leads to a high rate of implementation, as in the case of the Outdoor Recreation Resources Review Commission. Perry R. Hagenstein, who was appointed senior staff member of the Public Land Law Review Commission in 1965, believes that having members of Congress on a commission is no guarantee that legislative proposals may ensue.

In a paper "Commissions and Public Land Policies: Setting the Stage for Change" (presented at an April 1977 Denver Conference on the Public Land Law Review Commissions), Hagenstein wrote:

Being party to a commission's report does not bind a member to support its recommendations. Within 48 hours of the release of the [1970] Public Land Law Review Commission report, one of the Commission's influential congressional members had already denounced the report roundly and disassociated himself from some of its major recommendations. In addition, members of Congress face the realities of change too. Although only one of the 13 congressional members of the Public Land Law Review Commission failed to serve in the Congress following release of the Commission's report, six more, including the Chairman, had dropped by the wayside in the next Congress, the 93rd. Today (seven years later) only two members of the PLLRC, the Chairmen of the Senate Energy and Natural Resources Committee and the House Interior and Insular Affairs Committee, remain in Congress.

Hagenstein notes that the Public Land Law Review Commission, although structured along the lines of the Outdoor Recreation Resources Review Commission, was actually not a presidential commission. Twelve of its members, plus the chairman, were chosen by Congress from Congress; there were only six presidential appointees. Hagenstein added:

Participation by the Executive Branch in this predominately congressional effort was necessary to give the Commission credibility with recreation and preservation interests and to gain a semblance of commitment to its recommendations from the Executive Branch itself. Some congressional members found it difficult to separate their public posture in committee hearings and with constituents from the private deliberations at the Commission meetings.

Timing and the political atmosphere also played a part in hampering follow-up to the Public Land Law Review Commission:

It was conceived during President Kennedy's

term, the public members were appointed by President Johnson, and it reported to President Nixon. It had no home in the White House, and its recommendations, many of which were based on criticism of the way in which the laws were being administered, did not have the enthusiastic support of the public land management agencies.
. . .

Chairman [Wayne] Aspinall stated at various times that once the Commission finished its work, the next step would be up to the Congress. . . . Some three months after the 92nd Congress convened and nine months after the Commission's report had been filed, H.R. 7211, a bill that put a number of the Commission recommendations in a cumbersome package, was introduced by Chairman Aspinall. The bill in its entirety had a constituency of one, although that one, Aspinall, was in a position as Chairman of the Interior and Insular Affairs Committee to make the bill move. . . . Power in the Congress accumulates slowly, but erodes rapidly, and Aspinall was unable to bring H.R. 7211 to a floor vote following his defeat in a primary some weeks before the 92nd Congress adjourned. Faced with its own problems of timing, elections and politics, the Congress is not the place to center responsibility for follow-up.

Toward a Social Report (1967) and Other Studies of the Mid-1960s. Johnson's Secretary of Health, Education, and Welfare John Gardner became interested in social indicators and persuaded the President to assign to his Department the task of developing "the necessary social statistics and indicators to supplement those prepared by the Bureau of Labor Statistics and the Council of Economic Advisers. With these yardsticks we can better measure the distance we have come and plan the way ahead." Johnson so directed in his Message to Congress on Domestic Health and Education.

Under prodding from HEW Under Secretary Wilbur J. Cohen, Assistant Secretary for Planning William Gorham hired Mancur Olson in 1967 as Deputy Assistant Secretary for Social Indicators, to lead in preparing a social report. With the help of a panel cochaired by social scientist Daniel Bell and HEW Assistant Secretary Alice M. Rivlin, Olson sought to devise a system of social indicators—which he defined as measures of the level of well-being in a society—for measuring the social progress or retrogression of the nation. The study was scheduled to be completed in mid-1969, but when President Johnson announced he would not run again and Richard M. Nixon was elected, Olson rushed the study to completion ahead of schedule so it could be published before Johnson left office. The document, "Toward a Social

Report," was submitted to the President by HEW Secretary Wilbur Cohen nine days before Johnson left office.

Three of its seven chapters were titled: "Health and Illness" (Are we becoming healthier?); "Our Physical Environment" (Are conditions improving?); and "Public Order and Safety" (What is the impact of crime on our lives?) A final chapter discussed the need for continuing studies of social indicators and how to apply them in formulating policy.

Although no institutional apparatus for policy-making resulted from "Toward a Social Report," one of the members of the Panel on Social Indicators, Daniel Patrick Moynihan, continued to advocate social reporting when appointed Counselor to President Nixon in 1969. Also, the Census Bureau representative to the Social Indicators Panel, Julius Shiskin, went on to the Office of Management and Budget (OMB), where he headed the staff that produced the OMB report "Social Indicators of 1973." (An updated version, "Social Indicators of 1976," was issued by OMB in December 1977.)

The mid-1960s saw two other efforts in the social area. In 1967, Senator Walter G. Mondale, supported by 10 other senators, introduced "The Full Opportunity and Social Accounting Act," which proposed a Council of Social Advisers in the Executive Office of the President, and the publication for transmittal to Congress of an annual Social Report by the President, similar to the yearly Economic Report of the Council of Economic Advisers. The Mondale bill twice passed the Senate (in 1970 and 1972), but no action was ever taken by the House.

In the private sector, Daniel Bell organized the Commission on the Year 2000, funded by the Carnegie Corporation and run by the American Academy of Arts and Sciences. About 30 prominent social scientists and other experts concerned about preparations for the future and alternative policy choices held working sessions for three days in 1965 and for two days in 1966. During 1967 they contributed papers and participated in the discussions of eight working parties. The Commission's 350-page report, "Toward the Year 2000: Work in Progress," was widely distributed after publication as the entire Summer 1967 issue of *Daedalus,* the journal of the American Academy of Arts and Sciences.

This private-sector commission made no formal recommendations, however. According to Bell, the Commission avoided issues related to natural resources, environment, and population because there were too many variables. Instead, the Commission tried to identify technological trends in terms of a 10-year lead time. And they also looked at changes in social frameworks, such as those in a postindustrial society.

The Last Decade

National Environmental Policy Act of 1969

Improving the quality of the environment has been the objective of a number of laws passed by Congress and executive orders issued by Presidents in the last two decades. Only one law, however, served to provide for a long-range, holistic approach to decision-making throughout the government and established an institution that had the potential, on paper at least, for advising the President on how to prepare for some of the problems of the future. This law, the National Environmental Policy Act of 1969, required "environmental impact statements" by the responsible official for all major federal actions "significantly affecting the quality of the human environment." It also provided for establishing in the Executive Office of the President a three-member Council on Environmental Quality.

The legislation was developed by congressional committees without assistance from the Nixon White House. While Congress was considering the legislation, President Nixon had established by executive order his own Cabinet-level Environmental Quality Council in May 1969.

Nixon's Council consisted of the President as Chairman, the Vice President (serving as Chairman in the President's absence), the Secretaries of six Departments—Agriculture; Commerce; Health, Education, and Welfare; Housing and Urban Development; Interior; and Transportation—and the Science Adviser to the President, who was named Executive Secretary. The general purpose of the Council was to "assist the President with respect to environmental quality matters." One of its specific duties was to "review the adequacy of existing systems for monitoring and predicting environmental changes so as to achieve effective coverage and efficient use of facilities and other resources." The Cabinet-level Council met only a few times and accomplished very little.

Congress ignored White House opposition and passed the National Environmental Policy Act in December 1969. The Act was signed into law on January 1, 1970, by the President, who subsequently dropped his Cabinet-level council and appointed three members to the new Council on Environmental Quality required by the Act.

Council on Environmental Quality

As a declaration of national environmental policy, Section 101 (b) of the 1969 Act provided that:

it is the continuing responsibility of the Federal Government to use all practicable means, consistent with other essential considerations of national policy, to improve and coordinate Federal plans, functions, programs, and resources to the end that the Nation may—

(1) fulfill the responsibilities of each generation as trustee of the environment for succeeding generations;

(2) assure for all Americans safe, healthful, productive, and esthetically and culturally pleasing surroundings;

(3) attain the widest range of beneficial uses of the environment without degradation, risk to health or safety, or other undesirable and unintended consequences;

(4) preserve important historic, cultural, and natural aspects of our national heritage, and maintain, wherever possible, an environment which supports diversity and variety of individual choice;

(5) achieve a balance between population and resource use which will permit high standards of living and a wide sharing of life's amenities;

(6) enhance the quality of renewable resources and approach the maximum attainable recycling of depletable resources.

In preparing environmental impact statements, responsible federal officials were required to include:

- The environmental impact of the proposed action;
- Any adverse environmental effects which cannot be avoided should the proposal be implemented;
- Alternatives to the proposed action;
- The relationship between local short-term uses of man's environment and the maintenance and enhancement of long-term productivity;
- Any irreversible and irretrievable commitments of resources which would be involved in the proposed action should it be implemented.

The Council on Environmental Quality was specifically given the duty "to develop and recommend to the President national policies to foster and promote the improvement of environmental quality to meet the conservation, social, economic, health, and other requirements and goals of the Nation" and also to assist and advise the President in the preparation of an annual Environmental Quality Report.

The annual report was to set forth such things as

• Current and foreseeable trends in the quality, management and utilization of such environments and the effects of those trends on the social, economic, and other requirements of the Nation; and

• The adequacy of available natural resources for fulfilling human and economic requirements of the Nation in the light of expected population pressures.

Another section of the National Environmental Policy Act required that all agencies of the federal government should

recognize the worldwide and long-range character of environmental problems and, where consistent with the foreign policy of the United States, lend appropriate support to initiatives, resolutions, and programs designed to maximize international cooperation in anticipating and preventing a decline in the quality of the environment.

While there have been efforts over the past seven years to carry out these basic provisions of the Act, its implementation has been far less than its framers intended. Federal officials have in most cases followed the letter of the law's requirement that they consider the environmental impact of major decisions and alternative courses of action that might be better for the nation. However, only rarely have officials submitted such statements *before a decision is made,* as the law requires.

While President Nixon did not include the Council on Environmental Quality among his foremost advisers, he relied on it to prepare his environmental legislative program. The Council performed other useful functions in developing major new studies, reviewing international environmental activities, coordinating domestic environmental activities, and overseeing the environmental impact statement process.

National Goals Research Staff (1969)

In July 1969, President Nixon established a National Goals Research Staff in the White House. The impetus came largely from Daniel Patrick Moynihan, then counselor to the President and head of the newly created Urban Affairs Council, operating out of the White House basement.*

The National Goals Research Staff consisted of a small group of experts, whose primary task was to prepare a report annually, at least until 1976, setting forth some of the key policy choices facing the nation, together with the consequences of those choices. The goals group was not a planning agency; it was to provide information and analysis so that those making decisions "might have a better idea of the direction in which events are moving, the seeming pace of those movements, and alternative directions and speeds that possibly could be achieved, were policies to be shifted in one direction or another." That statement, by Moynihan, prefaced the first report of the Goals Research Staff, published on July 4, 1970, under the title "Toward Balanced Growth; Quantity with Quality."

Moynihan had conceived of the report as a social report, rather than an inventory of natural resources or collection of statistics. In the announcement of July 1969, President Nixon said the new Goals Staff would for the first time create within the White House "a unit specifically charged with the long perspective; it promises to provide the research tools with which we at last can deal with the future in an informed and informative way." The President also said the Goals Staff would provide for "new mechanisms which can enable government to respond to emerging needs early enough so that the response can be effective."

The functions of the National Goals Research Staff were to include

forecasting future developments, and assessing the longer-range consequences of present social trends; measuring the probable future impact of alternative courses of action, including measuring the degree to which change in one area would be likely to affect another; estimating the actual range of social choice—that is, what alternative sets of goals might be attainable, in light of the availability of resources and possible rates of progress; developing and monitoring social indicators that can reflect the present and future quality of American life, and the direction and rate of its change; summarizing, integrating, and correlating the results of related research activities being carried on within the various Federal agencies, and by State and local governments and private organizations.

The President announced that the first assignment of the new group would be to assemble data

---

*Moynihan had been aiming at such a futures study since his first days in office, when he had appointed an Urban Affairs Research Committee to develop projections and forecasts with a comprehensive, long-range perspective on

trends and to study the most probable longer-range consequences of major policy alternatives, as well as to anticipate developments for "an improved assessment of current priorities . . . useful in articulating feasible national goals."

that could help illumine the possible range of national goals for the nation's 1976 Bicentennial. The public report to be delivered by July 4, 1970—and annually thereafter— would make possible discussion of key choices and their consequences

while there still is time to make the choices effective. . . . Only shortly beyond the 200th anniversary lies the year 2000. These dates, together, can be targets for our aspirations. Our need now is to seize on the future as the key dimension in our decisions, and to chart that future as consciously as we are accustomed to charting the past.

Even before release of the President's statement, a power struggle had arisen within the White House over who would direct this goals research: Would it be Moynihan as Executive Secretary of the Council for Urban Affairs? Or would it be Arthur Burns, also a Counselor to the President and head of the Office of Program Development? Nixon solved the controversy by naming his Special Consultant, Leonard Garment, director of the National Goals Research Staff. Garment found out about his new "job" shortly before leaving on a long trip to the Soviet Union to set up a cultural exchange program. When he returned, he brought in some futures experts, including the Hudson Institute's Herman Kahn, the Harvard Business School's Raymond Bauer, and Brookings Institution's Director Charles Schultz, to assist him in setting up the group.

Garment soon encountered difficulties in implementing his task, as funds for the project were limited, and it was necessary to borrow some of the 10 members of the staff from federal agencies. He hired Bauer as senior consultant and staff report coordinator and appointed Charles Williams of the National Science Foundation as staff director. Garment, who modestly claimed "my main job was to protect the work," had the President's ear and was able to maintain Mr. Nixon's support, although he had to bypass the normal channels to keep the President informed of the Goals Staff's activities.

One of the early ideas was to build a network among state, regional, and local planning groups in order to obtain ideas about national goals through interaction with citizens. This effort was discontinued after one public hearing because of opposition from the White House staff. The Goals Staff, however, was able to bring in consultants in various fields.

Some work was done with the Bureau of the Budget's Office of Statistical Policy in developing regularly published social statistics using available data, but this work was not published in the 1970 report. No efforts were made to include foreign policy issues, as in the Eisenhower Commission on National Goals.

The Goals Staff worked instead on a relatively few issues; it tried to define the questions, analyze the "emerging" debates, and examine the alternative sets of consequences. Garment believes that the main strength of the goals work was its bringing forward for debate some issues which were ahead of their time, such as national growth policy, revenue sharing, and technology assessment. Civil rights, the Vietnam war, and other issues with which the public was already preoccupied were entirely ignored.

Even with the program's shortcomings, the July 4, 1970, "Toward Balanced Growth" provided a springboard for national debate on a number of vital issues. The report concentrated on population growth and distribution, environment, education, basic natural science, technology assessment, consumerism and economic choice, and balanced growth:

Confronted with the trend toward ever greater concentration of a growing population in already crowded metropolitan regions, should we accept the present trend? Or, if not, to what extent should the focus of public policy be on encouraging the spread of population into sparsely populated areas, fostering the growth of existing middle-sized cities and towns, or experimenting with the development of new cities outside of existing metropolitan areas? Given the present threat to our natural environment, how should we balance changes in patterns of production and consumption with new means of waste disposal or recycling—and how should be allocate the costs? Should they be borne by producers, by consumers, by the general public—or by what combination of these? How can consumer protection best be advanced without so interfering with the market mechanism as to leave the consumer worse off in the long run?

The report, published without White House or Bureau of the Budget interference, made some bold statements. For instance:

FHA and VA mortgage insurance, the interstate highway system, Federal and State tax policies, State and local land use programs, all contributed to the massive suburbanization of the last 25 years.

Defense contract awards have accelerated the population booms in Southern California and along the Gulf Coast.

Agricultural research and support programs have accelerated depletion of the rural population.

These policies make individually positive contributions to society, but their collective impact may not be desirable from the standpoint of distribution of population and economic opportunity.

The discussion in the population section was even more bold:

A considerable number of population experts strongly endorse the goal of a zero rate of increase—that is, a stationary population—as soon as we can achieve it. This means that in the interest of society, all American families should have an average of two children. Even many of those who do not see the problem as pressing see this as a desirable goal.

This choice implies a significant change in public policy. It calls for a deliberate government effort to promote the reduction in the growth rate until population stability is achieved. It also implies that we must not leave the possibility of population stability to chance. It means we may have to do more than rely upon liberalized abortion laws in the States, and upon the distribution of free contraceptives to the poor, who are the focus of most U.S. family-planning programs. We may also have to devise ways of changing individual and social attitudes, governmental policies and incentives, and through these, the motivation of young people and adults in all socio-economic groups.

Even if the country elects the goal of arresting the growth of U.S. population by the end of the century, it is not at all clear whether or not the Government can bring about a societal consensus voluntarily to control the growth of the U.S. population within a generation. More active public policies might be required than "moral encouragement." Changes in tax laws and health insurance programs might help. An extreme form of an active public policy would be to regulate family size by fiat. Some persons have even gone so far as to suggest enforced sterilization when each family reaches its maximum allowance. Less drastic forms of coercion could be devised. But whatever the form, coercion in the regulation of family size is likely to be unacceptable to the American people."

Several months before publication of the report, Garment and Williams formed an ad hoc committee to evaluate the possibilities for setting up an institute or organization in the private sector that would be the equivalent of the governmental goals effort. Williams discovered that the Senior Executive Council of the Conference Board was already considering something along similar lines. At a White House meeting chaired by Garment in March 1970 and attended by a half dozen private

sector leaders, the Conference Board's Executive Council agreed to study the possibility of putting together a Center for National Goals. White House officials said that President Nixon would announce formation of the institution when he issued the first National Goals Report on July 4, 1970. The private sector representatives did not believe that they could get a structure ready in so short a time. The timing problem did not develop, however, because no presidential statement was issued on July 4.

In June, a month before the Goals Research Staff's report was due to be published, the staff found out that its first report would also be its last. The President had decided to create a Domestic Council under John Ehrlichman, who felt the Domestic Council could carry on any additional goals and alternatives work. (In fact, however, it did not perform truly long-range policy analysis.)

The National Goals Research Staff was disbanded when the July 4, 1970, report was completed. Moynihan had prepared an introductory statement for the President to sign, but the President decided he should not be so directly associated with the report, and the Moynihan introduction appeared as a "statement of the Counselor to the President." The document emerged, finally, as a report from the National Goals Research Staff to the President.

The report was published just before the Fourth of July, while the President was in California, and no presidential statement was issued. Press coverage was accordingly light.

Proposal for a Center for National Goals and Alternatives (1970)

With the White House goals mission apparently ended, the Senior Executives Council, an advisory group to the Conference Board (an independent nonprofit business research organization) nevertheless decided to continue its investigation of the possibilities for a private sector effort for establishing national goals. The Council is composed of 36 chief executives, 25 of them from business and the rest from universities, foundations, and public institutions. They finance their own studies and activities and operate independently of the Conference Board. Board President H. Bruce Palmer was interested in the subject, having been one of the sponsors for the formation of the Institute for the Future. The Senior Executives Council put up $60,000 to study the best design for such an organization, and the National Endowment for the Humanities contributed $9,800 for the study. Willis W. Harman of the Stanford Research Institute was selected to do a 4-month analysis, assisted by representatives from Arthur D. Little Company, the Institute for the Future, the Center for a Voluntary Society, the Senior Executives Council, and Anthony Wiener of the Hudson Institute, who had been a research consultant for the National Goals Research Staff.

In December 1970, the Harman group submitted its report to the steering committee of the Senior Executives Council. The report proposed forming a Center for National Goals and Alternatives. The essential function of the proposed Center would be to address four basic issues: (1) how to understand the processes of social change, interpret the present moment in history, and anticipate the consequences of alternative actions; (2) how to explore the range of attainable social choices; (3) how best to clarify bases for value choices and goals selection; and (4) how to identify, evaluate, and implement alternative policies and strategies. The Center, at least in theory, would be free of domination by any power group; it would foster an interdisciplinary approach and would have a permanent staff as well as visiting fellows, scholars, and interns. Joint involvement of public, private, and voluntary sectors would be provided through the mechanism of a Forum that would give a broad representational base for steering the Center and would ensure objectivity and promote credibility. Forum members would select a third of the members of the Board of Trustees. The estimated budget was $7.5 million for the first three years, and $5 million per year after that. Two-thirds of the budget would be obtained from nongovernment sources, one-third from the federal government.

The Conference Board's Senior Executive's Council asked Erik Jonsson of Texas Instruments, former Mayor of Dallas and head of Goals for Dallas, to assess the viability of the proposal for a Center. In answer to questions raised by Jonsson's assessment, Harman prepared a paper justifying the need to discover whether the future would be more or less an unbroken extrapolation of the past, or whether, after a tumultuous period of a few decades, radical societal change would be required.

In the absence of any solid knowledge on which the nation could base its choice of a course to follow, Harman felt the Center should formulate means with which to examine national goals, priorities, and policies in both contexts. In support of the need for approaches to meet radical societal changes, he presented a table showing how "successes" of the technological era had resulted in

problems for the future because they had been "too successful," inferring, that we had not prepared in advance to cope with the results. For instance:

Prolonging the life span had resulted in overpopulation and problems of the aged.

Weapons for national defense had resulted in the hazard of mass destruction through nuclear and biological weapons.

Replacement of manual and routine labor by machines had exacerbated unemployment; efficiency had resulted in dehumanization of the world of work.

Growth in the power of systematized knowledge produced threats to privacy and freedom, and erected a knowledge barrier to the underprivileged.

Affluence had increased per capita environmental impact, pollution and energy shortages.

Satisfaction of basic needs had produced a worldwide revolution of rising expectations, rebellion against nonmeaningful work, and unrest among affluent students.

Although Jonsson's review of the Harman proposal approved the technical basis of the proposed organization, some members of the Senior Executives Council raised questions, and further study was ordered in 1971 under the guidance of Robert O. Anderson, chairman of the Board of the Atlantic Richfield Company and new head of the Senior Executives Council. The proposal was accordingly refined to create an Institute for National Objectives—A Center for Integrative Studies of National Policies, Priorities, and Alternatives. Its 12- to 30-man Board of Trustees would include representatives from the Administration, Congress, and the National Science Foundation, and perhaps one or more governors or mayors. Involvement of public, private, and voluntary sectors would be reinforced through an Advisory Council of up to 50 members elected for 3-year terms, plus about 20 members elected by the Advisory Council itself. Business, foundations, and labor and voluntary organizations would be asked to participate in funding; half the initial $10 million would be sought from the National Science Foundation, the National Institutes of Health, Congress, and other federal sources.

Robert O. Anderson and Erik Jonsson presented the proposal for the new Institute to the President in January 1972. Nixon agreed that something should be done. He felt that a government effort would be viewed as political, but if the Institute originated as a private organization, he would see that government funds were made available. He put John Ehrlichman in charge of Administration cooperation for the project. Nixon said that the Institute's sponsors would have to be credible and outside of politics, and that the money would have to come from several pockets.

Although some members of the Senior Executives Council still expressed reservations, $115,000 was raised initially. Robert Anderson placed the project under Joseph Slater, head of the Aspen Institute for Humanistic Studies (Anderson serves as board chairman of the Institute), but Slater was unable to get the necessary additional funding from foundations, and the project, as proposed by the Senior Executives Council, was terminated. However, the Aspen Institute developed the concept in its own way, proposing an Institute for Analysis of Public Choices, free of all federal ties. The proposal was submitted to Nelson Rockefeller in 1973 and, according to Slater, influenced the direction Rockefeller took when he started his Commission on Critical Choices for Americans. The Aspen Institute is now seeking to turn many of its own programs toward developing analysis of choices in decision-making.

Commission on Population Growth and the American Future (1970)

In July 1969 President Nixon sent to Congress a historic first population message, recommending the establishment by legislation of a blue-ribbon commission to examine the growth of the nation's population and the impact it will have on the American future. John D. Rockefeller III, who had started the Population Council, had been urging since the early days of the Eisenhower Administration that such a commission be established. Lyndon Johnson had refused to see Rockefeller in 1964, but by 1968, he was ready to yield to pressure and established the President's Committee on Population and Family Planning, co-chaired by Rockefeller and HEW Secretary Wilbur Cohen.

The Committee established by President Johnson was not a full-blown commission. Its report, sent to the President at the end of 1968, "Population and Family Planning: The Transition from Concern to Action," suggested the establishment of a presidential commission to give the problem further study. It recommended that family planning services be extended to every American woman unable to afford them. It also recommended an increase in the budgets of HEW and the Office of Economic Opportunity for the purpose of population research. The report was released without publicity in January 1969, just

before Johnson left office. He did not meet with the Committee to receive the report, nor make a statement on it.

In early 1969, Rockefeller's pressure for a presidential commission was abetted by presidential Counselor Moynihan, who convinced Nixon that the time had come to face the problems of population. The President asked in his message to Congress that a Commission be assigned to develop population projections and estimate the impact of an anticipated 100 million increase in U.S. population by the year 2000. For the interim, the President called for more research "on birth control methods" and for the establishment, as a national goal, of "the provision of adequate family planning services within the next five years for all those who want them but cannot afford them." In his message to Congress, Nixon stated:

One of the most serious challenges to human destiny in the last third of this century will be the growth of the population. Whether man's response to that challenge will be a cause for pride or for despair in the year 2000 will depend very much on what we do today. If we now begin our work in an appropriate manner, and if we continue to devote a considerable amount of attention and energy to this problem, then mankind will be able to surmount this challenge as it has surmounted so many during the long march of civilization.

When the Congress passed a bill in March 1970 creating the Commission on Population Growth and the American Future, President Nixon named John D. Rockefeller III chairman of the 24-member group, which included four women, two college students, three blacks, two senators, and two representatives. About 20 full-time professionals and 10 consultants supervised a 2-year effort which resulted in the release of a controversial final report in March 1972, plus seven volumes of research papers. More than 100 research projects were conducted, and more than 100 witnesses testified at public hearings in Washington, Los Angeles, Little Rock, Chicago, and New York. Additional information concerning public attitudes was obtained through a special detailed public opinion poll.

The Commission's conclusion was that no substantial benefits would result from continued growth of the nation's population:

The population problem, and the growth ethic with which it is intimately connected, reflect deeper external conditions and more fundamental political, economic, and philosophical values. Consequently, to improve the quality of our existence while slowing growth, will require nothing less than a basic recasting of American values.

The more than 60 Population Commission recommendations included:

- Creation of an Office of Population Growth and Distribution within the Executive Office of the President;
- Establishment, within the National Institutes of Health, of a National Institute of Population Sciences to provide an adequate institutional framework for implementing a greatly expanded program of population research;
- Legislation by Congress establishing a Council of Social Advisers, with one of the main functions the monitoring of demographic variables;
- The addition of a mid-decade census of the population; and
- National planning for a stabilized population.

These recommendations were overshadowed, at least in the publicity given them, by the recommendations that states adopt legislation permitting minors "to receive contraceptive and prophylactic information and services in appropriate settings sensitive to their needs and concerns" and "that present state laws restricting abortion be liberalized along the lines of the New York statute, such abortion to be performed on request by duly licensed physicians under conditions of medical safety." The Commission also recommended that abortion be covered by health insurance benefits, and that federal, state, and local governments make funds available to support abortion in states with liberalized statutes.

President Nixon was unhappy with the Commission report, released in March 1972 at the beginning of his re-election campaign, largely because of the recommendations on liberalized abortion and the furnishing of contraceptives to teen-agers (which in 1972 was a bigger issue than abortion). The President met only a few minutes with Mr. Rockefeller. He perfunctorily received the Commission report, but issued a statement repudiating it. No word of support was forthcoming for the stabilized population concept that he had backed in 1969.

Although all members of the Commission showed their support for the report by signing it, several members wrote minority statements about certain recommendations, especially the one on abortion. The Commission debated whether to finesse the two controversial issues, since these recommendations were not of major demographic importance. But Chairman Rockefeller felt it was only right that the majority of the Commission be able to state an opinion on all relevant issues.

"We went ahead, realizing we would get our heads cut off," said the staff director, Charles Westoff. "But we hadn't quite appreciated how much these recommendations were going to dominate the response to the report."

The timing of the report was unfortunate in that during the three years since Nixon's population message, the public had come to agree on stabilizing population growth, and the goal of the two-child family was already being achieved in the statistics.

No recommendations were made by the Commission in the resources and environment areas.

The Commission staff chose a basis methodology for its extensive research efforts, which were published in six large volumes. The research was organized basically around one simple question: What difference will it make if the U.S. population grows at a two-child per family rate, or if it grows at a three-child per family rate? This approach was adopted in all research efforts except where it was not appropriate, as in migration studies. The research documents used U.S. Bureau of the Census statistics in its projections, and extensive new data on these assumptions was supplied by the Bureau of Economic Analysis of the Department of Commerce.

Volume III, *Population, Resources and the Environment*, contained extensive research on the relative impacts of the two growth scenarios on resources and the environment. Chapters were devoted to: the economy; resource requirements and pollution levels; energy; outdoor recreation and congestion; agriculture, population, and the environment; future water needs and supplies; urban scale and environmental quality; and ecological perspectives.

The other volumes covered: *Demographic and Social Aspects of Population Growth* (Vol. I); *Economic Aspects of Population Change* (II); *Governance and Population: The Governmental Implications of Population Change* (IV); *Population Distribution and Policy* (V); *Aspects of Population Growth Policy* (VI). Research on global population and resources was not a part of the Commission mandate.

Despite the lack of White House support, Commission members and staff sought ways to disseminate to the public the findings of the report and the research materials. Chairman Rockefeller testified before congressional hearings. A privately financed Citizens Committee on Population and the American Future, formed after release of the report, took the leading role in spreading the findings; it tried to create a dialogue on the issues and lobbied in Congress for passage of some of the recommendations. It also sponsored two large conferences.

A privately financed film version of the Population Commission report, which had been in preparation for more than a year, was issued about six months after the Commission made its report and received wide distribution. It was shown over the National Educational Television network, a number of individual TV stations, and by many schools. A set of teaching materials was prepared for the classroom use. The film stressed the impacts of too much population and did not dwell on the Commission's recommendations.

The deputy director of the Population Commission staff, Robert Parke, felt that the report and the research volumes made a strong base for future efforts at meeting population growth problems. And he believed the Commission and its staff had learned at least one valuable lesson: A commission studying a controversial subject should not publish its report during a presidential campaign.

National Commission on Materials Policy (1970)

Congress legislated a new National Commission on Materials Policy in the fall of 1970 as a part of the Resources Recovery Act. Although the chief sponsor of the Commission was a Republican, J. Caleb Boggs, of Delaware, the White House did not look with favor on the Commission, and President Nixon delayed almost a year before appointing the five public members to join the Secretaries of Interior and Commerce. There were three Secretaries of Commerce during the term of the Commission. Only the first, Maurice Stans, attended Commission meetings; the last, Frederick Dent, issued a separate statement disagreeing with many of the Commission's major recommendations. Secretary of the Interior Rogers Morton did not personally attend meetings.

Commission Chairman Jerome Klaff was head of a secondary materials processing company; Staff Director James Boyd was a former director of the Bureau of Mines and, at the time, head of a mining company. A full-time staff of 25 was hired.

The Materials Policy Commission did not attempt a materials resources inventory and update of the Paley Commission but rather concentrated its attention on the policy area and emphasized the environmental aspects of resources problems, an area which the Paley Commission had ignored. The new Commission contracted for a study of the estimated demand for 10 commodities to the year 2000. A report was made on basic mineral stocks, reserves, production data, consumption, and exports for selected foreign countries, including the People's Republic of China, the Soviet Union, and the East European countries, none of which had been considered by the Paley Commission of 1951. A number of other reports were prepared by independent contractors.

Advisory panels from industry participated by submitting information and assisting with more than a dozen meetings and hearings conducted around the nation. Federal agencies also supplied data and analysis.

The summary report of the National Materials Policy Commission and its special publications have proved useful to a number of federal agencies and to industry. As with earlier studies, the involvement of several hundred public officials and industry participants helped to educate a sizable cadre in the need for forward-looking analyses.

The major recommendations of the Commission, when it reported to the President and Congress in June 1973, were mostly general policy directives:

Strike a balance between the "need to produce goods" and the "need to protect the environment" by modifying the materials system so that all resources, including environmental, are paid for by users. Strive for an equilibrium between the supply of materials and the demand for their use by increasing primary materials production and by conserving materials through accelerated waste recycling and greater efficiency-of-use of materials. Manage materials policy more effectively by recognizing the complex interrelationships of the materials—energy—environment system so that laws, executive orders, and administrative practices reinforce policy and not counteract it.

More specific recommendations of the Commission included creation of a comprehensive Cabinet-level agency for materials, energy, and the environment, and the formation of a joint committee of Congress having legislative jurisdiction roughly parallel to the proposed new agency.

By the time the Commission report was completed, the Commission's chief sponsor in the Senate had been defeated in a bid for re-election, and the White House, for its part, showed no interest in publicizing the report.

After release of the report in June 1973, Staff Director Boyd set up a small office on his own (with some financial help from his company) to follow through on the Commission study and to try to get some of the recommendations implemented. Much of the follow-up was done by working with members of Congress, congressional staffs, and federal agencies, with Boyd testifying at congressional hearings on the usefulness of the report and the need for implementation of some of the recommendations.

Because the report had appeared after passage of the Federal Advisory Committee Act, the Administration was required by law to at least respond to the findings. A task group and subcommittee of the President's Domestic Council drafted an executive branch response which noted that some of the recommendations were simplistic and subjective, that some were inappropriately worded or did not reflect ongoing activities in the executive agencies, and that there was no clear ordering of priorities in the report. The White House position was that regular program activities of the Department of the Interior and the Environmental Protection Agency would accomplish most of the actions recommended by the Commission, and that a separate mechanism to insure their implementation was unnecessary. An Interior Department spokesman pointed out at a congressional hearing that many of the Commission's 177 recommendations were encompassed by nine broader recommendations in the Secretary of the Interior's June 1973 Second Annual Report under the Mining and Minerals Policy Act of 1970.

A report by the General Accounting Office (GAO) entitled "Better Followup System Needed to Deal with Recommendations by Study Commissions in the Federal Government" (RED–76–33, Dec. 4, 1975), used the Materials Policy Commission as one of its four examples.

GAO criticized the White House response document for not being specific regarding the nature and timing of the action to be taken "and therefore it cannot be considered an effective vehicle for implementing the recommendations." It pointed to one recommendation in the Commission report calling for "improved utilization and conservation of groundwater through early completion of surveys of the Nation's major aquifers, using them for planning the optimum management of ground and surface supplies, and monitoring aquifers from which substantial withdrawals are being made." The executive branch response, according to GAO, was confined to its concurrence in principle and stated that "Interior and Agriculture are working toward these ends. Increased activity will be required."

GAO added that other responses to recommendations with which the executive branch expressed concurrence or concurrence in principle described the actions to be taken in general language such as "current efforts are under way," "efforts are being made," or "interested agencies are fully involved in the question," but gave no further particulars. GAO concluded:

We believe that the results of the study on a national materials policy could have been more beneficial if it had been directed to more specific problem areas and had specified recommended actions. Also, preparation of an executive branch response, as required by the Federal Advisory Committee Act, is not enough to insure successful implementation of a study commission's report. Effective machinery for implementation and follow through must be established and monitored at the highest level in the executive branch.

One of the Commission members, University of Indiana political scientist Lynton K. Caldwell, disagreed that this Commission, or any other, should try to be too specific or try to dictate legislation. "Anyone who has been around Government knows that the surest way to kill something is to make it so specific that no one else can ever adopt it as his own," Caldwell has said. "People feel inclined to reject specific recommendations so they can come up with something that reflects exactly what they want to do."

Some observers felt that the report would have been more influential if the Commission's chairman had been more nationally prominent. The general problem of a commission having been imposed on the President by legislation without his concurrence also worked against its effectiveness. The stated disagreements of Commission member Frederick Dent (the Secretary of Commerce) were detrimental.

National Growth Policy Reports (1972, 1974, and 1976)

Section 703(a) of the 1970 Housing and Urban Development Act directed the President, "in order to assist in the development of a National Urban Growth Policy, to prepare every even-numbered year beginning with 1972 a 'Report on Urban Growth.'" The Act called for the report to include identification of significant trends and developments, a summary of significant problems facing the nation as a result of these trends, a statement of current and foreseeable needs in the areas served by policies, plans, and programs designed to carry out an urban growth policy, and recommendations for programs and policies for carrying out the urban growth policy.

Members of the Nixon Administration opposed this part of the legislation, claiming they were working out policy for urban and national growth in their own way, chiefly through the Cabinet Committee on National Growth Policy, appointed by President Nixon and chaired by the Secretary of Housing and Urban Development (HUD) and including the Secretaries of Agriculture, Commerce, Labor, and Transportation, the Chairman of the Council of Economic Advisers, and the Director of the Office of Economic Opportunity. The Administration also disliked the Act's specific provision that the Domestic Council was to be "adequately organized and staffed for the purpose [of carrying out the legislative mandate]."

John Ehrlichman, as head of the Domestic Council, decided early in 1971 that the biennial report should be assigned to the Department of Housing and Urban Development. The resulting draft report featured a number of new housing and urban initiatives that HUD Secretary George Romney hoped to institute, with a budget-busting price tag. Ehrlichman rejected the report and had the Domestic Council revise it completely. The report the President submitted to Congress in February 1972 bore little resemblance to what Congress had envisioned. It was called a "Report on National Growth." The introductory statement explained that the term "national urban growth policy" was too narrow. Instead, the report would cover national growth policy, "recognizing that rural and urban community development are inseparably linked." The report also interpreted the 1970 Act narrowly, pointing out that the statute required only that the report "assist in the development" of national policy; it was not required to "enunciate" such policy.

Most of the 1972 report featured Census Bureau statistics about population growth and distribution, a recitation of the Nixon Administration's achievements in its first two years, and promotional descriptions of White House proposals then before Congress, including a proposed Department of Community Development, general and special revenue sharing, national land use planning, powerplant siting, and welfare reform.

Before the 1974 report was prepared, Ehrlichman sent a detailed questionnaire to the Secretaries of HUD, Transportation, HEW, and Commerce. Among the 135 questions were these:

Is there any reliable estimate of alternative futures for the country in the absence of a national growth policy?

Are there growth objectives which can safely be said to have widespread or universal support which are not being promoted by present Federal policy?

How do we define the national interest—how do we balance the relative weights of economic, social, and other considerations?

To what extent should a national growth policy attempt to achieve welfare and social goals?

The small group at HUD preparing the 1974 report was never furnished the answers to this questionnaire. They were told by the White House, only to avoid putting in any new policy recommendations. The draft went from HUD to the White House late in 1973, but no action was taken for almost a year. Then the Domestic Council under President Gerald Ford revised the draft and submitted it to Congress under the title "Report on National Growth and Development." It came out early in 1975, almost a year late, and contributed little to any analysis of future national growth problems or preparations to meet them. It listed 13 "national goals related to growth" (one sentence per goal), and stated that the policymakers' task was to understand how and whether present and proposed actions would affect these goals. This would require "systematic review in the course of decision-making of the possible effects, not just on the mission goal of each decision-maker, but on other national goals as well; and improved evaluation of existing activities with emphasis on both attainment of the mission goal and effects on other goals."

The report concluded that such evaluation was "much easier said than done." It then suggested developing an agreed-upon set of guidelines for the decision-making process. It did not, however, produce any such guidelines.

The 1976 report, without measuring up to congressional expectations, was a decided improvement over the two earlier reports. HUD convened a technical research program and selected a 25-member federal interagency task force to help delineate growth trends, identify problems and present broad policy options. For the first time, public participation was permitted through seminars on regional growth and development held in Washington, D.C., Kansas City, and San Francisco. Also, HUD received funding with which it let a number of contracts for preparation of technical materials as the basis for public and interagency discussion. A draft report was circulated for review and comment to 35 public-interest groups, trade groups, state and local government representatives, areawide organizations and Congress, and HUD publicized the comments in a separate volume.

The 1976 report was subtitled "The Changing Issues for National Growth." While the report identified ongoing problems, it did not offer detailed analyses of their relation to the future, nor did it adequately identify the options and alternatives available. The principal recommendations for addressing the issues, the report stated, "can be found in the Budget Message, the State of the Union Message and legislative proposals now before the Congress."

The report did, however, make suggestions for increased public participation "to provide for orderly and direct communication to the President and the Congress of a wide range of perceptions of national growth issues," and "to increase public awareness of future implications of the present policies and of the necessity to plan for the future." The report also suggested that, because federal assistance for state and local growth planning efforts is fragmented and uncoordinated, "a designated element of the Executive Branch under the auspices of the Domestic Council should accomplish the rationalization of Federal planning assistance programs and requirements across department and agency lines."

The first four chapters of the 1976 report described national trends and the changes that were appearing in the national economy and society. Another nine chapters examined broad policy alternatives in several areas of growth (such as energy impacts and promises and problems of alternative energy sources), growth consequences of environmental regulations and environmental impacts on the location of growth, choices in natural resources, transportation policy, housing policy, and balanced economic growth.

The National Forum on Growth Policy, a private organization, comprising over 40 organizations involved in business, the design professions, public interest matters, public affairs, the environment, civil rights, banking, and state and local government, sponsored a critique of the 1976 report, pointing out that the report did "not contain recommended national goals, policy or programs." It was said that the report lacked a "theoretical framework needed to interpret the meaning of the analytical information" and that it failed "to clearly articulate its assumptions and define its terms." The Forum recommended that the 1978 report should evaluate and recommend new institutions to improve the process of policy development and should focus on revitalization of the central city, national housing policy, environmental quality, and growth policy.

Hubert Humphrey, as cochairman of the Senate Joint Economic Committee's Subcommittee on Economic Growth and Stabilization, submitted to HUD a detailed critique of the 1976 report, which was longer than the report itself. Although he saw it as an improvement over the 1972 and 1974 reports, Senator Humphrey wrote that it had two great flaws:

First, even though it contains considerably more information than earlier reports, it does not really help us to understand the meaning of the information it presents.

Second, as in the past the report does not confront the high priority problem presented by the structure of decisionmaking processes that impede the formulation of growth and development policy for the United States.

Humphrey recommended that the timing of the report be changed so that it would be ready for each new Congress, that future reports contain important research findings and relevant policy recommendations presented elsewhere by the Administration, that the growth report receive wider distribution, and that future reports give increased attention to the problem of improving public access to the growth policy planning process.

"The fundamental issue in growth policy today is that the Federal Government, in both its legislative and executive branches, is not structured in such a way that it can systematically assess long-range policy and program questions or estimate long-range impacts of current decisions," stated Humphrey and Senator Jacob Javits in a Joint Economic Committee document that reviewed the 1976 report. They added: "There is growing public concern about the performance of Government, in part because of Government promising more than it can deliver. We believe that this public concern is the result of an awareness on the part of the public that the Federal Government has failed to develop the capacity to make public policy decisions in a rational, informed, future-oriented, and coherent way."

One HUD official involved in the biennial reports said that such one-shot studies were highly inadequate. An institution vested close to the President, he believed, should be created for long-range studies and planning. The institution should be in a position to cycle major presidential initiatives, like the state of the union address and the budget, through its members for response and policy suggestions. The group should also be in a position to consult with state and corporate leaders and with members of Congress.

For the 1978 report, the Democratic Administration recommended a revision of the 1970 Housing and Urban Development Act in order to convert the biennial urban *growth* report into a national urban *policy* report. This change was made to reflect the patterns of population and job movements and the continuing decline of some older established cities since the 1970 Act.

The President appointed the HUD Secretary in March 1977 to head a federal working group that would formulate the urban policy and recommendations for national government action. Participating agencies included HUD, The Departments of Treasury, Labor, Transportation, and Commerce, The Environmental Protection Agency, Community Services Administration, ACTION, and The Law Enforcement Assistance Administration. Involvement of nonfederal groups was extensively sought and encompassed the views of state and local officials, civil-rights, labor, and corporate leaders, public-interest and volunteer groups, businessmen and businesswomen, and private citizens.

The President announced on March 27, 1978, a comprehensive urban policy, based on the working group's recommendations and extensive White House discussion with many interest groups, congressional representatives, and the public.

The urban policy set forth a framework of concern for urban areas with special emphasis on remedial actions to help the older, more distressed communities as well as preventative actions to avoid hurting them in the future.

Workshop on Alternative Energy Strategies (1974)

The Workshop on Alternative Energy Strategies (WAES) was a private sector initiative that included government and business decision-makers from 15 countries. It is included here as one of two nongovernmental examples of such a group because it offers some valuable insights into organizing for effectiveness on an international scale.

Over a 3-year period ending in 1977, the Workshop produced the first energy assessment to the year 2000 on a nearly global scale (communist countries were not included). The project was led by Carroll L. Wilson of the Massachusetts Institute of Technology and supported by a number of private philanthropic foundations, three corporate foundations, and the National Science Foundation.

Wilson had, in recent years, initiated and led a number of other studies such as the "Study of Critical Environmental Problems" (1969) and "Man's Impact on Climate" (1970). He concluded, however, that while these and similar studies received recognition in academic circles, they were not adequately presented to decision-makers.

The Workshop on Alternative Energy Strategies was born of Wilson's belief that more effective mechanisms were needed for the study of critical global problems. He selected energy as the study topic because he felt the world was moving steadily, and with little apparent concern, toward a new and massive energy crisis. The catalytic ingredient of this new study was its use of people who had major standing in their own communities and who had access to a network of influence in their own country.

Wilson assembled people who, rather than being technical experts in energy, were high-level representatives of large energy users or producers or government officials having some responsibility for energy policy. Participants were from Canada, Denmark, Finland, France, Germany, Iran, Italy, Japan, Mexico, the Netherlands, Norway, Sweden, the United Kingdom, the United States, and Venezuela. One-third of all the participants were from government.

Each participant was required to choose and provide funding for at least one associate who could work nearly full-time for the Workshop and secure the necessary data and technical expertise for his country. Associates met 13 times for 1–2 week sessions over a period of 28 months. Participants met seven times, 2–4 days at a time. The goals of the study were:

- To develop a useful method of projecting national supply and demand for energy;

- To study supply and demand to 1985 and 2000 for the countries participating in the Workshop, which, together, consume most of the world's energy;

- To develop a method for estimating global production of oil, gas, coal and nuclear power; and

- To determine whether and when prospective global shortages of certain fuels are likely to occur and how rapidly they might grow.

The report, published in a book, *Energy: Global Prospects 1985–2000*, contained conclusions but did not make recommendations.

From the start, the project participants kept in mind the need for adequate dissemination of the findings. Most members briefed the editorial boards of the leading newspapers in their countries in advance of the release of the report. Press conferences were held on the same day in the capitals of the countries. Wilson testified before energy hearings in Congress, and participants from several other countries communicated the information to their governments or to the private sector.

International Institute for Applied Systems Anaylsis (1972)

A unique institution with a holistic approach to common problems that cannot be solved by any single country alone is the International Institute for Applied Systems Analysis (IIASA). The Institute is situated near Vienna, Austria, and supports about 100 research scientists. It is considered nongovernmental because its members are scientific institutions from the participating nations and not the political entitites of the governments themselves. It was founded in October 1972 on the initiative of the academies of science or equivalent institutions in 12 industrial nations, both East and West (institutions from five other countries have since joined the the the institute). The Academy of Science of the U.S.S.R. and the U.S. National Academy of Sciences (funded through the National Science Foundation) contribute the largest part of the financial support, and private sources such as philanthropic or corporate foundations contribute about $1 million a year.

IIASA's programs are classified as either "global" (programs that affect and can be resolved only by the actions of more than one nation) and "universal" (those that affect and can be resolved by actions of individual nations but which all nations share). As the name of the Institution indicates, its scientific research and study concentrate on applying modern methods of analysis to contemporary problems of society, using the tools of modern management, such as systems theory, operations research, and cybernetics. Emphasis is placed on attempting to bridge the gap between scientists and decision-makers. The results of studies are widely communicated through publications distributed by member scientific institutions, and an effort is made to inform the nonexpert of the results of studies of international problems.

Two current major global projects are on energy systems and on food and agriculture. The energy project is concentrating on finding strategies for the transition over the next 15 to 50 years from an energy economy based on oil, gas, and conventional coal to an economy based on the virtually inexhaustible resources—solar, nuclear, and geothermal—as well as to some extent on new sources of coal. Research activities include studying systems implications of the exploitation of scarce energy resources; energy demand studies, such as one that projects global energy demand with regard to the development of regions, world population growth, and changes in lifestyle; and a study of strategies relating the nuclear-risk problem to decision-making. The final energy project report is expected in 1979.

Although IIASA is composed of scientific representatives from industrial nations, the food and agriculture program is concerned also with a number of less developed countries (LDCs) that have agricultural economies. The program objectives are to evaluate the nature and dimensions of the world food situation, to study alternative policy actions at the national, regional, and global level that may alleviate existing and emerging food problems, and to determine how to meet the nutritional needs of the growing global population.

Typical projects include developing a model of the dynamic interdependence between migration and human settlement patterns and agricultural technology, identifying and measuring the environmental consequences of water use in agriculture as constraints on agricultural production, and modeling the agricultural structures of some pilot LDCs—describing their agricultural policy objectives and devising planning models suitable for estimating the consequences of alternative national policies.

National Commission on Supplies and Shortages; Advisory Committee on National Growth Policy Processes (1975)

Another Nixon-Ford era initiative in the materials field with a major institutional objective was the National Commission on Supplies and Shortages and its separate Advisory Committee on National Growth Policy Processes. These activites, like the 1971–73 National Commission on Materials Policy, were conceived by Congress. During 1974 Senate Majority Leader Mike Mansfield pushed for legislation that resulted in creation of the National Commission on Supplies and Shortages. He drew support from other members of Congress concerned with the 1973–74 oil crisis as well as shortages of other materials in the early 1970s. They believed that the shortages were a symptom of inadequate preparation by government and that existing institutions were not doing enough to identify and anticipate such shortages. They were also concerned that the data on materials being collected in various agencies of the government, were not being systematically coordinated and transmitted to the appropriate agencies and to Congress.

However, Senator Mansfield's concern reached beyond shortages of materials. As Majority Leader, he had become increasingly troubled and frustrated over the inability of government to identify resource availability problems in a timely fashion and to suggest alternatives for dealing with them. Mansfield felt so strongly about this that he worked with Republican Senate leader Hugh Scott to get cooperation from the White House for the legislation and to work out an arrangement for making appointments to the Commission in a way that would be satisfactory to President Nixon, who was not enthusiastic over the new Commission. After a number of meetings, the White House agreed to back the bill, which would give the President the opportunity to appoint 9 of the Commission's 14 members, 4 to be senior officials from the executive branch and 5 private citizens selected in consultation with the Majority and Minority Leaders of the Senate.

The original idea was for a 6-month study using existing data but focusing on institutional changes that could aid in examination and anticipation of shortages. When the enabling legislation went to the floor for passage, however, it provided for a one-year study. On the day the bill was to be voted on in the Senate, Hubert Humphrey introduced an amendment to add a Citizens Advisory Committee and expand the list of study areas beyond materials and into almost all parts of the Government. Humphrey's purpose was to develop recommendations for establishing a more adequate economic policymaking process and structure within the executive and legislative branches.

For years, Humphrey had been interested in getting better institutional arrangements for developing economic policies and alternatives to deal with future problems. Earlier in 1974, as part of a Humphrey legislative proposal for a Balanced National Growth and Development Act, the Senator had proposed a National Citizens Council on the American Future.

When Humphrey introduced his amendment to the Mansfield bill, the Majority Leader opposed the surprise amendment because he thought it would unnecessarily burden his bill. But Humphrey was insistent, and Mansfield eventually agreed to a watered-down version of the amendment. When the amended bill was approved by the Senate, many observers believed the Humphrey-proposed Advisory Committee would be eliminated in a Senate-House Conference.

For several weeks a good deal of political maneuvering took place as presidential support for the Mansfield bill waned. White House officials felt that another presidential commission was unnecessary. Late in September, however, Mansfield used the tactic of offering the entire bill, which already had passed the House, in the form of an amendment to another bill to change the

Defense Production Act of 1950. The strategy worked, and the Congress approved the Mansfield-proposed National Commission on Supplies and Shortages, along with its Advisory Committee on National Growth Policy Processes, as part of the defense bill. President Ford signed the legislation in September 1974, a few weeks after taking office.

After almost a year's delay, resulting from the inability of the White House to come up with selections for the five private-sector members, the Commission finally got under way in September 1975. Donald Rice, president of the Rand Corporation (a former assistant director of the Office of Management and Budget), became chairman.

Many of the administration and congressional members of the Commission did not personally attend Commission meetings, which were held every six weeks or so; they sent delegates instead. The early Commission meetings were not announced in the *Federal Register,* although ostensibly they were open to the public. Later meetings, at which decisions were made, were open only to Commission members.

The Commission did not attempt any new data collection or make supply-and-demand projections into the future. Instead it analyzed available information, concluding that "we see little reason to fear that the world will run out of natural resources during the [next] quarter century."

Nine case studies were prepared that examined the causes of shortages in certain materials during the 1973–74 period. The Commission's major recommendations were for improvement of data collection and analysis in specific government agencies, with emphasis on line agencies. On the subject so important to Senator Mansfield—a new institution for policymaking—the Commission wound up recommending the creation within the Office of Management and Budget of a unit of 20–30 "sectoral and industry specialists" to monitor key materials industries and sectors, to develop a framework for analyzing the comprehensive effects of proposed major federal policy actions, and to monitor the basic data collection, data analysis, and policy analysis activities of the line agencies and departments. They also recommended adding 10 senior staff positions to to the President's Council of Economic Advisers to build up sectoral and industry analysis capabilities in the materials area.

The Commission's report, "Government and the Nation's Resources," was released the first week of 1977. The timing could not have been worse. Not only had Senator Mansfield left office, but both of the senators who served on the

Commission had been defeated, and one of the two House members had left office. The Administration was changing, and the mining industry was upset over one of the recommendations concerning the U.S. Bureau of Mines. Staff Director George Eads spent January 1977 working at the Council of Economic Advisers, seeking to get some of the Commission's ideas implemented. The only bright spot was a hearing held by the Senate Subcommittee on Science, Technology, and Space (of the Commerce Committee), which gave some visibility to the report's findings and recommendations.

While the National Commission on Supplies and Shortages was making its year-long study and preparing its report, its Advisory Committee on National Growth Policy Processes had been at work along separate and sometimes conflicting lines. The Advisory Committee's 19 members all came from outside Government and included a former Cabinet member and a noted presidential historian. Industrialist Arnold A. Saltzman was named Advisory Committee Chairman. The staff director, James E. Thornton, had been the author of the Humphrey amendment that established the Committee, and while working on the Senate Agriculture and Forestry Committee, had helped Humphrey on his proposal for achieving balanced national growth and development.

The legislation authorizing the Advisory Committee provided a wide-ranging mandate ("to develop recommendations as to the establishment of a policymaking process and structure within the executive and legislative branches of the Federal Government as a means to integrate the study of supplies and shortages of resources and commodities into the total problem of balanced national growth and development"). The Advisory Committee, however, had a sparse budget that supported only a staff director and one assistant, and many of the Committee members paid their own expenses when attending monthly meetings. Members wrote their own papers and worked up proposals between meetings. The issue that received most attention was the attempt to determine how to improve the long-range policymaking processes of government in both the executive and legislative branches.

In its report to the President and Congress, the Advisory Committee urged that the nation become not a *planned* society, but a *planning* society. Adequate and open planning for the future would result in less governmental interference, and the necessary government intervention would be more considered, more timely, and less heavy-handed. The report's prime recommendation was for the

institutionalization of the planning process in an independent executive branch agency to be created by Congress and called the National Growth and Development Commission. The new Commission would have the mandate "to examine emerging issues of middle- to long-range growth and development, and to suggest feasible alternatives for the Congress, the President, and the public." The Commission would provide an early warning system that would identify and examine policy issues before they surfaced as crises. It would have no executive, legislative, or judicial powers. The Advisory Committee recommended that enabling legislation to establish the National Growth and Development Commission should require the President and Congress to respond in some fashion to the Commission's reports. The proposed Commission would conduct its affairs openly and hold public hearings. It would submit an annual report to Congress and the President, setting forth its proposed research agenda, the status of ongoing work, and a summary of the reaction from Congress, the President, and the public to previous reports. The new Commission would receive an initial budget authorization for eight years to ensure its continuity. To balance presidential and congressional influence, the chairman of the Commission would be appointed by the President, but the President would be required to consult with the congressional leadership before making Commission appointments. The Advisory Committee report also suggested that the new Commission consist of nine people, five full-time and four part-time (allowing for participation by those not able to accept full-time appointments). Terms of office would run for five years. No member could be removed except for cause, and all appointments would require Senate confirmation.

The Advisory Committee was not unanimous on this recommendation. One Committee member argued that it would give too much power to "the group of wise men," as the Committee members informally referred to the members of the proposed Commission.

Another institutional recommendation of the Advisory Committee was the creation of a Center for Statistical Policy and Analysis to coordinate statistical support for the work of the President and Congress. The Center would be an independent agency in the executive branch, but outside the Executive Office of the President.

Among recommendations of the Advisory Committee that dealt with Congress was one that would require each congressional committee report accompanying proposed legislation to include an outline of the bill's foreseeable indirect middle-to long-range effects, as well as a concise statement of the general goals and specific objectives of the bill.

Reflecting one of the major differences of approach between the parent National Commission on Supplies and Shortages and its Advisory Committee, the Commission in its report expressed doubts concerning creation of an independent new National Growth and Development Commission, as recommended by the Advisory Committee. In the formal letter to the President and to Congress submitting the Advisory Committee's report, Commission Chairman Rice stated that the Commission believed that the proposed new institution "fails the test of feasibility and that the aims sought would be better met by the proposals we have made in our own report for improving the analytical capabilities of existing agencies and departments." The impact of the two groups' reports was marred by this disagreement.

Conclusions

Some Observations

1. For the past 70 years the nation's leadership has perceived periodically a need for long-term analysis of problems relating to natural resources, population, or the environment. For the most part, these issues have been addressed on an ad hoc basis by appointing presidential commissions or other temporary groups to study the situation, make their reports, and then disband. As a result, decision-makers continue to deal primarily with immediate problems, while consideration of how to prepare for conditions that might exist 10, 20, or 30 years in the future is postponed for lack of adequate and systematic information on the options available and on the social, economic, and environmental impacts of alternate choices.

2. Future-oriented commissions or study groups have generally studied natural resources problems separately from problems related to population and the environment. There has been insufficient recognition of the interrelation of these three issues. Each succeeding year, as the problems become more complex and the interrelationships more involved, the need for a holistic approach to decision-making becomes more urgent.

3. Most analyses of future problems in population, natural resources, and the environment have been made only on a national basis. President Truman recognized the need for assessing global implications of natural resources when he instructed his Materials Policy Commission in 1951 to make its study of materials policy international

in scope, at least to the extent of considering the needs and resources of friendly nations. But while the harmful effects of population growth, resource consumption, and pollution spread across borders and oceans, the international approach to long-range planning for solutions to these problems continues to be neglected.

4. When commissions or other bodies have been formed to consider long-term problems in population, natural resources, and the environment, their effectiveness has been hampered by lack of provisions for following up on their recommendations. In several cases the heads of commissions felt so strongly about the need for ongoing institutions that they set up private organizations on their own to follow up with their group's recommendations, which have led to some efforts of ongoing analysis.

5. One recommendation has been made by virtually every presidential commission on population, natural resources, or the environment: the establishment of a permanent body somewhere high in the executive branch for performing continuous futures research and analysis. Although ideas for location of such a permanent group have varied, proposals have generally indicated that a statutorily created institution with access to the President could explore potential goals, watch for trends, and look at alternate possibilities for accomplishing stated objectives.

Lessons from the Past

The recommendation of President Truman's Materials Policy Commission for an advisory body in the Executive Office of the President to frame recommendations for policy up to 25 years ahead went unheeded. The National Goals Research Staff was terminated by President Nixon after completing only one of its scheduled annual reports on goals, and before it could complete its work of setting up in the private sector a National Center for Goals and Alternatives to work with the governmental efforts at decision-making for the future. The National Materials Policy Commission (appointed by President Nixon in 1971), recommended creation of a comprehensive Cabinet-level agency for looking at the future in terms of materials, energy, and the environment, but the recommendation produced no results. And the 1976 recommendation of the National Commission on Supplies and Shortages' Advisory Committee on National Growth Policy Processes, calling for a permanent National Growth and Development Commission, was submitted in the last few weeks of the outgoing Ford Administration, too late to be acted upon. The Advisory Committee had urged that a permanent institution for planning conduct its affairs openly, hold public hearings, and submit an annual report setting forth its proposed research agenda, the status of ongoing work, and a summary of reactions from Congress and the President to previous reports.

In the one case in which a President did establish—without congressional authorization—a mechanism for long-range planning and advice, the institution was often at odds with other agencies and with the Congress and was finally legislated out of existence by Congress. This was Franklin D. Roosevelt's National Resources Planning Board and its earlier entities. When the Board helped to coordinate activities of some Cabinet agencies and to get their ideas before the President, it had some success. But when it tried to establish its own field staff and do its own planning, it incurred hostility from regular line agencies. Roosevelt's Board also did most of its work in secret, which aroused further antagonism.

On the other hand, in the one case in which Congress enacted legislation (the National Environmental Policy Act of 1969) to establish a permanent Council on Environmental Quality to advise the President regularly on long-term national environmental policies, the results were indecisive and the Council has not yet been used to its statutory potential.

A permanent advisory group could provide early warning of problems so that public officials and private citizens would have time to prepare contingency plans. As demonstrated by the presidential commissions, research and analysis of long-term impacts can have a significant educational influence, even if no actions are taken immediately as a result of recommendations. Truman's Materials Policy Commission and the 1961–62 National Academy of Sciences Committee on Natural Resources brought large numbers of scientists and other experts together to work on future problems and thus formed a cadre of individuals who continued to enlighten others. The study groups also helped to coordinate research efforts among government, universities, and industry. An unmeasurable educational factor was present in the activity of the Commission on Population Growth and the American Future (1970–72) through Commission-sponsored seminars with experts, public hearings, a film, and brochures. The research work directed by the Commission also resulted in extensive new knowledge and its dissemination through publication of its research papers. The same has been true of all the other commissions and groups dealing with future problems.

Involvement of the private sector in the activities of a permanent future-oriented high-level advisory group would serve both to educate citizens and build a constituency for carrying out recommendations. This was demonstrated by the 1958 Outdoor Recreation Resources Review Commission when it formed an advisory council that included 25 citizen leaders representing varied citizen organizations. The Commission held joint meetings and field trips with the advisory council, and Commission recommendations were submitted in draft form to the advisory council for consideration. A Citizens Committee that was formed after completion of the Commission report helped obtain support for implementing the recommendations. The seminars and public hearings held by the 1970 Commission on Population Growth and the American Future served an educational purpose. And the Commission's Citizens Committee, which promoted a film and an education program on the Commission's work, provided new avenues for dissemination of the findings. Public participation in the 1976 National Growth and Development report through seminars in San Francisco, Kansas City, and Washington, provided advisory assistance to the HUD team preparing the report. A draft of the report was circulated for review and comment to 35 public groups and Congress. These activities proved helpful to a report which previously had inputs only from a few people in the White House Domestic Council and the Department of Housing and Urban Development.

The Matter of Timing

A permanent institution would have much more freedom in choosing the moment to present new ideas, and thus avoid the timing and politics-related problems that have often hindered activities of temporary presidential commissions. The interest of a President or Congress or the public proved to be much greater at the time a study is started than when it is completed. The Materials Policy Commission was appointed by President Truman in January 1951, when military involvement in Korea had reintroduced fears of shortages that were still fresh in the minds of administrators and the public following World War II. But when the Commission's report went to the President in June 1952, the scarcity issue had lost its priority and public concern. When President Nixon sent a Message to Congress in 1969 asking for creation of a commission to study population growth, the subject was politically attractive inasmuch as people were concerned about rising birthrates. But by the time the Population Commission's report was submitted, statistics showed that the birthrate in the nation had already declined to a stability rate—two children per family—and the subject had less political importance. Another unfavorable timing factor was that the report was sent to the President at the start of his 1972 reelection campaign; some of the Commission's recommendations raised controversy, causing the President to repudiate the Commission's work. On the other hand, the release of the report of the Outdoor Recreation Resources Review Commission came at a time when the popularity of outdoor recreation was booming, and Congress welcomed help in devising solutions to the problems connected with the growing recreation use of public lands, national parks, and national forests.

Another problem of timing was the frequent long delays between the request for a commission and its creation, or between the time the law was passed and the President appointed the public members. Sometimes the period allowed for a study was too short, as with the preparation of "Toward a Social Report." That study also ran into a frequent timing problem: having been started by one President, the study is then submitted either at the end of his term or to his successor.

For all of these reasons, many observers have urged the establishment by law of a permanent group in the Executive Office of the President to institutionalize the coordination of long-term global and holistic considerations of population, resources, environment, and their related issues.

INDEX